MW00582371

HOLT SCIENCE & TECHNOLOGY

Integrated Science

level GREEN

HOLT, RINEHART AND WINSTON

A Harcourt Education Company

Orlando • **Austin** • New York • San Diego • London

Acknowledgments

Contributing Authors

Mapi Cuevas, Ph.D.
Professor of Chemistry
Department of Natural Sciences
Santa Fe Community College
Gainesville, Florida

Katy Z. Allen
Science Writer
Wayland, Massachusetts

Linda Ruth Berg, Ph.D.
Adjunct Professor of Natural Sciences
St. Petersburg College
St. Petersburg, Florida

Leila Dumas, MA
Former Physics Teacher
Lago Vista, Texas

Jennie Dusheck, MA
Science Writer
Santa Cruz, California

Robert H. Fronk, Ph.D.
Chair of Science and Mathematics Education
Florida Institute of Technology
West Melbourne, Florida

Kathleen Kaska
Life and Earth Science Teacher
Oak Harbor Middle School
Oak Harbor, Washington

William G. Lamb, Ph.D.
Winningstad Chair in the Physical Sciences
Oregon Episcopal School
Portland, Oregon

Karen J. Meech, Ph.D.
Associate Astronomer
Institute for Astronomy
University of Hawaii
Honolulu, Hawaii

Gregory K. Pregill, Ph.D.
Professor
Department of Biology
University of San Diego
San Diego, California

Robert J. Sager, Ph.D.
Chair and Professor of Earth Sciences
Pierce College
Lakewood, Washington

Lee Summerlin, Ph.D.
Professor of Chemistry (retired)
University of Alabama
Birmingham, Alabama

Mark F. Taylor, Ph.D.
Associate Professor of Biology
Biology Department
Baylor University
Waco, Texas

Safety Reviewer

Jack Gerlovich, Ph.D.
Associate Professor
School of Education
Drake University
Des Moines, Iowa

Inclusion Specialist

Karen Clay
Inclusion Consultant
Boston, Massachusetts

Ellen McPeek Glisan
Special Needs Consultant
San Antonio, Texas

Academic Reviewers

Glenn Adelson, Ph.D.
Instructor
Department of Organismic and Evolutionary Biology
Harvard University
Cambridge, Massachusetts

Katy Z. Allen
Science Writer
Wayland, Massachusetts

David M. Armstrong, Ph.D.
Professor
Ecology and Evolutionary Biology
University of Colorado
Boulder, Colorado

Linda Ruth Berg, Ph.D.
Adjunct Professor of Natural Sciences
St. Petersburg College
St. Petersburg, Florida

Acknowledgments
continued on page 869

ISBN-13: 978-0-03-095870-0
ISBN-10: 0-03-095870-9

5 6 7 0868 10 09

Contents in Brief

Contents

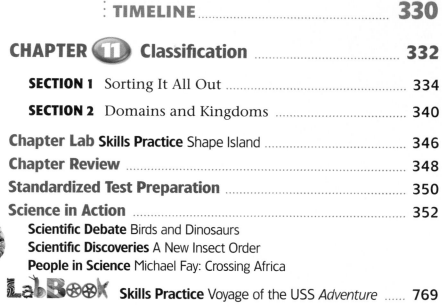
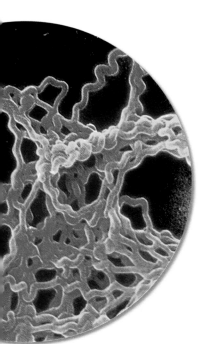
Contents   **ix**

Chapter Labs

Make science a "hands on" experience.

Each chapter ends with a chapter lab designed to help you experience science firsthand. But please don't forget to be safe. Read the **Safety First!** section before starting any of the labs.

Labs

LabBook Labs

The more labs, the better!
Additional labs appear within a special **LabBook** in the back of the textbook. Use these labs to help you extend your lab skills. Don't forget to read the **Safety First!** section before starting any of the labs.

Quick Labs

Not all laboratory investigations have to be long and involved.
The **Quick Labs** found throughout the chapters of this textbook require only a small amount of time and limited equipment. But just because they are quick, don't skimp on safety.

Pre-Reading Activities

FOLDNOTES

Start your engines with an activity!

Get motivated to learn by doing the two activities at the beginning of each chapter. The **Pre-Reading Activity** helps you organize information as you read the chapter. The **Start-Up Activity** helps you gain scientific understanding of the topic through hands-on experience.

Graphic Organizer

Start-Up Activities

Reading Strategies

Activities

Remembering what you read doesn't have to be hard!

A **Reading Strategy** at the beginning of every section provides tips to help you remember and/or organize the information covered in the section.

Internet Activities

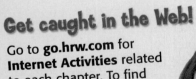

Get caught in the Web!

Go to **go.hrw.com** for **Internet Activities** related to each chapter. To find the Internet Activity for a particular chapter, just type in the keyword listed above.

School to Home

Math Practice

Math Focus

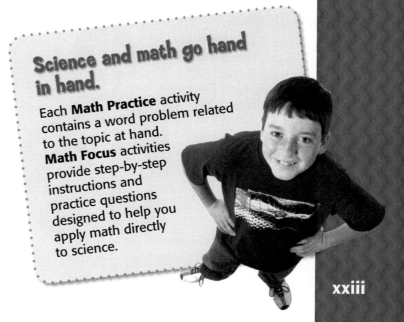

Science and math go hand in hand.

Each **Math Practice** activity contains a word problem related to the topic at hand. **Math Focus** activities provide step-by-step instructions and practice questions designed to help you apply math directly to science.

Connection to...

One subject leads to another.

You may not realize it at first, but different subjects are related to each other in many ways. Each **Connection** explores a topic from the viewpoint of another discipline. In this way, all of the subjects you learn about in school merge to improve your understanding of the world around you.

Science In Action

Science moves beyond the classroom!
Read **Science in Action** articles to learn more about science in the real world. These articles will give you an idea of how interesting, strange, helpful, and action-packed science is. At the end of each chapter, you will find three short articles. And if your thirst is still not quenched, go to **go.hrw.com** for in-depth coverage.

How to Use Your Textbook

Your Roadmap for Success with Holt Science and Technology

What You Will Learn

At the beginning of every section you will find the section's objectives and vocabulary terms. The objectives tell you what you'll need to know after you finish reading the section.

Vocabulary terms are listed for each section. Learn the definitions of these terms because you will most likely be tested on them. Each term is highlighted in the text and is defined at point of use and in the margin. You can also use the glossary to locate definitions quickly.

STUDY TIP Reread the objectives and the definitions to the terms when studying for a test to be sure you know the material.

Get Organized

A Reading Strategy at the beginning of every section provides tips to help you organize and remember the information covered in the section. Keep a science notebook so that you are ready to take notes when your teacher reviews the material in class. Keep your assignments in this notebook so that you can review them when studying for the chapter test.

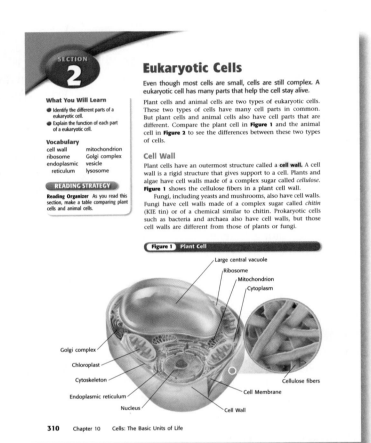

Be Resourceful—Use the Web

SciLinks boxes in your textbook take you to resources that you can use for science projects, reports, and research papers. Go to **scilinks.org** and type in the **SciLinks code** to find information on a topic.

Visit go.hrw.com
Check out the **Current Science®** magazine articles and other materials that go with your textbook at **go.hrw.com.** Click on the textbook icon and the table of contents to see all of the resources for each chapter.

Cell Membrane

All cells have a cell membrane. The *cell membrane* is a protective barrier that encloses a cell. It separates the cell's contents from the cell's environment. The cell membrane is the outermost structure in cells that lack a cell wall. In cells that have a cell wall, the cell membrane lies just inside the cell wall.

The cell membrane contains proteins, lipids, and phospholipids. *Lipids*, which include fats and cholesterol, are a group of compounds that do not dissolve in water. The cell membrane has two layers of phospholipids (FAHS foh LIP idz), shown in **Figure 2.** A *phospholipid* is a lipid that contains phosphorus. Lipids are "water fearing," or *hydrophobic.* Lipid ends of phospholipids form the inner part of the membrane. Phosphorus-containing ends of the phospholipids are "water loving," or *hydrophilic.* These ends form the outer part of the membrane.

Some of the proteins and lipids control the movement of materials into and out of the cell. Some of the proteins form passageways. Nutrients and water move into the cell, and wastes move out of the cell, through these protein passageways.

Reading Check What are two functions of a cell membrane?

CONNECTION TO Language Arts

WRITING SKILL **The Great Barrier** In your **science** journal, write a science fiction story about tiny travelers inside a person's body. These little explorers need to find a way into or out of a cell to solve a problem. You may need to do research to find out more about how the cell membrane works. Illustrate your story.

cell wall a rigid structure that surrounds the cell membrane and provides support to the cell

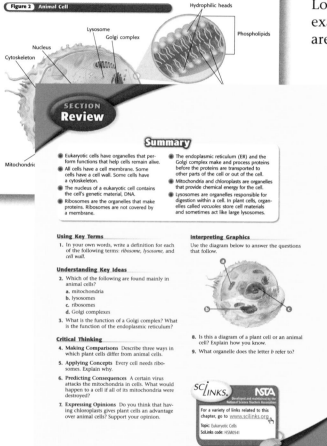

Figure 2 Animal Cell

Lysosome
Golgi complex
Nucleus
Cytoskeleton
Mitochondria
Hydrophilic heads
Phospholipids

SECTION Review

Summary

- Eukaryotic cells have organelles that perform functions that help cells remain alive.
- All cells have a cell membrane. Some cells have a cell wall. Some cells have a cytoskeleton.
- The nucleus of a eukaryotic cell contains the cell's genetic material, DNA.
- Ribosomes are the organelles that make proteins. Ribosomes are not covered by a membrane.
- The endoplasmic reticulum (ER) and the Golgi complex make and process proteins before the proteins are transported to other parts of the cell or out of the cell.
- Mitochondria and chloroplasts are organelles that provide chemical energy for the cell.
- Lysosomes are organelles responsible for digestion within a cell. In plant cells, organelles called *vacuoles* store cell materials and sometimes act like large lysosomes.

Using Key Terms

1. In your own words, write a definition for each of the following terms: *ribosome, lysosome,* and *cell wall.*

Understanding Key Ideas

2. Which of the following are found mainly in animal cells?
   a. mitochondria
   b. lysosomes
   c. ribosomes
   d. Golgi complexes
3. What is the function of a Golgi complex? What is the function of the endoplasmic reticulum?

Critical Thinking

4. **Making Comparisons** Describe three ways in which plant cells differ from animal cells.
5. **Applying Concepts** Every cell needs ribosomes. Explain why.
6. **Predicting Consequences** A certain virus attacks the mitochondria in cells. What would happen to a cell if all of its mitochondria were destroyed?
7. **Expressing Opinions** Do you think that having chloroplasts gives plant cells an advantage over animal cells? Support your opinion.

Interpreting Graphics

Use the diagram below to answer the questions that follow.

8. Is this a diagram of a plant cell or an animal cell? Explain how you know.
9. What organelle does the letter b refer to?

SCLINKS. **NSTA**
Developed and maintained by the National Science Teachers Association

For a variety of links related to this chapter, go to www.scilinks.org
Topic: Eukaryotic Cells
SciLinks code: HSM0541

317

Use the Illustrations and Photos

Art shows complex ideas and processes. Learn to analyze the art so that you better understand the material you read in the text.

Tables and graphs display important information in an organized way to help you see relationships.

A picture is worth a thousand words. Look at the photographs to see relevant examples of science concepts that you are reading about.

Answer the Section Reviews

Section Reviews test your knowledge of the main points of the section. Critical Thinking items challenge you to think about the material in greater depth and to find connections that you infer from the text.

STUDY TIP When you can't answer a question, reread the section. The answer is usually there.

Do Your Homework

Your teacher may assign worksheets to help you understand and remember the material in the chapter.

STUDY TIP Don't try to answer the questions without reading the text and reviewing your class notes. A little preparation up front will make your homework assignments a lot easier. Answering the items in the Chapter Review will help prepare you for the chapter test.

Holt Online Learning

Visit Holt Online Learning
If your teacher gives you a special password to log onto the **Holt Online Learning** site, you'll find your complete textbook on the Web. In addition, you'll find some great learning tools and practice quizzes. You'll be able to see how well you know the material from your textbook.

SAFETY FIRST!

Exploring, inventing, and investigating are essential to the study of science. However, these activities can also be dangerous. To make sure that your experiments and explorations are safe, you must be aware of a variety of safety guidelines. You have probably heard of the saying, "It is better to be safe than sorry." This is particularly true in a science classroom where experiments and explorations are being performed. Being uninformed and careless can result in serious injuries. Don't take chances with your own safety or with anyone else's.

The following pages describe important guidelines for staying safe in the science classroom. Your teacher may also have safety guidelines and tips that are specific to your classroom and laboratory. Take the time to be safe.

Safety Rules!

Start Out Right

Always get your teacher's permission before attempting any laboratory exploration. Read the procedures carefully, and pay particular attention to safety information and caution statements. If you are unsure about what a safety symbol means, look it up or ask your teacher. You cannot be too careful when it comes to safety. If an accident does occur, inform your teacher immediately regardless of how minor you think the accident is.

If you are instructed to note the odor of a substance, wave the fumes toward your nose with your hand. Never put your nose close to the source.

Safety Symbols

All of the experiments and investigations in this book and their related worksheets include important safety symbols to alert you to particular safety concerns. Become familiar with these symbols so that when you see them, you will know what they mean and what to do. It is important that you read this entire safety section to learn about specific dangers in the laboratory.

Eye protection

Clothing protection

Hand safety

Heating safety

Electric safety

Chemical safety

Animal safety

Sharp object

Plant safety

Eye Safety

Wear safety goggles when working around chemicals, acids, bases, or any type of flame or heating device. Wear safety goggles any time there is even the slightest chance that harm could come to your eyes. If any substance gets into your eyes, notify your teacher immediately and flush your eyes with running water for at least 15 minutes. Treat any unknown chemical as if it were a dangerous chemical. Never look directly into the sun. Doing so could cause permanent blindness.

Avoid wearing contact lenses in a laboratory situation. Even if you are wearing safety goggles, chemicals can get between the contact lenses and your eyes. If your doctor requires that you wear contact lenses instead of glasses, wear eye-cup safety goggles in the lab.

Safety Equipment

Know the locations of the nearest fire alarms and any other safety equipment, such as fire blankets and eyewash fountains, as identified by your teacher, and know the procedures for using the equipment.

Neatness

Keep your work area free of all unnecessary books and papers. Tie back long hair, and secure loose sleeves or other loose articles of clothing, such as ties and bows. Remove dangling jewelry. Don't wear open-toed shoes or sandals in the laboratory. Never eat, drink, or apply cosmetics in a laboratory setting. Food, drink, and cosmetics can easily become contaminated with dangerous materials.

Certain hair products (such as aerosol hair spray) are flammable and should not be worn while working near an open flame. Avoid wearing hair spray or hair gel on lab days.

Sharp/Pointed Objects

Use knives and other sharp instruments with extreme care. Never cut objects while holding them in your hands. Place objects on a suitable work surface for cutting.

Be extra careful when using any glassware. When adding a heavy object to a graduated cylinder, tilt the cylinder so that the object slides slowly to the bottom.

Heat

Wear safety goggles when using a heating device or a flame. Whenever possible, use an electric hot plate as a heat source instead of using an open flame. When heating materials in a test tube, always angle the test tube away from yourself and others. To avoid burns, wear heat-resistant gloves whenever instructed to do so.

Electricity

Be careful with electrical cords. When using a microscope with a lamp, do not place the cord where it could trip someone. Do not let cords hang over a table edge in a way that could cause equipment to fall if the cord is accidentally pulled. Do not use equipment with damaged cords. Be sure that your hands are dry and that the electrical equipment is in the "off" position before plugging it in. Turn off and unplug electrical equipment when you are finished.

Chemicals

Wear safety goggles when handling any potentially dangerous chemicals, acids, or bases. If a chemical is unknown, handle it as you would a dangerous chemical. Wear an apron and protective gloves when you work with acids or bases or whenever you are told to do so. If a spill gets on your skin or clothing, rinse it off immediately with water for at least 5 minutes while calling to your teacher.

Never mix chemicals unless your teacher tells you to do so. Never taste, touch, or smell chemicals unless you are specifically directed to do so. Before working with a flammable liquid or gas, check for the presence of any source of flame, spark, or heat.

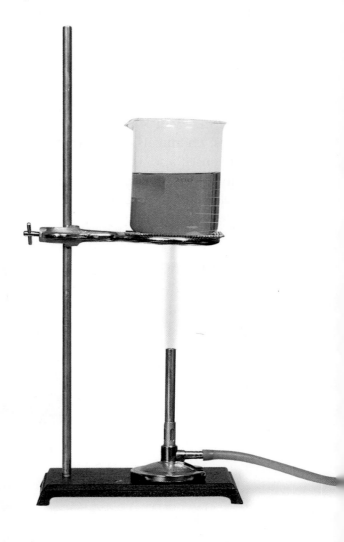

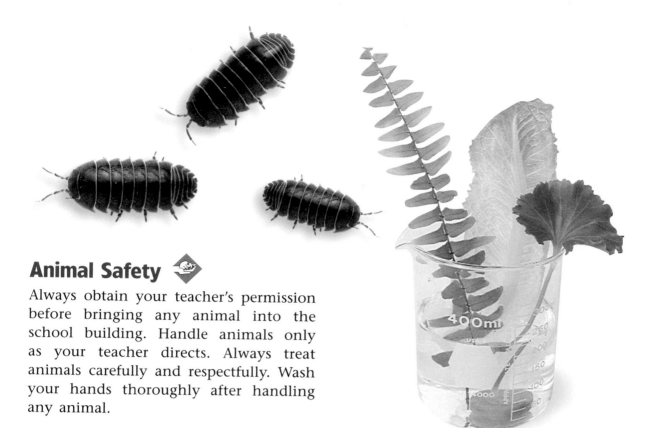

Animal Safety

Always obtain your teacher's permission before bringing any animal into the school building. Handle animals only as your teacher directs. Always treat animals carefully and respectfully. Wash your hands thoroughly after handling any animal.

Plant Safety

Do not eat any part of a plant or plant seed used in the laboratory. Wash your hands thoroughly after handling any part of a plant. When in nature, do not pick any wild plants unless your teacher instructs you to do so.

Glassware

Examine all glassware before use. Be sure that glassware is clean and free of chips and cracks. Report damaged glassware to your teacher. Glass containers used for heating should be made of heat-resistant glass.

1

Science in Our World

The Big Idea

Scientists use careful observations and clear reasoning to understand processes and patterns in nature.

About the Photo

What is that man doing? Ricardo Alonso, a geologist in Argentina, is measuring the footprints left by a dinosaur millions of years ago. Taking measurements is just one way that scientists collect data to answer questions and test hypotheses.

PRE-READING ACTIVITY

FOLDNOTES **Key-Term Fold** Before you read the chapter, create the FoldNote entitled "Key-Term Fold" described in the **Study Skills** section of the Appendix. Write a key term from the chapter on each tab of the key-term fold. Under each tab, write the definition of the key term.

START-UP ACTiViTY

Mission Impossible?

In this activity, you will do some creative thinking to solve what might seem like an impossible problem.

Procedure

1. Examine an **index card.** Your mission is to fit yourself through the card. You can only tear and fold the card. You cannot use tape, glue, or anything else to hold the card together.

2. Brainstorm with a partner ways to complete your mission. Then, record your plan.

3. Test your plan. Did it work? If necessary, get **another index card** and try again. Record your new plan and the results.

4. Share your plans and results with your classmates.

Analysis

1. Why was it helpful to come up with a plan in advance?

2. How did testing your plan help you complete your mission?

3. How did sharing your ideas with your classmates help you complete your mission? What did your classmates do differently?

science the knowledge obtained by observing natural events and conditions in order to discover facts and formulate laws or principles that can be verified or tested

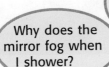

How are a frog and a lizard different?

Why does the mirror fog when I shower?

How do birds know where to go when they migrate?

Science and Scientists

You are on a hike in the mountains when you see something strange. You pick it up. It looks like a shell. You are curious. How could a shell be up on this mountain?

Congratulations! You just completed the first steps of being a scientist. How did you do it? You observed the world around you. Then, you asked a question about your observations. And that's part of what science is all about.

Science Starts with a Question

Science is the knowledge gained by observing the natural world. Asking a question can help you gather knowledge. The world around you is full of amazing things that can lead you to ask questions, such as those in **Figure 1**.

✓ **Reading Check** What is science? (*See the Appendix for answers to Reading Checks.*)

In Your Own Neighborhood

Take a look around your school and around your neighborhood. Most of the time, you take things that you use or see every day for granted. However, one day you might look at something in a new way. That's when a question hits you! You might sit under the tree in front of your school every day. At some point, you may wonder how the leaves change color.

The World and Beyond

Do you think that you might get tired of asking questions about things in your neighborhood? Then just remember that the world is a big place. You could ask questions about deserts, forests, or sandy beaches. Many different plants and animals live in each of these places, and the environment is full of rocks, soil, and water.

But the Earth is not the final place to look for questions. You can look outward to the moon, sun, and planets in our solar system. And beyond that, you have the rest of the universe! There seems to be enough questions to keep scientists busy for a long time.

Figure 1 *Part of science is asking questions about the world around you.*

Investigation: The Search for Answers

Once you ask a question, it's time to look for an answer. But how do you start your investigation? Well, there are several methods that you can use.

Research

You can find answers to some of your questions by doing research, as shown in **Figure 2.** You can ask someone who knows a lot about the subject of your question. You can look up information in textbooks, encyclopedias, and magazines. You could also search on the Internet. You might learn more about your subject if you find the report of an experiment that someone did. But be sure to think about the source of the information that you find. Scientists use information only from reliable sources.

Observation

You can also find answers to questions by making careful observations. For example, if you want to know which birds live around you, you could go for a walk and look for them. Or you could hang a bird feeder outside your window and observe the birds that use it.

Experimentation

You can even answer some of your questions by doing an experiment, as shown in **Figure 3.** Your research might help you plan your experiment. And, of course, you'll need to make careful observations during the experiment. What do you do if your experiment needs materials or conditions that are hard to get? For example, what do you do if you want to see how crystals grow in space? Don't give up! Do more research to see if you can find the results from someone else's experiment!

Figure 2 *A library is a good place to begin your search for answers.*

CONNECTION TO Language Arts

Reading and Research
Think of a scientific question you'd like to research. Look for the answer to your question by reading books, newspapers, scientific journals, and articles on the Internet. Did all of your different sources provide similar information? Which of your sources were the most useful and reliable? Did any resources contradict each other? What is the answer to your scientific question?

Figure 3 *This student is doing an experiment to find out the hardness of a mineral.*

Why Ask Why?

Although people cannot use science to answer every question, many questions can be answered by science. But do any of the answers really matter? Absolutely! Here are just a few ways that science affects our lives.

Saving Lives

Using science, people have answered the question, "How can bicycle riding be made safer?" Science has helped people develop new materials and designs for safer helmets. Effective helmets help protect a rider's head if it hits the ground. These helmets can prevent injuries that lead to brain damage or even death. Scientific research has led to many life-saving discoveries, such as medicines, weather predicting, and disease prevention.

Using Resources Wisely

Science has also helped answer the question, "How can resources be made to last longer?" For example, by recycling paper, people can save trees, as shown in **Figure 4.** Recycling helps protect forests and saves fuel and chemicals used to make paper from trees. Also, scientists have learned to plan ahead so that resources are not used up. For example, many areas where trees are cut down are also sites where new trees are planted. Scientists help determine how to help these trees remain healthy and grow quickly.

✓ **Reading Check** What are the benefits of recycling paper?

Figure 4 **Resources Saved Through Recycling**

 Compared with making the paper originally, recycling 1 metric ton (1.1 tons) of paper:

 produces 30 kg (66 lb) less air pollution

 uses 2.5 m³ (3.3 yd³) less landfill space

 uses 18.7 fewer trees

 uses 4,500 kWh less energy

 uses 29,100 L (7,700 gal) less water

 uses 1,800 L (470 gal) less oil

Healthy Surroundings

Science has helped people answer the question, "How can we reduce the threat of a polluted environment?" Pollution in our surroundings can harm our health and the health of other living things. Air pollution can lead to acid precipitation (pree SIP uh TAY shuhn), which can hurt plants and damage buildings. Pollution in the oceans harms plants and animals that live there. By making less pollution, people can protect the environment and reduce the threat to their health.

One way that scientists have helped reduce pollution is by finding ways that cars can produce less exhaust. Scientists have developed lightweight materials that can be used to make lighter cars. Lighter cars are easier to move than heavier cars, so they burn less fuel. Therefore, lighter cars make less pollution. Science has also helped people develop new types of cars, such as the one in **Figure 5.**

Figure 5 *This car makes less air pollution than most cars do because it runs on batteries.*

Scientists All Around You

Scientists work in many places. If you think about it, any person who asks questions and looks for answers could be called a scientist! Keep reading to take a look at just a few people who use science in their jobs.

Environmental Scientist

To protect the environment, people need to know how and where they are damaging the world around them. An *environmental scientist* is a person who studies how humans interact with their environment. As shown in **Figure 6,** environmental scientists can find out if humans are damaging the environment. Environmental scientists are helping people save Earth's resources and use these resources more wisely.

Figure 6 *This environmental scientist is testing water quality.*

Figure 7 *The Mississippi River helped St. Louis, Missouri, become the large city that it is today. Boats were able to carry supplies and people to and from St. Louis.*

Figure 8 *These zoologists are working to preserve populations of endangered red wolves.*

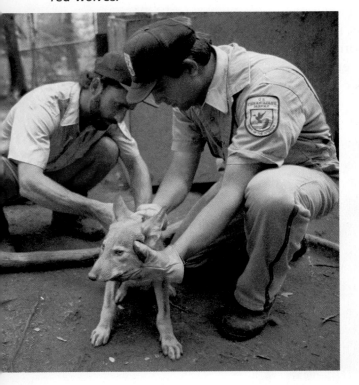

Cartographer

A *cartographer* (kahr TAHG ruh fuhr) makes maps of the surface of the Earth. These maps can be used to plan how cities can grow. Have you ever wondered why cities were built where they are? Often, a city is built in a place because of the features of the land. Many cities, such as the one in **Figure 7,** were built near rivers. Others were built near lakes or oceans. Bodies of water allow the use of boats to move people and things. Rivers and lakes also provide water for drinking and for raising crops. Maps help people keep track of these natural resources.

Engineer

An *engineer* (EN juh NIR) puts scientific knowledge to practical use. Some engineers design and build the buildings, roads, and bridges that make up cities, such as the city in **Figure 7.** Others design and build electronic things, such as computers and televisions. Some even design processes and equipment to make chemicals and medicines. Engineers may work for universities, governments, and private companies.

Zoologist

A *zoologist* (zoh AHL uh jist) studies animals. The men shown in **Figure 8** are part of a study on how to protect an endangered species. Some animals are in danger of becoming extinct because of the loss of habitats where the animals live. By learning about animals' needs, zoologists hope to make a plan to help protect many species from dying out.

Science Educator

A *science educator* is a person who teaches others about science. Learning about science can help people understand how the world works. With education, people can be aware of the effects of their actions. As a result, people can act in ways that are healthy for themselves and others around them. Many science educators teach at schools. Others work at zoos, at aquariums, or in national parks, as shown in **Figure 9.**

✓ **Reading Check** Where do science educators work?

Figure 9 *Some science educators work as park rangers in national parks.*

SECTION Review

Summary

- Science is the knowledge gained by observing the natural world.
- Scientists answer questions by using research, observation, and experimentation to collect data. Often, there is more than one good way to analyze and interpret data.
- Knowledge gained through science helps people protect lives, resources, and the environment.
- People use science in many types of jobs. Some people who use science in their jobs are environmental scientists, cartographers, engineers, zoologists, and science educators.

Using Key Terms

1. In your own words, write a definition for the term *science*.

Understanding Key Ideas

2. How do scientists investigate their questions?

3. What are three ways that knowledge gained through scientific discoveries can benefit the world around you?

4. Which of the following careers does NOT rely on science?
   a. environmental science
   b. cartography
   c. zoology
   d. None of the above

5. What are some resources that you can use to do research?

Math Skills

6. If recycling 1 metric ton of paper saves 4,500 kWh of energy, how much energy is saved by recycling 2.75 metric tons of paper?

7. Imagine that you are a cartographer who needs to draw a map that has the following scale: 1 cm = 1 m. How long would the line representing a wall that is 8.5 m long be?

Critical Thinking

8. **Consumer Focus** Your family usually buys the leading brand of toothpaste. A 5 oz tube of this toothpaste costs $3.00. You notice that a 5 oz tube of another brand costs $2. Which brand is cheaper? What other information would you need in order to decide which brand was a better value?

9. **Applying Concepts** Imagine that you were camping during a meteor shower. You were amazed at what you saw, and you wanted to know what causes a shooting star. Name two ways that you could investigate the cause of a shooting star.

SC**L**INKS®

NSTA
Developed and maintained by the
National Science Teachers Association

For a variety of links related to this chapter, go to www.scilinks.org

Topic: Recycling; Careers in Science
SciLinks code: HSM1277; HSM0225

What You Will Learn

- Identify the steps used in scientific methods.
- Formulate testable hypotheses.
- Explain how scientific methods are used to answer questions and solve problems.

Vocabulary

scientific methods
observation
hypothesis
data

READING STRATEGY

Reading Organizer As you read this section, make a flowchart of the possible steps in scientific methods.

scientific methods a series of steps followed to solve problems

Scientific Methods

Standing by a river, several long-necked dinosaurs quietly chew on plants. Through the trees, they see an allosaurus (AL oh SAWR uhs), the most common meat-eating dinosaur of the Jurassic period.

This scene is not based on imagination alone. Even though scientists have never seen a dinosaur, they have been studying dinosaurs for years! How can that be? Scientists gather bits of information about dinosaurs and their environment from fossils. Then, they re-create what the Earth might have been like long ago. They use imagination and scientific methods.

What Are Scientific Methods?

When scientists observe the natural world, they often think of a question or problem. But scientists don't just guess at answers. **Scientific methods** are the ways in which scientists answer questions and solve problems.

As scientists look for answers, they often use the same steps. But there is more than one way to use the steps. Look at **Figure 1.** Scientists may use all of the steps or just some of the steps during an investigation. They may even repeat some of the steps or do the steps in a different order. It all depends on what works best to answer their question.

Figure 1 Scientific methods often involve the same steps, but the steps are not always used in the same order.

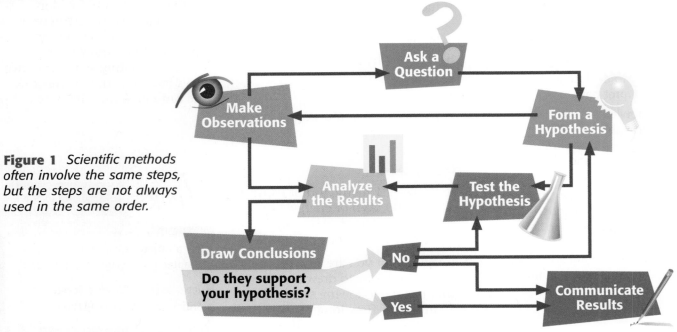

Ask a Question

Asking a question helps focus the purpose of an investigation. Scientists often ask a question after making observations. An **observation** is the act of using the senses to gather information. Observations can be made at any point in an investigation.

There are many kinds of observations. Observations may describe the hardness or softness of a rock. They may describe the color of a substance. Even the patterns in behavior of an animal can be described by observations. Measurements are observations that are made with tools, such as metersticks, stopwatches, and thermometers. Observations lead to answers only when they are accurate and carefully recorded.

observation the process of obtaining information by using the senses

A Dinosaur-Sized Question

In 1979, two people on a hike found dinosaur bones in the area of northwestern New Mexico shown in **Figure 2.** Soon after, David D. Gillette, a scientist who studies fossils, went to see the bones. After observing the bones, Gillette may have asked, "What kind of dinosaur did these bones come from?" Gillette would have to use scientific methods to come up with an answer that he could trust.

✓ **Reading Check** Why do scientists use scientific methods to answer questions? (*See the Appendix for answers to Reading Checks.*)

Figure 2 *Bones were found in this part of New Mexico.*

Form a Hypothesis

hypothesis an explanation that is based on prior scientific research or observations and that can be tested

When scientists want to investigate a question, they form a hypothesis. A **hypothesis** is a possible explanation or answer to a question. It is sometimes called an educated guess. The hypothesis is a scientist's best answer to the question. But a hypothesis can't be just any answer. Someone must be able to test the hypothesis to see if it is true.

From his observations and previous knowledge about dinosaurs, Gillette formed a hypothesis about the bones. He said that the bones, seen in **Figure 3,** came from a kind of dinosaur not yet known to scientists. This hypothesis was Gillette's best testable explanation. To test it, Gillette would have to do a lot of research.

Make Predictions

Before scientists test a hypothesis, they often make predictions. To make a prediction, you say what you think will happen in your experiment or investigation. Predictions are usually stated in an if-then format. For example, Gillette could make the following prediction: If the bones are from a dinosaur not yet known to science, then at least some of the bones will not match any dinosaur bones that have been studied before. Sometimes, scientists make many predictions about one experiment. After predictions are made, scientists can do experiments to see which predictions, if any, support the hypothesis.

Figure 3 *Gillette and his team had to dig out the bones carefully before studying them.*

Test the Hypothesis

A hypothesis must be tested for scientists to learn whether an idea can be supported scientifically. Scientists test hypotheses by gathering data. **Data** are any pieces of information gathered through experimentation. The data can help scientists tell if the hypotheses are valid.

To test his hypothesis, Gillette took hundreds of measurements of the bones, as shown in **Figure 4.** He compared his measurements with those of bones from known dinosaurs. He visited museums and talked with other scientists. After gathering all of these data, Gillette was ready for the next step toward answering his question.

Under Control

To test a hypothesis, a scientist may conduct a controlled experiment. A *controlled experiment* tests only one factor at a time. The one factor that is changed in a controlled experiment is called a *variable.* By changing only the variable, scientists can see the results of just that one change.

Not all investigations are made by doing controlled experiments. Sometimes, it is not possible to use a controlled experiment to test something. Also, some scientists depend on observations more than they depend on experiments to test their hypotheses. By observing nature, scientists can often collect large amounts of data about their hypotheses. When large amounts of data support a hypothesis, the hypothesis is probably valid.

data any pieces of information acquired through observation or experimentation

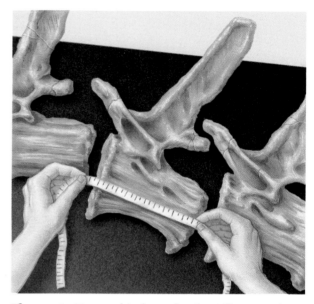

Figure 4 *To test his hypothesis, Gillette took hundreds of measurements of the bones.*

✓ **Reading Check**   What is a variable?

CONNECTION TO Geology

Laguna Colorada In some parts of the world, lake water doesn't look blue. In parts of Bolivia, the lakes may be green, yellow, or red! One Bolivian lake, Laguna Colorada, is a deep-red body of water surrounded by a white stretch of flat land. The land around the lake is white because of all of the salty minerals in the rock there. Some of the lakes are colored by minerals. Others are colored by the microorganisms that live there. How could you find out why Laguna Colorada is red?

Analyze the Results

After they finish their tests, scientists must analyze the results. Analyzing the results helps scientists construct reasonable explanations based on the evidence that has been collected. Scientists often make tables and graphs to arrange their data. **Figure 5** shows how Gillette organized his data. When Gillette analyzed his results, he found that the bones of the mystery dinosaur did not match the bones of any known dinosaur. The bones were either too large or too different in shape.

✓ Reading Check What are two ways that scientists can organize their data?

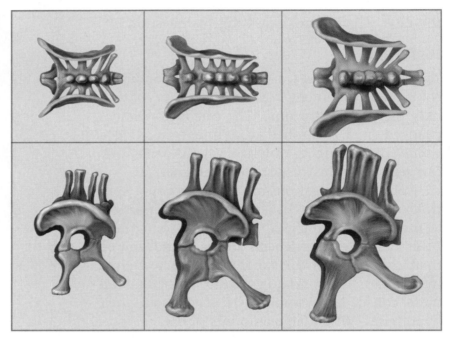

Figure 5 *By organizing his measurements in a chart, Gillette could analyze his results more easily.*

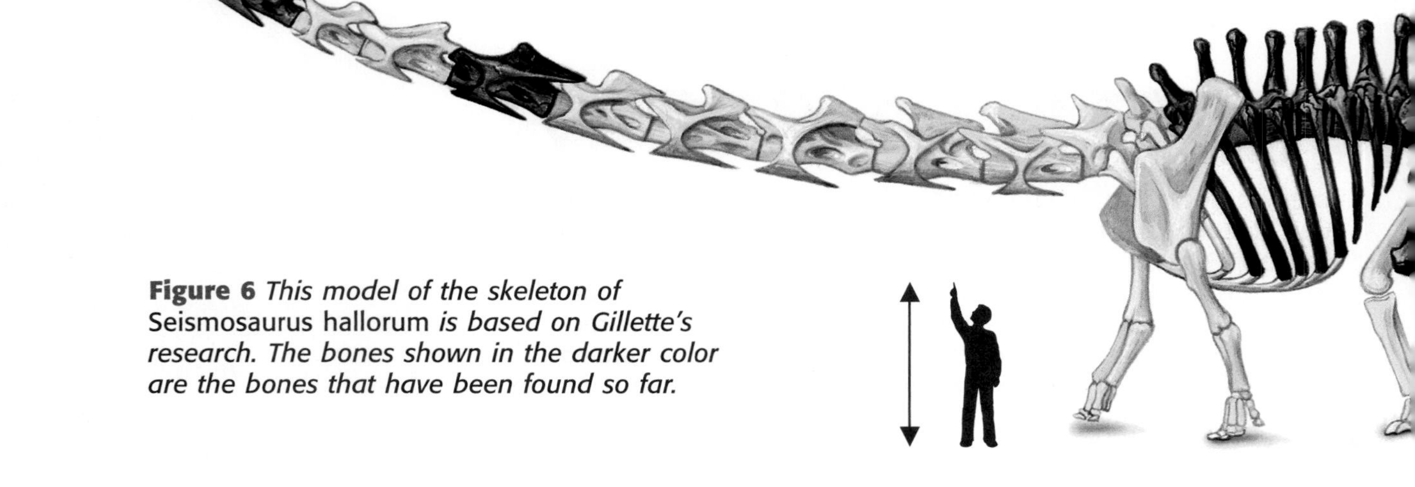

Figure 6 *This model of the skeleton of* Seismosaurus hallorum *is based on Gillette's research. The bones shown in the darker color are the bones that have been found so far.*

Mapping a Sphere

1. Examine a **soccer ball,** and notice the patterns on the ball.

2. Place different **stickers** on each pentagon of the ball.

3. Now, try mapping the images from the soccer ball onto a **flat piece of paper.**

4. What problems came up when you tried to represent a sphere on a flat piece of paper?

5. Use your experience to draw a conclusion about why maps of the entire Earth are often represented on a globe. Then, explain why flat maps of the entire Earth are often distorted.

Draw Conclusions

After analyzing the results of their tests, scientists must conclude if the results support the hypothesis. Proving that a hypothesis is not true can be as valuable as proving that it is true. If the hypothesis is not supported, scientists may repeat the investigation to check for mistakes. Or, scientists may look at the original question in a new way, ask new questions, and form new hypotheses. New questions and hypotheses can lead to new investigations and discoveries.

From all of his work, Gillette concluded that the bones found in New Mexico, shown in the model in **Figure 6,** were indeed from a yet unknown dinosaur. The dinosaur was about 45 m (148 ft) long and had a mass of almost 100 metric tons. The creature certainly fit the name that Gillette gave it— *Seismosaurus hallorum,* the "earth shaker."

For another activity related to this chapter, go to **go.hrw.com** and type in the keyword **HZ5WESW.**

Communicate Results

After finishing an investigation, scientists communicate their results. By doing so, scientists share what they have learned. Scientists communicate by writing reports for scientific journals and by giving talks. They can also put their results on the Internet. In fact, scientists use computers to prepare research reports as well as to share data with other scientists.

Science depends on sharing information. Sharing allows other scientists to repeat experiments to see if they get the same results. Also, by sharing, scientists can compare hypotheses and form consistent explanations. Sometimes, new data lead scientists to change their hypotheses.

Gillette shared his discovery of *Seismosaurus hallorum* at a press conference at the New Mexico Museum of Natural History and Science. He later sent a report that described his investigation to the *Journal of Vertebrate Paleontology*.

✓ Reading Check Name three ways that scientists share results.

Case Closed?

All of the bones that Gillette found have been dug up from the ground. But as **Figure 7** shows, the fun is not over yet! The work on *Seismosaurus hallorum* continues. The remains of one of the largest dinosaurs ever discovered are still being studied. Like so many other investigations, Gillette's work led to new questions to be answered.

CONNECTION TO Physics

Defining Technology As technologies are developed, scientists are able to investigate questions in new ways. How would you define the word *technology*? Consider the pros and cons of the following definitions: 1) artifact or hardware; 2) methodology or technique; 3) system of production; or 4) social-technical system. Can you find evidence to support the use of any of these definitions? Give an example of a technology that fits each definition.

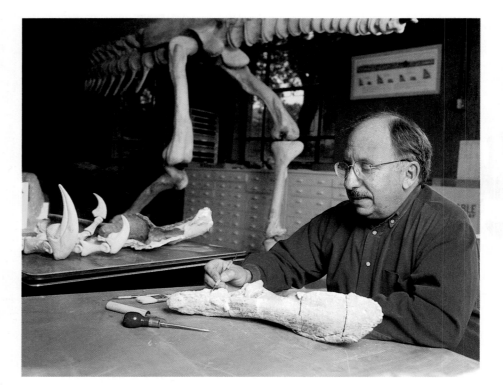

Figure 7 *David Gillette continues to study the bones of* Seismosaurus hallorum *for new views into the past.*

Summary

- Scientific methods are the ways in which scientists follow steps to answer questions and solve problems.

- Any information gathered through the senses is an observation. Observations often lead to the formation of questions and hypotheses.

- A hypothesis is a possible explanation or answer to a question. A well-formed hypothesis can be tested by experiments.

- A controlled experiment tests only one factor at a time in order to determine the effects of changes to just that one factor.

- After testing a hypothesis, scientists analyze the results and draw conclusions about whether the hypothesis is supported.

- Communicating results allows others to check the results, add to their knowledge, form new hypotheses, and design new experiments.

Using Key Terms

1. Use the following terms in the same sentence: *scientific methods, observations, hypothesis,* and *data*.

Understanding Key Ideas

2. Which of the following statements about the steps of scientific methods is true?
   a. Steps must always be used in the same order.
   b. All steps must be used.
   c. Steps are repeated sometimes.
   d. The steps must support the hypothesis.

3. The following statements could have been made during Gillette's field investigation. Which statement is a testable hypothesis?
   a. Dinosaur bones were found in New Mexico.
   b. The bones are from a known dinosaur.
   c. One of the ribs is 2 m long.
   d. The first step in studying the bones is to dig them out of the ground.

4. What is an observation? Write down one observation about the room that you are in at this moment.

5. What is a controlled experiment?

Critical Thinking

6. **Analyzing Processes** How could two scientists working to answer the same question draw different conclusions?

7. **Applying Concepts** What are two ways that you could analyze data about temperature changes over many years? What are the benefits and limitations of each method?

Interpreting Graphics

8. The table below shows how long one bacterium takes to divide into two bacteria. Plot the data on a graph. Put temperature on the *x*-axis and the time to double on the *y*-axis. Do not graph values for which there is no growth. What temperature allows the bacteria to grow the fastest?

Temperature (°C)	Time to double (min)
10	130
20	60
25	40
30	29
37	17
40	19
45	32
50	no growth

SCI**LINKS**®

N**STA**
Developed and maintained by the
National Science Teachers Association

For a variety of links related to this chapter, go to www.scilinks.org

Topic: Scientific Methods
SciLinks code: HSM1359

Scientific Models

Imagine you are studying volcanoes. How do you think baking soda, vinegar, and some clay could help you?

You might not think these things alone could help you. But you could use them to build a model of a volcano. Then they might help you understand volcanoes a little better.

Types of Scientific Models

A **model** is a representation of an object or system. Models often use familiar objects or ideas that stand for other things. That's how a model can be a tool for understanding the natural world. A model uses something familiar to help you understand something that is not familiar. Models can be used to explain the past and the present. They can even be used to predict future events. However, keep in mind that models have limitations. Three major kinds of scientific models are physical, mathematical, and conceptual models.

Physical Models

Model airplanes, maps, and dolls are physical models. Some physical models, such as a doll, look like the thing they model. However, a limitation of a doll as the model of a baby is that the doll doesn't act like a baby. Other models, such as the one shown in **Figure 1,** look and act at least somewhat like the real thing.

What You Will Learn

● Use models to represent the natural world.
● Identify the limitations of models.
● Describe theories and laws.

Vocabulary

model
theory
law

READING STRATEGY

Paired Summarizing Read this section silently. In pairs, take turns summarizing the material. Stop to discuss ideas that seem confusing.

model a pattern, plan, representation, or description designed to show the structure or workings of an object, system, or concept

Figure 1 *The model volcano looks a little bit like the real volcano, but it has its limitations. The model lava is not formed in the same way or at the same temperature as the real lava.*

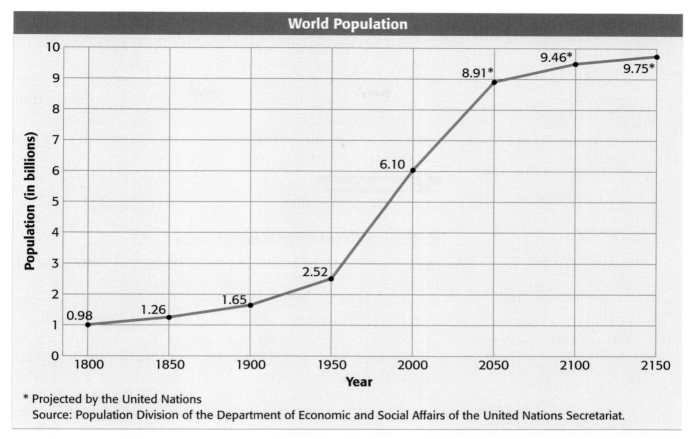

World Population

Population (in billions) vs *Year*

0.98 (1800)
1.26 (1850)
1.65 (1900)
2.52 (1950)
6.10 (2000)
8.91* (2050)
9.46* (2100)
9.75* (2150)

* Projected by the United Nations
Source: Population Division of the Department of Economic and Social Affairs of the United Nations Secretariat.

Mathematical Models

A mathematical model is made up of mathematical equations and data. Simple mathematical models allow you to calculate things such as how far a car will go in an hour. Other models are so complex that only computers can handle them. Look at **Figure 2.** Scientists use a mathematical model to help predict how fast the number of people on Earth will grow and how many resources people will use. Some of these very complex models have many variables. Using the most correct data does not make the prediction correct. A change in a variable that was not predicted could cause the model to fail.

Conceptual Models

The third kind of model is a conceptual model. Some conceptual models are systems of ideas. Others are based on making comparisons with familiar things to help illustrate or explain an idea. One example of a conceptual model is the system that scientists use to classify living things. By using a system of ideas, scientists can group living things by what they have in common. This type of model allows scientists to better understand each group of living things.

Reading Check **What are three kinds of models?** (*See the Appendix for answers to Reading Checks.*)

Figure 2 *This graph shows human population growth predicted by a mathematical model run on a computer.*

CONNECTION TO Language Arts

Analogies Many writers use analogies. An analogy points to similarities between two things that are otherwise unlike each other. Do you think scientists use analogies? What could be some strengths and weaknesses of using analogies to describe events and objects in scientific explorations?

Just the Right Size

Models are often used to represent things that are very small or very large. Particles of matter are too small to see. The Earth or the solar system is too large to see completely. In these cases, a model can help you picture the thing in your mind. Models can even help you observe features that are not easily observed in real life. With a model, you can examine each of the layers inside the Earth.

✓ Reading Check How can people picture in their minds objects that are too small or too large to see completely?

Building Scientific Knowledge

Models are often used to help illustrate and explain scientific theories. In science, a **theory** is a unifying explanation for a range of hypotheses and observations that have been supported by testing. A theory not only can explain an observation you've made but also can predict what might happen in the future.

Scientists use models to help guide their search for new information. This information can help support a theory or show it to be wrong. Keep in mind that models can be changed or replaced. These changes happen because new observations cause scientists to change their theories. You can compare an old model with a current one in **Figure 3.**

theory an explanation that ties together many hypotheses and observations

law a summary of many experimental results and observations; a law tells how things work

Figure 3 *Scientists' model of Earth changed as new information was gathered.*

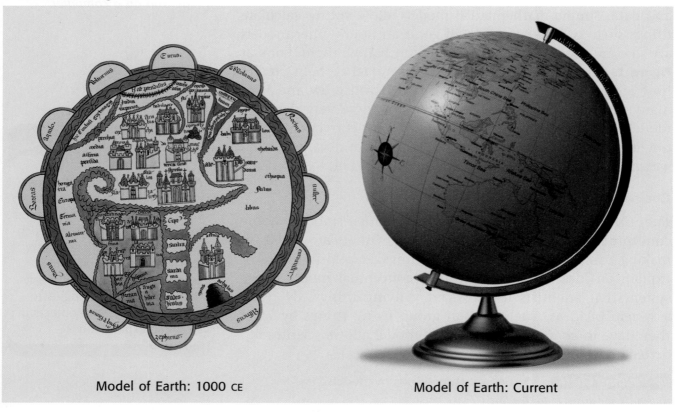

Model of Earth: 1000 CE

Model of Earth: Current

Scientific Laws

What happens when a theory and its models correctly predict the results of many different experiments? A scientific law could be formed. In science, a **law** is a summary of many experimental results and observations. A law tells you how things work.

A law tells you to expect the same thing to happen every time. Look at **Figure 4.** Every object in the universe is attracted to every other object. This fact is summed up by the *law of universal gravitation.* This law says that you can always expect two objects to be attracted to one another. It also helps you calculate the size of the attraction. The size of the attraction depends on the masses of the objects and the distance between them. However, the law does not explain why there is an attraction.

Force of attraction on small book

Force of attraction on large book

Figure 4 *Each of these books has a different attraction between it and Earth. The attraction is larger between the more massive book and Earth.*

SECTION Review

Summary

- Three main types of models are physical, mathematical, and conceptual.
- A model is a representation of an object or system. Models often use familiar things to represent unfamiliar things that may be difficult to observe.
- Scientific knowledge is built as scientists form laws and revise scientific hypotheses, models, and theories.

Using Key Terms

In each of the following sentences, replace the incorrect term with the correct term from the word bank.

theory   model   law

1. A conclusion is an explanation that matches many hypotheses but may still change.

2. A hypothesis tells you exactly what to expect in a situation.

3. A variable represents an object or a system.

Understanding Key Ideas

4. What are the three main types of models?

5. How do scientists form theories and laws?

Math Skills

6. If Jerry is 2.1 m tall, how tall is a scale model of Jerry that is 10% of his size?

Critical Thinking

7. **Applying Concepts** Draw a map showing the way from your school to your home. What type of model have you made? Identify any symbols that you used to represent things on your map. What are some limitations of your model?

8. **Forming Hypotheses** How could you use a solar system model to hypothesize why the moon appears to change shape?

SCiLINKS

NSTA
Developed and maintained by the National Science Teachers Association

For a variety of links related to this chapter, go to www.scilinks.org

Topic: Using Models
SciLinks code: HSM1588

Tools, Measurement, and Safety

Would you use a hammer to tighten a bolt on a bicycle? You probably wouldn't. To be successful in many tasks, you need the correct tools.

What You Will Learn

- Describe three kinds of tools.
- Explain the importance of the International System of Units.
- Describe how to measure length, area, mass, volume, and temperature.
- Identify lab safety symbols, and demonstrate safe practices during lab investigations.

Vocabulary

meter	volume
area	temperature
mass	

READING STRATEGY

Reading Organizer As you read this section, make a concept map by using the terms above.

Tools for Science

Scientists use many tools. A *tool* is anything that helps you do a task. If you observe a jar of pond water, you may see a few creatures swimming around. But a microscope can help you see many creatures that you couldn't see before. And a graduated cylinder can help you measure the water in the jar. Different tools help scientists gather specific kinds of data.

Tools for Seeing

Microscopes help you make careful observations of things that are too small to see with just your eyes. The compound light microscope in **Figure 1** is made up of three main parts—a tube that has lenses at each end, a stage, and a light. When you place what you want to see on the stage, light passes through it. The lenses magnify the image.

✓ **Reading Check**   Name the three main parts of a compound light microscope. (*See the Appendix for answers to Reading Checks.*)

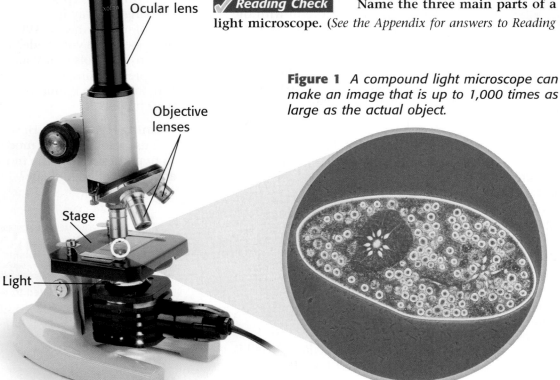

Ocular lens

Objective lenses

Stage

Light

Figure 1 *A compound light microscope can make an image that is up to 1,000 times as large as the actual object.*

Figure 2 Measurement Tools

You can use a **graduated cylinder** to measure volume.

You can use a **stopwatch** to measure time.

You can use a **meterstick** to measure length.

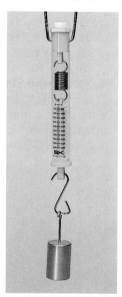

You can use a **spring scale** to measure force.

You can use a **thermometer** to measure temperature.

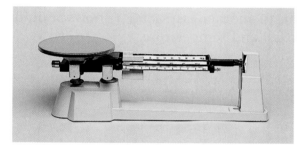

You can use a **balance** to measure mass.

Tools for Measuring

You might remember that one way to collect data during an experiment is to take measurements. To have the best measurements possible, you need to use the proper tools. Stopwatches, metersticks, and balances are some of the tools you can use to make measurements. Thermometers, spring scales, and graduated cylinders are also helpful tools. **Figure 2** explains what characteristics these tools can be used to measure.

Tools for Analyzing

After you collect data, you need to analyze them. Perhaps you need to find the average of your data. Calculators are handy tools that help you do calculations quickly. Or you might show your data in a graph or a figure. A computer that has the correct software can help you make neat, colorful figures. In fact, computers have become invaluable tools for collecting, storing, and analyzing data. Of course, even a pencil and graph paper are tools that you can use to graph your data.

See for Yourself

1. Use a **metric ruler** to measure the length and width of one of your fingernails. Draw and describe the details of your fingernail.

2. Look at the same fingernail through a **magnifying lens.** Now, draw the details of your fingernail as seen with magnification.

3. How does using a magnifying lens change what details you can see?

Units of Measurement

Measure the width of your desk, but do not use a ruler. Pick an object to use as your unit of measurement. It could be a pencil, your hand, or anything else. Find how many units wide your desk is. Compare your measurement with those of your classmates. In your **science journal,** explain why using standard units of measurement is important.

ACTIVITY

Measurement

Hundreds of years ago, different countries used different systems of measurement. At one time in England, the standard for an inch was three grains of barley placed end to end. Other modern standardized units were originally based on parts of the body, such as the foot. Such systems were not very reliable. Their units were based on objects that had different sizes.

The International System of Units

In time, people realized that they needed a simple and reliable measurement system. In the late 1700s, the French Academy of Sciences set out to make that system. Over the next 200 years, the metric system was formed. This system is now called the *International System of Units* (SI).

Today, most scientists and almost all countries use the International System of Units. One advantage of using the SI measurements is that they help all scientists share and compare their observations and results. Another advantage of the SI is that all units are based on the number 10. This feature makes changing from one unit to another easy. **Table 1** shows SI units for length, volume, mass, and temperature.

Table 1 **Common SI Units and Conversions**		
Length	**meter (m)** kilometer (km) decimeter (dm) centimeter (cm) millimeter (mm) micrometer (µm) nanometer (nm)	1 km = 1,000 m 1 dm = 0.1 m 1 cm = 0.01 m 1 mm = 0.001 m 1 µm = 0.000001 m 1 nm = 0.000000001 m
Volume	**cubic meter (m^3)** cubic centimeter (cm^3) liter (L) milliliter (mL)	1 cm^3 = 0.000001 m^3 1 L = 1 dm^3 = 0.001 m^3 1 mL = 0.001 L = 1 cm^3
Mass	**kilogram (kg)** gram (g) milligram (mg)	1 g = 0.001 kg 1 mg = 0.000001 kg
Temperature	**Kelvin (K)** Celsius (°C)	0°C = 273 K 100°C = 373 K

Length

How long is your arm? The student in **Figure 3** could describe the length of her arm by using the **meter** (m), the basic SI unit of length. Remember that SI units are based on the number 10. If you divide 1 m into 100 parts, each part equals 1 cm. In other words, 1 cm is one-hundredth of a meter. To describe the length of microscopic objects, micrometers (μm) or nanometers (nm) are used. To describe the length of larger objects, kilometers (km) are used.

Area

How much carpet would it take to cover the floor of your classroom? To answer this question, you must find the area of the floor. **Area** is a measure of how much surface an object has. Area is based on two measurements. To calculate the area of a square or rectangle, first measure the length and width. Then, use the following equation:

$$area = length \times width$$

The units for area are square units, such as square meters (m^2), square centimeters (cm^2), and square kilometers (km^2).

✓ **Reading Check** What does area measure?

Mass

How many sacks of grain can a mule carry? The answer depends on the strength of the mule and the mass of the sacks of grain. **Mass** is the amount of matter that makes up an object. Scientists often use a balance to measure mass, as shown in **Figure 4.** The kilogram (kg) is the basic unit for mass. The kilogram is used to describe the mass of things such as sacks of grain. Many common objects are not so large, however. The mass of smaller objects, such as an apple, can be described by using grams. One thousand grams equals 1 kg. The mass of large objects, such as an elephant, is given in metric tons. A metric ton equals 1,000 kg.

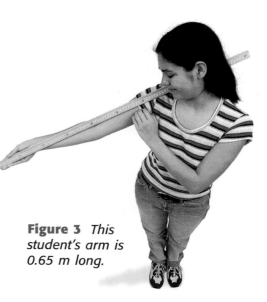

Figure 3 *This student's arm is 0.65 m long.*

meter the basic unit of length in the SI (symbol, m)

area a measure of the size of a surface or a region

mass a measure of the amount of matter in an object

Figure 4 *This boy is using a balance to measure the mass of an apple.*

70 mL

80 mL

Figure 5 *Adding the rock changes the water level from 70 mL to 80 mL. So, the rock displaces 10 mL of water. Because 1 mL = 1 cm³, the volume of the rock is 10 cm³.*

volume a measure of the size of a body or region in three-dimensional space

temperature a measure of how hot (or cold) something is

Figure 6 *This thermometer shows the relationship between degrees Fahrenheit and degrees Celsius.*

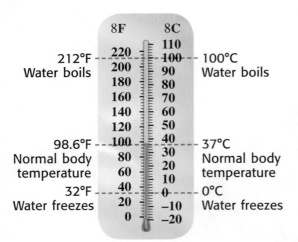

°F	°C
	110
212°F --- 220 --- 100 --- 100°C
Water boils 200 90 Water boils
180 80
160 70
140 60
120 50
98.6°F --- 100 --- 40 --- 37°C
Normal body 80 30 Normal body
temperature 60 20 temperature
32°F --- 40 --- 0 --- 0°C
Water freezes 20 −10 Water freezes
0 −20

Volume

Suppose that some hippos born in a zoo are being moved to Africa. How many hippos will fit into a cage? The answer depends on volume. **Volume** is the amount of space that something occupies or, as in the case of the cage, the amount of space that something contains.

The volume of a liquid is often given in liters (L). Liters are based on the meter. A cubic meter (1 m³) is equal to 1,000 L. So, 1,000 L will fit into a box measuring 1 m on each side. A milliliter (mL) will fit into a box measuring 1 cm on each side. So, 1 mL = 1 cm³. Graduated cylinders are used to measure liquid volume in milliliters.

The volume of a large, solid object is given in cubic meters (m³). The volumes of smaller objects can be given in cubic centimeters (cm³) or cubic millimeters (mm³). To calculate the volume of a box-shaped object, multiply the object's length by its width and then by its height. To find the volume of an irregularly shaped object, measure the volume of liquid that the object displaces. This process is shown in **Figure 5.**

Temperature

How hot is a lava flow? To answer this question, scientists need to measure temperature. **Temperature** is a measure of how hot (or cold) something is. You probably use degrees Fahrenheit (°F) to describe temperature. Scientists often use degrees Celsius (°C). However, the kelvin (K), the SI base unit for temperature, is also used. The thermometer in **Figure 6** shows how two of these units are related.

Safety Rules!

Science can be exciting, fun, and safe if you follow your teacher's instructions. You should get your teacher's permission before starting any science investigation. Read lab procedures carefully, and pay special attention to safety information. **Figure 7** shows the safety symbols used in this book. Be sure you know these symbols and their meanings. You should also read the safety information at the beginning of this book. If you still have safety-related questions, ask your teacher for help.

✓ Reading Check What should you do if you don't understand what a safety symbol means?

Figure 7 **Safety Symbols**

 Eye Protection

 Clothing Protection

 Hand Safety

 Heating Safety

Electric Safety

 Sharp Object

 Chemical Safety

 Animal Safety

 Plant Safety

SECTION Review

Summary

- Scientists use tools that help them see, measure and analyze. Microscopes, metersticks, and computers are a few tools that scientists use in their investigations.
- Scientists use the International System of Units so that they can share and compare their observations and results.
- Scientists have determined standard ways to measure length, area, mass, volume, and temperature.
- Students and anyone doing science investigations should follow safety instructions and should be able to understand safety icons.

Using Key Terms

Complete each of the following sentences by choosing the correct term from the word bank.

area   mass
volume   temperature

1. The measure of the surface of an object is called ____.

2. Scientists use kilograms when measuring an object's ____.

3. The ____ of a liquid is usually described in liters.

Understanding Key Ideas

4. SI units are
   a. always based on standardized measurements of body parts.
   b. almost always based on the number 10.
   c. used to measure only length.
   d. used only in France.

5. What are three units that are used to measure temperature?

6. If you were going to measure the mass of a fly, which SI unit would be most appropriate?

7. Describe three kinds of tools, and give an example of each kind of tool.

Math Skills

8. What is the area of a garden that is 12 m long and 8 m wide?

9. What is the volume of a box if the sides of the box are each 1 m in length?

Critical Thinking

10. **Predicting Consequences** Give an example of what could happen if you do not follow safety rules about animal safety.

11. **Applying Concepts** During an experiment, you must mix chemicals in a glass beaker. What should you wear to protect yourself during this experiment?

SCLINKS®

NSTA
Developed and maintained by the National Science Teachers Association

For a variety of links related to this chapter, go to www.scilinks.org

Topic: Tools of Science; SI Units
SciLinks code: HSM1535; HSM1390

Model-Making Lab

OBJECTIVES

Design a model to demonstrate core sampling.

Create a diagram of a classmate's model by using the core sample method.

MATERIALS

- knife, plastic
- modeling clay, three or four colors
- pan or box, opaque
- pencil, unsharpened
- pencils or markers, three or four colors
- PVC pipe, 1/2 in.

SAFETY

Using Scientific Methods

Geologists often use a technique called core sampling to learn what underground rock layers look like. This technique involves drilling several holes in the ground in different places and taking samples of the underground rock or soil. Geologists then compare the samples from each hole at each depth to construct a diagram that shows the bigger picture.

In this activity, you will model the process geologists use to diagram underground rock layers. You will first use modeling clay to form a rock-layer model. You will then exchange models with a classmate, take core samples, and draw a diagram of your classmate's rock layers.

- Form a plan for your rock layers. Make a sketch of the layers. Your sketch should include the colors of clay in several layers of varying thicknesses. Note: Do not let the classmates who will be using your model see your plan.

- In the pan or box, mold the clay into the shape of the lowest layer in your sketch.

- Repeat the procedure described in the second bullet for each additional layer of clay. Exchange your rock-layer model with a classmate.

Ask a Question

1 Can unseen features be revealed by sampling parts of the whole?

Form a Hypothesis

2 Form a hypothesis about whether taking core samples from several locations will give a good indication of the entire hidden feature.

Test the Hypothesis

3 Choose three places on the surface of the clay to drill holes. The holes should be far apart and in a straight line. (Do not remove the clay from the pan or box.)

4 Slowly push the PVC pipe through all the layers of clay. Slowly remove the pipe.

5 Gently push the clay out of the pipe with an unsharpened pencil. This clay is a core sample.

6 Draw the core sample, and record your observations. Be sure to use a different color of pencil or marker for each layer.

7 Repeat steps 4–6 for the next two core samples. Make sure your drawings are side by side and in the same order as the samples in the model.

Analyze the Results

1 **Examining Data** Look at the pattern of rock layers in each of your core samples. Think about how the rock layers between the core samples might look. Then, make a diagram of the rock layers.

2 **Organizing Data** Complete your diagram by coloring the rest of each rock layer.

Draw Conclusions

3 **Evaluating Models** Use the plastic knife to cut the clay model along a line connecting the three holes. Remove one side of the model so that you can see the layers. How well does your rock-layer diagram match the model? Explain your answer.

4 **Evaluating Methods** What are some limitations of your diagram as a model of the rock layers?

5 **Drawing Conclusions** Do your conclusions support your hypothesis? Explain your answer.

Applying Your Data

List two ways that the core-sampling method could be improved.

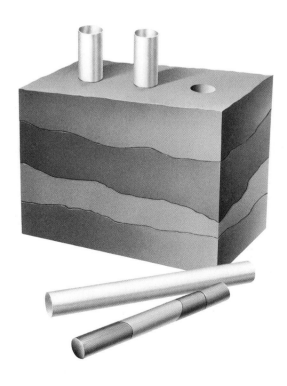

Chapter Review

USING KEY TERMS

Complete each of the following sentences by choosing the correct term from the word bank.

models   science
scientific methods   hypothesis

1 The process of gathering knowledge about the natural world is called ___.

2 An explanation that is based on prior scientific research or observations and that can be tested is called a ___.

3 ___ are a series of steps followed to solve problems.

UNDERSTANDING KEY IDEAS

Multiple Choice

4 A good way to investigate answers to scientific questions is to

a. do research only.

b. make observations only.

c. do experiments only.

d. do research, make observations, and do experiments.

5 A pencil measures 14 cm long. How many millimeters long is it?

a. 1.4 mm   c. 1,400 mm

b. 140 mm   d. 1,400,000 mm

6 Which of the following units is NOT an SI unit?

a. meter   c. liter

b. foot   d. degree Celsius

7 Which of the following statements describes a limitation of models?

a. Models are large enough to be seen.

b. Models do not act exactly like the things that they model.

c. Models are smaller than the thing that they model.

d. Models use familiar things to model unfamiliar things.

8 What kind of model is a map?

a. physical model

b. conceptual model

c. mathematical model

d. hypothesis model

Short Answer

9 How could a hypothesis that is proven to be false lead to new scientific investigations?

10 How and why do scientists use models?

11 What are three types of models? Give an example of each type.

12 What problems could occur if scientists did not communicate the results of their investigations?

13 What problems could occur if the International System of Units were not used?

14 Which safety symbols would you expect to see for an experiment that requires the use of acid?

CRITICAL THINKING

15 **Concept Mapping** Use the following terms to create a concept map: *science, scientific methods, hypothesis, problems, questions, experiments,* and *observations*.

16 **Analyzing Processes** What are the steps of scientific methods? Why don't you need to complete the steps of scientific methods in a specific order?

17 **Evaluating Conclusions** How could a scientist respond to another scientist who questioned her conclusion?

18 **Identifying Relationships** Science helps us save lives, use resources wisely, and have healthy surroundings. How can healthy surroundings help save lives?

19 **Making Comparisons** Why might a person who wanted to protect the environment have trouble deciding between being a science educator or an environmental scientist?

INTERPRETING GRAPHICS

Use the graph below to answer the questions that follow.

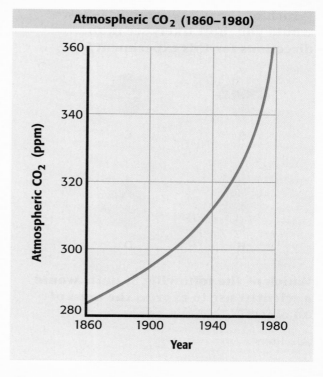

Atmospheric CO$_2$ (1860–1980)

Year

Atmospheric CO$_2$ (ppm)

20 Has the amount of CO$_2$ in the atmosphere increased or decreased since 1860?

21 The line on the graph is curved. What does this curve indicate?

22 Was the rate of change in the level of CO$_2$ between 1940 and 1960 higher or lower than it was between 1880 and 1900? How can you tell?

23 What conclusions can you draw from reading this graph?

Multiple Choice

1. You are preparing for an experiment in which you will test how different types of rock react to an acid solution. Which of the safety symbols below would you most likely see in the directions for this experiment?

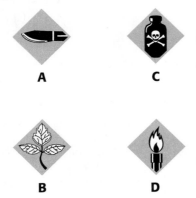

A   C

B   D

2. Which of the following SI units would a scientist use to express the mass of an object?

A. liters

B. kilograms

C. cubic meters

D. meters

3. What must a scientist always be sure of when testing a hypothesis?

A. that observations meet expectations

B. that records of observations are accurate

C. that observations are supported by opinions

D. that observations prove that a hypothesis is true

4. Which of the following physical properties does a graduated cylinder measure?

A. the density of an object

B. the mass of an object

C. the volume of an object

D. the temperature of an object

5. Which of the following types of models is based on making comparisons with familiar things to help illustrate or explain an idea?

A. conceptual models

B. climate models

C. physical models

D. mathematical model

The diagram below shows the steps of the scientific method.

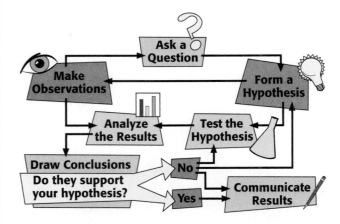

6. During which step would scientists organize the data they have collected?

A. Make Observations

B. Draw Conclusions

C. Test the Hypothesis

D. Analyze the Results

7. **How have mathematics and technology changed the way scientists create models?**

   A. Scientists can create models that prevent natural catastrophes.

   B. Scientists can create models that make exact predictions about the future.

   C. Scientists can create models from large amounts of data from many different variables.

   D. Scientists can create models that no longer require them to use scientific methods.

8. **When does the scientific community accept the results of a scientific experiment?**

   A. when other scientists have carefully reviewed the completed experiment

   B. before the results of an experiment have been communicated

   C. after a hypothesis has been developed

   D. during data gathering

9. **Why do scientists sometimes communicate different results about the same topic?**

   A. Not all scientists use scientific methods.

   B. The results of scientific experiments can never be reproduced.

   C. Scientists support only their own opinions.

   D. Scientific data can be interpreted in different ways.

10. **What do scientists do when the results of an experiment do not support a theory?**

   A. Scientists conduct further experiments.

   B. Scientists reject the results of the experiment.

   C. Scientists reject the theory.

   D. Scientists change the scientific method.

11. **Why do scientists keep accurate records of their data and share their data with other scientists?**

   A. The data support the scientists' hypothesis.

   B. The data can be analyzed by other scientists.

   C. The data prevent experiments from having to be repeated.

   D. The data will help all scientists to reach the same conclusions.

Open Response

12. **Geologists at state universities often study the properties of common local minerals and mineral deposits. Why is it important for researchers to study mineral resources found in their own states?**

13. **The U.S. National Hurricane Center has developed the SLOSH model to estimate the height of storm surges caused by hurricanes. A storm surge is water that is pushed onto the shore by high winds. The surge height is predicted using information about local shorelines and the hurricane. What kind of model is the SLOSH model? What characteristics of the shoreline and the hurricane would scientists study to create a SLOSH model?**

Science in Action

Science, Technology, and Society

A "Ship" That Flips?

Does your school's laboratory have doors on the floor or tables bolted sideways to the walls? A lab like this exists, and you can find it floating in the ocean. *FLIP,* or *Floating Instrument Platform,* is a 108 m long ocean research vessel that can tilt 90°. *FLIP* is towed to an area that scientists want to study. To flip the vessel, empty chambers within the vessel are filled with water. The *FLIP* begins tilting until almost all of the vessel is underwater. Having most of the vessel below the ocean's surface stabilizes the vessel against wind and waves. Scientists can collect accurate data from the ocean, even during a hurricane!

Social Studies ACTIVITY

Design your own *FLIP*. Make a map on poster board. Draw the layout of a living room, bathroom, and bedroom before your *FLIP* is tilted 90°. Include entrances and walkways to use when *FLIP* is not flipped.

Weird Science

It's Raining Fish and Frogs

What forms of precipitation have you seen fall from the sky? Rain, snow, hail, sleet, or fish? Wait a minute! Fish? Fish and frogs might not be a form of precipitation, but as early as the second century, they have been reported to fall from the sky during rainstorms. Scientists theorize that tornadoes or waterspouts that suck water into clouds can also suck up unsuspecting fish, frogs, or tadpoles that are near the surface of the water. After being sucked up into the clouds and carried a few miles, these reluctant travelers then rain down from the sky.

Language Arts ACTIVITY

WRITING SKILL You are a reporter for your local newspaper. On a rainy day in spring, while driving to work, you witness a downpour of frogs and fish. You pull off to the side of the road and interview other witnesses. Write an article describing this event for your local newspaper.

Sue Hendrickson

Paleontologist Could you imagine having a job in which you spent all day digging in the dirt? This is just one of Sue Hendrickson's job descriptions. But Hendrickson does not dig up flowers. Hendrickson is a paleontologist, and she digs up dinosaurs! Her most famous discovery is the bones of a *Tyrannosaurus rex*. *T. rex* is one of the largest meat-eating dinosaurs. It lived between 65 million and 85 million years ago. Walking tall at 6 m, *T. rex* was approximately 12.4 m long and weighed between 5 and 7 tons. Hendrickson's discovery is the most complete set of bones ever found of the *T. rex*. The dinosaur was named Sue to honor Hendrickson for her important find. From these bones, Hendrickson and other scientists have been able to learn more about the dinosaur, including how it lived millions of years ago. For example, Hendrickson and her team of scientists found the remains of Sue's last meal, part of a duck-billed, plant-eating dinosaur of the genus *Edmontosaurus* that weighed approximately 3.5 tons!

Math ACTIVITY

The *T. rex* named Sue weighed 7 tons and the *Edmontosaurus* dinosaur weighed 3.5 tons. How much smaller is *Edmontosaurus* than Sue? Express your answer as a percentage.

go.hrw.com

To learn more about these Science in Action topics, visit go.hrw.com and type in the keyword **HZ5WESF**.

Current Science

Check out Current Science® articles related to this chapter by visiting go.hrw.com. Just type in the keyword **HZ5CS01**.

UNIT 1

TIMELINE

Reshaping the Land

In this unit, you will learn about how the surface of the Earth is continuously reshaped. There is a constant struggle between the forces that build up the Earth's land features and the forces that break them down. This timeline shows some of the events that have occurred in this struggle as natural changes in the Earth's features took place.

320
Million years ago

Vast swamps along the western edge of the Appalachian Mountains are buried by sediment and form the largest coal fields in the world.

6
Million years ago

The Colorado River begins to carve the Grand Canyon, which is roughly 2 km deep today.

10,000
years ago

The Great Lakes form at the end of the last Ice Age.

1930

Carlsbad Caverns National Park is established. It features the nation's deepest limestone cave and one of the largest underground chambers in the world.

Carlsbad Caverns

280
Million years ago

The shallow inland sea that covered much of what is now the upper midwestern United States fills with sediment and disappears.

140
Million years ago

The mouth of the Mississippi River is near present-day Cairo, Illinois.

65
Million years ago

Dinosaurs become extinct.

1775

The Battle of Bunker Hill, a victory for the Colonials, takes place on a drumlin, a tear-shaped mound of sediment that was formed by an ice-age glacier 10,000 years earlier.

1879

Cleopatra's Needle, a granite obelisk, is moved from Egypt to New York City. Within the next 100 years, the weather and pollution severely damage the 3,000-year-old monument.

1987

An iceberg twice the size of Rhode Island breaks off the edge of Antarctica's continental glacier.

1998

Hong Kong opens a new airport on an artificially enlarged island. Almost 350 million cubic meters of rock and soil were deposited in the South China Sea to form the over 3,000-acre island.

2002

A NASA study finds that the arctic ice cap is melting at a rate of 9% per decade. At this rate, the ice cap could melt during this century.

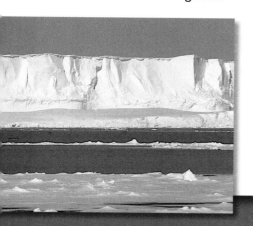

2

Weathering and Soil Formation

The Big Idea

Weathering is a continuous process that results in the formation of soil and the development of landforms.

About the Photo

Need a nose job, Mr. President? The carving of Thomas Jefferson that is part of the Mount Rushmore National Memorial is having its nose inspected by a National Parks worker. The process of weathering has caused cracks to form in the carving of President Jefferson. National Parks workers use a sealant to protect the memorial from moisture, which can cause further cracking.

PRE-READING ACTIVITY

FOLDNOTES **Key-Term Fold** Before you read the chapter, create the FoldNote entitled "Key-Term Fold" described in the **Study Skills** section of the Appendix. Write a key term from the chapter on each tab of the key-term fold. Under each tab, write the definition of the key term.

START-UP ACTIVITY

What's the Difference?

In this chapter, you will learn about the processes and rates of weathering. Complete this activity to learn about how the size and surface area of a substance affects how quickly the substance breaks down.

Procedure

1. Fill **two small containers** about half full with **water.**

2. Add **one sugar cube** to one container.

3. Add **1 tsp of granulated sugar** to the other container.

4. Using **one spoon for each container,** stir the water and sugar in each container at the same rate.

5. Using a **stopwatch,** measure how long it takes for the sugar to dissolve in each container.

Analysis

1. Did the sugar dissolve at the same rate in both containers? Explain why or why not.

2. Do you think one large rock or several smaller rocks would wear away faster? Explain your answer.

Weathering

If you have ever walked along a trail, you might have noticed small rocks lying around. Where did these rocks come from?

These smaller rocks came from larger rocks that were broken down. **Weathering** is the process by which rock materials are broken down by the action of physical or chemical processes.

Mechanical Weathering

If you were to crush one rock with another rock, you would be demonstrating one type of mechanical weathering. **Mechanical weathering** is the breakdown of rock into smaller pieces by physical means. Agents of mechanical weathering include ice, wind, water, gravity, plants, and even animals.

Ice

The alternate freezing and thawing of soil and rock, called *frost action,* is a form of mechanical weathering. One type of frost action, *ice wedging,* is shown in **Figure 1.** Ice wedging starts when water seeps into cracks during warm weather. When temperatures drop, the water freezes and expands. The ice then pushes against the sides of the crack. This causes the crack to widen.

weathering the process by which rock materials are broken down by the action of physical and chemical processes

mechanical weathering the breakdown of rock into smaller pieces by physical means

Figure 1 **Ice Wedging**

The granite in the photo has been broken down by repeated ice wedging, which is shown below.

Water

Ice

Water

Ice

Figure 2 Three Forms of Abrasion

These river rocks are rounded because they have been tumbled in the riverbed by fast-moving water for many years.

This rock has been shaped by blowing sand. Such rocks are called ventifacts.

Rocks grind against each other in a rock slide, which creates smaller and smaller rock fragments.

Abrasion

As you scrape a piece of chalk against a board, particles of the chalk rub off to make a line on the board and the piece of chalk wears down and becomes smaller. The same process, called *abrasion,* happens with rocks. **Abrasion** is the grinding and wearing away of rock surfaces through the mechanical action of other rock or sand particles.

Wind, Water, and Gravity

Abrasion can happen in many ways, as shown in **Figure 2.** When rocks and pebbles roll along the bottom of swiftly flowing rivers, they bump into and scrape against each other. The weathering that occurs eventually causes these rocks to become rounded and smooth.

Wind also causes abrasion. When wind blows sand and silt against exposed rock, the sand eventually wears away the rock's surface. The figure above (center) shows what this kind of sandblasting can do to a rock.

Abrasion also occurs when rocks fall on one another. You can imagine the forces rocks exert on each other as they tumble down a mountainside. In fact, anytime one rock hits another, abrasion takes place.

Reading Check Name three things that can cause abrasion. (*See the Appendix for answers to Reading Checks.*)

abrasion the grinding and wearing away of rock surfaces through the mechanical action of other rock or sand particles

Plants

You may not think of plants as being strong, but some plants can easily break rocks. Have you ever seen sidewalks and streets that are cracked because of tree roots? Roots don't grow fast, but they certainly are powerful! Plants often send their roots into existing cracks in rocks. As the plant grows, the force of the expanding root becomes so strong that the crack widens. Eventually, the entire rock can split apart, as shown in **Figure 3.**

Animals

Believe it or not, earthworms cause a lot of weathering! They burrow through the soil and move soil particles around. This exposes fresh surfaces to continued weathering. Would you believe that some kinds of tropical worms move an estimated 100 metric tons of soil per acre every year? Almost any animal that burrows causes mechanical weathering. Ants, worms, mice, coyotes, and rabbits are just some of the animals that contribute to weathering. **Figure 4** shows some of these animals in action. The mixing and digging that animals do often contribute to another type of weathering, called *chemical weathering.* You will learn about this type of weathering next.

✓ Reading Check List three animals that can cause weathering.

Figure 3 *Although they grow slowly, tree roots are strong enough to break solid rock.*

Figure 4 *Animals that live in the soil, such as moles, prairie dogs, insects, worms, and gophers, cause a lot of weathering. When the animals burrow in the ground, they break up soil and loosen rocks to be exposed to further weathering.*

Figure 5 Chemical Weathering of Granite

After thousands of years of chemical weathering, even hard rock, such as granite, can turn to sediment.

① Rain, weak acids, and air chemically weather granite.

② The bonds between mineral grains weaken as weathering proceeds.

③ When granite is weathered, it makes sand and clay, also called sediment.

Chemical Weathering

The process by which rocks break down as a result of chemical reactions is called **chemical weathering.** Common agents of chemical weathering are water, weak acids, and air.

Water

If you drop a sugar cube into a glass of water, the sugar cube will dissolve after a few minutes. This process is an example of chemical weathering. Even hard rock, such as granite, can be broken down by water. But, it just may take thousands of years. **Figure 5** shows how granite is chemically weathered.

Acid Precipitation

Rain, sleet, or snow, that contains a high concentration of acids is called **acid precipitation.** Precipitation is naturally acidic. However, acid precipitation contains more acid than normal precipitation. The high level of acidity can cause very rapid weathering of rock. Small amounts of sulfuric and nitric acids from natural sources, such as volcanoes, can make precipitation acidic. However, acid precipitation can also be caused by air pollution from the burning of fossil fuels, such as coal and oil. When these fuels are burned, they give off gases, including sulfur oxides, nitrogen oxides, and carbon oxides. When these compounds combine with water in the atmosphere, they form weak acids, which then fall back to the ground in rain and snow. When the acidity is too high, acid precipitation can be harmful to plants and animals.

chemical weathering the process by which rocks break down as a result of chemical reactions

acid precipitation rain, sleet, or snow, that contains a high concentration of acids

CONNECTION TO Chemistry

Acidity of Precipitation
Acidity is measured by using a pH scale, the units of which range from 0 to 14. Solutions that have a pH of less than 7 are acidic. Research some recorded pH levels of acid rain. Then, compare these pH levels with the pH levels of other common acids, such as lemon juice and acetic acid.

Figure 6 *Acid in groundwater has weathered limestone to form Carlsbad Caverns, in New Mexico.*

Acids in Groundwater

In certain places groundwater contains weak acids, such as carbonic or sulfuric acid. These acids react with rocks in the ground, such as limestone. When groundwater comes in contact with limestone, a chemical reaction occurs. Over a long period of time, the dissolving of limestone forms karst features, such as caverns. The caverns, like the one shown in **Figure 6,** form from the eating away of the limestone.

Acids in Living Things

Another source of acids that cause weathering might surprise you. Take a look at the lichens in **Figure 7.** Lichens produce acids that can slowly break down rock. If you have ever taken a walk in a park or forest, you have probably seen lichens growing on the sides of trees or rocks. Lichens can also grow in places where some of the hardiest plants cannot. For example, lichens can grow in deserts, in arctic areas, and in areas high above timberline, where even trees don't grow.

Figure 7 *Lichens, which consist of fungi and algae living together, contribute to chemical weathering.*

Quick Lab

Acids React!

1. Ketchup is one example of a food that contains weak acids, which react with certain substances. Take a **penny** that has a dull appearance, rub **ketchup** on it for several minutes.

2. Rinse the penny.

3. Where did all the grime on the penny go?

4. How is this process similar to what happens to a rock when it is exposed to natural acids during weathering?

Air

The car shown in **Figure 8** is undergoing chemical weathering due to the air. The oxygen in the air is reacting with the iron in the car, causing the car to rust. Water speeds up the process. But the iron would rust even if no water were present. Scientists call this process oxidation.

Oxidation is a chemical reaction in which an element, such as iron, combines with oxygen to form an oxide. This common form of chemical weathering is what causes rust. Old cars, aluminum cans, and your bike can experience oxidation if left exposed to air and rain for long periods of time.

Reading Check What can cause oxidation?

Figure 8 *Rust is a result of chemical weathering.*

SECTION Review

Summary

- Ice wedging is a form of mechanical weathering in which water seeps into rock cracks and then freezes and expands.
- Wind, water, and gravity cause mechanical weathering by abrasion.
- Animals and plants cause mechanical weathering by turning the soil and breaking apart rocks.
- Water, acids, and air chemically weather rock by weakening the bonds between mineral grains of the rock.

Using Key Terms

1. In your own words, write a definition for each of the following terms: *weathering, mechanical weathering, abrasion, chemical weathering* and *acid precipitation*.

Understanding Key Ideas

2. Which of the following things cannot cause mechanical weathering?
   a. water
   b. acid
   c. wind
   d. animals

3. List three things that cause chemical weathering of rocks.

4. Describe three ways abrasion occurs in nature.

5. Describe the similarity in the ways tree roots and ice mechanically weather rock.

6. Describe five sources of chemical weathering.

Critical Thinking

7. **Making Inferences** Why does acid precipitation weather rocks faster than normal precipitation?

8. **Making Comparisons** Compare the weather processes that affect a rock on top of a mountain and a rock buried beneath the ground.

Math Skills

9. Substances that have a pH of less than 7 are acidic. For each pH unit lower, the acidity is ten times greater. For example, normal precipitation is slightly acidic at a 5.6 pH. If acid precipitation were measured at 4.6 pH, it would be 10 times more acidic than normal precipitation. How many times more acidic would precipitation at 3.6 pH be than normal precipitation?

SCiLINKS®

NSTA
Developed and maintained by the
National Science Teachers Association

For a variety of links related to this chapter, go to www.scilinks.org

Topic: Weathering
SciLinks code: HSM1648

Rates of Weathering

Have you ever seen a cartoon in which a character falls off a cliff and lands on a ledge? Ledges exist in nature because the rock that the ledge is made of weathers more slowly than the surrounding rock.

Weathering is a process that takes a long time. However, some rock will weather faster than other rock. The rate at which a rock weathers depends on climate, elevation, and the makeup of the rock.

Differential Weathering

Hard rocks, such as granite, weather more slowly than softer rocks, such as limestone. **Differential weathering** is a process by which softer, less weather resistant rocks wear away and leave harder, more weather resistant rocks behind.

Figure 1 shows a landform that has been shaped by differential weathering. Devils Tower was once a mass of molten rock deep inside an active volcano. When the molten rock cooled and hardened, it was protected from weathering by the outer rock of the volcano. After thousands of years of weathering, the soft outer parts of the volcano have worn away. The harder, more resistant rock is all that remains.

Figure 1 *The illustration is an artist's idea of how the original volcano may have looked. The photo inset shows Devils Tower as it appears today.*

The Shape of Rocks

Weathering takes place on the outer surface of rocks. Therefore, the more surface area that is exposed to weathering, the faster the rock will be worn down. A large rock has a large surface area. But a large rock also has a large volume. Because of the large rock's volume, the large rock will take a long time to wear down.

If a large rock is broken into smaller fragments, weathering of the rock happens much more quickly. The rate of weathering increases because a smaller rock has more surface area to volume than a larger rock has. So, more of a smaller rock is exposed to the weathering process. **Figure 2** shows this concept in detail.

differential weathering the process by which softer, less weather resistant rocks wear away and leave harder, more weather resistant rocks behind

✓ **Reading Check** How does an increase in surface area affect the rate of weathering? (*See the Appendix for answers to Reading Checks.*)

Figure 2 Total Surface Area to Volume

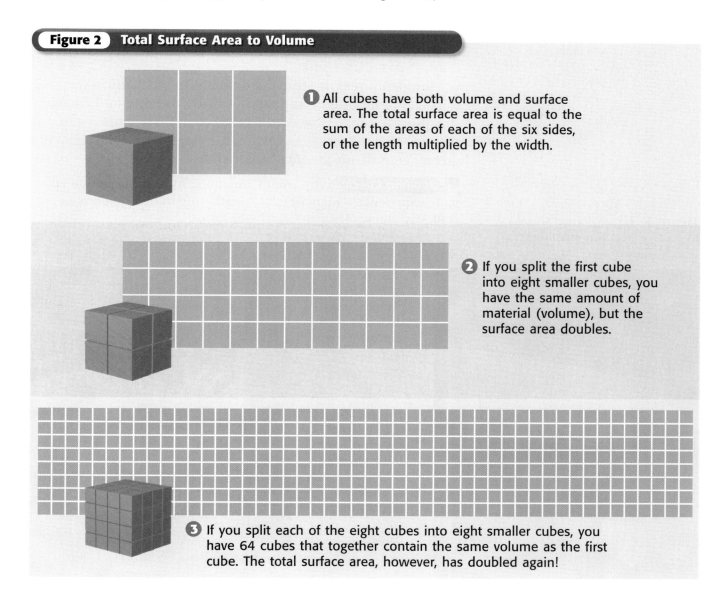

❶ All cubes have both volume and surface area. The total surface area is equal to the sum of the areas of each of the six sides, or the length multiplied by the width.

❷ If you split the first cube into eight smaller cubes, you have the same amount of material (volume), but the surface area doubles.

❸ If you split each of the eight cubes into eight smaller cubes, you have 64 cubes that together contain the same volume as the first cube. The total surface area, however, has doubled again!

Weathering and Climate

The rate of weathering in an area is greatly affected by the climate of that area. *Climate* is the average weather condition in an area over a long period of time. For example, the two mailboxes shown in **Figure 3** are in two different climates. The mailbox on the left is in a dry climate. The mailbox on the right is in a warm, humid climate. As you can see, the mailbox in the warm, humid climate is rusty.

Temperature and Water

The rate of chemical weathering is faster in warm, humid climates. The rusty mailbox has experienced a type of chemical weathering called oxidation. Oxidation, like other chemical reactions, happens at a faster rate when temperatures are higher and when water is present.

Water also increases the rate of mechanical weathering. The freezing of water that seeps into the cracks of rocks is the process of ice wedging. Ice wedging causes rocks to break apart. Over time, this form of weathering can break down even the hardest rocks into soil.

Temperature is another major factor in mechanical weathering. The more often temperatures cause freezing and thawing, the more often ice wedging takes place. Therefore, climatic regions that experience frequent freezes and thaws have a greater rate of mechanical weathering.

✓ Reading Check Why would a mailbox in a warm, humid climate experience a higher rate of weathering than a mailbox in a cold, dry climate?

Figure 3 *These photos show the effects different climates can have on rates of weathering.*

This mailbox is in a dry climate and does not experience a high rate of weathering.

This mailbox ▶ *is in a warm, humid climate. It experiences a high rate of chemical weathering called oxidation.*

Weathering and Elevation

Just like everything else, mountains are exposed to air and water. As a result, mountain ranges are weathered down. Weathering happens on mountains in the same way it does everywhere else. However, as shown in **Figure 4,** rocks at higher elevations, as on a mountain, are exposed to more wind, rain, and ice than the rocks at lower elevations are. This increase in wind, rain, and ice at higher elevations causes the peaks of mountains to weather faster.

Gravity affects weathering, too. The steepness of mountain slopes increases the effects of mechanical and chemical weathering. Steep slopes cause rainwater to quickly run off the sides of mountains. The rainwater carries the sediment down the mountain's slope. This continual removal of sediment exposes fresh rock surfaces to the effects of weathering. New rock surfaces are also exposed to weathering when gravity causes rocks to fall away from the sides of mountains. The increased surface area means weathering happens at a faster rate.

Reading Check Why do mountaintops weather faster than rocks at sea level?

Figure 4 *The ice, rain, and wind that these mountain peaks are exposed to cause them to weather at a fast rate.*

SECTION Review

Summary

- Hard rocks weather more slowly than softer rocks.
- The more surface area of a rock that is exposed to weathering, the faster the rock will be worn down.
- Chemical weathering occurs faster in warm, humid climates.
- Weathering occurs faster at high elevations because of an increase in ice, rain, and wind.

Using Key Terms

1. In your own words, write a definition for the term *differential weathering*.

Understanding Key Ideas

2. A rock will have a lower rate of weathering when the rock
   a. is in a humid climate.
   b. is a very hard rock, such as granite.
   c. is at a high elevation.
   d. has more surface area exposed to weathering.

3. How does surface area affect the rate of weathering?

4. How does climate affect the rate of weathering?

5. Why does the peak of a mountain weather faster than the rocks at the bottom of the mountain?

Math Skills

6. The surface area of an entire cube is 96 cm². If the length and width of each side are equal, what is the length of one side of the cube?

Critical Thinking

7. **Making Inferences** Does the rate of chemical weathering increase or stay the same when a rock becomes more mechanically weathered? Why?

SCiLINKS

NSTA
Developed and maintained by the National Science Teachers Association

For a variety of links related to this chapter, go to www.scilinks.org

Topic: Rates of Weathering
SciLinks code: HSM1269

From Bedrock to Soil

Most plants need soil to grow. But what exactly is soil? Where does it come from?

What You Will Learn

● Describe the source of soil.
● Explain how the different properties of soil affect plant growth.
● Describe how various climates affect soil.

Vocabulary

soil	soil structure
parent rock	humus
bedrock	leaching
soil texture	

READING STRATEGY

Prediction Guide Before you read this section, write the title of each heading in this section. Next, under each heading, write what you think you will learn.

The Source of Soil

To a scientist, **soil** is a loose mixture of small mineral fragments, organic material, water, and air that can support the growth of vegetation. But not all soils are the same. Because soils are made from weathered rock fragments, the type of soil that forms depends on the type of rock that weathers. The rock formation that is the source of mineral fragments in the soil is called **parent rock.**

Bedrock is the layer of rock beneath soil. In this case, the bedrock is the parent rock because the soil above it formed from the bedrock below. Soil that remains above its parent rock is called *residual soil.*

Soil can be blown or washed away from its parent rock. This soil is called *transported soil.* **Figure 1** shows one way that soil is moved from one place to another. Both wind and the movement of glaciers are also responsible for transporting soil.

✓ **Reading Check** What is soil formed from? (*See the Appendix for answers to Reading Checks.*)

soil a loose mixture of rock fragments, organic material, water, and air that can support the growth of vegetation

parent rock a rock formation that is the source of soil

bedrock the layer of rock beneath soil

Figure 1 *Transported soil may be moved long distances from its parent rock by rivers, such as this one.*

Figure 2 Soil Texture

The proportion of these different-sized particles in soil determine the soil's texture.

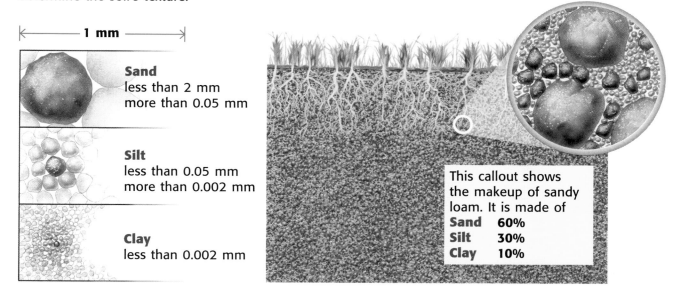

← 1 mm →

Sand
less than 2 mm
more than 0.05 mm

Silt
less than 0.05 mm
more than 0.002 mm

Clay
less than 0.002 mm

This callout shows the makeup of sandy loam. It is made of
Sand   60%
Silt   30%
Clay   10%

Soil Properties

Some soils are great for growing plants. Other soils can't support the growth of plants. To better understand soil, you will next learn about its properties, such as soil texture, soil structure, and soil fertility.

Soil Texture and Soil Structure

Soil is made of different-sized particles. These particles can be as large as 2 mm, such as sand. Other particles can be too small to see without a microscope. **Soil texture** is the soil quality that is based on the proportions of soil particles. **Figure 2** shows the soil texture for a one type of soil.

Soil texture affects the soil's consistency. Consistency describes a soil's ability to be worked and broken up for farming. For example, soil texture that has a large proportion of clay can be hard and difficult for farmers to break up.

Soil texture influences the *infiltration,* or ability of water to move through soil. Soil should allow water to get to the plants' roots without causing the soil to be completely saturated.

Water and air movement through soil is also influenced by soil structure. **Soil structure** is the arrangement of soil particles. Soil particles are not always evenly spread out. Often, one type of soil particle will clump in an area. A clump of one type of soil can either block water flow or help water flow, which affects soil moisture.

soil texture the soil quality that is based on the proportions of soil particles.

soil structure the arrangement of soil particles

Soil Fertility

Nutrients in soil, such as iron, are necessary for plants to grow. Some soils are rich in nutrients. Other soils may not have many nutrients or are not able to supply the nutrients to the plants. A soil's ability to hold nutrients and to supply nutrients to a plant is described as *soil fertility*. Many nutrients in soil come from the parent rock. Other nutrients come from **humus,** which is the organic material formed in soil from the decayed remains of plants and animals. These remains are broken down into nutrients by decomposers, such as bacteria and fungi.

Soil Horizons

Because of the way soil forms, soil often ends up in a series of layers, with humus-rich soil on top, sediment below that, and bedrock on the bottom. Geologists call these layers *horizons*. The word *horizon* tells you that the layers are horizontal. **Figure 3** shows what these horizons can look like. You can see these layers in some road cuts.

The top layer of soil is often called the *topsoil*. Topsoil contains more humus than the layers below it. The humus is rich in the nutrients plants need to be healthy. This is why good topsoil is necessary for farming.

humus the dark, organic material formed in soil from the decayed remains of plants and animals

leaching the removal of substances that can be dissolved from rock, ore, or layers of soil due to the passing of water

Figure 3   Soil Horizons

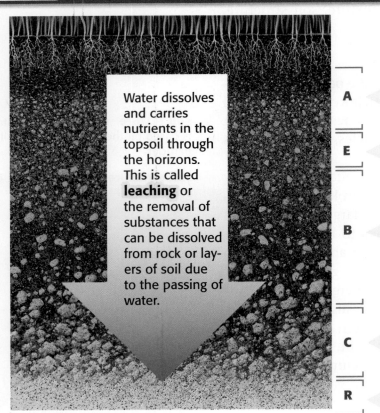

Water dissolves and carries nutrients in the topsoil through the horizons. This is called **leaching** or the removal of substances that can be dissolved from rock or layers of soil due to the passing of water.

A This horizon consists of the topsoil. Topsoil contains more humus than any other soil horizon. Soil in forests often has an O horizon. The O horizon is made up of litter from dead plants and animals.

E This horizon experiences intense leaching of nutrients.

B This horizon collects the dissolved substances and nutrients deposited from the upper horizons.

C This horizon is made of partially weathered bedrock.

R This horizon is made of bedrock that has little or no weathering.

Soil pH

Soils can be acidic or basic. The pH scale is used to measure how acidic or basic a soil is and ranges from 0 to 14. The midpoint, which is 7, is neutral. Soil that has a pH below 7 is acidic. Soil that has a pH above 7 is basic.

The pH of a soil influences how nutrients dissolve in the soil. For example, plants are unable to take up certain nutrients from soils that are basic, or that have a high pH. Soils that have a low pH can restrict other important nutrients from hungry plants. Because different plants need different nutrients, the right pH for a soil depends on the plants growing in it.

Soil and Climate

Soil types vary from place to place. One reason for this is the differences in climate. As you read on, you will see that climate can make a difference in the types of soils that develop around the world.

Tropical Rain Forest Climates

Take a look at **Figure 4.** In tropical rain forest climates, the air is very humid and the land receives a large amount of rain. Because of warm temperatures, crops can be grown year-round. The warm soil temperature also allows dead plants and animals to decay easily. This provides rich humus to the soil.

Because of the lush plant growth, you may think that tropical rain forest soils are the most nutrient-rich in the world. However, tropical rain forest soils are nutrient poor. The heavy rains in this climate leach precious nutrients from the topsoil into deeper layers of soil. The result is that tropical topsoil is very thin. Another reason tropical rain forest soil is nutrient poor is that the lush vegetation has a great demand for nutrients. The nutrients that aren't leached away are quickly taken up by plants and trees that live off the soil.

✓ **Reading Check** Why is the topsoil in tropical rain forests thin?

CONNECTION TO
Social Studies

WRITING SKILL **Deforestation in Brazil** In Brazil, rain forests have been cut down at an alarmingly high rate, mostly by farmers. However, tropical rain forest topsoil is very thin and is not suitable for long-term farming. Research the long-term effects of deforestation on the farmers and indigenous people of Brazil. Then, write a one page report on your findings.

Figure 4 *Lush tropical rain forests have surprisingly thin topsoil.*

Figure 5 *The salty conditions of desert soils make it difficult for many plants to survive.*

INTERNET ACTIVITY

For another activity related to this chapter, go to **go.hrw.com** and type in the keyword **HZ5WSFW.**

Desert Climates

While tropical climates get a lot of rain, deserts get less than 25 cm a year. Leaching of nutrients is not a problem in desert soils. But the lack of rain causes many other problems, such as very low rates of chemical weathering and less ability to support plant and animal life. A low rate of weathering means soil is created at a slower rate.

Some water is available from groundwater. Groundwater can trickle in from surrounding areas and seep to the surface. But as soon as the water is close to the surface, it evaporates. So, any materials that were dissolved in the water are left behind in the soil. Without the water to dissolve the minerals, the plants are unable to take them up. Often, the chemicals left behind are various types of salts. These salts can sometimes become so concentrated that the soil becomes toxic, or poisonous, even to desert plants! Death Valley, shown in **Figure 5,** is a desert that has toxic levels of salt in the soil.

Temperate Forest and Grassland Climates

Much of the continental United States has a temperate climate. An abundance of weathering occurs in temperate climates. Temperate areas get enough rain to cause a high level of chemical weathering, but not so much that the nutrients are leached out of the soil. Frequent changes in temperature lead to frost action. As a result, thick, fertile soils develop, as shown in **Figure 6.**

Temperate soils are some of the most-productive soils in the world. In fact, the midwestern part of the United States has earned the nickname "breadbasket" for the many crops the region's soil supports.

Reading Check Which climate has the most-productive soil?

Figure 6 *The rich soils in areas that have a temperate climate support a vast farming industry.*

Arctic Climates

Arctic areas have so little precipitation that they are like cold deserts. In arctic climates, as in desert climates, chemical weathering occurs very slowly. So, soil formation also occurs slowly. Slow soil formation is why soil in arctic areas, as shown in **Figure 7,** is thin and unable to support many plants.

Arctic climates also have low soil temperatures. At low temperatures, decomposition of plants and animals happens more slowly or stops completely. Slow decomposition limits the amount of humus in the soil, which limits the nutrients available. These nutrients are necessary for plant growth.

Figure 7 *Arctic soils, such as the soil along Denali Highway, in Alaska, cannot support lush vegetation.*

SECTION Review

Summary

- Soil is formed from the weathering of bedrock.
- Soil texture affects how soil can be worked for farming and how well water passes through it.
- The ability of soil to provide nutrients so that plants can survive and grow is called *soil fertility*.
- The pH of a soil influences which nutrients plants can take up from the soil.
- Different climates have different types of soil, depending on the temperature and rainfall.

Using Key Terms

1. Use each of the following terms in a separate sentence: *soil, parent rock, bedrock, soil texture, soil structure, humus,* and *leaching.*

Understanding Key Ideas

2. Which of the following soil properties influences soil moisture?
   a. soil horizon
   b. soil fertility
   c. soil structure
   d. soil pH

3. Which of the following soil properties influences how nutrients can be dissolved in soil?
   a. soil texture
   b. soil fertility
   c. soil structure
   d. soil pH

4. When is parent rock the same as bedrock?

5. What is the difference between residual and transported soils?

6. Which climate has the most thick, fertile soil?

7. How does soil temperature influence arctic soil?

Math Skills

8. If a soil sample is 60% sand particles and has 30 million particles of soil, how many of those soil particles are sand?

Critical Thinking

9. **Identifying Relationships** In which type of climate would leaching be more common—tropical rain forest or desert?

10. **Making Comparisons** Although arctic climates are extremely different from desert climates, their soils may be somewhat similar. Explain why.

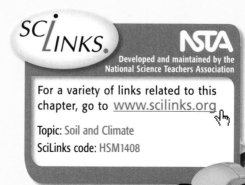

SCI LINKS®

NSTA

Developed and maintained by the National Science Teachers Association

For a variety of links related to this chapter, go to www.scilinks.org

Topic: Soil and Climate
SciLinks code: HSM1408

Soil Conservation

Believe it or not, soil can be endangered, just like plants and animals. Because soil takes thousands of years to form, it is not easy to replace.

What You Will Learn

● Describe three important benefits that soil provides.
● Describe four methods of preventing soil damage and loss.

Vocabulary

soil conservation
erosion

READING STRATEGY

Reading Organizer As you read this section, make a table comparing the four methods of preventing soil damage and loss.

soil conservation a method to maintain the fertility of the soil by protecting the soil from erosion and nutrient loss

If we do not take care of our soils, we can ruin them or even lose them. Soil is a resource that must be conserved. **Soil conservation** is a method to maintain the fertility of the soil by protecting the soil from erosion and nutrient loss.

The Importance of Soil

Soil provides minerals and other nutrients for plants. If the soil loses these nutrients, then plants will not be able to grow. Take a look at the plants shown in **Figure 1.** The plants on the right look unhealthy because they are not getting enough nutrients. There is enough soil to support the plant's roots, but the soil is not providing them with the food they need. The plants on the left are healthy because the soil they live in is rich in nutrients.

All animals get their energy from plants. The animals get their energy either by eating the plants or by eating animals that have eaten plants. So, if plants can't get their nutrients from the soil, animals can't get their nutrients from plants.

✓ **Reading Check** Why is soil important? (*See the Appendix for answers to Reading Checks.*)

Housing

Soil also provides a place for animals to live. The region where a plant or animal lives is called its *habitat*. Earthworms, grubs, spiders, ants, moles, and prairie dogs all live in soil. If the soil disappears, so does the habitat for these animals.

Figure 1 *Both of these photos show the same crop, but the soil in the photo on the right is poor in nutrients.*

Water Storage

Soil is also extremely important to plants for water storage. Without soil to hold water, plants would not get the moisture or the nutrients they need. Soil also keeps water from running off, flowing elsewhere, and possibly causing flooding.

Soil Damage and Loss

What would happen if there were no soil? Soil loss is a serious problem around the world. Soil damage can lead to soil loss. Soil can be damaged from overuse by poor farming techniques or by overgrazing. Overused soil can lose its nutrients and become infertile. Plants can't grow in soil that is infertile. Without plants to hold and help cycle water, the area can become a desert. This process, formally known as *desertification,* is called *land degradation*. Without plants and moisture, the soil can be blown or washed away.

Soil Erosion

When soil is left unprotected, it can be exposed to erosion. **Erosion** is the process by which wind, water, or gravity transport soil and sediment from one location to another. **Figure 2** shows Providence Canyon, which was formed from the erosion of soil when trees were cut down to clear land for farming. Roots from plants and trees are like anchors to the soil. Roots keep topsoil from being eroded. Therefore, plants and trees protect the soil. By taking care of the vegetation, you also take care of the soil.

Making Soil

Suppose it takes 500 years for 2 cm of new soil to form in a certain area. But the soil is eroding at a rate of 1 mm per year. Is the soil eroding faster than it can be replaced? Explain.

erosion the process by which wind, water, ice, or gravity transport soil and sediment from one location to another

Figure 2 *Providence Canyon has suffered soil erosion from the cutting of forests for farmland.*

Figure 3 Soil Conservation Techniques

Contour plowing helps prevent erosion from heavy rains.

Terracing prevents erosion from heavy rains on steep hills.

No-till farming prevents erosion by providing cover that reduces water runoff.

Soybeans are a **cover crop** which restores nutrients to soil.

Contour Plowing and Terracing

If farmers plowed rows so that they ran up and down hills, what might happen during a heavy rain? The rows would act as river valleys and channel the rainwater down the hill, which would erode the soil. To prevent erosion in this way, a farmer could plow across the slope of the hills. This is called contour plowing. In *contour plowing,* the rows act as a series of dams instead of a series of rivers. **Figure 3** shows contour plowing and three other methods of soil conservation. If the hills are really steep, farmers can use *terracing.* Terracing changes one steep field into a series of smaller, flatter fields. *No-till farming,* which is the practice of leaving old stalks, provides cover from rain. The cover reduces water runoff and slows soil erosion.

Cover Crop and Crop Rotation

In the southern United States, during the early 1900s, the soil had become nutrient poor by the farming of only one crop, cotton. George Washington Carver, the scientist shown in **Figure 4,** urged farmers to plant soybeans and peanuts instead of cotton. Some plants, such as soybeans and peanuts, helped to restore important nutrients to the soil. These plants are called cover crops. *Cover crops* are crops that are planted between harvests to replace certain nutrients and prevent erosion. Cover crops prevent erosion by providing cover from wind and rain.

Another way to slow down nutrient depletion is through *crop rotation.* If the same crop is grown year after year in the same field, certain nutrients become depleted. To slow this process, a farmer can plant different crops. A different crop will use up less nutrients or different nutrients from the soil.

✓ **Reading Check** What can soybeans and peanuts do for nutrient-poor soil?

Figure 4 *George Washington Carver taught soil conservation techniques to farmers.*

SECTION Review

Summary

- Soil is important for plants to grow, for animals to live in, and for water to be stored.
- Soil erosion and soil damage can be prevented by no-till farming, contour plowing, terracing, using cover crop, and practicing crop rotation.

Using Key Terms

1. In your own words, write a definition for each of the following terms: *soil conservation* and *erosion.*

Understanding Key Ideas

2. What are three important benefits that soil provides?

3. Practicing which of the following soil conservation techniques will replace nutrients in the soil?
   a. cover crop use
   b. no-till farming
   c. terracing
   d. contour plowing

4. How does crop rotation benefit soil?

5. List five methods of soil conservation, and describe how each helps prevent the loss of soil.

Math Skills

6. Suppose it takes 500 years to form 2 cm of new soil without erosion. If a farmer needs at least 35 cm of soil to plant a particular crop, how many years will the farmer need to wait before planting his or her crop?

Critical Thinking

7. **Applying Concepts** Why do land animals, even meat eaters, depend on soil to survive?

For a variety of links related to this chapter, go to www.scilinks.org

Topic: Soil Conservation
SciLinks code: HSM1409

Model-Making Lab

Rockin' Through Time

Wind, water, and gravity constantly change rocks. As wind and water rush over the rocks, the rocks may be worn smooth. As rocks bump against one another, their shapes change. The form of mechanical weathering that occurs as rocks collide and scrape together is called *abrasion*. In this activity, you will shake some pieces of limestone to model the effects of abrasion.

OBJECTIVES

Design a model to understand how abrasion breaks down rocks.

Evaluate the effects of abrasion.

MATERIALS

- bottle, plastic, wide-mouthed, with lid, 3 L
- graph paper or computer
- markers
- pieces of limestone, all about the same size (24)
- poster board
- tap water

SAFETY

Ask a Question

1 How does abrasion break down rocks? How can I use this information to identify rocks that have been abraded in nature?

Form a Hypothesis

2 Formulate a hypothesis that answers the questions above.

Test the Hypothesis

3 Copy the chart on the next page onto a piece of poster board. Allow enough space to place rocks in each square.

4 Lay three of the limestone pieces on the poster board in the area marked "0 shakes." Be careful not to bump the poster board after you have added the rocks.

5 Place the remaining 21 rocks in the 3 L bottle. Then, fill the bottle halfway with water.

6 Close the lid of the bottle securely. Shake the bottle vigorously 100 times.

7 Remove three rocks from the bottle, and place them on the poster board in the box that indicates the number of times the rocks have been shaken.

8 Repeat steps 6 and 7 six times until all of the rocks have been added to the board.

Analyze the Results

1 **Examining Data** Describe the surface of the rocks that you placed in the area marked "0 shakes." Are they smooth or rough?

2 **Describing Events** How did the shape of the rocks change as you performed this activity?

3 **Constructing Graphs** Using graph paper or a computer, construct a graph, table, or chart that describes how the shapes of the rocks changed as a result of the number of times they were shaken.

Draw Conclusions

4 **Drawing Conclusions** Why did the rocks change?

5 **Evaluating Results** How did the water change during the activity? Why did it change?

6 **Making Predictions** What would happen if you used a much harder rock, such as granite, for this experiment?

7 **Interpreting Information** How do the results of this experiment compare with what happens in a river?

Rocks Table	
0 shakes	100 shakes
200 shakes	300 shakes
400 shakes	500 shakes
600 shakes	700 shakes

Chapter Review

USING KEY TERMS

1 In your own words, write a definition for each of the following terms: *abrasion* and *soil texture*.

2 Use each of the following terms in a separate sentence: *soil conservation* and *erosion*.

For each pair of terms, explain how the meanings of the terms differ.

3 *mechanical weathering* and *chemical weathering*

4 *soil* and *parent rock*

UNDERSTANDING KEY IDEAS

Multiple Choice

5 Which of the following processes is a possible effect of water?

  a. mechanical weathering
  b. chemical weathering
  c. abrasion
  d. All of the above

6 In which climate would you find the fastest rate of chemical weathering?

  a. a warm, humid climate
  b. a cold, humid climate
  c. a cold, dry climate
  d. a warm, dry climate

7 Which of the following properties does soil texture affect?

  a. soil pH
  b. soil temperature
  c. soil consistency
  d. None of the above

8 Which of the following properties describes a soil's ability to supply nutrients?

  a. soil structure
  b. infiltration
  c. soil fertility
  d. consistency

9 Soil is important because it provides

  a. housing for animals.
  b. nutrients for plants.
  c. storage for water.
  d. All of the above

10 Which of the following soil conservation techniques prevents erosion?

  a. contour plowing
  b. terracing
  c. no-till farming
  d. All of the above

Short Answer

11 Describe the two major types of weathering.

12 Why is Devils Tower higher than the surrounding area?

13 Why is soil in temperate forests thick and fertile?

14 What can happen to soil when soil conservation is not practiced?

15 Describe the process of land degradation.

16 How do cover crops help prevent soil erosion?

CRITICAL THINKING

17 Concept Mapping Use the following terms to create a concept map: *weathering, chemical weathering, mechanical weathering, abrasion, ice wedging, oxidation,* and *soil.*

18 Analyzing Processes Heat generally speeds up chemical reactions. But weathering, including chemical weathering, is usually slowest in hot, dry climates. Why?

19 Making Inferences Mechanical weathering, such as ice wedging, increases surface area by breaking larger rocks into smaller rocks. Draw conclusions about how mechanical weathering can affect the rate of chemical weathering.

20 Evaluating Data A scientist has a new theory. She believes that climates that receive heavy rains all year long have thin topsoil. Given what you have learned, decide if the scientist's theory is correct. Explain your answer.

21 Analyzing Processes What forms of mechanical and chemical weathering would be most common in the desert? Explain your answer.

22 Applying Concepts If you had to plant a crop on a steep hill, what soil conservation techniques would you use to prevent erosion?

23 Making Comparisons Compare the weathering processes in a warm, humid climate with those in a dry, cold climate.

INTERPRETING GRAPHICS

The graph below shows how the density of water changes when temperature changes. The denser a substance is, the less volume it occupies. In other words, as most substances get colder, they contract and become denser. But water is unlike most other substances. When water freezes, it expands and becomes less dense. Use the graph below to answer the questions that follow.

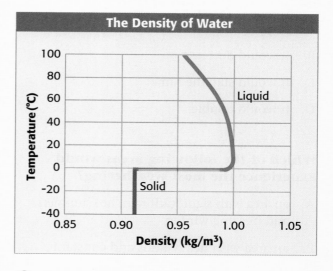

The Density of Water

24 Which has the greater density: water at 40°C or water at –20°C?

25 How would the line in the graph look if water behaved like most other liquids?

26 Which substance would be a more effective agent of mechanical weathering: water or another liquid? Why?

Standardized Test Preparation

Multiple Choice

1. Water chemically breaks down rock because

  A. water expands when it freezes.

  B. acids in the water react with substances in the rock.

  C. materials dissolved in the water are deposited.

  D. water is not affected by wind.

2. If a region's average annual precipitation changed from moderate to a very low level, what would probably happen to the rate of chemical weathering?

  A. It would increase slightly.

  B. It would decrease.

  C. It would stay the same.

  D. It would double.

3. Which of the following areas would experience the most weathering?

  A. an area with significant rain, hot summers, and freezing winters

  B. an area with heavy rains and constant temperatures

  C. an area with constant heat and minimal rain

  D. All areas are subject to the same amounts of weathering.

4. Which of the following statements describes how a rock changes after it is in a riverbed for a long time?

  A. The rock rapidly breaks into smaller pieces.

  B. Chunks of the rock break off, and the rock becomes rougher.

  C. The edges of the rock are worn away, so its surface becomes smoother.

  D. The rock absorbs water from the riverbed and becomes softer.

Use the picture below to answer question 5.

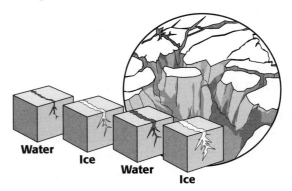

5. The picture above shows the process of mechanical weathering that can cause cracks in rocks in Georgia's northern mountains to widen. What is this process called?

  A. abrasion

  B. dissolution

  C. ice wedging

  D. oxidation

6. How is it possible for air to chemically weather rock?

A. The air molecules are abrasive.

B. Air fills cracks in the rock and later expands, causing the cracks to enlarge.

C. The oxygen in the air combines with elements in the rock in a process called oxidation.

D. The rock cracks after absorbing too much oxygen in a process called oxidation.

7. If a granite statue is moved from a desert town in Arizona to a warm and humid coastal town in Florida, what would most likely happen to the statue's rate of chemical weathering?

A. It would decrease.

B. It would increase.

C. It would remain the same.

D. Not enough information is given to determine the rates of weathering.

8. Which of the following is an everyday example of a chemical phenomenon?

A. Fast-moving river water rushes over rocks.

B. Organic acids produced by lichens break down rock.

C. Rocks tumble down a mountain during a rockslide.

D. Ice forms in a crack in a rock and makes the crack larger.

Use the chart below to answer question 9.

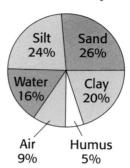

9. Naomi made the pie chart above during a laboratory experiment in which she analyzed the composition of soil found in Georgia. Based on this chart, which of the following is a valid conclusion?

A. Approximately 95% of loam's composition is useless to plants in terms of their survival.

B. Decayed organic matter is the least abundant component of loam.

C. Only about 9% of loam's composition is beneficial to plants.

D. Only about 16% of loam's composition is beneficial to plants.

Open Response

10. When people clear tropical rain forests, the ecological impact can be very negative. If cleared land is not replanted very quickly with trees and crops, the soil will wash away. Why might farmers move from one plot of this land to another, increasing the negative impact?

11. Why is the soil of tropical rain forests nutrient-poor?

Standardized Test Preparation

Science in Action

Science, Technology, and Society

Flying Fertilizer

Would you believe that dust from storms in large deserts can be transported over the oceans to different continents? Dust from the Gobi Desert in China has traveled all the way to Hawaii! In many cases, the dust is a welcome guest. Iron in dust from the Sahara, a desert in Africa, fertilizes the canopies of South American rain forests. In fact, research has shown that the canopies of Central and South American rain forests get much of their nutrients from dust from the Sahara!

Social Studies ACTiViTY

Find pictures on the Internet or in magazines that show how people in rain forests live. Make a poster by using the pictures you find.

Scientific Discoveries

Strange Soil

Mysterious patterns of circles, polygons, and stripes were discovered in the soil in remote areas in Alaska and the Norwegian islands. At first, scientists were puzzled by these strange designs in remote areas. Then, the scientists discovered that these patterns were created by the area's weathering process, which includes cycles of freezing and thawing. When the soil freezes, the soil expands. When the soil thaws, the soil contracts. This process moves and sorts the particles of the soil into patterns.

Language Arts ACTiViTY

WRITING SKILL Write a creative short story describing what life would be like if you were a soil circle on one of these remote islands.

J. David Bamberger

Habitat Restoration J. David Bamberger knows how important taking care of the environment is. Therefore, he has turned his ranch into the largest habitat restoration project in Texas. For Bamberger, restoring the habitat started with restoring the soil. One way Bamberger restored the soil was to manage the grazing of the grasslands and to make sure that grazing animals didn't expose the soil. Overgrazing causes soil erosion. When cattle clear the land of its grasses, the soil is exposed to wind and rain, which can wash the topsoil away.

Bamberger also cleared his land of most of the shrub, *juniper*. Juniper requires so much water per day that it leaves little water in the soil for the grasses and wildflowers. The change in the ranch since Bamberger first bought it in 1959 is most obvious at the fence-line border of his ranch. Beyond the fence is a small forest of junipers and little other vegetation. On Bamberger's side, the ranch is lush with grasses, wildflowers, trees, and shrubs.

Math Activity

Bamberger's ranch is 2,300 hectares. There are 0.405 hectares in 1 acre. How many acres is Bamberger's ranch?

go.hrw.com

To learn more about these Science in Action topics, visit **go.hrw.com** and type in the keyword **HZ5WSFF**.

Current Science

Check out Current Science® articles related to this chapter by visiting **go.hrw.com**. Just type in the keyword **HZ5CS10**.

3

The Flow of Fresh Water

The Big Idea

The flow of water on Earth's surface and underground is the dominant process in shaping the landscape.

About the Photo

You can hear the roar of Iguaçu (EE gwah SOO) Falls for miles. The Iguaçu River travels more than 500 km across Brazil before it tumbles off the edge of a volcanic plateau in a series of 275 individual waterfalls. Over the past 20,000 years, erosion has caused the falls to move 28 km upstream.

PRE-READING ACTIVITY

FOLDNOTES **Booklet** Before you read the chapter, create the FoldNote entitled "Booklet" described in the **Study Skills** section of the Appendix. Label each page of the booklet with a main idea from the chapter. As you read the chapter, write what you learn about each main idea on the appropriate page of the booklet.

Stream Weavers

Do the following activity to learn how streams and river systems develop.

Procedure

1. Begin with enough **sand** and **gravel** to fill the bottom of a **rectangular plastic washtub.**

2. Spread the gravel in a layer at the bottom of the washtub. On top of the gravel, place a layer of sand that is 4 cm to 6 cm deep. Add more sand to one end of the washtub to form a slope.

3. Make a small hole in the bottom of a **paper cup.** Attach the cup to the inside wall of the tub with a **clothespin.** The cup should be placed at the end that has more sand.

4. Fill the cup with **water,** and observe the water as it moves over the sand. Use a **magnifying lens** to observe features of the stream more closely.

5. Record your observations.

Analysis

1. At the start of your experiment, how did the moving water affect the sand?

2. As time passed, how did the moving water affect the sand?

3. Explain how this activity modeled the development of streams. In what ways was the model accurate? How was it inaccurate?

The Active River

If you had fallen asleep with your toes dangling in the Colorado River 6 million years ago and you had woken up today, your toes would be hanging about 1.6 km (about 1 mi) above the river!

The Colorado River carved the Grand Canyon, shown in **Figure 1,** by washing billions of tons of soil and rock from its riverbed. The Colorado River made the Grand Canyon by a process that can take millions of years.

Rivers: Agents of Erosion

Six million years ago, the area now known as the Grand Canyon was nearly as flat as a pancake. The Colorado River cut down into the rock and formed the Grand Canyon over millions of years through a process called erosion. **Erosion** is the process by which soil and sediment are transported from one location to another. Rivers are not the only agents of erosion. Wind, rain, ice, and snow can also cause erosion.

Because of erosion caused by water, the Grand Canyon is now about 1.6 km deep and 446 km long. In this section, you will learn about stream development, river systems, and the factors that affect the rate of stream erosion.

✓ Reading Check Describe the process that created the Grand Canyon. (*See the Appendix for answers to Reading Checks.*)

What You Will Learn

● Describe how moving water shapes the surface of the Earth by the process of erosion.
● Explain how water moves through the water cycle.
● Describe a watershed.
● Explain three factors that affect the rate of stream erosion.
● Identify four ways that rivers are described.

Vocabulary

erosion	divide
water cycle	channel
tributary	load
watershed	

READING STRATEGY

Reading Organizer As you read this section, create an outline of the section. Use the headings from the section in your outline.

erosion the process by which wind, water, ice, or gravity transports soil and sediment from one location to another

Figure 1 *The Grand Canyon is located in northwestern Arizona. The canyon formed over millions of years as running water eroded the rock layers. (In some places, the canyon is now 29 km wide.)*

The Water Cycle

Have you ever wondered how rivers keep flowing? Where do rivers get their water? Learning about the water cycle, shown in **Figure 2,** will help you answer these questions. The **water cycle** is the continuous movement of Earth's water from the ocean to the atmosphere to the land and back to the ocean. The water cycle is driven by energy from the sun.

water cycle the continuous movement of water from the ocean to the atmosphere to the land and back to the ocean

Figure 2 The Water Cycle

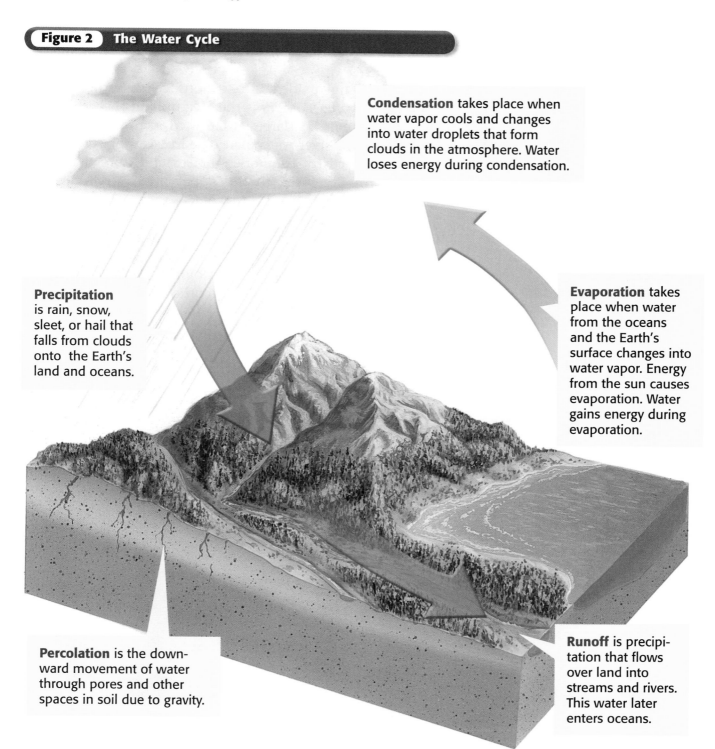

Condensation takes place when water vapor cools and changes into water droplets that form clouds in the atmosphere. Water loses energy during condensation.

Precipitation is rain, snow, sleet, or hail that falls from clouds onto the Earth's land and oceans.

Evaporation takes place when water from the oceans and the Earth's surface changes into water vapor. Energy from the sun causes evaporation. Water gains energy during evaporation.

Percolation is the downward movement of water through pores and other spaces in soil due to gravity.

Runoff is precipitation that flows over land into streams and rivers. This water later enters oceans.

River Systems

The next time you take a shower, notice that individual drops of water join together to become small streams. These streams join other small streams and form larger ones. Eventually, all of the water flows down the drain. Every time you shower, you create a model river system—a network of streams and rivers that drains an area of its runoff. Just as the shower forms a network of flowing water, streams and rivers form a network of flowing water on land. A stream that flows into a lake or into a larger stream is called a **tributary.**

Watersheds

River systems are divided into regions called watersheds. A **watershed,** or *drainage basin,* is the area of land that is drained by a water system. The largest watershed in the United States is the Mississippi River watershed. The Mississippi River watershed has hundreds of tributaries that extend from the Rocky Mountains, in the West, to the Appalachian Mountains, in the East.

The satellite image in **Figure 3** shows that the Mississippi River watershed covers more than one-third of the United States. Other major watersheds in the United States are the Columbia River, Rio Grande, and Colorado River watersheds. Watersheds are separated from each other by an area of higher ground called a **divide.**

✓ **Reading Check** Describe the difference between a watershed and a divide.

Figure 3 *The Continental Divide runs through the Rocky Mountains. It separates the watersheds that flow into the Atlantic Ocean and the Gulf of Mexico from those that flow into the Pacific Ocean.*

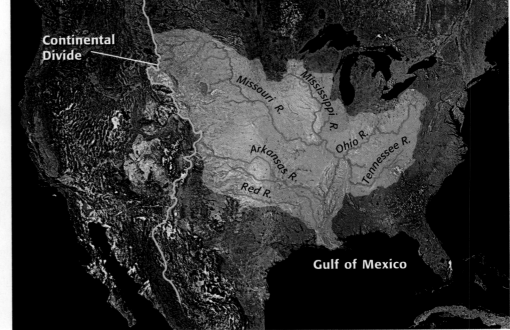

Figure 4 *A mountain stream, such as the one at left, at Kenai Peninsula in Alaska, flows rapidly and has more erosive energy. A river on a flat plain, such as the Kuskokwim River in Alaska, shown below, flows slowly and has less erosive energy.*

Stream Erosion

As a stream forms, it erodes soil and rock to make a channel. A **channel** is the path that a stream follows. When a stream first forms, its channel is usually narrow and steep. Over time, the stream transports rock and soil downstream and makes the channel wider and deeper. When streams become longer and wider, they are called *rivers*. A stream's ability to erode is influenced by three factors: gradient, discharge, and load.

Gradient

Figure 4 shows two photos of rivers with very different gradients. *Gradient* is the measure of the change in elevation over a certain distance. A high gradient gives a stream or river more erosive energy to erode rock and soil. A river or stream that has a low gradient has less energy for erosion.

Discharge

The amount of water that a stream or river carries in a given amount of time is called *discharge*. The discharge of a stream increases when a major storm occurs or when warm weather rapidly melts snow. As the stream's discharge increases, its erosive energy and speed and the amount of materials that the stream can carry also increase.

 **Reading Check** What factors cause a stream to flow faster?

tributary a stream that flows into a lake or into a larger stream

watershed the area of land that is drained by a water system

divide the boundary between drainage areas that have streams that flow in opposite directions

channel the path that a stream follows

MATH PRACTICE

Calculating a Stream's Gradient

If a stream starts at an elevation of 4,900 m and travels 450 km downstream to a lake that is at an elevation of 400 m, what is the stream's gradient? (Hint: Subtract the final elevation from the starting elevation, and divide by 450. Don't forget to keep track of the units.)

Load

load the materials carried by a stream

The materials carried by a stream are called the stream's **load.** The size of a stream's load is affected by the stream's speed. Fast-moving streams can carry large particles. Rocks and pebbles bounce and scrape along the bottom and sides of the stream bed. Thus, the size of a stream's load also affects its rate of erosion. The illustration below shows the three ways that a stream can carry its load.

A stream can bounce large materials, such as pebbles and boulders, along the stream bed. These rocks are called the **bed load.**

A stream can carry small rocks and soil in suspension. These materials, called the **suspended load,** make the river look muddy.

The **dissolved load** is material carried in solution, which means that the material is dissolved in the water. Sodium and calcium are some of the materials in the dissolved load.

The Stages of a River

In the early 1900s, William Morris Davis developed a model for the stages of river development. According to his model, rivers evolve from a youthful stage to an old-age stage. He thought that all rivers erode in the same way and at the same rate.

Today, scientists support a different model that considers factors of stream development that differ from those considered in Davis's model. For example, because different materials erode at different rates, one river may develop more quickly than another river. Many factors, including climate, gradient, and load, influence the development of a river. Scientists no longer use Davis's model to explain river development, but they still use many of his terms to describe a river. These terms describe a river's general features, not a river's actual age.

Youthful Rivers

A youthful river, such as the one shown in **Figure 5,** erodes its channel deeper rather than wider. The river flows quickly because of its steep gradient. Its channel is narrow and straight. The river tumbles over rocks in rapids and waterfalls. Youthful rivers have very few tributaries.

Mature Rivers

A mature river, as shown in **Figure 6,** erodes its channel wider rather than deeper. The gradient of a mature river is not as steep as that of a youthful river. Also, a mature river has fewer falls and rapids. A mature river is fed by many tributaries. Because of its good drainage, a mature river has more discharge than a youthful river.

Reading Check What are the characteristics of a mature river?

CONNECTION TO Language Arts

Huckleberry Finn Mark Twain's famous book, *The Adventures of Huckleberry Finn,* describes the life of a boy who lived on the Mississippi River. Mark Twain's real name was Samuel Clemens. Do research to find out why Clemens chose to use the name Mark Twain and how the name relates to the Mississippi River.

▲ **Figure 5** *This youthful river is located in Yellowstone National Park in Wyoming. Rapids and falls are found where the river flows over hard, resistant rock.*

◀ **Figure 6** *A mature river, such as this one in the Amazon basin of Peru, curves back and forth. The bends in the river's channel are called* meanders.

Figure 7 *This old river is located in New Zealand.*

Old Rivers

An old river has a low gradient and little erosive energy. Instead of widening and deepening its banks, the river deposits rock and soil in and along its channel. Old rivers, such as the one in **Figure 7,** are characterized by wide, flat *flood plains*, or valleys, and many bends. Also, an old river has fewer tributaries than a mature river because the smaller tributaries have joined together.

Rejuvenated Rivers

Rejuvenated (ri JOO vuh NAYT ed) rivers are found where the land is raised by tectonic activity. When land rises, the river's gradient becomes steeper, and the river flows more quickly. The increased gradient of a rejuvenated river allows the river to cut more deeply into the valley floor. Steplike formations called *terraces* often form on both sides of a stream valley as a result of rejuvenation. Can you find the terraces in **Figure 8**?

✓ Reading Check How do rejuvenated rivers form?

Figure 8 *This rejuvenated river is located in Canyonlands National Park in Utah.*

Summary

- Rivers cause erosion by removing and transporting soil and rock from the riverbed.

- The water cycle is the movement of Earth's water from the ocean to the atmosphere to the land and back to the ocean.

- A river system is made up of a network of streams and rivers.

- A watershed is a region that collects runoff water that then becomes part of a river or a lake.

- A stream with a high gradient has more energy for eroding soil and rock.

- When a stream's discharge increases, its erosive energy also increases.

- A stream with a load of large particles has a higher rate of erosion than a stream with a dissolved load.

- A developing river can be described as youthful, mature, old, or rejuvenated.

Using Key Terms

1. Use each of the following terms in a separate sentence: *erosion, water cycle, tributary, watershed, divide, channel,* and *load.*

Understanding Key Ideas

2. Which of the following drains a watershed?
   a. a divide
   b. a drainage basin
   c. a tributary
   d. a water system

3. Describe how the Grand Canyon was formed.

4. Draw the water cycle. In your drawing, label *condensation, precipitation,* and *evaporation.*

5. What are three factors that affect the rate of stream erosion?

6. Which stage of river development is characterized by flat flood plains?

Critical Thinking

7. **Making Inferences** How does the water cycle help develop river systems?

8. **Making Comparisons** How do youthful rivers, mature rivers, and old rivers differ?

Interpreting Graphics

Use the pie graph below to answer the questions that follow.

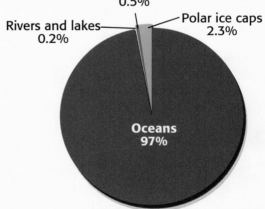

Distribution of Water in the World

Water underground, in soil, and in air
0.5%

Rivers and lakes
0.2%

Polar ice caps
2.3%

Oceans
97%

9. Where is most of the water in the world found?

10. In what form is the majority of the world's fresh water?

What You Will Learn

● Describe the four different types of stream deposits.
● Describe how the deposition of sediment affects the land.

Vocabulary

deposition   alluvial fan
delta   floodplain

READING STRATEGY

Prediction Guide Before reading this section, write the title of each heading in this section. Next, under each heading, write what you think you will learn.

Stream and River Deposits

If your job were to carry millions of tons of soil across the United States, how would you do it? You might use a bulldozer or a dump truck, but it would still take you a long time. Did you know that rivers do this job every day?

Rivers erode and move enormous amounts of material, such as soil and rock. Acting as liquid conveyor belts, rivers often carry fertile soil to farmland and wetlands. Although erosion is a serious problem, rivers also renew soils and form new land. As you will see in this section, rivers create some of the most impressive landforms on Earth.

Deposition in Water

You have learned how flowing water erodes the Earth's surface. After rivers erode rock and soil, they drop, or *deposit*, their load downstream. **Deposition** is the process in which material is laid down or dropped. Rock and soil deposited by streams are called *sediment*. Rivers and streams deposit sediment where the speed of the water current decreases. **Figure 1** shows this type of deposition.

Figure 1 *This photo shows erosion and deposition at a bend, or meander, of a river in Alaska.*

Deposition occurs along the inside bank of the bend, where the water flows slower.

Erosion occurs along the outside bank of the bend, where the water flows faster.

Placer Deposits

Heavy minerals are sometimes deposited at places in a river where the current slows down. This kind of sediment is called a *placer deposit* (PLAS uhr dee PAHZ it). Some placer deposits contain gold. During the California gold rush, which began in 1849, many miners panned for gold in the placer deposits of rivers, as shown in **Figure 2.**

Delta

A river's current slows when a river empties into a large body of water, such as a lake or an ocean. As its current slows, a river often deposits its load in a fan-shaped pattern called a **delta.** In **Figure 3,** you can see an astronaut's view of the Nile Delta. A delta usually forms on a flat surface and is made mostly of mud. These mud deposits form new land and cause the coastline to grow. The world's deltas are home to a rich diversity of plant and animal life.

If you look back at the map of the Mississippi River watershed, you can see where the Mississippi Delta has formed. It has formed where the Mississippi River flows into the Gulf of Mexico. Each of the fine mud particles in the delta began its journey far upstream. Parts of Louisiana are made up of particles that were transported from places as far away as Montana, Minnesota, Ohio, and Illinois!

✓ Reading Check What are deltas made of? (*See the Appendix for answers to Reading Checks.*)

Figure 2 *Miners rushed to California in the 1850s to find gold. They often found it in the bends of rivers in placer deposits.*

deposition the process in which material is laid down

delta a fan-shaped mass of material deposited at the mouth of a stream

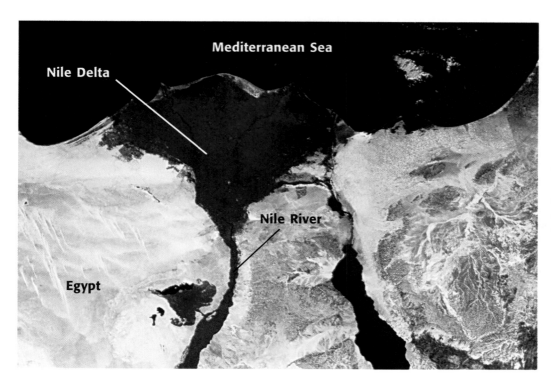

Mediterranean Sea

Nile Delta

Nile River

Egypt

Figure 3 *As sediment is dropped at the mouth of the Nile River, in Egypt, a delta forms.*

Figure 4 *An alluvial fan, like this one at Death Valley in California, forms when an eroding stream changes rapidly into a depositing stream.*

Alluvial fan

Deposition on Land

When a fast-moving mountain stream flows onto a flat plain, the stream slows down very quickly. As the stream slows down, it deposits sediment. The sediment forms an alluvial fan, such as the one shown in **Figure 4. Alluvial fans** are fan-shaped deposits that, unlike deltas, form on dry land.

alluvial fan a fan-shaped mass of material deposited by a stream when the slope of the land decreases sharply

floodplain an area along a river that forms from sediments deposited when the river overflows its banks

Floodplains

During periods of high rainfall or rapid snow melt, a sudden increase in the volume of water flowing into a stream can cause the stream to overflow its banks. The area along a river that forms from sediment deposited when a river overflows its banks is called a **floodplain.** When a stream floods, a layer of sediment is deposited across the flood plain. Each flood adds another layer of sediment.

Flood plains are rich farming areas because periodic flooding brings new soil to the land. However, flooding can cause damage, too. When the Mississippi River flooded in 1993, farms were destroyed, and entire towns were evacuated. **Figure 5** shows an area north of St. Louis, Missouri, that was flooded.

Figure 5 *The normal flow of the Mississippi River and Missouri River is shown in black. The area that was flooded when both rivers spilled over their banks in 1993 is shaded red.*

Mississippi River

Missouri River

Flooding Dangers

The flooding of the Mississippi River in 1993 caused damage in nine states. But floods can damage more than property. Many people have lost their lives to powerful floods. As shown in **Figure 6,** flash flooding can take a driver by surprise. However, there are ways that floods can be controlled.

One type of barrier that can be built to help control flooding is called a *dam*. A dam is a barrier that can redirect the flow of water. A dam can prevent flooding in one area and create an artificial lake in another area. The water stored in the artificial lake can be used to irrigate farmland during droughts and provide drinking water to local towns and cities. The stored water can also be used to generate electricity.

Overflow from a river can also be controlled by a barrier called a *levee*. A levee is the buildup of sediment deposited along the channel of a river. This buildup helps keep the river inside its banks. People often use sandbags to build artificial levees to control water during serious flooding.

✓ Reading Check List two ways that the flow of water can be controlled.

Figure 6 *Cars driven on flooded roads can easily be carried down to deeper, more dangerous water.*

SECTION Review

Summary

● Sediment forms several types of deposits.

● Sediments deposited where a river's current slows are called *placer deposits.*

● A delta is a fan-shaped deposit of sediment where a river meets a large body of water.

● Alluvial fans can form when a river deposits sediment on land.

● Flooding brings rich soil to farmland but can also lead to property damage and death.

Using Key Terms

1. In your own words, write a definition for each of the following terms: *deposition* and *flood plain*.

Understanding Key Ideas

2. Which of the following forms at places in a river where the current slows?
   a. a placer deposit
   b. a delta
   c. a flood plain
   d. a levee

3. Which of the following can help to prevent a flood?
   a. a placer deposit
   b. a delta
   c. a flood plain
   d. a levee

4. Where do alluvial fans form?

5. Explain why flood plains are both good and bad areas for farming.

Math Skills

6. A river flows at a speed of 8 km/h. If you floated on a raft in this river, how far would you have traveled after 5 h?

Critical Thinking

7. **Identifying Relationships** What factors increase the likelihood that sediment will be deposited?

8. **Making Comparisons** How are alluvial fans and deltas similar?

SCILINKS

NSTA
Developed and maintained by the National Science Teachers Association

For a variety of links related to this chapter, go to www.scilinks.org

Topic: Stream Deposits
SciLinks code: HSM1458

Water Underground

Imagine that instead of turning on a faucet to get a glass of water, you pour water from a chunk of solid rock! This idea may sound crazy, but millions of people get their water from within rock that is deep underground.

Although you can see some of Earth's water in streams and lakes, you cannot see the large amount of water that flows underground. The water located within the rocks below the Earth's surface is called *groundwater*. Groundwater not only is an important resource but also plays an important role in erosion and deposition.

The Location of Groundwater

Surface water seeps underground into the soil and rock. This underground area is divided into two zones. Rainwater passes through the upper zone, called the *zone of aeration*. Farther down, the water collects in an area called the *zone of saturation*. In this zone, the spaces between the rock particles are filled with water.

These two zones meet at a boundary known as the **water table,** shown in **Figure 1.** The water table rises during wet seasons and falls during dry seasons. In wet regions, the water table can be at or just beneath the soil's surface. In dry regions, such as deserts, the water table may be hundreds of meters beneath the ground.

> ✓ **Reading Check** Describe where the zone of aeration is located. *(See the Appendix for answers to Reading Checks.)*

What You Will Learn

- Identify and describe the location of the water table.
- Describe an aquifer.
- Explain the difference between a spring and a well.
- Explain how caves and sinkholes form as a result of erosion and deposition.

Vocabulary

water table
aquifer
porosity
permeability
recharge zone
artesian spring

READING STRATEGY

Discussion Read this section silently. Write down questions that you have about this section. Discuss your questions in a small group.

water table the upper surface of underground water; the upper boundary of the zone of saturation

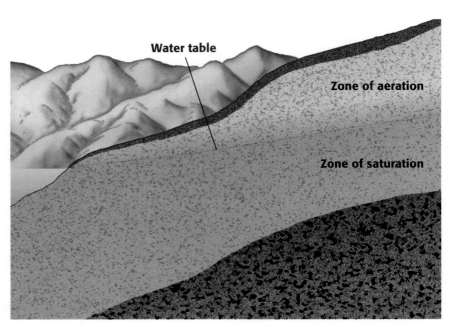

Figure 1 *The water table is the upper surface of the zone of saturation.*

Water table

Zone of aeration

Zone of saturation

Aquifers

A rock layer that stores groundwater and allows the flow of groundwater is called an **aquifer.** An aquifer can be described by its ability to hold water and its ability to allow water to pass freely through it.

Porosity

The more open spaces, or pores, between particles in an aquifer, the more water the aquifer can hold. The percentage of open space between individual rock particles in a rock layer is called **porosity.**

Porosity is influenced by the differences in sizes of the particles in the rock layer. If a rock layer contains many particles of different sizes, it is likely that small particles will fill up the different-sized empty spaces between large particles. Therefore, a rock layer with particles of different sizes has a low percentage of open space between particles and has low porosity. On the other hand, a rock layer containing same-sized particles has high porosity. This rock layer has high porosity because smaller particles are not present to fill the empty space between particles. So, there is more open space between particles.

Permeability

If the pores of a rock layer are connected, groundwater can flow through the rock layer. A rock's ability to let water pass through is called **permeability.** A rock that stops the flow of water is *impermeable.*

The larger the particles are, the more permeable the rock layer is. Because large particles have less surface area relative to their volume than small particles do, large particles cause less friction. *Friction* is a force that causes moving objects to slow down. Less friction allows water to flow more easily through the rock layer, as shown in **Figure 2.**

aquifer a body of rock or sediment that stores groundwater and allows the flow of groundwater

porosity the percentage of the total volume of a rock or sediment that consists of open spaces

permeability the ability of a rock or sediment to let fluids pass through its open spaces, or pores

For another activity related to this chapter, go to **go.hrw.com** and type in the keyword **HZ5DEPW.**

Figure 2 *Large particles, shown at left, have less total surface area—and so cause less friction—than small particles, shown at right, do.*

Figure 3 *This map shows aquifers in the United States (excluding Alaska and Hawaii).*

Aquifers

recharge zone an area in which water travels downward to become part of an aquifer

Water Conservation

Did you know that water use in the United States has been reduced by 15% in the last 20 years? This decrease is due in part to the conservation efforts of people like you. Work with a parent or guardian to create a water budget for your household. Figure out how much water your family uses every day. Identify ways to reduce your water use, and then set a goal to limit your water use over the course of a week.

Aquifer Geology and Geography

The best aquifers usually form in permeable materials, such as sandstone, limestone, or layers of sand and gravel. Some aquifers cover large underground areas and are an important source of water for cities and agriculture. The map in **Figure 3** shows the location of the major aquifers in the United States.

Recharge Zones

Like rivers, aquifers depend on the water cycle to maintain a constant flow of water. The ground surface where water enters an aquifer is called the **recharge zone.** The size of the recharge zone depends on how permeable rock is at the surface. If the surface rock is permeable, water can seep down into the aquifer. If the aquifer is covered by an impermeable rock layer, water cannot reach the aquifer. Construction of buildings on top of the recharge zone can also limit the amount of water that enters an aquifer.

Reading Check What factors affect the size of the recharge zone?

Springs and Wells

Groundwater movement is determined by the slope of the water table. Like surface water, groundwater tends to move downslope, toward lower elevations. If the water table reaches the Earth's surface, water will flow out from the ground and will form a *spring*. Springs are an important source of drinking water. In areas where the water table is higher than the Earth's surface, lakes will form.

Artesian Springs

A sloping layer of permeable rock sandwiched between two layers of impermeable rock is called an *artesian formation*. The permeable rock is an aquifer, and the top layer of impermeable rock is called a *cap rock*, as shown in **Figure 4.** Artesian formations are the source of water for artesian springs. An **artesian spring** is a spring whose water flows from a crack in the cap rock of the aquifer. Artesian springs are sometimes found in deserts, where they are often the only source of water.

Most springs have cool water. However, some springs have hot water. The water becomes hot when it flows deep in the Earth, because Earth's temperature increases with depth. The temperature of some hot springs can reach 50°C!

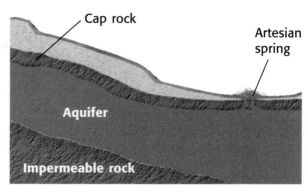

Figure 4 *Artesian springs form when water from an aquifer flows through cracks in the cap rock of an artesian formation.*

Wells

A human-made hole that is deeper than the level of the water table is called a *well*. If a well is not deep enough, as shown in **Figure 5,** it will dry up when the water table falls below the bottom of the well. Also, if an area has too many wells, groundwater can be removed too rapidly. If groundwater is removed too rapidly, the water table will drop, and all of the wells will run dry.

artesian spring a spring whose water flows from a crack in the cap rock over the aquifer

> ✓ **Reading Check** How deep must a well be to reach water?

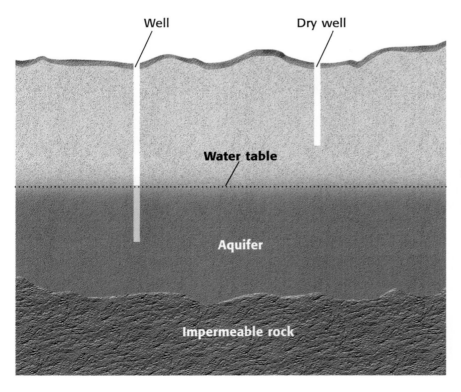

Figure 5 *A well must be drilled deep enough so that when the water table drops, the well still contains water.*

Underground Erosion and Deposition

As you have learned, rivers cause erosion when water removes and transports rock and soil from its banks. Groundwater can also cause erosion. However, groundwater causes erosion by dissolving rock. Some groundwater contains weak acids, such as carbonic acid, that dissolve the rock. Also, some types of rock, such as limestone, dissolve in groundwater more easily than other types do.

When underground erosion happens, caves can form. Most of the world's caves formed over thousands of years as groundwater dissolved the limestone of the cave sites. Some caves, such as the one shown in **Figure 6,** reach spectacular proportions.

Cave Formations

Although caves are formed by erosion, they also show signs of deposition. Water that drips from a crack in a cave's ceiling leaves behind deposits of calcium carbonate. Sharp, icicle-shaped features that form on cave ceilings are known as *stalactites* (stuh LAK tiets). Water that falls to the cave's floor adds to cone-shaped features known as *stalagmites* (stuh LAG miets). If water drips long enough, the stalactites and stalagmites join to form a *dripstone column*.

Reading Check What process causes the formation of stalactites and stalagmites?

Figure 6 *At Carlsbad Caverns in New Mexico, underground passages and enormous "rooms" have been eroded below the surface of the Earth.*

Stalactite

Stalagmite

Sinkholes

When the water table is lower than the level of a cave, the cave is no longer supported by the water underneath. The roof of the cave can then collapse, which leaves a circular depression called a *sinkhole*. Surface streams can "disappear" into sinkholes and then flow through underground caves. Sinkholes often form lakes in areas where the water table is high. Central Florida is covered with hundreds of round sinkhole lakes. **Figure 7** shows how the collapse of an underground cave can affect a landscape.

Figure 7 *The damage to this city block shows the effects of a sinkhole in Winter Park, Florida.*

SECTION Review

Summary

- The water table is the boundary between the zone of aeration and the zone of saturation.

- Porosity and permeability describe an aquifer's ability to hold water and ability to allow water to flow through.

- Springs are a natural way that water reaches the surface. Wells are made by humans.

- Caves and sinkholes form from the erosion of limestone by groundwater.

Using Key Terms

1. Use the following terms in the same sentence: *water table, aquifer, porosity,* and *artesian spring.*

Understanding Key Ideas

2. Which of the following describes an aquifer's ability to allow water to flow through?
   a. porosity
   b. permeability
   c. geology
   d. recharge zone

3. What is the water table?

4. Describe how particles affect the porosity of an aquifer.

5. Explain the difference between an artesian spring and other springs.

6. Name a feature that is formed by underground erosion.

7. Name two features that are formed by underground deposition.

8. What type of weathering process causes underground erosion?

Math Skills

9. Groundwater in an area flows at a speed of 4 km/h. How long would it take the water to flow 10 km to its spring?

Critical Thinking

10. **Predicting Consequences** Explain how urban growth might affect the recharge zone of an aquifer.

11. **Making Comparisons** Explain the difference between a spring and a well.

12. **Analyzing Relationships** What is the relationship between the zone of aeration, the zone of saturation, and the water table?

SCILINKS®

NSTA
Developed and maintained by the
National Science Teachers Association

For a variety of links related to this chapter, go to www.scilinks.org

Topic: Water Underground
SciLinks code: HSM1633

What You Will Learn

● Identify two forms of water pollution.
● Explain how the properties of water influence the health of a water system.
● Describe two ways that wastewater can be treated.
● Describe how water is used and how water can be conserved in industry, in agriculture, and at home.

Vocabulary

point-source pollution
nonpoint-source pollution
sewage treatment plant
septic tank

READING STRATEGY

Paired Summarizing Read this section silently. In pairs, take turns summarizing the material. Stop to discuss ideas that seem confusing.

point-source pollution pollution that comes from a specific site

nonpoint-source pollution pollution that comes from many sources rather than from a single, specific site

Using Water Wisely

Did you know that you are almost 65% water? You depend on clean, fresh drinking water to maintain that 65% of you. But there is a limited amount of fresh water available on Earth. Only 3% of Earth's water is drinkable.

And of the 3% of Earth's water that is drinkable, 75% is frozen in the polar icecaps. This frozen water is not readily available for our use. Therefore, it is important that we protect our water resources.

Water Pollution

Surface water, such as the water in rivers and lakes, and groundwater can be polluted by waste from cities, factories, and farms. Pollution is the introduction of harmful substances into the environment. Water can become so polluted that it can no longer be used or can even be deadly.

Point-Source and Nonpoint-Source Pollution

Pollution that comes from one specific site is called **point-source pollution.** For example, a leak from a sewer pipe is point-source pollution. In most cases, this type of pollution can be controlled because its source can be identified.

Nonpoint-source pollution, another type of pollution, is pollution that comes from many sources. This type of pollution is much more difficult to control because it does not come from a single source. Most nonpoint-source pollution reaches bodies of water by runoff. The main sources of nonpoint-source pollution are street gutters, fertilizers, eroded soils and silt from farming and logging, drainage from mines, and salts from irrigation. **Figure 1** shows an example of a source of nonpoint-source pollution.

✓ Reading Check What type of pollution is the hardest to control? (*See the Appendix for answers to Reading Checks.*)

Figure 1 *The runoff from this irrigation system could collect pesticides and other pollutants. The result would be nonpoint-source pollution.*

Figure 2 *Waste from farm animals can seep into groundwater and cause nitrate pollution.*

Health of a Water System

You might not realize it, but water quality affects your quality of life as well as other organisms that depend on water. Therefore, it is important to understand how the properties of water influence water quality.

Dissolved Oxygen

Just as you need oxygen to live, so do fish and other organisms that live in lakes and streams. The oxygen dissolved in water is called *dissolved oxygen,* or DO. Levels of DO that are below 4.0 mg/L in fresh water can cause stress and possibly death for organisms in the water.

Pollutants such as sewage, fertilizer runoff, and animal waste can decrease DO levels. Temperature changes also affect DO levels. For example, cold water holds more oxygen than warm water does. Facilities such as nuclear power plants can increase the temperature of lakes and rivers when they use the water as a cooling agent. Such an increase in water temperature is called *thermal pollution*, which causes a decrease in DO levels.

Nitrates

Nitrates are naturally occurring compounds of nitrogen and oxygen. Small amounts of nitrates in water are normal. However, elevated nitrate levels in water can be harmful to organisms. An excess of nitrates in lakes and rivers can also lower DO levels. As shown in **Figure 2,** nitrate pollution can come from animal wastes or fertilizers that seep into groundwater.

Alkalinity

Alkalinity refers to the water's ability to neutralize acid. Acid rain and other acid wastes can harm aquatic life. A pH below 6.0 is too acidic for most aquatic life. Water with a higher alkalinity can better protect organisms from acid.

Measuring Alkalinity

1. Identify two water sources from which to collect water samples.

2. Fill a **plastic cup** with water from one source. Fill a **second plastic cup** with water from the second source. Label each cup with its source.

3. Using a **pH test kit,** test the pH of each sample.

4. Follow the instructions in the test kit, and determine the pH of each of the two samples. Record your observations.

5. What did the results for the two samples indicate about the two sources?

6. Use **water test kits** to measure DO and nitrate levels in the two water samples, and discuss your results.

Cleaning Polluted Water

When you flush the toilet or watch water go down the shower drain, do you ever wonder where the water goes? If you live in a city or large town, the water flows through sewer pipes to a sewage treatment plant. **Sewage treatment plants** are facilities that clean the waste materials out of water. These plants help protect the environment from water pollution. They also protect us from diseases that are easily transmitted through dirty water.

sewage treatment plant a facility that cleans the waste materials found in water that comes from sewers or drains

Primary Treatment

When water reaches a sewage treatment plant, it is cleaned in two ways. First, it goes through a series of steps known as *primary treatment*. In primary treatment, dirty water is passed through a large screen to catch solid objects, such as paper, rags, and bottle caps. The water is then placed in a large tank, where smaller particles, or sludge, can sink and be filtered out. These particles include things such as food, coffee grounds, and soil. Any floating oils and scum are skimmed off the surface.

Secondary Treatment

After undergoing primary treatment, the water is ready for *secondary treatment*. In secondary treatment, the water is sent to an aeration tank, where it is mixed with oxygen and bacteria. The bacteria feed on the wastes and use the oxygen. The water is then sent to another settling tank, where chlorine is added to disinfect the water. The water is finally released into a water source—a river, a lake, or the ocean. **Figure 3** shows the major components of a sewage treatment plant.

Figure 3 *If you live in a city, the water used in your home most likely ends up at a sewage treatment plant, where the water is cleaned.*

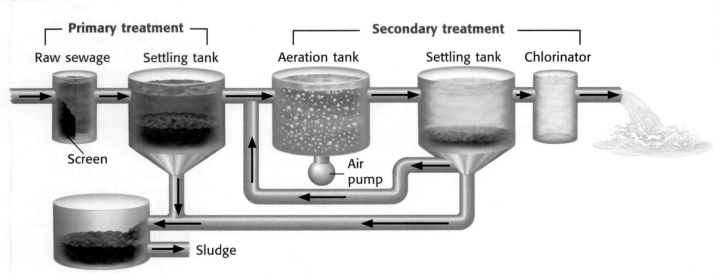

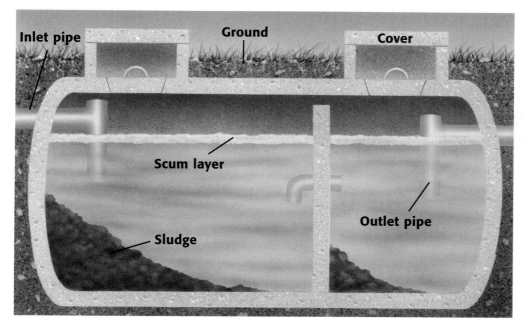

Figure 4 *Most septic tanks must be cleaned out every few years in order to work properly.*

Labels: Inlet pipe, Ground, Cover, Scum layer, Sludge, Outlet pipe

Another Way to Clean Wastewater

If you live in an area that does not have a sewage treatment plant, your house probably uses a septic tank. **Figure 4** shows an example of a septic tank. A **septic tank** is a large underground tank that cleans the wastewater from a household. Wastewater flows from the house into the tank, where the solids sink to the bottom. Bacteria break down these wastes on the bottom of the tank. The water flows from the tank into a group of buried pipes. Then, the buried pipes, called a *drain field,* distribute the water. Distributing the water enables the water to soak into the ground.

septic tank a tank that separates solid waste from liquids and that has bacteria that break down the solid waste

Where the Water Goes

Think of some ways that you use water in your home. Do you water the lawn? Do you do the dishes? The graph in **Figure 5** shows how an average household in the United States uses water. Notice that less than 8% of the water we use in our homes is used for drinking. The rest is used for flushing toilets, doing laundry, bathing, and watering lawns and plants.

The water we use in our homes is not the only way water is used. More water is used in industry and agriculture than in homes.

✓ Reading Check What percentage of water in our homes is used for drinking?

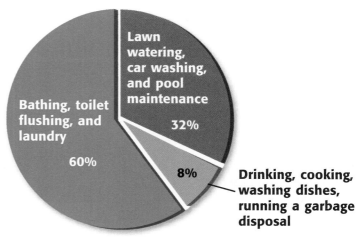

Labels: Lawn watering, car washing, and pool maintenance 32%; Bathing, toilet flushing, and laundry 60%; 8% Drinking, cooking, washing dishes, running a garbage disposal

Figure 5 *The average household in the United States uses about 100 gal of water per day. This pie graph shows some common uses of these 100 gal.*

Water in Industry

About 19% of water used in the world is used for industrial purposes. Water is used to manufacture goods, cool power stations, clean industrial products, extract minerals, and generate energy for factories.

Because water resources have become expensive, many industries are trying to conserve, or use less, water. One way industries conserve water is by recycling it. In the United States, most of the water used in factories is recycled at least once. At least 90% of this recycled water can be treated and returned to surface water.

Water in Agriculture

The Ogallala aquifer is the largest known aquifer in North America. The map in **Figure 6** shows that the Ogallala aquifer runs beneath the ground through eight states, from South Dakota to Texas. The Ogallala aquifer provides water for approximately one-fifth of the cropland in the United States. Farming is the largest user of water in the Western United States. Recently, the water table in the aquifer has dropped so low that some scientists say that it would take at least 1,000 years to replenish the aquifer if it were no longer used.

Most of the water that is lost during farming is lost through evaporation and runoff. New technology, such as drip irrigation systems, has helped conserve water in agriculture. A drip irrigation system delivers small amounts of water directly to plant roots. This system allows plants to absorb the water before the water has a chance to evaporate or become runoff.

Reading Check How does the drip irrigation system help conserve water?

Agriculture in Israel

From 1950 to 1980, Israel reduced the amount of water used in agriculture from 83% to 5%. Israel did so primarily by switching from overhead sprinklers to drip irrigation. A small farm uses 10,000 L of water per day for overhead sprinkler irrigation. How much water would the farm save in 1 year by using a drip irrigation system that uses 75% less water than a sprinkler system?

Figure 6 *Because the Ogallala aquifer has been such a good source of groundwater, it has become overused. The water table has dropped more than 30 m in some areas.*

Conserving Water at Home

There are many ways that people can conserve water at home. For example, many people save water by installing low-flow shower heads and low-flush toilets, because these items use much less water. To avoid watering lawns, some people plant only native plants in their yards. Native plants grow well in the local climate and don't need extra watering.

Your behavior can also help you conserve water. For example, you can take shorter showers. You can avoid running the water while brushing your teeth. And when you run the dishwasher, make sure it is full, as shown in **Figure 7.**

✔ **Reading Check** List ways in which you can conserve water in your home.

Figure 7 *Run the dishwasher only when it is full.*

SECTION Review

Summary

- Point-source pollution and nonpoint-source pollution are two kinds of water pollution.

- Pollutants can decrease oxygen levels and increase nitrate levels in water. These changes can cause harm to plants, animals, and humans.

- Wastewater can be treated by sewage treatment plants and septic systems.

- Water can be conserved by using only the water that is needed, by recycling water, and by using drip irrigation systems.

Using Key Terms

1. Use each of the following terms in a separate sentence: *point-source pollution, nonpoint-source pollution, sewage treatment plant,* and *septic tank*.

Understanding Key Ideas

2. Which of the following can help protect fish from acid rain?
   - **a.** dissolved oxygen
   - **b.** nitrates
   - **c.** alkalinity
   - **d.** point-source pollution

3. What type of wastewater treatment can be used for an individual home?
   - **a.** sewage treatment plant
   - **b.** primary treatment
   - **c.** secondary treatment
   - **d.** septic tank

4. Which kind of water pollution is often caused by runoff of fertilizers?

5. Describe what DO is.

6. What factors affect the level of dissolved oxygen in water?

7. Describe how water is conserved in industry.

Math Skills

8. If 25% of water used in your home is used to water the lawn and you used a total of 95 gal of water today, how many gallons of water did you use to water the lawn?

Critical Thinking

9. **Making Inferences** How do bacteria help break down the waste in water treatment plants?

10. **Applying Concepts** Other than examples listed in this section, what are some ways you can conserve water?

11. **Making Inferences** Why is it better to water your lawn at night instead of during the day?

Developed and maintained by the National Science Teachers Association

For a variety of links related to this chapter, go to www.scilinks.org
Topic: Water Pollution and Conservation
SciLinks code: HSM1630

Model-Making Lab

Water Cycle—What Goes Up . . .

Why does a bathroom mirror fog up? Where does water go when it dries up? Where does rain come from? These questions relate to the major parts of the water cycle—condensation, evaporation, and precipitation. In this activity, you will make a model of the water cycle.

OBJECTIVES

Design a model that follows the same processes as those of the water cycle.

Identify each stage of the water cycle in the model.

MATERIALS

- beaker
- gloves, heat-resistant
- graduated cylinder
- hot plate
- plate, glass, or watch glass
- tap water, 50 mL
- tongs or forceps

SAFETY

Procedure

1. Use the graduated cylinder to pour 50 mL of water into the beaker. Note the water level in the beaker.

2. Put on your safety goggles and gloves. Place the beaker securely on the hot plate. Turn the heat to medium, and bring the water to a boil.

3. While waiting for the water to boil, practice picking up and handling the glass plate or watch glass with the tongs. Hold the glass plate a few centimeters above the beaker, and tilt it so that the lowest edge of the glass is still above the beaker.

4. Observe the glass plate as the water in the beaker boils. Record the changes you see in the beaker, in the air above the beaker, and on the glass plate held over the beaker. Write down any changes you see in the water.

5 Continue until you have observed steam rising off the water, the glass plate becoming foggy, and water dripping from the glass plate.

6 Carefully set the glass plate on a counter or other safe surface as directed by your teacher.

7 Turn off the hot plate, and allow the beaker to cool. Move the hot beaker with gloves or tongs if you are directed to do so by your teacher.

Analyze the Results

1 **Constructing Charts** Copy the illustration shown above. On your sketch, draw and label the water cycle as it happened in your model. Include arrows and labels for *evaporation, condensation,* and *precipitation*.

2 **Analyzing Results** Compare the water level in the beaker now with the water level at the beginning of the experiment. Was there a change? Explain why or why not.

Draw Conclusions

3 **Making Predictions** If you had used a scale or a balance to measure the mass of the water in the beaker before and after this activity, would the mass have changed? Explain.

4 **Analyzing Charts** How is your model similar to the Earth's water cycle? On your sketch of the illustration, label where the processes shown in the model reflect the Earth's water cycle.

5 **Drawing Conclusions** When you finished this experiment, the water in the beaker was still hot. What stores much of the energy in the Earth's water cycle?

Applying Your Data

As rainwater runs over the land, the water picks up minerals and salts. Do these minerals and salts evaporate, condense, and precipitate as part of the water cycle? Where do they go?

Chapter Review

USING KEY TERMS

The statements below are false. For each statement, replace the underlined term to make a true statement.

1 A stream that flows into a lake or into a larger stream is a <u>water cycle</u>.

2 The area along a river that forms from sediment deposited when the river overflows is a <u>delta</u>.

3 A rock's ability to let water pass through it is called <u>porosity</u>.

For each pair of terms, explain how the meanings of the terms differ.

4 *divide* and *watershed*

5 *artesian springs* and *wells*

6 *point-source pollution* and *nonpoint-source pollution*

UNDERSTANDING KEY IDEAS

Multiple Choice

7 Which of the following processes is not part of the water cycle?

a. evaporation

b. percolation

c. condensation

d. deposition

8 Which features are common in youthful river channels?

a. meanders

b. flood plains

c. rapids

d. sandbars

9 Which depositional feature is found at the coast?

a. delta

b. flood plain

c. alluvial fan

d. placer deposit

10 Caves are mainly a product of

a. erosion by rivers.

b. river deposition.

c. water pollution.

d. erosion by groundwater.

11 Which of the following is necessary for aquatic life to survive?

a. dissolved oxygen

b. nitrates

c. alkalinity

d. point-source pollution

12 During primary treatment at a sewage treatment plant,

a. water is sent to an aeration tank.

b. water is mixed with bacteria and oxygen.

c. dirty water is passed through a large screen.

d. water is sent to a settling tank where chlorine is added.

Short Answer

13 Identify and describe the location of the water table.

14 Explain how surface water enters an aquifer.

15 Why are caves usually found in limestone-rich regions?

CRITICAL THINKING

16 Concept Mapping Use the following terms to create a concept map: *zone of aeration, zone of saturation, water table, gravity, porosity,* and *permeability.*

17 Identifying Relationships What is water's role in erosion and deposition?

18 Analyzing Processes What are the features of a river channel that has a steep gradient?

19 Analyzing Processes Why is groundwater hard to clean?

20 Evaluating Conclusions How can water be considered both a renewable and a nonrenewable resource? Give an example of each case.

21 Analyzing Processes Does water vapor lose or gain energy during the process of condensation? Explain.

The hydrograph below illustrates data collected on river flow during field investigations over a period of 1 year. The discharge readings are from the Yakima River, in Washington. Use the hydrograph below to answer the questions that follow.

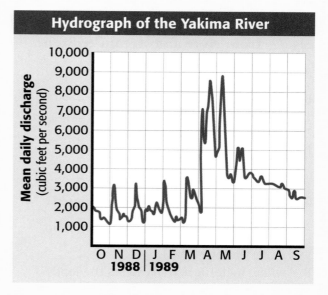

Hydrograph of the Yakima River

22 In which months is there the highest river discharge?

23 Why is there such a high river discharge during these months?

24 What might cause the peaks in river discharge between November and March?

Standardized Test Preparation

Multiple Choice

1. **In the water cycle, the sun's energy causes**

   A. evaporation.

   B. condensation.

   C. precipitation.

   D. percolation.

2. **Which one of the following landforms results from river and stream erosion?**

   A. glaciers

   B. aquifers

   C. mountains

   D. river channels

3. **Where is a rejuvenated river formed?**

   A. where the land is raised by the buildup of groundwater pressure

   B. where tectonic activity raises the land

   C. where the land sinks due to gravitational forces

   D. where new tributaries feed into an old river

4. **The Savannah River watershed covers parts of Georgia, North Carolina, and South Carolina. What are the streams and rivers that flow into the Savannah River called?**

   A. deltas

   B. aquifers

   C. gradients

   D. tributaries

Use the table below to answer question 5.

ANNUAL LEVELS OF DISSOLVED OXYGEN IN A LAKE

Year	Amount of Dissolved Oxygen (mg/L)
1950	8.1 mg/L
1960	7.6 mg/L
1970	7.0 mg/L
1980	6.4 mg/L
1990	5.8 mg/L
2000	5.0 mg/L

5. **The table above shows the levels of dissolved oxygen (DO) in one lake over a period of 50 years. Since 1950, the DO level in the lake has decreased from 8.1 milligrams per liter (mg/L) to 5.0 mg/L. What is the average decrease in the DO level per 10 year period?**

   A. 3.1 mg/L

   B. 0.62 mg/L

   C. 6.65 mg/L

   D. 0.52 mg/L

6. **Lakes form in areas where**

   A. wells are drilled.

   B. the water table is below the Earth's surface.

   C. the water table is above the Earth's surface.

   D. there are placer deposits.

7. In which step(s) of the water cycle does water lose energy?

   A. evaporation

   B. condensation

   C. transpiration

   D. all steps

8. In a shower, many small streams of water combine to form larger streams, which eventually combine and flow down the drain. What is this a simple model of?

   A. a youthful river

   B. a divide

   C. a river delta

   D. a watershed

9. Which of these situations could produce a natural spring?

   A. where water enters an aquifer

   B. where the zone of aeration meets Earth's surface

   C. where the water table meets Earth's surface

   D. where the zone of aeration meets the zone of saturation

Use the diagram below to answer question 10.

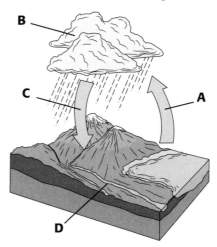

10. At which point in the diagram above is precipitation most likely taking place?

   A. point A

   B. point B

   C. point C

   D. point D

Open Response

11. Water in an artesian formation flows downhill through an aquifer under pressure. Where there are cracks in the cap rock, water flows freely through the cracks, forming artesian springs. If a number of water wells were drilled into an aquifer, what would be the *most likely* effect on the aquifer? How will the rate of flow through an artesian spring or the water level of the aquifer be affected?

12. Mammoth Cave, near Cave City, Kentucky, is the longest cave in the world. How do caves form in existing layers of limestone?

Science in Action

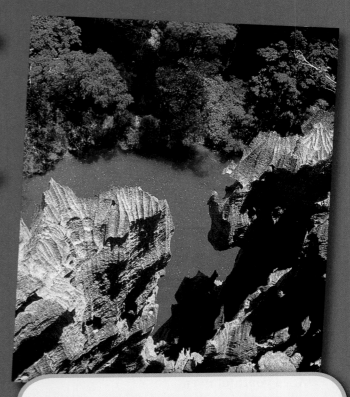

Weird Science

Secret Lake

Would you believe there is a freshwater lake more than 3 km below an Antarctic glacier near the South Pole? It is surprising that Lake Vostok can remain in a liquid state at a place where the temperature can fall below −50°C. Scientists believe that the intense pressure from the overlying ice heats the lake and keeps it from freezing. Geothermal energy, which is the energy within the surface of the Earth, also contributes to warmer temperatures. The other unique thing about Lake Vostok is the discovery of living microbes under the glacier that covers the lake!

Language Arts ACTiViTY

Look up the word *geothermal* in the dictionary. What is the meaning of the roots *geo-* and *-thermal*? Find other words in the dictionary that begin with the root *geo-*.

Scientific Discoveries

Sunken Forests

Imagine having your own little secret forest. In Ankarana National Park, in Madagascar, there are plenty of them. Within the limestone mountain of the park, caves have formed from the twisting path of the flowing groundwater. In many places in the caves, the roof has collapsed to form a sinkhole. The light that now shines through the collapsed roof of the cave has allowed miniature sunken forests to grow. Each sunken forest has unique characteristics. Some have crocodiles. Others have blind cavefish. You can even find some species that can't be found anywhere else in the world!

Social Studies ACTiViTY

Find out how Madagascar's geography contributes to the biodiversity of the island nation. Make a map of the island that highlights some of the unique forms of life found there.

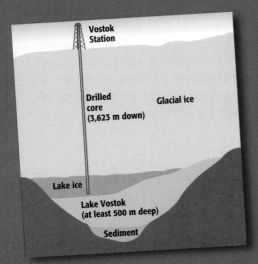

Vostok Station

Drilled core (3,623 m down)

Glacial ice

Lake ice

Lake Vostok (at least 500 m deep)

Sediment

Rita Colwell

A Water Filter for All Did you ever drink a glass of water through a piece of cloth? Dr. Rita Colwell, director of the National Science Foundation, has found that filtering drinking water through a cloth can actually decrease the number of disease-causing bacteria in the water. This discovery is very important for the people of Bangladesh, where deadly outbreaks of cholera are frequent. People are usually infected by the cholera bacteria by drinking contaminated water. Colwell knew that filtering the water would remove the bacteria. The water would then be safe to drink. Unfortunately, filters were too expensive for most of the people to buy. Colwell tried filtering the water with a sari. A sari is a long piece of colorful cloth that many women in Bangladesh wear as skirtlike cloth. Filtering the water with the sari cloth did the trick. The amount of cholera bacteria in the water was reduced. Fewer people contracted cholera, and many lives were saved!

Math ACTIVITY

With the cloth water-filter method, there was a 48% reduction in the occurrence of cholera. If there were 125 people out of 100,000 who contracted cholera before the cloth-filter method was used, how many people per 100,000 contracted cholera after using the cloth-filter method?

go.hrw.com

To learn more about these Science in Action topics, visit **go.hrw.com** and type in the keyword **HZ5DEPF.**

Current Science

Check out Current Science® articles related to this chapter by visiting go.hrw.com. Just type in the keyword HZ5CS11.

4

Agents of Erosion and Deposition

The Big Idea

Earth's surface is reshaped by the erosion of rock and soil and by the transportation and deposition of sediment.

SECTION

PRE-READING ACTIVITY

FOLDNOTES **Layered Book** Before you read the chapter, create the FoldNote entitled "The Layered Book" described in the **Study Skills** section of the Appendix. Label the tabs of the layered book with "Shoreline erosion and deposition," "Wind erosion and deposition," and "Erosion and deposition by ice." As you read the chapter, write information you learn about each category under the appropriate tab.

About the Photo

The results of erosion can often be dramatic. For example, this sinkhole formed in a parking lot in Atlanta, Georgia, when water running underground eventually caused the surface of the land to collapse.

Making Waves

Above ground or below, water plays an important role in the erosion and deposition of rock and soil. A shoreline is a good example of how water shapes the Earth's surface by erosion and deposition. Did you know that shorelines are shaped by crashing waves? Build a model shoreline, and see for yourself!

Procedure

1. Make a shoreline by adding **sand** to one end of a **washtub**. Fill the washtub with **water** to a depth of 5 cm. Sketch the shoreline profile (side view), and label it "A."

2. Place a **block** at the end of the washtub opposite the beach.

3. Move the block up and down very slowly to create small waves for 2 min. Sketch the new shoreline profile, and label it "B."

4. Now, move the block up and down more rapidly to create large waves for 2 min. Sketch the new shoreline profile, and label it "C."

Analysis

1. Compare the three shoreline profiles. What is happening to the shoreline?

2. How do small waves and large waves erode the shoreline differently?

What You Will Learn

● Explain how energy from waves affects a shoreline.
● Identify six shoreline features created by wave erosion.
● Explain how wave deposits form beaches.
● Describe how sand moves along a beach.

Vocabulary

shoreline
beach

READING STRATEGY

Reading Organizer As you read this section, create an outline of the section. Use the headings from the section in your outline.

Shoreline Erosion and Deposition

Think about the last time you were at a beach. Where did all of the sand come from?

Two basic ingredients are necessary to make sand: rock and energy. The rock is usually available on the shore. The energy is provided by waves that travel through water. When waves crash into rocks over long periods of time, the rocks are broken down into smaller and smaller pieces until they become sand.

As you read on, you will learn how wave erosion and deposition shape the shoreline. A **shoreline** is simply the place where land and a body of water meet. Waves usually play a major role in building up and breaking down the shoreline.

Wave Energy

As the wind moves across the ocean surface, it produces ripples called *waves*. The size of a wave depends on how hard the wind is blowing and how long the wind blows. The harder and longer the wind blows, the bigger the wave.

The wind that results from summer hurricanes and severe winter storms produces large waves that cause dramatic shoreline erosion. Waves may travel hundreds or even thousands of kilometers from a storm before reaching the shoreline. Some of the largest waves to reach the California coast are produced by storms as far away as Australia. So, the California surfer in **Figure 1** can ride a wave that formed on the other side of the Pacific Ocean!

Figure 1 *Waves produced by storms on the other side of the Pacific Ocean propel this surfer toward a California shore.*

Wave Trains

When you drop a pebble into a pond, is there just one ripple? Of course not. Waves, like ripples, don't move alone. As shown in **Figure 2,** waves travel in groups called *wave trains*. As wave trains move away from their source, they travel through the ocean water uninterrupted. But when waves reach shallow water, the bottom of the wave drags against the sea floor, slowing the wave down. The upper part of the wave moves more rapidly and grows taller. When the top of the wave becomes so tall that it cannot support itself, it begins to curl and break. These breaking waves are known as *surf*. Now you know how surfers got their name. The *wave period* is the time interval between breaking waves. Wave periods are usually 10 to 20 s long.

The Pounding Surf

Look at **Figure 3,** and you will get an idea of how sand is made. A tremendous amount of energy is released when waves break. A crashing wave can break solid rock and throw broken rocks back against the shore. As the rushing water in breaking waves enters cracks in rock, it helps break off large boulders and wash away fine grains of sand. The loose sand picked up by waves wears down and polishes coastal rocks. As a result of these actions, rock is broken down into smaller and smaller pieces that eventually become sand.

✓ Reading Check How do waves help break down rock into sand? (*See the Appendix for answers to Reading Checks.*)

Figure 2 *Because waves travel in wave trains, they break at regular intervals.*

shoreline the boundary between land and a body of water

Counting Waves

If the wave period is 10 s, approximately how many waves reach a shoreline in a day? (Hint: Calculate how many waves occur in an hour, and multiply that number by the number of hours in a day.)

Figure 3 *Breaking waves crash against the rocky shore, releasing their energy.*

Wave Erosion

Wave erosion produces a variety of features along a shoreline. *Sea cliffs* are formed when waves erode and undercut rock to produce steep slopes. Waves strike the base of the cliff, which wears away the soil and rock and makes the cliff steeper. The rate at which the sea cliffs erode depends on the hardness of the rock and the energy of the waves. Sea cliffs made of hard rock, such as granite, erode very slowly. Sea cliffs made of soft rock, such as shale, erode more rapidly, especially during storms.

Figure 4 Coastal Landforms Created by Wave Erosion

Sea stacks are offshore columns of resistant rock that were once connected to the mainland. In these instances, waves have eroded the mainland, leaving behind isolated columns of rock.

Sea arches form when wave action continues to erode a sea cave, cutting completely through the rock.

Sea caves form when waves cut large holes into fractured or weak rock along the base of sea cliffs. Sea caves are common in cliffs composed of sedimentary rock.

Shaping a Shoreline

Much of the erosion responsible for landforms you might see along the shoreline takes place during storms. Large waves generated by storms release far more energy than normal waves do. This energy is so powerful that it is capable of removing huge chunks of rock. **Figure 4** shows some of the major landscape features that result from wave erosion.

✓ **Reading Check** Why are large waves more capable of removing large chunks of rock from a shoreline than normal waves are?

INTERNET ACTIVITY

For another activity related to this chapter, go to **go.hrw.com** and type in the keyword **HZ5ICEW**.

Headlands are finger-shaped projections that form when cliffs made of hard rock erode more slowly than surrounding rock. On many shorelines, hard rock will form headlands, and the softer rock will form beaches or bays.

Wave-cut terraces form when a sea cliff is worn back, producing a nearly level platform beneath the water at the base of the cliff.

England

U.S. Virgin Islands

Hawaii

Figure 5 *Beaches are made of different types of material deposited by waves.*

beach an area of the shoreline made up of material deposited by waves

Wave Deposits

Waves carry a variety of materials, including sand, rock fragments, dead coral, and shells. Often, this material is deposited on a shoreline, where it forms a beach.

Beaches

You would probably recognize a beach if you saw one. However, scientifically speaking, a **beach** is any area of the shoreline made up of material deposited by waves. Some beach material is also deposited by rivers.

Compare the beaches shown in **Figure 5.** Notice that the colors and textures vary. They vary because the type of material found on a beach depends on its source. Light-colored sand is the most common beach material. Much of this sand comes from the mineral quartz. But not all beaches are made of light-colored sand. For example, on many tropical islands, such as the Virgin Islands, beaches are made of fine, white coral material. Some Florida beaches are made of tiny pieces of broken seashells. Black sand beaches in Hawaii are made of eroded volcanic lava. In areas where stormy seas are common, beaches are made of pebbles and boulders.

✓ Reading Check Where does beach material come from?

Wave Angle and Sand Movement

The movement of sand along a beach depends on the angle at which the waves strike the shore. Most waves approach the beach at a slight angle and retreat in a direction more perpendicular to the shore. This movement of water is called a longshore current. A *longshore current* is a water current that moves the sand in a zigzag pattern along the beach, as you can see in **Figure 6.**

Figure 6 *When waves strike the shoreline at an angle, sand migrates along the beach in a zigzag path.*

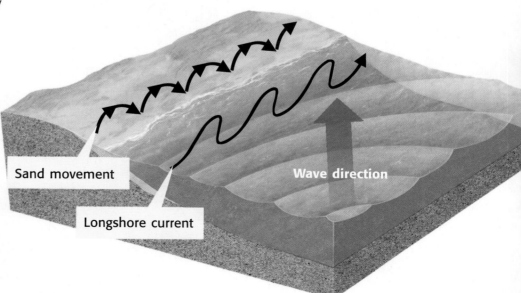

Sand movement

Longshore current

Wave direction

Offshore Deposits

Waves moving at an angle to the shoreline push water along the shore and create longshore currents. When waves erode material from the shoreline, longshore currents can transport and deposit this material offshore, which creates landforms in open water. A *sandbar* is an underwater or exposed ridge of sand, gravel, or shell material. A *barrier spit* is an exposed sandbar that is connected to the shoreline. Cape Cod, Massachusetts, shown in **Figure 7,** is an example of a barrier spit. A barrier island is a long, narrow island usually made of sand that forms offshore parallel to the shoreline.

Figure 7 *A barrier spit, such as Cape Cod, Massachusetts, occurs when an exposed sandbar is connected to the shoreline.*

SECTION Review

Summary

- As waves break against a shoreline, rock is broken down into sand.
- Six shoreline features created by wave erosion include sea cliffs, sea stacks, sea caves, sea arches, headlands, and wave-cut terraces.
- Beaches are made from material deposited by waves.
- Longshore currents cause sand to move in a zigzag pattern along the shore.

Using Key Terms

Complete each of the following sentences by choosing the correct term from the word bank.

shoreline   beach

1. A ___ is an area made up of material deposited by waves.

2. An area in which land and a body of water meet is a ___.

Understanding Key Ideas

3. Which of the following is a result of wave deposition?
   a. sea arch
   b. sea cave
   c. barrier spit
   d. headland

4. How do wave deposits affect a shoreline?

5. Describe how sand moves along a beach.

6. What are six shoreline features created by wave erosion?

7. How can the energy of waves traveling through water affect a shoreline?

8. Would a small wave or a large wave have more energy? Explain your answer.

Math Skills

9. Imagine that there is a large boulder on the edge of a shoreline. If the wave period is 15 s long, how many times is the boulder hit in a year?

Critical Thinking

10. **Applying Concepts** Not all beaches are made from light-colored sand. Explain why this statement is true.

11. **Making Inferences** How can severe storms over the ocean affect shoreline erosion and deposition?

12. **Making Predictions** How could a headland change in 250 years? Describe some of the features that may form.

Developed and maintained by the National Science Teachers Association

For a variety of links related to this chapter, go to www.scilinks.org

Topic: Wave Erosion
SciLinks code: HSM1638

Wind Erosion and Deposition

What You Will Learn

- Explain why some areas are more affected by wind erosion than other areas are.
- Describe the process of saltation.
- Identify three landforms that result from wind erosion and deposition.
- Explain how dunes move.

Vocabulary

saltation   loess
deflation   dune
abrasion

READING STRATEGY

Reading Organizer As you read this section, make a table comparing deflation and abrasion.

Have you ever been working outside and had a gusty wind blow an important stack of papers all over the place?

Do you remember how fast and far the papers traveled and how long it took to pick them up? Every time you caught up with them, they were on the move again. If this has happened to you, then you have seen how wind erosion works. As an agent of erosion, the wind removes soil, sand, and rock particles and transports them from one place to another.

Certain locations are more vulnerable to wind erosion than others. An area with little plant cover can be severely affected by wind erosion because plant roots anchor sand and soil in place. Deserts and coastlines that are made of fine, loose rock material and have little plant cover are shaped most dramatically by the wind.

The Process of Wind Erosion

Wind moves material in different ways. In areas where strong winds occur, material is moved by saltation. **Saltation** is the skipping and bouncing movement of sand-sized particles in the direction the wind is blowing. As you can see in **Figure 1,** the wind causes the particles to bounce. When moving sand grains knock into one another, some grains bounce up in the air, fall forward, and strike other sand grains. These impacts cause other grains to roll and bounce forward.

Figure 1 *The wind causes sand grains to move by saltation.*

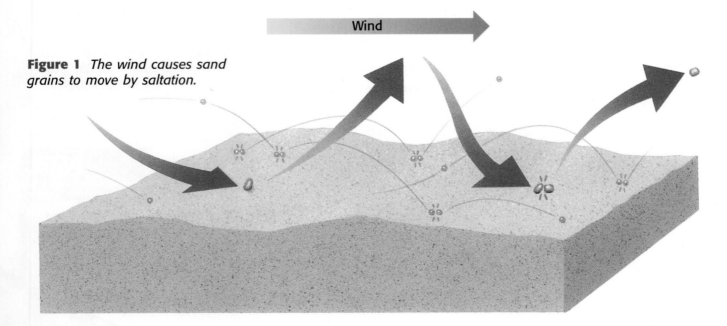

Wind

Figure 2 *Desert pavement, such as that found in the Painted Desert in Arizona, forms when wind removes all the fine materials.*

Deflation

The removal of fine sediment by wind is called **deflation.** During deflation, wind removes the top layer of fine sediment or soil and leaves behind rock fragments that are too heavy to be lifted by the wind. Deflation may cause *desert pavement*, which is a surface consisting of pebbles and small broken rocks. An example of desert pavement is shown in **Figure 2.**

Have you ever blown on a layer of dust while cleaning off a dresser? If you have, you may have noticed that in addition to your face getting dirty, a little scooped-out depression formed in the dust. Similarly, in areas where there is little vegetation, the wind may scoop out depressions in the landscape. These depressions are called *deflation hollows*.

Reading Check Where do deflation hollows form? (*See the Appendix for answers to Reading Checks.*)

Abrasion

The grinding and wearing down of rock surfaces by other rock or sand particles is called **abrasion.** Abrasion commonly happens in areas where there are strong winds, loose sand, and soft rocks. The blowing of millions of sharp sand grains creates a sandblasting effect. This effect helps to erode, smooth, and polish rocks.

saltation the movement of sand or other sediments by short jumps and bounces that is caused by wind or water

deflation a form of wind erosion in which fine, dry soil particles are blown away

abrasion the grinding and wearing away of rock surfaces through the mechanical action of other rock or sand particles

Making Desert Pavement

1. Spread a mixture of **dust, sand,** and **gravel** on an **outdoor table.**
2. Place an **electric fan** at one end of the table.
3. Put on **safety goggles** and a **filter mask.** Aim the fan across the sediment. Start the fan on its lowest speed. Record your observations.
4. Turn the fan to a medium speed. Record your observations.
5. Finally, turn the fan to a high speed to imitate a desert windstorm. Record your observations.
6. What is the relationship between the wind speed and the size of the sediment that is moved?
7. Does the remaining sediment fit the definition of desert pavement?

loess very fine sediments deposited by the wind

dune a mound of wind-deposited sand that keeps its shape even though it moves

Wind-Deposited Materials

Much like rivers, the wind also carries sediment. And just as rivers deposit their loads, the wind eventually drops all the material it carries. The amount and the size of particles the wind can carry depend on the wind speed. The faster the wind blows, the more material and the heavier the particles it can carry. As wind speed slows, heavier particles are deposited first.

Loess

Wind can deposit extremely fine material. Thick deposits of this windblown, fine-grained sediment are known as **loess** (LOH es). Loess feels like the talcum powder a person may use after a shower.

Because wind carries fine-grained material much higher and farther than it carries sand, loess deposits are sometimes found far away from their source. Many loess deposits came from glacial sources during the last Ice Age. In the United States, loess is present in the Midwest, along the eastern edge of the Mississippi Valley, and in eastern Oregon and Washington.

Dunes

When the wind hits an obstacle, such as a plant or a rock, the wind slows down. As it slows, the wind deposits, or drops, the heavier material. The material collects, which creates an additional obstacle. This obstacle causes even more material to be deposited, forming a mound. Eventually, the original obstacle becomes buried. The mounds of wind-deposited sand are called **dunes.** Dunes are common in sandy deserts and along the sandy shores of lakes and oceans. **Figure 3** shows a large dune in a desert area.

Figure 3 *Dunes migrate in the direction of the wind.*

The Movement of Dunes

Dunes tend to move in the direction of strong winds. Different wind conditions produce dunes in various shapes and sizes. A dune usually has a gently sloped side and a steeply sloped side, or *slip face,* as shown in **Figure 4.** In most cases, the gently sloped side faces the wind. The wind is constantly transporting material up this side of the dune. As sand moves over the crest, or peak, of the dune, it slides down the slip face, creating a steep slope.

✓ Reading Check In what direction do dunes move?

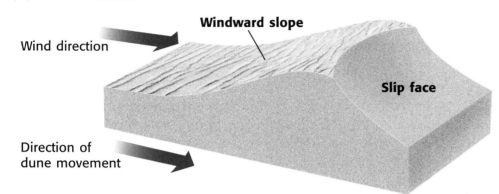

Wind direction

Windward slope

Slip face

Direction of dune movement

Figure 4 *Dunes are formed from material deposited by wind.*

Using Key Terms

In each of the following sentences, replace the incorrect term with the correct term from the word bank.

dune   saltation
deflation   abrasion

1. <u>Deflation hollows</u> are mounds of wind-deposited sand.

2. The removal of fine sediment by wind is called <u>abrasion</u>.

Understanding Key Ideas

3. Which of the following landforms is the result of wind deposition?
   a. deflation hollow
   b. desert pavement
   c. dune
   d. abrasion

4. Describe how material is moved in areas where strong winds blow.

5. Explain the process of abrasion.

Math Skills

6. If a dune moves 40 m per year, how far does it move in 1 day?

Critical Thinking

7. **Identifying Relationships** Explain the relationship between plant cover and wind erosion.

8. **Applying Concepts** If you climbed up the steep side of a sand dune, is it likely that you traveled in the direction the wind was blowing?

SCI_{LINKS}

NSTA
Developed and maintained by the National Science Teachers Association

For a variety of links related to this chapter, go to www.scilinks.org

Topic: Wind Erosion
SciLinks code: HSM1669

113

Erosion and Deposition by Ice

What You Will Learn

- Explain the difference between alpine glaciers and continental glaciers.
- Describe two ways in which glaciers move.
- Identify five landscape features formed by alpine glaciers.
- Identify four types of moraines.

Vocabulary

glacier   till
glacial drift   stratified drift

READING STRATEGY

Discussion Read this section silently. Write down questions that you have about this section. Discuss your questions in a small group.

glacier a large mass of moving ice

Can you imagine an ice cube that is the size of a football stadium? Well, glaciers can be even bigger than that.

A **glacier** is an enormous mass of moving ice. Because glaciers are very heavy and have the ability to move across the Earth's surface, they are capable of eroding, moving, and depositing large amounts of rock materials. And while you will never see a glacier chilling a punch bowl, you might one day visit some of the spectacular landscapes carved by glacial activity!

Glaciers—Rivers of Ice

Glaciers form in areas so cold that snow stays on the ground year-round. In polar regions and at high elevations, snow piles up year after year. Over time, the weight of the snow on top causes the deep-packed snow to become ice crystals. These ice crystals eventually form a giant ice mass. Because glaciers are so massive, the pull of gravity causes them to flow slowly, like "rivers of ice." In this section, you will learn about two main types of glaciers, alpine and continental.

Alpine Glaciers

Alpine glaciers form in mountainous areas. One common type of alpine glacier is a valley glacier. Valley glaciers form in valleys originally created by stream erosion. As these glaciers slowly flow downhill, they widen and straighten the valleys into broad U shapes as shown in **Figure 1.**

✓ **Reading Check** Where do alpine glaciers form? (*See the Appendix for answers to Reading Checks.*)

Figure 1 *Alpine glaciers start as snowfields in mountainous areas.*

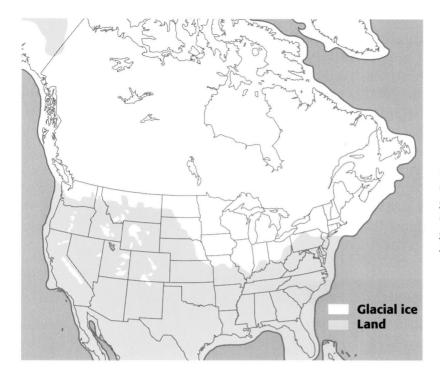

Figure 2 *Eleven U.S. states were covered by ice during the last glacial ice period. Because much of the Earth's water was frozen in glaciers, sea levels fell. Blue lines show the coastline at that time.*

Glacial ice
Land

Continental Glaciers

Not all glaciers are true "rivers of ice." In fact, some glaciers spread across entire continents. These glaciers, called *continental glaciers*, are huge, continuous masses of ice. The largest continental glacier in the world covers almost all of Antarctica. This ice sheet is approximately one and a half times the size of the United States. It is so thick—more than 4,000 m in places—that it buries everything but the highest mountain peaks.

Glaciers on the Move

When enough ice builds up on a slope, the ice begins to move downhill. Thick glaciers move faster than thin glaciers, and the steeper the slope is, the faster the glaciers will move. Glaciers move in two ways: by sliding and by flowing. A glacier slides when its weight causes the ice at the bottom of the glacier to melt. As the water from a melting ice cube causes the ice cube to travel across a table, the water from the melting ice causes a glacier to move forward. A glacier also flows slowly as ice crystals within the glacier slip over each other. Think of placing a deck of cards on a table and then tilting the table. The top cards will slide farther than the lower cards. Similarly, the upper part of the glacier flows faster than the base.

Glacier movement is affected by climate. As the Earth cools, glaciers grow. About 10,000 years ago, a continental glacier covered most of North America, as shown in **Figure 2.** In some places, the ice sheet was several kilometers thick!

The *Titanic*

WRITING SKILL An area where an ice sheet is resting on open water is called an *ice shelf*. When pieces of the ice shelf break off, they are called *icebergs*. How far do you think the iceberg that struck the *Titanic* drifted before the two met that fateful night in 1912? Together with an adult, plot on a map of the North Atlantic Ocean the route of the *Titanic* from Southampton, England, to New York. Then, plot a possible route of the drifting iceberg from Greenland to where the ship sank, just south of the Canadian island province of Newfoundland. Describe your findings in your **science journal.**

ACTIVITY

Speed of a Glacier

An alpine glacier is estimated to be moving forward at 5 m per day. Calculate how long the ice will take to reach a road and campground located 0.5 km from the front of the advancing glacier. (Hint: 1 km = 1,000 m)

Landforms Carved by Glaciers

Continental glaciers and alpine glaciers produce landscapes that are very different from one another. Continental glaciers smooth the landscape by scraping and eroding features that existed before the ice appeared. Alpine glaciers carve out rugged features in the mountain rocks through which they flow. **Figure 3** shows the very different landscapes that each type of glacier produces.

Alpine glaciers, such as those in the Rocky Mountains and the Alps, carve out large amounts of rock material and create spectacular landforms. **Figure 4** shows the kinds of landscape features that are sculpted by alpine glaciers.

Figure 3 Landscapes Created by Glaciers

◀ Continental glaciers smooth and flatten the landscape.

Alpine glaciers carved out this rugged landscape. ▶

Figure 4 Landscape Features Carved by Alpine Glaciers

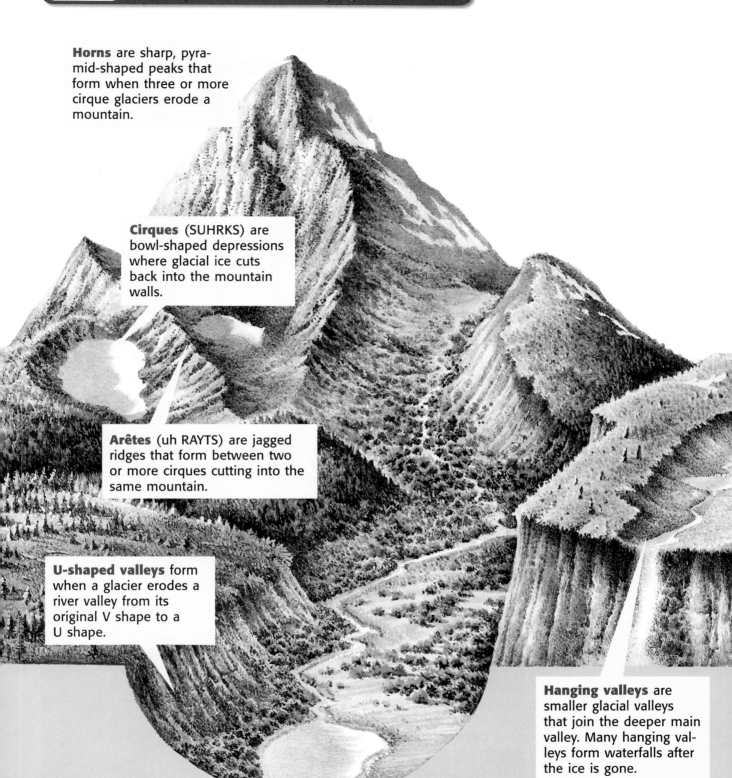

Horns are sharp, pyramid-shaped peaks that form when three or more cirque glaciers erode a mountain.

Cirques (SUHRKS) are bowl-shaped depressions where glacial ice cuts back into the mountain walls.

Arêtes (uh RAYTS) are jagged ridges that form between two or more cirques cutting into the same mountain.

U-shaped valleys form when a glacier erodes a river valley from its original V shape to a U shape.

Hanging valleys are smaller glacial valleys that join the deeper main valley. Many hanging valleys form waterfalls after the ice is gone.

Types of Glacial Deposits

As a glacier melts, it drops all the material it is carrying. **Glacial drift** is the general term used to describe all material carried and deposited by glaciers. Glacial drift is divided into two main types, *till* and *stratified drift*.

Till Deposits

Unsorted rock material that is deposited directly by the ice when it melts is called **till.** *Unsorted* means that the till is made up of rock material of different sizes—from large boulders to fine sediment. When the glacier melts, the unsorted material is deposited on the surface of the ground.

The most common till deposits are *moraines*. Moraines generally form ridges along the edges of glaciers. Moraines are produced when glaciers carry material to the front of and along the sides of the ice. As the ice melts, the sediment and rock it is carrying are dropped, which forms different types of moraines. The various types of moraines are shown in **Figure 5.**

glacial drift the rock material carried and deposited by glaciers

till unsorted rock material that is deposited directly by a melting glacier

stratified drift a glacial deposit that has been sorted and layered by the action of streams or meltwater

Figure 5 Types of Moraines

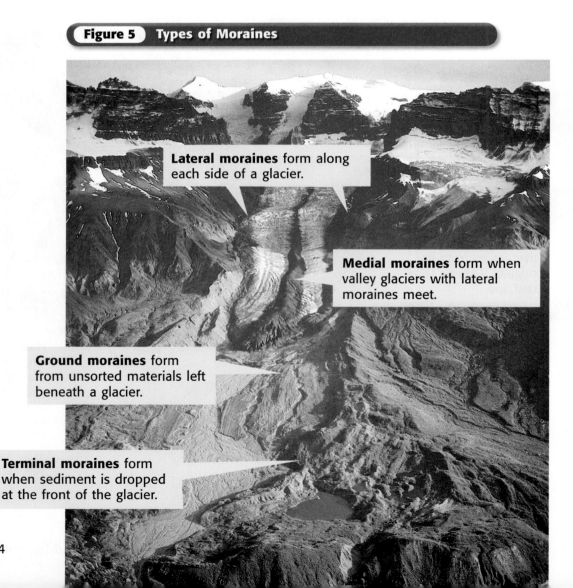

Lateral moraines form along each side of a glacier.

Medial moraines form when valley glaciers with lateral moraines meet.

Ground moraines form from unsorted materials left beneath a glacier.

Terminal moraines form when sediment is dropped at the front of the glacier.

Stratified Drift

When a glacier melts, streams form that carry rock material away from the shrinking glacier. A glacial deposit that is sorted into layers based on the size of the rock material is called **stratified drift.** Streams carry sorted material and deposit it in front of the glacier in a broad area called an *outwash plain*. Sometimes, a block of ice is left in the outwash plain when a glacier retreats. As the ice melts, sediment builds up around the block of ice, and a depression called a *kettle* forms. Kettles commonly fill with water to form lakes or ponds, as **Figure 6** shows.

✓ **Reading Check** Explain the difference between a till deposit and stratified drift.

Figure 6 *Kettle lakes form in outwash plains and are common in states such as Minnesota.*

SECTION
Review

Summary

- Alpine glaciers form in mountainous areas. Continental glaciers spread across entire continents.
- Glaciers can move by sliding or by flowing.
- Alpine glaciers can carve cirques, arêtes, horns, U-shaped valleys, and hanging valleys.
- Two types of glacial drift are till and stratified drift.
- Four types of moraines are lateral, medial, ground, and terminal moraines.

Using Key Terms

Complete each of the following sentences by choosing the correct term from the word bank.

glacial drift   glacier
stratified drift   till

1. A glacial deposit that is sorted into layers based on the size of the rock material is called ___.

2. ___ is all of the material carried and deposited by glaciers.

3. Unsorted rock material that is deposited directly by the ice when it melts is ___.

4. A ___ is an enormous mass of moving ice.

Understanding Key Ideas

5. Which of the following is not a type of moraine?
   a. lateral
   b. horn
   c. ground
   d. medial

6. Explain the difference between alpine and continental glaciers.

7. Name five landscape features formed by alpine glaciers.

8. Describe two ways in which glaciers move.

Math Skills

9. A recent study shows that a glacier in Alaska is melting at a rate of 23 ft per year. At what rate is the glacier melting in meters? (Hint: 1 ft = 0.3 m)

Critical Thinking

10. **Analyzing Ideas** Explain why continental glaciers smooth the landscape and alpine glaciers create a rugged landscape.

11. **Applying Concepts** How can a glacier deposit both sorted and unsorted material?

12. **Applying Concepts** Why are glaciers such effective agents of erosion and deposition?

SCi LINKS®

Developed and maintained by the National Science Teachers Association

For a variety of links related to this chapter, go to www.scilinks.org

Topic: Glaciers
SciLinks code: HSM0675

The Effect of Gravity on Erosion and Deposition

Did you know that the Appalachian Mountains may have once been almost five times as tall as they are now? Why are they shorter now? Part of the answer lies in the effect that gravity has on all objects on Earth.

Although you can't see it, the force of gravity is also an agent of erosion and deposition. Gravity not only influences the movement of water and ice but also causes rocks and soil to move downslope. **Mass movement** is the movement of any material, such as rock, soil, or snow, downslope. Whether mass movement happens rapidly or slowly, it plays a major role in shaping the Earth's surface.

Angle of Repose

If dry sand is piled up, it will move downhill until the slope becomes stable. The *angle of repose* is the steepest angle, or slope, at which loose material will not slide downslope. This is demonstrated in **Figure 1.** The angle of repose is different for each type of surface material. Characteristics of the surface material, such as its size, weight, shape, and moisture level, determine at what angle the material will move downslope.

mass movement a movement of a section of land down a slope

Figure 1 *If the slope on which material rests is less than the angle of repose, the material will stay in place. If the slope is greater than the angle of repose, the material will move downslope.*

Rapid Mass Movement

The most destructive mass movements happen suddenly and rapidly. Rapid mass movement can be very dangerous and can destroy everything in its path.

Rock Falls

While driving along a mountain road, you may have noticed signs along the road that warn of falling rocks. A **rock fall** happens when loose rocks fall down a steep slope. Steep slopes are sometimes created to make room for a road in mountainous areas. Loosened and exposed rocks above the road tend to fall as a result of gravity. The rocks in a rock fall can range in size from small fragments to large boulders.

Landslides

Another type of rapid mass movement is a landslide. A **landslide** is the sudden and rapid movement of a large amount of material downslope. A *slump,* shown in **Figure 2,** is the most common type of landslide. Slumping occurs when a block of material moves downslope over a curved surface. Heavy rains, deforestation, construction on unstable slopes, and earthquakes increase the chances that a landslide will happen. **Figure 3** shows a landslide in India.

Reading Check What is a slump? (*See the Appendix for answers to Reading Checks.*)

Figure 2 *A slump is a type of landslide that occurs when a block of land becomes detached and slides downhill.*

rock fall a group of loose rocks that fall down a steep slope

landslide the sudden movement of rock and soil down a slope

Figure 3 *This landslide in Bombay, India, happened after heavy monsoon rains.*

Figure 4 *This photo shows one of the many mudflows that have occurred in California during rainy winters.*

mudflow the flow of a mass of mud or rock and soil mixed with a large amount of water

Figure 5 *This lahar overtook the city of Kyushu in Japan.*

Mudflows

A rapid movement of a large mass of mud is a **mudflow.** Mudflows happen when a large amount of water mixes with soil and rock. The water causes the slippery mass of mud to flow rapidly downslope. Mudflows commonly happen in mountainous regions when a long dry season is followed by heavy rains. Deforestation and the removal of ground cover can often result in devastating mudflows. As you can see in **Figure 4,** a mudflow can carry trees, houses, cars, and other objects that lie in its path.

Lahars

Volcanic eruptions or heavy rains on volcanic ash can produce some of the most dangerous mudflows. Mudflows of volcanic origin are called *lahars*. Lahars can travel at speeds greater than 80 km/h and can be as thick as cement. On volcanoes with snowy peaks, an eruption can suddenly melt a great amount of ice. The water from the ice liquefies the soil and volcanic ash to produce a hot mudflow that rushes downslope. **Figure 5** shows the effects of a massive lahar in Japan.

Reading Check Explain how a lahar occurs.

Slow Mass Movement

Sometimes, you don't even notice mass movement happening. Although rapid mass movements are visible and dramatic, slow mass movements happen a little at a time. However, because slow mass movements occur more frequently, more material is moved collectively over time.

Creep

Even though most slopes appear to be stable, they are actually undergoing slow mass movement, as shown in **Figure 6.** The extremely slow movement of material downslope is called **creep.** Many factors contribute to creep. Water loosens soil and allows it to move freely. In addition, plant roots act as a wedge that forces rocks and soil particles apart. Burrowing animals, such as gophers and groundhogs, also loosen rock and soil particles. In fact, rock and soil on every slope travels slowly downhill.

Figure 6 *Bent tree trunks are evidence that creep is happening.*

creep the slow downhill movement of weathered rock material

SECTION Review

Summary

- Gravity causes rocks and soil to move downslope.
- If the slope on which material rests is greater than the angle of repose, mass movement will occur.
- Four types of rapid mass movement are rock falls, landslides, mudflows, and lahars.
- Water, plant roots, and burrowing animals can cause creep.

Using Key Terms

Complete each of the following sentences by choosing the correct term from the word bank.

creep   mass movement
mudflow   rock fall

1. A ___ occurs when a large amount of water mixes with soil and rock.

2. The extremely slow movement of material downslope is called ___.

Understanding Key Ideas

3. Which of the following is a factor that affects creep?

   a. water

   b. burrowing animals

   c. plant roots

   d. All of the above.

4. How is the angle of repose related to mass movement?

Math Skills

5. If a lahar is traveling at 80 km/h, how long will it take the lahar to travel 20 km?

Critical Thinking

6. **Identifying Relationships** Which types of mass movement are most dangerous to humans? Explain your answer.

7. **Making Inferences** How does deforestation increase the likelihood of mudflows?

SCI**LINKS**®

NSTA
Developed and maintained by the National Science Teachers Association

For a variety of links related to this chapter, go to www.scilinks.org

Topic: Mass Movements
SciLinks code: HSM0917

Model-Making Lab

Gliding Glaciers

A glacier is a large, moving mass of ice. Glaciers are responsible for shaping many of Earth's natural features. Glaciers are set in motion by the pull of gravity and by the gradual melting of the glacier. As a glacier moves, it changes the landscape by eroding the surface over which it passes.

Part A: Getting in the Groove

Procedure

The material that is carried by a glacier erodes Earth's surface by gouging out grooves called *striations*. Different materials have varying effects on the landscape. In this activity, you will create a model glacier with which to demonstrate the effects of glacial erosion by various materials.

1. Fill one margarine container with sand to a depth of 1 cm. Fill another margarine container with gravel to a depth of 1 cm. Leave the third container empty. Fill the containers with water.

2. Put the three containers in a freezer, and leave them there overnight.

3. Retrieve the containers from the freezer, and remove the three ice blocks from the containers.

4. Use a rolling pin to flatten the modeling clay.

5. Hold the ice block from the third container firmly with a towel, and press as you move the ice along the length of the clay. Do this three times. In a notebook, sketch the pattern that the ice block makes in the clay.

OBJECTIVES

Build a model of a glacier.

Demonstrate the effects of glacial erosion by various materials.

Observe the effect of pressure on the melting rate of a glacier.

MATERIALS

- brick (3)
- clay, modeling (2 lb)
- container, empty large margarine (3)
- freezer
- graduated cylinder, 50 mL
- gravel (1 lb)
- pan, aluminum rectangular (3)
- rolling pin, wood
- ruler, metric
- sand (1 lb)
- stopwatch
- towel, small hand
- water

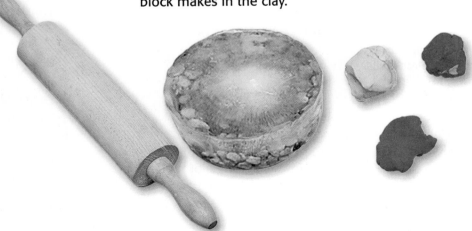

6 Repeat steps 4 and 5 using the ice block that contains sand.

7 Repeat steps 4 and 5 using the ice block that contains gravel.

Analyze the Results

1 **Describing Events** Did any material from the clay become mixed with the material in the ice blocks? Explain.

2 **Describing Events** Was any material from the ice blocks deposited on the clay surface? Explain.

3 **Examining Data** What glacial features are represented in your clay model?

Draw Conclusions

4 **Evaluating Data** Compare the patterns formed by the three model glaciers. Do the patterns look like features carved by alpine glaciers or by continental glaciers? Explain.

Part B: Melting Away

Procedure

As the layers of ice build up and a glacier gets larger, a glacier will eventually begin to melt. The water from the melted ice allows a glacier to move forward. In this activity, you'll explore the effect of pressure on the melting rate of a glacier.

1 If possible, make three identical ice blocks without any sand or gravel in them. If that is not possible, use the ice blocks from Part A. Place one ice block upside down in each pan.

2 Place one brick on top of one of the ice blocks. Place two bricks on top of another ice block. Do not put any bricks on the third ice block.

3 After 15 min, remove the bricks from the ice blocks.

4 Using the graduated cylinder, measure the amount of water that has melted from each ice block.

5 Observe and record your findings.

Analyze the Results

1 **Analyzing Data** Which ice block produced the most water?

2 **Explaining Events** What did the bricks represent?

3 **Analyzing Results** What part of the ice blocks melted first? Explain.

Draw Conclusions

4 **Interpreting Information** How could you relate this investigation to the melting rate of glaciers? Explain.

Applying Your Data

Replace the clay with different materials, such as soft wood or sand. How does each ice block affect the different surface materials? What types of surfaces do the different materials represent?

Chapter Review

USING KEY TERMS

For each pair of terms, explain how the meanings of the terms differ.

1. *shoreline* and *longshore current*

2. *beaches* and *dunes*

3. *deflation* and *saltation*

4. *continental glacier* and *alpine glacier*

5. *stratified drift* and *till*

6. *mudflow* and *creep*

UNDERSTANDING KEY IDEAS

Multiple Choice

7. *Surf* refers to
   a. large storm waves in the open ocean.
   b. giant waves produced by hurricanes.
   c. breaking waves near the shoreline.
   d. small waves on a calm sea.

8. When waves cut completely through a headland, a ___ is formed.
   a. sea cave
   b. sea arch
   c. wave-cut terrace
   d. sandbar

9. A narrow strip of sand that is formed by wave deposition and is connected to the shore is called a
   a. barrier spit.
   b. sandbar.
   c. wave-cut terrace.
   d. headland.

10. A wind-eroded depression is called a
    a. deflation hollow.
    b. desert pavement.
    c. dune.
    d. dust bowl.

11. What term describes all types of glacial deposits?
    a. glacial drift
    b. dune
    c. till
    d. outwash

12. Which of the following is NOT a landform created by an alpine glacier?
    a. cirque
    b. deflation hollow
    c. horn
    d. arête

13. What is the term for a mass movement that is of volcanic origin?
    a. lahar
    b. slump
    c. creep
    d. rock fall

14. Which of the following is a slow mass movement?
    a. mudflow
    b. landslide
    c. creep
    d. rock fall

Short Answer

15. Why do waves break when they near the shore?

16. Why are some areas more affected by wind erosion than other areas are?

17 What kind of mass movement happens continuously, day after day?

18 In what direction do sand dunes move?

19 Describe the different types of glacial moraines.

CRITICAL THINKING

20 Concept Mapping Use the following terms to create a concept map: *deflation*, *strong winds*, *saltation*, *dune*, and *desert pavement*.

21 Making Inferences How do humans increase the likelihood that wind erosion will occur?

22 Identifying Relationships If the large ice sheet covering Antarctica were to melt completely, what type of landscape would you expect Antarctica to have?

23 Applying Concepts You are a geologist who is studying rock to determine the direction of flow of an ancient glacier. What clues might help you determine the glacier's direction of flow?

24 Applying Concepts You are interested in purchasing a home that overlooks the ocean. The home that you want to buy sits atop a steep sea cliff. Given what you have learned about shoreline erosion, what factors would you take into consideration when deciding whether to buy the home?

INTERPRETING GRAPHICS

The graph below illustrates coastal erosion and deposition at an imaginary beach over a period of 8 years. Use the graph below to answer the questions that follow.

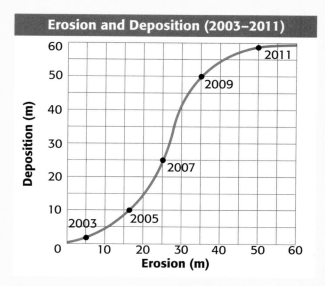

Erosion and Deposition (2003–2011)

25 What is happening to the beach over time?

26 In what year does the amount of erosion equal the amount of deposition?

27 Based on the erosion and deposition data for 2005, what might happen to the beach in the years that follow 2005?

Standardized Test Preparation

Multiple Choice

1. On a geology research trip, Jeff finds a deposit of till that is located along the side of an active glacier. Which type of deposit did Jeff find?

   A. terminal moraine

   B. ground moraine

   C. medial moraine

   D. lateral moraine

2. Which of the following best describes how a sea arch forms in a coastal area?

   A. Salt water dissolves the rock, so a hole is created in the rock formation.

   B. Energy from a strong storm hits the rocks and creates a hole in the rock formation.

   C. The shifting of tectonic plates creates cracks in the rock formation.

   D. The repeated action of waves slowly wears a hole in the rock formation.

3. A lahar forms during a volcanic eruption and moves toward a village that is 28 km away. If the lahar is moving at a rate of 92 km/h, how much time do the people in the village have to evacuate?

   A. about 3 minutes

   B. about 18 minutes

   C. about 30 minutes

   D. about 180 minutes

Use the illustrations below to answer question 4.

 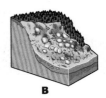 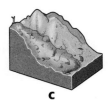

A   B   C

4. During a classroom activity, Andrea made the illustrations above of various types of mass movement. Which of the following is a valid conclusion about the processes shown in Andrea's illustrations?

   A. The amount of plant coverage in an area does not affect the likelihood of each process occurring.

   B. The process in illustration B is caused by plant coverage.

   C. The process shown in illustration A is generally the most deadly, because it involves the most mass.

   D. Gravity is a factor that plays a major role in these mass movement processes.

5. How does the energy from a wave in one part of the world reach another part of the world?

   A. Convection currents carry the energy across the ocean.

   B. The energy travels because it is transferred from wave to wave across the ocean.

   C. The energy travels in undersea currents across the ocean.

   D. Water particles carry energy and form waves close to the coast.

6. Which of the following areas would be most strongly affected by wind erosion?

   A. pine forest

   B. rocky beach

   C. desert

   D. grassland

7. Which of the following best describes the process responsible for the formation of sand?

   A. rocks + waves = sand

   B. wind + waves = sand

   C. beach + longshore current = sand

   D. surf + wave train = sand

8. Where would you be most likely to observe saltation on a sand dune?

   A. slip face

   B. crest

   C. windward slope

   D. in any area of the dune

Use the table below to answer question 9.

Rocky Beaches Along a Coastline	Average Wave Period
Beach A	13 S
Beach B	18 S
Beach C	10 S
Beach D	21 S

9. The table shows the average wave period for four beaches along a coastline. Which beach will have the largest (highest) waves hitting the beach?

   A. Beach A

   B. Beach B

   C. Beach C

   D. Beach D

Open Response

10. The Outer Banks are a series of barrier islands that are located along North Carolina's Atlantic coastline. They were formed by wave action over many centuries. Along the Outer Banks, the beaches that face east tend to erode away, and south-facing shorelines tend to grow. Explain how this pattern of shoreline erosion and deposition might occur?

11. Around 10,000 years ago, a continental glacier covered the areas that are now Canada and the northern United States. What kinds of landscape features caused by this glacier would you expect to see in the northern U.S. now?

Standardized Test Preparation

Science in Action

Weird Science

Long-Runout Landslides

At 4:10 A.M. on April 29, 1903, the town of Frank, Canada, was changed forever when disaster struck without warning. An enormous chunk of limestone fell suddenly from the top of nearby Turtle Mountain. In less than two minutes, the huge mass of rock buried most of the town! Landslides such as the Frank landslide are now known as *long-runout landslides*. Most landslides travel a horizontal distance that is less than twice the vertical distance that they have fallen. But long-runout landslides carry enormous amounts of rock and thus can travel many times farther than they fall. The physics of long-runout landslides are still a mystery to scientists.

Scientific Discoveries

The Lost Squadron

During World War II, an American squadron of eight planes crash-landed on the ice of Greenland. The crew was rescued, but the planes were lost. After the war, several people tried to find the "Lost Squadron." Finally, in 1988, a team of adventurers found the planes by using radar. The planes were buried by 40 years of snowfall and had become part of the Greenland ice sheet! When the planes were found, they were buried under 80 m of glacial ice. Incredibly, the team tunneled down through the ice and recovered a plane. The plane is now named Glacier Girl, and it still flies today!

Math ACTIVITY

The Frank landslide traveled 4 km in 100 s. Calculate this speed in meters per second.

Language Arts ACTIVITY

WRITING SKILL The crew of the Lost Squadron had to wait 10 days to be rescued by dog sled. Imagine that you were part of the crew—what would you have done to survive? Write a short story describing your adventure on the ice sheet of Greenland.

Johan Reinhard

High-Altitude Anthropologist Imagine discovering the mummified body of a girl from 500 years ago! In 1995, while climbing Mount Ampato, one of the tallest mountains in the Andes, Johan Reinhard made an incredible discovery—the well-preserved mummy of a young Inca girl. The recent eruption of a nearby volcano had caused the snow on Mount Ampato to melt and uncover the mummy. The discovery of the "Inca Ice Maiden" gave scientists a wealth of new information about Incan culture. Today, Reinhard considers the discovery of the Inca Ice Maiden his most exciting moment in the field.

Johan Reinhard is an anthropologist. Anthropologists study the physical and cultural characteristics of human populations. Reinhard studied anthropology at the University of Arizona and at the University of Vienna, in Austria. Early in his career, Reinhard worked on underwater archeology projects in Austria and Italy and on projects in the mountains of Nepal and Tibet. He soon made mountains and mountain peoples the focus of his career as an anthropologist. Reinhard spent 10 years in the highest mountains on Earth, the Himalayas. There, he studied the role of sacred mountains in Tibetan religions. Now, Reinhard studies the culture of the ancient Inca in the Andes of South America.

Social Studies ACTIVITY

Find out more about the Inca Ice Maiden or about Ötzi, a mummy that is more than 5,000 years old that was found in a glacier in Italy. Create a poster that summarizes what scientists have learned from these discoveries.

The Inca Ice Maiden was buried under ice and snow for more than 500 years.

To learn more about these Science in Action topics, visit go.hrw.com and type in the keyword **HZ5ICEF.**

Current Science

Check out Current Science® articles related to this chapter by visiting go.hrw.com. Just type in the keyword **HZ5CS12.**

UNIT 2

TIMELINE

Weather, Climate, and Space

In this unit, you will learn about Earth's atmosphere, including how it affects conditions on the Earth's surface. The constantly changing weather is always a good topic for conversation, but forecasting the weather is not an easy task. Climate, on the other hand, is much more predictable. This timeline shows some of the events that have occurred as scientists have tried to better understand Earth's atmosphere, weather, and climate.

1281

A sudden typhoon destroys a fleet of Mongolian ships about to reach Japan. This "divine wind," or *kamikaze* in Japanese, saves the country from invasion and conquest.

1778

Carl Scheele concludes that air is mostly made of nitrogen and oxygen.

1838

John James Audubon publishes *The Birds of America*.

1974

Chlorofluorocarbons (CFCs) are recognized as harmful to the ozone layer.

1982

Weather information becomes available 24 hours a day, 7 days a week, on commercial TV.

1655

Saturn's rings are recognized as such. Galileo Galilei had seen them in 1610, but his telescope was not strong enough to show that they were rings.

1718

Gabriel Fahrenheit builds the first mercury thermometer.

1749

Benjamin Franklin explains how updrafts of air are caused by the sun's heating of the local atmosphere.

1920

Serbian scientist Milutin Milankovitch determines that over tens of thousands of years, changes in the Earth's motion through space have profound effects on climate.

1945

The first atmospheric test of an atomic bomb takes place near Alamogordo, New Mexico.

1985

Scientists discover an ozone hole over Antarctica.

1986

The world's worst nuclear accident takes place at Chernobyl, Ukraine, and spreads radiation through the atmosphere as far as the western United States.

1999

The first nonstop balloon trip around the world is successfully completed when Brian Jones and Bertrand Piccard land in Egypt.

2003

A record 393 tornadoes are observed in the United States during one week in May.

The path of radioactive material released from Chernobyl

The Breitling Orbiter 3 *lands in Egypt on March 21, 1999.*

5

The Atmosphere

The Big Idea

Earth's atmosphere is a mixture of gases that distributes heat and enables life to exist on Earth.

About the Photo

Imagine climbing a mountain and taking only one out of three breaths! As altitude increases, the density of the atmosphere decreases. At the heights shown in this picture, the atmosphere is so thin that it contains only 30% of the amount of oxygen found in the atmosphere at sea level. So, most mountaineers carry part of their atmosphere with them—in the form of oxygen tanks.

PRE-READING ACTIVITY

FOLDNOTES **Booklet** Before you read the chapter, create the FoldNote entitled "Booklet" described in the **Study Skills** section of the Appendix. Label each page of the booklet with a main idea from the chapter. As you read the chapter, write what you learn about each main idea on the appropriate page of the booklet.

START-UP ACTIVITY

Does Air Have Mass?

In this activity, you will compare an inflated balloon with a deflated balloon to find out if air has mass.

Procedure

1. In a **notebook,** answer the following questions: Does air have mass? Will an inflated balloon weigh more than a deflated balloon?

2. Inflate **two large balloons,** and tie the balloons closed. Attach each balloon to opposite ends of a **meterstick** using identical **pushpins.** Balance the meterstick on a **pencil** held by a volunteer. Check that the meterstick is perfectly balanced.

3. Predict what will happen when you pop one balloon. Record your predictions.

4. Put on **safety goggles,** and carefully pop one of the balloons with a **pushpin.**

5. Record your observations.

Analysis

1. Explain your observations. Was your prediction correct?

2. Based on your results, does air have mass? If air has mass, is the atmosphere affected by Earth's gravity? Explain your answers.

The Atmosphere   **135**

Characteristics of the Atmosphere

READING STRATEGY

Mnemonics As you read this section, create a mnemonic device to help you remember the layers of the Earth's atmosphere.

If you were lost in the desert, you could survive for a few days without food and water. But you wouldn't last more than five minutes without the atmosphere.

The **atmosphere** is a mixture of gases that surrounds Earth. In addition to containing the oxygen you need to breathe, the atmosphere protects you from the sun's damaging rays. The atmosphere is always changing. Every breath you take, every tree that is planted, and every vehicle you ride in affects the atmosphere's composition.

The Composition of the Atmosphere

As you can see in **Figure 1,** the atmosphere is made up mostly of nitrogen gas. The oxygen you breathe makes up a little more than 20% of the atmosphere. In addition to containing nitrogen and oxygen, the atmosphere contains small particles, such as dust, volcanic ash, sea salt, dirt, and smoke. The next time you turn off the lights at night, shine a flashlight, and you will see some of these tiny particles floating in the air.

Water is also found in the atmosphere. Liquid water (water droplets) and solid water (snow and ice crystals) are found in clouds. But most water in the atmosphere exists as an invisible gas called *water vapor*. When atmospheric conditions change, water vapor can change into solid or liquid water, and rain or snow might fall from the sky.

✓ **Reading Check** Describe the three physical states of water in the atmosphere. (*See the Appendix for answers to Reading Checks.*)

Figure 1 **Composition of the Atmosphere**

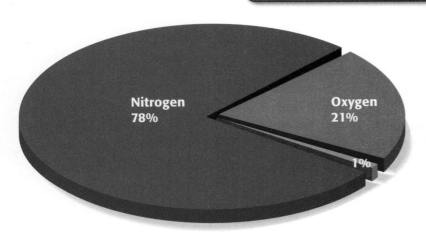

Nitrogen, the most common atmospheric gas, is released when dead plants and dead animals break down and when volcanoes erupt.

Oxygen, the second most common atmospheric gas, is made by phytoplankton and plants.

The remaining 1% of the atmosphere is made up of argon, carbon dioxide, water vapor, and other gases.

Atmospheric Pressure and Temperature

What would carrying a column of air that is 700 km high feel like? You may be surprised to learn that you carry this load every day. While air is not very heavy, its weight adds up. At sea level, a square inch of surface area is under almost 15 lb of air. Carrying that much air on such a small surface area is like carrying a large bowling ball on the tip of your finger!

As Altitude Increases, Air Pressure Decreases

The atmosphere is held around the Earth by gravity. Gravity pulls gas molecules in the atmosphere toward the Earth's surface, causing air pressure. **Air pressure** is the measure of the force with which air molecules push on a surface. Air pressure is strongest at the Earth's surface because more air is above you. As you move farther away from the Earth's surface, fewer gas molecules are above you. So, as altitude (distance from sea level) increases, air pressure decreases. Think of air pressure as a human pyramid, as shown in **Figure 2.** The people at the bottom of the pyramid can feel all the weight and pressure of the people on top. Air pressure works in a similar way.

Atmospheric Composition Affects Air Temperature

Air temperature also changes as altitude increases. The temperature differences result mainly from the way solar energy is absorbed as it moves through the atmosphere. Some parts of the atmosphere are warmer because they contain a high percentage of gases that absorb solar energy. Other parts of the atmosphere contain less of these gases and are cooler.

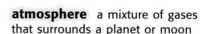

CONNECTION TO Physics

Air-Pressure Experiment
Does air pressure push only downward? Try this experiment to find out. Fill a plastic cup to the brim with water. Firmly hold a piece of cardboard over the mouth of the cup. Quickly invert the glass over a sink, and observe what happens. How do the effects of air pressure explain your observations?

ACTIVITY

atmosphere a mixture of gases that surrounds a planet or moon

air pressure the measure of the force with which air molecules push on a surface

Lower pressure

Higher pressure

Figure 2 *As in a human pyramid, air pressure increases closer to the Earth's surface.*

Modeling the Atmosphere
In teams, use a metric ruler to create an illustrated scale model of the atmosphere similar to the one shown on this page. Assume that the atmosphere is about 700 km high. If you reduced the height of the atmosphere by a factor of 100,000, your scale model would be 7 m long, and the troposphere would be 16 cm long. Think of a creative way to display your model. You could use sidewalk chalk, stakes and string, poster board, or other materials approved by your teacher. Do some research to add interesting information about each layer.

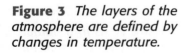

Figure 3 *The layers of the atmosphere are defined by changes in temperature.*

Layers of the Atmosphere

Based on temperature changes, the Earth's atmosphere is divided into four layers, as shown in **Figure 3.** These layers are the *troposphere, stratosphere, mesosphere,* and *thermosphere.* Although these words might sound complicated, the name of each layer gives you clues about its features.

For example, *-sphere* means "ball," which suggests that each layer of the atmosphere surrounds the Earth like a hollow ball. *Tropo-* means "turning" or "change," and the troposphere is the layer where gases turn and mix. *Strato-* means "layer," and the stratosphere is the sphere where gases are layered and do not mix very much. *Meso-* means "middle," and the mesosphere is the middle layer. Finally, *thermo-* means "heat," and the thermosphere is the sphere where temperatures are highest.

Reading Check What does the name of each atmospheric layer mean?

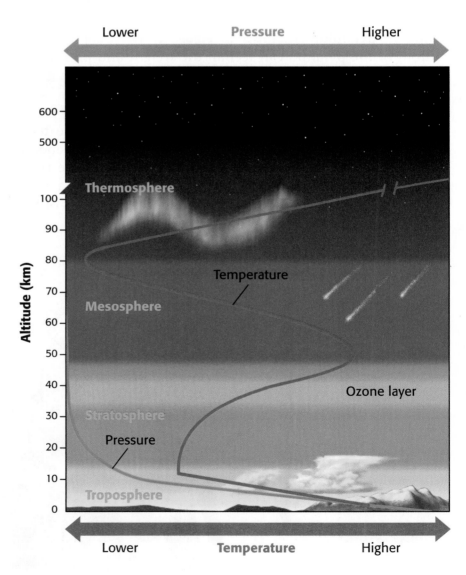

The Troposphere: The Layer in Which We Live

The lowest layer of the atmosphere, which lies next to the Earth's surface, is called the **troposphere.** The troposphere is also the densest atmospheric layer. It contains almost 90% of the atmosphere's total mass! Almost all of the Earth's carbon dioxide, water vapor, clouds, air pollution, weather, and life-forms are in the troposphere. As shown in **Figure 4,** temperatures vary greatly in the troposphere. Differences in air temperature and density cause gases in the troposphere to mix continuously.

The Stratosphere: Home of the Ozone Layer

The atmospheric layer above the troposphere is called the **stratosphere. Figure 5** shows the boundary between the stratosphere and the troposphere. Gases in the stratosphere are layered and do not mix as much as gases in the troposphere. The air is also very thin in the stratosphere and contains little moisture. The lower stratosphere is extremely cold. Its temperature averages –60°C. But temperature rises as altitude increases in the stratosphere. This rise happens because ozone in the stratosphere absorbs ultraviolet radiation from the sun, which warms the air. Almost all of the ozone in the stratosphere is contained in the ozone layer. The *ozone layer* protects life on Earth by absorbing harmful ultraviolet radiation.

The Mesosphere: The Middle Layer

Above the stratosphere is the mesosphere. The **mesosphere** is the middle layer of the atmosphere. It is also the coldest layer. As in the troposphere, the temperature decreases as altitude increases in the mesosphere. Temperatures can be as low as –93°C at the top of the mesosphere.

Figure 4 *As altitude increases in the troposphere, temperature decreases. Snow remains all year on this mountaintop.*

troposphere the lowest layer of the atmosphere, in which temperature decreases at a constant rate as altitude increases

stratosphere the layer of the atmosphere that is above the troposphere and in which temperature increases as altitude increases

mesosphere the layer of the atmosphere between the stratosphere and the thermosphere and in which temperature decreases as altitude increases

Figure 5 *This photograph of Earth's atmosphere was taken from space. The troposphere is the yellow layer; the stratosphere is the white layer.*

The Thermosphere: The Edge of the Atmosphere

The uppermost atmospheric layer is called the **thermosphere.** In the thermosphere, temperature again increases with altitude. Atoms of nitrogen and oxygen absorb high-energy solar radiation and release thermal energy, which causes temperatures in the thermosphere to be 1,000°C or higher.

When you think of an area that has high temperatures, you probably think of a place that is very hot. Although the thermosphere has very high temperatures, it does not feel hot. Temperature is different from heat. Temperature is a measure of the average energy of particles in motion. The high temperature of the thermosphere means that particles in that layer are moving very fast. Heat, however, is the transfer of thermal energy between objects of different temperatures. Particles must touch one another to transfer thermal energy. The space between particles in the thermosphere is so great that particles do not transfer much energy. In other words, the density of the thermosphere is so low that particles do not often collide and transfer energy. **Figure 6** shows how air density affects the heating of the troposphere and the thermosphere.

Reading Check Why doesn't the thermosphere feel hot?

thermosphere the uppermost layer of the atmosphere, in which temperature increases as altitude increases

Figure 6 Temperature in the Troposphere and the Thermosphere

The **thermosphere** is less dense than the troposphere. So, although particles are moving very fast, they do not transfer much thermal energy.

The **troposphere** is denser than the thermosphere. So, although particles in the troposphere are moving much slower than particles in the thermosphere, they can transfer much more thermal energy.

The Ionosphere: Home of the Auroras

In the upper mesosphere and the lower thermosphere, nitrogen and oxygen atoms absorb harmful solar energy. As a result, the thermosphere's temperature rises, and gas particles become electrically charged. Electrically charged particles are called *ions*. Therefore, this part of the thermosphere is called the *ionosphere*. As shown in **Figure 7,** in polar regions these ions radiate energy as shimmering lights called *auroras*. The ionosphere also reflects AM radio waves. When conditions are right, an AM radio wave can travel around the world by reflecting off the ionosphere. These radio signals bounce off the ionosphere and are sent back to Earth.

Figure 7 *Charged particles in the ionosphere cause auroras, or northern and southern lights.*

SECTION Review

Summary

- Nitrogen and oxygen make up most of Earth's atmosphere.
- Air pressure decreases as altitude increases.
- The composition of atmospheric layers affects their temperature.
- The troposphere is the lowest atmospheric layer. It is the layer in which we live.
- The stratosphere contains the ozone layer, which protects us from harmful UV radiation.
- The mesosphere is the coldest atmospheric layer.
- The thermosphere is the uppermost layer of the atmosphere.

Using Key Terms

1. Use each of the following terms in a separate sentence: *air pressure, atmosphere, troposphere, stratosphere, mesosphere,* and *thermosphere*.

Understanding Key Ideas

2. Why does the temperature of different layers of the atmosphere vary?
   a. because air temperature increases as altitude increases
   b. because the amount of energy radiated from the sun varies
   c. because of interference by humans
   d. because of the composition of gases in each layer

3. Why does air pressure decrease as altitude increases?

4. How can the thermosphere have high temperatures but not feel hot?

5. What determines the temperature of atmospheric layers?

6. What two gases make up most of the atmosphere?

Math Skills

7. If an average cloud has a density of 0.5 g/m^3 and has a volume of 1,000,000,000 m^3, what is the weight of an average cloud?

Critical Thinking

8. **Applying Concepts** Apply what you know about the relationship between altitude and air pressure to explain why rescue helicopters have a difficult time flying at altitudes above 6,000 m.

9. **Making Inferences** If the upper atmosphere is very thin, why do space vehicles heat up as they enter the atmosphere?

10. **Making Inferences** Explain why gases such as helium can escape Earth's atmosphere.

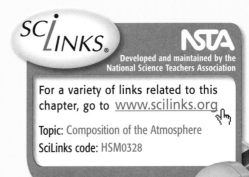

SCiLINKS®

Developed and maintained by the National Science Teachers Association

For a variety of links related to this chapter, go to www.scilinks.org

Topic: Composition of the Atmosphere
SciLinks code: HSM0328

Atmospheric Heating

You are lying in a park. Your eyes are closed, and you feel the warmth of the sun on your face. You may have done this before, but have you ever stopped to think that it takes a little more than eight minutes for the energy that warms your face to travel from a star that is 149,000,000 km away?

What You Will Learn

● Describe what happens to solar energy that reaches Earth.
● Summarize the processes of radiation, thermal conduction, and convection.
● Explain the relationship between the greenhouse effect and global warming.

Vocabulary

radiation
thermal conduction
convection
global warming
greenhouse effect

READING STRATEGY

Reading Organizer As you read this section, make a table comparing radiation, conduction, and convection.

Energy in the Atmosphere

In the scenario above, your face was warmed by energy from the sun. Earth and its atmosphere are also warmed by energy from the sun. In this section, you will find out what happens to solar energy as it enters the atmosphere.

Radiation: Energy Transfer by Waves

The Earth receives energy from the sun by radiation. **Radiation** is the transfer of energy as electromagnetic waves. Although the sun radiates a huge amount of energy, Earth receives only about two-billionths of this energy. But this small fraction of energy is enough to drive the weather cycle and make Earth habitable. **Figure 1** shows what happens to solar energy once it enters the atmosphere.

Figure 1 *Energy from the sun is absorbed by the atmosphere, land, and water and is changed into thermal energy.*

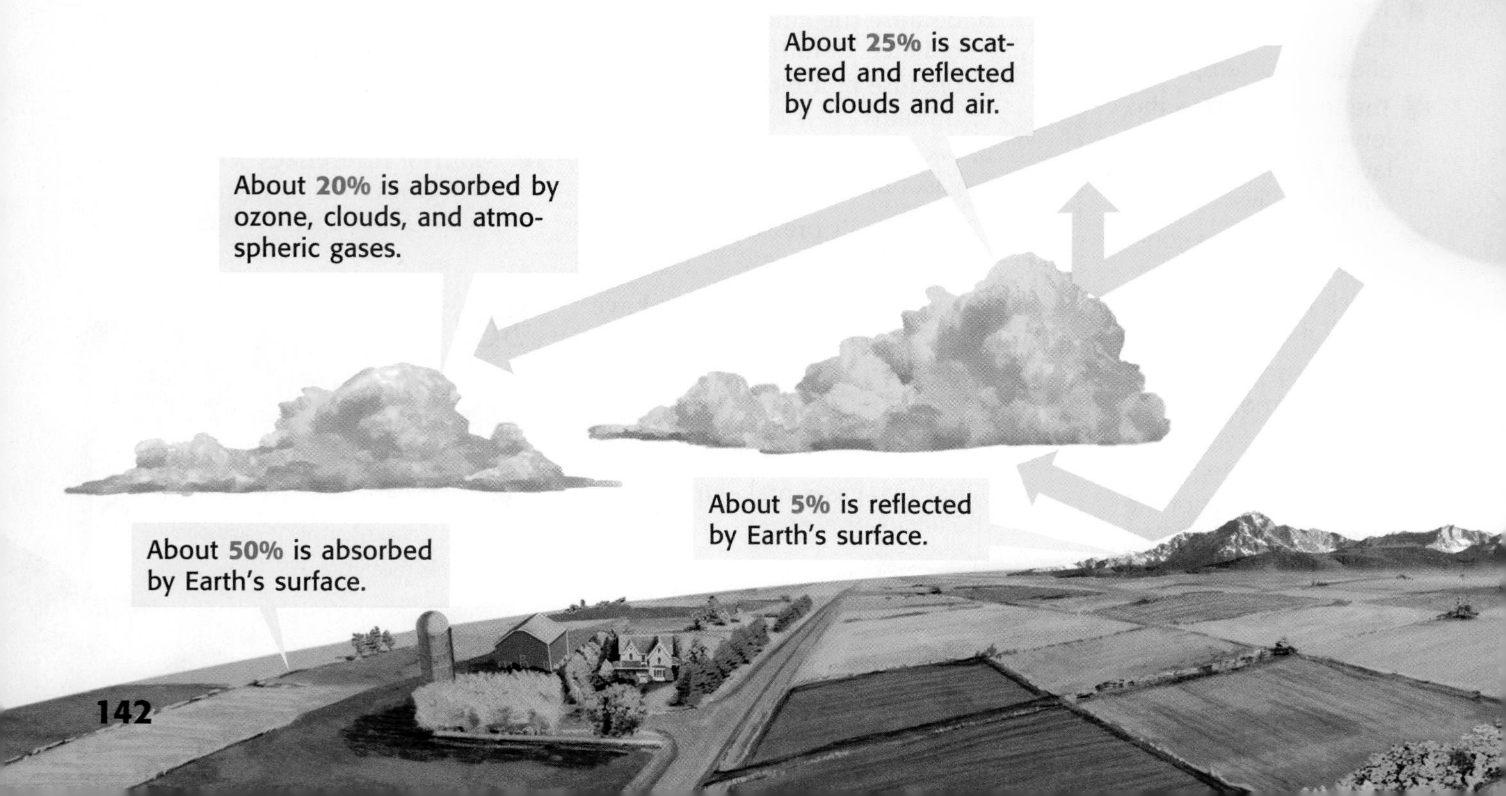

About **25%** is scattered and reflected by clouds and air.

About **20%** is absorbed by ozone, clouds, and atmospheric gases.

About **5%** is reflected by Earth's surface.

About **50%** is absorbed by Earth's surface.

Conduction: Energy Transfer by Contact

If you have ever touched something hot, you have experienced the process of conduction. **Thermal conduction** is the transfer of thermal energy through a material. Thermal energy is always transferred from warm to cold areas. When air molecules come into direct contact with the warm surface of Earth, thermal energy is transferred to the atmosphere.

Convection: Energy Transfer by Circulation

If you have ever watched a pot of water boil, you have observed convection. **Convection** is the transfer of thermal energy by the circulation or movement of a liquid or gas. Most thermal energy in the atmosphere is transferred by convection. For example, as air is heated, it becomes less dense and rises. Cool air is denser, so it sinks. As the cool air sinks, it pushes the warm air up. The cool air is eventually heated by the Earth's surface and begins to rise again. This cycle of warm air rising and cool air sinking causes a circular movement of air, called a *convection current,* as shown in **Figure 2.**

✓ Reading Check How do differences in air density cause convection currents? (*See the Appendix for answers to Reading Checks.*)

radiation the transfer of energy as electromagnetic waves

thermal conduction the transfer of energy as heat through a material

convection the transfer of thermal energy by the circulation or movement of a liquid or gas

Figure 2 *The processes of radiation, thermal conduction, and convection heat Earth and its atmosphere.*

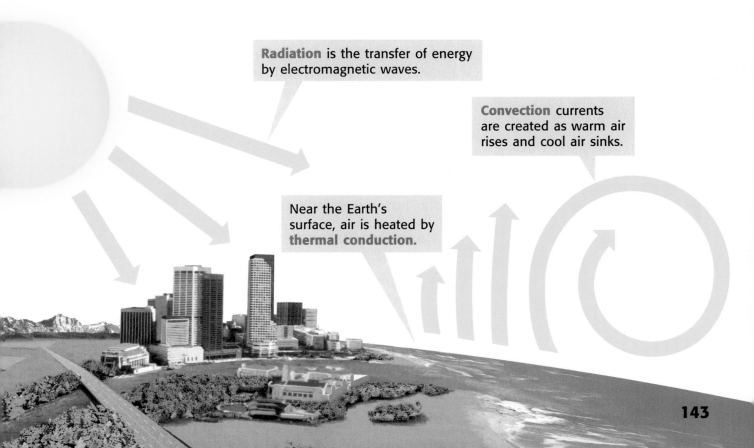

Radiation is the transfer of energy by electromagnetic waves.

Convection currents are created as warm air rises and cool air sinks.

Near the Earth's surface, air is heated by **thermal conduction.**

Figure 3   **The Greenhouse Effect**

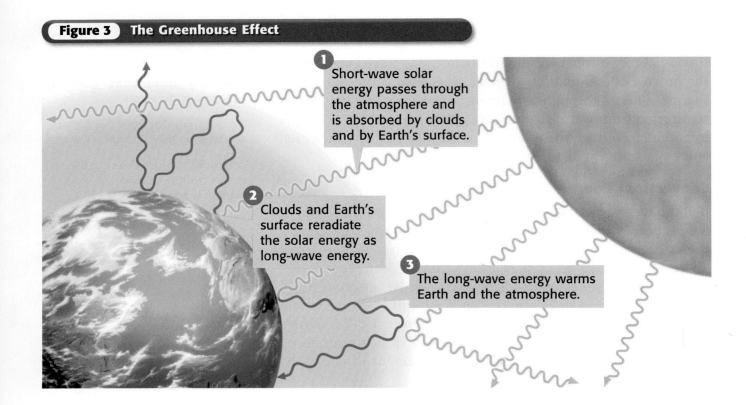

1 Short-wave solar energy passes through the atmosphere and is absorbed by clouds and by Earth's surface.

2 Clouds and Earth's surface reradiate the solar energy as long-wave energy.

3 The long-wave energy warms Earth and the atmosphere.

greenhouse effect the warming of the surface and lower atmosphere of Earth that occurs when water vapor, carbon dioxide, and other gases absorb and reradiate thermal energy

The Greenhouse Effect and Life on Earth

As you have learned, about 70% of the radiation that enters Earth's atmosphere is absorbed by clouds and by the Earth's surface. This energy is converted into thermal energy that warms the planet. In other words, short-wave visible light is absorbed and reradiated into the atmosphere as long-wave thermal energy. So, why doesn't this thermal energy escape back into space? Most of it does, but the atmosphere is like a warm blanket that traps enough energy to make Earth livable. This process, shown in **Figure 3,** is called the greenhouse effect. The **greenhouse effect** is the process by which gases in the atmosphere, such as water vapor and carbon dioxide, absorb thermal energy and radiate it back to Earth. This process is called the greenhouse effect because the gases function like the glass walls and roof of a greenhouse, which allow solar energy to enter but prevent thermal energy from escaping.

The Radiation Balance: Energy In, Energy Out

For Earth to remain livable, the amount of energy received from the sun and the amount of energy returned to space must be approximately equal. Solar energy that is absorbed by the Earth and its atmosphere is eventually reradiated into space as thermal energy. Every day, the Earth receives more energy from the sun. The balance between incoming energy and outgoing energy is known as the *radiation balance*.

Greenhouse Gases and Global Warming

Many scientists have become concerned about data that show that average global temperatures have increased in the past 100 years. Such an increase in average global temperatures is called **global warming.** Some scientists have hypothesized that an increase of greenhouse gases in the atmosphere may be the cause of this warming trend. Greenhouse gases are gases that absorb thermal energy in the atmosphere.

Human activity, such as the burning of fossil fuels and deforestation, may be increasing levels of greenhouse gases, such as carbon dioxide, in the atmosphere. If this hypothesis is correct, increasing levels of greenhouse gases may cause average global temperatures to continue to rise. If global warming continues, global climate patterns could be disrupted. Plants and animals that are adapted to live in specific climates would be affected. However, climate models are extremely complex, and scientists continue to debate whether the global warming trend is the result of an increase in greenhouse gases.

global warming a gradual increase in average global temperature

✔ **Reading Check** What is a greenhouse gas?

SECTION Review

Summary

● Energy from the sun is transferred through the atmosphere by radiation, thermal conduction, and convection.

● Radiation is energy transfer by electromagnetic waves. Thermal conduction is energy transfer by direct contact. Convection is energy transfer by circulation.

● The greenhouse effect is Earth's natural heating process. Increasing levels of greenhouse gases could cause global warming.

Using Key Terms

1. Use each of the following terms in a separate sentence: *thermal conduction, radiation, convection, greenhouse effect,* and *global warming.*

Understanding Key Ideas

2. Which of the following is the best example of thermal conduction?
   a. a light bulb warming a lampshade
   b. an egg cooking in a frying pan
   c. water boiling in a pot
   d. gases circulating in the atmosphere

3. Describe three ways that energy is transferred in the atmosphere.

4. What is the difference between the greenhouse effect and global warming?

5. What is the radiation balance?

Math Skills

6. Find the average of the following temperatures: 73.2°F, 71.1°F, 54.6°F, 65.5°F, 78.2°F, 81.9°F, and 82.1°F.

Critical Thinking

7. **Identifying Relationships** How does the process of convection rely on radiation?

8. **Applying Concepts** Describe global warming in terms of the radiation balance.

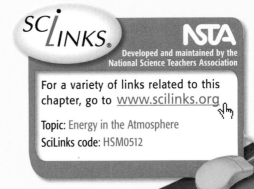

SCiLINKS® NSTA
Developed and maintained by the National Science Teachers Association

For a variety of links related to this chapter, go to www.scilinks.org

Topic: Energy in the Atmosphere
SciLinks code: HSM0512

Global Winds and Local Winds

What You Will Learn

● Explain the relationship between air pressure and wind direction.
● Describe global wind patterns.
● Explain the causes of local wind patterns.

Vocabulary

wind
Coriolis effect
polar easterlies
westerlies
trade winds
jet stream

READING STRATEGY

Prediction Guide Before reading this section, write the title of each heading in this section. Next, under each heading, write what you think you will learn.

wind the movement of air caused by differences in air pressure

If you open the valve on a bicycle tube, the air rushes out. Why? The air inside the tube is at a higher pressure than the air is outside the tube. In effect, letting air out of the tube created a wind.

Why Air Moves

The movement of air caused by differences in air pressure is called **wind.** The greater the pressure difference, the faster the wind moves. The devastation shown in **Figure 1** was caused by winds that resulted from extreme differences in air pressure.

Air Rises at the Equator and Sinks at the Poles

Differences in air pressure are generally caused by the unequal heating of the Earth. The equator receives more direct solar energy than other latitudes, so air at the equator is warmer and less dense than the surrounding air. Warm, less dense air rises and creates an area of low pressure. This warm, rising air flows toward the poles. At the poles, the air is colder and denser than the surrounding air, so it sinks. As the cold air sinks, it creates areas of high pressure around the poles. This cold polar air then flows toward the equator.

Figure 1 *In 1992, Hurricane Andrew became the most destructive hurricane in U.S. history. The winds from the hurricane reached 264 km/h.*

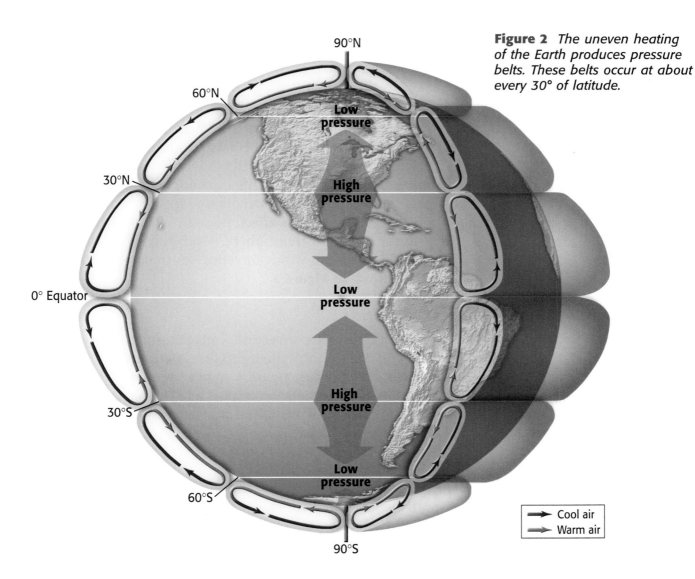

Figure 2 *The uneven heating of the Earth produces pressure belts. These belts occur at about every 30° of latitude.*

90°N
60°N
Low pressure
30°N
High pressure
0° Equator
Low pressure
High pressure
30°S
Low pressure
60°S
90°S

→ Cool air
→ Warm air

Pressure Belts Are Found Every 30°

You may imagine that wind moves in one huge, circular pattern from the poles to the equator. In fact, air travels in many large, circular patterns called *convection cells*. Convection cells are separated by *pressure belts,* bands of high pressure and low pressure found about every 30° of latitude, as shown in **Figure 2.** As warm air rises over the equator and moves toward the poles, the air begins to cool. At about 30° north and 30° south latitude, some of the cool air begins to sink. Cool, sinking air causes high pressure belts near 30° north and 30° south latitude. This cool air flows back to the equator, where it warms and rises again. At the poles, cold air sinks and moves toward the equator. Air warms as it moves away from the poles. Around 60° north and 60° south latitude, the warmer air rises, which creates a low pressure belt. This air flows back to the poles.

✓ Reading Check Why does sinking air cause areas of high pressure? (*See the Appendix for answers to Reading Checks.*)

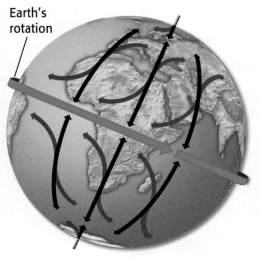

Earth's rotation

➡ Path of wind without Coriolis effect
➡ Approximate path of wind

Figure 3 *The Coriolis effect in the Northern Hemisphere causes winds traveling north to appear to curve to the east and winds traveling south to appear to curve to the west.*

Coriolis effect the apparent curving of the path of a moving object from an otherwise straight path due to the Earth's rotation

polar easterlies prevailing winds that blow from east to west between 60° and 90° latitude in both hemispheres

westerlies prevailing winds that blow from west to east between 30° and 60° latitude in both hemispheres

trade winds prevailing winds that blow northeast from 30° north latitude to the equator and that blow southeast from 30° south latitude to the equator

The Coriolis Effect

As you have learned, pressure differences cause air to move between the equator and the poles. But try spinning a globe and using a piece of chalk to trace a straight line from the equator to the North Pole. The chalk line curves because the globe was spinning. Like the chalk line, winds do not travel directly north or south, because the Earth is rotating. The apparent curving of the path of winds and ocean currents due to the Earth's rotation is called the **Coriolis effect.** Because of the Coriolis effect in the Northern Hemisphere, winds traveling north curve to the east, and winds traveling south curve to the west, as shown in **Figure 3.**

Global Winds

The combination of convection cells found at every 30° of latitude and the Coriolis effect produces patterns of air circulation called *global winds.* **Figure 4** shows the major global wind systems: polar easterlies, westerlies, and trade winds. Winds such as easterlies and westerlies are named for the direction from which they blow.

Polar Easterlies

The wind belts that extend from the poles to 60° latitude in both hemispheres are called the **polar easterlies.** The polar easterlies are formed as cold, sinking air moves from the poles toward 60° north and 60° south latitude. In the Northern Hemisphere, polar easterlies can carry cold arctic air over the United States, producing snow and freezing weather.

Westerlies

The wind belts found between 30° and 60° latitude in both hemispheres are called the **westerlies.** The westerlies flow toward the poles from west to east. The westerlies can carry moist air over the United States, producing rain and snow.

Trade Winds

In both hemispheres, the winds that blow from 30° latitude almost to the equator are called **trade winds.** The Coriolis effect causes the trade winds to curve to the west in the Northern Hemisphere and to the east in the Southern Hemisphere. Early traders used the trade winds to sail from Europe to the Americas. As a result, the winds became known as "trade winds."

✓ Reading Check If the trade winds carried traders from Europe to the Americas, what wind system carried traders back to Europe?

The Doldrums

The trade winds of the Northern and Southern Hemispheres meet in an area around the equator called the *doldrums*. In the doldrums, there is very little wind because the warm, rising air creates an area of low pressure. The name *doldrums* means "dull" or "sluggish."

The Horse Latitudes

At about 30° north and 30° south latitude, sinking air creates an area of high pressure. The winds at these locations are weak. These areas are called the *horse latitudes*. According to legend, this name was given to these areas when sailing ships carried horses from Europe to the Americas. When the ships were stuck in this windless area, horses were sometimes thrown overboard to save drinking water for the sailors. Most of the world's deserts are located in the horse latitudes because the sinking air is very dry.

INTERNET ACTIVITY

For another activity related to this chapter, go to **go.hrw.com** and type in the keyword **HZ5ATMW**.

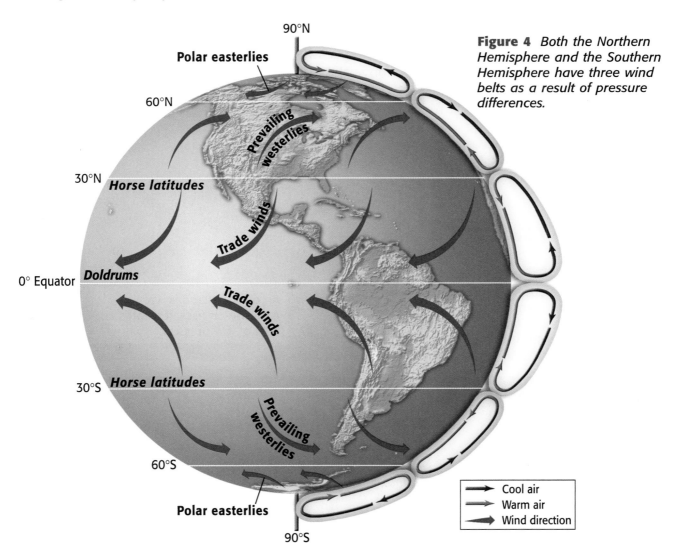

Figure 4 *Both the Northern Hemisphere and the Southern Hemisphere have three wind belts as a result of pressure differences.*

90°N
Polar easterlies
60°N
Prevailing westerlies
30°N Horse latitudes
Trade winds
0° Equator Doldrums
Trade winds
30°S Horse latitudes
Prevailing westerlies
60°S
Polar easterlies
90°S

→ Cool air
→ Warm air
→ Wind direction

Jet Streams: Atmospheric Conveyor Belts

The flight from Seattle to Boston can be 30 minutes faster than the flight from Boston to Seattle. Why? Pilots take advantage of a jet stream similar to the one shown in **Figure 5.** The **jet streams** are narrow belts of high-speed winds that blow in the upper troposphere and lower stratosphere. These winds can reach maximum speeds of 400 km/h. Unlike other global winds, the jet streams do not follow regular paths around the Earth. Knowing the path of a jet stream is important not only to pilots but also to meteorologists. Because jet streams affect the movement of storms, meteorologists can track a storm if they know the location of a jet stream.

Local Winds

Local winds generally move short distances and can blow from any direction. Local geographic features, such as a shoreline or a mountain, can produce temperature differences that cause local winds. For example, the formation of sea and land breezes is shown in **Figure 6.** During the day, the land heats up faster than the water, so the air above the land becomes warmer than the air above the ocean. The warm land air rises, and the cold ocean air flows in to replace it. At night, the land cools faster than water, so the wind blows toward the ocean.

Figure 5 *The jet stream forms this band of clouds as it flows above the Earth.*

jet stream a narrow belt of strong winds that blow in the upper troposphere

Figure 6 Sea and Land Breezes

During the day, air over the ocean is cooler and forms an area of high pressure. The cool air flows to the land, producing a sea breeze.

Air over the land is warmer. As warm air rises, it creates an area of low pressure.

At night, air over the ocean is warmer. As the warm air rises, it forms an area of low pressure.

Air over land is cooler and forms an area of high pressure. The cool air moves toward the ocean, producing a land breeze.

Mountain Breezes and Valley Breezes

Mountain and valley breezes are other examples of local winds caused by an area's geography. Campers in mountainous areas may feel a warm afternoon quickly change into a cold night soon after the sun sets. During the day, the sun warms the air along the mountain slopes. This warm air rises up the mountain slopes, creating a valley breeze. At nightfall, the air along the mountain slopes cools. This cool air moves down the slopes into the valley, producing a mountain breeze.

✓ Reading Check Why does the wind tend to blow down from mountains at night?

CONNECTION TO Social Studies

Local Breezes The chinook, the shamal, the sirocco, and the Santa Ana are all local winds. Find out about an interesting local wind, and create a poster-board display that shows how the wind forms and how it affects human cultures.

ACTIVITY

SECTION Review

Summary

- Winds blow from areas of high pressure to areas of low pressure.
- Pressure belts are found approximately every 30° of latitude.
- The Coriolis effect causes wind to appear to curve as it moves across the Earth's surface.
- Global winds include the polar easterlies, the westerlies, and the trade winds.
- Local winds include sea and land breezes and mountain and valley breezes.

Using Key Terms

1. In your own words, write a definition for each of the following terms: *wind, Coriolis effect, jet stream, polar easterlies, westerlies,* and *trade winds.*

Understanding Key Ideas

2. Why does warm air rise and cold air sink?
   a. because warm air is less dense than cold air
   b. because warm air is denser than cold air
   c. because cold air is less dense than warm air
   d. because warm air has less pressure than cold air does

3. What are pressure belts?

4. What causes winds?

5. How does the Coriolis effect affect wind movement?

6. How are sea and land breezes similar to mountain and valley breezes?

7. Would there be winds if the Earth's surface were the same temperature everywhere? Explain your answer.

Math Skills

8. Flying an airplane at 500 km/h, a pilot plans to reach her destination in 5 h. But she finds a jet stream moving 250 km/h in the direction she is traveling. If she gets a boost from the jet stream for 2 h, how long will the flight last?

Critical Thinking

9. **Making Inferences** In the Northern Hemisphere, why do westerlies flow from the west but trade winds flow from the east?

10. **Applying Concepts** Imagine you are near an ocean in the daytime. You want to go to the ocean, but you don't know how to get there. How might a local wind help you find the ocean?

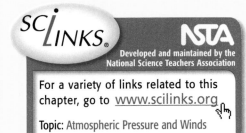

SCILINKS

NSTA Developed and maintained by the National Science Teachers Association

For a variety of links related to this chapter, go to www.scilinks.org

Topic: Atmospheric Pressure and Winds
SciLinks code: HSM0115

Secondary Pollutants

Pollutants that form when primary pollutants react with other primary pollutants or with naturally occurring substances, such as water vapor, are *secondary pollutants*. Ozone and smog are examples of secondary pollutants. Ozone is produced when sunlight reacts with vehicle exhaust and air. You may have heard of "Ozone Action Day" warnings in your community. When such a warning is issued, people are discouraged from outdoor physical activity because ozone can damage their lungs. In the stratosphere, ozone forms a protective layer that absorbs harmful radiation from the sun. Near the Earth's surface, however, ozone is a dangerous pollutant that negatively affects the health of organisms.

The Formation of Smog

Smog forms when ozone and vehicle exhaust react with sunlight, as shown in **Figure 2.** Local geography and weather patterns can also contribute to smog formation. Los Angeles, shown in **Figure 3,** is almost completely surrounded by mountains that trap pollutants and contribute to smog formation. Although pollution controls have reduced levels of smog in Los Angeles, smog remains a problem for Los Angeles and many other large cities.

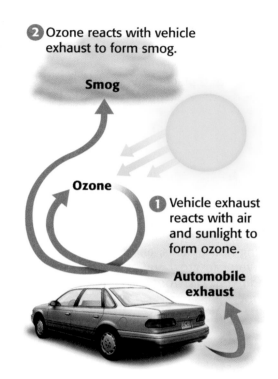

2 Ozone reacts with vehicle exhaust to form smog.

Smog

Ozone

1 Vehicle exhaust reacts with air and sunlight to form ozone.

Automobile exhaust

Figure 2 *Smog forms when sunlight reacts with ozone and vehicle exhaust.*

Figure 3 *Smog levels in Los Angeles can vary dramatically. During summer, a layer of warm air can trap smog near the ground. However, in the winter, a storm can quickly clear the air.*

Figure 4 *There are many sources of indoor air pollution. Indoor air pollution can be difficult to detect because it is often invisible.*

Sources of Human-Caused Air Pollution

Human-caused air pollution comes from a variety of sources. A major source of air pollution today is transportation. Cars contribute about 10% to 20% of the human-caused air pollution in the United States. Vehicle exhaust contains nitrogen oxide, which contributes to smog formation and acid precipitation. However, pollution controls and cleaner gasoline have greatly reduced air pollution from vehicles.

Industrial Air Pollution

Many industrial plants and electric power plants burn fossil fuels, such as coal, to produce energy. Burning some types of coal without pollution controls can release large amounts of air pollutants. Some industries also produce chemicals that can pollute the air. Oil refineries, chemical manufacturing plants, dry-cleaning businesses, furniture refinishers, and auto body shops are all potential sources of air pollution.

Indoor Air Pollution

Sometimes, the air inside a building can be more polluted than the air outside. Some sources of indoor air pollution are shown in **Figure 4.** *Ventilation,* or the mixing of indoor air with outdoor air, can reduce indoor air pollution. Another way to reduce indoor air pollution is to limit the use of chemical solvents and cleaners.

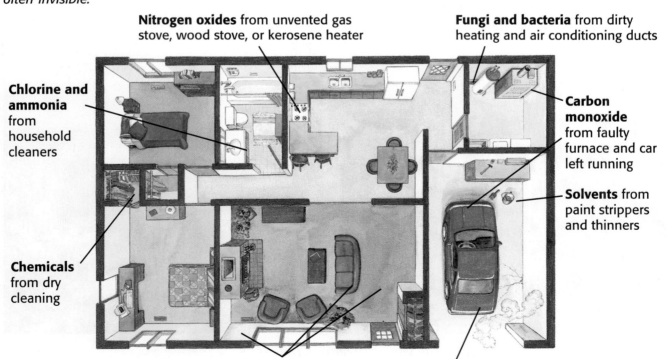

Nitrogen oxides from unvented gas stove, wood stove, or kerosene heater

Fungi and bacteria from dirty heating and air conditioning ducts

Chlorine and ammonia from household cleaners

Carbon monoxide from faulty furnace and car left running

Solvents from paint strippers and thinners

Chemicals from dry cleaning

Formaldehyde from furniture, carpeting, particleboard, and foam insulation

Gasoline from car and lawn mower

Acid Precipitation

Precipitation such as rain, sleet, or snow that contains acids from air pollution is called **acid precipitation.** When fossil fuels are burned, they can release sulfur dioxide and nitrogen oxide into the atmosphere. When these pollutants combine with water in the atmosphere, they form sulfuric acid and nitric acid. Precipitation is naturally acidic, but sulfuric acid and nitric acid can make it so acidic that it can negatively affect the environment. In most areas of the world, pollution controls have helped reduce acid precipitation.

Acid Precipitation and Plants

Plant communities have adapted over long periods of time to the natural acidity of the soil in which they grow. Acid precipitation can cause the acidity of soil to increase. This process, called *acidification*, changes the balance of a soil's chemistry in several ways. When the acidity of soil increases, some nutrients are dissolved. Nutrients that plants need for growth get washed away by rainwater. Increased acidity also causes aluminum and other toxic metals to be released. Some of these toxic metals are absorbed by the roots of plants.

Reading Check How does acid precipitation affect plants?

The Effects of Acid Precipitation on Forests

Forest ecology is complex. Scientists are still trying to fully understand the long-term effects of acid precipitation on groups of plants and their habitats. In some areas of the world, however, acid precipitation has damaged large areas of forest. The effects of acid precipitation are most noticeable in Eastern Europe, as shown in **Figure 5.** Forests in the northeastern United States and in eastern Canada have also been affected by acid precipitation.

acid precipitation rain, sleet, or snow that contains a high concentration of acids

Testing for Particulates

1. Particulates are pollutants such as dust that are extremely small. In this lab, you will measure the amount of particulates in the air. Begin by covering **ten 5 in. × 7 in. index cards** with a thin coat of **petroleum jelly.**

2. Hang the cards in various locations inside and outside your school.

3. One day later, use a **magnifying lens** to count the number of particles on the cards. Which location had the fewest number of particulates? Which location had the highest number of particulates? Hypothesize why.

Figure 5 *This forest in Poland was damaged by acid precipitation.*

Acid Precipitation and Aquatic Ecosystems

Aquatic organisms have adapted to live in water with a particular range of acidity. If acid precipitation increases the acidity of a lake or stream, aquatic plants, fish, and other aquatic organisms may die. The effects of acid precipitation on lakes and rivers are worst in the spring, when the acidic snow that built up in the winter melts and acidic water flows into lakes and rivers. A rapid change in a body of water's acidity is called *acid shock*. Acid shock can cause large numbers of fish to die. Acid shock can also affect the delicate eggs of fish and amphibians.

To reduce the effects of acid precipitation on aquatic ecosystems, some communities spray powdered lime on acidified lakes in the spring, which reduces the acidity of the lakes. Lime, a base, neutralizes the acid in the water. Unfortunately, lime cannot be spread to offset all acid damage to lakes.

✔ Reading Check Why is powdered lime sprayed on lakes in the spring instead of the fall?

The Ozone Hole

In 1985, scientists reported an alarming discovery about the Earth's protective ozone layer. Over the Antarctic regions, the ozone layer was thinning, particularly during the spring. This change was also noted over the Arctic. Chemicals called *CFCs* were causing ozone to break down into oxygen, which does not block the sun's harmful ultraviolet (UV) rays. The thinning of the ozone layer creates an ozone hole, shown in **Figure 6.** The ozone hole allows more UV radiation to reach the Earth's surface. UV radiation is dangerous to organisms because it damages genes and can cause skin cancer.

Cooperation to Reduce the Ozone Hole

In 1987, a group of nations met in Canada and agreed to take action against ozone depletion. Agreements were made to reduce and eventually ban CFC use, and CFC alternatives were quickly developed. Because many countries agreed to take swift action to control CFC use, and because a technological solution was quickly found, many people consider ozone protection an environmental success story. The battle to protect the ozone layer is not over, however. CFC molecules can remain active in the stratosphere for 60 to 120 years. So, CFCs released 30 years ago are still destroying ozone today. Thus, it will take many years for the ozone layer to completely recover.

Figure 6 *Polar weather conditions cause the size of the ozone hole (shown in blue) to vary. In the 2001 image, the ozone hole is larger than North America. One year later, it was 40% smaller.*

September 2001

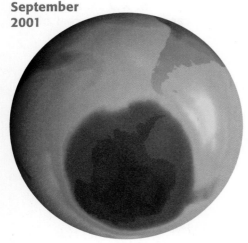

September 2002

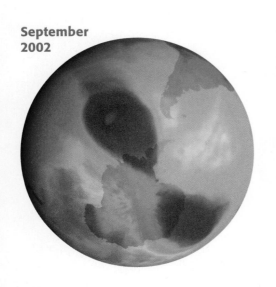

Air Pollution and Human Health

Daily exposure to small amounts of air pollution can cause serious health problems. Children, elderly people, and people with asthma, allergies, lung problems, and heart problems are especially vulnerable to the effects of air pollution. **Table 1** shows some of the effects of air pollution on the human body. The short-term effects of air pollution are immediately noticeable. Coughing, headaches, and increase in asthma-related problems are only a few short-term effects. The long-term effects of air pollution, such as lung cancer, are more dangerous because they may not be noticed until many years after an individual has been exposed to pollutants.

Table 1	Effects of Air Pollution on Human Health
Short-term effects	headache; nausea; irritation of eyes, nose, and throat; coughing; upper respiratory infections; worsening of asthma and emphysema
Long-term effects	emphysema; lung cancer; permanent lung damage; heart disease

Cleaning Up Air Pollution

Much progress has been made in reducing air pollution. For example, in the United States the Clean Air Act was passed by Congress in 1970. The Clean Air Act is a law that gives the Environmental Protection Agency (EPA) the authority to control the amount of air pollutants that can be released from any source, such as cars and factories. The EPA also checks air quality. If air quality worsens, the EPA can set stricter standards. The Clean Air Act was strengthened in 1990.

Controlling Air Pollution from Industry

The Clean Air Act requires many industries to use pollution-control devices such as scrubbers. A *scrubber* is a device that is used to remove some pollutants before they are released by smokestacks. Scrubbers in coal-burning power plants remove particles such as ash from the smoke. Other industrial plants, such as the power plant shown in **Figure 7,** focus on burning fuel more efficiently so that fewer pollutants are released.

Figure 7 *This power plant in Florida is leading the way in clean-coal technology. The plant turns coal into a gas before it is burned, so fewer pollutants are released.*

The Allowance Trading System

The Allowance Trading System is another initiative to reduce air pollution. In this program, the EPA establishes allowances for the amount of a pollutant that companies can release. If a company exceeds their allowance, they must pay a fine. A company that releases less than its allowance can sell some of its allowance to a company that releases more. Allowances are also available for the public to buy. So, organizations seeking to reduce air pollution can buy an allowance of 1,000 tons of sulfur dioxide, thus reducing the total amount of sulfur dioxide released by industries.

Reading Check How does the Allowance Trading System work?

Reducing Air Pollution from Vehicles

A large percentage of air pollution in the United States comes from the vehicles we drive. To reduce air pollution from vehicles, the EPA requires car makers to meet a certain standard for vehicle exhaust. Devices such as catalytic converters remove many pollutants from exhaust and help cars meet this standard. Cleaner fuels and more-effient engines have also helped reduce air pollution from vehicles. Car manufacturers are also making cars that run on fuels other than gasoline. Some of these cars run on hydrogen or natural gas. Hybrid cars, which are becoming more common, use gasoline and electric power to reduce emissions. Another way to reduce air pollution is to carpool, use public transportation, or bike or walk to your destination, as shown in **Figure 8.**

Figure 8 *In Copenhagen, Denmark, companies loan free bicycles in exchange for publicity. The program helps reduce air pollution and auto traffic.*

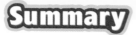

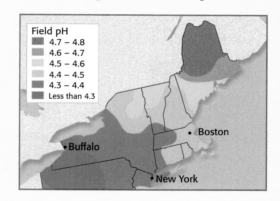

Summary

- Primary pollutants are pollutants that are put directly into the air by human or natural activity.

- Secondary pollutants are pollutants that form when primary pollutants react with other primary pollutants or with naturally occurring substances.

- Transportation, industry, and natural sources are the main sources of air pollution.

- Air pollution can be reduced by legislation, such as the Clean Air Act; by technology, such as scrubbers; and by changes in lifestyle.

Using Key Terms

The statements below are false. For each statement, replace the underlined term to make a true statement.

1. Air pollution is a sudden change in the acidity of a stream or lake.

2. Smog is rain, sleet, or snow that has a high concentration of acid.

Understanding Key Ideas

3. Which of the following results in the formation of smog?
   a. Acids in the air react with ozone.
   b. Ozone reacts with vehicle exhaust.
   c. Vehicle exhaust reacts with sunlight and ozone.
   d. Water vapor reacts with sunlight and ozone.

4. What is the difference between primary and secondary pollutants?

5. Describe five sources of indoor air pollution. Is all air pollution caused by humans? Explain.

6. What is the ozone hole, and why does it form?

7. Describe five effects of air pollution on human health. How can air pollution be reduced?

Critical Thinking

8. **Expressing Opinions** How do you think that nations should resolve air-pollution problems that cross national boundaries?

9. **Making Inferences** Why might establishing a direct link between air pollution and health problems be difficult?

Interpreting Graphics

The map below shows the pH of precipitation measured at field stations in the northeastern U.S. On the pH scale, lower numbers indicate solutions that are more acidic than solutions with higher numbers. Use the map to answer the questions below.

Field pH
- 4.7 – 4.8
- 4.6 – 4.7
- 4.5 – 4.6
- 4.4 – 4.5
- 4.3 – 4.4
- Less than 4.3

Boston
Buffalo
New York

10. Which areas have the most acidic precipitation? Hypothesize why.

11. Boston is a larger city than Buffalo is, but the precipitation measured in Buffalo is more acidic than the precipitation in Boston. Explain why.

SCI**LINKS**

NSTA
Developed and maintained by the
National Science Teachers Association

For a variety of links related to this chapter, go to www.scilinks.org

Topic: Air Pollution
SciLinks code: HSM0033

Skills Practice Lab

Under Pressure!

OBJECTIVES

Predict how changes in air pressure affect a barometer.

Build a barometer to test your hypothesis.

MATERIALS

- balloon
- can, coffee, large, empty, 10 cm in diameter
- card, index
- scissors
- straw, drinking
- tape, masking, or rubber band

SAFETY

Imagine that you are planning a picnic with your friends, so you look in the newspaper for the weather forecast. The temperature this afternoon should be in the low 80s. This temperature sounds quite comfortable! But you notice that the newspaper's forecast also includes the barometer reading. What's a barometer? And what does the reading tell you? In this activity, you will build your own barometer and will discover what this tool can tell you.

Ask a Question

1. How can I use a barometer to detect changes in air pressure?

Form a Hypothesis

2. Write a few sentences that answer the question above.

Test the Hypothesis

3. Stretch the balloon a few times. Then, blow up the balloon, and let the air out. This step will make your barometer more sensitive to changes in atmospheric pressure.

4. Cut off the open end of the balloon. Next, stretch the balloon over the open end of the coffee can. Then, attach the balloon to the can with masking tape or a rubber band.

5. Cut one end of the straw at an angle to make a pointer.

6. Place the straw on the stretched balloon so that the pointer is directed away from the center of the balloon. Five centimeters of the end of the straw should hang over the edge of the can. Tape the straw to the balloon as shown in the illustration at right.

7. Tape the index card to the side of the can as shown in the illustration at right. Congratulations! You have just made a barometer!

8. Now, use your barometer to collect and record information about air pressure. Place the barometer outside for 3 or 4 days. On each day, mark on the index card where the tip of the straw points.

Analyze the Results

1. **Explaining Events** What atmospheric factors affect how your barometer works? Explain your answer.

2. **Recognizing Patterns** What does it mean when the straw moves up?

3. **Recognizing Patterns** What does it mean when the straw moves down?

Draw Conclusions

4. **Applying Conclusions** Compare your results with the barometric pressures listed in your local newspaper. What kind of weather is associated with high pressure? What kind of weather is associated with low pressure?

5. **Evaluating Results** Does the barometer you built support your hypothesis? Explain your answer.

Applying Your Data

Now, you can use your barometer to measure the actual air pressure! Get the weather section from your local newspaper for the same 3 or 4 days that you were testing your barometer. Find the barometer reading in the newspaper for each day, and record the reading beside that day's mark on your index card. Use these markings on your card to create a scale with marks at regular intervals. Transfer this scale to a new card and attach it to your barometer.

Chapter Review

USING KEY TERMS

For each pair of terms, explain how the meanings of the terms differ.

1 *air pressure* and *wind*

2 *troposphere* and *thermosphere*

3 *greenhouse effect* and *global warming*

4 *convection* and *thermal conduction*

5 *global wind* and *local wind*

6 *stratosphere* and *mesosphere*

UNDERSTANDING KEY IDEAS

Multiple Choice

7 What is the most abundant gas in the atmosphere?

a. oxygen

b. hydrogen

c. nitrogen

d. carbon dioxide

8 A major source of oxygen for the Earth's atmosphere is

a. sea water.

b. the sun.

c. plants.

d. animals.

9 The bottom layer of the atmosphere, where almost all weather occurs, is the

a. stratosphere.

b. troposphere.

c. thermosphere.

d. mesosphere.

10 What percentage of the solar energy that reaches the outer atmosphere is absorbed at the Earth's surface?

a. 20%   **c.** 50%

b. 30%   **d.** 70%

11 The ozone layer is located in the

a. stratosphere.

b. troposphere.

c. thermosphere.

d. mesosphere.

12 By which method does most thermal energy in the atmosphere circulate?

a. conduction

b. convection

c. advection

d. radiation

13 The balance between incoming and outgoing energy is called

a. the convection balance.

b. the conduction balance.

c. the greenhouse effect.

d. the radiation balance.

14 In which wind belt is most of the United States located?

a. westerlies

b. northeast trade winds

c. southeast trade winds

d. doldrums

15 Which of the following pollutants is NOT a primary pollutant?

a. car exhaust

b. acid precipitation

c. smoke from a factory

d. fumes from burning plastic

16 The Clean Air Act

    a. controls the amount of air pollutants that can be released from many sources.

    b. requires cars to run on fuels other than gasoline.

    c. requires many industries to use scrubbers.

    d. Both (a) and (c)

Short Answer

17 Why does the atmosphere become less dense as altitude increases?

18 Explain why air rises when it is heated.

19 What is the main cause of temperature changes in the atmosphere?

20 What are secondary pollutants, and how do they form? Give an example of a secondary pollutant.

CRITICAL THINKING

21 **Concept Mapping** Use the following terms to create a concept map: *mesosphere, stratosphere, layers, temperature, troposphere,* and *atmosphere.*

22 **Identifying Relationships** What is the relationship between the greenhouse effect and global warming?

23 **Applying Concepts** How do you think the Coriolis effect would change if the Earth rotated twice as fast as it does? Explain.

24 **Making Inferences** The atmosphere of Venus has a very high level of carbon dioxide. How might this fact influence the greenhouse effect on Venus?

INTERPRETING GRAPHICS

Use the diagram below to answer the questions that follow. When answering the questions that follow, assume that ocean currents do not affect the path of the boats.

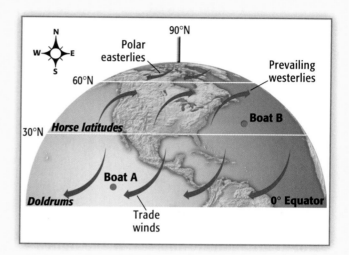

25 If Boat A traveled to 50°N, from which direction would the prevailing winds blow?

26 If Boat B sailed with the prevailing westerlies in the Northern Hemisphere, in which direction would the boat be traveling?

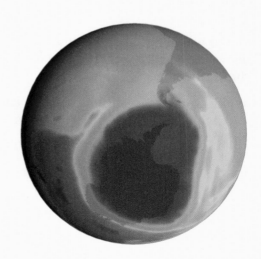

Standardized Test Preparation

Multiple Choice

Use the illustration below to answer question 1.

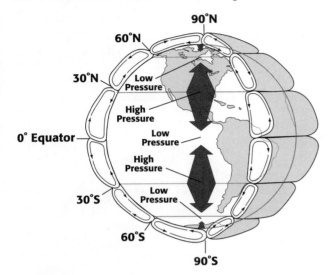

1. **The map above shows the locations of low- and high-pressure belts across North and South America. If the figure shows the pressure belts during April, how might the winds between the 0° and 30°N latitude pressure belts be different in July?**

   A. Winds would be stronger because more heat from the sun would create a larger difference in pressure.

   B. Winds would stay about the same because most of the sun's energy would heat the air at the equator.

   C. Winds would be lighter because the area above the equator would receive more direct sunlight.

   D. Winds would be stronger during the day and lighter at night due to changes in air pressure.

2. **Which causes winter snow and summer rain at higher latitudes?**

   A. the Earth's rotation and the Coriolis effect

   B. changes in evaporation and cloud cover

   C. changes in pressure belts and winds

   D. change in amount of direct sunlight

3. **How might burning fossil fuels contribute to global warming?**

   A. by polluting water that then becomes acid precipitation in the water cycle

   B. by breaking down the atmosphere and allowing more radiation in

   C. by producing carbon dioxide that traps heat in the atmosphere

   D. by producing pollution that blocks sunlight from reaching Earth

4. **As solar radiation hits Earth's surface, it transfers thermal energy. If the same amount of radiation hit the following surfaces, which surface would transfer the most thermal energy to the air above it?**

   A. a maple forest

   B. an asphalt or blacktop parking lot

   C. an ocean bay

   D. a cornfield

5. **Asthma is worsened by smog. What type of pollutants should be reduced in order to reduce the amount of smog in cities?**

   A. CFCs

   B. carbon dioxide

   C. nitrogen oxide

   D. dihydrogen monoxide

6. Why is the top of the mesosphere colder than the top of the troposphere?

A. There are fewer gases that absorb solar energy in the mesosphere.

B. The troposphere is closer to the sun than the mesosphere is.

C. Particles are far apart in the mesosphere, so they do not transfer energy.

D. The mesosphere contains less ozone than the troposphere does.

7. Area A, which has high pressure, is next to area B, which has low pressure. The wind is blowing hard toward area B. Which is most likely to occur if the temperature in area B decreases slightly?

A. The wind will blow harder toward area B.

B. The wind will blow more softly toward area B.

C. The wind will stop blowing.

D. The wind will start blowing toward area A.

8. As the sun heats the surface of the ocean, some of the water evaporates and enters the air. How is this water vapor carried in the atmosphere?

A. by waves

B. by clouds

C. by conduction

D. by convection currents

Use the illustration below to answer question 9.

Layer of the Atmosphere	Temperature in Celsius (°C)	Altitude in Kilometers (km)	Amount of Heat Energy
Troposphere	Varies greatly	10	High levels
Stratosphere	−60	40	Moderate levels
Mesosphere	−93	65	Low levels
Thermosphere	1000	100	Very low levels

9. At which altitude would the most thermal energy be transferred to a slow moving weather balloon?

A. 10 km

B. 40 km

C. 65 km

D. 100 km

Open Response

10. Hikers are exploring mountaintops and valleys in the Appalachians during the hot month of July. In order to stay cool, where should they camp at night? Explain your answer.

11. How is the greenhouse effect related to the water cycle? What might happen to the water cycle as greenhouse gases increase?

Standardized Test Preparation

Science in Action

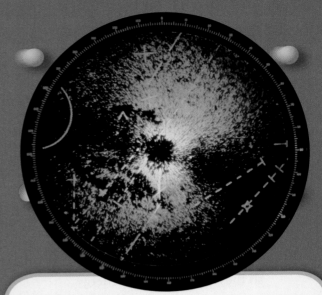

Science, Technology, and Society

The HyperSoar Jet

Imagine traveling from Chicago to Tokyo in 72 minutes. If the HyperSoar jet becomes a reality, you may be able to travel to the other side of the world in less time than it takes to watch a movie! To accomplish this amazing feat, the jet would "skip" across the upper stratosphere. To begin skipping, the jet would climb above the stratosphere, turn off its engines, and glide for about 60 km. Then, gravity would pull the jet down to where the air is denser. The denser air would cause the jet to soar upward. In this way, the jet would skip across a layer of dense air until it was ready to land. Each 2-minute skip would cover about 450 km, and the HyperSoar would be able to fly at Mach 10—a speed of 3 km/s!

Math ACTIVITY

A trip on the HyperSoar from Chicago to Tokyo would require about 18 "skips." Each skip is 450 km. If the trip is 10,123 km, how many kilometers will the jet travel when it is not skipping?

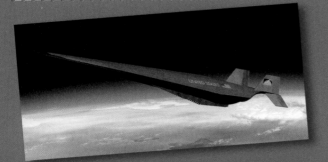

Weird Science

Radar Zoology

"For tonight's forecast, expect a light shower of mayflies. A wave of warblers will approach from the south. Tomorrow will be cloudy, and a band of free-tailed bats will move to the south in the early evening." Such a forecast may not make the evening news, but it is a familiar scenario for radar zoologists. Radar zoologists use a type of radar called *NEXRAD* to track migrating birds, bands of bats, and swarms of insects. NEXRAD tracks animals in the atmosphere in the same way that it tracks storms. The system sends out a microwave signal. If the signal hits an object, some of the energy reflects back to a receiver. NEXRAD has been especially useful to scientists who study bird migration. Birds tend to migrate at night, when the atmosphere is more stable, so until now, nighttime bird migration has been difficult to observe. NEXRAD has also helped identify important bird migration routes and critical stopovers. For example, scientists have discovered that many birds migrate over the Gulf of Mexico instead of around it.

Social Studies ACTIVITY

Geography plays an important role in bird migration. Many birds ride the "thermals" produced by mountain ranges. Find out what thermals are, and create a map of bird migration routes over North America.

Ellen Paneok

Bush Pilot For Ellen Paneok, understanding weather patterns is a matter of life and death. As a bush pilot, she flies mail, supplies, and people to remote villages in Alaska that can be reached only by plane. Bad weather is one of the most serious challenges Paneok faces. "It's beautiful up here," she says, "but it can also be harsh." One dangerous situation is landing a plane in mountainous regions. "On top of a mountain you can't tell which way the wind is blowing," Paneok says. In this case, she flies in a rectangular pattern to determine the wind direction. Landing a plane on the frozen Arctic Ocean is also dangerous. In white-out conditions, the horizon can't be seen because the sky and the ground are the same color. "It's like flying in a milk bottle full of milk," Paneok says. In these conditions, she fills black plastic garbage bags and drops them from the plane to help guide her landing.

Paneok had to overcome many challenges to become a pilot. As a child, she lived in seven foster homes before being placed in an all-girls' home at the age of 14. In the girls' home, she read a magazine about careers in aviation and decided then and there that she wanted to become a pilot. At first, she faced a lot of opposition from people telling her that she wouldn't be able to become a pilot. Now, she encourages young people to pursue their goals. "If you decide you want to go for it, go for it. There may be obstacles in your way, but you've just got to find a way to go over them, get around them, or dig under them," she says.

Ellen Paneok is shown at right with two of her Inupiat passengers.

Language Arts ACTiViTY

Beryl Markham lived an exciting life as a bush pilot delivering mail and supplies to remote areas of Africa. Read about her life or the life of Bessie Coleman, one of the most famous African American women in the history of flying.

To learn more about these Science in Action topics, visit go.hrw.com and type in the keyword **HZ5ATMF.**

Current Science

Check out Current Science® articles related to this chapter by visiting go.hrw.com. Just type in the keyword HZ5CS15.

6

Understanding Weather

The Big Idea

Weather results from differences in pressure, heat, air movement, and humidity.

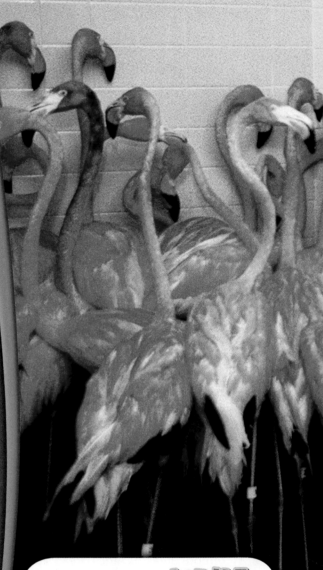

About the Photo

Flamingos in the bathroom? This may look like someone's idea of a practical joke, but in fact, it's a practical idea! These flamingos reside at the Miami-Metro Zoo in Florida. They were put in the bathroom for protection against the incredibly dangerous winds of Hurricane Floyd in September of 1999.

PRE-READING ACTIVITY

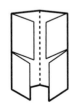

FOLDNOTES **Four-Corner Fold**
Before you read the chapter, create the FoldNote entitled "Four-Corner Fold" described in the **Study Skills** section of the Appendix. Label the flaps of the four-corner fold with "Water in the air," "Air masses and fronts," "Severe weather," and "Forecasting the weather." Write what you know about each topic under the appropriate flap. As you read the chapter, add other information that you learn.

STARTUP ACTIVITY

Meeting of the Masses

In this activity, you will model what happens when two air masses that have different temperature characteristics meet.

Procedure

1. Pour **500 mL of water** into a **beaker.** Pour **500 mL of cooking oil** into a **second beaker.** The water represents a dense cold air mass. The cooking oil represents a less dense warm air mass.

2. Predict what would happen to the two liquids if you tried to mix them.

3. Pour the contents of both beakers into a **clear, plastic, rectangular container** at the same time from opposite ends of the container.

4. Observe the interaction of the oil and water.

Analysis

1. What happens when the liquids meet?

2. Does the prediction that you made in step 2 of the Procedure match your results?

3. Using your results, hypothesize what would happen if a cold air mass met a warm air mass.

Water in the Air

What will the weather be this weekend? Depending on what you have planned, knowing the answer to this question could be important. A picnic in the rain can be a mess!

Have you ever wondered what weather is? **Weather** is the condition of the atmosphere at a certain time and place. The condition of the atmosphere is affected by the amount of water in the air. So, to understand weather, you need to understand how water cycles through Earth's atmosphere.

The Water Cycle

Water in liquid, solid, and gaseous states is constantly being recycled through the water cycle. The *water cycle* is the continuous movement of water from sources on Earth's surface—such as lakes, oceans, and plants—into the air, onto and over land, into the ground, and back to the surface. The movement of water through the water cycle is shown in **Figure 1.**

☑ **Reading Check** What is the water cycle? (*See the Appendix for answers to Reading Checks.*)

What You Will Learn

● Explain how water moves through the water cycle.
● Describe how relative humidity is affected by temperature and levels of water vapor.
● Describe the relationship between dew point and condensation.
● List three types of cloud forms.
● Identify four kinds of precipitation.

Vocabulary

weather
humidity
relative humidity
condensation
cloud
precipitation

READING STRATEGY

Paired Summarizing Read this section silently. In pairs, take turns summarizing the material. Stop to discuss ideas that seem confusing.

Figure 1 The Water Cycle

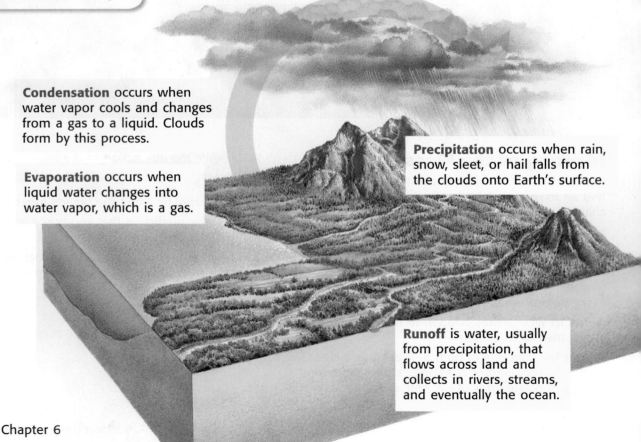

Condensation occurs when water vapor cools and changes from a gas to a liquid. Clouds form by this process.

Evaporation occurs when liquid water changes into water vapor, which is a gas.

Precipitation occurs when rain, snow, sleet, or hail falls from the clouds onto Earth's surface.

Runoff is water, usually from precipitation, that flows across land and collects in rivers, streams, and eventually the ocean.

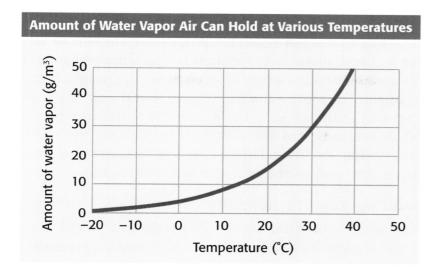

Amount of Water Vapor Air Can Hold at Various Temperatures

Figure 2 *This graph shows that as air gets warmer, the amount of water vapor that the air can hold increases.*

Humidity

As water evaporates from lakes, oceans, and plants, it becomes *water vapor,* or moisture in the air. Water vapor is invisible. The amount of water vapor in the air is called **humidity.** As water evaporates and becomes water vapor, the humidity of the air increases. The air's ability to hold water vapor changes as the temperature of the air changes. **Figure 2** shows that as the temperature of the air increases, the air's ability to hold water vapor also increases.

Relative Humidity

One way to express humidity is through relative humidity. **Relative humidity** is the amount of water vapor in the air compared with the maximum amount of water vapor that the air can hold at a certain temperature. So, relative humidity is given as a percentage. When air holds all of the water that it can at a given temperature, it is said to be *saturated.* Saturated air has a relative humidity of 100%. But how do you find the relative humidity of air that is not saturated? If you know the maximum amount of water vapor that air can hold at a given temperature and the actual amount of water vapor in the air, you can calculate the relative humidity.

Suppose that 1 m³ of air at a certain temperature can hold 24 g of water vapor. However, you know that the air actually contains 18 g of water vapor. You can calculate the relative humidity by using the following formula:

$$\frac{\textit{actual water vapor content (g/m}^3)}{\textit{saturation water vapor content (g/m}^3)} \times 100 = \textit{relative humidity (\%)}$$

$$\frac{18 \text{ g/m}^3}{24 \text{ g/m}^3} = 75\%$$

weather the short-term state of the atmosphere, including temperature, humidity, precipitation, wind, and visibility

humidity the amount of water vapor in the air

relative humidity the ratio of the amount of water vapor in the air to the maximum amount of water vapor the air can hold at a set temperature

Relative Humidity

Assume that 1 m³ of air at 25°C contains 11 g of water vapor. At this temperature, the air can hold 24 g/m³ of water vapor. Calculate the relative humidity of the air.

INTERNET ACTIVITY

For another activity related to this chapter, go to **go.hrw.com** and type in the keyword **HZ5WEAW**.

Factors Affecting Relative Humidity

Two factors that affect relative humidity are amount of water vapor and temperature. At constant temperature and pressure, as the amount of water vapor in air changes, the relative humidity changes. The more water vapor there is in the air, the higher the relative humidity is. If the amount of water vapor in the air stays the same but the temperature changes, the relative humidity changes. The relative humidity decreases as the temperature rises and increases as the temperature drops.

Measuring Relative Humidity

A *psychrometer* (sie KRAHM uht uhr) is an instrument that is used to measure relative humidity. A psychrometer consists of two thermometers, one of which is a wet-bulb thermometer. The bulb of a wet-bulb thermometer is covered with a damp cloth. The other thermometer is a dry-bulb thermometer.

The difference in temperature readings between the thermometers indicates the amount of water vapor in the air. The larger the difference between the two readings is, the less water vapor the air contains and thus the lower the humidity is. **Figure 3** shows how to use a table of differences between wet-bulb and dry-bulb readings to determine relative humidity.

✓ **Reading Check** What tool is used to measure relative humidity?

Figure 3 **Determining Relative Humidity**

Find the relative humidity by locating the column head that is equal to the difference between the wet-bulb and dry-bulb readings. Then, locate the row head that equals the temperature reading on the dry-bulb thermometer. The value that lies where the column and row intersect equals the relative humidity. You can see a psychrometer below.

Relative Humidity (%)								
Dry-bulb reading (°C)	Difference between wet-bulb reading and dry-bulb reading (°C)							
	1	2	3	4	5	6	7	8
0	81	64	46	29	13			
2	84	68	52	37	22	7		
4	85	71	57	43	29	16		
6	86	73	60	48	35	24	11	
8	87	75	63	51	40	29	19	8
10	88	77	66	55	44	34	24	15
12	89	78	68	58	48	39	29	21
14	90	79	70	60	51	42	34	26
16	90	81	71	63	54	46	38	30
18	91	82	73	65	57	49	41	34
20	91	83	74	66	59	51	44	37

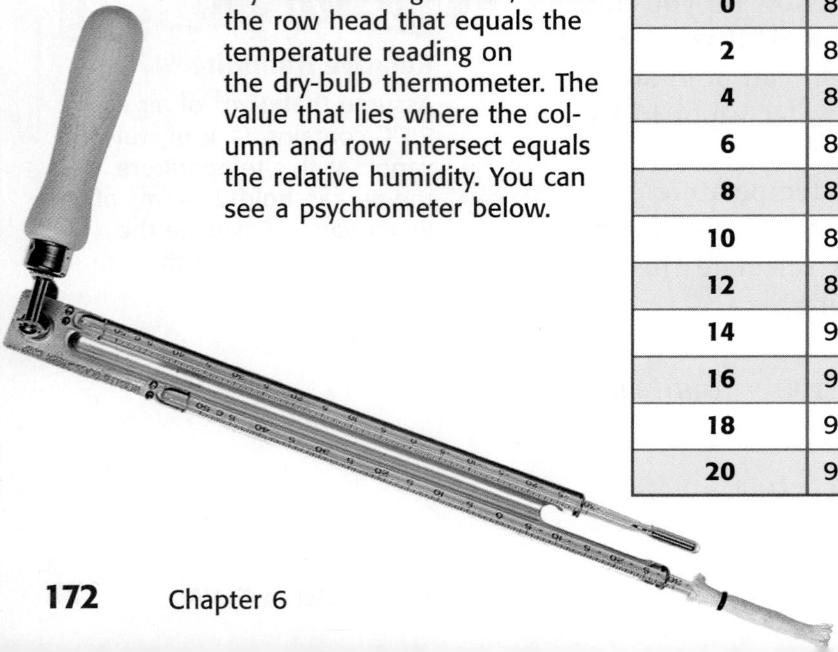

How a Wet-Bulb Thermometer Works

A wet-bulb thermometer works differently than a dry-bulb thermometer, which measures only air temperature. As air passes over the wet-bulb thermometer, the water in the cloth evaporates. As the water evaporates, the cloth cools. If the humidity is low, the water will evaporate more quickly and the temperature reading on the wet-bulb thermometer will drop. If the humidity is high, only a small amount of water will evaporate from the cloth of the wet-bulb thermometer and the change in temperature will be small.

Reading Check Explain how a wet-bulb thermometer works.

Condensation

You have probably seen water droplets form on the outside of a glass of ice water, as shown in **Figure 4.** Where did those water drops come from? The water came from the surrounding air, and droplets formed as a result of condensation. **Condensation** is the process by which a gas, such as water vapor, becomes a liquid. Before condensation can occur, the air must be saturated, which means that the air must have a relative humidity of 100%. Condensation occurs when saturated air cools.

Figure 4 *Condensation occurred when the air next to the glass cooled to its dew point.*

Dew Point

Air can become saturated when water vapor is added to the air through evaporation. Air can also become saturated when it cools to its dew point. The *dew point* is the temperature at which a gas condenses into a liquid. At its dew point, air is saturated. The ice in the glass of water causes the air surrounding the glass to cool to its dew point.

Before water vapor can condense, though, it must have a surface to condense on. In the case of the glass of ice water, water vapor condenses on the outside of the glass.

condensation the change of state from a gas to a liquid

Out of Thin Air

1. Pour **room-temperature water** into a **plastic container,** such as a drinking cup, until the water level is near the top of the cup.
2. Observe the outside of the container, and record your observations.
3. Add **one or two ice cubes** to the container of water.
4. Watch the outside of the container for any changes.
5. What happened to the outside of the container?
6. What is the liquid on the container?
7. Where did the liquid come from? Explain your answer.

Figure 5 Three Forms of Clouds

Cumulus clouds look like piles of cotton balls.

Stratus clouds are not as tall as cumulus clouds, but they cover more area.

Cirrus clouds are made of ice crystals.

cloud a collection of small water droplets or ice crystals suspended in the air, which forms when the air is cooled and condensation occurs

CONNECTION TO Language Arts

Cloud Clues Did you know that the name of a cloud actually describes the characteristics of the cloud? For example, the word *cumulus* comes from the Latin word meaning "heap." A cumulus cloud is a puffy, white cloud, which could be described as a "heap" of clouds. Use a dictionary or the Internet to find the word origins of the names of the other cloud types you learn about in this section.

Clouds

Have you ever wondered what clouds are and how they form? A **cloud** is a collection of millions of tiny water droplets or ice crystals. Clouds form as warm air rises and cools. As the rising air cools, it becomes saturated. When the air is saturated, the water vapor changes to a liquid or a solid, depending on the air temperature. At temperatures above freezing, water vapor condenses on small particles in the air and forms tiny water droplets. At temperatures below freezing, water vapor changes to a solid to form ice crystals. Clouds are classified by form, as shown in **Figure 5,** and by altitude.

Cumulus Clouds

Puffy, white clouds that tend to have flat bottoms are called *cumulus clouds* (KYOO myoo luhs KLOWDZ). Cumulus clouds form when warm air rises. These clouds generally indicate fair weather. However, when these clouds get larger, they produce thunderstorms. Thunderstorms come from a kind of cumulus cloud called a *cumulonimbus cloud* (KYOO myoo loh NIM buhs KLOWD). Clouds that have names that include *-nimbus* or *nimbo-* are likely to produce precipitation.

Stratus Clouds

Clouds called *stratus clouds* (STRAYT uhs KLOWDZ) are clouds that form in layers. Stratus clouds cover large areas of the sky and often block out the sun. These clouds can be caused by a gentle lifting of a large body of air into the atmosphere. *Nimbostratus clouds* (NIM boh STRAYT uhs KLOWDZ) are dark stratus clouds that usually produce light to heavy, continuous rain. *Fog* is a stratus cloud that has formed near the ground.

Cirrus Clouds

As you can see in **Figure 5,** *cirrus clouds* (SIR uhs KLOWDZ) are thin, feathery, white clouds found at high altitudes. Cirrus clouds form when the wind is strong. If they get thicker, cirrus clouds indicate that a change in the weather is coming.

Clouds and Altitude

Clouds are also classified by the altitude at which they form. **Figure 6** shows two altitude groups used to describe clouds and the altitudes at which they form in the middle latitudes. The prefix *cirro-* is used to describe clouds that form at high altitudes. For example, a cumulus cloud that forms high in the atmosphere is called a *cirrocumulus cloud*. The prefix *alto-* describes clouds that form at middle altitudes. Clouds that form at low altitudes do not have a specific prefix to describe them.

Reading Check At what altitude does an altostratus cloud form?

Figure 6 Cloud Types Based on Form and Altitude

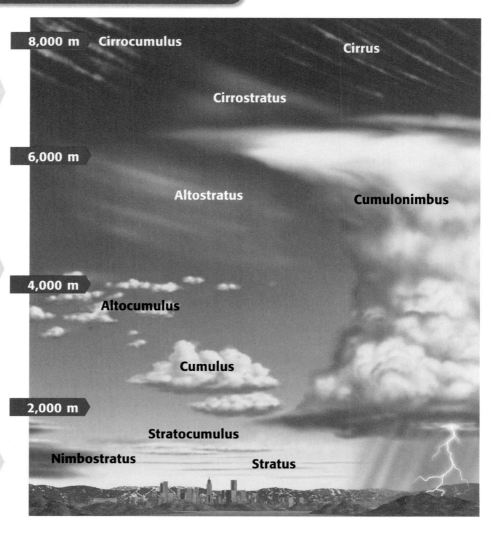

High Clouds Because of the cold temperatures at high altitude, high clouds are made up of ice crystals. The prefix *cirro-* is used to describe high clouds.

Middle Clouds Middle clouds can be made up of both water drops and ice crystals. The prefix *alto-* is used to describe middle clouds.

Low Clouds Low clouds are made up of water drops. There is no specific prefix used to describe low clouds.

8,000 m Cirrocumulus   Cirrus

Cirrostratus

6,000 m

Altostratus   Cumulonimbus

4,000 m

Altocumulus

Cumulus

2,000 m

Stratocumulus

Nimbostratus   Stratus

Figure 7 *Snowflakes are six-sided ice crystals that can be several millimeters to several centimeters in size.*

precipitation any form of water that falls to the Earth's surface from the clouds

Precipitation

When water from the air returns to Earth's surface, it returns as precipitation. **Precipitation** is water, in solid or liquid form, that falls from the air to Earth. There are four major forms of precipitation—rain, snow, sleet, and hail.

Rain

The most common form of precipitation is *rain*. A cloud produces rain when the water drops in the cloud become a certain size. A water drop in a cloud begins as a droplet that is smaller than the period at the end of this sentence. Before such a water drop falls as rain, it must become about 100 times its original size.

Sleet and Snow

Sleet forms when rain falls through a layer of freezing air. The rain freezes in the air, which produces falling ice. *Snow* forms when temperatures are so cold that water vapor changes directly to a solid. Snow can fall as single ice crystals or can join to form snowflakes, as shown in **Figure 7.**

Hail

Balls or lumps of ice that fall from clouds are called *hail*. Hail forms in cumulonimbus clouds. When updrafts of air in the clouds carry raindrops high in the clouds, the raindrops freeze and hail forms. As hail falls, water drops coat it. Another updraft of air can send the hail up again. Here, the water drops collected on the hail freeze to form another layer of ice on the hail. This process can happen many times. Eventually, the hail becomes too heavy to be carried by the updrafts and so falls to Earth's surface, as shown in **Figure 8.**

Figure 8 *The impact of large hailstones can damage property and crops. The inset photograph shows layers inside of a hailstone, which reveal how it formed.*

Summary

- Weather is the condition of the atmosphere at a certain time and place. Weather is affected by the amount of water vapor in the air.

- The water cycle describes the movement of water above, on, and below Earth's surface.

- Humidity describes the amount of water vapor in the air. Relative humidity is a way to express humidity.

- When the temperature of the air cools to its dew point, the air has reached saturation and condensation occurs.

- Clouds form as air cools to its dew point. Clouds are classified by form and by the altitude at which they form.

- Precipitation occurs when the water vapor that condenses in the atmosphere falls back to Earth in solid or liquid form.

Using Key Terms

1. In your own words, write a definition for each of the following terms: *relative humidity, condensation, cloud,* and *precipitation*.

Understanding Key Ideas

2. Which of the following clouds is most likely to produce light to heavy, continuous rain?
   a. cumulus cloud
   b. cumulonimbus cloud
   c. nimbostratus cloud
   d. cirrus cloud

3. How is relative humidity affected by the amount of water vapor in the air?

4. What does a relative humidity of 75% mean?

5. Describe the path of water through the water cycle.

6. What are four types of precipitation?

Critical Thinking

7. **Applying Concepts** Why are some clouds formed from water droplets, while others are made up of ice crystals?

8. **Applying Concepts** How can rain and hail fall from the same cumulonimbus cloud?

9. **Identifying Relationships** What happens to relative humidity as the air temperature drops below the dew point?

Interpreting Graphics

Use the image below to answer the questions that follow.

10. What type of cloud is shown in the image?

11. How is this type of cloud formed?

12. What type of weather can you expect when you see this type of cloud? Explain.

SCILINKS®

NSTA
Developed and maintained by the
National Science Teachers Association

For a variety of links related to this chapter, go to www.scilinks.org

Topic: The Water Cycle
SciLinks code: HSM1626

Air Masses and Fronts

Have you ever wondered how the weather can change so quickly? For example, the weather may be warm and sunny in the morning and cold and rainy by afternoon.

Changes in weather are caused by the movement and interaction of air masses. An **air mass** is a large body of air where temperature and moisture content are similar throughout. In this section, you will learn about air masses and their effect on weather.

Air Masses

Air masses are characterized by their moisture content and temperature. The moisture content and temperature of an air mass are determined by the area over which the air mass forms. These areas are called *source regions*. An example of a source region is the Gulf of Mexico. An air mass that forms over the Gulf of Mexico is warm and wet because this area is warm and has a lot of water that evaporates. There are many types of air masses, each of which is associated with a particular source region. The characteristics of these air masses are represented on maps by a two-letter symbol, as shown in **Figure 1.** The first letter indicates the moisture content that is characteristic of the air mass. The second letter represents the temperature that is characteristic of the air mass.

What You Will Learn

- Identify the four kinds of air masses that influence weather in the United States.
- Describe the four major types of fronts.
- Explain how fronts cause weather changes.
- Explain how cyclones and anticyclones affect the weather.

Vocabulary

air mass   cyclone
front   anticyclone

READING STRATEGY

Reading Organizer As you read this section, make a table comparing cold, warm, occluded, and stationary fronts.

Figure 1 Air Masses That Affect Weather in North America

maritime (m) forms over water; wet

continental (c) forms over land; dry

polar (P) forms over the polar regions; cold

tropical (T) develops over the Tropics; warm

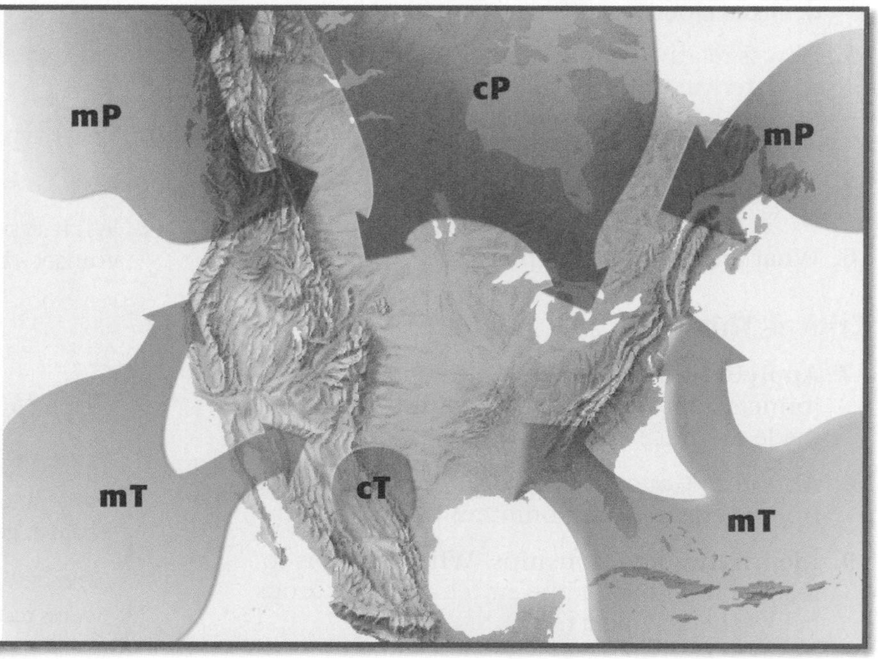

Figure 2 *Cold air masses that form over the North Atlantic Ocean can bring severe weather, such as blizzards, in the winter.*

Cold Air Masses

Most of the cold winter weather in the United States is influenced by three polar air masses. A continental polar (cP) air mass forms over northern Canada, which brings extremely cold winter weather to the United States. In the summer, a cP air mass generally brings cool, dry weather.

A maritime polar (mP) air mass that forms over the North Pacific Ocean is cool and very wet. This air mass brings rain and snow to the Pacific Coast in the winter and cool, foggy weather in the summer.

A maritime polar air mass that forms over the North Atlantic Ocean brings cool, cloudy weather and precipitation to New England in the winter, as shown in **Figure 2.** In the summer, the air mass brings cool weather and fog.

air mass a large body of air where temperature and moisture content are constant throughout

Warm Air Masses

Four warm air masses influence the weather in the United States. A maritime tropical (mT) air mass that develops over warm areas in the Pacific Ocean is milder than the maritime polar air mass that forms over the Pacific Ocean.

Other maritime tropical air masses develop over the warm waters of the Gulf of Mexico and the Atlantic Ocean. These air masses move north across the East Coast and into the Midwest. In the summer, they bring hot and humid weather, hurricanes, and thunderstorms, as shown in **Figure 3.** In the winter, they bring mild, often cloudy weather.

A continental tropical (cT) air mass forms over the deserts of northern Mexico and the southwestern United States. This air mass moves northward and brings clear, dry, and hot weather in the summer.

Figure 3 *Warm air masses that develop over the Gulf of Mexico bring thunderstorms in the summer.*

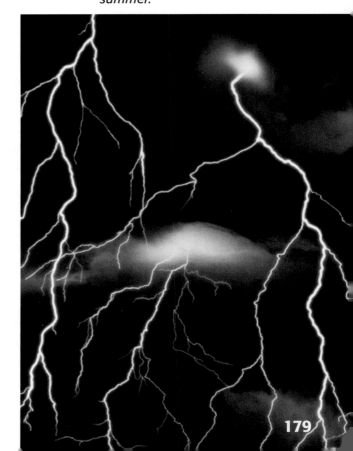

✔ *Reading Check* **What type of air mass contributes to the hot and humid summer weather in the midwestern United States?** (*See the Appendix for answers to Reading Checks.*)

179

Figure 4 **Fronts That Affect Weather in North America**

Cold Front

Warm Front

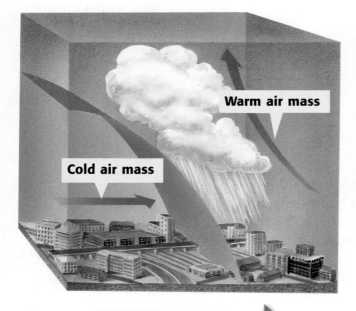

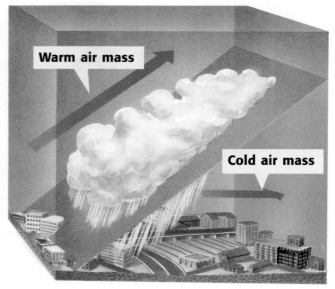

Warm air mass

Cold air mass

Direction of front

Warm air mass

Cold air mass

Direction of front

Fronts

Air masses that form from different areas often do not mix. The reason is that the air masses have different densities. For example, warm air is less dense than cold air. So, when two types of air masses meet, warm air generally rises. The area in which two types of air masses meet is called a **front.** The four kinds of fronts—cold fronts, warm fronts, occluded fronts, and stationary fronts—are shown in **Figure 4.** Fronts are associated with weather in the middle latitudes.

front the boundary between air masses of different densities and usually different temperatures

Cold Front

A cold front forms where cold air moves under warm air, which is less dense, and pushes the warm air up. Cold fronts can move quickly and bring thunderstorms, heavy rain, or snow. Cooler weather usually follows a cold front because the air mass behind the cold front is cooler and drier than the air mass that it is replacing.

Warm Front

A warm front forms where warm air moves over cold, denser air. In a warm front, the warm air gradually replaces the cold air. Warm fronts generally bring drizzly rain and are followed by clear and warm weather.

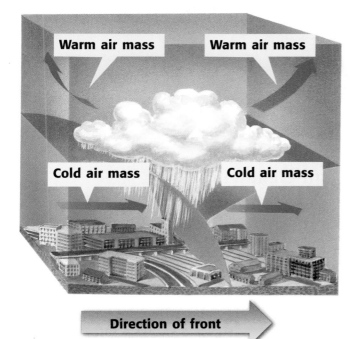

Occluded Front

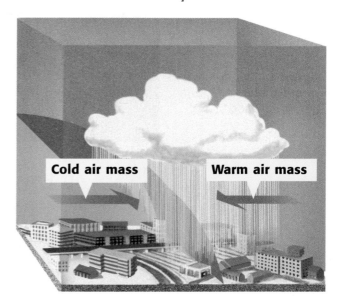

Stationary Front

Occluded Front

An occluded front forms when a warm air mass is caught between two colder air masses. The coldest air mass moves under and pushes up the warm air mass. The coldest air mass then moves forward until it meets a cold air mass that is warmer and less dense. The colder of these two air masses moves under and pushes up the warmer air mass. Sometimes, though, the two colder air masses mix. An occluded front has cool temperatures and large amounts of rain and snow.

✓ Reading Check What type of weather would you expect an occluded front to produce?

Stationary Front

A stationary front forms when a cold air mass meets a warm air mass. In this case, however, both air masses do not have enough force to lift the warm air mass over the cold air mass. So, the two air masses remain separated. This may happen because there is not enough wind to keep the air masses pushing against each other. A stationary front often brings many days of cloudy, wet weather.

Figure 5 *This satellite image shows a cyclone system forming.*

Air Pressure and Weather

You may have heard a weather reporter on TV or radio talking about areas of low pressure and high pressure. These areas of different pressure affect the weather.

Cyclones

Areas that have lower pressure than the surrounding areas do are called **cyclones.** Cyclones are areas where air masses come together, or converge, and rise. **Figure 5** shows a satellite image of the formation of a cyclone system.

Anticyclones

Areas that have high pressure are called **anticyclones.** Anticyclones are areas where air moves apart, or diverges, and sinks. The sinking air is denser than the surrounding air, and the pressure is higher. Cooler, denser air moves out of the center of these high-pressure areas toward areas of lower pressure. **Figure 6** shows how wind can spiral out of an anticyclone and into a cyclone.

cyclone an area in the atmosphere that has lower pressure than the surrounding areas and has winds that spiral toward the center

anticyclone the rotation of air around a high-pressure center in the direction opposite to Earth's rotation

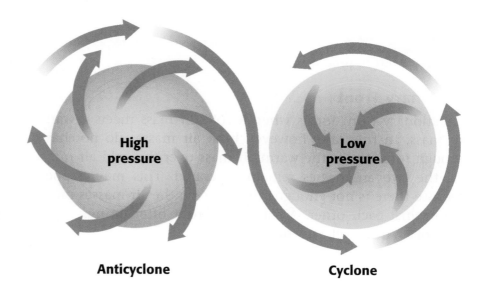

Figure 6 *As the colder, denser air spirals out of the anticyclone, it moves towards areas of low pressure, which sometimes forms a cyclone.*

Cyclones, Anticyclones, and Weather

You have learned what cyclones and anticyclones are. So, now you might be wondering how do cyclones and anticyclones affect the weather? As the air in the center of a cyclone rises, it cools and forms clouds and rain. The rising air in a cyclone causes stormy weather. In an anticyclone, the air sinks. As the air sinks, it gets warmer and absorbs moisture. The sinking air in an anticyclone brings dry, clear weather. By keeping track of cyclones and anticyclones, meteorologists can predict the weather.

✓ Reading Check Describe the different types of weather that a cyclone and an anticyclone can produce.

CONNECTION TO Astronomy

Storms on Jupiter Cyclones and anticyclones occur on Jupiter, too! Generally, cyclones on Jupiter appear as dark ovals, and anticyclones appear as bright ovals. Jupiter's Great Red Spot is an anticyclone that has existed for centuries. Research the existence of cyclones and anticyclones on other bodies in our solar system.

SECTION Review

Summary

- Air masses are characterized by moisture content and temperature.
- A front occurs where two air masses meet.
- Four major types of fronts are cold, warm, occluded, and stationary fronts.
- Differences in air pressure cause cyclones, which bring stormy weather, and anticyclones, which bring dry, clear weather.

Using Key Terms

For each pair of terms, explain how the meanings of the terms differ.

1. *front* and *air mass*

2. *cyclone* and *anticyclone*

Understanding Key Ideas

3. What kind of front forms when a cold air mass displaces a warm air mass?
   a. a cold front
   b. a warm front
   c. an occluded front
   d. a stationary front

4. What are the major air masses that influence the weather in the United States?

5. What is one source region of a maritime polar air mass?

6. What are the characteristics of an air mass whose two-letter symbol is cP?

7. What are the four major types of fronts?

8. How do fronts cause weather changes?

9. How do cyclones and anticyclones affect the weather?

Math Skills

10. A cold front is moving toward the town of La Porte at 35 km/h. The front is 200 km away from La Porte. How long will it take the front to get to La Porte?

Critical Thinking

11. **Applying Concepts** How do air masses that form over the land and ocean affect weather in the United States?

12. **Identifying Relationships** Why does the Pacific Coast have cool, wet winters and warm, dry summers? Explain.

13. **Applying Concepts** Which air masses influence the weather where you live? Explain.

SCILINKS®

NSTA
Developed and maintained by the National Science Teachers Association

For a variety of links related to this chapter, go to www.scilinks.org

Topic: Air Masses and Fronts
SciLinks code: HSM0032

What You Will Learn

● Describe how lightning forms.
● Describe the formation of thunderstorms, tornadoes, and hurricanes.
● Describe the characteristics of thunderstorms, tornadoes, and hurricanes.
● Explain how to stay safe during severe weather.

Vocabulary

thunderstorm   tornado
lightning   hurricane
thunder

READING STRATEGY

Reading Organizer As you read this section, create an outline of the section. Use the headings from the section in your outline.

thunderstorm a usually brief, heavy storm that consists of rain, strong winds, lightning, and thunder

Severe Weather

CRAAAACK! BOOM! What made that noise? You didn't expect it, and it sure made you jump.

A big boom of thunder has probably surprised you at one time or another. And the thunder was probably followed by a thunderstorm. A thunderstorm is an example of severe weather. *Severe weather* is weather that can cause property damage and sometimes death.

Thunderstorms

Thunderstorms can be very loud and powerful. **Thunderstorms,** such as the one shown in **Figure 1,** are small, intense weather systems that produce strong winds, heavy rain, lightning, and thunder. Thunderstorms can occur along cold fronts. But thunderstorms can develop in other places, too. There are only two atmospheric conditions required to produce thunderstorms: warm and moist air near Earth's surface and an unstable atmosphere. The atmosphere is unstable when the surrounding air is colder than the rising air mass. The air mass will continue to rise as long as the surrounding air is colder than the air mass.

When the rising warm air reaches its dew point, the water vapor in the air condenses and forms cumulus clouds. If the atmosphere is extremely unstable, the warm air will continue to rise, which causes the cloud to grow into a dark, cumulonimbus cloud. Cumulonimbus clouds can reach heights of more than 15 km.

Figure 1 *A typical thunderstorm, such as this one over Dallas, Texas, generates an enormous amount of electrical energy.*

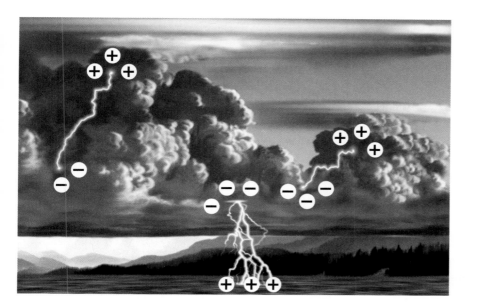

Figure 2 *The upper part of a cloud usually carries a positive electric charge, while the lower part of the cloud carries mainly negative charges.*

Lightning

Thunderstorms are very active electrically. **Lightning** is an electric discharge that occurs between a positively charged area and a negatively charged area, as shown in **Figure 2.** Lightning can happen between two clouds, between Earth and a cloud, or even between two parts of the same cloud. Have you ever touched someone after scuffing your feet on the carpet and received a mild shock? If so, you have experienced how lightning forms. While you walk around, friction between the floor and your shoes builds up an electric charge in your body. When you touch someone else, the charge is released.

When lightning strikes, energy is released. This energy is transferred to the air and causes the air to expand rapidly and send out sound waves. **Thunder** is the sound that results from the rapid expansion of air along the lightning strike.

lightning an electric discharge that takes place between two oppositely charged surfaces, such as between a cloud and the ground, between two clouds, or between two parts of the same cloud

thunder the sound caused by the rapid expansion of air along an electrical strike

Severe Thunderstorms

Severe thunderstorms can produce one or more of the following conditions: high winds, hail, flash floods, and tornadoes. Hailstorms damage crops, dent the metal on cars, and break windows. Flash flooding that results from heavy rains causes millions of dollars in property damage annually. And every year, flash flooding is a leading cause of weather-related deaths.

Lightning, as shown in **Figure 3,** happens during all thunderstorms and is very powerful. Lightning is responsible for starting thousands of forest fires each year and for killing or injuring hundreds of people a year in the United States.

Figure 3 *Lightning often strikes the tallest object in an area, such as the Eiffel Tower in Paris, France.*

✔ Reading Check **What is a severe thunderstorm?** (*See the Appendix for answers to Reading Checks.*)

Tornadoes

tornado a destructive, rotating column of air that has very high wind speeds, is visible as a funnel-shaped cloud, and touches the ground

Tornadoes happen in only 1% of all thunderstorms. A **tornado** is a small, spinning column of air that has high wind speeds and low central pressure and that touches the ground. A tornado starts out as a funnel cloud that pokes through the bottom of a cumulonimbus cloud and hangs in the air. The funnel cloud becomes a tornado when it makes contact with Earth's surface. **Figure 4** shows how a tornado forms.

Figure 4 How a Tornado Forms

❶ Wind moving in two directions causes a layer of air in the middle to begin to spin like a roll of toilet paper.

❷ The spinning column of air is turned to a vertical position by strong updrafts of air in the cumulonimbus cloud. The updrafts of air also begin to spin.

❸ The spinning column of air moves to the bottom of the cumulonimbus cloud and forms a funnel cloud.

❹ The funnel cloud becomes a tornado when it touches the ground.

Figure 5 *The tornado that hit Kissimmee, Florida, in 1998 had wind speeds of up to 416 km/h.*

Twists of Terror

About 75% of the world's tornadoes occur in the United States. Most of these tornadoes happen in the spring and early summer when cold, dry air from Canada meets warm, moist air from the Tropics. The size of a tornado's path of destruction is usually about 8 km long and 10 to 60 m wide. Although most tornadoes last only a few minutes, they can cause a lot of damage. Their ability to cause damage is due to their strong spinning winds. The average tornado has wind speeds between 120 and 180 km/h, but rarer, more violent tornadoes can have spinning winds of up to 500 km/h. The winds of tornadoes have been known to uproot trees and destroy buildings, as shown in **Figure 5.** Tornadoes are capable of picking up heavy objects, such as mobile homes and cars, and hurling them through the air.

hurricane a severe storm that develops over tropical oceans and whose strong winds of more than 120 km/h spiral in toward the intensely low-pressure storm center

Hurricanes

A large, rotating tropical weather system that has wind speeds of at least 120 km/h is called a **hurricane,** shown in **Figure 6.** Hurricanes are the most powerful storms on Earth. Hurricanes have different names in different parts of the world. In the western Pacific Ocean, hurricanes are called *typhoons.* Hurricanes that form over the Indian Ocean are called *cyclones.*

Most hurricanes form in the areas between 5° and 20° north latitude and between 5° and 20° south latitude over warm, tropical oceans. At higher latitudes, the water is too cold for hurricanes to form. Hurricanes vary in size from 160 to 1,500 km in diameter and can travel for thousands of kilometers.

✔ Reading Check What are some other names for hurricanes?

Figure 6 *This photograph of Hurricane Fran was taken from space.*

How a Hurricane Forms

A hurricane begins as a group of thunderstorms moving over tropical ocean waters. Winds traveling in two different directions meet and cause the storm to spin. Because of the Coriolis effect, the storm turns counterclockwise in the Northern Hemisphere and clockwise in the Southern Hemisphere.

A hurricane gets its energy from the condensation of water vapor. Once formed, the hurricane is fueled through contact with the warm ocean water. Moisture is added to the warm air by evaporation from the ocean. As the warm, moist air rises, the water vapor condenses and releases large amounts of energy. The hurricane continues to grow as long as it is over its source of warm, moist air. When the hurricane moves into colder waters or over land, it begins to die because it has lost its source of energy. **Figure 7** and **Figure 8** show two views of a hurricane.

✓ **Reading Check** Where do hurricanes get their energy?

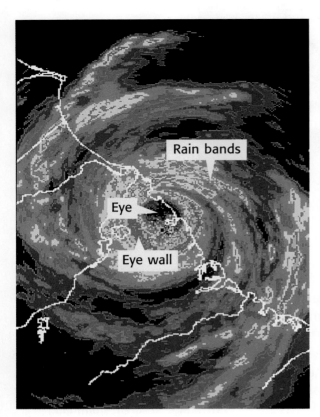

Figure 7 *The photo above gives you a bird's-eye view of a hurricane.*

Figure 8 **Cross Section of a Hurricane**

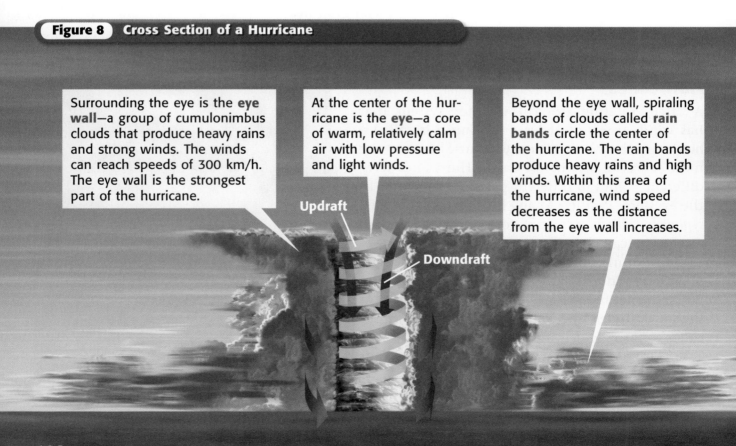

Surrounding the eye is the **eye wall**—a group of cumulonimbus clouds that produce heavy rains and strong winds. The winds can reach speeds of 300 km/h. The eye wall is the strongest part of the hurricane.

At the center of the hurricane is the **eye**—a core of warm, relatively calm air with low pressure and light winds.

Beyond the eye wall, spiraling bands of clouds called **rain bands** circle the center of the hurricane. The rain bands produce heavy rains and high winds. Within this area of the hurricane, wind speed decreases as the distance from the eye wall increases.

Updraft

Downdraft

Damage Caused by Hurricanes

Hurricanes can cause a lot of damage when they move near or onto land. Wind speeds of most hurricanes range from 120 to 150 km/h. Some can reach speeds as high as 300 km/h. Hurricane winds can knock down trees and telephone poles and can damage and destroy buildings and homes.

While high winds cause a great deal of damage, most hurricane damage is caused by flooding associated with heavy rains and storm surges. A *storm surge* is a wall of water that builds up over the ocean because of the strong winds and low atmospheric pressure. The wall of water gets bigger as it nears the shore, and it reaches its greatest height when it crashes onto the shore. Depending on the hurricane's strength, a storm surge can be 1 to 8 m high and 65 to 160 km long. Flooding causes tremendous damage to property and lives when a storm surge moves onto shore, as shown in **Figure 9.**

Severe Weather Safety

Severe weather can be very dangerous, so it is important to keep yourself safe. One way to stay safe is to turn on the radio or TV during a storm. Your local radio and TV stations will let you know if a storm has gotten worse.

Thunderstorm Safety

Lightning is one of the most dangerous parts of a thunderstorm. Lightning is attracted to tall objects. If you are outside, stay away from trees, which can get struck down. If you are in the open, crouch down. Otherwise, you will be the tallest object in the area! Stay away from bodies of water. If lightning hits water while you are in it, you could be hurt or could even die.

Figure 9 *A hurricane's storm surge can cause severe damage to homes near the shoreline.*

Natural Disaster Plan

WRITING SKILL Every family should have a plan to deal with weather emergencies. With an adult, discuss what your family should do in the event of severe weather. Together, write up a plan for your family to follow in case of a natural disaster. Also, make a disaster supply kit that includes enough food and water to last several days.

Figure 10 *During a tornado warning, it is best to protect yourself by crouching against a wall and covering the back of your head and neck with your hands or a book.*

Tornado Safety

Weather forecasters use watches and warnings to let people know about tornadoes. A *watch* is a weather alert that lets people know that a tornado may happen. A *warning* is a weather alert that lets people know that a tornado has been spotted.

If there is a tornado warning for your area, find shelter quickly. The best place to go is a basement or cellar. Or you can go to a windowless room in the center of the building, such as a bathroom, closet, or hallway, as **Figure 10** shows. If you are outside, lie down in a large, open field or a deep ditch.

Flood Safety

An area can get so much rain that it begins to flood. So, like tornadoes, floods have watches and warnings. However, little warning can usually be given. A flash flood is a flood that rises and falls very suddenly. The best thing to do during a flood is to find a high place to wait out the flood. You should always stay out of floodwaters. Even shallow water can be dangerous if it is moving fast.

Hurricane Safety

If a hurricane is in your area, your local TV or radio station will keep you updated on its condition. People living on the shore may be asked to evacuate the area. If you live in an area where hurricanes strike, your family should have a disaster supply kit that includes enough water and food to last several days. To protect the windows in your home, you should cover them with plywood, as shown in **Figure 11.** Most important, you must stay indoors during the storm.

Figure 11 *These store owners are boarding up their windows to protect the windows from strong winds during a hurricane.*

Summary

- Thunderstorms are intense weather systems that produce strong winds, heavy rain, lightning, and thunder.

- Lightning is a large electric discharge that occurs between two oppositely charged surfaces. Lightning releases a great deal of energy and can be very dangerous.

- Tornadoes are small, rotating columns of air that touch the ground and can cause severe damage.

- A hurricane is a large, rotating tropical weather system. Hurricanes cause strong winds and can cause severe property damage.

- In the event of severe weather, it is important to stay safe. Listening to your local TV or radio station for updates and remaining indoors and away from windows are good rules to follow.

Using Key Terms

Complete each of the following sentences by choosing the correct term from the word bank.

hurricane	storm surge
tornado	lightning

1. Thunderstorms are very active electrically and often cause ___.

2. A ___ forms when a funnel cloud pokes through the bottom of a cumulonimbus cloud and makes contact with the ground.

Understanding Key Ideas

3. The safest thing to do if you are caught outdoors during a tornado is to
   a. stay near buildings and roads.
   b. head for an open area.
   c. seek shelter near a large tree.
   d. None of the above

4. Describe how tornadoes form.

5. At what latitudes do hurricanes usually form?

6. What is lightning? What happens when lightning strikes?

Critical Thinking

7. **Applying Concepts** What items do you think you would need in a disaster kit? Explain.

8. **Identifying Relationships** What happens to a hurricane as it moves over land? Explain.

Interpreting Graphics

Use the diagram below to answer the questions that follow.

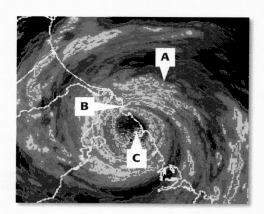

9. Describe what is happening at point C.

10. What is point B?

11. What kind of weather can you expect at point A?

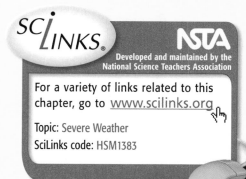

SCILINKS

NSTA
Developed and maintained by the
National Science Teachers Association

For a variety of links related to this chapter, go to www.scilinks.org

Topic: Severe Weather
SciLinks code: HSM1383

Forecasting the Weather

You watch the weather forecast on the evening news. The news is good—there's no rain in sight. But how can the weather forecasters tell that it won't rain?

Weather affects how you dress and how you plan your day, so it is important to get accurate weather forecasts. But where do weather reporters get their information? And how do they predict the weather? A *weather forecast* is a prediction of weather conditions over the next 3 to 5 days. A *meteorologist* is a person who observes and collects data on atmospheric conditions to make weather predictions. In this section, you will learn how weather data are collected and shown.

Weather-Forecasting Technology

To accurately forecast the weather, meteorologists need to measure various atmospheric conditions, such as air pressure, humidity, precipitation, temperature, wind speed, and wind direction. Meteorologists use special instruments to collect data on weather conditions both near and far above Earth's surface.

High in the Sky

Weather balloons carry electronic equipment that can measure weather conditions as high as 30 km above Earth's surface. Weather balloons, such as the one in **Figure 1,** carry equipment that measures temperature, air pressure, and relative humidity. By tracking the balloons, meteorologists can also measure wind speed and direction.

✓ **Reading Check** How do meteorologists gather data on atmospheric conditions above Earth's surface? (*See the Appendix for answers to Reading Check.*)

What You Will Learn

- Describe the different types of instruments used to take weather measurements.
- Explain how radar and weather satellites help meteorologists forecast the weather.
- Explain how to interpret a weather map.

Vocabulary

thermometer
barometer
anemometer

READING STRATEGY

Reading Organizer As you read this section, make a table comparing the different instruments used to collect weather data.

Figure 1 *Weather balloons carry radio transmitters that send measurements to stations on the ground.*

Figure 2 *Meteorologists use these tools to collect atmospheric data.*

Measuring Air Temperature and Pressure

A tool used to measure air temperature is called a **thermometer.** Most thermometers use a liquid sealed in a narrow glass tube, as shown in **Figure 2.** When air temperature increases, the liquid expands and moves up the glass tube. As air temperature decreases, the liquid shrinks and moves down the tube.

A **barometer** is an instrument used to measure air pressure. A mercurial barometer consists of a glass tube that is sealed at one end and placed in a container full of mercury. As the air pressure pushes on the mercury inside the container, the mercury moves up the glass tube. The greater the air pressure is, the higher the mercury will rise.

Measuring Wind Direction

Wind direction can be measured by using a windsock or a wind vane. A windsock, shown in **Figure 2,** is a cone-shaped cloth bag open at both ends. The wind enters through the wide end and leaves through the narrow end. Therefore, the wide end points into the wind. A wind vane is shaped like an arrow with a large tail and is attached to a pole. As the wind pushes the tail of the wind vane, the wind vane spins on the pole until the arrow points into the wind.

Measuring Wind Speed

An instrument used to measure wind speed is called an **anemometer.** An anemometer, as shown in **Figure 2,** consists of three or four cups connected by spokes to a pole. The wind pushes on the hollow sides of the cups and causes the cups to rotate on the pole. The motion sends a weak electric current that is measured and displayed on a dial.

thermometer an instrument that measures and indicates temperature

barometer an instrument that measures atmospheric pressure

anemometer an instrument used to measure wind speed

Figure 3 *Using Doppler radar, meteorologists can predict a tornado up to 20 minutes before it touches the ground.*

CONNECTION TO Biology

WRITING SKILL **Predicting the Weather** Throughout history, people have predicted approaching weather by interpreting natural signs. Animals and plants are usually more sensitive to changes in atmospheric conditions, such as air pressure, humidity, and temperature, than humans are. To find out more about natural signs, research this topic at the library or on the Internet. Write a short paper on your findings to share with the class.

Radar and Satellites

Radar is used to find the location, movement, and amount of precipitation. It can also detect what form of precipitation a weather system is carrying. You might have seen a kind of radar called *Doppler radar* used in a local TV weather report. **Figure 3** shows how Doppler radar is used to track precipitation. *Weather satellites* that orbit Earth provide the images of weather systems that you see on TV weather reports. Satellites can track storms and measure wind speeds, humidity, and temperatures at different altitudes.

Weather Maps

In the United States, the National Weather Service (NWS) and the National Oceanic and Atmospheric Administration (NOAA) collect and analyze weather data. The NWS produces weather maps based on information gathered from about 1,000 weather stations across the United States. On these maps, each station is represented by a station model. A *station model* is a small circle that shows the location of the weather station. As shown in **Figure 4,** surrounding the small circle is a set of symbols and numbers, which represent the weather data.

Figure 4 **A Station Model**

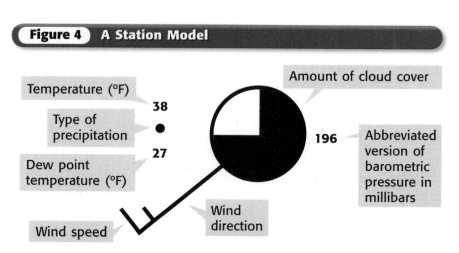

Temperature (°F)

Type of precipitation

Dew point temperature (°F)

Wind speed

Amount of cloud cover

Abbreviated version of barometric pressure in millibars

Wind direction

38

27

196

Reading a Weather Map

Weather maps that you see on TV include lines called *isobars*. Isobars are lines that connect points of equal air pressure. Isobars that form closed circles represent areas of high or low pressure. These areas are usually marked on a map with a capital *H* or *L*. Fronts are also labeled on weather maps, as you can see on the weather map in **Figure 5.**

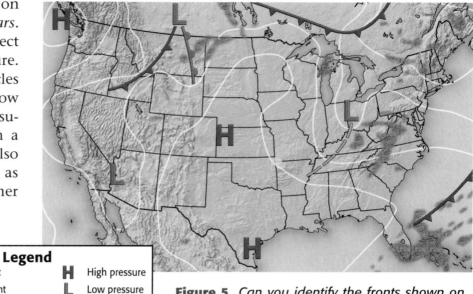

Legend

▽▽▽	Cold front	**H**	High pressure
▲▲▲	Warm front	**L**	Low pressure
—•—•—	Low pressure trough	▬	Rain
～～～	Isobar		Fog

Figure 5 *Can you identify the fronts shown on the weather map?*

SECTION Review

Summary

- Meteorologists use several instruments, such as weather balloons, thermometers, barometers, anemometers, windsocks, weather vanes, radar, and weather satellites, to forecast the weather.

- Station models show the weather conditions at various points across the United States.

- Weather maps show areas of high and low pressure as well as the location of fronts.

Using Key Terms

1. In your own words, write a definition for each of the following terms: *thermometer, barometer,* and *anemometer.*

Understanding Key Ideas

2. Which of the following instruments measures air pressure?

   a. thermometer

   b. barometer

   c. anemometer

   d. windsock

3. How does radar help meteorologists forecast the weather?

4. What does a station model represent?

Math Skills

5. If it is 75°F outside, what is the temperature in degrees Celsius? (Hint: °F = (°C × 9/5) + 32)

Critical Thinking

6. **Applying Concepts** Why would a meteorologist compare a new weather map with one that is 24 h old?

7. **Making Inferences** In the United States, why is weather data gathered from a large number of station models?

8. **Making Inferences** How might several station models from different regions plotted on a map help a meteorologist?

SC*L*INKS®

NSTA

Developed and maintained by the National Science Teachers Association

For a variety of links related to this chapter, go to www.scilinks.org

Topic: Forecasting the Weather
SciLinks code: HSM0606

OBJECTIVES

Construct a device that uses water to measure temperature.

Calibrate the new device by using a mercury thermometer.

MATERIALS

- bottle, plastic
- can, aluminum soda
- card, index, 3 in. × 5 in.
- clay, modeling (1 lb)
- container, yogurt, with lid
- cup, plastic-foam, large (2)
- film canister
- food coloring, red (1 bottle)
- funnel, plastic or paper cone
- gloves, heat-resistant
- hot plate
- ice, cube (5 or 6)
- pan, aluminum pie
- pitcher
- plastic tubing, 5 mm diameter, 30 cm long
- ruler, metric
- straw, plastic, inflexible, clear (1)
- tape, transparent (1 roll)
- thermometer, Celsius
- water, tap

SAFETY

Boiling Over!

Safety Industries, Inc., would like to produce and sell thermometers that are safer than mercury thermometers. The company would like your team of inventors to design a thermometer that uses water instead of mercury. The company will offer a contract to the team that creates the best design of a water thermometer. Good luck!

Ask a Question

1 What causes the liquid in a thermometer to rise? How can I use this information to make a thermometer?

Form a Hypothesis

2 Brainstorm with a classmate to design a thermometer that uses only water to measure temperature. Sketch your design. Write a one-sentence hypothesis that describes how your thermometer will work.

Test the Hypothesis

3 Following your design, build a thermometer by using only materials from the materials list. Like a mercury thermometer, your thermometer needs a bulb and a tube. However, the liquid in your thermometer will be water.

4 To test your design, place the aluminum pie pan on a hot plate. Use the pitcher to carefully pour water into the pan until the pan is half full. Turn on the hot plate, and heat the water.

5 Put on your safety goggles and heat-resistant gloves, and carefully place the "bulb" of your thermometer in the hot water. Observe the water level in the tube. Does the water level rise?

6 If the water level does not rise, change your design as necessary and repeat steps 3–5. When the water level in your thermometer does rise, sketch the design of this thermometer as your final design.

7 After you decide on your final design, you must calibrate your thermometer by using a laboratory thermometer. Tape an index card to your thermometer's tube so that the part of the tube that sticks out from the "bulb" of your thermometer touches the card.

8. Place the plastic funnel or the cone-shaped paper funnel into a plastic-foam cup. Carefully pour hot water from the pie pan into the funnel. Be sure that no water splashes or spills.

9. Place your thermometer and a laboratory thermometer in the hot water. As your thermometer's water level rises, mark the level on the index card. At the same time, observe and record the temperature of the laboratory thermometer, and write this value beside your mark on the card.

10. Repeat steps 8–9 using warm tap water.

11. Repeat steps 8–9 using ice water.

12. Draw evenly spaced scale markings between your temperature markings on the index card. Write the temperatures that correspond to the scale marks on the index card.

Analyze the Results

1. **Analyzing Results** How well does your thermometer measure temperature?

Draw Conclusions

2. **Drawing Conclusions** Compare your thermometer design with other students' designs. How would you change your design to make your thermometer measure temperature better?

3. **Applying Conclusions** Take a class vote to see which design should be used by Safety Industries. Why was this thermometer design chosen? How did it differ from other designs in the class?

Chapter Review

USING KEY TERMS

For each pair of terms, explain how the meanings of the terms differ.

1. *relative humidity* and *dew point*

2. *condensation* and *precipitation*

3. *air mass* and *front*

4. *lightning* and *thunder*

5. *tornado* and *hurricane*

6. *barometer* and *anemometer*

UNDERSTANDING KEY IDEAS

Multiple Choice

7. The process in which water changes from a liquid to gas is called

   a. precipitation.

   b. condensation.

   c. evaporation.

   d. water vapor.

8. What is the relative humidity of air at its dew point?

   a. 0%   c. 75%

   b. 50%   d. 100%

9. Which of the following is NOT a type of condensation?

   a. fog   c. snow

   b. cloud   d. dew

10. High clouds made of ice crystals are called ___ clouds.

    a. stratus   c. nimbostratus

    b. cumulus   d. cirrus

11. Large thunderhead clouds that produce precipitation are called ___ clouds.

    a. nimbostratus   c. cumulus

    b. cumulonimbus   d. stratus

12. Strong updrafts within a thunderhead can produce

    a. snow.   c. sleet.

    b. rain.   d. hail.

13. A maritime tropical air mass contains

    a. warm, wet air.   c. warm, dry air.

    b. cold, moist air. d. cold, dry air.

14. A front that forms when a warm air mass is trapped between cold air masses and is forced to rise is a(n)

    a. stationary front. c. occluded front.

    b. warm front.   d. cold front.

15. A severe storm that forms as a rapidly rotating funnel cloud is called a

    a. hurricane.   c. typhoon.

    b. tornado.   d. thunderstorm.

16. The lines connecting points of equal air pressure on a weather map are called

    a. contour lines.   c. isobars.

    b. highs.   d. lows.

Short Answer

17. Explain the relationship between condensation and dew point.

18 Describe the conditions along a stationary front.

19 What are the characteristics of an air mass that forms over the Gulf of Mexico?

20 Explain how a hurricane develops.

21 Describe the water cycle, and explain how it affects weather.

22 List the major similarities and differences between hurricanes and tornadoes.

23 Explain how a tornado forms.

24 Describe an interaction between weather and ocean systems.

25 What is a station model? What types of information do station models provide?

26 What type of technology is used to locate and measure the amount of precipitation in an area?

27 List two ways to keep yourself informed during severe weather.

28 Explain why staying away from flood-water is important even when the water is shallow.

CRITICAL THINKING

29 **Concept Mapping** Use the following terms to create a concept map: *evaporation, relative humidity, water vapor, dew, psychrometer, clouds,* and *fog.*

30 **Making Inferences** If both the air temperature and the amount of water vapor in the air change, is it possible for the relative humidity to stay the same? Explain.

31 **Applying Concepts** What can you assume about the amount of water vapor in the air if there is no difference between the wet- and dry-bulb readings of a psychrometer?

32 **Identifying Relationships** Explain why the concept of relative humidity is important to understanding weather.

INTERPRETING GRAPHICS

Use the weather map below to answer the questions that follow.

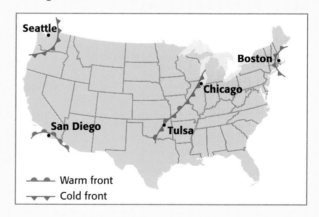

33 Where are thunderstorms most likely to occur? Explain your answer.

34 What are the weather conditions in Tulsa, Oklahoma? Explain your answer.

Multiple Choice

Use the diagram below to answer questions 1–2.

1. **The diagram above represents the meeting of two air masses. One formed over a polar region and the other formed over a tropical region. Which type of front is pictured in the diagram?**

    A. cold front

    B. warm front

    C. occluded front

    D. stationary front

2. **What kind of weather is associated with this type of front?**

    A. sunny skies

    B. drizzly rain

    C. thunderstorms, heavy rain, or snow

    D. hot, muggy weather

3. **Under which of the following conditions is a hurricane most likely to form?**

    A. when high and low pressure zones meet over warm land

    B. when thunderstorms meet over warm ocean water

    C. when thunderstorms meet over cool ocean water

    D. when warm and cold fronts meet over warm water

4. **Clouds are observed in a high-pressure area over Kentucky, and clear skies are observed in a low-pressure area directly to the east. Which of the following is most likely to occur?**

    A. Wind will blow the clouds in a westerly direction.

    B. The warm air will cause the clouds to evaporate.

    C. The clouds will move east to the low-pressure area.

    D. A thunderstorm will occur between the two areas.

5. **The sun's radiant energy is NOT a major factor in producing**

    A. the water cycle.

    B. humidity of air.

    C. air temperature.

    D. motion of tides.

Use the graph below to answer question 6.

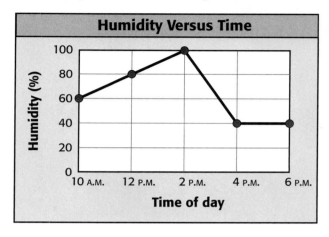

Humidity Versus Time

Humidity (%)

Time of day

6. **Which of the following events most likely occurred at 2:00 P.M. in the graph above?**

   A. a cold front

   B. a warm front

   C. rain showers

   D. evaporations

7. **Jane filled one glass with warm water and one with ice water. After 10 minutes, she observed that water drops were forming on the outside of the glass with ice water in it. What conclusion can Jane draw about her observations?**

   A. The ice water caused the air around the glass to cool to its dew point.

   B. The ice water caused the humidity around the glass to increase.

   C. The ice water leaked through the glass.

   D. The temperature of the warm water was below the dew point.

8. **Which term describes a swelling wall of water that develops over the ocean because of low atmospheric pressure and heavy winds?**

   A. tsunami

   B. tornado

   C. thunderstorm

   D. storm surge

9. **Which of the following conditions contributes to the decrease in a hurricane's strength as it moves from the ocean onto land?**

   A. the lack of warm, moist air over land

   B. the uneven land surface

   C. rising hot air from the land

   D. falling cool air over land

10. **Where are fronts associated with weather?**

    A. over the North Pole

    B. in the middle latitudes

    C. only over the middle of a landmass

    D. only over the Pacific Ocean

Open Response

11. **What are the components of a hurricane, and where is the most energy released?**

12. **Water droplets form on the outside of a lemonade glass on a hot day. How could you substantially reduce the amount of condensation that forms on the outside of the glass? Why would this work?**

Standardized Test Preparation

Science in Action

Science Fiction

"All Summer in a Day" by Ray Bradbury

It is raining, just as it has been for seven long years. For the people who live on Venus, constant rain is a fact of life. But today is a special day—a day when the rain stops and the sun shines. This day comes once every seven years. At school, the students have been looking forward to this day for weeks. But Margot longs to see the sun even more than the others do. The reason for her longing makes the other kids jealous, and jealous kids can be cruel. What happens to Margot? Find out by reading Ray Bradbury's "All Summer in a Day" in the *Holt Anthology of Science Fiction*.

Weird Science

Can Animals Forecast the Weather?

Before ways of making sophisticated weather forecasts were developed, people observed animals and insects for evidence of changing weather. By observing the behavior of certain animals and insects, you, too, can detect changing weather! For example, did you know that birds fly higher when fair weather is coming? And a robin's song is high pitched in fair weather and low pitched as rain approaches. Ants travel in lines when rain is coming and scatter when the weather is clear. You can tell how hot the weather is by listening for the chirping of crickets—crickets chirp faster as the temperature rises!

Language Arts ACTiViTY

WRITING SKILL What would living in a place where it rained all day and every day for seven years be like? Write a short story describing what your life would be like if you lived in such a place. In your story, describe what you and your friends would do for fun after school.

Math ACTiViTY

To estimate the outdoor temperature in degrees Fahrenheit, count the number of times that a cricket chirps in 15 s and add 37. If you count 40 chirps in 15 s, what is the estimated temperature?

Cristy Mitchell

Meteorologist Predicting floods, observing a tornado develop inside a storm, watching the growth of a hurricane, and issuing flood warnings are all in a day's work for Cristy Mitchell. As a meteorologist for the National Weather Service, Mitchell spends each working day observing the powerful forces of nature. When asked what made her job interesting, Mitchell replied, "There's nothing like the adrenaline rush you get when you see a tornado coming!"

Perhaps the most familiar field of meteorology is weather forecasting. However, meteorology is also used in air-pollution control, weather control, agricultural planning, and even criminal and civil investigations. Meteorologists also study trends in Earth's climate.

Meteorologists such as Mitchell use high-tech tools—computers and satellites—to collect data. By analyzing such data, Mitchell is able to forecast the weather.

Social Studies ACTIVITY

An almanac is a type of calendar that contains various information, including weather forecasts and astronomical data, for every day of the year. Many people used almanacs before meteorologists started to forecast the weather on TV. Use an almanac from the library to find out what the weather was on the day that you were born.

To learn more about these Science in Action topics, visit go.hrw.com and type in the keyword **HZ5WEAF**.

Current Science

Check out Current Science® articles related to this chapter by visiting **go.hrw.com**. Just type in the keyword **HZ5CS16**.

Climate

The Big Idea

Earth's atmosphere and oceans distribute energy from the sun, which results in different climates.

About the Photo

Would you like to hang out on this ice with the penguins? You probably would not. You would be shivering, and your teeth would be chattering. However, these penguins feel comfortable. They have thick feathers and lots of body fat to keep them warm. Like other animals, penguins have adapted to their climate, which allows them to live comfortably in that climate. So, you will never see one of these penguins living comfortably on a hot, sunny beach in Florida!

PRE-READING ACTIVITY

Pyramid Before you read the chapter, create the FoldNote entitled "Pyramid" described in the **Study Skills** section of the Appendix. Label the sides of the pyramid with "Tropical climate," "Temperate climate," and "Polar climate." As you read the chapter, define each climate zone, and write characteristics of each climate zone on the appropriate pyramid side.

START-UP ACTIVITY

What's Your Angle?

Try this activity to see how the angle of the sun's solar rays influences temperatures on Earth.

Procedure

1. Place a **lamp** 30 cm from a **globe.**
2. Point the lamp so that the light shines directly on the globe's equator.
3. Using **adhesive putty,** attach a **thermometer** to the globe's equator in a vertical position. Attach **another thermometer** to the globe's North Pole so that the tip points toward the lamp.
4. Record the temperature reading of each thermometer.

5. Turn on the lamp, and let the light shine on the globe for 3 minutes.
6. After 3 minutes, turn off the lamp and record the temperature reading of each thermometer again.

Analysis

1. Was there a difference between the final temperature at the globe's North Pole and the final temperature at the globe's equator? If so, what was it?
2. Explain why the temperature readings at the North Pole and the equator may be different.

What Is Climate?

Suppose you receive a call from a friend who is coming to visit you tomorrow. To decide what clothing to bring, he asks about the current weather in your area.

You step outside to see if rain clouds are in the sky and to check the temperature. But what would you do if your friend asked you about the climate in your area? What is the difference between weather and climate?

Climate Vs. Weather

The main difference between weather and climate is the length of time over which both are measured. **Weather** is the condition of the atmosphere at a particular time. Weather conditions vary from day to day and include temperature, humidity, precipitation, wind, and visibility. **Climate,** on the other hand, is the average weather condition in an area over a long period of time. Climate is mostly determined by two factors—temperature and precipitation. Different parts of the world can have different climates, as shown in **Figure 1.** But why are climates so different? The answer is complicated. It includes factors in addition to temperature and precipitation, such as latitude, wind patterns, mountains, large bodies of water, and ocean currents.

✓ **Reading Check** How is climate different from weather? (*See the Appendix for answers to Reading Checks.*)

Figure 1 *How does the climate in northern Africa differ from the climate where you live?*

North America

Africa

South America

Latitude

Think of the last time you looked at a globe. Do you recall the thin, horizontal lines that circle the globe? Those lines are called lines of latitude. **Latitude** is the distance north or south, measured in degrees, from the equator. In general, the temperature of an area depends on its latitude. The higher the latitude is, the colder the climate tends to be. One of the coldest places on Earth, the North Pole, is 90° north of the equator. However, the equator, at latitude 0°, is usually hot.

As shown in **Figure 2,** if you were to take a trip to different latitudes in the United States, you would experience different climates. For example, the climate in Washington, D.C., which is at a higher latitude, is different from the climate in Texas.

Solar Energy and Latitude

Solar energy, which is energy from the sun, heats the Earth. The amount of direct solar energy a particular area receives is determined by latitude. **Figure 3** shows how the curve of the Earth affects the amount of direct solar energy at different latitudes. Notice that the sun's rays hit the equator directly, at almost a 90° angle. At this angle, a small area of the Earth's surface receives more direct solar energy than at a lesser angle. As a result, that area has high temperatures. However, the sun's rays strike the poles at a lesser angle than they do the equator. At this angle, the same amount of direct solar energy that hits the area at the equator is spread over a larger area at the poles. The result is lower temperatures at the poles.

Figure 2 *Winter in south Texas (top) is different from winter in Washington D.C. (bottom).*

weather the short-term state of the atmosphere, including temperature, humidity, precipitation, wind, and visibility

climate the average weather condition in an area over a long period of time

latitude the distance north or south from the equator; expressed in degrees

Figure 3 The sun's rays strike the Earth's surface at different angles because the surface is curved.

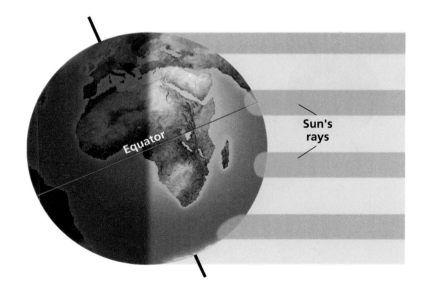

Seasons and Latitude

In most places in the United States, the year consists of four seasons. But there are places in the world that do not have such seasonal changes. For example, areas near the equator have approximately the same temperatures and same amount of daylight year-round. Seasons happen because the Earth is tilted on its axis at a 23.5° angle. This tilt affects how much solar energy an area receives as Earth moves around the sun. **Figure 4** shows how latitude and the tilt of the Earth determine the seasons and the length of the day in a particular area.

✓ Reading Check Why is there less seasonal change near the equator?

Figure 4 **The Seasons**

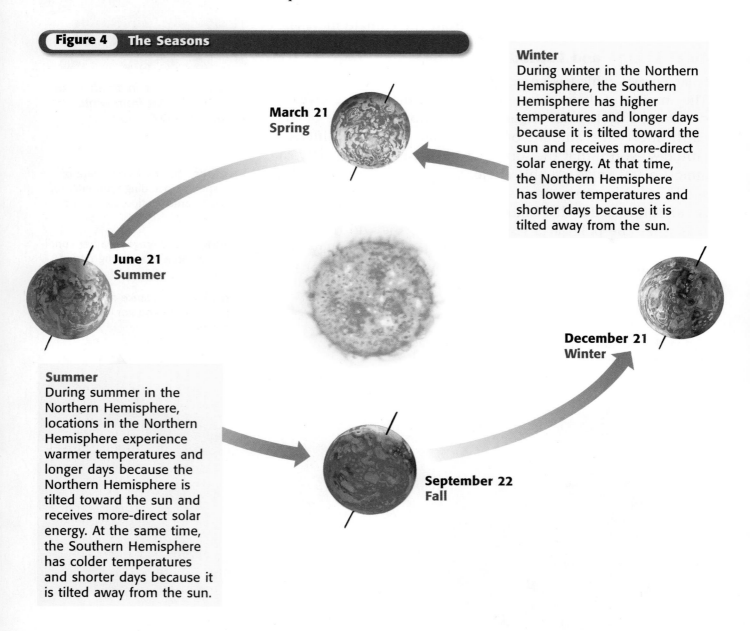

March 21 Spring

June 21 Summer

September 22 Fall

December 21 Winter

Winter
During winter in the Northern Hemisphere, the Southern Hemisphere has higher temperatures and longer days because it is tilted toward the sun and receives more-direct solar energy. At that time, the Northern Hemisphere has lower temperatures and shorter days because it is tilted away from the sun.

Summer
During summer in the Northern Hemisphere, locations in the Northern Hemisphere experience warmer temperatures and longer days because the Northern Hemisphere is tilted toward the sun and receives more-direct solar energy. At the same time, the Southern Hemisphere has colder temperatures and shorter days because it is tilted away from the sun.

Figure 5   The Circulation of Warm Air and Cold Air

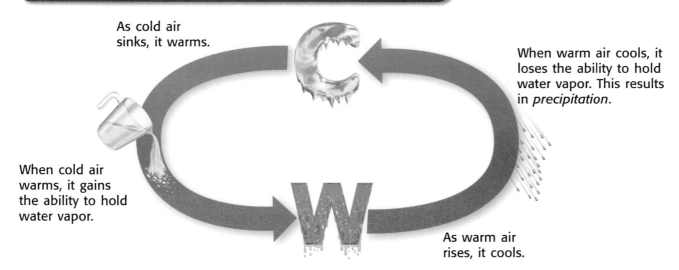

As cold air
sinks, it warms.

When warm air cools, it
loses the ability to hold
water vapor. This results
in *precipitation*.

When cold air
warms, it gains
the ability to hold
water vapor.

As warm air
rises, it cools.

Prevailing Winds

Winds that blow mainly from one direction are **prevailing winds**. Before you learn how the prevailing winds affect climate, take a look at **Figure 5** to learn about some of the basic properties of air.

Prevailing winds affect the amount of precipitation that a region receives. If the prevailing winds form from warm air, they may carry moisture. If the prevailing winds form from cold air, they will probably be dry.

The amount of moisture in prevailing winds is also affected by whether the winds blow across land or across a large body of water. Winds that travel across large bodies of water absorb moisture. Winds that travel across land tend to be dry. Even if a region borders the ocean, the area might be dry. **Figure 6** shows an example of how dry prevailing winds can cause the land to be dry though the land is near an ocean.

prevailing winds winds that blow mainly from one direction during a given period

A Cool Breeze

1. Hold a **thermometer** next to the top edge of a **cup** of **water** containing two **ice cubes**. Record the temperature next to the cup.

2. Have your lab partner fan the surface of the cup with a **paper fan**. Record the temperature again. Has the temperature changed? Why or why not?

Figure 6 *The Sahara Desert, in northern Africa, is extremely dry because of the dry prevailing winds that blow across the continent.*

Using a Map

With an adult, use a physical map to locate the mountain ranges in the United States. Does climate vary from one side of a mountain range to the other? If so, what does this tell you about the climatic conditions on either side of the mountain? From what direction are the prevailing winds blowing?

Mountains

Mountains can influence an area's climate by affecting both temperature and precipitation. Kilimanjaro is the tallest mountain in Africa. It has snow-covered peaks year-round, even though it is only about 3° (320 km) south of the equator. Temperatures on Kilimanjaro and in other mountainous areas are affected by elevation. **Elevation** is the height of surface landforms above sea level. As the elevation increases, the ability of air to transfer energy from the ground to the atmosphere decreases. Therefore, as elevation increases, temperature decreases.

Mountains also affect the climate of nearby areas by influencing the distribution of precipitation. **Figure 7** shows how the climates on two sides of a mountain can be very different.

Reading Check Why does the atmosphere become cooler at higher elevations?

Figure 7 *Mountains block the prevailing winds and affect the climate on the other side.*

The Wet Side
Mountains force air to rise. The air cools as it rises, releasing moisture as snow or rain. The land on the windward side of the mountain is usually green and lush because the air releases its moisture.

The Dry Side
After dry air crosses the mountain, the air begins to sink. As the air sinks, it is warmed and absorbs moisture. The dry conditions created by the sinking, warm air usually produce a desert. This side of the mountain is in a *rain shadow*.

Large Bodies of Water

Large bodies of water can influence an area's climate. Water absorbs and releases heat slower than land does. Because of this quality, water helps to moderate the temperatures of the land around it. So, sudden or extreme temperature changes rarely take place on land near large bodies of water. For example, the state of Michigan, which is surrounded by the Great Lakes, has more-moderate temperatures than other places at the same latitude. The lakes also increase the moisture content of the air, which leads to heavy snowfall in the winter. This "lake effect" can cause 350 inches of snow to drop in one year!

Ocean Currents

The circulation of ocean surface currents has a large effect on an area's climate. **Surface currents** are streamlike movements of water that occur at or near the surface of the ocean. **Figure 8** shows the pattern of the major ocean surface currents.

As surface currents move, they carry warm or cool water to different locations. The surface temperature of the water affects the temperature of the air above it. Warm currents heat the surrounding air and cause warmer temperatures. Cool currents cool the surrounding air and cause cooler temperatures. The Gulf Stream current carries warm water northward off the east coast of North America and past Iceland. Iceland is an island country located just below the Arctic Circle. The warm water from the Gulf Stream heats the surrounding air and creates warmer temperatures in southern Iceland. Iceland experiences milder temperatures than Greenland, its neighboring island. Greenland's climate is cooler because Greenland is not influenced by the Gulf Stream.

✓ Reading Check Why does Iceland experience milder temperatures than Greenland?

elevation the height of an object above sea level

surface current a horizontal movement of ocean water that is caused by wind and that occurs at or near the ocean's surface

Figure 8 *The red arrows represent the movement of warm surface currents. The blue arrows represent the movement of cold surface currents.*

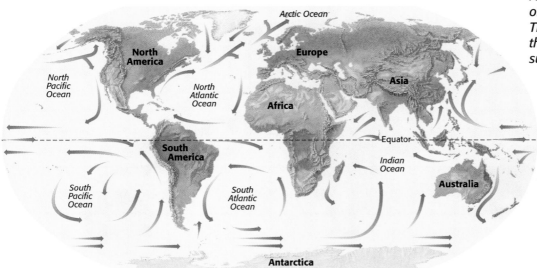

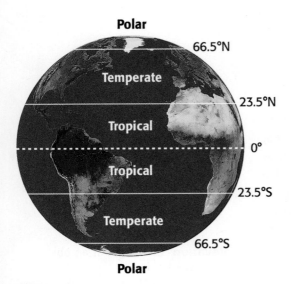

Polar

66.5°N

Temperate

23.5°N

Tropical

0°

Tropical

23.5°S

Temperate

66.5°S

Polar

Figure 9 *The three major climate zones are determined by latitude.*

biome a large region characterized by a specific type of climate and certain types of plant and animal communities

Climates of the World

Have you seen any polar bears in your neighborhood lately? You probably have not. That's because polar bears live only in very cold arctic regions. Why are the animals in one part of the world so different from the animals in other parts? One of the differences has to do with climate. Plants and animals that have adapted to one climate may not be able to live in another climate. For example, frogs would not be able to survive at the North Pole.

Climate Zones

The Earth's three major climate zones—tropical, temperate, and polar—are shown in **Figure 9.** Each zone has a temperature range that relates to its latitude. However, in each of these zones, there are several types of climates because of differences in the geography and the amount of precipitation. Because of the various climates in each zone, there are different biomes in each zone. A **biome** is a large region characterized by a specific type of climate and certain types of plant and animal communities. **Figure 10** shows the distribution of the Earth's land biomes. In which biome do you live?

✓ Reading Check What factors distinguish one biome from another biome?

Figure 10 **The Earth's Land Biomes**

Tundra Temperate grassland Chaparral

Taiga Tropical savanna Mountains

Temperate forest Temperate desert

Tropical rain forest Tropical desert

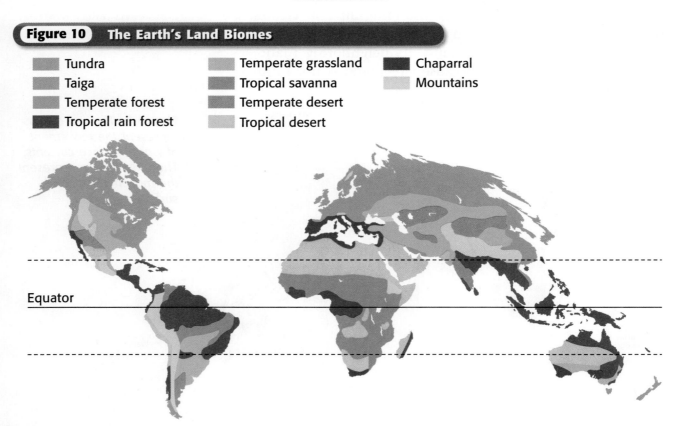

Equator

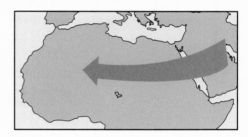

Summary

- Weather is the condition of the atmosphere at a particular time. This condition includes temperature, humidity, precipitation, wind, and visibility.

- Climate is the average weather condition in an area over a long period of time.

- The higher the latitude, the cooler the climate.

- Prevailing winds affect the climate of an area by the amount of moisture they carry.

- Mountains influence an area's climate by affecting both temperature and precipitation.

- Large bodies of water and ocean currents influence the climate of an area by affecting the temperature of the air over the water.

- The three climate zones of the world are the tropical zone, the temperate zone, and the polar zone.

Using Key Terms

1. In your own words, write a definition for each of the following terms: *weather, climate, latitude, prevailing winds, elevation, surface currents,* and *biome.*

Understanding Key Ideas

2. Which of the following affects climate by causing the air to rise?
   a. mountains
   b. ocean currents
   c. large bodies of water
   d. latitude

3. What is the difference between weather and climate?

4. List five factors that determine climates.

5. Explain why there is a difference in climate between areas at 0° latitude and areas at 45° latitude.

6. List the three climate zones of the world.

Critical Thinking

7. **Analyzing Relationships** How would seasons be different if the Earth did not tilt on its axis?

8. **Applying Concepts** During what months does Australia have summer? Explain.

Interpreting Graphics

Use the map below to answer the questions that follow.

9. Would you expect the area that the arrow points to to be moist or dry? Explain your answer.

10. Describe how the climate of the same area would change if the prevailing winds traveled from the opposite direction. Explain how you came to this conclusion.

SCiLINKS®

NSTA
Developed and maintained by the
National Science Teachers Association

For a variety of links related to this chapter, go to www.scilinks.org

Topic: What Is Climate?
SciLinks code: HSM1659

The Tropics

Where in the world do you think you could find a flying dragon gliding above you from one treetop to the next?

Don't worry. This flying dragon, or tree lizard, is only about 20 cm long, and it eats only insects. With winglike skin flaps, the flying dragon can glide from one treetop to the next. But, you won't find this kind of animal in the United States. These flying dragons live in Southeast Asia, which is in the tropical zone.

The Tropical Zone

The region that surrounds the equator and that extends from about 23.5° north latitude to 23.5° south latitude is called the **tropical zone.** The tropical zone is also known as the Tropics. Latitudes in the tropical zone receive the most solar radiation. Temperatures are therefore usually hot, except at high elevations.

Within the tropical zone, there are three major types of biomes—tropical rain forest, tropical desert, and tropical savanna. These three biomes have high temperatures. But they differ in the amount of precipitation, soil characteristics, vegetation, and kinds of animals. **Figure 1** shows the distribution of these biomes.

✔ **Reading Check** At what latitudes would you find the tropical zone? (*See the Appendix for answers to Reading Checks.*)

What You Will Learn

● Locate and describe the tropical zone.
● Describe the biomes found in the tropical zone.

Vocabulary
tropical zone

READING STRATEGY

Reading Organizer As you read this section, make a table comparing *tropical rain forests, tropical savannas,* and *tropical deserts.*

Figure 1 Biomes of the Tropical Zone

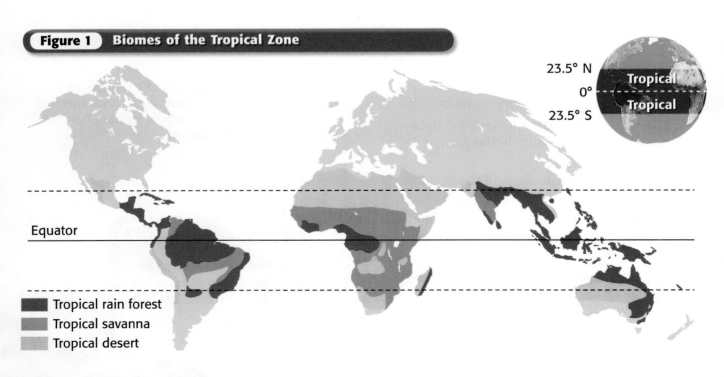

23.5° N
0°
23.5° S
Tropical
Tropical

Equator

■ Tropical rain forest
■ Tropical savanna
■ Tropical desert

Tropical Rain Forest

- **Average Temperature Range**
  25°C to 28°C (77°F to 82°F)
- **Average Yearly Precipitation**
  200 cm or more
- **Soil Characteristics**
  thin and nutrient poor

Tropical Rain Forests

Tropical rain forests are always warm and wet. Because they are located near the equator, they receive strong sunlight year-round. So, there is little difference between seasons in tropical rain forests.

Tropical rain forests contain the greatest number of animal and plant species of any biome. Animals found in tropical rain forests include monkeys, parrots, tree frogs, tigers, and leopards. Plants found in tropical rain forests include mahogany, vines, ferns, and bamboo. But in spite of the lush vegetation, shown in **Figure 2,** the soil in rain forests is poor. The rapid decay of plants and animals returns nutrients to the soil. But these nutrients are quickly absorbed and used by the plants. The nutrients that are not immediately used by the plants are washed away by the heavy rains. The soil is left thin and nutrient poor.

Figure 2 *In tropical rain forests, many of the trees form above-ground roots that provide extra support for the trees in the thin, nutrient-poor soil.*

tropical zone the region that surrounds the equator and that extends from about 23.5° north latitude to 23.5° south latitude

CONNECTION TO Social Studies

WRITING SKILL **Living in the Tropics** The tropical climate is very hot and humid. People who live in the Tropics have had to adapt to feel comfortable in that climate. For example, in the country of Samoa, some people live in homes that have no walls, which are called *fales*. Fales have only a roof, which provides shade. The openness of the home allows cool breezes to flow through the home. Research other countries in the Tropics. See how the climate influences the way the people live in those countries. Then, in your **science journal,** describe how the people's lifestyle helps them adapt to the climate.

Figure 3 *The grass of a tropical savanna can be as tall as 5 m.*

Tropical Savannas

Tropical savannas, or grasslands, are composed of tall grasses and a few scattered trees. The climate is usually very warm. Tropical savannas have a dry season that lasts four to eight months and that is followed by short periods of rain. Savanna soils are generally nutrient poor. However, grass fires, which are common during the dry season, leave the soils nutrient enriched. An African savanna is shown in **Figure 3.**

Many plants have adapted to fire and use it to promote development. For example, some species need fire to break open their seeds' outer skin. Only after this skin is broken can each seed grow. For other species, heat from the fire triggers the plants to drop their seeds into the newly enriched soil.

Animals that live in tropical savannas include giraffes, lions, crocodiles, and elephants. Plants include tall grasses, trees, and thorny shrubs.

CONNECTION TO
Biology

WRITING SKILL **Animal and Plant Adaptations** Animals and plants adapt to the climate in which they live. These adaptations cause certain animals and plants to be unique to particular biomes. For example, the camel, which is unique to the desert, has adapted to going for long periods of time without water. Research other animals or plants that live in the Tropics. Then, in your **science journal,** describe the characteristics that help them survive in the Tropics.

Tropical Deserts

A desert is an area that receives less than 25 cm of rainfall per year. Because of this low yearly rainfall, deserts are the driest places on Earth. Desert plants, such as those shown in **Figure 4,** are adapted to survive in places that have little water. Animals such as rats, lizards, snakes, and scorpions have also adapted to survive in these deserts.

There are two kinds of deserts—hot deserts and cold deserts. Hot deserts are caused by cool, sinking air masses. Many hot deserts, such as the Sahara, in Africa, are tropical deserts. Daily temperatures in tropical deserts often vary from very hot daytime temperatures (50°C) to cool nighttime temperatures (20°C). Because of the dryness of deserts, the soil is poor in organic matter, which is needed for plants to grow.

✔ Reading Check What animals would you find in a tropical desert?

Tropical Desert

- **Average Temperature Range 16°C to 50°C (61°F to 120°F)**
- **Average Yearly Precipitation 0–25 cm**
- **Soil Characteristics poor in organic matter**

Figure 4 *This oasis, surrounded by sand dunes, is located in Libya.*

SECTION Review

Summary

- The tropical zone is located around the equator, between 23.5° north and 23.5° south latitude.
- Temperatures are usually hot in the tropical zone.
- Tropical rain forests are warm and wet. They have the greatest number of plant and animal species of any biome.
- Tropical savannas are grasslands that have a dry season.
- Tropical deserts are hot and receive little rain.

Using Key Terms

1. In your own words, write a definition for the term *tropical zone*.

Understanding Key Ideas

2. Which of the following tropical biomes has less than 50 cm of precipitation a year?
   - **a.** rain forest
   - **c.** grassland
   - **b.** desert
   - **d.** savanna

3. What are the soil characteristics of a tropical rain forest?

4. In what ways have savanna vegetation adapted to fire?

Math Skills

5. Suppose that in a tropical savanna, the temperature was recorded every hour for 4 h. The recorded temperatures were 27°C, 28°C, 29°C, and 29°C. Calculate the average temperature for this 4 h period.

Critical Thinking

6. **Analyzing Relationships** How do the tropical biomes differ?

7. **Making Inferences** How would you expect the adaptations of a plant in a tropical rain forest to differ from the adaptations of a tropical desert plant? Explain.

8. **Analyzing Data** An area has a temperature range of 30°C to 40°C and received 10 cm of rain this year. What biome is this area in?

SCILINKS.

NSTA
Developed and maintained by the National Science Teachers Association

For a variety of links related to this chapter, go to www.scilinks.org

Topic: Climates of the World
SciLinks code: HSM0302

Temperate and Polar Zones

Which season is your favorite? Do you like the change of colors in the fall, the flowers in the spring, or do you prefer the hot days of summer?

If you live in the continental United States, chances are you live in a biome that experiences seasonal change. Seasonal change is one characteristic of the temperate zone. Most of the continental United States is in the temperate zone, which is the climate zone between the Tropics and the polar zone.

What You Will Learn

● Locate and describe the temperate zone and the polar zone.
● Describe the different biomes found in the temperate zone and the polar zone.
● Explain what a microclimate is.

Vocabulary

temperate zone
polar zone
microclimate

READING STRATEGY

Reading Organizer As you read this section, create an outline of the section. Use the headings from the section in your outline.

The Temperate Zone

The climate zone between the Tropics and the polar zone is the **temperate zone.** Latitudes in the temperate zone receive less solar energy than latitudes in the Tropics do. Because of this, temperatures in the temperate zone tend to be lower than in the Tropics. Some biomes in the temperate zone have a mild change of seasons. Other biomes in the country can experience freezing temperatures in the winter and very hot temperatures in the summer. The temperate zone consists of the following four biomes—temperate forest, temperate grassland, chaparral, and temperate desert. Although these biomes have four distinct seasons, the biomes differ in temperature and precipitation and have different plants and animals. **Figure 1** shows the distribution of the biomes found in the temperate zone.

✓ **Reading Check** **Where is the temperate zone?** (*See the Appendix for answers to Reading Checks.*)

Figure 1 **Biomes of the Temperate Zone**

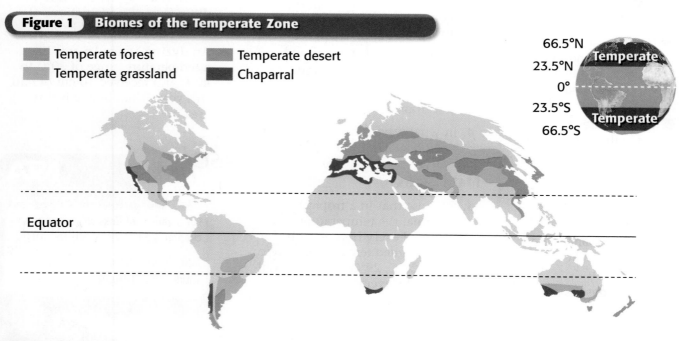

- Temperate forest
- Temperate grassland
- Temperate desert
- Chaparral

66.5°N
23.5°N
0°
23.5°S
66.5°S

Temperate
Temperate

Equator

Temperate Forest

- Average Temperature Range
  0°C to 28°C (32°F to 82°F)
- Average Yearly Precipitation
  76 to 250 cm
- Soil Characteristics
  very fertile, organically rich

Temperate Forests

The temperate forest biomes tend to have high amounts of rainfall and seasonal temperature differences. Summers are often warm, and winters are often cold. Animals such as deer, bears, and foxes live in temperate forests. **Figure 2** shows deciduous trees in a temperate forest. *Deciduous* describes trees that lose their leaves at the end of the growing season. The soils in deciduous forests are usually fertile because of the high organic content from decaying leaves that drop every winter. Another type of tree found in the temperate forest is the evergreen. *Evergreens* are trees that keep their leaves year-round.

Figure 2 *Deciduous trees have leaves that change color and drop when temperatures become cold.*

temperate zone the climate zone between the Tropics and the polar zone

Temperate Grasslands

Temperate grasslands, such as those shown in **Figure 3,** are regions that receive too little rainfall for trees to grow. This biome has warm summers and cold winters. Examples of animals that are found in temperate grasslands include bison in North America and kangaroo in Australia. Grasses are the most common kind of plant found in this biome. Because grasslands have the most-fertile soils of all biomes, much of the grassland has been plowed to make room for croplands.

Figure 3 *At one time, the world's grasslands covered about 42% of Earth's total land surface. Today, they occupy only about 12% of the Earth's total land surface.*

Temperate Grassland

- Average Temperature Range
  −6°C to 26°C (21°F to 78°F)
- Average Yearly Precipitation
  38 to 76 cm
- Soil Characteristics
  most-fertile soils of all biomes

- **Average Temperature Range 11°C to 26°C (51°F to 78°F)**
- **Average Yearly Precipitation 48 to 56 cm**
- **Soil Characteristics rocky, nutrient-poor soils**

Figure 4 *Some plant species found in chaparral require fire to reproduce.*

Chaparrals

Chaparral regions, as shown in **Figure 4,** have cool, wet winters and hot, dry summers. Animals, such as coyotes and mountain lions live in chaparrals. The vegetation is mainly evergreen shrubs. These shrubs are short, woody plants with thick, waxy leaves. The waxy leaves are adaptations that help prevent water loss in dry conditions. These shrubs grow in rocky, nutrient-poor soil. Like tropical-savanna vegetation, chaparral vegetation has adapted to fire. In fact, some plants, such as chamise, can grow back from their roots after a fire.

Temperate Deserts

The temperate desert biomes, like the one shown in **Figure 5,** tend to be cold deserts. Like all deserts, cold deserts receive less than 25 cm of precipitation yearly. Examples of animals that live in temperate deserts are lizards, snakes, bats, and toads. And the types of plants found in temperate deserts include cacti, shrubs, and thorny trees.

Temperate deserts can be very hot in the daytime. But, unlike hot deserts, they are often very cold at night. This large change in temperature between day and night is caused by low humidity and cloudless skies. These conditions allow for a large amount of energy to heat the Earth's surface during the day. However, these same characteristics allow the energy to escape at night. This causes temperatures to drop. You probably rarely think of snow and deserts together. But temperate deserts often receive light snow during the winter.

Figure 5 *The desert in Death Valley is in the rain shadow of the Sierra Nevada.*

✔ **Reading Check** Why are temperate deserts cold at night?

Temperate Desert

- **Average Temperature Range 1°C to 50°C (34°F to 120°F)**
- **Average Yearly Precipitation 0 to 25 cm**
- **Soil Characteristics poor in organic matter**

Figure 6   Biomes of the Polar Zone

Polar
66.5°N
0°
66.5°S
Polar

Equator

■ Tundra
■ Taiga

The Polar Zone

The climate zone located at the North or South Pole and its surrounding area is called the **polar zone.** Polar climates have the coldest average temperatures of all the climate zones. Temperatures in the winter stay below freezing. The temperatures during the summer remain cool. **Figure 6** shows the distribution of the biomes found in the polar zone.

polar zone the North or South Pole and its surrounding area

Tundra

The tundra biome, as shown in **Figure 7,** has long, cold winters with almost 24 hours of night. It also has short, cool summers with almost 24 hours of daylight. In the summer, only the top meter of soil thaws. Underneath the thawed soil lies a permanently frozen layer of soil, called *permafrost.* This frozen layer prevents the water in the thawed soil from draining. Because of the poor drainage, the upper soil layer is muddy. This muddy layer of soil makes a great breeding ground for insects, such as mosquitoes. Many birds migrate to the tundra during the summer to feed on the insects. Other animals that live in the tundra are caribou, reindeer, and polar bears. Plants in this biome include mosses and lichens.

Tundra

• **Average Temperature Range** −27°C to 5°C (−17°F to 41°F)

• **Average Yearly Precipitation** 0 to 25 cm

• **Soil Characteristics** frozen

Figure 7 *In the tundra, mosses and lichens cover rocks.*

Figure 8 *The taiga, such as this one in Washington, have mostly evergreens for trees.*

microclimate the climate of a small area

Taiga (Northern Coniferous Forest)

Just south of the tundra lies the taiga biome. The taiga, as shown in **Figure 8,** has long, cold winters and short, warm summers. Animals commonly found here are moose, bears, and rabbits. The majority of the trees are evergreen needle-leaved trees called *conifers,* such as pine, spruce, and fir trees. The needles and flexible branches allow these trees to shed heavy snow before they can be damaged. Conifer needles are made of acidic substances. When the needles die and fall to the soil, they make the soil acidic. Most plants cannot grow in acidic soil. Because of the acidic soil, the forest floor is bare except for some mosses and lichens.

Microclimates

The climate and the biome of a particular place can also be influenced by local conditions. **Microclimate** is the climate of a small area. The alpine biome is a cold biome found on mountains all around the world. The alpine biome can even be found on mountains in the Tropics! How is this possible? The high elevation affects the area's climate and therefore its biome. As the elevation increases, the air's ability to transfer heat from the ground to the atmosphere by conduction decreases, which causes temperatures to decrease. In winter, the temperatures are below freezing. In summer, average temperatures range from 10°C to 15°C. Plants and animals have had to develop special adaptations to live in this severe climate.

Cities

Cities are also microclimates. In a city, temperatures can be 1°C to 2°C warmer than the surrounding rural areas. Have you ever walked barefoot on a black asphalt street on a hot summer day? Doing so burns your feet because buildings and pavement made of dark materials absorb solar radiation instead of reflecting it. There is also less vegetation in a city to take in the sun's rays. This absorption and re-radiation of heat by buildings and pavement heats the surrounding air. In turn, the temperatures rise.

Reading Check Why do cities have higher temperatures than the surrounding rural areas?

CONNECTION TO Physics

Hot Roofs! Scientists studied roofs on a sunny day when the air temperature was 13°C. They recorded roof temperatures ranging from 18°C to 61°C depending on color and material of the roof. Place thermometers on outside objects that are made of different types of materials and that are different colors. Please stay off the roof! Is there a difference in temperatures?

ACTIVITY

SECTION Review

Summary

- The temperate zone is located between the Tropics and the polar zone. It has moderate temperatures.
- Temperate forests, temperate grasslands, and temperate deserts are biomes in the temperate zone.
- The polar zone includes the North or South Pole and its surrounding area. The polar zone has the coldest temperatures.
- The tundra and the taiga are biomes within the polar zone.

Using Key Terms

1. In your own words, write a definition for the term *microclimate*.

Complete each of the following sentences by choosing the correct term from the word bank.

temperate zone   polar zone
microclimate

2. The coldest temperatures are found in the ___.

3. The ___ has moderate temperatures.

Understanding Key Ideas

4. Which of the following biomes has the driest climate?
   a. temperate forests
   b. temperate grasslands
   c. chaparrals
   d. temperate deserts

5. Explain why the temperate zone has lower temperatures than the Tropics.

6. Describe how the latitude of the polar zone affects the climate in that area.

7. Explain why the tundra can sometimes experience 24 hours of daylight or 24 hours of night.

8. How do conifers make the soil they grow in too acidic for other plants to grow?

Math Skills

9. Texas has an area of about 700,000 square kilometers. Grasslands compose about 20% of this area. About how many square kilometers of grassland are there in Texas?

Critical Thinking

10. **Identifying Relationships** Which biome would be more suitable for growing crops, temperate forest or taiga? Explain.

11. **Making Inferences** Describe the types of animals and vegetation you might find in the Alpine biome.

SCILINKS

NSTA
Developed and maintained by the National Science Teachers Association

For a variety of links related to this chapter, go to www.scilinks.org

Topic: Modeling Earth's Climate
SciLinks code: HSM0976

Changes in Climate

As you have probably noticed, the weather changes from day to day. Sometimes, the weather can change several times in one day! But have you ever noticed the climate change?

On Saturday, your morning baseball game was canceled because of rain, but by that afternoon the sun was shining. Now, think about the climate where you live. You probably haven't noticed a change in climate, because climates change slowly. What causes climatic change? Studies indicate that human activity may cause climatic change. However, natural factors also can influence changes in the climate.

Ice Ages

The geologic record indicates that the Earth's climate has been much colder than it is today. In fact, much of the Earth was covered by sheets of ice during certain periods. An **ice age** is a period during which ice collects in high latitudes and moves toward lower latitudes. Scientists have found evidence of many major ice ages throughout the Earth's geologic history. The most recent ice age began about 2 million years ago.

Glacial Periods

During an ice age, there are periods of cold and periods of warmth. These periods are called glacial and interglacial periods. During *glacial periods,* the enormous sheets of ice advance. As they advance, they get bigger and cover a larger area, as shown in **Figure 1.** Because a large amount of water is frozen during glacial periods, the sea level drops.

ice age a long period of climate cooling during which ice sheets cover large areas of Earth's surface; also known as a glacial period

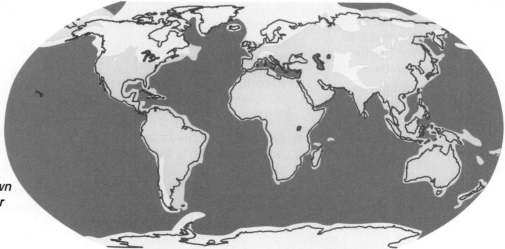

Figure 1 *During glacial periods, ice sheets (as shown in light blue), cover a larger portion of the Earth.*

Interglacial Periods

Warmer times that happen between glacial periods are called *interglacial periods*. During an interglacial period, the ice begins to melt and the sea level rises again. The last interglacial period began 10,000 years ago and is still happening. Why do these periods occur? Will the Earth have another glacial period in the future? These questions have been debated by scientists for the past 200 years.

Motions of the Earth

There are many theories about the causes of ice ages. Each theory tries to explain the gradual cooling that begins an ice age. This cooling leads to the development of large ice sheets that periodically cover large areas of the Earth's surface.

The *Milankovitch theory* explains why an ice age isn't just one long cold spell. Instead, the ice age alternates between cold and warm periods. Milutin Milankovitch, a Yugoslavian scientist, proposed that changes in the Earth's orbit and in the tilt of the Earth's axis cause ice ages. His theory is shown in **Figure 2.** In a 100,000 year period, the Earth's orbit changes from elliptical to circular. This changes the Earth's distance from the sun. In turn, it changes the temperature on Earth. Changes in the tilt of the Earth also influence the climate. The more the Earth is tilted, the closer the poles are to the sun.

✓ Reading Check What are the two things Milankovitch says causes ice ages? (*See the Appendix for answers to Reading Checks.*)

INTERNET ACTIVITY

For another activity related to this chapter, go to **go.hrw.com** and type in the keyword **HZ5CLMW**.

Figure 2 The Milankovitch Theory

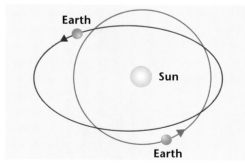

Eccentricity Earth encounters more variation in the energy that it receives from the sun when Earth's orbit is elongated than it does when Earth's orbit is circular.

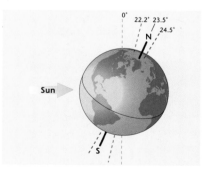

Tilt Over a period of 41,000 years, the tilt of Earth's axis varies between 22.2° and 24.5°. The poles receive more solar energy when the tilt angle is greater.

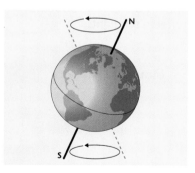

Precession The wobble of Earth's axis affects the amount of solar radiation that reaches different parts of Earth's surface at different times of the year.

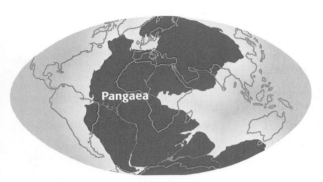

Figure 3 *Much of Pangaea—the part that is now Africa, South America, India, Antarctica, Australia, and Saudi Arabia—was covered by continental ice sheets.*

Plate Tectonics

The Earth's climate is further influenced by plate tectonics and continental drift. One theory proposes that ice ages happen when the continents are positioned closer to the polar regions. About 250 million years ago, all the continents were connected near the South Pole in one giant landmass called *Pangaea,* as shown in **Figure 3.** During this time, ice covered a large area of the Earth's surface. As Pangaea broke apart, the continents moved toward the equator, and the ice age ended. During the last ice age, many large landmasses were positioned in the polar zones. Antarctica, northern North America, Europe, and Asia were covered by large sheets of ice.

Volcanic Eruptions

Many natural factors can affect global climate. Catastrophic events, such as volcanic eruptions, can influence climate. Volcanic eruptions send large amounts of dust, ash, and smoke into the atmosphere. Once in the atmosphere, the dust, smoke, and ash particles act as a shield. This shield blocks some of the sun's rays, which causes the Earth to cool. **Figure 4** shows how dust particles from a volcanic eruption block the sun.

✓ *Reading Check* **How can volcanoes change the climate?**

Figure 4 **Volcanic Dust in the Atmosphere**

Volcanic eruptions, such as the 1980 eruption of Mount St. Helens, as shown at right, produce dust that reflects sunlight.

Sun's rays

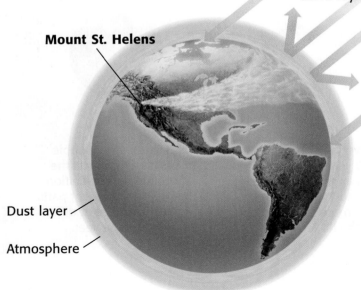

Mount St. Helens

Dust layer

Atmosphere

Figure 5 *Some scientists believe that a 10 km chunk of rock smashed into the Earth 65 million years ago, which caused the climatic change that resulted in the extinction of dinosaurs.*

Asteroid Impact

Imagine a rock the size of a car flying in from outer space and crashing in your neighborhood. This rock, like the one shown in **Figure 5,** is called an asteroid. An *asteroid* is a small, rocky object that orbits the sun. Sometimes, asteroids enter our atmosphere and crash into the Earth. What would happen if an asteroid 1 km wide, which is more than half a mile long, hit the Earth? Scientists believe that if an asteroid this big hit the Earth, it could change the climate of the entire world.

When a large piece of rock slams into the Earth, it causes debris to shoot into the atmosphere. *Debris* is dust and smaller rocks. This debris can block some of the sunlight and thermal energy. This would lower average temperatures, which would change the climate. Plants wouldn't get the sunlight they needed to grow, and animals would find surviving difficult. Scientists believe such an event is what caused dinosaurs to become extinct 65 million years ago when a 10 km asteroid slammed into the Earth and changed the Earth's climate.

The Sun's Cycle

Some changes in the climate can be linked to changes in the sun. You might think that the sun always stays the same. However, the sun follows an 11-year cycle. During this cycle, the sun changes from a solar maximum to a solar minimum. During a solar minimum, the sun produces a low percentage of high-energy radiation. But when the sun is at its solar maximum, it produces a larger percentage of high-energy radiation than when it is at its solar minimum. This increase in high-energy radiation warms the winds in the atmosphere. This change in turn affects climate patterns around the world.

CONNECTION TO Astronomy

Sunspots Sunspots are dark areas on the sun's surface. The number of sunspots changes with the sun's cycle. When the cycle is at a solar maximum, there are many sunspots. When the cycle is at a solar minimum, there are fewer sunspots. If the number of sunspots was low in 1997, in what year will the next low point in the cycle happen?

The Ride to School

1. The round-trip distance from your home to school is 20 km.

2. You traveled from home to school and from school to home 23 times in a month.

3. The vehicle in which you took your trips travels 30 km/gal.

4. If burning 1 gal of gasoline produces 9 kg of carbon dioxide, how much carbon dioxide did the vehicle release during the month?

global warming a gradual increase in the average global temperature

greenhouse effect the warming of the surface and lower atmosphere of Earth that occurs when carbon dioxide, water vapor, and other gases in the air absorb and trap thermal energy

Global Warming

A gradual increase in the average global temperature that is due to a higher concentration of gases, such as carbon dioxide in the atmosphere, is called **global warming.** To understand how global warming works, you must first learn about the greenhouse effect.

Greenhouse Effect

The Earth's natural heating process, in which gases in the atmosphere trap thermal energy, is called the **greenhouse effect.** The car in **Figure 6** shows how the greenhouse effect works. The car's windows stop most of the thermal energy from escaping, and the inside of the car gets hot. On Earth, instead of glass stopping the thermal energy, atmospheric gases absorb the thermal energy. When this happens, the thermal energy stays in the atmosphere and keeps the Earth warm. Many scientists believe that the rise in global temperatures is due to an increase of carbon dioxide, an atmospheric gas. Most evidence shows that the increase in carbon dioxide is caused by the burning of fossil fuels.

Another factor that may add to global warming is the clearing of forests. In many countries, forests are being burned to clear land for farming. Burning of the forests releases more carbon dioxide. Because plants use carbon dioxide to make food, destroying the trees decreases a natural way of removing carbon dioxide from the atmosphere.

Figure 6 *Sunlight streams into the car through the clear, glass windows. The seats absorb the radiant energy and change it into thermal energy. The energy is then trapped in the car.*

Consequences of Global Warming

Many scientists think that if the global temperature continues to rise, the ice caps will melt and cause flooding. Melted ice-caps would raise the sea level and flood low-lying areas, such as the coasts.

Areas that receive little rainfall, such as deserts, might receive even less because of increased evaporation. Desert animals and plants would find surviving harder. Warmer and drier climates could harm crops in the Midwest of the United States. But farther north, such as in Canada, weather conditions for farming could improve.

✓ Reading Check How would warmer temperatures affect deserts?

Reducing Pollution
Your city just received a warning from the Environmental Protection Agency for exceeding the automobile fuel emissions standards. Discuss with an adult ways that the city can reduce the amount of automobile emissions.

SECTION Review

Summary

- The Earth's climate experiences glacial and inter-glacial periods.
- The Milankovitch theory states that the Earth's climate changes as its orbit and the tilt of its axis change.
- Climate changes can be caused by volcanic eruptions, asteroid impact, the sun's cycle, and by global warming.
- Excess carbon dioxide is believed to contribute to global warming.

Using Key Terms

1. Use the following term in a sentence: *ice age*.

2. In your own words, write a definition for each of the following terms: *global warming* and *greenhouse effect*.

Understanding Key Ideas

3. Describe the possible causes of an ice age.

4. Which of the following can cause a change in the climate due to dust particles?
   a. volcanic eruptions
   b. plate tectonics
   c. solar cycles
   d. ice ages

5. How has the Earth's climate changed over time?

6. What might have caused the Earth's climate to change?

7. Which period of an ice age are we in currently? Explain.

8. Explain how the greenhouse effect warms the Earth.

Math Skills

9. After a volcanic eruption, the average temperature in a region dropped from 30° to 18°C. By how many degrees Celsius did the temperature drop?

Critical Thinking

10. **Analyzing Relationships** How will the warming of the Earth affect agriculture in different parts of the world? Explain.

11. **Predicting Consequences** How would deforestation (the cutting of trees) affect global warming?

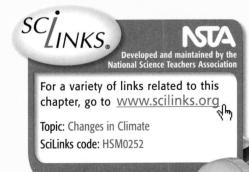

Developed and maintained by the
National Science Teachers Association

For a variety of links related to this chapter, go to www.scilinks.org

Topic: Changes in Climate
SciLinks code: HSM0252

Skills Practice Lab

Biome Business

You have just been hired as an assistant to a world-famous botanist. You have been provided with climatographs for three biomes. A *climatograph* is a graph that shows the monthly temperature and precipitation of an area in a year.

You can use the information provided in the three graphs to determine what type of climate each biome has. Next to the climatograph for each biome is an unlabeled map of the biome. Using the maps and the information provided in the graphs, you must figure out what the environment is like in each biome. You can find the exact location of each biome by tracing the map of the biome and matching it to the map at the bottom of the page.

Procedure

1 Look at each climatograph. The shaded areas show the average precipitation for the biome. The red line shows the average temperature.

2 Use the climatographs to determine the climate patterns for each biome. Compare the map of each biome with the map below to find the exact location of each biome.

- Tundra
- Taiga
- Temperate forest
- Tropical rain forest
- Temperate grassland
- Tropical savanna
- Temperate desert
- Tropical desert
- Chaparral
- Mountains

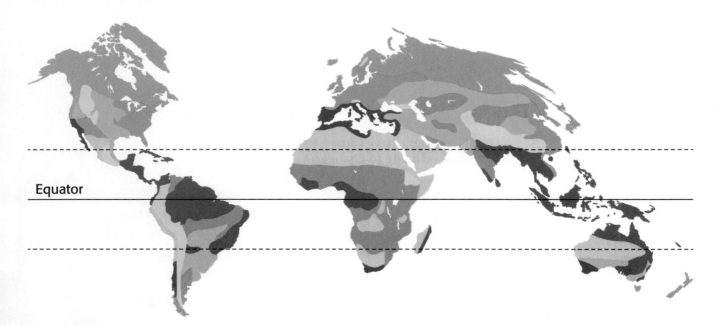

Equator

Analyze Results

1 **Analyzing Data** Describe the precipitation patterns of each biome by answering the following questions:

a. In which month does the biome receive the most precipitation?

b. Do you think that the biome is dry, or do you think that it is wet from frequent rains?

2 **Analyzing Data** Describe the temperature patterns of each biome by answering the following questions:

a. In the biome, which months are warmest?

b. Does the biome seem to have temperature cycles, like seasons, or is the temperature almost always the same?

c. Do you think that the biome is warm or cold? Explain.

Draw Conclusions

3 **Drawing Conclusions** Name each biome.

4 **Applying Conclusions** Where is each biome located?

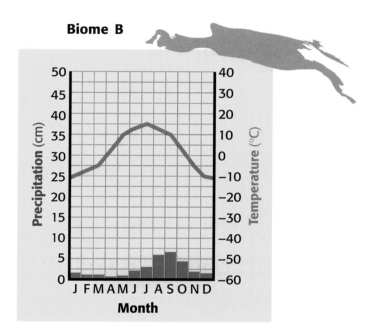

Biome B

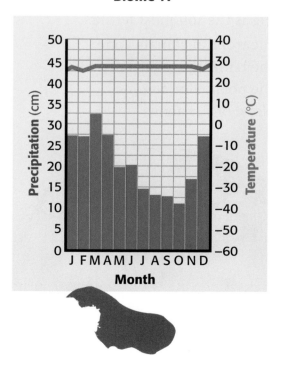

Biome A

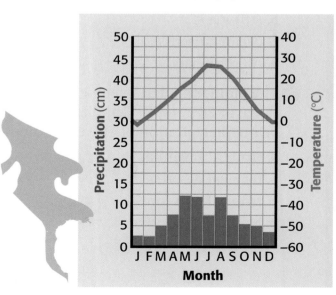

Biome C

Chapter Review

USING KEY TERMS

For each pair of terms, explain how the meanings of the terms differ.

1 *biome* and *tropical zone*

2 *weather* and *climate*

3 *temperate zone* and *polar zone*

Complete each of the following sentences by choosing the correct term from the word bank.

biome   microclimate
ice age   global warming

4 One factor that could add to ___ is an increase in pollution.

5 A city is an example of a(n) ___.

UNDERSTANDING KEY IDEAS

Multiple Choice

6 Which of the following is a factor that affects climate?

a. prevailing winds

b. latitude

c. ocean currents

d. All of the above

7 The biome that has a temperature range of 28°C to 32°C and an average yearly precipitation of 100 cm is the

a. tropical savanna.

b. tropical desert.

c. tropical rain forest.

d. None of the above

8 Which of the following biomes is NOT found in the temperate zone?

a. temperate forest

b. taiga

c. chaparral

d. temperate grassland

9 In which of the following is the tilt of the Earth's axis considered to have an effect on climate?

a. global warming

b. the sun's cycle

c. the Milankovitch theory

d. asteroid impact

10 Which of the following substances contributes to the greenhouse effect?

a. smoke

b. smog

c. carbon dioxide

d. All of the above

11 In which of the following climate zones is the soil most fertile?

a. the tropical climate zone

b. the temperate climate zone

c. the polar climate zone

d. None of the above

Short Answer

12 Why do higher latitudes receive less solar radiation than lower latitudes do?

13 How does wind influence precipitation patterns?

14 Give an example of a microclimate. What causes the unique temperature and precipitation characteristics of this area?

15 How are tundras and deserts similar?

16 How does deforestation influence global warming?

CRITICAL THINKING

17 **Concept Mapping** Use the following terms to create a concept map: *global warming, deforestation, changes in climate, greenhouse effect, ice ages,* and *the Milankovitch theory.*

18 **Analyzing Processes** Explain how ocean surface currents cause milder climates.

19 **Identifying Relationships** Describe how the tilt of the Earth's axis affects seasonal changes in different latitudes.

20 **Evaluating Conclusions** Explain why the climate on the eastern side of the Rocky Mountains differs drastically from the climate on the western side.

21 **Applying Concepts** What are some steps you and your family can take to reduce the amount of carbon dioxide that is released into the atmosphere?

22 **Applying Concepts** If you wanted to live in a warm, dry area, which biome would you choose to live in?

23 **Evaluating Data** Explain why the vegetation in areas that have a tundra climate is sparse even though these areas receive precipitation that is adequate to support life.

INTERPRETING GRAPHICS

Use the diagram below to answer the questions that follow.

24 At what position—1, 2, 3, or 4—is it spring in the Southern Hemisphere?

25 At what position does the South Pole receive almost 24 hours of daylight?

26 Explain what is happening in each climate zone in both the Northern and Southern Hemispheres at position 4.

Multiple Choice

Use the map below to answer question 1.

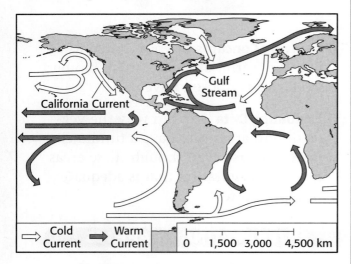

Cold Current ⇒   Warm Current →   0   1,500 3,000   4,500 km

1. Use the map to analyze the California Current. Which of the following is a reasonable inference?

A. The California Current warms the air off the West Coast, making California warmer than it would otherwise be.

B. The cool California Current causes most of California to be a desert.

C. The California Current cools the air off the coast, making California cooler than it otherwise would be.

D. The California Current brings warm, moist air inland, providing most of California with substantial rainfall.

2. When Earth's axis is tilted with the North Pole toward the sun, what season is it in South America?

A. spring

B. summer

C. fall

D. winter

3. Which of the following natural events would most likely have an effect on the global climate?

A. tornado

B. volcanic eruption

C. earthquake

D. thunderstorm

4. Which biome is characterized by very low rainfall, frozen ground, and a large insect population?

A. chaparral

B. temperate desert

C. tundra

D. tropical savanna

Use the diagram below to answer questions 5–6.

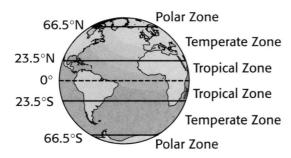

5. **Look at the illustration of Earth's climate zones above. Where are biomes containing the largest number of plant and animal species located?**

   A. in the polar zones

   B. only in the northern portion of the tropical zone

   C. in the tropical zones

   D. in the temperate zones

6. **Deciduous trees lose their leaves in the winter. Which climate zone shown above contains forests of deciduous trees?**

   A. the northern polar zone

   B. the southern polar zone

   C. the temperate zones

   D. the tropical zones

7. **Carbon dioxide in the atmosphere can lead to global warming. How can carbon dioxide do this?**

   A. It absorbs heat and keeps heat in the atmosphere.

   B. It creates warm fronts that heat Earth.

   C. Its natural radiation heats Earth.

   D. It causes warm ocean currents that heat Earth.

8. **What effect does a volcanic eruption have on climate?**

   A. The eruption releases the Earth's thermal energy, which makes the Earth cooler.

   B. The ash traps the Earth's thermal energy, which makes the Earth hotter.

   C. The large amounts of lava released make the Earth much hotter.

   D. The dust and ash block the sun's rays from entering the atmosphere, which makes the Earth cooler.

Open Response

9. **Earth's axis tilts at an angle of approximately 23.5°. If Earth's tilt were reduced to zero, how would the seasons on Earth be affected?**

10. **Why is the climate at the North Pole cooler than it is at the equator?**

Science in Action

Scientific Debate

Global Warming

Many scientists believe that pollution from burning fossil fuels is causing temperatures on Earth to rise. Higher average temperatures can cause significant changes in climate. These changes may make survival difficult for animals and plants that have adapted to a biome.

However, other scientists believe that there isn't enough evidence to prove that global warming exists. They argue that any increase in temperatures around the world can be caused by a number of factors other than pollution, such as the sun's cycle.

Science, Technology, and Society

Ice Cores

How do scientists know what Earth's climate was like thousands of years ago? Scientists learn about Earth's past climates by studying ice cores. An ice core is collected by drilling a tube of ice from glaciers and polar ice sheets. Layers in the ice core contain substances that landed in the snow during a particular year or season, such as dust from desert storms, ash from volcanic eruptions, and carbon dioxide from pollution. By studying the layers of the ice cores, scientists can learn what factors influenced the past climates.

Language Arts ACTiViTY

WRITING SKILL Read articles that present a variety of viewpoints on global warming. Then, write your own article supporting your viewpoint on global warming.

Math ACTiViTY

An area has an average yearly rainfall of 20 cm. In 1,000 years, if the average yearly rainfall decreases by 6%, what would the new average yearly rainfall be?

Mercedes Pascual

Climate Change and Disease Mercedes Pascual is a theoretical ecologist at the University of Michigan. Pascual has been able to help the people of Bangladesh save lives by using information about climate changes to predict outbreaks of the disease cholera. Cholera can be a deadly disease that people usually contract by drinking contaminated water. Pascual knew that in Bangladesh, outbreaks of cholera peak every 3.7 years. She noticed that this period matches the frequency of the El Niño Southern Oscillations, which is a weather event that occurs in the Pacific Ocean. El Niño affects weather patterns in many regions of the world, including Bangladesh. El Niño increases the temperatures of the sea off the coast of Bangladesh. Pascual found that increased sea temperatures lead to higher numbers of the bacteria that cause cholera. In turn, more people contract cholera. But because of the research conducted by Pascual and other scientists, the people of Bangladesh can better predict and prepare for outbreaks of cholera.

Social Studies ACTiViTy

WRITING SKILL Research the effects of El Niño. Write a report describing El Niño and its affect on a country other than Bangladesh.

go.hrw.com

To learn more about these Science in Action topics, visit go.hrw.com and type in the keyword **HZ5CLMF.**

Current Science

Check out Current Science® articles related to this chapter by visiting go.hrw.com. Just type in the keyword HZ5CS17.

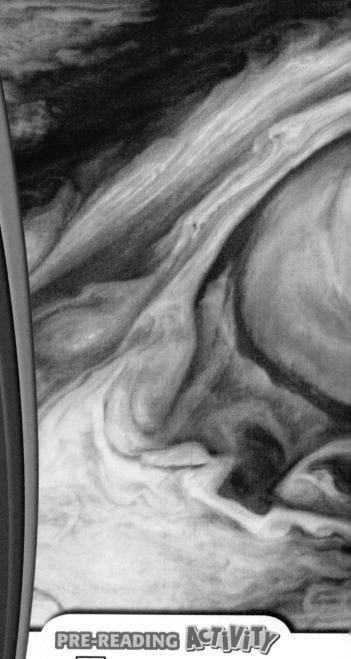

8

A Family of Planets

The Big Idea

The solar system contains a variety of objects that differ in size, appearance, and composition and that move in predictable ways.

About the Photo

These rich swirls of color may remind you of a painting you might see in an art museum. But this photograph is of the planet Jupiter. The red swirl, called the Great Red Spot, is actually a hurricane-like storm system that is 3 times the diameter of Earth!

PRE-READING ACTIVITY

FOLDNOTES **Booklet** Before you read the chapter, create the FoldNote entitled "Booklet" described in the **Study Skills** section of the Appendix. Label each page of the booklet with a name of a planet in our solar system. As you read the chapter, write what you learn about each planet on the appropriate page of the booklet.

Measuring Space

Do the following activity to get a better idea of your solar neighborhood.

Procedure

1. Use a **meterstick** and some **chalk** to draw a line 2 m long on a **chalkboard.** Draw a large dot at one end of the line. This dot represents the sun.

2. Draw smaller dots on the line to represent the relative distances of each of the bodies from the sun, based on information in the table.

Analysis

1. What do you notice about how the bodies are spaced?

Body	Distance from sun	
	Millions of km	**Scaled to cm**
Mercury	57.9	2
Venus	108.2	4
Earth	149.6	5
Mars	227.9	8
Jupiter	778.4	26
Saturn	1,424.0	48
Uranus	2,827.0	97
Neptune	4,499.0	151
Pluto	5,943.0	200

Our Solar System

Did you know that planets, when viewed from Earth, look like stars to the naked eye? Ancient astronomers were intrigued by these "stars" which seemed to wander in the sky.

Ancient astronomers named these "stars" planets, which means "wanderers" in Greek. These astronomers knew planets were physical bodies and could predict their motions. But scientists did not begin to explore these worlds until the 17th century, when Galileo used the telescope to study planets and stars. Now, scientists have completed more than 150 successful missions to moons, planets, comets, and asteroids in our cosmic neighborhood.

A Combination of Systems

Our *solar system*, shown in **Figure 1**, includes the sun, the planets, and many smaller objects. In some cases, these bodies may be organized into smaller systems of their own. For example, the Saturn system is made of the planet Saturn and the several moons that orbit Saturn. In this way, our solar system is a combination of many smaller systems.

What You Will Learn

- List the planets in the order in which they orbit the sun.
- Explain how scientists measure distances in space.
- Describe how the planets in our solar system were discovered.
- Describe three ways in which the inner planets and outer planets differ.

Vocabulary

astronomical unit

READING STRATEGY

Paired Summarizing Read this section silently. In pairs, take turns summarizing the material. Stop to discuss ideas that seem confusing.

Figure 1 *These images show the relative diameters of the planets and the sun.*

Mercury
4,879 km

Venus
12,104 km

Earth
12,756 km

Mars
6,794 km

Sun
1,392,000 km

Jupiter
142,984 km

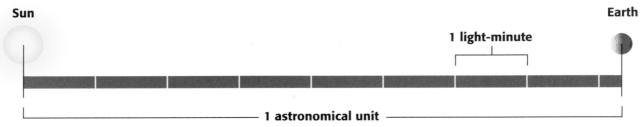

Sun   **Earth**

1 light-minute

1 astronomical unit

Figure 2 *One astronomical unit equals about 8.3 light-minutes.*

Measuring Interplanetary Distances

One way that scientists measure distances in space is by using the astronomical unit. One **astronomical unit** (AU) is the average distance between the sun and Earth, or approximately 150,000,000 km. Another way to measure distances in space is by using the speed of light. Light travels at about 300,000 km/s in space. This means that in 1 s, light travels 300,000 km.

In 1 min, light travels nearly 18,000,000 km. This distance is also called a *light-minute*. Look at **Figure 2**. Light from the sun takes 8.3 min to reach Earth. So, the distance from Earth to the sun, or 1 AU, is 8.3 light-minutes. Distances in the solar system can be measured in light-minutes and light-hours.

☑ **Reading Check** **How far does light travel in 1 s?** (*See the Appendix for answers to Reading Checks.*)

astronomical unit the average distance between the Earth and the sun; approximately 150 million kilometers (symbol, AU)

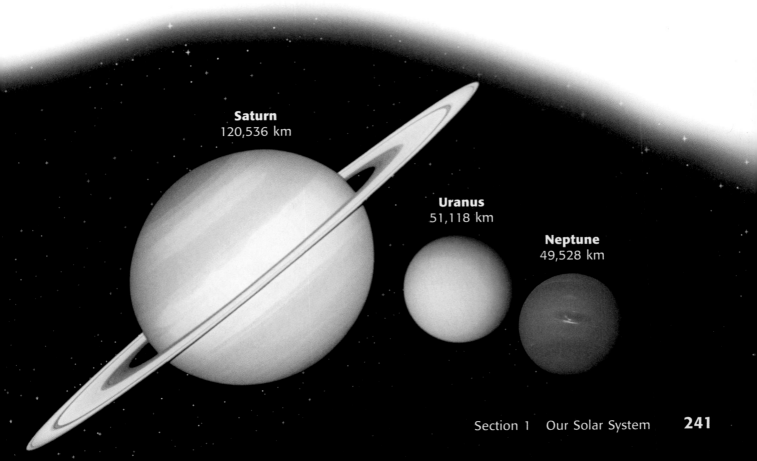

Saturn
120,536 km

Uranus
51,118 km

Neptune
49,528 km

The Discovery of the Solar System

Up until the 17th century, the universe was thought to have only eight bodies. These bodies included the planets Earth, Mercury, Venus, Mars, Jupiter, and Saturn, the sun, and the Earth's moon. These bodies are the only ones that can be seen from Earth without using a telescope.

After the telescope was invented in the 17th century, however, more discoveries were made. By the end of the 17th century, nine more large bodies were discovered. These bodies were moons of Jupiter and Saturn.

By the 18th century, the planet Uranus, along with two of its moons and two more of Saturn's moons, was discovered. In the 19th century, Neptune, as well as moons of several other planets, was discovered. Finally, in the 20th century, Pluto and many other bodies were discovered.

The Inner and Outer Solar Systems

The solar system is divided into two main parts: the inner solar system and the outer solar system. The inner solar system contains the four planets that are closest to the sun. The outer solar system contains the planets that are farthest from the sun.

The Inner Planets

The planets of the inner solar system, shown in **Figure 3,** are more closely spaced than the planets of the outer solar system. The inner planets are also known as the *terrestrial planets* because their surfaces are dense and rocky. However, each of the inner planets is unique.

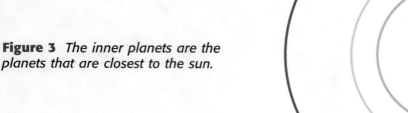

Figure 3 *The inner planets are the planets that are closest to the sun.*

The Outer Planets

The planets of the outer solar system include Jupiter, Saturn, Uranus, and Neptune. The outer planets are very different from the inner planets, as you will soon find out.

Unlike the inner planets, the outer planets are large and are composed mostly of gases. Because of this, Jupiter, Saturn, Uranus, and Neptune are known as gas giants. The atmospheres of these planets blend smoothly into the denser layers of their interiors. You can see a diagram of the orbits of the outer planets in **Figure 4.**

Several smaller bodies, including Pluto, are located beyond the orbit of Neptune. These bodies are made of rock and ice and may be leftover material from the formation of the early solar system.

Reading Check Which planets are in the outer solar system?

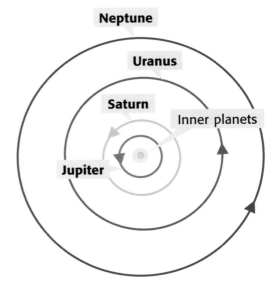

Figure 4 The planets of the outer solar system are the farthest from the sun.

SECTION Review

Summary

- In the order in which they orbit the sun, the eight planets are Mercury, Venus, Earth, Mars, Jupiter, Saturn, Uranus, and Neptune.

- Two ways in which scientists measure distances in space are to use astronomical units and to use light-years.

- The inner planets are spaced more closely together, are smaller, and are rockier than the outer planets.

Using Key Terms

1. In your own words, write a definition for the term *astronomical unit.*

Understanding Key Ideas

2. When was the planet Uranus discovered?
   a. before the 17th century
   b. in the 18th century
   c. in the 19th century
   d. in the 20th century

3. The invention of what instrument helped early scientists discover more bodies in the solar system?

4. Which of the eight planets are included in the outer solar system?

5. Describe how the inner planets are different from the outer planets.

Math Skills

6. If Venus is 6.0 light-minutes from the sun, what is Venus's distance from the sun in astronomical units?

Critical Thinking

7. **Analyzing Methods** The distance between Earth and the sun is measured in light-minutes, but the distance between Neptune and the sun is measured in light-hours. Explain why.

What You Will Learn

● Explain the difference between a planet's period of rotation and period of revolution.
● Describe the difference between prograde and retrograde rotation.
● Describe the individual characteristics of Mercury, Venus, Earth, and Mars.
● Identify the characteristics that make Earth suitable for life.

Vocabulary

terrestrial planet
prograde rotation
retrograde rotation

READING STRATEGY

Reading Organizer As you read this section, create an outline of the section. Use the headings from the section in your outline.

terrestrial planet one of the highly dense planets nearest to the sun; Mercury, Venus, Mars, and Earth

The Inner Planets

In the inner solar system, you will find one of the hottest places in our solar system as well as the only planet known to support life.

The inner planets are also called **terrestrial planets** because, like Earth, they are very dense and rocky. The inner planets are smaller, denser, and rockier than the outer planets. In this section, you will learn more about the individual characteristics of Mercury, Venus, Earth, and Mars.

Mercury: Closest to the Sun

If you visited the planet Mercury, shown in **Figure 1,** you would find a very strange world. For one thing, on Mercury you would weigh only 38% of what you weigh on Earth. The weight you have on Earth is due to surface gravity, which is less on less massive planets. Also, because of Mercury's slow rotation, a day on Mercury is almost 59 Earth days long! The amount of time that an object takes to rotate once is called its *period of rotation*. So, Mercury's period of rotation is almost 59 Earth days long.

A Year on Mercury

Another curious thing about Mercury is that its year is only 88 Earth days long. As you know, a *year* is the time that a planet takes to go around the sun once. The motion of a body orbiting another body in space is called *revolution*. The time an object takes to revolve around the sun once is called its *period of revolution*. Every 88 Earth days, or 1.5 Mercurian days, Mercury revolves once around the sun.

Figure 1 *This image of Mercury was taken by the* Mariner 10 *spacecraft on March 24, 1974, from a distance of 5,380,000 km.*

Mercury Statistics	
Distance from sun	3.2 light-minutes
Period of rotation	58 days, 19 h
Period of revolution	88 days
Diameter	4,879 km
Density	5.43 g/cm³
Surface temperature	−173°C to 427°C
Surface gravity	38% of Earth's

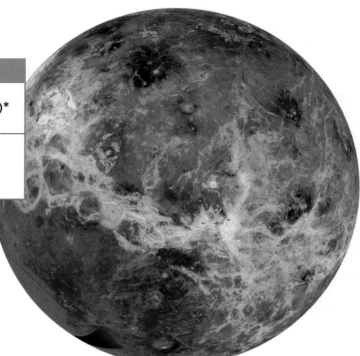

Venus Statistics	
Distance from sun	6.0 light-minutes
Period of rotation	243 days, 16 h (R)*
Period of revolution	224 days, 17 h
Diameter	12,104 km
Density	5.24 g/cm³
Surface temperature	464°C
Surface gravity	91% of Earth's

*R = retrograde rotation

Figure 2 *This image of Venus was taken by* Mariner 10 *on February 5, 1974. The uppermost layer of clouds contains sulfuric acid.*

Venus: Earth's Twin?

Look at **Figure 2.** In many ways, Venus is more like Earth than any other planet. Venus is only slightly smaller, less massive, and less dense than Earth. But in other ways, Venus is very different from Earth. On Venus, the sun rises in the west and sets in the east. The reason is that Venus and Earth rotate in opposite directions. Earth is said to have **prograde rotation** because it appears to spin in a *counterclockwise* direction when it is viewed from above its North Pole. If a planet spins in a *clockwise* direction, the planet is said to have **retrograde rotation.**

The Atmosphere of Venus

Of the terrestrial planets, Venus has the densest atmosphere. Venus's atmosphere has 90 times the pressure of Earth's atmosphere! The air on Venus is mostly carbon dioxide, but the air is also made of some of the most destructive acids known. The carbon dioxide traps thermal energy from sunlight in a process called the *greenhouse effect.* The greenhouse effect causes Venus's surface temperature to be very high. At 464°C, Venus has the hottest surface of any planet in the solar system.

Mapping Venus's Surface

Between 1990 and 1992, the *Magellan* spacecraft mapped the surface of Venus by using radar waves. The radar waves traveled through the clouds and bounced off the planet's surface. Data gathered from the radar waves showed that Venus, like Earth, has volcanoes.

Reading Check What technology was used to map the surface of Venus? (*See the Appendix for answers to Reading Checks.*)

prograde rotation the counterclockwise spin of a planet or moon as seen from above the planet's North Pole; rotation in the same direction as the sun's rotation

retrograde rotation the clockwise spin of a planet or moon as seen from above the planet's North Pole

Figure 3 *Earth is the only planet known to support life.*

Earth: An Oasis in Space

As viewed from space, Earth is like a sparkling blue oasis in a black sea of stars. Constantly changing weather patterns create the swirls of clouds that blanket the blue and brown sphere we call home. Look at **Figure 3.** Why did Earth have such good fortune, while its two nearest neighbors, Venus and Mars, are unsuitable for life as we know it?

Water on Earth

Earth formed at just the right distance from the sun. Earth is warm enough to keep most of its water from freezing. But unlike Venus, Earth is cool enough to keep its water from boiling away. Liquid water is a vital part of the chemical processes that living things depend on for survival.

The Earth from Space

The picture of Earth shown in **Figure 4** was taken from space. You might think that the only goal of space exploration is to make discoveries beyond Earth. But the National Aeronautics and Space Administration (NASA) has a program to study Earth by using satellites in the same way that scientists study other planets. This program is called the Earth Science Enterprise. Its goal is to study the Earth as a global system that is made of smaller systems. These smaller systems include the atmosphere, land, ice, the oceans, and life. The program will also help us understand how humans affect the global environment. By studying Earth from space, scientists hope to understand how different parts of the global system interact.

✓ Reading Check What is the Earth Science Enterprise?

Earth Statistics	
Distance from sun	8.3 light-minutes
Period of rotation	23 h, 56 min
Period of revolution	365 days, 6 h
Diameter	12,756 km
Density	5.52 g/cm³
Surface temperature	−13°C to 37°C
Surface gravity	100% of Earth's

Figure 4 *This image of Earth was taken on December 7, 1972, by the crew of the* Apollo 17 *spacecraft while on their way to the moon.*

Mars Statistics	
Distance from sun	12.7 light-minutes
Period of rotation	24 h, 40 min
Period of revolution	1 year, 322 days
Diameter	6,794 km
Density	3.93 g/cm³
Surface temperature	−123°C to 37°C
Surface gravity	38% of Earth's

Mars: Our Intriguing Neighbor

Mars, shown in **Figure 5,** is perhaps the most studied planet in the solar system other than Earth. Much of our knowledge of Mars has come from information gathered by spacecraft. *Viking 1* and *Viking 2* landed on Mars in 1976, and *Mars Pathfinder* landed on Mars in 1997.

The Atmosphere of Mars

Because of its thinner atmosphere and greater distance from the sun, Mars is a cold planet. Midsummer temperatures recorded by the *Mars Pathfinder* range from –13°C to –77°C. Martian air is so thin that the air pressure on the surface of Mars is about the same as it is 30 km above Earth's surface. This distance is about 3 times higher than most planes fly! The air pressure is so low that any liquid water would quickly boil away. The only water found on the surface of Mars is in the form of ice.

Figure 5 *This Viking orbiter image shows the eastern hemisphere of Mars. The large circular feature in the center is the impact crater Schiaparelli, which has a diameter of 450 km.*

Water on Mars

Even though liquid water cannot exist on Mars's surface today, there is strong evidence that it existed there in the past. **Figure 6** shows an area on Mars with features that might have resulted from deposition of sediment in a lake. This finding means that in the past Mars might have been a warmer place and had a thicker atmosphere.

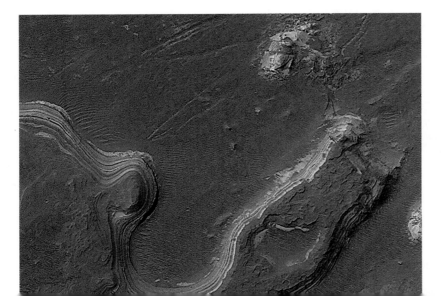

Figure 6 *The origin of the features shown in this image is unknown. The features might have resulted from deposition of sediment in a lake.*

CONNECTION TO Physics

WRITING SKILL **Boiling Point on Mars** At sea level on Earth's surface, water boils at 100°C. But if you try to boil water on top of a high mountain, you will find that the boiling point is lower than 100°C. Do some research to find out why. Then, in your own words, explain why liquid water cannot exist on Mars, based on what you learned.

Where Is the Water Now?

Mars has two polar icecaps made of both frozen water and frozen carbon dioxide. But the polar icecaps do not have enough water to create a thick atmosphere or rivers. Looking closely at the walls of some Martian craters, scientists have found that the debris around the craters looks as if it were made by the flow of mud rather than by dry soil. In this case, where might some of the "lost" Martian water have gone? Many scientists think that it is frozen beneath the Martian soil.

Martian Volcanoes

Mars has a rich volcanic history. Unlike Earth, where volcanoes exist in many places, Mars has only two large volcanic systems. The largest, the Tharsis region, stretches 8,000 km across the planet. The largest mountain in the solar system, Olympus Mons, is an extinct shield volcano similar to Mauna Kea on the island of Hawaii. Mars not only is smaller and cooler than Earth but also has a slightly different chemical makeup. This makeup may have kept the Martian crust from moving around as Earth's crust does. As a result, the volcanoes kept building up in the same spots on Mars. Images and data sent back by probes such as the *Sojourner* rover, shown in **Figure 7,** are helping to explain Mars's mysterious past.

Reading Check What characteristics of Mars may explain why Mars has only two large volcanic systems?

Figure 7 *The* Sojourner *rover, part of the Mars Pathfinder mission, is shown here creeping up to a rock named Yogi to measure its composition. The solar panel on the rover's back collected the solar energy used to power the rover's motor.*

Missions to Mars

Scientists are still intrigued by the mysteries of Mars. Several recent missions to Mars were launched to gain a better understanding of the Martian world. **Figure 8** shows the *Mars Express Orbiter,* which was launched by the European Space Agency (ESA) in 2003, and was designed to help scientists determine the composition of the Martian atmosphere and Martian climate. Also, in 2003, NASA launched the Twin Rover mission to Mars. These exploration rovers are designed to gather information that may help scientists determine if life ever existed on Mars. In addition, information collected by these rovers may help scientists prepare for human exploration on Mars.

Figure 8 *The* Mars Express Orbiter *will help scientists study Mars's atmosphere.*

SECTION
Review

Summary

- A period of rotation is the length of time that an object takes to rotate once on its axis.

- A period of revolution is the length of time that an object takes to revolve around the sun.

- Mercury is the planet closest to the sun. Of all the terrestrial planets, Venus has the densest atmosphere. Earth is the only planet known to support life. Mars has a rich volcanic history and shows evidence of once having had water.

Using Key Terms

1. In your own words, write a definition for the term *terrestrial planet.*

For the pair of terms below, explain how the meanings of the terms differ.

2. *prograde rotation* and *retrograde rotation*

Understanding Key Ideas

3. Scientists believe that the water on Mars now exists as
   a. polar icecaps.
   b. dry riverbeds.
   c. ice beneath the Martian soil.
   d. Both (a) and (c)

4. List three differences between and three similarities of Venus and Earth.

5. What is the difference between a planet's period of rotation and its period of revolution?

6. What are some of the characteristics of Earth that make it suitable for life?

7. Explain why the surface temperature of Venus is higher than the surface temperatures of the other planets in our solar system.

Math Skills

8. Mercury has a period of rotation equal to 58.67 Earth days. Mercury's period of revolution is equal to 88 Earth days. How many times does Mercury rotate during one revolution around the sun?

Critical Thinking

9. **Making Inferences** What type of information can we get by studying Earth from space?

10. **Analyzing Ideas** What type of evidence found on Mars suggests that Mars may have been a warmer place and had a thicker atmosphere?

SC**LINKS**®

N**STA**

Developed and maintained by the National Science Teachers Association

For a variety of links related to this chapter, go to www.scilinks.org

Topic: The Inner Planets
SciLinks code: HSM0798

SECTION 3

The Outer Planets

What two characteristics do all of the outer planets have in common? The outer planets are very large planets that are made mostly of gases.

What You Will Learn

- Explain how gas giants are different from terrestrial planets.
- Describe the individual characteristics of Jupiter, Saturn, Uranus, Neptune, and Pluto.

Vocabulary

gas giant

READING STRATEGY

Prediction Guide Before reading this section, write the title of each heading in this section. Next, under each heading write what you think you will learn.

Because they are so much larger than the inner planets, the outer planets are called gas giants. **Gas giants** are planets that have deep, massive atmospheres rather than hard and rocky surfaces like those of the inner planets.

gas giant a planet that has a deep, massive atmosphere, such as Jupiter, Saturn, Uranus, or Neptune

Jupiter: A Giant Among Giants

Jupiter is the largest planet in our solar system. Like the sun, Jupiter is made mostly of hydrogen and helium. The outer part of Jupiter's atmosphere is made of layered clouds of water, methane, and ammonia. The beautiful colors you see in **Figure 1** are probably due to small amounts of organic compounds. At a depth of about 10,000 km into Jupiter's atmosphere, the pressure is high enough to change hydrogen gas into a liquid. Deeper still, the pressure changes the liquid hydrogen into a liquid, metallic state. Unlike most planets, Jupiter radiates much more energy into space than it receives from the sun. The reason is that Jupiter's interior is very hot. Another striking feature of Jupiter is the Great Red Spot, a storm system that is more than 400 years old and is about 3 times the diameter of Earth!

NASA Missions to Jupiter

NASA has sent five missions to Jupiter. These include two Pioneer missions, two Voyager missions, and the recent Galileo mission. The *Voyager 1* and *Voyager 2* spacecraft sent back images that revealed a thin, faint ring around Jupiter. The Voyager missions also gave us the first detailed images of Jupiter's moons. The *Galileo* spacecraft reached Jupiter in 1995 and sent a probe into Jupiter's atmosphere. The probe sent back data on Jupiter's composition, temperature, and pressure.

Figure 1 *This* Voyager 2 *image of Jupiter was taken at a distance of 28.4 million kilometers. Io, one of Jupiter's largest moons, can also be seen in this image.*

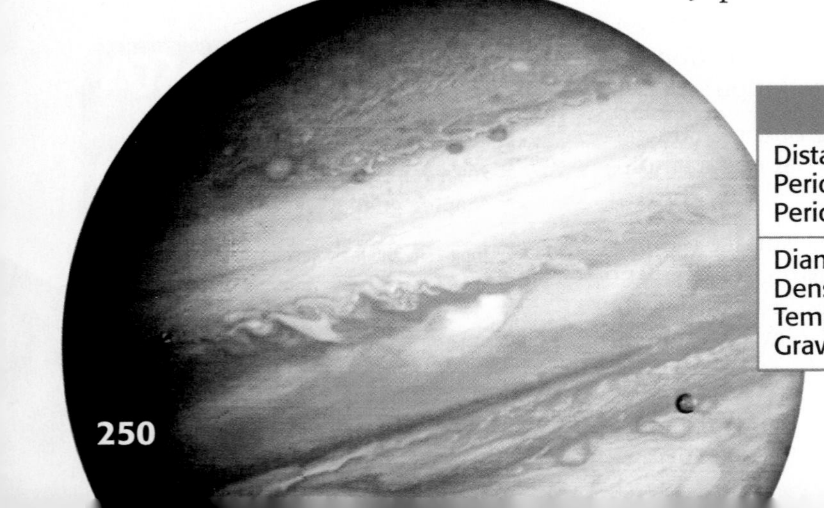

Jupiter Statistics	
Distance from sun	43.3 light-minutes
Period of rotation	9 h, 54 min
Period of revolution	11 years, 313 days
Diameter	142,984 km
Density	1.33 g/cm^3
Temperature	−110°C
Gravity	236% of Earth's

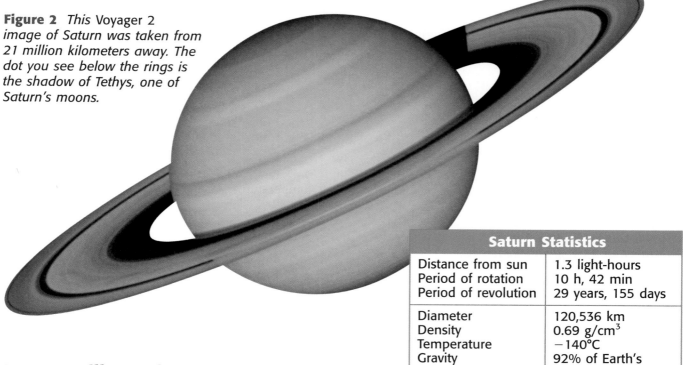

Figure 2 *This* Voyager 2 *image of Saturn was taken from 21 million kilometers away. The dot you see below the rings is the shadow of Tethys, one of Saturn's moons.*

Saturn Statistics	
Distance from sun	1.3 light-hours
Period of rotation	10 h, 42 min
Period of revolution	29 years, 155 days
Diameter	120,536 km
Density	0.69 g/cm^3
Temperature	−140°C
Gravity	92% of Earth's

Saturn: Still Forming

Saturn, shown in **Figure 2,** is the second-largest planet in the solar system. Saturn has roughly 764 times the volume of Earth and is 95 times more massive than Earth. Its overall composition, like Jupiter's, is mostly hydrogen and helium. But methane, ammonia, and ethane are found in the upper atmosphere. Saturn's interior is probably much like Jupiter's. Also, like Jupiter, Saturn gives off much more energy than it receives from the sun. Scientists think that Saturn's extra energy comes from helium falling out of the atmosphere and sinking to the core. In other words, Saturn is still forming!

The Rings of Saturn

Although all of the gas giants have rings, Saturn's rings are the largest. Saturn's rings have a total diameter of 272,000 km. Yet, Saturn's rings are only a few hundred meters thick. The rings are made of icy particles that range in size from a few centimeters to several meters wide. **Figure 3** shows a close-up view of Saturn's rings.

✔ Reading Check What are Saturn's rings made of? (*See the Appendix for answers to Reading Checks.*)

NASA's Exploration of Saturn

Launched in 1997, the *Cassini* spacecraft is designed to study Saturn's rings, moons, and atmosphere. The spacecraft is also designed to return more than 300,000 color images of Saturn.

Figure 3 *The different colors in this* Voyager 2 *image of Saturn's rings show differences in the rings' chemical composition.*

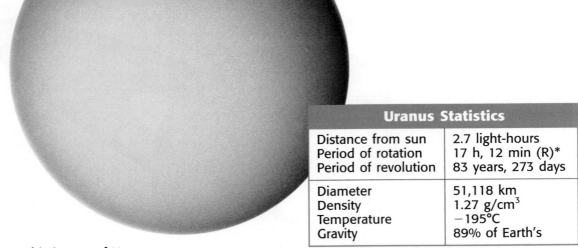

Uranus Statistics	
Distance from sun	2.7 light-hours
Period of rotation	17 h, 12 min (R)*
Period of revolution	83 years, 273 days
Diameter	51,118 km
Density	1.27 g/cm³
Temperature	−195°C
Gravity	89% of Earth's

*R = retrograde rotation

Figure 4 *This image of Uranus was taken by* Voyager 2 *at a distance of 9.1 million kilometers.*

Uranus: A Small Giant

Uranus (YOOR uh nuhs) was discovered by the English amateur astronomer William Herschel in 1781. The atmosphere of Uranus is mainly hydrogen and methane. Because these gases absorb the red part of sunlight very strongly, Uranus appears blue-green in color, as shown in **Figure 4.** Uranus and Neptune have much less mass than Jupiter, but their densities are similar. This suggests that their compositions are different from Jupiter's. They may have lower percentages of light elements and a greater percentage of water.

A Tilted Planet

Unlike most other planets, Uranus is tipped over on its side. So, its axis of rotation is tilted by almost 90° and lies almost in the plane of its orbit, as shown in **Figure 5.** For part of a Uranus year, one pole points toward the sun while the other pole is in darkness. At the other end of Uranus's orbit, the poles are reversed. Some scientists think that early in its history, Uranus may have been hit by a massive object that tipped the planet over.

Figure 5 *Uranus's axis of rotation is tilted so that the axis is nearly parallel to the plane of Uranus's orbit. In contrast, the axes of most other planets are closer to being perpendicular to the plane of the planets' orbits.*

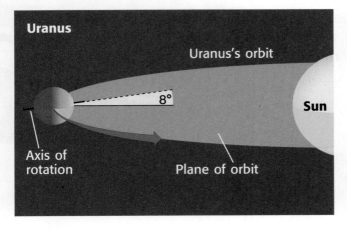

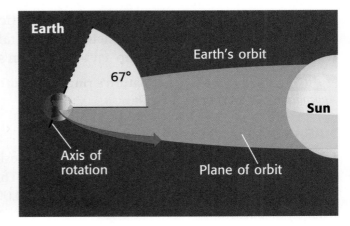

Neptune: The Blue World

Irregularities in the orbit of Uranus suggested to early astronomers that there must be another planet beyond it. They thought that the gravity of this new planet pulled Uranus off its predicted path. By using the predictions of the new planet's orbit, astronomers discovered the planet Neptune in 1846. Neptune is shown in **Figure 6.**

The Atmosphere of Neptune

The *Voyager 2* spacecraft sent back images that provided much new information about Neptune's atmosphere. Although the composition of Neptune's atmosphere is similar to that of Uranus's atmosphere, Neptune's atmosphere has belts of clouds that are much more visible. At the time of *Voyager 2*'s visit, Neptune had a Great Dark Spot like the Great Red Spot on Jupiter. And like the interiors of Jupiter and Saturn, Neptune's interior releases thermal energy to its outer layers. This release of energy helps the warm gases rise and the cool gases sink, which sets up the wind patterns in the atmosphere that create the belts of clouds. *Voyager 2* images also revealed that Neptune has a set of very narrow rings.

Reading Check What characteristic of Neptune's interior accounts for the belts of clouds in Neptune's atmosphere?

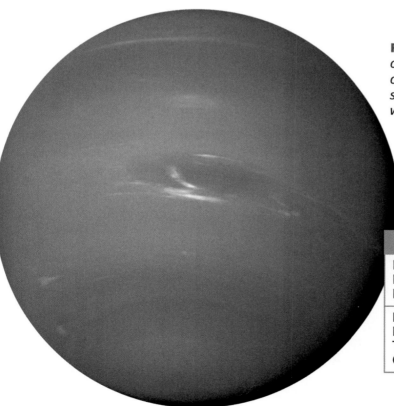

Figure 6 *This* Voyager 2 *image of Neptune, taken at a distance of more than 7 million kilometers, shows the Great Dark Spot as well as some bright cloud bands.*

Neptune Statistics	
Distance from sun	4.2 light-hours
Period of rotation	16 h, 6 min
Period of revolution	163 years, 263 days
Diameter	49,528 km
Density	1.64 g/cm^3
Temperature	−200°C
Gravity	112% of Earth's

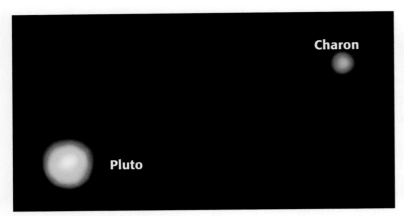

Pluto Statistics	
Distance from sun	5.4 light-hours
Period of rotation	6 days, 10 h (R)*
Period of revolution	248 years, 4 days
Diameter	2,390 km
Density	1.75 g/cm^3
Surface temperature	−225°C
Surface gravity	6% of Earth's

*R = retrograde rotation

Figure 7 *This Hubble Space Telescope image is one of the clearest ever taken of Pluto (left) and its moon, Charon (right).*

Pluto: A Dwarf Planet

Since its discovery in 1930, Pluto has been called the ninth planet. However, in 2006, astronomers created a new definition of *planet*. Because Pluto does not fit all of the conditions necessary for it to be considered a planet, Pluto has been reclassified as a dwarf planet.

A Small World

Pluto differs a lot from the nearby gas giants. Pluto is less than half the size of Mercury and is made mainly of ice and rock. Scientists think that Pluto is covered by frozen nitrogen and has a thin atmosphere of methane. Pluto's moon, Charon (KER uhn), is covered by frozen water and is more than half Pluto's size! In fact, Charon is the largest satellite relative to its planet in the solar system. **Figure 7** shows Pluto and Charon together. **Figure 8** shows how far from the sun Pluto and Charon really are. From Pluto, the sun looks like a very distant bright star.

Pluto and Charon have not been visited by a NASA mission. However, plans are underway to visit these bodies soon. During this mission, scientists hope to map the surfaces of both Pluto and Charon.

Figure 8 *An artist's view of the sun and Charon from Pluto shows just how little light and heat Pluto receives from the sun.*

Other Dwarf Planets

Because Pluto is so small and is so unusual, its classification as a planet has been questioned for many years. The discovery of an object called Eris challenged that classification even more. Eris is larger than Pluto. However, like Pluto, Eris has not cleared its orbit of debris. Because these objects are so similar, they are now also classified as dwarf planets. A *dwarf planet* is any object that orbits the sun, is round because of its own gravity, but has not cleared its orbital path. Ceres is another object that has been reclassified as a dwarf planet. Ceres was previously classified as an asteroid.

SCHOOL to HOME

Surviving Space

WRITING SKILL Imagine it is the year 2150 and you are flying a spacecraft to Pluto. Suddenly, your systems fail, giving you only one chance to land safely. You can't head back to Earth. With a parent or guardian, write a paragraph explaining which planet you would choose to land on.

ACTIVITY

SECTION Review

Summary

- Jupiter is the largest planet in our solar system. Energy from the interior of Jupiter is transferred to its exterior.

- Saturn is the second-largest planet and, in some ways, is still forming as a planet.

- Uranus's axis of rotation is tilted by almost 90°.

- Neptune has a faint ring, and its atmosphere contains belts of clouds.

- Pluto is a dwarf planet, and its moon, Charon, is more than half its size.

Using Key Terms

1. In your own words, write a definition for the term *gas giant*.

Understanding Key Ideas

2. The many colors of Jupiter's atmosphere are probably caused by _____ in the atmosphere.
   a. clouds of water
   b. methane
   c. ammonia
   d. organic compounds

3. Why do scientists claim that Saturn, in a way, is still forming?

4. Why does Uranus have a blue green color?

5. What is unusual about Pluto's moon, Charon?

6. What is the Great Red Spot?

7. Explain why Jupiter radiates more energy into space than it receives from the sun.

8. How do the gas giants differ from the terrestrial planets?

9. What is so unusual about Uranus's axis of rotation?

Math Skills

10. Pluto is 5.5 light-hours from the sun. How far is Pluto from the sun in astronomical units? (Hint: 1 AU = 8.3 light-minutes)

11. If Jupiter is 43.3 light-minutes from the sun and Neptune is 4.2 light-hours from the sun, how far from Jupiter is Neptune?

Critical Thinking

12. **Evaluating Data** What conclusions can your draw about the properties of a planet just by knowing how far it is from the sun?

13. **Applying Concepts** Why isn't the word *surface* included in the statistics for the gas giants?

SCILINKS®

NSTA

Developed and maintained by the National Science Teachers Association

For a variety of links related to this chapter, go to www.scilinks.org

Topic: The Outer Planets
SciLinks code: HSM1091

Moons

If you could, which moon would you visit? With volcanoes, craters, and possible underground oceans, the moons in our solar system would be interesting places to visit.

Natural or artificial bodies that revolve around larger bodies such as planets are called **satellites.** Except for Mercury and Venus, all of the planets have natural satellites called *moons.*

Luna: The Moon of Earth

Scientists have learned a lot from studying Earth's moon, which is also called *Luna.* The lunar rocks brought back during the Apollo missions were found to be about 4.6 billion years old. Because these rocks have hardly changed since they formed, scientists know the solar system itself is about 4.6 billion years old.

The Surface of the Moon

As you can see in **Figure 1,** the moon's history is written on its face. The surfaces of bodies that have no atmospheres preserve a record of almost all of the impacts that the bodies have had. Because scientists now know the age of the moon, they can count the number of impact craters to find the rate of cratering since the birth of our solar system. By knowing the rate of cratering, scientists are able to use the number of craters on any body to estimate how old the body's surface is. That way, scientists don't need to bring back rock samples.

What You Will Learn

- Describe the current theory of the origin of Earth's moon.
- Explain what causes the phases of Earth's moon.
- Describe the difference between a solar eclipse and a lunar eclipse.
- Describe the individual characteristics of the moons of other planets.

Vocabulary

satellite
phase
eclipse

READING STRATEGY

Reading Organizer As you read this section, make a table comparing solar eclipses and lunar eclipses.

Figure 1 *This image of the moon was taken by the* Galileo *spacecraft while on its way to Jupiter. The large, dark areas are lava plains called* maria.

Moon Statistics	
Period of rotation	27 days, 9 hours
Period of revolution	27 days, 7 hours
Diameter	3,475 km
Density	3.34 g/cm^3
Surface temperature	−170 to 134°C
Surface gravity	16% of Earth's

Lunar Origins

Before scientists had rock samples from the moon, there were three popular explanations for the moon's formation: (1) The moon was a separate body captured by Earth's gravity, (2) the moon formed at the same time and from the same materials as the Earth, and (3) the newly formed Earth was spinning so fast that a piece flew off and became the moon.

When rock samples of the moon were brought back from the Apollo mission, the mystery was solved. Scientists found that the composition of the moon was similar to that of Earth's mantle. This evidence from the lunar rock samples supported the third explanation for the moon's formation.

The current theory is that a large, Mars-sized object collided with Earth while the Earth was still forming, as shown in **Figure 2.** The collision was so violent that part of the Earth's mantle was blasted into orbit around Earth to form the moon.

✓ Reading Check What is the current explanation for the formation of the moon? (*See the Appendix for answers to Reading Checks.*)

satellite a natural or artificial body that revolves around a planet

---

Figure 2 **Formation of the Moon**

❶ Impact
About 4.6 billion years ago, when Earth was still mostly molten, a large body collided with Earth. Scientists reason that the object must have been large enough to blast part of Earth's mantle into space, because the composition of the moon is similar to that of Earth's mantle.

❷ Ejection
The resulting debris began to revolve around the Earth within a few hours of the impact. This debris consisted of mantle material from Earth and from the impacting body as well as part of the iron core of the impacting body.

❸ Formation
Soon after the giant impact, the clumps of material ejected into orbit around Earth began to join together to form the moon. Much later, as the moon cooled, additional impacts created deep basins and fractured the moon's surface. Lunar lava flowed from those cracks and flooded the basins to form the lunar maria that we see today.

Phases of the Moon

From Earth, one of the most noticeable aspects of the moon is its continually changing appearance. Within a month, the moon's Earthward face changes from a fully lit circle to a thin crescent and then back to a circle. These different appearances of the moon result from its changing position relative to Earth and the sun. As the moon revolves around Earth, the amount of sunlight on the side of the moon that faces Earth changes. The different appearances of the moon due to its changing position are called **phases.** The phases of the moon are shown in **Figure 3.**

phase the change in the sunlit area of one celestial body as seen from another celestial body

Waxing and Waning

When the moon is *waxing,* the sunlit fraction that we can see from Earth is getting larger. When the moon is *waning,* the sunlit fraction is getting smaller. Notice in **Figure 3** that even as the phases of the moon change, the total amount of sunlight that the moon gets remains the same. Half the moon is always in sunlight, just as half the Earth is always in sunlight. But because the moon's period of rotation is the same as its period of revolution, on Earth you always see the same side of the moon. If you lived on the far side of the moon, you would see the sun for half of each lunar day, but you would never see the Earth!

Figure 3 *The positions of the moon, sun, and Earth determine which phase the moon is in. The photo insets show how the moon looks from Earth at each phase.*

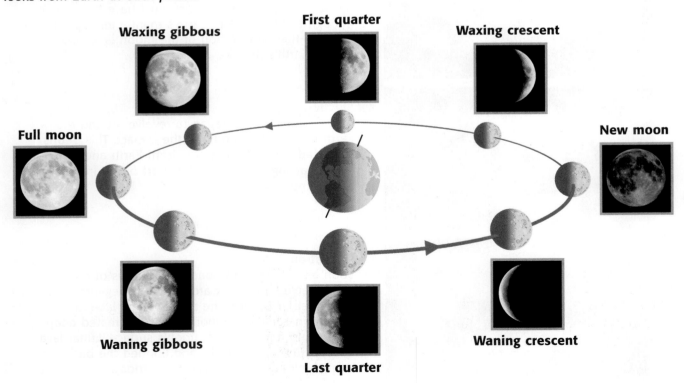

Waxing gibbous

First quarter

Waxing crescent

Full moon

New moon

Waning gibbous

Last quarter

Waning crescent

Solar eclipse

NEVER look directly at the sun! You can permanently damage your eyes.

Eclipses

When the shadow of one celestial body falls on another, an **eclipse** occurs. A *solar eclipse* happens when the moon comes between Earth and the sun and the shadow of the moon falls on part of Earth. A *lunar eclipse* happens when Earth comes between the sun and the moon and the shadow of Earth falls on the moon.

Solar Eclipses

Because the moon's orbit is elliptical, the distance between the moon and the Earth changes. During an *annular eclipse*, the moon is farther from the Earth. The disk of the moon does not completely cover the disk of the sun. A thin ring of the sun shows around the moon's outer edge. When the moon is closer to the Earth, the moon appears to be the same size as the sun. During a *total solar eclipse*, the disk of the moon completely covers the disk of the sun, as shown in **Figure 4.**

Reading Check Describe what happens during a solar eclipse.

Figure 4 *On the left is a diagram of the positions of the Earth and the moon during a solar eclipse. On the right is a picture of the sun's outer atmosphere, or corona, which is visible only when the entire disk of the sun is blocked by the moon.*

eclipse an event in which the shadow of one celestial body falls on another

Clever Insight

1. Cut out a circle of **heavy, white paper.** This circle will represent Earth.
2. Find **two spherical objects** and **several other objects** of different shapes.
3. Hold up each object in front of a **lamp** (which represents the sun) so that the object's shadow falls on the white paper circle.
4. Rotate your objects in all directions, and record the shapes of the shadows that the objects make.
5. Which objects always cast a curved shadow?

Lunar eclipse

Figure 5 *On the left, you can see that the moon can have a reddish color during a lunar eclipse. On the right, you can see the positions of Earth and the moon during a lunar eclipse.*

Lunar Eclipses

As shown in **Figure 5,** the view during a lunar eclipse is spectacular. Earth's atmosphere acts like a lens and bends some of the sunlight into the Earth's shadow. When sunlight hits the particles in the atmosphere, blue light is filtered out. As a result, most of the remaining light that lights the moon is red.

The Tilted Orbit of the Moon

You may be wondering why you don't see solar and lunar eclipses every month. The reason is that the moon's orbit around Earth is tilted—by about 5°—relative to the orbit of Earth around the sun. This tilt is enough to place the moon out of Earth's shadow for most full moons and Earth out of the moon's shadow for most new moons.

✓ Reading Check Explain why you don't see solar and lunar eclipses every month.

The Moons of Other Planets

The moons of the other planets range in size from very small to as large as terrestrial planets. All of the gas giants have multiple moons, and scientists are still discovering new moons. Some moons have very elongated, or elliptical, orbits, and some moons even orbit their planet backward! Many of the very small moons may be captured asteroids. As scientists are learning from recent space missions, moons may be some of the most bizarre and interesting places in the solar system!

The Moons of Mars

Mars's two moons, Phobos and Deimos, are small, oddly shaped satellites. Both moons are very dark. Their surface materials are much like those of some asteroids—large, rocky bodies in space. Scientists think that these two moons are asteroids caught by Mars's gravity.

The Moons of Jupiter

Jupiter has dozens of moons. The four largest moons—Ganymede, Callisto, Io, and Europa—were discovered in 1610 by Galileo. They are known as the *Galilean satellites*. The largest moon, Ganymede, is even larger than the planet Mercury! Many of the smaller moons probably are captured asteroids.

The Galilean satellite closest to Jupiter is Io, a truly bizarre world. Io is caught in a gravitational tug of war between Jupiter and Io's nearest neighbor, the moon Europa. This constant tugging stretches Io a little and causes it to heat up. As a result, Io is the most volcanically active body in the solar system!

Recent pictures of the moon Europa, shown in **Figure 6,** support the idea that liquid water may lie beneath the moon's icy surface. This idea makes many scientists wonder if life could have evolved in the underground oceans of Europa.

Figure 6 *Europa, Jupiter's fourth largest moon, might have liquid water beneath the moon's icy surface.*

The Moons of Saturn

Like Jupiter, Saturn has dozens of moons. Most of these moons are small bodies that are made mostly of frozen water but contain some rocky material. The largest satellite, Titan, was discovered in 1655 by Christiaan Huygens. In 1980, the *Voyager 1* spacecraft flew past Titan and discovered a hazy orange atmosphere, as shown in **Figure 7.** Earth's early atmosphere may have been much like Titan's is now. In 1997, NASA launched the *Cassini* spacecraft to study Saturn and its moons, including Titan. By studying Titan, scientists hope to learn more about how life began on Earth.

✓ Reading Check How can scientists learn more about how life began on Earth by studying Titan?

Figure 7 *Titan is Saturn's largest moon.*

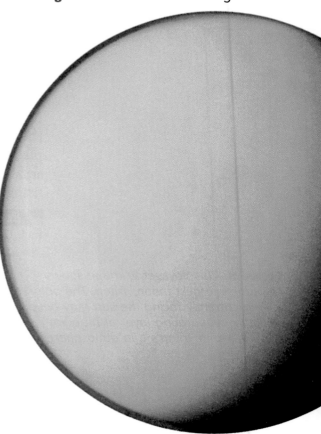

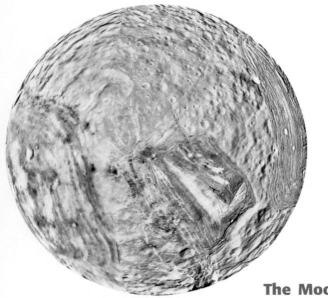

Figure 8 *This* Voyager 2 *image shows Miranda, the most unusual moon of Uranus. Its patchwork terrain indicates that it has had a violent history.*

The Moons of Uranus

Uranus has several moons. Like the moons of Saturn, Uranus's largest moons are made of ice and rock and are heavily cratered. The small moon Miranda, shown in **Figure 8,** has some of the strangest features in the solar system. Miranda's surface has smooth, cratered plains as well as regions that have grooves and cliffs. Scientists think that Miranda may have been hit and broken apart in the past. Gravity pulled the pieces together again, leaving a patchwork surface.

The Moons of Neptune

Neptune has several known moons, only one of which is large. This large moon, Triton, is shown in **Figure 9.** It revolves around the planet in a *retrograde,* or "backward," orbit. This orbit suggests that Triton may have been captured by Neptune's gravity. Triton has a very thin atmosphere made mostly of nitrogen gas. Triton's surface is mostly frozen nitrogen and methane. *Voyager 2* images reveal that Triton is geologically active. "Ice volcanoes," or geysers, eject nitrogen gas high into the atmosphere. The other moons of Neptune are small, rocky worlds much like the smaller moons of Saturn and Jupiter.

The Moons of Pluto

Although Pluto is not considered a planet, it does have at least three moons. Charon is the largest moon and is almost half the size of Pluto. Charon's period of revolution is the same as Pluto's period of rotation—about 6.4 days. So, one side of Pluto always faces Charon. In other words, if you stood on the surface of Pluto, Charon would always occupy the same place in the sky. Pluto's other moons, Hydra and Nix, are much smaller. These moons were discovered in 2005 by astronomers using the *Hubble Space Telescope.*

Reading Check Why does the same side of Pluto always face Charon?

Figure 9 *This* Voyager 2 *image shows Neptune's largest moon, Triton. The polar icecap currently facing the sun may have a slowly evaporating layer of nitrogen ice, adding to Triton's thin atmosphere.*

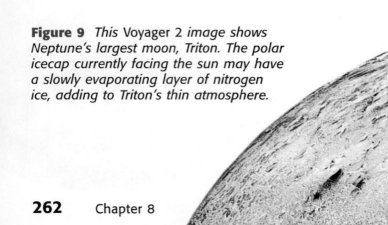

SECTION Review

Summary

- Scientists reason that the moon formed from the debris that was created after a large body collided with Earth.
- As the moon revolves around Earth, the amount of sunlight on the side of the moon changes. Because the amount of sunlight on the side of the moon changes, the moon's appearance from Earth changes. These changes in appearance are the phases of the moon.
- A solar eclipse happens when the shadow of the moon falls on Earth.

- A lunar eclipse happens when the shadow of Earth falls on the moon.
- Mars has 2 moons: Phobos and Deimos.
- Jupiter has dozens of moons. Ganymede, Io, Callisto, and Europa are the largest.
- Saturn has dozens of moons. Titan is the largest.
- Uranus has several moons.
- Neptune has several moons. Triton is the largest.
- Pluto has 3 known moons.

Using Key Terms

Complete each of the following sentences by choosing the correct term from the word bank.

satellite   eclipse

1. A(n) _____, or a body that revolves around a larger body, can be either artificial or natural.

2. A(n) _____ occurs when the shadow of one body in space falls on another body.

Understanding Key Ideas

3. Which of the following is a Galilean satellite?
   a. Phobos
   b. Deimos
   c. Ganymede
   d. Charon

4. Describe the current theory for the origin of Earth's moon.

5. What is the difference between a solar eclipse and a lunar eclipse?

6. What causes the phases of Earth's moon?

Critical Thinking

7. **Analyzing Methods** How can astronomers use the age of a lunar rock to estimate the age of the surface of a planet such as Mercury?

8. **Identifying Relationships** Charon stays in the same place in Pluto's sky, but the moon moves across Earth's sky. What causes this difference?

Interpreting Graphics

Use the diagram below to answer the questions that follow.

9. What type of eclipse is shown in the diagram?

10. Describe what is happening in the diagram.

11. Make a sketch of the type of eclipse that is not shown in the diagram.

SCILINKS®

NSTA
Developed and maintained by the National Science Teachers Association

For a variety of links related to this chapter, go to www.scilinks.org

Topic: Moons of Other Planets
SciLinks code: HSM0993

Small Bodies in the Solar System

Imagine you are traveling in a spacecraft to explore the edge of our solar system. You see several small bodies, as well as the planets and their satellites, moving through space.

The solar system contains not only planets and moons but other small bodies, including comets, asteroids, and meteoroids. Scientists study these objects to learn about the composition of the solar system.

Comets

A small body of ice, rock, and cosmic dust loosely packed together is called a **comet**. Some scientists refer to comets as "dirty snowballs" because of their composition. Comets formed in the cold, outer solar system. Nothing much has happened to comets since the birth of the solar system 4.6 billion years ago. Comets are probably left over from the time when the planets formed. As a result, each comet is a sample of the early solar system. Scientists want to learn more about comets to piece together the history of our solar system.

Comet Tails

When a comet passes close enough to the sun, solar radiation heats the ice so that the comet gives off gas and dust in the form of a long tail, as shown in **Figure 1.** Sometimes, a comet has two tails—an *ion tail* and a *dust tail*. The ion tail is made of electrically charged particles called *ions*. The solid center of a comet is called its *nucleus*. Comet nuclei can range in size from less than half a kilometer to more than 100 km in diameter.

What You Will Learn

● Explain why comets, asteroids, and meteoroids are important to the study of the formation of the solar system.
● Describe the similarities of and differences between asteroids and meteoroids.
● Explain how cosmic impacts may affect life on Earth.

Vocabulary

comet	meteoroid
asteroid	meteorite
asteroid belt	meteor

READING STRATEGY

Discussion Read this section silently. Write down questions that you have about this section. Discuss your questions in a small group.

Figure 1 *This image shows the physical features of a comet when it is close to the sun. The nucleus of a comet is hidden by brightly lit gases and dust.*

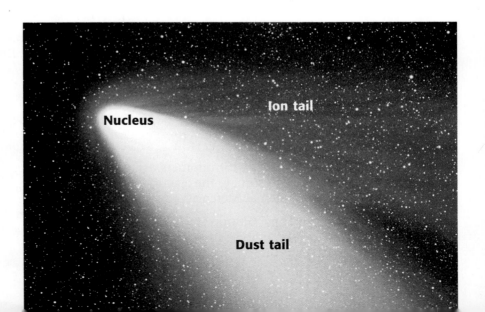

Nucleus

Ion tail

Dust tail

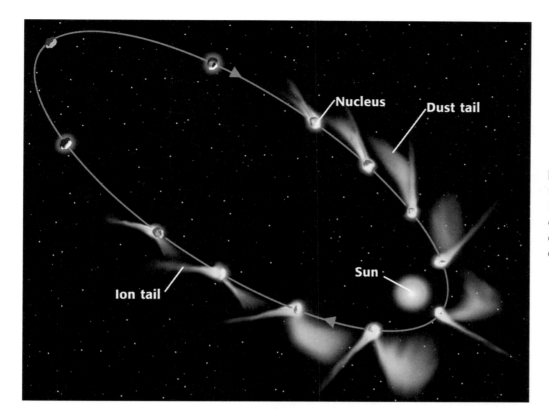

Figure 2 *Comets have very elongated orbits. When a comet gets close to the sun, the comet can develop one or two tails.*

Comet Orbits

The orbits of all bodies that move around the sun are ellipses. *Ellipses* are circles that are somewhat stretched out of shape. The orbits of most planets are close to perfect circles, but the orbits of comets are very elongated.

Notice in **Figure 2** that a comet's ion tail always points away from the sun. The reason is that the ion tail is blown away from the sun by *solar wind*, which is also made of ions. The dust tail tends to follow the comet's orbit around the sun. Dust tails do not always point away from the sun. When a comet is close to the sun, its tail can extend millions of kilometers through space!

Comet Origins

Where do comets come from? Many scientists think that comets come from the Oort (AWRT) cloud, a spherical region that surrounds the solar system. When the gravity of a passing planet or star disturbs part of this cloud, comets can be pulled toward the sun. Another recently discovered region where comets exist is the Kuiper (KIE puhr) belt, which is the region outside the orbit of Neptune.

✓ **Reading Check** From which two regions do comets come? (*See the Appendix for answers to Reading Checks*.)

comet a small body of ice, rock, and cosmic dust that follows an elliptical orbit around the sun and that gives off gas and dust in the form of a tail as it passes close to the sun

CONNECTION TO Language Arts

WRITING SKILL **Interplanetary Journalist** In 1994, the world watched in awe as parts of the comet Shoemaker-Levy 9 collided with Jupiter, which caused enormous explosions. Imagine you were an interplanetary journalist who traveled through space to observe the comet during this time. Write an article describing your adventure.

Asteroids

asteroid a small, rocky object that orbits the sun, usually in a band between the orbits of Mars and Jupiter

asteroid belt the region of the solar system that is between the orbits of Mars and Jupiter and in which most asteroids orbit

Small, rocky bodies that revolve around the sun are called **asteroids.** They range in size from a few meters to more than 900 km in diameter. Asteroids have irregular shapes, although some of the larger ones are spherical. Most asteroids orbit the sun in the asteroid belt. The **asteroid belt** is a wide region between the orbits of Mars and Jupiter. Like comets, asteroids are thought to be material left over from the formation of the solar system.

Types of Asteroids

The composition of asteroids varies depending on where they are located within the asteroid belt. In the outermost region of the asteroid belt, asteroids have dark reddish brown to black surfaces. This coloring may indicate that the asteroids are rich in organic material. Asteroids that have dark gray surfaces are rich in carbon. In the innermost part of the asteroid belt are light gray asteroids that have either a stony or metallic composition. **Figure 3** shows two asteroids: Hektor and Vesta.

Figure 3 The Asteroid Belt

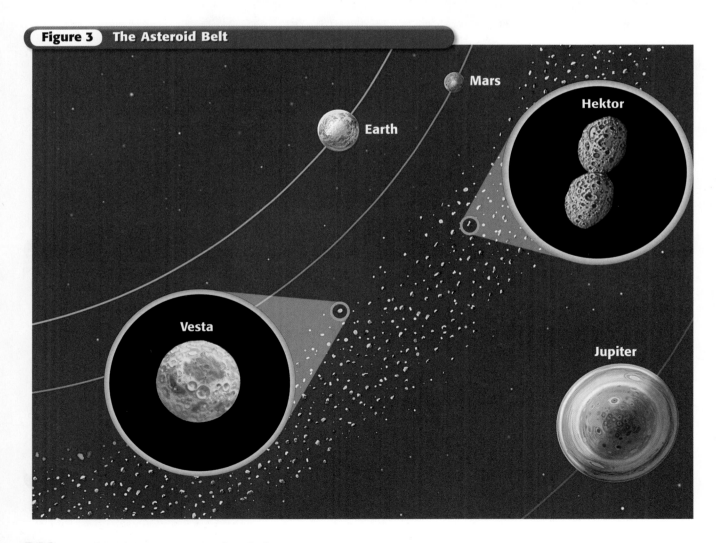

Meteoroids

Meteoroids are similar to but much smaller than asteroids. A **meteoroid** is a small, rocky body that revolves around the sun. Most meteoroids are probably pieces of asteroids. A meteoroid that enters Earth's atmosphere and strikes the ground is called a **meteorite.** As a meteoroid falls into Earth's atmosphere, the meteoroid moves so fast that its surface melts. As the meteoroid burns up, it gives off an enormous amount of light and thermal energy. From the ground, you see a spectacular streak of light, or a shooting star. A **meteor** is the bright streak of light caused by a meteoroid or comet dust burning up in the atmosphere.

meteoroid a relatively small, rocky body that travels through space

meteorite a meteoroid that reaches the Earth's surface without burning up completely

meteor a bright streak of light that results when a meteoroid burns up in the Earth's atmosphere

Meteor Showers

Many of the meteors that we see come from very small (dust-sized to pebble-sized) rocks. Even so, meteors can be seen on almost any night if you are far enough away from a city to avoid the glare of its lights. At certain times of the year, you can see large numbers of meteors, as shown in **Figure 4.** These events are called *meteor showers*. Meteor showers happen when Earth passes through the dusty debris that comets leave behind.

Types of Meteorites

Like their asteroid relatives, meteorites have different compositions. The three major types of meteorites—stony, metallic, and stony-iron meteorites—are shown in **Figure 5.** Many of the stony meteorites probably come from carbon-rich asteroids. Stony meteorites may contain organic materials and water. Scientists use meteorites to study the early solar system. Like comets and asteroids, meteorites are some of the building blocks of planets.

Figure 4 *Meteors are the streaks of light caused by meteoroids as they burn up in Earth's atmosphere.*

✓ Reading Check What are the major types of meteorites?

Figure 5 **Three Major Types of Meteorites**

Stony meteorite rocky material	Metallic meteorite iron and nickel	Stony-iron meteorite rocky material, iron, and nickel

The Role of Impacts in the Solar System

An impact happens when an object in space collides with another object in space. Often, the result of such a collision is an impact crater. Many planets and moons have visible impact craters. In fact, several planets and moons have many more impact craters than Earth does. Planets and moons that do not have atmospheres have more impact craters than do planets and moons that have atmospheres.

Look at **Figure 6.** Earth's moon has many more impact craters than the Earth does because the moon has no atmosphere to slow objects down. Fewer objects strike Earth because Earth's atmosphere acts as a shield. Smaller objects burn up before they ever reach the surface. Also, most craters left on Earth are no longer visible because of weathering, erosion, and tectonic activity.

Future Impacts on Earth?

Most objects that come close to Earth are small and usually burn up in the atmosphere. However, larger objects are more likely to strike Earth's surface. Scientists estimate that impacts that are powerful enough to cause a natural disaster might happen once every few thousand years. An impact that is large enough to cause a global catastrophe is estimated to happen once every few hundred thousand years, on average.

Reading Check How often do large objects strike Earth?

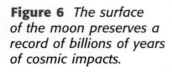

CONNECTION TO Biology

WRITING SKILL **Mass Extinctions** Throughout Earth's history, there have been times when large numbers of species suddenly became extinct. Many scientists think that these mass extinctions may have been caused by impacts of large objects on Earth. However, other scientists are not so sure. Use the Internet or another source to research this idea. In your **science journal,** write a paragraph describing the different theories scientists have for past mass extinctions.

Figure 6 *The surface of the moon preserves a record of billions of years of cosmic impacts.*

The Torino Scale

The Torino scale is a system that allows scientists to rate the hazard level of an object moving toward Earth. The object is carefully observed and then assigned a number from the scale. The scale ranges from 0 to 10. Zero indicates that the object has a very small chance of striking Earth. Ten indicates that the object will definitely strike Earth and cause a global disaster. The Torino scale is also color coded. White represents 0, and green represents 1. White and green objects rarely strike Earth. Yellow represents 2, 3, and 4 and indicates a higher chance that objects will hit Earth. Orange, which represents 5, 6, and 7, refers to objects highly likely to hit Earth. Red refers to objects that will definitely hit Earth.

SECTION Review

Summary

- Studying comets, asteroids, and meteoroids can help scientists understand more about the formation of the solar system.

- Asteroids are small bodies that orbit the sun. Meteoroids are similar to but smaller than asteroids. Most meteoroids come from asteroids.

- Most objects that collide with Earth burn up in the atmosphere. Large impacts, however, may cause a global catastrophe.

Using Key Terms

For each pair of terms, explain how the meanings of the terms differ.

1. *comet* and *asteroid*

2. *meteor* and *meteorite*

Understanding Key Ideas

3. Which of the following is NOT a type of meteorite?
   a. stony meteorite
   b. rocky-iron meteorite
   c. stony-iron meteorite
   d. metallic meteorite

4. Why is the study of comets, asteroids, and meteoroids important in understanding the formation of the solar system?

5. Why do a comet's two tails often point in different directions?

6. How can a cosmic impact affect life on Earth?

7. What is the difference between an asteroid and a meteoroid?

8. Where is the asteroid belt located?

9. What is the Torino scale?

10. Describe why we see several impact craters on the moon but few on Earth.

Math Skills

11. The diameter of comet A's nucleus is 55 km. If the diameter of comet B's nucleus is 30% larger than comet A's nucleus, what is the diameter of comet B's nucleus?

Critical Thinking

12. **Expressing Opinions** Do you think the government should spend money on programs to search for asteroids and comets that have Earth-crossing orbits? Explain.

13. **Making Inferences** What is the likelihood that scientists will discover an object belonging in the red category of the Torino scale in the next 500 years? Explain your answer.

Inquiry Lab

Create a Calendar

Imagine that you live in the first colony on Mars. You have been trying to follow the Earth calendar, but it just isn't working anymore. Mars takes almost 2 Earth years to revolve around the sun—almost 687 Earth days to be exact! That means that there are only two Martian seasons for every Earth calendar year. On Mars, in one Earth year, you get winter and spring, but the next year, you get only summer and fall! And Martian days are longer than Earth days. Mars takes 24.6 Earth hours to rotate on its axis. Although they are similar, Earth days and Martian days just don't match. You need a new calendar!

OBJECTIVES

Create a calendar based on the Martian cycles of rotation and revolution.

Describe why it is useful to have a calendar that matches the cycles of the planet on which you live.

MATERIALS

- calculator (optional)
- marker
- pencils, assorted colors
- poster board
- ruler, metric

Ask a Question

1 How can I create a calendar based on the Martian cycles of rotation and revolution that includes months, weeks, and days?

Form a Hypothesis

2 Write a few sentences that answer your question.

Test the Hypothesis

3 Use the following formulas to determine the number of Martian days in a Martian year:

$$\frac{687 \text{ Earth days}}{1 \text{ Martian year}} \times \frac{24 \text{ Earth hours}}{1 \text{ Earth day}} = \text{ Earth hours per Martian year}$$

$$\text{Earth hours per Martian year} \times \frac{1 \text{ Martian day}}{24.6 \text{ Earth hours}} = \text{ Martian days per Martian year}$$

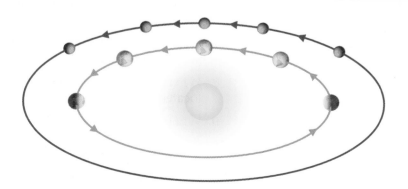

4 Decide how to divide your calendar into a system of Martian months, weeks, and days. Will you have a leap day, a leap week, a leap month, or a leap year? How often will it occur?

5 Choose names for the months and days of your calendar. Explain why you chose each name. If you have time, explain how you would number the Martian years. For instance, would the first year correspond to a certain Earth year?

6 Follow your design to create your own calendar for Mars. Construct your calendar by using a computer to help organize your data. Draw the calendar on your piece of poster board. Make sure it is brightly colored and easy to follow.

7 Present your calendar to the class. Explain how you chose your months, weeks, and days.

Analyze the Results

1 **Analyzing Results** What advantages does your calendar design have? Are there any disadvantages to your design?

2 **Classifying** Which student or group created the most original calendar? Which design was the most useful? Explain.

3 **Analyzing Results** What might you do to improve your calendar?

Draw Conclusions

4 **Evaluating Models** Take a class vote to decide which design should be chosen as the new calendar for Mars. Why was this calendar chosen? How did it differ from the other designs?

5 **Drawing Conclusions** Why is it useful to have a calendar that matches the cycles of the planet on which you live?

Chapter Review

USING KEY TERMS

For each pair of terms, explain how the meanings of the terms differ.

1 *terrestrial planet* and *gas giant*

2 *asteroid* and *comet*

3 *meteor* and *meteorite*

Complete each of the following sentences by choosing the correct term from the word bank.

astronomical unit	meteorite
meteoroid	prograde
retrograde	satellite

4 The average distance between the sun and Earth is 1 ___.

5 A small rock in space is called a(n) ___.

6 When viewed from above its north pole, a body that moves in a counter-clockwise direction is said to have ___ rotation.

7 A(n) ___ is a natural or artificial body that revolves around a planet.

UNDERSTANDING KEY IDEAS

Multiple Choice

8 Of the following, which is the largest body?

a. the moon

b. Pluto

c. Mercury

d. Ganymede

9 Which of the following planets have retrograde rotation?

a. the terrestrial planets

b. the gas giants

c. Mercury and Venus

d. Venus and Uranus

10 Which of the following planets does NOT have any moons?

a. Mercury

b. Mars

c. Uranus

d. None of the above

11 Why can liquid water NOT exist on the surface of Mars?

a. The temperature is too high.

b. Liquid water once existed there.

c. The gravity of Mars is too weak.

d. The atmospheric pressure is too low.

Short Answer

12 List the names of the planets in the order the planets orbit the sun.

13 Describe three ways in which the inner planets are different from the outer planets.

14 What are the gas giants? How are the gas giants different from the terrestrial planets?

15 What is the difference between asteroids and meteoroids?

16 What is the difference between a planet's period of rotation and period of revolution?

17 Explain the difference between pro-grade rotation and retrograde rotation.

18 Which characteristics of Earth make it suitable for life?

19 Describe the current theory for the origin of Earth's moon.

20 What causes the phases of the moon?

CRITICAL THINKING

21 **Concept Mapping** Use the following terms to create a concept map: *solar system, terrestrial planets, gas giants, moons, comets, asteroids,* and *meteoroids.*

22 **Applying Concepts** Even though we haven't yet retrieved any rock samples from Mercury's surface for radiometric dating, scientists know that the surface of Mercury is much older than that of Earth. How do scientists know this?

23 **Making Inferences** Where in the solar system might scientists search for life, and why?

24 **Analyzing Ideas** Is the far side of the moon always dark? Explain your answer.

25 **Predicting Consequences** If scientists could somehow bring Europa as close to the sun as the Earth is, 1 AU, how do you think Europa would be affected?

26 **Identifying Relationships** How did variations in the orbit of Uranus help scientists discover Neptune?

INTERPRETING GRAPHICS

The graph below shows density versus mass for Earth, Uranus, and Neptune. Mass is given in Earth masses—the mass of Earth is equal to 1 Earth mass. The relative volumes for the planets are shown by the size of each circle. Use the graph below to answer the questions that follow.

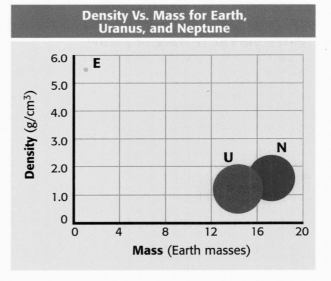

Density Vs. Mass for Earth, Uranus, and Neptune

27 Which planet is denser, Uranus or Neptune? How can you tell?

28 You can see that although Earth has the smallest mass, it has the highest density of the three planets. How can Earth be the densest of the three when Uranus and Neptune have so much more mass than Earth does?

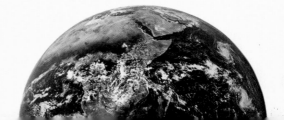

Multiple Choice

1. **Why do scientists think that liquid water may have once existed on Mars?**

   A. Surface features on Mars suggest erosion and deposition by water.

   B. Mars had an atmosphere that contained clouds.

   C. Mars has two polar icecaps that contain frozen carbon dioxide.

   D. Fossils of marine organisms have been discovered on the surface of Mars.

2. **As part of a field investigation, Mercedes learns that there are more craters on the surface of planet A than there are on the surface of planet B. Both planets have about the same mass, and neither planet has an atmosphere. Which of the following is a valid conclusion about the planets?**

   A. Planet A has had several recent lava flows.

   B. Planet B has a much stronger gravitational field than planet A does.

   C. Planet A has an older surface than planet B does.

   D. Planet B lies in the path of an asteroid belt.

3. **Scientists observe a planet in a distant galaxy. This planet appears to have similar features to Earth. Which feature would the scientists be most interested in if they were looking for life on this planet?**

   A. thick atmosphere

   B. liquid water

   C. active volcanoes

   D. long day length

Use the illustrations below to answer questions 4–5.

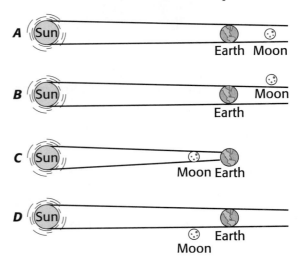

4. **Mara made the illustrations above as part of a field investigation of moon phases and eclipses. Which illustration depicts a lunar eclipse?**

   A. illustration A

   B. illustration B

   C. illustration C

   D. illustration D

5. **Which of Mara's illustrations depicts a solar eclipse?**

   A. illustration A

   B. illustration B

   C. illustration C

   D. illustration D

6. Which of the following would travel the farthest during one revolution around the sun?

 A. the planet Mars

 B. the asteroid Vesta

 C. the moon Titan

 D. the comet Wild 2

7. The distance from Earth to the sun is 1 astronomical unit (AU), or 8.3 light-minutes. If Saturn is located about 9.4 AU away from the sun, how many light-hours from the sun is it?

 A. 0.3 light-hours

 B. 1.3 light-hours

 C. 17.7 light-hours

 D. 78.0 light-hours

Use the diagram below to answer question 8.

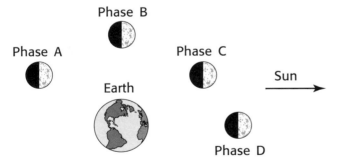

Phase B

Phase A

Phase C

Earth

Sun

Phase D

8. The diagram above shows different phases of the moon in relation to Earth and the sun. In which phase will an observer on Earth see a crescent moon?

 A. phase A

 B. phase B

 C. phase C

 D. phase D

9. Which of the following events takes the longest period of time to occur?

 A. Earth orbits the sun once.

 B. The moon orbits Earth twice.

 C. Earth rotates on its axis five times.

 D. Eleven full moons are seen from Earth.

10. The full moon occurs on Wednesday, January 3rd. On what day could a lunar eclipse occur during January?

 A. Wednesday the 3rd

 B. Thursday the 11th

 C. Thursday the 18th

 D. Thursday the 25th

Open Response

11. The moon is much smaller than the sun. Explain why the sun and the moon appear to be approximately the same size when they are viewed from Earth.

12. Carrie explained to her little brother that a solar eclipse happens when the moon blocks the sun. Was she correct? Explain your answer.

Science in Action

Science Fiction

"The Mad Moon" by Stanley Weinbaum

The third largest moon of Jupiter, called Io, can be a hard place to live. Grant Calthorpe is finding this out the hard way. Although living comfortably is possible in the small cities at the polar regions of Io, Grant has to spend most of his time in the moon's hot and humid jungles. Grant treks into the jungles of Io to gather ferva leaves so that they can be converted into useful medications for humans. During Grant's quest, he encounters loonies and slinkers, and he has to avoid blancha, a kind of tropical fever that causes hallucinations, weakness, and vicious headaches. Without proper medication a person with blancha can go mad or even die. In "The Mad Moon," you'll discover a dozen adventures with Grant Calthorpe as he struggles to stay alive—and sane.

Language Arts ACTiViTY

WRITING SKILL Read "The Mad Moon" by Stanley Weinbaum. Write a short story describing the adventures that you would have on Io if you were chosen as Grant Calthorpe's assistant.

HOLT ANTHOLOGY OF
Science Fiction

HOLT, RINEHART AND WINSTON

Scientific Debate

Is Pluto a Planet?

Technology has allowed scientists to discover many objects beyond the orbit of Neptune. Some of those objects are the same size as Pluto or are larger than Pluto. Since its discovery in 1930, Pluto has been included as one of the nine planets in our solar system. However, because these objects are similar to Pluto, some scientists thought the objects would all have to be classified as planets. As a result, astronomers around the world began to debate the definition of a planet. The International Astronomical Union (IAU) met in 2006 and voted on a definition for *planet*. Because Pluto has not cleared the debris from the area around its orbital path, it does not meet the full requirements of the definition. Therefore, Pluto was reclassified as a *dwarf planet*. Some astronomers disagree with this change in Pluto's status. As scientists continue to debate the definition of *planet*, it is possible that in the future, Pluto may be considered a planet again!

Math ACTiViTY

How many more kilometers is Earth's diameter compared to Pluto's diameter if Earth's diameter is 12,756 km and Pluto's diameter is 2,390 km?

Adriana C. Ocampo

Planetary Geologist Sixty-five million years ago, in what is now Mexico, a giant meteor at least six miles wide struck Earth. The meteor made a hole nine miles deep and over 100 miles wide. The meteor sent billions of tons of dust into Earth's atmosphere. This dust formed thick clouds. After forming, these clouds may have left the planet in total darkness for six months, and the temperature near freezing for ten years. Some scientists think that this meteor crash and its effect on the Earth's climate led to the extinction of the dinosaurs. Adriana Ocampo studies the site in Mexico made by the crater known as the Chicxulub (cheeks OO loob) impact crater. Ocampo is a planetary geologist and has been interested in space exploration since she was young. Ocampo's specialty is studying "impact craters." "Impact craters are formed when an asteroid or a comet collides with the Earth or any other terrestrial planet," explains Ocampo. Ocampo visits crater sites around the world to collect data. She also uses computers to create models of how the impact affected the planet. Ocampo has worked for NASA and has helped plan space exploration missions to Mars, Jupiter, Saturn, and Mercury. Ocampo currently works for the European Space Agency (ESA) and is part of the team getting ready to launch the next spacecraft that will go to Mars.

Social Studies ACTIVITY

Research information about impact craters. Find the different locations around the world where impact craters have been found. Make a world map that highlights these locations.

The circle on the map shows the site in Mexico made by the Chicxulub impact crater.

To learn more about these Science in Action topics, visit go.hrw.com and type in the keyword **HZ5FAMF.**

Current Science

Check out Current Science® articles related to this chapter by visiting go.hrw.com. Just type in the keyword HZ5CS21.

UNIT 3

TIMELINE

Cells

Cells are everywhere. Even though most cells can't be seen with the naked eye, they make up every living thing. Your body alone contains trillions of cells.

In this unit, you will learn about cells. You will learn the difference between animal cells, plant cells, and bacterial cells. You will learn about the parts of a cell and will see how they work together.

Since cells were discovered in 1665, we have learned a lot about cells and the way they work. This timeline shows some of the discoveries that have been made along the way, but there is still a lot to learn about the fascinating world of cells!

1620
The Pilgrims settle Plymouth Colony.

1665
Robert Hooke discovers cells after observing a thin piece of cork under a microscope.

1861
The American Civil War begins.

1952
Martha Chase and Alfred Hershey demonstrate that DNA is the hereditary material.

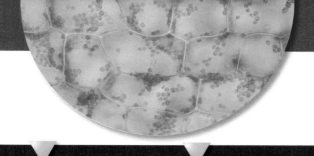

1831
Robert Brown discovers the nucleus in a plant cell.

1838
Matthias Schleiden discovers that all plant tissue is made up of cells.

1839
Theodor Schwann shows that all animal tissue is made up of cells.

1858
Rudolf Virchow determines that all cells are produced from cells.

1873
Anton Schneider observes and accurately describes mitosis.

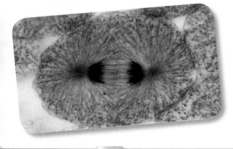

1937
The Golden Gate Bridge opens in San Francisco.

1941
George Beadle and Edward Tatum discover that genes control the chemical reactions in cells by directing protein production.

1956
The manufacture of protein in the cell is found to occur in ribosomes.

1971
Lynn Margulis proposes the endosymbiotic theory of the origin of cell organelles.

1997
A sheep named Dolly becomes the first animal to be cloned from a single body cell.

2002
Scientists test a cancer vaccine that can be given orally. Tests on mice lead scientists to be hopeful that the vaccine can be tested on humans.

It's Alive!! Or Is It?

The Big Idea

Living things must be able to obtain and use resources, grow, reproduce, and maintain stable internal conditions.

About the Photo

What does it mean to say something is *alive*? Machines have some of the characteristics of living things, but machines do not have all of these characteristics. This amazing robot insect can respond to changes in its environment. It can walk over obstacles. It can perform some tasks. But it is still not alive. How is it like and unlike a living insect?

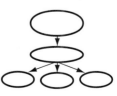

PRE-READING ACTIVITY

Graphic Organizer

Concept Map Before you read the chapter, create the graphic organizer entitled "Concept Map" described in the **Study Skills** section of the Appendix. As you read the chapter, fill in the concept map with details about the characteristics of living things.

Lights On!

In this activity, you will work with a partner to see how eyes react to changes in light.

Procedure

1. Observe a classmate's eyes in a lighted room. Note the size of your partner's pupils.

2. Have your partner keep both eyes open. Ask him or her to cover each one with a cupped hand. Wait about one minute.

3. Instruct your partner to pull away both hands quickly. Immediately, look at your partner's pupils. Record what happens.

4. Now, briefly shine a **flashlight** into your partner's eyes. Record how this affects your partner's pupils. **Caution:** Do not use the sun as the source of the light.

5. Change places with your partner, and repeat steps 1–4 so that your partner can observe your eyes.

Analysis

1. How did your partner's eyes respond to changes in the level of light?

2. How did changes in the size of your pupils affect your vision? What does this tell you about why pupils change size?

It's Alive!! Or Is It?   **281**

Characteristics of Living Things

What You Will Learn

● Describe the six characteristics of living things.

● Describe how organisms maintain stable internal conditions.

● Explain how asexual reproduction differs from sexual reproduction.

Vocabulary

cell
stimulus
homeostasis
sexual
  reproduction
asexual
  reproduction
heredity
metabolism

READING STRATEGY

Prediction Guide Before reading this section, write the title of each heading in this section. Next, under each heading, write what you think you will learn.

While outside one day, you notice something strange in the grass. It's slimy, bright yellow, and about the size of a dime. You have no idea what it is. Is it a plant part that fell from a tree? Is it alive? How can you tell?

An amazing variety of living things exists on Earth. But living things are all alike in several ways. What does a dog have in common with a bacterium? What does a fish have in common with a mushroom? And what do *you* have in common with a slimy, yellow blob, known as a *slime mold*? Read on to find out about the six characteristics that all organisms share.

Living Things Have Cells

All living things, such as those in **Figure 1,** are composed of one or more cells. A **cell** is a membrane-covered structure that contains all of the materials necessary for life. The membrane that surrounds a cell separates the contents of the cell from the cell's environment. Most cells are too small to be seen with the naked eye.

Some organisms are made up of trillions of cells. In an organism with many cells, different kinds of cells perform specialized functions. For example, your nerve cells transport signals, and your muscle cells are specialized for movement.

In an organism made up of only one cell, different parts of the cell perform different functions. For example, a one-celled paramecium needs to eat. So, some parts of the cell take in food. Other parts of the cell break down the food. Still other parts of the cell excrete wastes.

Figure 1 *Some organisms, such as the protists on the right, are made of one cell or a few cells. The monkeys on the left are made up of trillions of cells.*

Figure 2 *The touch of an insect triggers the Venus' flytrap to close its leaves quickly.*

Living Things Sense and Respond to Change

All organisms have the ability to sense change in their environment and to respond to that change. When your pupils are exposed to light, they respond by becoming smaller. A change that affects the activity of the organism is called a **stimulus** (plural, *stimuli*).

Stimuli can be chemicals, gravity, light, sounds, hunger, or anything that causes organisms to respond in some way. A gentle touch causes a response in the plant shown in **Figure 2.**

Homeostasis

Even though an organism's outside environment may change, conditions inside an organism's body must stay the same. Many chemical reactions keep an organism alive. These reactions can take place only when conditions are exactly right, so an organism must maintain stable internal conditions to survive. The maintenance of a stable internal environment is called **homeostasis** (HOH mee OH STAY sis).

Responding to External Changes

Your body maintains a temperature of about 37°C. When you get hot, your body responds by sweating. When you get cold, your muscles twitch in an attempt to warm you up. This twitching is called *shivering*. Whether you are sweating or shivering, your body is trying to return itself to normal.

Other animals also need to have stable internal conditions. But many cannot respond the way you do. They have to control their body temperature by moving from one environment to another. If they get too warm, they move to the shade. If they get too cool, they move out into the sunlight.

> **Reading Check** How do some animals maintain homeostasis?
> (*See the Appendix for answers to Reading Checks.*)

cell the smallest unit that can perform all life processes; cells are covered by a membrane and have DNA and cytoplasm

stimulus anything that causes a reaction or change in an organism or any part of an organism

homeostasis the maintenance of a constant internal state in a changing environment

---

CONNECTION TO Physics

Temperature Regulation
Your body temperature does not change very much throughout the day. When you exercise, you sweat. Sweating helps keep your body temperature stable. As your sweat evaporates, your skin cools. Given this information, why do you think you feel cooler faster when you stand in front of a fan?

Figure 3 *Like most animals, bears produce offspring by sexual reproduction.*

Figure 4 *The hydra can reproduce asexually by forming buds that break off and grow into new individuals.*

sexual reproduction reproduction in which the sex cells from two parents unite, producing offspring that share traits from both parents

asexual reproduction reproduction that does not involve the union of sex cells and in which one parent produces offspring identical to itself

heredity the passing of genetic traits from parent to offspring

metabolism the sum of all chemical processes that occur in an organism

Living Things Reproduce

Organisms make other organisms similar to themselves. They do so in one of two ways: by sexual reproduction or by asexual reproduction. In **sexual reproduction,** two parents produce offspring that will share characteristics of both parents. Most animals and plants reproduce in this way. The bear cubs in **Figure 3** were produced sexually by their parents.

In **asexual reproduction,** a single parent produces offspring that are identical to the parent. **Figure 4** shows an organism that reproduces asexually. Most single-celled organisms reproduce in this way.

Living Things Have DNA

The cells of all living things contain the molecule **d**eoxyribo**n**ucleic (dee AHKS uh RIE boh noo KLEE ik) **a**cid, or DNA. *DNA* controls the structure and function of cells. When organisms reproduce, they pass copies of their DNA to their offspring. Passing DNA ensures that offspring resemble parents. The passing of traits from one generation to the next is called **heredity.**

Living Things Use Energy

Organisms use energy to carry out the activities of life. These activities include such things as making food, breaking down food, moving materials into and out of cells, and building cells. An organism's **metabolism** (muh TAB uh LIZ uhm) is the total of all of the chemical activities that the organism performs.

✔ Reading Check Name four chemical activities in living things that require energy.

Living Things Grow and Develop

All living things, whether they are made of one cell or many cells, grow during periods of their lives. In a single-celled organism, the cell gets larger and divides, making other organisms. In organisms made of many cells, the number of cells gets larger, and the organism gets bigger.

In addition to getting larger, living things may develop and change as they grow. Just like the organisms in **Figure 5,** you will pass through different stages in your life as you develop into an adult.

Figure 5 *Over time, acorns develop into oak seedlings, which become oak trees.*

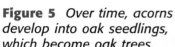
SECTION
Review

Summary

- All living things share six characteristics that are also used to classify organisms.
- Organisms are made of one or more cells.
- Organisms detect and respond to stimuli.
- Organisms reproduce.
- Organisms have DNA.
- Organisms use energy for their metabolism.
- Organisms grow and develop.
- Homeostasis is the maintenance of a stable internal environment.

Using Key Terms

Complete each of the following sentences by choosing the correct term from the word bank.

> cells   stimulus
> homeostasis   metabolism

1. Sunlight can be a ___.
2. Living things are made of ___.

Understanding Key Ideas

3. Homeostasis means maintaining
   a. stable internal conditions.
   b. varied internal conditions.
   c. similar offspring.
   d. varied offspring.

4. Explain the difference between asexual and sexual reproduction.

5. Describe the six characteristics of living things.

Math Skills

6. Bacteria double every generation. One bacterium is in the first generation. How many are in the sixth generation?

Critical Thinking

7. **Applying Concepts** How do you respond to some stimuli in your environment?

8. **Identifying Relationships** What does the fur coat of a bear have to do with homeostasis?

SCI**LINKS**.

NSTA
Developed and maintained by the National Science Teachers Association

For a variety of links related to this chapter, go to www.scilinks.org

Topic: Characteristics of Living Things
SciLinks code: HSM0258

The Necessities of Life

Would it surprise you to learn that you have the same basic needs as a tree, a frog, and a fly?

What You Will Learn

● Explain why organisms need food, water, air, and living space.
● Describe the chemical building blocks of cells.

Vocabulary

producer   lipid
consumer   phospholipid
decomposer   ATP
protein   nucleic acid
carbohydrate

READING STRATEGY

Discussion   Read this section silently. Write down questions that you have about this section. Discuss your questions in a small group.

In fact, almost every organism has the same basic needs: water, air, a place to live, and food.

Water

You may know that your body is made mostly of water. In fact, your cells and the cells of almost all living organisms are approximately 70% water. Most of the chemical reactions involved in metabolism require water.

Organisms differ greatly in terms of how much water they need and how they get it. You could survive for only about three days without water. You get water from the fluids you drink and the food you eat. The desert-dwelling kangaroo rat never drinks. It gets all of its water from its food.

Air

Air is a mixture of several different gases, including oxygen and carbon dioxide. Most living things use oxygen in the chemical process that releases energy from food. Oxygen may come from the air or may be dissolved in water. The European diving spider in **Figure 1** goes to great lengths to get oxygen. Green plants, algae, and some bacteria need carbon dioxide gas in addition to oxygen. These organisms produce food and oxygen by using photosynthesis (FOHT oh SIN thuh sis). In *photosynthesis*, green organisms convert the energy in sunlight to energy stored in food.

Although almost all living things need air, some do not. Organisms that can live without air are *anaerobic organisms*. *Clostridium botulinum* is an anaerobic bacterium that causes sickness in humans. It will not grow in the presence of air.

Reading Check   What process do plants use to make food? (*See the Appendix for answers to Reading Checks.*)

Figure 1   *This spider surrounds itself with an air bubble that provides the spider with a source of oxygen underwater.*

A Place to Live

All organisms need a place to live that contains all of the things they need to survive. Some organisms, such as elephants, require a large amount of space. Other organisms may live their entire life in one place.

Space on Earth is limited. So, organisms often compete with each other for food, water, and other necessities. Many animals, including the warbler in **Figure 2,** will claim a particular space. After claiming a space, they try to keep other animals away.

Figure 2 *A warbler's song is more than just a pretty tune. The warbler is protecting its home by telling other warblers to stay out of its territory.*

Food

All living things need food. Food gives organisms energy and the raw materials needed to carry on life processes. Organisms use nutrients from food to replace cells and build body parts. But not all organisms get food in the same way. In fact, organisms can be grouped into three different groups based on how they get their food.

producer an organism that can make its own food by using energy from its surroundings

consumer an organism that eats other organisms or organic matter

decomposer an organism that gets energy by breaking down the remains of dead organisms or animal wastes and consuming or absorbing the nutrients

Making Food

Some organisms, such as plants, are called producers. **Producers** can make their own food. Like most producers, plants use energy from the sun to make food from water and carbon dioxide. Some producers get energy and food from the chemicals in their environment.

Taking Food

Other organisms are called **consumers** because they must eat (consume) other organisms to get food. The frog in **Figure 3** is an example of a consumer. It gets the energy it needs by eating insects and other organisms.

Some consumers are decomposers. **Decomposers** are organisms that get their food by breaking down the nutrients in dead organisms or animal wastes. The mushroom in **Figure 3** is a decomposer.

Figure 3 *The frog is a consumer. The mushroom is a decomposer. The green plants are producers.*

protein a molecule that is made up of amino acids and that is needed to build and repair body structures and to regulate processes in the body

Putting It All Together

Some organisms make their own food. Some organisms get food from eating other organisms. But all organisms need to break down that food in order to use the nutrients in it.

Nutrients are made up of molecules. A *molecule* is a substance made when two or more atoms combine. Molecules made of different kinds of atoms are *compounds*. Molecules found in living things are usually made of different combinations of six elements: carbon, hydrogen, nitrogen, oxygen, phosphorus, and sulfur. These elements combine to form proteins, carbohydrates, lipids, ATP, and nucleic acids.

Proteins

Almost all of the life processes of a cell involve proteins. **Proteins** are large molecules that are made up of smaller molecules called *amino acids*.

Making Proteins

Organisms break down the proteins in food to supply their cells with amino acids. These amino acids are then linked together to form new proteins. Some proteins are made up of only a few amino acids, but others contain more than 10,000 amino acids.

Proteins in Action

Proteins have many different functions. Some proteins form structures that are easy to see, such as those in **Figure 4.** Other proteins are very small and help cells do their jobs. Inside red blood cells, the protein hemoglobin (HEE moh GLOH bin) binds to oxygen to deliver and release oxygen throughout the body. Some proteins protect cells. Other proteins, called *enzymes* (EN ZIEMZ), start or speed up chemical reactions in cells.

Figure 4 *Spider webs, hair, horns, and feathers are all made from proteins.*

Figure 5 *The extra sugar in a potato plant is stored in the potato as starch, a complex carbohydrate.*

Carbohydrates

Molecules made of sugars are called **carbohydrates.** Cells use carbohydrates as a source of energy and for energy storage. An organism's cells break down carbohydrates to release the energy stored in them. There are two kinds of carbohydrates—simple carbohydrates and complex carbohydrates.

carbohydrate a class of energy-giving nutrients that includes sugars, starches, and fiber; contains carbon, hydrogen, and oxygen

Simple Carbohydrates

Simple carbohydrates are made up of one sugar molecule or a few sugar molecules linked together. Table sugar and the sugar in fruits are examples of simple carbohydrates.

Complex Carbohydrates

When an organism has more sugar than it needs, its extra sugar may be stored as complex carbohydrates. *Complex carbohydrates* are made of hundreds of sugar molecules linked together. Plants, such as the potato plant in **Figure 5,** store extra sugar as starch. When you eat mashed potatoes, you are eating a potato plant's stored starch. Your body then breaks down this complex carbohydrate to release the energy stored in the potato.

How Much Oxygen?
Each red blood cell carries about 250 million molecules of hemoglobin. How many molecules of oxygen could a single red blood cell deliver throughout the body if every hemoglobin molecule attached to four oxygen molecules?

✓ **Reading Check** What is the difference between simple carbohydrates and complex carbohydrates?

Starch Search

1. Obtain several **food samples** from your teacher.
2. Put **a few drops of iodine** on each sample. Record your observations. **Caution:** Iodine can stain clothing.
3. When iodine comes into contact with starch, a black substance appears. Which samples contain starch?

Figure 6   **Phospholipid Membranes**

The head of a phospholipid molecule is attracted to water, but the tail is not. ▶

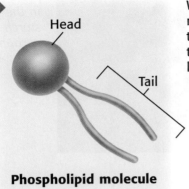

Head

Tail

Phospholipid molecule

When phospholipid molecules come together in water, they form two layers. ▶

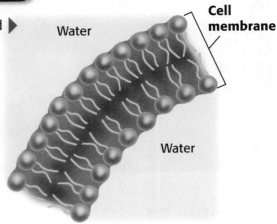

Water

Cell membrane

Water

Lipids

Lipids are compounds that cannot mix with water. Lipids have many important jobs in the cell. Like carbohydrates, some lipids store energy. Other lipids form the membranes of cells.

Phospholipids

All cells are surrounded by a cell membrane. The cell membrane helps protect the cell and keep the internal conditions of the cell stable. **Phospholipids** (FAHS foh LIP idz) are the molecules that form much of the cell membrane. The head of a phospholipid molecule is attracted to water. The tail is not. Cells are mostly water. When phospholipids are in water, the tails come together, and the heads face out into the water. **Figure 6** shows how phospholipid molecules form two layers in water.

Fats and Oils

Fats and oils are lipids that store energy. When an organism has used up most of its carbohydrates, it can get energy from these lipids. The structures of fats and oils are almost the same, but at room temperature, most fats are solid, and most oils are liquid. Most of the lipids stored in plants are oils. Most of the lipids stored in animals are fats.

✓ **Reading Check**   What is one difference between oils and fats?

ATP

Adenosine **tri**phosphate (uh DEN uh SEEN trie FAHS FAYT), also called ATP, is another important molecule. **ATP** is the major energy-carrying molecule in the cell. The energy in carbohydrates and lipids must be transferred to ATP, which then provides fuel for cellular activities.

lipid a type of biochemical that does not dissolve in water; fats and steroids are lipids

phospholipid a lipid that contains phosphorus and that is a structural component in cell membranes

ATP **a**denosine **t**ri**p**hosphate, a molecule that acts as the main energy source for cell processes

CONNECTION TO
Social Studies

Whaling In the 1900s, whales were hunted and killed for their oil. Whale oil was often used as fuel for oil lamps. Most of the oil taken from whales was taken from their fat, or *blubber*. Some whales had blubber over 18 in. thick, producing over 40 barrels of oil per whale. Research whether anyone still hunts whales or uses whale oil. Make a presentation to the class on your findings.

Nucleic Acids

Nucleic acids are sometimes called the blueprints of life because they have all the information needed for a cell to make proteins. **Nucleic acids** are large molecules made up of molecules called *nucleotides* (NOO klee oh TIEDZ). A nucleic acid may have thousands of nucleotides. The order of those nucleotides stores information. DNA is a nucleic acid. A DNA molecule is like a recipe book entitled *How to Make Proteins*. When a cell needs to make a certain protein, the cell gets information from the order of the nucleotides in DNA. This order of nucleotides tells the cell the order of the amino acids that are linked together to make that protein.

nucleic acid a molecule made up of subunits called *nucleotides*

INTERNET ACTIVITY

For another activity related to this chapter, go to **go.hrw.com** and type in the keyword **HL5ALVW**.

SECTION Review

Summary

- Organisms need water for cellular processes.
- Most organisms use oxygen to release the energy contained in their food.
- Organisms must have a place to live.
- Cells store energy in carbohydrates, which are made of sugars.
- Proteins are made up of amino acids. Some proteins are enzymes.
- Fats and oils store energy and make up cell membranes.
- Cells use molecules of ATP to fuel their activities.
- Nucleic acids, such as DNA, are made up of nucleotides.

Using Key Terms

For each pair of terms, explain how the meanings of the terms differ.

1. *producer* and *consumer*

2. *lipid* and *phospholipid*

Understanding Key Ideas

3. Plants store extra sugar as
   a. proteins.
   b. starch.
   c. nucleic acids.
   d. phospholipids.

4. Explain why organisms need food, water, air, and living space.

5. Describe the chemical building blocks of cells.

6. Why are decomposers categorized as consumers? How do they differ from producers?

7. What are the subunits of proteins?

Math Skills

8. Protein A is a chain of 660 amino acids. Protein B is a chain of 11 amino acids. How many times more amino acids does protein A have than protein B?

Critical Thinking

9. **Making Inferences** Could life as we know it exist on Earth if air contained only oxygen? Explain.

10. **Identifying Relationships** How might a cave, an ant, and a lake each meet the needs of an organism?

11. **Predicting Consequences** What would happen to the supply of ATP in your cells if you did not eat enough carbohydrates? How would this affect your cells?

12. **Applying Concepts** Which resource do you think is most important to your survival: water, air, a place to live, or food? Explain your answer.

SCILINKS

NSTA
Developed and maintained by the National Science Teachers Association

For a variety of links related to this chapter, go to www.scilinks.org

Topic: The Necessities of Life
SciLinks code: HSM1018

Inquiry Lab

Roly-Poly Races

Have you ever watched a bug run? Did you wonder why it was running? The bug you saw running was probably reacting to a stimulus. In other words, something happened to make the bug run! One characteristic of living things is that they respond to stimuli. In this activity, you will study the movement of roly-polies. Roly-polies are also called *pill bugs*. But they are not really bugs; they are land-dwelling animals called *isopods*. Isopods live in dark, moist areas under rocks or wood. You will provide stimuli to determine how fast your isopod can move and what affects its speed and direction. Remember that isopods are living things and must be treated gently and respectfully.

OBJECTIVES

Observe responses to stimuli.

Analyze responses to stimuli.

MATERIALS

- chalk (1 stick)
- container, plastic, small, with lid
- gloves, protective
- isopod (4)
- potato, raw (1 small slice)
- ruler, metric
- soil (8 oz)
- stopwatch

SAFETY

Ask a Question

1. Ask a question such as, "Which stimuli cause pill bugs to run?"

Form a Hypothesis

2. Using your question as a guide, form a hypothesis. For example, you could form the following hypothesis: "Light, sound, and touch stimulate pill bugs to run."

Test the Hypothesis

3. Choose a partner, and decide together how you will run your roly-poly race. Discuss some gentle ways to stimulate your isopods to move. Choose five or six things that might cause movement, such as a gentle nudge or a change in temperature, sound, or light. Check your choices with your teacher.

4. Make a data table similar to the table below. Label the columns with the stimuli that you've chosen. Label the rows "Isopod 1," "Isopod 2," "Isopod 3," and "Isopod 4."

Isopod Responses			
	Stimulus 1	**Stimulus 2**	**Stimulus 3**
Isopod 1			
Isopod 2			
Isopod 3			
Isopod 4			

DO NOT WRITE IN BOOK

5. Place a layer of soil that is 1 cm or 2 cm deep in a small plastic container. Add a small slice of potato and a piece of chalk. Your isopods will eat these items.

6. Place four isopods in your container. Observe them for a minute or two before you perform your tests. Record your observations.

7. Decide which stimulus you want to test first. Carefully arrange the isopods at the "starting line." The starting line can be an imaginary line at one end of the container.

8. Gently stimulate each isopod at the same time and in the same way. In your data table, record the isopods' responses to the stimulus. Be sure to record the distance that each isopod travels. Don't forget to time the race.

9. Repeat steps 7–8 for each stimulus. Be sure to wait at least 2 min between trials.

Analyze the Results

1. **Describing Events** Describe the way that isopods move. Do their legs move together?

2. **Analyzing Results** Did your isopods move before or between the trials? Did the movement seem to have a purpose, or were the isopods responding to a stimulus? Explain.

Draw Conclusions

3. **Interpreting Information** Did any of the stimuli make the isopods move faster or go farther? Explain.

Applying Your Data

Like isopods and all other living things, humans react to stimuli. Describe three stimuli that might cause humans to run.

Chapter Review

USING KEY TERMS

Complete each of the following sentences by choosing the correct term from the word bank.

lipid   carbohydrate
consumer heredity
homeostasis producer

1 The process of maintaining a stable internal environment is known as ___.

2 Offspring resemble their parents because of ___.

3 A ___ obtains food by eating other organisms.

4 Starch is a ___ and is made up of sugars.

5 Fat is a ___ that stores energy for an organism.

UNDERSTANDING KEY IDEAS

Multiple Choice

6 Which of the following statements about cells is true?

 a. Cells are the structures that contain all of the materials necessary for life.

 b. Cells are found in all organisms.

 c. Cells are sometimes specialized for particular functions.

 d. All of the above

7 Which of the following statements about all living things is true?

 a. All living things reproduce sexually.

 b. All living things have one or more cells.

 c. All living things must make their own food.

 d. All living things reproduce asexually.

8 Organisms must have food because

 a. food is a source of energy.

 b. food supplies cells with oxygen.

 c. organisms never make their own food.

 d. All of the above

9 A change in an organism's environment that affects the organism's activities is a

 a. response. **c.** metabolism.

 b. stimulus. **d.** producer.

10 Organisms store energy in

 a. nucleic acids. **c.** lipids.

 b. phospholipids. **d.** water.

11 The molecule that contains the information about how to make proteins is

 a. ATP.

 b. a carbohydrate.

 c. DNA.

 d. a phospholipid.

12 The subunits of nucleic acids are

 a. nucleotides.

 b. oils.

 c. sugars.

 d. amino acids.

Short Answer

13 What is the difference between asexual reproduction and sexual reproduction?

14 In one or two sentences, explain why most living things must have air.

15 What is ATP, and why is it important to a cell?

CRITICAL THINKING

16 **Concept Mapping** Use the following terms to create a concept map: *cell, carbohydrates, protein, enzymes, DNA, sugars, lipids, nucleotides, amino acids,* and *nucleic acid*.

17 **Analyzing Ideas** A flame can move, grow larger, and give off heat. Is a flame alive? Explain.

18 **Applying Concepts** Based on what you know about carbohydrates, lipids, and proteins, why is it important for you to eat a balanced diet?

19 **Evaluating Hypotheses** Your friend tells you that the stimulus of music makes his goldfish swim faster. How would you design a controlled experiment to test your friend's claim?

INTERPRETING GRAPHICS

The pictures below show the same plant over a period of 3 days. Use the pictures below to answer the questions that follow.

Day 1

Day 2

Day 3

20 What is the plant doing?

21 What characteristic(s) of living things is the plant exhibiting?

Multiple Choice

Use the diagram below to answer question 1.

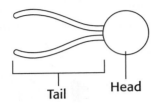

Tail   Head

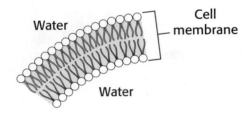

Water   Cell membrane

Water

1. **Membranes allow cells to maintain stable internal conditions in a changing external environment. The phospholipids that make up the membrane in the diagram can form this protective layer because**

   A. the tails are attracted to water and the heads are not.

   B. the tails are attracted to the heads of other phospholipids.

   C. the heads and the tails are attracted to water.

   D. the heads are attracted to water and the tails are not.

2. **New organisms are produced either by sexual or asexual reproduction. How are offspring that are produced sexually and offspring that are produced asexually similar?**

   A. Both are identical to one parent.

   B. Both have DNA.

   C. Both have multiple cells.

   D. Both share traits of two parents.

3. **Which of the following make up molecules that speed up cell reactions?**

   A. amino acids

   B. lipids

   C. nucleic acids

   D. carbohydrates

4. **Kai's dog gets a thicker coat in the winter and sheds its hair in the spring and summer. This process relates to which of the following characteristics of living things?**

   A. It has cells.

   B. It has DNA.

   C. It uses energy.

   D. It responds to change.

5. To make food, what materials do plants need?

A. oxygen and carbon dioxide

B. water and glucose

C. oxygen and sucrose

D. water and carbon dioxide

6. Which of the following describes the passing of biological traits from one generation to the next?

A. sexual reproduction

B. heredity

C. budding

D. asexual reproduction

7. Plants, such as potato plants, store extra sugar as starch. What type of molecule is starch?

A. enzyme

B. ATP

C. simple carbohydrate

D. complex carbohydrate

8. To grow and divide, the cells of all organisms need nutrients. What type of organism gets nutrients from eating other organisms?

A. a producer

B. a lipid

C. a consumer

D. a carbohydrate

Craig got sick this week. The graph below shows how his temperature changed.

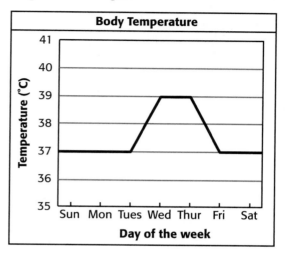

Body Temperature

9. Based on the graph, which of the following statements about homeostasis in Craig's body is true?

A. Homeostasis was disrupted on Wednesday and Thursday.

B. Homeostasis was maintained every day of the week.

C. Homeostasis was disrupted on Sunday, Monday, and Tuesday.

D. Homeostasis was maintained on Thursday, Friday, and Saturday.

Open Response

10. An amoeba is made up of one cell. Humans are made up of trillions of cells. How are the life functions of each the same? How do they differ?

11. Describe how living things respond to change in their external environment. Use the following terms in your answer: stimuli, homeostasis, and internal response.

Science in Action

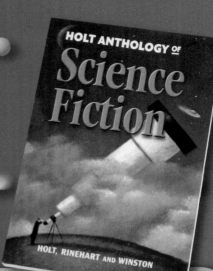

HOLT ANTHOLOGY OF
Science Fiction

HOLT, RINEHART AND WINSTON

Science, Technology, and Society

Chess-Playing Computers

Computers can help us explore how humans think. One way to explore how humans think is to study how people and computers play chess against each other.

A computer's approach to chess is straightforward. By calculating each piece's possible board position for the next few moves, a computer creates what is called a *position tree*. A position tree shows how each move can lead to other moves. This way of playing requires millions of calculations.

Human chess champions play differently. Humans calculate only three or four moves every minute. Even so, human champions are still a match for computer opponents. By studying the ways that people and computers play chess, scientists are learning how people think and make choices.

Science Fiction

"They're Made Out of Meat" by Terry Bisson

Two space explorers millions of light-years from home are visiting an uncharted sector of the universe to find signs of life. Their mission is to contact, welcome, and log any and all beings in this part of the universe.

During their mission, they encounter a life-form quite unlike anything they have ever seen before. It looked too strange and, well, disgusting. The explorers have very strong doubts about adding this new organism to the list. But the explorers' official duty is to contact and welcome all life-forms no matter how ugly they are. Can the explorers bring themselves to perform their duty?

You'll find out by reading "They're Made Out of Meat," a short story by Terry Bisson. This story is in the *Holt Anthology of Science Fiction*.

Math ACTIVITY

A chess-playing computer needs to evaluate 3 million positions before a move. If you could evaluate two positions in 1 min, how long would it take you to evaluate 3 million possible positions?

Language Arts ACTIVITY

WRITING SKILL Write a story about what happens when the explorers next meet the creatures on the star in G445 zone.

Janis Davis-Street

NASA Nutritionist Do astronauts eat shrimp cocktail in space? Yes, they do! Shrimp cocktail is nutritious and tastes so good that it is one of the most popular foods in the space program. And eating a proper diet helps astronauts stay healthy while they are in space.

But who figures out what astronauts need to eat? Janis Davis-Street is a nutritionist and laboratory supervisor for the Nutritional Biochemistry Laboratory at the Johnson Space Center in Houston, Texas. She was born in Georgetown, Guyana, on the northeastern coast of South America. She was educated in Canada.

Davis-Street is part of a team that uses their knowledge of nutrition, biology, and chemistry to figure out the nutritional requirements for spaceflight. For example, they determine how many calories and other nutrients each astronaut needs per day during spaceflight.

The Nutritional Biochemistry Laboratory's work on the space shuttle missions and *Mir* space station developed into tests that allow NASA to help ensure astronaut health before, during, and after flight. These tests are important for understanding how the human body adapts to long space missions, and for determining whether treatments for preventing bone and muscle loss during spaceflight are working.

Social Studies ACTiViTY

Scientists from more than 30 countries have been on space missions. Research which countries have provided astronauts or cosmonauts for space missions. Using a map, place self-stick notes on countries that have provided scientists for space missions. Write the names of the appropriate scientists on the self-stick notes.

To learn more about these Science in Action topics, visit go.hrw.com and type in the keyword HL5ALVF.

Current Science

Check out Current Science® articles related to this chapter by visiting go.hrw.com. Just type in the keyword HL5CS02.

10

Cells: The Basic Units of Life

The Big Idea

All organisms are composed of one or more cells.

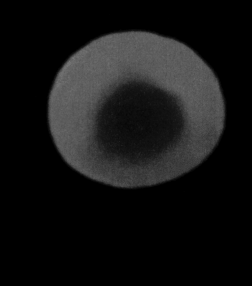

About the Photo

Harmful bacteria may invade your body and make you sick. But wait—your white blood cells come to the rescue! In this image, a white blood cell (the large, yellowish cell) reaches out its pseudopod to destroy bacteria (the purple cells). The red discs are red blood cells.

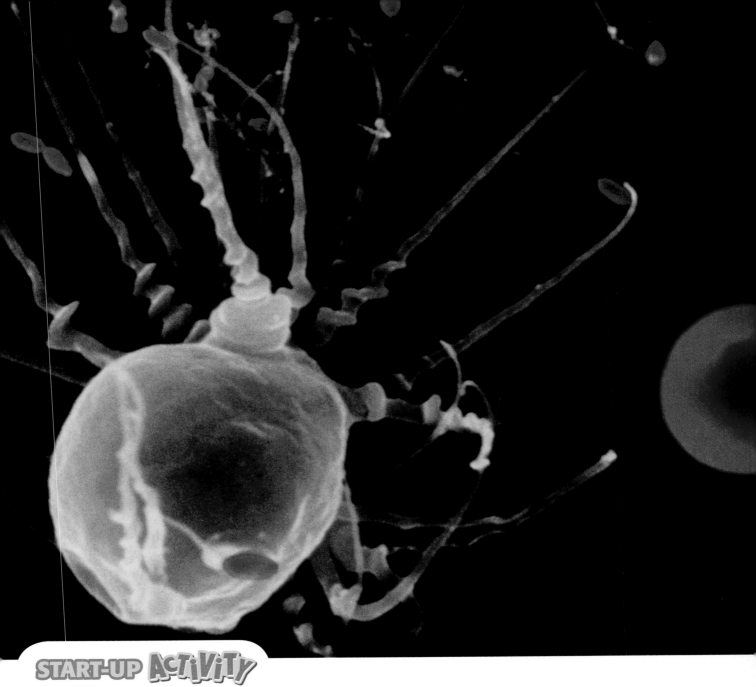

What Are Plants Made Of?

All living things, including plants, are made of cells. What do plant cells look like? Do this activity to find out.

Procedure

1. Tear off a **small leaf** from near the tip of an **Elodea sprig.**

2. Using **forceps,** place the whole leaf in a **drop of water** on a **microscope slide.**

3. Place a **coverslip** on top of the water drop by putting one edge of the coverslip on the slide near the water drop. Next, lower the coverslip slowly so that the coverslip does not trap air bubbles.

4. Place the slide on your **microscope.**

5. Using the lowest-powered lens first, find the plant cells. When you can see the cells under the lower-powered lens, switch to a higher-powered lens.

6. Draw a picture of what you see.

Analysis

1. Describe the shape of the *Elodea* cells. Are all of the cells in the *Elodea* the same?

2. Do you think human cells look like *Elodea* cells? How do you think they are different? How might they be similar?

What You Will Learn

- State the parts of the cell theory.
- Explain why cells are so small.
- Describe the parts of a cell.
- Describe how bacteria are different from archaea.
- Explain the difference between prokaryotic cells and eukaryotic cells.

Vocabulary

cell   nucleus
cell membrane   prokaryote
organelle   eukaryote

READING STRATEGY

Reading Organizer As you read this section, create an outline of the section. Use the headings from the section in your outline.

The Diversity of Cells

Most cells are so small they can't be seen by the naked eye. So how did scientists find cells? By accident, that's how! The first person to see cells wasn't even looking for them.

All living things are made of tiny structures called cells. A **cell** is the smallest unit that can perform all the processes necessary for life. Because of their size, cells weren't discovered until microscopes were invented in the mid-1600s.

Cells and the Cell Theory

Robert Hooke was the first person to describe cells. In 1665, he built a microscope to look at tiny objects. One day, he looked at a thin slice of cork. Cork is found in the bark of cork trees. The cork looked like it was made of little boxes. Hooke named these boxes *cells,* which means "little rooms" in Latin. Hooke's cells were really the outer layers of dead cork cells. Hooke's microscope and his drawing of the cork cells are shown in **Figure 1.**

Hooke also looked at thin slices of living plants. He saw that they too were made of cells. Some cells were even filled with "juice." The "juicy" cells were living cells.

Hooke also looked at feathers, fish scales, and the eyes of houseflies. But he spent most of his time looking at plants and fungi. The cells of plants and fungi have cell walls. This makes them easy to see. Animal cells do not have cell walls. This absence of cell walls makes it harder to see the outline of animal cells. Because Hooke couldn't see their cells, he thought that animals weren't made of cells.

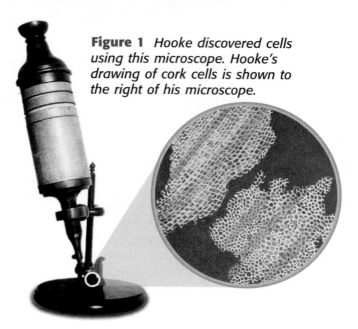

Figure 1 *Hooke discovered cells using this microscope. Hooke's drawing of cork cells is shown to the right of his microscope.*

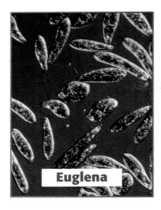
Euglena

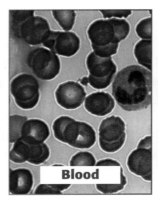
Blood

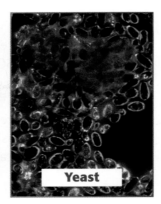
Yeast

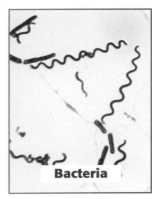
Bacteria

Finding Cells in Other Organisms

In 1673, Anton van Leeuwenhoek (LAY vuhn HOOK), a Dutch merchant, made his own microscopes. Leeuwenhoek used one of his microscopes to look at pond scum. Leeuwenhoek saw small organisms in the water. He named these organisms *animalcules,* which means "little animals." Today, we call these single-celled organisms protists (PROH tists).

Leeuwenhoek also looked at animal blood. He saw differences in blood cells from different kinds of animals. For example, blood cells in fish, birds, and frogs are oval. Blood cells in humans and dogs are round and flat. Leeuwenhoek was also the first person to see bacteria. And he discovered that yeasts that make bread dough rise are single-celled organisms. Examples of the types of cells Leeuwenhoek examined are shown in **Figure 2.**

The Cell Theory

Almost 200 years passed before scientists concluded that cells are present in all living things. Scientist Matthias Schleiden (mah THEE uhs SHLIE duhn) studied plants. In 1838, he concluded that all plant parts were made of cells. Theodor Schwann (TAY oh dohr SHVAHN) studied animals. In 1839, Schwann concluded that all animal tissues were made of cells. Soon after that, Schwann wrote the first two parts of what is now known as the *cell theory*.

- All organisms are made of one or more cells.
- The cell is the basic unit of all living things.

Later, in 1858, Rudolf Virchow (ROO dawlf FIR koh), a doctor, stated that all cells could form only from other cells. Virchow then added the third part of the cell theory.

- All cells come from existing cells.

✓ **Reading Check** What are the three parts of the cell theory?
(*See the Appendix for answers to Reading Checks.*)

Figure 2 *Leeuwenhoek examined many types of cells, including protists such as* Euglena *and the other types of cells shown above. The bacteria cells in the photo have been enlarged more than the other cells. Bacterial cells are usually much smaller than most other types of cells.*

cell in biology, the smallest unit that can perform all life processes; cells are covered by a membrane and have DNA and cytoplasm

CONNECTION TO Physics

Microscopes The microscope Hooke used to study cells was much different from microscopes today. Research different kinds of microscopes, such as light microscopes, scanning electron microscopes (SEMs), and transmission electron microscopes (TEMs). Select one type of microscope. Make a poster or other presentation to show to the class. Describe how the microscope works and how it is used. Be sure to include images.

ACTIVITY

Cell Size

Most cells are too small to be seen without a microscope. It would take 50 human cells to cover the dot on this letter *i*.

A Few Large Cells

Most cells are small. A few, however, are big. The yolk of a chicken egg, shown in **Figure 3,** is one big cell. The egg can be this large because it does not have to take in more nutrients.

Many Small Cells

There is a physical reason why most cells are so small. Cells take in food and get rid of wastes through their outer surface. As a cell gets larger, it needs more food and produces more waste. Therefore, more materials pass through its outer surface.

As the cell's volume increases, its surface area grows too. But the cell's volume grows faster than its surface area. If a cell gets too large, the cell's surface area will not be large enough to take in enough nutrients or pump out enough wastes. So, the area of a cell's surface—compared with the cell's volume—limits the cell's size. The ratio of the cell's outer surface area to the cell's volume is called the *surface area–to-volume ratio,* which can be calculated by using the following equation:

$$\textit{surface area–to–volume ratio} = \frac{\textit{surface area}}{\textit{volume}}$$

✓ Reading Check Why are most cells small?

Figure 3 *The white and yolk of this chicken egg provide nutrients for the development of a chick.*

MATH FOCUS

Surface Area–to-Volume Ratio Calculate the surface area–to-volume ratio of a cube whose sides measure 2 cm.

Step 1: Calculate the surface area.

surface area of cube = number of sides ×
area of side

surface area of cube = 6 × (2 cm × 2 cm)

surface area of cube = 24 cm²

Step 2: Calculate the volume.

volume of cube = side × side × side

volume of cube = 2 cm × 2 cm × 2 cm

volume of cube = 8 cm³

Step 3: Calculate the surface area–to-volume ratio.

$$\textit{surface area–to–volume ratio} = \frac{\textit{surface area}}{\textit{volume}} = \frac{24}{8} = \frac{3}{1}$$

Now It's Your Turn

1. Calculate the surface area–to-volume ratio of a cube whose sides are 3 cm long.

2. Calculate the surface area–to-volume ratio of a cube whose sides are 4 cm long.

3. Of the cubes from questions 1 and 2, which has the greater surface area–to-volume ratio?

4. What is the relationship between the length of a side and the surface area–to-volume ratio of a cell?

Parts of a Cell

Cells come in many shapes and sizes. Cells have many different functions. But all cells have the following parts in common.

The Cell Membrane and Cytoplasm

All cells are surrounded by a cell membrane. The **cell membrane** is a protective layer that covers the cell's surface and acts as a barrier. It separates the cell's contents from its environment. The cell membrane also controls materials going into and out of the cell. Inside the cell is a fluid. This fluid and almost all of its contents are called the *cytoplasm* (SIET oh PLAZ uhm).

Organelles

Cells have organelles that carry out various life processes. **Organelles** are structures that perform specific functions within the cell. Different types of cells have different organelles. Most organelles are surrounded by membranes. For example, the algal cell in **Figure 4** has membrane-bound organelles. Some organelles float in the cytoplasm. Other organelles are attached to membranes or other organelles.

✓ **Reading Check** What are organelles?

Genetic Material

All cells contain DNA (**d**eoxyribo**n**ucleic **a**cid) at some point in their life. *DNA* is the genetic material that carries information needed to make new cells and new organisms. DNA is passed on from parent cells to new cells and controls the activities of a cell. **Figure 5** shows the DNA of a bacterium.

In some cells, the DNA is enclosed inside an organelle called the **nucleus.** For example, your cells have a nucleus. In contrast, bacterial cells do not have a nucleus.

In humans, mature red blood cells lose their DNA. Red blood cells are made inside bones. When red blood cells are first made, they have a nucleus with DNA. But before they enter the bloodstream, red blood cells lose their nucleus and DNA. They survive with no new instructions from their DNA.

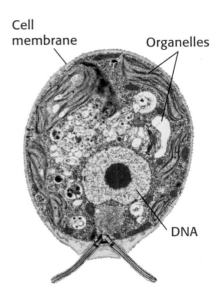

Cell membrane   Organelles

DNA

Figure 4 *This green alga has organelles. The organelles and the fluid surrounding them make up the cytoplasm.*

cell membrane a phospholipid layer that covers a cell's surface; acts as a barrier between the inside of a cell and the cell's environment

organelle one of the small bodies in a cell's cytoplasm that are specialized to perform a specific function

nucleus in a eukaryotic cell, a membrane-bound organelle that contains the cell's DNA and that has a role in processes such as growth, metabolism, and reproduction

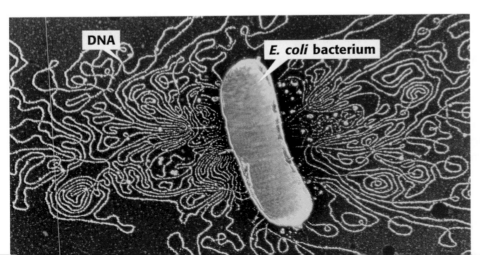

DNA

E. coli **bacterium**

Figure 5 *This photo shows an* Escherichia coli *bacterium. The bacterium's cell membrane has been treated so that the cell's DNA is released.*

prokaryote an organism that consists of a single cell that does not have a nucleus

Two Kinds of Cells

All cells have cell membranes, organelles, cytoplasm, and DNA. But there are two basic types of cells—cells without a nucleus and cells with a nucleus. Cells with no nucleus are *prokaryotic* (proh KAR ee AHT ik) *cells*. Cells that have a nucleus are *eukaryotic* (yoo KAR ee AHT ik) *cells*. Prokaryotic cells are further classified into two groups: *bacteria* (bak TIR ee uh) and *archaea* (AHR kee uh).

Prokaryotes: Bacteria and Archaea

Bacteria and archaea are prokaryotes (pro KAR ee OHTS). **Prokaryotes** are single-celled organisms that do not have a nucleus or membrane-bound organelles.

Bacteria

The most common prokaryotes are bacteria (singular, *bacterium*). Bacteria are the smallest cells known. These tiny organisms live almost everywhere. Bacteria do not have a nucleus, but they do have DNA. A bacteria's DNA is a long, circular molecule, shaped like a twisted rubber band. Bacteria have no membrane-covered organelles. But they do have ribosomes. *Ribosomes* are tiny, round organelles made of protein and other material.

Bacteria also have a strong, weblike exterior cell wall. This wall helps the cell retain its shape. A bacterium's cell membrane is just inside the cell wall. Together, the cell wall and cell membrane allow materials into and out of the cell.

Some bacteria live in the soil and water. Others live in, or on, other organisms. For example, you have bacteria living on your skin and teeth. You also have bacteria living in your digestive system. These bacteria help the process of digestion. A typical bacterial cell is shown in **Figure 6.**

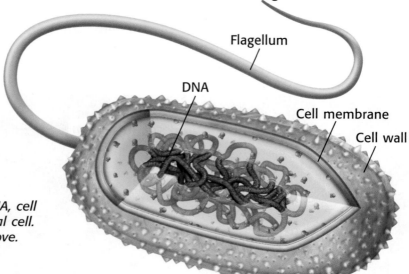

Figure 6 *This diagram shows the DNA, cell membrane, and cell wall of a bacterial cell. The flagellum helps the bacterium move.*

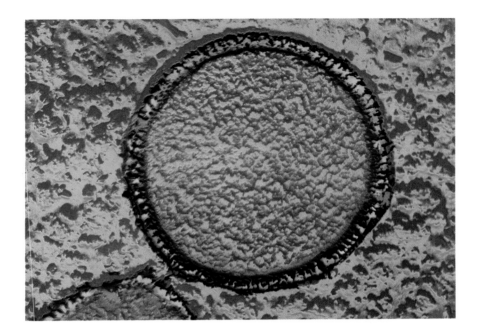

Figure 7 *This photograph, taken with an electron microscope, is of an archaeon that lives in the very high temperatures of deep-sea volcanic vents. The photograph has been colored so that the cell wall is green and the cell contents are pink.*

Archaea

The second kind of prokaryote are the archaea (singular, *archaeon*). Archaea are similar to bacteria in some ways. For example, both are single-celled organisms. Both have ribosomes, a cell membrane, and circular DNA. And both lack a nucleus and membrane-bound organelles. But archaea differ from bacteria in some way, too. For example, archaeal ribosomes are different from bacterial ribosomes.

Archaea are similar to eukaryotic cells in some ways, too. For example, archaeal ribosomes are more like the ribosomes of eukaryotic cells. But archaea also have some features that no other cells have. For example, the cell wall and cell membranes of archaea are different from the cell walls of other organisms. And some archaea live in places where no other organisms could live.

Three types of archaea are *heat-loving,* s*alt-loving,* and *methane-making.* Methane is a kind of gas frequently found in swamps. Heat-loving and salt-loving archaea are sometimes called extremophiles. *Extremophiles* live in places where conditions are extreme. They live in very hot water, such as in hot springs, or where the water is extremely salty. **Figure 7** shows one kind of methane-making archaea that lives deep in the ocean near volcanic vents. The temperature of the water from those vents is extreme: it is above the boiling point of water at sea level.

Reading Check What is one difference between bacteria and archaea?

CONNECTION TO
Social Studies

Where Do They Live? While most archaea live in extreme environments, scientists have found that archaea live almost everywhere. Do research about archaea. Select one kind of archaea. Create a poster showing the geographical location where the organism lives, describing its physical environment, and explaining how it survives in its environment.

ACTIVITY

Eukaryotic Cells and Eukaryotes

Eukaryotic cells are the largest cells. Most eukaryotic cells are still microscopic, but they are about 10 times larger than most bacterial cells. A typical eukaryotic cell is shown in **Figure 8.**

Unlike bacteria and archaea, eukaryotic cells have a nucleus. The nucleus is one kind of membrane-bound organelle. A cell's nucleus holds the cell's DNA. Eukaryotic cells have other membrane-bound organelles as well. Organelles are like the different organs in your body. Each kind of organelle has a specific job in the cell. Together, organelles, such as the ones shown in **Figure 8,** perform all the processes necessary for life.

All living things that are not bacteria or archaea are made of one or more eukaryotic cells. Organisms made of eukaryotic cells are called **eukaryotes.** Many eukaryotes are multicellular. *Multicellular* means "many cells." Multicellular organisms are usually larger than single-cell organisms. So, most organisms you see with your naked eye are eukaryotes. There are many types of eukaryotes. Animals, including humans, are eukaryotes. So are plants. Some protists, such as amoebas, are single-celled eukaryotes. Other protists, including some types of green algae, are multicellular eukaryotes. Fungi are organisms such as mushrooms or yeasts. Mushrooms are multicellular eukaryotes. Yeasts are single-celled eukaryotes.

✓ Reading Check How are eukaryotes different from prokaryotes?

eukaryote an organism made up of cells that have a nucleus enclosed by a membrane; eukaryotes include animals, plants, and fungi, but not archaea or bacteria

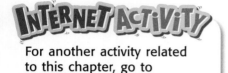

INTERNET ACTIVITY

For another activity related to this chapter, go to **go.hrw.com** and type in the keyword **HL5CELW.**

Figure 8   Organelles in a Typical Eukaryotic Cell

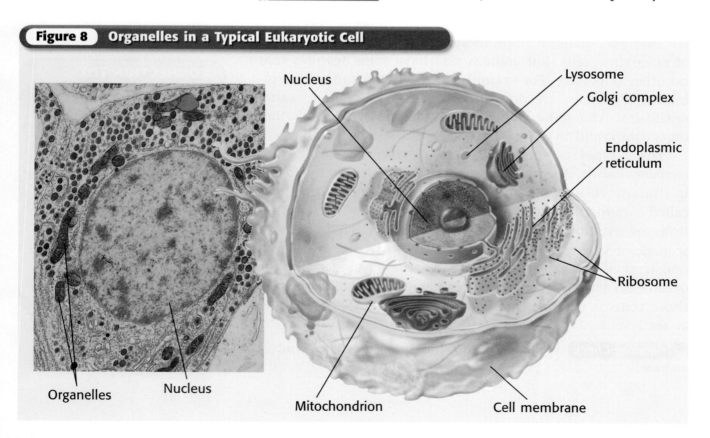

Nucleus

Lysosome

Golgi complex

Endoplasmic reticulum

Ribosome

Organelles

Nucleus

Mitochondrion

Cell membrane

Summary

- Cells were not discovered until microscopes were invented in the 1600s.

- Cell theory states that all organisms are made of cells, the cell is the basic unit of all living things, and all cells come from other cells.

- All cells have a cell membrane, cytoplasm, and DNA.

- Most cells are too small to be seen with the naked eye. A cell's surface area–to-volume ratio limits the size of a cell.

- The two basic kinds of cells are prokaryotic cells and eukaryotic cells. Eukaryotic cells have a nucleus and membrane-bound organelles. Prokaryotic cells do not.

- Prokaryotes are classified as archaea and bacteria.

- Archaeal cell walls and ribosomes are different from the cell walls and ribosomes of other organisms.

- Eukaryotes can be single-celled or multicellular.

Using Key Terms

1. In your own words, write a definition for the term *organelle*.

2. Use the following terms in the same sentence: *prokaryotic, nucleus,* and *eukaryotic.*

Understanding Key Ideas

3. Cell size is limited by the
   a. thickness of the cell wall.
   b. size of the cell's nucleus.
   c. cell's surface area–to-volume ratio.
   d. amount of cytoplasm in the cell.

4. What are the three parts of the cell theory?

5. Name three structures that every cell has.

6. Give two ways in which archaea are different from bacteria.

Critical Thinking

7. **Applying Concepts** You have discovered a new single-celled organism. It has a cell wall, ribosomes, and long, circular DNA. Is it a eukaryote or a prokaryote cell? Explain.

8. **Identifying Relationships** You are looking at a cell under a microscope. It is a single cell, but it also forms chains. What characteristics would this cell have if the organism is a eukaryote? If it is a prokaryote? What would you look for first?

Interpreting Graphics

The picture below shows a particular organism. Use the picture to answer the questions that follow.

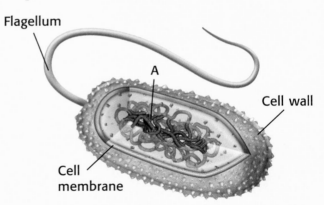

Flagellum

A

Cell wall

Cell membrane

9. What type of organism does the picture represent? How do you know?

10. Which structure helps the organism move?

11. What part of the organism does the letter *A* represent?

SCiLINKS®

NSTA

Developed and maintained by the
National Science Teachers Association

For a variety of links related to this chapter, go to www.scilinks.org

Topic: Prokaryotic Cells
SciLinks code: HSM1225

Eukaryotic Cells

Even though most cells are small, cells are still complex. A eukaryotic cell has many parts that help the cell stay alive.

Plant cells and animal cells are two types of eukaryotic cells. These two types of cells have many cell parts in common. But plant cells and animal cells also have cell parts that are different. Compare the plant cell in **Figure 1** and the animal cell in **Figure 2** to see the differences between these two types of cells.

Cell Wall

Plant cells have an outermost structure called a **cell wall.** A cell wall is a rigid structure that gives support to a cell. Plants and algae have cell walls made of a complex sugar called *cellulose.* **Figure 1** shows the cellulose fibers in a plant cell wall.

Fungi, including yeasts and mushrooms, also have cell walls. Fungi have cell walls made of a complex sugar called *chitin* (KIE tin) or of a chemical similar to chitin. Prokaryotic cells such as bacteria and archaea also have cell walls, but those cell walls are different from those of plants or fungi.

What You Will Learn

● Identify the different parts of a eukaryotic cell.
● Explain the function of each part of a eukaryotic cell.

Vocabulary

cell wall
ribosome
endoplasmic
  reticulum
mitochondrion
Golgi complex
vesicle
lysosome

READING STRATEGY

Reading Organizer As you read this section, make a table comparing plant cells and animal cells.

Figure 1 **Plant Cell**

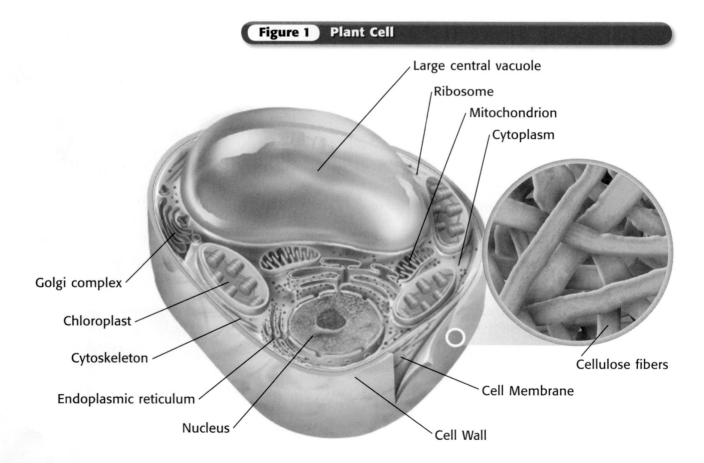

Large central vacuole
Ribosome
Mitochondrion
Cytoplasm
Golgi complex
Chloroplast
Cytoskeleton
Endoplasmic reticulum
Nucleus
Cell Wall
Cell Membrane
Cellulose fibers

Cell Membrane

All cells have a cell membrane. The *cell membrane* is a protective barrier that encloses a cell. It separates the cell's contents from the cell's environment. The cell membrane is the outermost structure in cells that lack a cell wall. In cells that have a cell wall, the cell membrane lies just inside the cell wall.

The cell membrane contains proteins, lipids, and phospholipids. *Lipids,* which include fats and cholesterol, are a group of compounds that do not dissolve in water. The cell membrane has two layers of phospholipids (FAHS foh LIP idz), shown in **Figure 2.** A *phospholipid* is a lipid that contains phosphorus. Lipids are "water fearing," or *hydrophobic.* Lipid ends of phospholipids form the inner part of the membrane. Phosphorus-containing ends of the phospholipids are "water loving," or *hydrophilic.* These ends form the outer part of the membrane.

Some of the proteins and lipids control the movement of materials into and out of the cell. Some of the proteins form passageways. Nutrients and water move into the cell, and wastes move out of the cell, through these protein passageways.

Reading Check What are two functions of a cell membrane?

cell wall a rigid structure that surrounds the cell membrane and provides support to the cell

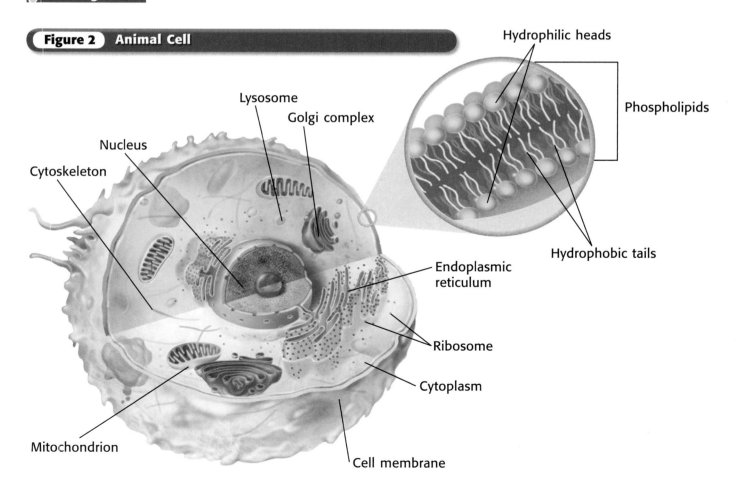

Figure 2 Animal Cell

Lysosome
Golgi complex
Nucleus
Cytoskeleton
Hydrophilic heads
Phospholipids
Hydrophobic tails
Endoplasmic reticulum
Ribosome
Cytoplasm
Mitochondrion
Cell membrane

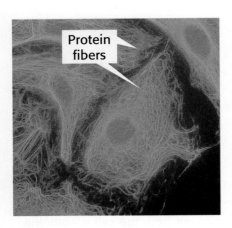

Figure 3 *The cytoskeleton, made of protein fibers, helps a cell retain its shape, move in its environment, and move its organelles.*

Cytoskeleton

The *cytoskeleton* (SIET oh SKEL uh tuhn) is a web of proteins in the cytoplasm. The cytoskeleton, shown in **Figure 3,** acts as both a muscle and a skeleton. It keeps the cell's membranes from collapsing. The cytoskeleton also helps some cells move.

The cytoskeleton is made of three types of protein. One protein is a hollow tube. The other two are long, stringy fibers. One of the stringy proteins is also found in muscle cells.

✓ *Reading Check* What is the cytoskeleton?

Nucleus

All eukaryotic cells have the same basic membrane-bound organelles, starting with the nucleus. The *nucleus* is a large organelle in a eukaryotic cell. It contains the cell's DNA, or genetic material. DNA contains the information on how to make a cell's proteins. Proteins control the chemical reactions in a cell. They also provide structural support for cells and tissues. But proteins are not made in the nucleus. Messages for how to make proteins are copied from the DNA. These messages are then sent out of the nucleus through the membranes.

The nucleus is covered by two membranes. Materials cross this double membrane by passing through pores. **Figure 4** shows a nucleus and nuclear pores. The nucleus of many cells has a dark area called the nucleolus (noo KLEE uh luhs). The *nucleolus* is where a cell begins to make its ribosomes.

Figure 4 *The nucleus contains the cell's DNA. Pores allow materials to move between the nucleus and the cytoplasm.*

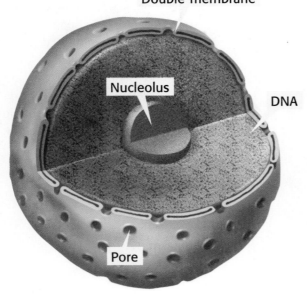

Double membrane

Nucleolus

DNA

Pore

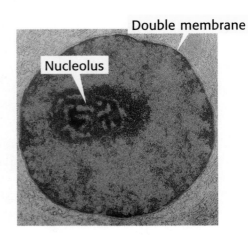

Double membrane

Nucleolus

Ribosomes

Organelles that make proteins are called **ribosomes.** Ribosomes are the smallest of all organelles. And there are more ribosomes in a cell than there are any other organelles. Some ribosomes float freely in the cytoplasm. Others are attached to membranes or the cytoskeleton. Unlike most organelles, ribosomes are not covered by a membrane.

Proteins are made within the ribosomes. Proteins are made of amino acids. An *amino acid* is any one of about 20 different organic molecules that are used to make proteins. All cells need proteins to live. All cells have ribosomes.

ribosome cell organelle composed of RNA and protein; the site of protein synthesis

endoplasmic reticulum a system of membranes that is found in a cell's cytoplasm and that assists in the production, processing, and transport of proteins and in the production of lipids

Endoplasmic Reticulum

Many chemical reactions take place in a cell. Many of these reactions happen on or in the endoplasmic reticulum (EN doh PLAZ mik ri TIK yuh luhm). The **endoplasmic reticulum,** or ER, is a system of folded membranes in which proteins, lipids, and other materials are made. The ER is shown in **Figure 5.**

The ER is part of the internal delivery system of the cell. Its folded membrane contains many tubes and passageways. Substances move through the ER to different places in the cell.

Endoplasmic reticulum is either rough ER or smooth ER. The part of the ER covered in ribosomes is rough ER. Rough ER is usually found near the nucleus. Ribosomes on rough ER make many of the cell's proteins. The ER delivers these proteins throughout the cell. ER that lacks ribosomes is smooth ER. The functions of smooth ER include making lipids and breaking down toxic materials that could damage the cell.

Figure 5 *The endoplasmic reticulum (ER) is a system of membranes. Rough ER is covered with ribosomes. Smooth ER does not have ribosomes.*

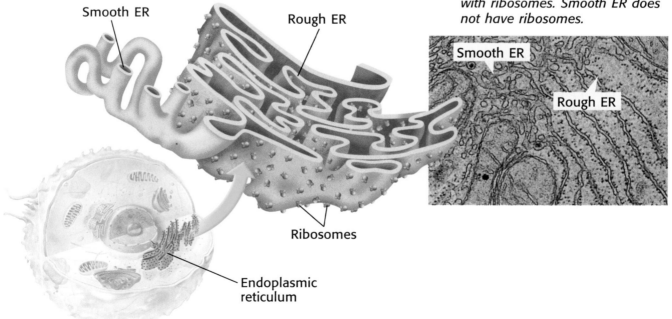

Smooth ER

Rough ER

Smooth ER

Rough ER

Ribosomes

Endoplasmic reticulum

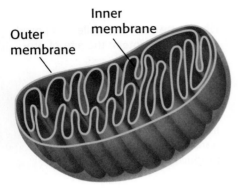

Outer membrane

Inner membrane

Outer membrane Inner membrane

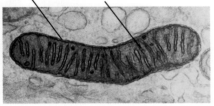

Figure 6 *Mitochondria break down sugar and make ATP. ATP is produced on the inner membrane.*

mitochondrion in eukaryotic cells, the cell organelle that is surrounded by two membranes and that is the site of cellular respiration

Mitochondria

A mitochondrion (MIET oh KAHN dree uhn) is the main power source of a cell. A **mitochondrion** is the organelle in which sugar is broken down to produce energy. Mitochondria are covered by two membranes, as shown in **Figure 6.** Energy released by mitochondria is stored in a substance called *ATP* (**a**denosine **t**ri**p**hosphate). The cell then uses ATP to do work. ATP can be made at several places in a cell. But most of a cell's ATP is made in the inner membrane of the cell's mitochondria.

Most eukaryotic cells have mitochondria. Mitochondria are the size of some bacteria. Like bacteria, mitochondria have their own DNA, and mitochondria can divide within a cell.

✓ **Reading Check** Where is most of a cell's ATP made?

Chloroplasts

Animal cells cannot make their own food. Plants and algae are different. They have chloroplasts (KLAWR uh PLASTS) in some of their cells. *Chloroplasts* are organelles in plant and algae cells in which photosynthesis takes place. Like mitochondria, chloroplasts have two membranes and their own DNA. A chloroplast is shown in **Figure 7.** *Photosynthesis* is the process by which plants and algae use sunlight, carbon dioxide, and water to make sugar and oxygen.

Chloroplasts are green because they contain *chlorophyll,* a green pigment. Chlorophyll is found inside the inner membrane of a chloroplast. Chlorophyll traps the energy of sunlight, which is used to make sugar. The sugar produced by photosynthesis is then used by mitochondria to make ATP.

Figure 7 *Chloroplasts harness and use the energy of the sun to make sugar. A green pigment—chlorophyll—traps the sun's energy.*

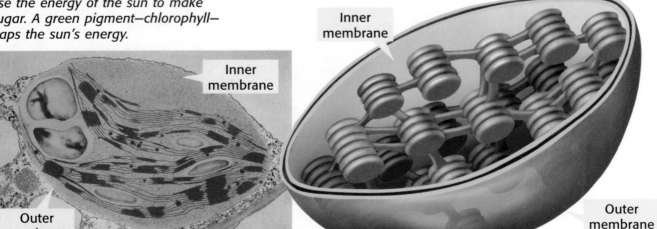

Inner membrane

Inner membrane

Outer membrane

Outer membrane

Golgi Complex

The organelle that packages and distributes proteins is called the **Golgi complex** (GOHL jee KAHM PLEKS). It is named after Camillo Golgi, the Italian scientist who first identified the organelle.

The Golgi complex looks like smooth ER, as shown in **Figure 8.** Lipids and proteins from the ER are delivered to the Golgi complex. There, the lipids and proteins may be modified to do different jobs. The final products are enclosed in a piece of the Golgi complex's membrane. This membrane pinches off to form a small bubble. The bubble transports its contents to other parts of the cell or out of the cell.

Cell Compartments

The bubble that forms from the Golgi complex's membrane is a vesicle. A **vesicle** (VES i kuhl) is a small sac that surrounds material to be moved into or out of a cell. All eukaryotic cells have vesicles. Vesicles also move material within a cell. For example, vesicles carry new protein from the ER to the Golgi complex. Other vesicles distribute material from the Golgi complex to other parts of the cell. Some vesicles form when part of the cell membrane surrounds an object outside the cell.

Golgi complex cell organelle that helps make and package materials to be transported out of the cell

vesicle a small cavity or sac that contains materials in a eukaryotic cell

Figure 8 *The Golgi complex processes proteins. It moves proteins to where they are needed, including out of the cell.*

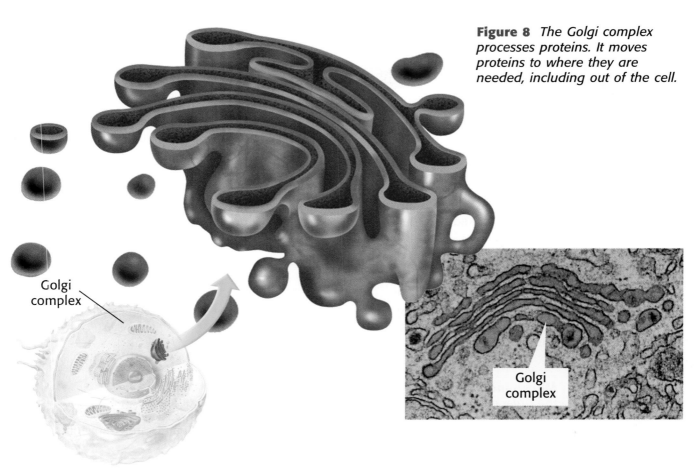

Golgi complex

Golgi complex

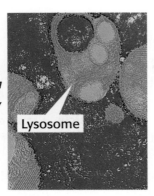

Figure 9
Lysosomes digest materials inside a cell. In plant cells, the large central vacuole stores water.

Lysosome

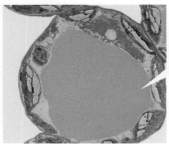

Large central vacuole

lysosome a cell organelle that contains digestive enzymes

Cellular Digestion

Lysosomes (LIE suh SOHMZ) are vesicles that are responsible for digestion inside a cell. **Lysosomes** are organelles that contain digestive enzymes. They destroy worn-out or damaged organelles, get rid of waste materials, and protect the cell from foreign invaders. Lysosomes, which come in a wide variety of sizes and shapes, are shown in **Figure 9.**

Lysosomes are found mainly in animal cells. When eukaryotic cells engulf particles, they enclose the particles in vesicles. Lysosomes bump into these vesicles and pour enzymes into them. These enzymes digest the particles in the vesicles.

✓ Reading Check Why are lysosomes important?

Vacuoles

A *vacuole* (VAK yoo OHL) is a vesicle. In plant and fungal cells, some vacuoles act like lysosomes. They store digestive enzymes and aid in digestion within the cell. The large central vacuole in plant cells stores water and other liquids. Large central vacuoles that are full of water, such as the one in **Figure 9,** help support the cell. Some plants wilt when their large central vacuoles lose water. **Table 1** shows some organelles and their functions.

Table 1 **Organelles and Their Functions**	
Nucleus the organelle that contains the cell's DNA and is the control center of the cell	**Chloroplast** the organelle that uses the energy of sunlight to make food
Ribosome the organelle in which amino acids are hooked together to make proteins	**Golgi complex** the organelle that processes and transports proteins and other materials out of cell
Endoplasmic reticulum the organelle that makes lipids, breaks down drugs and other substances, and packages proteins for Golgi complex	**Large central vacuole** the organelle that stores water and other materials
Mitochondrion the organelle that breaks down food molecules to make ATP	**Lysosome** the organelle that digests food particles, wastes, cell parts, and foreign invaders

Summary

- Eukaryotic cells have organelles that perform functions that help cells remain alive.
- All cells have a cell membrane. Some cells have a cell wall. Some cells have a cytoskeleton.
- The nucleus of a eukaryotic cell contains the cell's genetic material, DNA.
- Ribosomes are the organelles that make proteins. Ribosomes are not covered by a membrane.

- The endoplasmic reticulum (ER) and the Golgi complex make and process proteins before the proteins are transported to other parts of the cell or out of the cell.
- Mitochondria and chloroplasts are organelles that provide chemical energy for the cell.
- Lysosomes are organelles responsible for digestion within a cell. In plant cells, organelles called *vacuoles* store cell materials and sometimes act like large lysosomes.

Using Key Terms

1. In your own words, write a definition for each of the following terms: *ribosome, lysosome,* and *cell wall.*

Understanding Key Ideas

2. Which of the following are found mainly in animal cells?
   a. mitochondria
   b. lysosomes
   c. ribosomes
   d. Golgi complexes

3. What is the function of a Golgi complex? What is the function of the endoplasmic reticulum?

Critical Thinking

4. **Making Comparisons** Describe three ways in which plant cells differ from animal cells.

5. **Applying Concepts** Every cell needs ribosomes. Explain why.

6. **Predicting Consequences** A certain virus attacks the mitochondria in cells. What would happen to a cell if all of its mitochondria were destroyed?

7. **Expressing Opinions** Do you think that having chloroplasts gives plant cells an advantage over animal cells? Support your opinion.

Interpreting Graphics

Use the diagram below to answer the questions that follow.

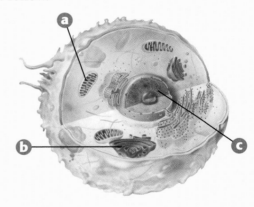

8. Is this a diagram of a plant cell or an animal cell? Explain how you know.

9. What organelle does the letter *b* refer to?

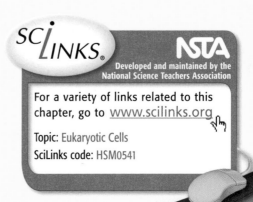

Developed and maintained by the National Science Teachers Association

For a variety of links related to this chapter, go to www.scilinks.org

Topic: Eukaryotic Cells
SciLinks code: HSM0541

The Organization of Living Things

In some ways, organisms are like machines. Some machines have just one part. But most machines have many parts. Some organisms exist as a single cell. Other organisms have many—even trillions—of cells.

Most cells are smaller than the period that ends this sentence. Yet, every cell in every organism performs all the processes of life. So, are there any advantages to having many cells?

The Benefits of Being Multicellular

You are a *multicellular organism.* This means that you are made of many cells. Multicellular organisms grow by making more small cells, not by making their cells larger. For example, an elephant is bigger than you are, but its cells are about the same size as yours. An elephant just has more cells than you do. Some benefits of being multicellular are the following:

● **Larger Size** Many multicellular organisms are small. But they are usually larger than single-celled organisms. Larger organisms are prey for fewer predators. Larger predators can eat a wider variety of prey.

● **Longer Life** The life span of a multicellular organism is not limited to the life span of any single cell.

● **Specialization** Each type of cell has a particular job. Specialization makes the organism more efficient. For example, the cardiac muscle cell in **Figure 1** is a specialized muscle cell. Heart muscle cells contract and make the heart pump blood.

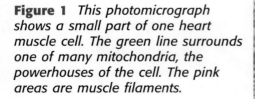 **Reading Check** List three advantages of being multicellular. *(See the Appendix for answers to Reading Checks.)*

Figure 1 *This photomicrograph shows a small part of one heart muscle cell. The green line surrounds one of many mitochondria, the powerhouses of the cell. The pink areas are muscle filaments.*

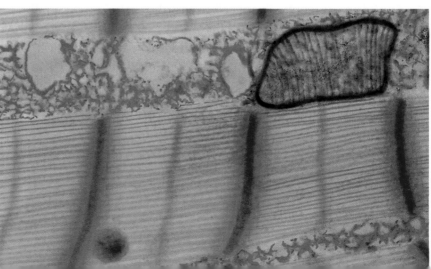

Figure 2 *This photomicrograph shows cardiac muscle tissue. Cardiac muscle tissue is made up of many cardiac cells.*

Cells Working Together

A **tissue** is a group of cells that work together to perform a specific job. The material around and between the cells is also part of the tissue. The cardiac muscle tissue, shown in **Figure 2,** is made of many cardiac muscle cells. Cardiac muscle tissue is just one type of tissue in a heart.

Animals have four basic types of tissues: nerve tissue, muscle tissue, connective tissue, and protective tissue. In contrast, plants have three types of tissues: transport tissue, protective tissue, and ground tissue. Transport tissue moves water and nutrients through a plant. Protective tissue covers the plant. It helps the plant retain water and protects the plant against damage. Photosynthesis takes place in ground tissue.

Tissues Working Together

A structure that is made up of two or more tissues working together to perform a specific function is called an **organ.** For example, your heart is an organ. It is made mostly of cardiac muscle tissue. But your heart also has nerve tissue and tissues of the blood vessels that all work together to make your heart the powerful pump that it is.

Another organ is your stomach. It also has several kinds of tissue. In the stomach, muscle tissue makes food move in and through the stomach. Special tissues make chemicals that help digest your food. Connective tissue holds the stomach together, and nervous tissue carries messages back and forth between the stomach and the brain. Other organs include the intestines, brain, and lungs.

Plants also have different kinds of tissues that work together as organs. A leaf is a plant organ that contains tissue that traps light energy to make food. Other examples of plant organs are stems and roots.

✓ Reading Check What is an organ?

tissue a group of similar cells that perform a common function

organ a collection of tissues that carry out a specialized function of the body

A Pet Protist
Imagine that you have a tiny box-shaped protist for a pet. To care for your pet protist properly, you have to figure out how much to feed it. The dimensions of your protist are roughly 25 μm × 20 μm × 2 μm. If seven food particles per second can enter through each square micrometer of surface area, how many particles can your protist eat in 1 min?

Organs Working Together

A group of organs working together to perform a particular function is called an **organ system.** Each organ system has a specific job to do in the body.

For example, the digestive system is made up of several organs, including the stomach and intestines. The digestive system's job is to break down food into small particles. Other parts of the body then use these small particles as fuel. In turn, the digestive system depends on the respiratory and cardiovascular systems for oxygen. The cardiovascular system, shown in **Figure 3,** includes organs and tissues such as the heart and blood vessels. Plants also have organ systems. They include leaf systems, root systems, and stem systems.

✓ **Reading Check** List the levels of organization in living things.

Organisms

Anything that can perform life processes by itself is an **organism.** An organism made of a single cell is called a *unicellular organism.* Prokaryotes, most protists, and some kinds of fungi are unicellular. Although some of these organisms live in colonies, they are still unicellular. They are unicellular organisms living together, and all of the cells in the colony are the same. Each cell must carry out all life processes in order for that cell to survive. In contrast, even the simplest multicellular organism has specialized cells that depend on each other for the organism to survive.

organ system a group of organs that work together to perform body functions

organism a living thing; anything that can carry out life processes independently

structure the arrangement of parts in an organism

function the special, normal, or proper activity of an organ or part

Figure 3 Levels of Organization in the Cardiovascular System

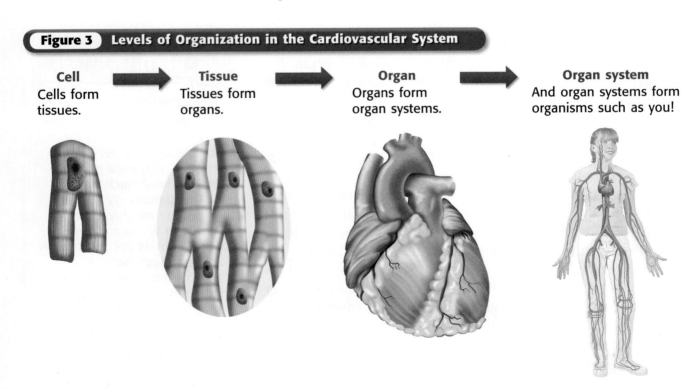

Cell
Cells form tissues.

Tissue
Tissues form organs.

Organ
Organs form organ systems.

Organ system
And organ systems form organisms such as you!

Structure and Function

In organisms, structure and function are related. **Structure** is the arrangement of parts in an organism. It includes the shape of a part and the material of which the part is made. **Function** is the job the part does. For example, the structure of the lungs is a large, spongy sac. In the lungs, there are millions of tiny air sacs called *alveoli*. Blood vessels wrap around the alveoli, as shown in **Figure 4.** Oxygen from air in the alveoli enters the blood. Blood then brings oxygen to body tissues. Also, in the alveoli, carbon dioxide leaves the blood and is exhaled.

The structures of alveoli and blood vessels enable them to perform a function. Together, they bring oxygen to the body and get rid of its carbon dioxide.

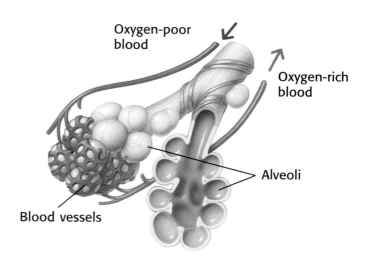

Figure 4 The Structure and Function of Alveoli

Oxygen-poor blood

Oxygen-rich blood

Alveoli

Blood vessels

SECTION Review

Summary

- Advantages of being multicellular are larger size, longer life, and cell specialization.

- Four levels of organization are cell, tissue, organ, and organ system.

- A *tissue* is a group of cells working together. An *organ* is two or more tissues working together. An *organ system* is two or more organs working together.

- In organisms, a part's structure and function are related.

Using Key Terms

1. Use each of the following terms in a separate sentence: *tissue, organ,* and *function.*

Understanding Key Ideas

2. What are the four levels of organization in living things?
   a. cell, multicellular, organ, organ system
   b. single cell, multicellular, tissue, organ
   c. larger size, longer life, specialized cells, organs
   d. cell, tissue, organ, organ system

Math Skills

3. One multicellular organism is a cube. Each of its sides is 3 cm long. Each of its cells is 1 cm³. How many cells does it have? If each side doubles in length, how many cells will it then have?

Critical Thinking

4. **Applying Concepts** Explain the relationship between structure and function. Use alveoli as an example. Be sure to include more than one level of organization.

5. **Making Inferences** Why can multicellular organisms be more complex than unicellular organisms? Use the three advantages of being multicellular to help explain your answer.

Model-Making Lab

OBJECTIVES

Explore why a single-celled organism cannot grow to the size of an elephant.

Create a model of a cell to illustrate the concept of surface area–to-volume ratio.

MATERIALS

- calculator (optional)
- cubic cell patterns
- heavy paper or poster board
- sand, fine
- scale or balance
- scissors
- tape, transparent

SAFETY

Elephant-Sized Amoebas?

An amoeba is a single-celled organism. Like most cells, amoebas are microscopic. Why can't amoebas grow as large as elephants? If an amoeba grew to the size of a quarter, the amoeba would starve to death. To understand how this can be true, build a model of a cell and see for yourself.

Procedure

1. Use heavy paper or poster board to make four cube-shaped cell models from the patterns supplied by your teacher. Cut out each cell model, fold the sides to make a cube, and tape the tabs on the sides. The smallest cell model has sides that are each one unit long. The next larger cell has sides of two units. The next cell has sides of three units, and the largest cell has sides of four units. These paper models represent the cell membrane, the part of a cell's exterior through which food and wastes pass.

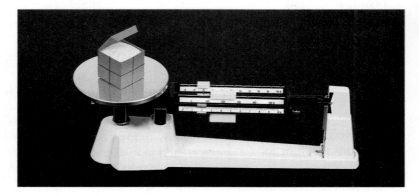

Data Table for Measurements						Key to Formula Symbols
Length of side	Area of one side (A = S × S)	Total surface area of cube cell (TA = S × S × 6)	Volume of cube cell (V = S × S × S)	Mass of filled cube cell		
1 unit	1 unit^2	6 unit^2	1 unit^3			S = the length of one side
2 unit						A = area
3 unit		DO NOT WRITE IN BOOK				6 = number of sides
4 unit						V = volume
						TA = total area

2. Copy the data table shown above. Use each formula to calculate the data about your cell models. Record your calculations in the table. Calculations for the smallest cell have been done for you.

3. Carefully fill each model with fine sand until the sand is level with the top edge of the model. Find the mass of the filled models by using a scale or a balance. What does the sand in your model represent?

4. Record the mass of each filled cell model in your Data Table for Measurements. (Always remember to use the appropriate mass unit.)

Analyze the Results

1. **Constructing Tables** Make a data table like the one shown at right.

2. **Organizing Data** Use the data from your Data Table for Measurements to find the ratios for each of your cell models. For each of the cell models, fill in the Data Table for Ratios.

Draw Conclusions

3. **Interpreting Information** As a cell grows larger, does the ratio of total surface area to volume increase, decrease, or stay the same?

4. **Interpreting Information** As a cell grows larger, does the total surface area–to-mass ratio increase, decrease, or stay the same?

5. **Drawing Conclusions** Which is better able to supply food to all the cytoplasm of the cell: the cell membrane of a small cell or the cell membrane of a large cell? Explain your answer.

6. **Evaluating Data** In the experiment, which is better able to feed all of the cytoplasm of the cell: the cell membrane of a cell that has high mass or the cell membrane of a cell that has low mass? You may explain your answer in a verbal presentation to the class, or you may choose to write a report and illustrate it with drawings of your models.

Data Table for Ratios		
Length of side	Ratio of total surface area to volume	Ratio of total surface area to mass
1 unit		
2 unit		
3 unit		
4 unit	DO NOT WRITE IN BOOK	

Chapter Review

USING KEY TERMS

Complete each of the following sentences by choosing the correct term from the word bank.

cell   organ
cell membrane   prokaryote
organelles   eukaryote
cell wall   tissue
structure   function

1 A(n) ___ is the most basic unit of all living things.

2 The job that an organ does is the ___ of that organ.

3 Ribosomes and mitochondria are types of ___.

4 A(n) ___ is an organism whose cells have a nucleus.

5 A group of cells working together to perform a specific function is a(n) ___.

6 Only plant cells have a(n) ___.

UNDERSTANDING KEY IDEAS

Multiple Choice

7 Which of the following best describes an organ?

  a. a group of cells that work together to perform a specific job

  b. a group of tissues that belong to different systems

  c. a group of tissues that work together to perform a specific job

  d. a body structure, such as muscles or lungs

8 The benefits of being multicellular include

  a. small size, long life, and cell specialization.

  b. generalized cells, longer life, and ability to prey on small animals.

  c. larger size, more enemies, and specialized cells.

  d. longer life, larger size, and specialized cells.

9 In eukaryotic cells, which organelle contains the DNA?

  a. nucleus   **c.** smooth ER

  b. Golgi complex   **d.** vacuole

10 Which of the following statements is part of the cell theory?

  a. All cells suddenly appear by themselves.

  b. All cells come from other cells.

  c. All organisms are multicellular.

  d. All cells have identical parts.

11 The surface area–to-volume ratio of a cell limits

  a. the number of organelles that the cell has.

  b. the size of the cell.

  c. where the cell lives.

  d. the types of nutrients that a cell needs.

12 Two types of organisms whose cells do not have a nucleus are

  a. prokaryotes and eukaryotes.

  b. plants and animals.

  c. bacteria and archaea.

  d. single-celled and multicellular organisms.

Short Answer

13 Explain why most cells are small.

14 Describe the four levels of organization in living things.

15 What is the difference between the structure of an organ and the function of the organ?

16 Name two functions of a cell membrane.

17 What are the structure and function of the cytoskeleton in a cell?

CRITICAL THINKING

18 **Concept Mapping** Use the following terms to create a concept map: *cells, organisms, Golgi complex, organ systems, organs, nucleus, organelle,* and *tissues.*

19 **Making Comparisons** Compare and contrast the functions of the endoplasmic reticulum and the Golgi complex.

20 **Identifying Relationships** Explain how the structure and function of an organism's parts are related. Give an example.

21 **Evaluating Hypotheses** One of your classmates states a hypothesis that all organisms must have organ systems. Is your classmate's hypothesis valid? Explain your answer.

22 **Predicting Consequences** What would happen if all of the ribosomes in your cells disappeared?

23 **Expressing Opinions** Scientists think that millions of years ago the surface of the Earth was very hot and that the atmosphere contained a lot of methane. In your opinion, which type of organism, a bacterium or an archaeon, is the older form of life? Explain your reasoning.

INTERPRETING GRAPHICS

Use the diagram below to answer the questions that follow.

24 What is the name of the structure identified by the letter *a*?

25 Which letter identifies the structure that digests food particles and foreign invaders?

26 Which letter identifies the structure that makes proteins, lipids, and other materials and that contains tubes and passageways that enable substances to move to different places in the cell?

Multiple Choice

Use the illustration below to answer question 1.

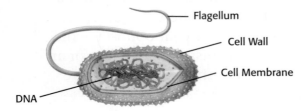

- Flagellum
- Cell Wall
- Cell Membrane
- DNA

1. **Which of the following statements is true about the organism that has the cell shown above?**

   A. It is made up of eukaryotic cells.

   B. It has many levels of organization.

   C. It undergoes cell division to repair damaged tissues.

   D. It has special structures to help it perform all its life functions.

2. **Which of the following comparisons between humans and Archaea is true?**

   A. Human cells contain DNA, but the cells of Archaea do not.

   B. Humans tissues, organs, and organ systems work together to perform life functions. In Archaea, each single cell must perform all life functions.

   C. Human cells perform life functions independently, but the cells of Archaea work together to perform life functions.

   D. Human cells have membranes but not walls. The cells of Archaea have walls but not membranes.

3. **What would most likely happen to a cell if its mitochondria were not functioning properly?**

   A. The cell would use lysosomes to release energy.

   B. The cell's level of ATP would decrease.

   C. The cell would create new mitochondria by cell division.

   D. The cell's level of sugar would decrease.

4. **Which of the following phrases describes the nucleus?**

   A. an organelle that has a double membrane and pores

   B. a system of folded membranes that is covered in ribosomes

   C. an organelle that has a membrane and a cell wall

   D. an organelle that has a folded inner membrane

5. **Which of the following describes the function of lungs?**

   A. Lungs are large, spongy sacs in the chest.

   B. Lungs move oxygen to body tissues.

   C. The lungs have many small sacs called *alveoli*.

   D. Lungs move oxygen from the air into the blood.

6. What type of cells differentiate?

A. cells of multicellular organisms

B. prokaryotic cells

C. bacterial cells

D. cells of unicellular organisms

Use the diagram below to answer question 7.

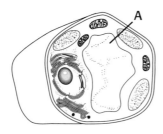

A

7. The figure above shows a basic plant cell. How does the organelle labeled A maintain the internal environment of a plant cell?

A. It makes food for the cell.

B. It contains the DNA of the cell.

C. It stores water and nutrients for the cell.

D. It moves materials into and out of the cell.

8. What is the function of transport tissue?

A. to move water and nutrients throughout a plant

B. to move blood, water, and materials to body cells

C. to carry messages between organs, such as the brain and the stomach

D. to make and carry glucose throughout a plant

9. What is the function of chloroplasts?

A. to convert sunlight, carbon dioxide, and water into ATP

B. to release the energy stored in sugar

C. to convert sunlight, sugar, and oxygen into carbon dioxide and water

D. to convert sunlight, carbon dioxide, and water into sugar and oxygen

10. Why are animal cells harder to see through a microscope than plant cells?

A. The cytoplasm of plant cells is green, but the cytoplasm of animal cells is colorless.

B. Plant cells have cell walls, but animal cells do not.

C. Plant cells are larger than animal cells.

D. Plant cells contain organelles, but animal cells do not.

Open Response

11. Describe the organization of multicellular organisms, such as humans, from the simplest unit of life to the level of the whole organism.

12. How does the membrane of a cell control the internal environment of the cell?

Standardized Test Preparation

Science in Action

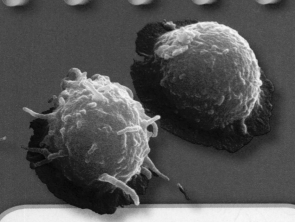

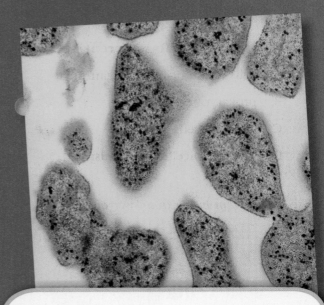

Scientific Discoveries

Discovery of the Stem Cell

What do Parkinson's disease, diabetes, aplastic anemia, and Alzheimer's disease have in common? All of these diseases are diseases for which stem cells may provide treatment or a cure. Stem cells are unspecialized cells from which all other kinds of cells can grow. And research on stem cells has been going on almost since microscopes were invented. But scientists have been able to culture, or grow, stem cells in laboratories for only about the last 20 years. Research during these 20 years has shown scientists that stem cells can be useful in treating—and possibly curing—a variety of diseases.

Weird Science

Extremophiles

Are there organisms on Earth that can give scientists clues about possible life elsewhere? Yes, there are! These organisms are called *extremophiles,* and they live where the environment is extreme. For example, some extremophiles live in the hot volcanic thermal vents deep in the ocean. Other extremophiles live in the extreme cold of Antarctica. But these organisms do not live only in extreme environments. Research shows that extremophiles may be abundant in plankton in the ocean. And not all extremophiles are archaea; some extremophiles are bacteria.

Language Arts

WRITING SKILL Imagine that you are a doctor who treats diseases such as Parkinson's disease. Design and create a pamphlet or brochure that you could use to explain what stem cells are. Include in your pamphlet a description of how stem cells might be used to treat one of your patients who has Parkinson's disease. Be sure to include information about Parkinson's disease.

Social Studies ACTIVITY

Choose one of the four types of extremophiles. Do some research about the organism you have chosen and make a poster showing what you learned about it, including where it can be found, under what conditions it lives, how it survives, and how it is used.

Caroline Schooley

Microscopist Imagine that your assignment is the following: Go outside. Look at 1 ft² of the ground for 30 min. Make notes about what you observe. Be prepared to describe what you see. If you look at the ground with just your naked eyes, you may quickly run out of things to see. But what would happen if you used a microscope to look? How much more would you be able to see? And how much more would you have to talk about? Caroline Schooley could tell you.

Caroline Schooley joined a science club in middle school. That's when her interest in looking at things through a microscope began. Since then, Schooley has spent many years studying life through a microscope. She is a microscopist. A *microscopist* is someone who uses a microscope to look at small things. Microscopists use their tools to explore the world of small things that cannot be seen by the naked eye. And with today's powerful electron microscopes, microscopists can study things we could never see before, things as small as atoms.

Math ACTIVITY

An average bacterium is about 0.000002 m long. A pencil point is about 0.001 m wide. Approximately how many bacteria would fit on a pencil point?

To learn more about these Science in Action topics, visit **go.hrw.com** and type in the keyword **HL5CELF.**

Current Science

Check out Current Science® articles related to this chapter by visiting go.hrw.com. Just type in the keyword HL5CS03.

UNIT 4

TIMELINE

Simple Organisms, Fungi, and Plants

Do you know how important plants are? Plants provide oxygen and food for other living things.

Throughout history, people have been trying to understand plants. In this unit, you will join them. You'll also learn about, some other fascinating organisms—bacteria, protists, and fungi. Some of these organisms cause disease, but others provide food and medicines. Read on, and be amazed!

Around 250

Mayan farmers build terraces to control the flow of water to crops.

1864

Louis Pasteur uses heat to eliminate microbes. This process is later called *pasteurization*.

1897

Beatrix Potter, the author of *The Tale of Peter Rabbit*, completes her collection of 270 watercolors of fungi. Today, she is considered an expert in mycology, the study of fungi.

1971

Ananda Chakrabarty uses genetics to design bacteria that can break down oil in oil spills.

1580

Prospero Alpini discovers that plants have both male structures and female structures.

1683

Anton van Leeuwenhoek is the first person to describe bacteria.

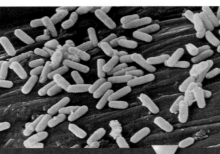

1763

Joseph Kolreuter studies orchid pollination and discovers that both parent plants contribute traits to the offspring.

E. coli under an electron microscope

1898

Martinus Beijerinck gives the name *virus* to infectious material that is smaller than a bacterium.

1928

Alexander Fleming observes that certain molds can eliminate bacterial growth, and he discovers penicillin.

1955

A vaccine for the polio virus developed by Dr. Jonas Salk becomes widely used.

1983

HIV, the virus responsible for AIDS, is isolated.

1995

An outbreak of the deadly Ebola virus occurs in Zaire.

2002

An international team decodes the DNA sequences for both the protist that causes malaria and the mosquito that carries this protist. As a result, the door to more-effective antimalaria drugs is opened.

Ebola virus

11

Classification

The Big Idea

Organisms are classified into groups based on their characteristics.

About the Photo

Look at the katydids, grasshoppers, and mantids in the photo. A scientist is classifying these insects. Every insect has a label describing the insect. These descriptions will be used to help the scientist know if each insect has already been discovered and named. When scientists discover a new insect or other organism, they have to give the organism a name. The name chosen is unique and should help other scientists understand some basic facts about the organism.

PRE-READING ACTIVITY

FOLDNOTES **Booklet** Before you read the chapter, create the FoldNote entitled "Booklet" described in the **Study Skills** section of the Appendix. Label each page of the booklet with a main idea from the chapter. As you read the chapter, write what you learn about each main idea on the appropriate page of the booklet.

START-UP ACTIVITY

Classifying Shoes

In this group activity, each group will develop a system of classification for shoes.

Procedure

1. Gather **10 shoes.** Number pieces of **masking tape** from 1 to 10. Label the sole of each shoe with a numbered piece of tape.

2. Make a list of shoe features. Make a table that has a column for each feature. Complete the table by describing each shoe.

3. Use the data in the table to make a shoe identification key.

4. The key should be a list of steps. Each step should have two contrasting statements about the shoes. The statements will lead you either to the next step or to a specific shoe.

5. If your shoe is not identified in one step, go on to the next step or steps until the shoe is identified.

6. Trade keys with another group. How did the other group's key help you identify the shoes?

Analysis

1. How was listing the shoe features before making the key helpful?

2. Were you able to identify the shoes using another group's key? Explain.

Sorting It All Out

Imagine that you live in a tropical rain forest and must get your own food, shelter, and clothing from the forest. What do you need to know to survive in the forest?

To survive in the rain forest, you need to know which plants are safe to eat and which are not. You need to know which animals you can eat and which might eat you. In other words, you need to study the living things around you and organize them into categories, or classify them. **Classification** is putting things into orderly groups based on similar characteristics.

Why Classify?

For thousands of years, humans have classified living things based on usefulness. The Chácabo people of Bolivia know of 360 types of plants that grow in the forest where they live. Of these 360 plant types, 305 are useful to the Chácabo.

Some biologists, such as those shown in **Figure 1,** classify living and extinct organisms. Scientists classify organisms to help make sense and order of the many kinds of living things in the world. Biologists use a system to classify living things. This system groups organisms according to the characteristics they share. The classification of living things makes it easier for biologists to answer many important questions, such as the following:

- How many known species are there?
- What are the defining characteristics of each species?
- What are the relationships between these species?

✓ Reading Check What are three questions that classifying organisms can help answer? (*See the Appendix for answers to Reading Checks.*)

What You Will Learn

- Explain why and how organisms are classified.
- List the eight levels of classification.
- Explain scientific names.
- Describe how dichotomous keys help in identifying organisms.

Vocabulary

classification
taxonomy
dichotomous key

READING STRATEGY

Reading Organizer As you read this section, create an outline of the section. Use the headings from the section in your outline.

classification the division of organisms into groups, or classes, based on specific characteristics

Figure 1 *These biologists are sorting rain-forest plant material.*

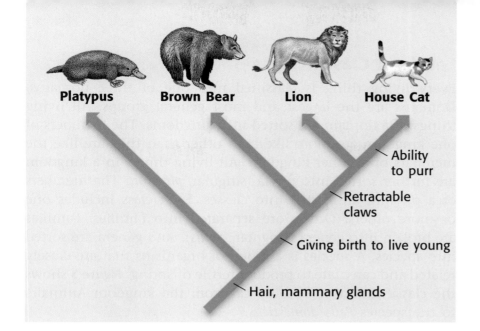

Figure 2 *This branching diagram shows the similarities and differences between four mammals.*

Ability to purr

Retractable claws

Giving birth to live young

Hair, mammary glands

How Do Scientists Classify Organisms?

Before the 1600s, many scientists divided organisms into two groups: plants and animals. But as more organisms were discovered, some did not fit into either group. In the 1700s, Carolus Linnaeus (KAR uh luhs li NAY uhs), a Swedish scientist, founded modern taxonomy. **Taxonomy** (taks AHN uh mee) is the science of describing, classifying, and naming living things. Linnaeus tried to classify all living things based on their shape and structure. Today, scientists use a system of classification that is very similar to the one that Linnaeus developed.

Classification Today

Taxonomists use an eight-level system to classify living things based on shared characteristics. Scientists also use shared characteristics to hypothesize how closely related living things are. The more characteristics the organisms share, the more closely related the organisms may be. For example, the platypus, brown bear, lion, and house cat are thought to be related because they share many characteristics. These animals have hair and mammary glands, so they are grouped together as mammals. But they can be further classified into more-specific groups.

Branching Diagrams

Look at the branching diagram in **Figure 2.** Several characteristics are listed along the line that points to the right. Each characteristic is shared by the animals to the right of it. All of the animals shown have hair and mammary glands. But only the bear, lion, and house cat give birth to live young. The lion and the house cat have retractable claws, but the other animals do not. Thus, the lion and the house cat are more closely related to each other than to the other animals.

taxonomy the science of describing, naming, and classifying organisms

A Branching Diagram

1. Construct a diagram similar to the one in **Figure 2.**

2. Use a frog, a snake, a kangaroo, and a rabbit in your diagram.

3. Think of one major change that happened before the frog evolved.

4. For the last three organisms, think of a change that happened between one of these organisms and the other two. Write all of these changes in your diagram.

Levels of Classification

Every living thing is classified into one of three domains. Domains are the largest and most general groups. All living things in a domain are sorted into kingdoms. The members of one kingdom are more like each other than they are like the members of another kingdom. All living things in a kingdom are further sorted into phyla (singular, *phylum*). The members of a phylum are sorted into classes. Each class includes one or more orders. Orders are separated into families. Families are broken into genera (singular, *genus*). And genera are sorted into species. A species is a group of organisms that are closely related and can mate to produce fertile offspring. **Figure 3** shows the classification of a house cat from the kingdom Animalia to the species *Felis domesticus.*

Scientific Names

By classifying organisms, biologists can give organisms scientific names. A scientific name remains the same for a specific kind of organism even if the organism has many common names. Before Linnaeus's time, scholars used names that were as long as 12 words to identify species. This system was hard to work with because the names were so long. The system was also hard to use because individual scientists named organisms differently. So, an organism could have more than one name.

INTERNET ACTIVITY

For another activity related to this chapter, go to **go.hrw.com** and type in the keyword **HL5CLSW.**

Figure 3 *The eight levels of classification are domain, kingdom, phylum, class, order, family, genus, and species.*

Kingdom Animalia	Phylum Chordata	Class Mammalia	Order Carnivora
All animals are in the **kingdom Animalia.** 	All animals in the **phylum Chordata** have a hollow nerve cord. Most have a backbone. 	Animals in the **class Mammalia** have a backbone. They also nurse their young. 	Animals in the **order Carnivora** have a backbone and nurse their young. They also have special teeth for tearing meat. 

Two-Part Names

Linnaeus simplified the naming of living things by giving each species a two-part scientific name. For example, the scientific name for the Asian elephant is *Elephas maximus* (EL uh fuhs MAK suh muhs). The first part of the name, *Elephas,* is the genus name. The second part, *maximus,* is the specific name. No other species has the name *Elephas maximus.* Naming rules help scientists communicate clearly about living things.

All genus names begin with a capital letter. All specific names begin with a lowercase letter. Usually, both words are underlined or italicized. But if the surrounding text is italicized, the scientific name is not, as **Figure 4** shows. These printing styles show a reader which words are the scientific name.

Scientific names, which are usually in Latin or Greek, contain information about an organism. The name of the animal shown in **Figure 4** is *Tyrannosaurus rex.* *Tyrannosaurus* is a combination of two Greek words and means "tyrant lizard." The word *rex* is Latin for "king." The name tells you that this animal was probably not a passive grass eater! Sometimes, *Tyrannosaurus rex* is referred to as *T. rex.* To be correct, the scientific name must consist of the genus name (or its abbreviation) and the specific name.

Figure 4 *You would never call* Tyrannosaurus rex *just* rex!

Reading Check What are the two parts of a scientific name?

Family Felidae	Genus *Felis*	Species *Felis domesticus*
Animals in the **family Felidae** are cats. They have a backbone, nurse their young, have special teeth for tearing meat, and have retractable claws.	Animals in the **genus *Felis*** have traits of other animals in the same family. However, these cats cannot roar; they can only purr.	The **species *Felis domesticus*** is the common house cat. The house cat shares traits with all of the organisms in the levels above the species level, but it also has unique traits.

Dichotomous Keys

You might someday turn over a rock and find an organism that you don't recognize. How would you identify the organism? Taxonomists have developed special guides to help scientists identify organisms. A **dichotomous key** (die KAHT uh muhs KEE) is an identification aid that uses sequential pairs of descriptive statements. There are only two alternative responses for each statement. From each pair of statements, the person trying to identify the organism chooses the statement that describes the organism. Either the chosen statement identifies the organism or the person is directed to another pair of statements. By working through the statements in the key in order, the person can eventually identify the organism. Using the simple dichotomous key in **Figure 5,** try to identify the two animals shown.

dichotomous key an aid that is used to identify organisms and that consists of the answers to a series of questions

✓ **Reading Check** What is a dichotomous key?

Figure 5 *A dichotomous key can help you identify organisms.*

Dichotomous Key to 10 Common Mammals in the Eastern United States

1. a. This mammal flies. Its "hand" forms a wing. **b.** This mammal does not fly. It's "hand" does not form a wing.	**little brown bat** Go to step 2.
2. a. This mammal has no hair on its tail. **b.** This mammal has hair on its tail.	Go to step 3. Go to step 4.
3. a. This mammal has a short, naked tail. **b.** This mammal has a long, naked tail.	**eastern mole** Go to step 5.
4. a. This mammal has a black mask across its face. **b.** This mammal does not have a black mask across its face.	**raccoon** Go to step 6.
5. a. This mammal has a tail that is flat and paddle shaped. **b.** This mammal has a tail that is not flat or paddle shaped.	**beaver** **opossum**
6. a. This mammal is brown and has a white underbelly. **b.** This mammal is not brown and does not have a white underbelly.	Go to step 7. Go to step 8.
7. a. This mammal has a long, furry tail that is black on the tip. **b.** This mammal has a long tail that has little fur.	**longtail weasel** **white-footed mouse**
8. a. This mammal is black and has a narrow white stripe on its forehead and broad white stripes on its back. **b.** This mammal is not black and does not have white stripes.	**striped skunk** Go to step 9.
9. a. This mammal has long ears and a short, cottony tail. **b.** This mammal has short ears and a medium-length tail.	**eastern cottontail** **woodchuck**

A Growing System

You may think that all of the organisms on Earth have already been classified. But people are still discovering and classifying organisms. Some newly discovered organisms fit into existing categories. But sometimes, someone discovers new evidence or an organism that is so different from other organisms that it does not fit existing categories. For example, in 1995, scientists studied an organism named *Symbion pandora* (SIM bee AHN pan DAWR uh). Scientists found *S. pandora* living on lobster lips! Scientists learned that *S. pandora* had some characteristics that no other known organism had. In fact, scientists trying to classify *S. pandora* found that it didn't fit in any existing phylum. So, taxonomists created a new phylum for *S. pandora*.

SECTION Review

Summary

- In classification, organisms are grouped according to the characteristics the organisms share. Classification lets scientists answer important questions about the relationships between organisms.
- The eight levels of classification are domain, kingdom, phylum, class, order, family, genus, and species.
- An organism has one two-part scientific name.
- A dichotomous key is a tool for identifying organisms that uses a series of paired descriptive statements.

Using Key Terms

1. In your own words, write a definition for each of the following terms: *classification* and *taxonomy*.

Understanding Key Ideas

2. The two parts of a scientific name are the names of the genus and the
   a. specific name.
   b. phylum name.
   c. family name.
   d. order name.

3. Why do scientists use scientific names for organisms?

4. List the eight levels of classification.

5. Describe how a dichotomous key helps scientists identify organisms.

Critical Thinking

6. **Analyzing Processes** Biologists think that millions of species are not classified yet. Why do you think so many species have not been classified yet?

7. **Applying Concepts** Both dolphins and sharks have a tail and fins. How can you determine if dolphins and sharks are closely related?

Interpreting Graphics

Use the figure below to answer the questions that follow.

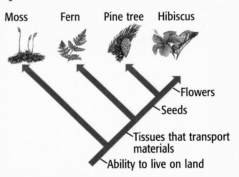

Moss   Fern   Pine tree   Hibiscus

Flowers
Seeds
Tissues that transport materials
Ability to live on land

8. Which plant is most similar to the hibiscus?

9. Which plant is least similar to the hibiscus?

SCiLINKS® NSTA

Developed and maintained by the National Science Teachers Association

For a variety of links related to this chapter, go to www.scilinks.org

Topic: Basis for Classification; Levels of Classification

SciLinks code: HSM0138; HSM0870

Domains and Kingdoms

What do you call an organism that is green, makes its own food, lives in pond water, and moves? Is it a plant, an animal, or something in between?

For hundreds of years, all living things were classified as either plants or animals. But over time, scientists discovered species that did not fit easily into these two kingdoms. For example, an organism of the genus *Euglena,* such as the one shown in **Figure 1,** has characteristics of both plants and animals. How would you classify such an organism?

What Is It?

Organisms are classified by their characteristics. For example, euglenoids, which include members of the genus *Euglena,* have the following characteristics:

- Euglenoids are single celled and live in pond water.
- Euglenoids are green and make their own food by photosynthesis.

These characteristics might lead you to conclude that euglenoids are plants. However, you should consider the following characteristics of euglenoids:

- Euglenoids move by whipping their "tails," which are called *flagella.*
- Euglenoids can feed on other organisms.

Plants do not move around and usually do not eat other organisms. So, are euglenoids animals? As you can see, euglenoids do not fit into plant or animal categories. Scientists solved this classification problem by adding another kingdom —kingdom Protista—to classify organisms such as euglenoids.

As scientists learned more about living things, they changed the classification system. Today, there are three domains in the classification system. Domains represent the largest differences between organisms. These domains are divided into several kingdoms.

What You Will Learn

- Explain how classification developed as greater numbers of organisms became known.
- Describe the three domains.
- Describe four kingdoms in the domain Eukarya.

Vocabulary

Archaea   Fungi
Bacteria   Plantae
Eukarya   Animalia
Protista

READING STRATEGY

Discussion Read this section silently. Write down questions that you have about this section. Discuss your questions in a small group.

Figure 1 *How would you classify this organism? This member of the genus* Euglena, *which is shown here highly magnified, has characteristics of both plants and animals.*

Figure 2 *The Grand Prismatic Spring in Yellowstone National Park contains water that is about 90°C (194°F). The spring is home to archaea that thrive in its hot water.*

Archaea in a modern taxonomic system, a domain made up of prokaryotes (most of which are known to live in extreme environments) that are distinguished from other prokaryotes by differences in their genetics and in the makeup of their cell wall; this domain aligns with the traditional kingdom Archaebacteria

Bacteria in a modern taxonomic system, a domain made up of prokaryotes that usually have a cell wall and that usually reproduce by cell division; this domain aligns with the traditional kingdom Eubacteria

Domain Archaea

The domain **Archaea** (ahr KEE uh) is made up entirely of archaea. Archaea are one of two kinds of prokaryotes (proh KAR ee OHTS). *Prokaryotes* are single-celled organisms that do not have a nucleus. Archaea were first discovered living in extreme environments, where other organisms could not survive. **Figure 2** shows a hot spring in Yellowstone National Park. The yellow and orange rings around the edge of the hot spring are made up of billions of archaea. Some archaea can also be found in moderate environments, such as the open ocean.

✔ Reading Check Describe one characteristic of an organism in the domain Archaea.

Domain Bacteria

All bacteria (bak TEER ee uh) belong to the domain **Bacteria.** Bacteria are another kind of prokaryote. Bacteria can be found in soil, water, and even on and inside the human body! For example, *Escherichia coli* (ESH uh RIK ee uh KOH LIE), shown in **Figure 3,** is present in large numbers in human intestines, where it produces vitamin K. One kind of bacterium converts milk into yogurt. Some bacteria cause diseases, such as pneumonia. Other bacteria make chemicals that help humans fight disease-causing bacteria.

Figure 3 *Specimens of* E. coli *are shown on the point of a pin under a scanning electron microscope. These bacteria live in the intestines of animals and decompose undigested food.*

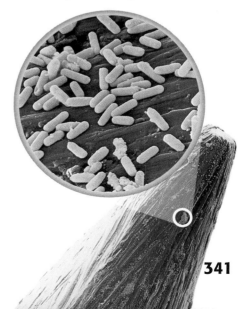

341

Domain Eukarya

All organisms whose cells have a nucleus and membrane-bound organelles are called *eukaryotes.* Eukaryotes belong to the domain **Eukarya.** Four kingdoms currently make up the domain Eukarya: Protista, Fungi, Plantae, and Animalia.

Kingdom Protista

Today, members of the kingdom **Protista** (proh TIST uh), commonly called *protists,* are single-celled or simple multicellular organisms. Scientists think that the first protists evolved from ancient bacteria about 2 billion years ago. Eventually, ancient protists gave rise to fungi, plants, and animals. The kingdom Protista contains many kinds of organisms. Some animal-like protists are called *protozoans.* Some plantlike protists are called *algae.* Protists also include slime molds, such as the one shown in **Figure 4,** and euglenoids.

Kingdom Fungi

Molds and mushrooms are examples of the complex, multicellular members of the kingdom **Fungi** (FUHN JIE). Unlike plants, fungi do not perform photosynthesis. Unlike animals, fungi do not eat food. Instead, fungi absorb nutrients from substances in their surroundings. They use digestive juices to break down the substances. **Figure 5** shows a very poisonous fungus. Never eat wild fungi.

Figure 4 *This slime mold is a protist.*

Eukarya in a modern taxonomic system, a domain made up of all eukaryotes; this domain aligns with the traditional kingdoms Protista, Fungi, Plantae, and Animalia

Protista a kingdom of mostly one-celled eukaryotic organisms that are different from plants, animals, bacteria, and fungi

Fungi a kingdom made up of nongreen, eukaryotic organisms that have no means of movement, reproduce by using spores, and get food by breaking down substances in their surroundings and absorbing the nutrients

Figure 5 *This beautiful fungus of the genus* Amanita *is poisonous.*

Figure 6 *Giant sequoias can measure 30 m around at the base and can grow to more than 91.5 m tall.*

Figure 7 *Plants such as these are common in the Tropics.*

Kingdom Plantae

Although plants vary remarkably in size and form, most people easily recognize the members of the kingdom Plantae. **Plantae** consists of organisms that are eukaryotic, have cell walls, and make food through photosynthesis. For photosynthesis to occur, plants must be exposed to sunlight. Plants can therefore be found on land and in water that light can penetrate.

The food that plants make is important not only for the plants but also for all of the organisms that get nutrients from plants. Most life on Earth is dependent on plants. For example, some fungi, protists, and bacteria consume plants. When these organisms digest the plant material, they get energy and nutrients made by the plants.

Plants also provide habitat for other organisms. The giant sequoias in **Figure 6** and the flowering plants in **Figure 7** provide birds, insects, and other animals with a place to live.

✓ **Reading Check** How do plants provide energy and nutrients to other organisms?

Plantae a kingdom made up of complex, multicellular organisms that are usually green, have cell walls made of cellulose, cannot move around, and use the sun's energy to make sugar by photosynthesis

Ring-Around-the-Sequoia
How many students would have to join hands to form a human chain around a giant sequoia that is 30 m in circumference? Assume for this calculation that the average student can extend his or her arms about 1.3 m.

Kingdom Animalia

Animalia a kingdom made up of complex, multicellular organisms that lack cell walls, can usually move around, and quickly respond to their environment

The kingdom **Animalia** contains complex, multicellular organisms that don't have cell walls, are usually able to move around, and have specialized sense organs. These sense organs help most animals quickly respond to their environment. Organisms in the kingdom Animalia are commonly called *animals*. You probably recognize many of the organisms in the kingdom Animalia. All of the organisms in **Figure 8** are animals.

Animals depend on the organisms from other kingdoms. For example, animals depend on plants for food. Animals also depend on bacteria and fungi to recycle the nutrients found in dead organisms.

Figure 8 *The kingdom Animalia contains many different organisms, such as eagles, tortoises, and beetles.*

CONNECTION TO Social Studies

WRITING SKILL **Animals That Help** Humans have depended on animals for thousands of years. Many people around the world still use oxen to farm. Camels, horses, donkeys, goats, and llamas are all still used as pack animals. Dogs still help herd sheep, protect property, and help people hunt. Scientists are even discovering new ways that animals can help us. For example, scientists are training bees to help find buried land mines. Using the library or the Internet, research an animal that helps people. Make a poster describing the animal and the animal's scientific name. The poster should show who uses the animal, how the animal is used, and how long people have depended on the animal. Find or draw pictures to put on your poster.

ACTIVITY

Strange Organisms

Classifying organisms is often not easy. Like animals, some plants can eat other organisms to obtain nutrients. Some protists can use photosynthesis as plants do and can move around as animals do. The kingdom Animalia also includes members that might surprise you, such as worms, insects, and corals.

The red cup sponge in **Figure 9** is also an animal. Sponges are usually considered the simplest animals. They lack sense organs, and most of them cannot move. Scientists used to classify sponges as plants. But sponges cannot make their own food. They must eat other organisms to get nutrients, which is one reason that sponges are classified as animals.

Reading Check Why were sponges once thought to be plants?

Figure 9 *This red cup sponge is a simple animal.*

SECTION Review

Summary

- In the past, organisms were classified as plants or animals. As scientists discovered more species, they found that organisms did not always fit into one of these two categories, so they changed the classification system.

- Today, domains are the largest groups of related organisms. The three domains are Archaea and Bacteria, both of which consist of prokaryotes, and Eukarya, which consists of eukaryotes.

- The kingdoms of the domain Eukarya are Protista, Fungi, Plantae, and Animalia.

Using Key Terms

For each pair of terms, explain how the meanings of the terms differ.

1. *Archaea* and *Bacteria*

2. *Plantae* and *Fungi*

Understanding Key Ideas

3. Biological classification schemes change
   a. as new evidence and more kinds of organisms are discovered.
   b. every 100 years.
   c. when scientists disagree.
   d. only once.

4. Describe the characteristics of each of the three domains.

5. Describe the four kingdoms of domain Eukarya.

Math Skills

6. A certain bacterium can divide every 30 min. If you begin with 1 bacterium, when will you have more than 1,000 bacteria?

Critical Thinking

7. **Identifying Relationships** How are bacteria similar to fungi? How are fungi similar to animals?

8. **Analyzing Methods** Why do you think Linnaeus did not include classification kingdoms for categories of archaea and bacteria?

9. **Applying Concepts** The Venus' flytrap does not move around. It can make its own food by using photosynthesis. It can also trap insects and digest the insects to get nutrients. The flytrap also has a cell wall. Into which kingdom would you place the Venus' flytrap? What makes this organism unusual in the kingdom you chose?

Skills Practice Lab

Shape Island

You are a biologist exploring uncharted parts of the world to look for new animal species. You sailed for days across the ocean and finally found Shape Island hundreds of miles south of Hawaii. Shape Island has some very unusual organisms. The shape of each organism is a variation of a geometric shape. You have spent more than a year collecting and classifying specimens. You have been able to assign a two-part scientific name to most of the species that you have collected. Now, you must assign a two-part scientific name to each of the last 12 specimens collected before you begin your journey home.

Procedure

1. Draw each of the organisms pictured on the facing page. Beside each organism, draw a line for its name, as shown on the top left of the following page. The first organism pictured has already been named, but you must name the remaining 12. Use the glossary of Greek and Latin prefixes, suffixes, and root words in the table to help you name the organisms.

Greek and Latin roots, prefixes, and suffixes	Meaning
ankylos	angle
antennae	external sense organs
bi-	two
cyclo-	circular
macro-	large
micro-	small
mono-	one
peri-	around
-plast	body
-pod	foot
quad-	four
stoma	mouth
tri-	three
uro-	tail

Analyze Results

1. **Analyzing Results** If you gave species 1 a common name, such as *round-face-no-nose,* would any other scientist know which of the newly discovered organisms you were referring to? Explain. How many others have a round face and no nose?

2. **Organizing Data** Describe two characteristics that are shared by all of your newly discovered specimens.

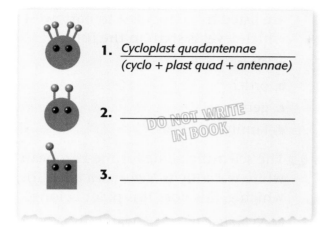

1. *Cycloplast quadantennae*
   (cyclo + plast quad + antennae)

2. _____

3. _____

DO NOT WRITE IN BOOK

Draw Conclusions

③ Applying Conclusions One more organism exists on Shape Island, but you have not been able to capture it. However, your supplies are running out, and you must start sailing for home. You have had a good look at the unusual animal and can draw it in detail. Draw an animal that is different from all of the others, and give it a two-part scientific name.

Applying Your Data

Look up the scientific names *Mertensia virginica* and *Porcellio scaber.* Answer the following questions as they apply to each organism: Is the organism a plant or an animal? How many common names does the organism have? How many scientific names does it have?

Think of the name of your favorite fruit or vegetable. Find out if it has other common names, and find out its two-part scientific name.

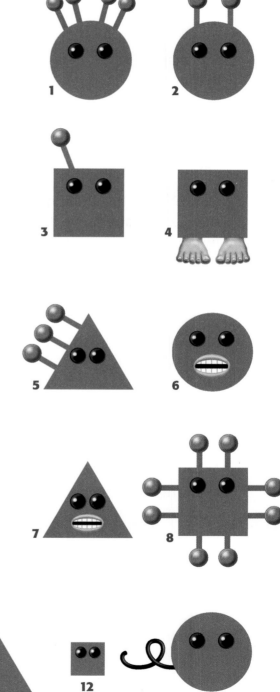

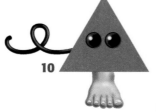

Chapter Review

USING KEY TERMS

Complete each of the following sentences by choosing the correct term from the word bank.

Animalia   Protista
Bacteria   Plantae
Archaea   classification
taxonomy

1 Linnaeus founded the science of ___.

2 Prokaryotes that live in extreme environments are in the domain ___.

3 Complex multicellular organisms that can usually move around and respond to their environment are in the kingdom ___.

4 A system of ___ can help group animals into categories.

5 Prokaryotes that can cause diseases are in the domain ___.

UNDERSTANDING KEY IDEAS

Multiple Choice

6 Scientists classify organisms by

  a. arranging the organisms in orderly groups.

  b. giving the organisms many common names.

  c. deciding whether the organisms are useful.

  d. using only existing categories of classification.

7 When the eight levels of classification are listed from broadest to narrowest, which level is sixth in the list?

  a. class

  b. order

  c. genus

  d. family

8 The scientific name for the European white waterlily is *Nymphaea alba*. To which genus does this plant belong?

  a. *Nymphaea*   **c.** water lily

  b. *alba*   **d.** alba lily

9 *Animalia, Protista, Fungi,* and *Plantae* are the

  a. scientific names of different organisms.

  b. names of kingdoms.

  c. levels of classification.

  d. scientists who organized taxonomy.

10 The simple, single-celled organisms that live in your intestines are classified in the domain

  a. Protista.   **c.** Archaea.

  b. Bacteria.   **d.** Eukarya.

11 What kind of organism thrives in hot springs and other extreme environments?

  a. fungus   **c.** archaean

  b. bacterium   **d.** protist

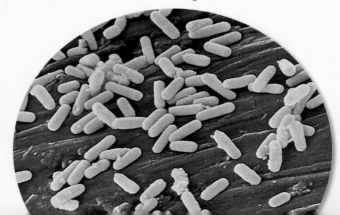

Short Answer

12 Why is the use of scientific names important in biology?

13 What kind of evidence is used by modern taxonomists to classify organisms based on evolutionary relationships?

14 Is a bacterium a type of eukaryote? Explain your answer

15 Scientists used to classify organisms as either plants or animals. Why doesn't that classification system work?

CRITICAL THINKING

16 **Concept Mapping** Use the following terms to create a concept map: *kingdom, fern, lizard, Animalia, Fungi, algae, Protista, Plantae,* and *mushroom.*

17 **Analyzing Methods** Explain how the levels of classification depend on the similarities and differences between organisms.

18 **Making Inferences** Explain why two species that belong to the same genus, such as white oak (*Quercus alba*) and cork oak (*Quercus suber*), also belong to the same family.

19 **Identifying Relationships** What characteristics do the members of the four kingdoms of the domain Eukarya have in common?

INTERPRETING GRAPHICS

Use the branching diagram of selected primates below to answer the questions that follow.

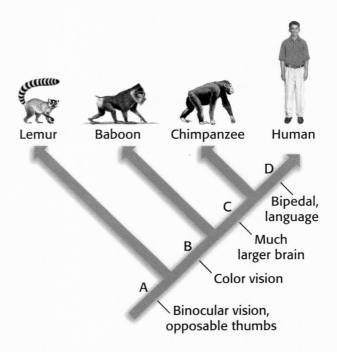

20 Which primate is the closest relative to the common ancestor of all primates?

21 Which primate shares the most traits with humans?

22 Do both lemurs and humans have the characteristics listed at point D? Explain your answer.

23 What characteristic do baboons have that lemurs do not have? Explain your answer.

Multiple Choice

1. The genus name of the rose Ryan is looking for is *rosa*. Its specific name is *alba*. What will it say on the tag identifying the plant?

   A. *alba rosa*

   B. *Alba rosa*

   C. *Rosa alba*

   D. *rosa alba*

Use the diagram below to answer question 2.

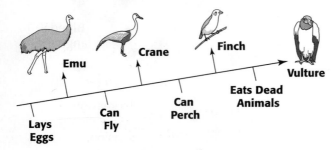

2. Which bird can fly but does not perch on trees or roost?

   A. crane

   B. emu

   C. finch

   D. vulture

3. What should a person do to find out where a new organism fits in the classification system used today?

   A. He should call a scientist to ask what to name the new organism.

   B. He should examine the organism directly.

   C. He should find other organisms that live in the same area.

   D. He should compare it with known organisms.

4. Drea is comparing three organisms. Two have many of the same characteristics. But they have very few characteristics in common with the third organism. What can Drea infer about the relatedness of these three organisms?

   A. The first two are equally related to the third.

   B. The first two are unrelated, but each is related to the third.

   C. Relatedness of the three organisms depends on the characteristics the first two share.

   D. The first two are more closely related to each other than they are to the third.

5. Kim is studying two types of chimpanzees: *Pan troglodytes* and *Pan paniscus*. Based on their names, Kim can conclude that they

   A. belong to different genera.

   B. belong to different species.

   C. belong to different domains.

   D. belong to different kingdoms.

6. At one time, scientists classified bacteria and protists together in one kingdom, but now they are in two separate domains. What evidence supported putting bacteria in a separate domain?

A. Protists have cytoplasm, but bacteria do not.

B. Bacteria have cell walls, but protists do not.

C. Bacteria consist of only one cell, but protists consist of many cells.

D. Protist cells have a nucleus and membrane-bound organelles, but bacteria cells do not.

7. Fungi were once classified as plants. Now they are placed in their own kingdom. Why were fungi removed from the plant kingdom?

A. Fungi live only on land, but plants live on land and in water.

B. Plants are made of many cells, but fungi consist of one cell.

C. Fungi can move around on their own, but plants cannot move.

D. Plants make their own food, but fungi absorb food from their surroundings.

8. An organism has many cells, but cannot move. It does not eat food, but cannot perform photosynthesis either. What kingdom does it belong to?

A. kingdom Fungi

B. kingdom Plantae

C. kingdom Protista

D. kingdom Animalia

Use the key below to answer question 9.

Dichotomous Key for Domains and Kingdoms	
1. a. one cell	Go to step 2.
b. many cells	Go to step 5.
2. a. no membrane-bound organelles	Go to step 3.
b. membrane-bound organelles	Go to step 4.
3. a. extreme environments	domain Archaea
b. throughout the environment and within larger living things	domain Bacteria
4. a. plantlike characteristics	kingdom Protista
b. absorbs nutrients from surroundings	kingdom Fungi
5. a. uses photosynthesis	kingdom Plantae
b. consumes other organisms	kingdom Animalia

9. An organism appears to be made up of one cell, doesn't move, and has mitochondria and chloroplasts. Using the dichotomous key above, determine the group to which the organism belongs.

A. domain Archaea

B. domain Bacteria

C. kingdom Plantae

D. kingdom Protista

Open Response

10. Compare kingdoms Plantae and Animalia.

11. Why are organisms such as sponges part of kingdom Animalia?

Standardized Test Preparation

Science in Action

Scientific Debate

Birds and Dinosaurs

Did birds evolve from dinosaurs? Some scientists think that birds evolved from small, carnivorous dinosaurs such as *Velociraptor* about 115 million to 150 million years ago. This idea is based on similarities of modern birds and these small dinosaurs. These similarities include the size, shape, and number of toes and "fingers," the location and shape of the breastbone and shoulder, and the presence of a hollow bone structure. Many scientists find this evidence convincing.

However, some scientists think that birds developed 100 million years before *Velociraptor* and its relatives did. These scientists point out that *Velociraptor* and its relatives were ground dwellers and were the wrong shape and size for flying.

Math ActiViTy

Velociraptor lived between 115 million and 150 million years ago. Find the average of these two numbers. Use that average to answer the following questions: How many weeks ago did *Velociraptor* live on Earth? How many days ago did *Velociraptor* live on Earth?

Scientific Discovery

A New Insect Order

In 2001, Oliver Zompro was studying a fossil insect preserved in amber. Although the fossil insect resembled a grasshopper or a walking stick, it was unique and could not be classified in the same group as either one. Zompro wondered if he might be seeing a new type of insect or an insect that was now thought to be extinct. The fossil insect was less than 4 cm long. Its spiny appearance earned the insect the nickname "gladiator." The gladiator bug that Zompro discovered is so unusual that it cannot be classified in any of the 30 existing orders of insects. Instead, the gladiator bug constitutes its own new order, which has been named *Mantophasmatodea*.

Language Arts ActiViTy

WRITING SKILL Give the gladiator bug a new nickname. Write a short essay about why you chose that particular name for the insect.

Michael Fay

Crossing Africa Finding and classifying wild animals takes a great deal of perseverance. Just ask Michael Fay, who spent 15 months crossing 2,000 miles of uninhabited rain forest in the Congo River Basin of West Africa. He used video, photography, and old-fashioned note taking to record the types of animals and vegetation that he encountered along the way.

To find and classify wild animals, Fay often had to think like an animal. When coming across a group of monkeys swinging high above him in the emerald green canopy, Fay would greet the monkeys with his imitation of the crowned eagle's high-pitched, whistling cry. When the monkeys responded with their own distinctive call, Fay could identify exactly what species they were and would jot it down in one of his 87 waterproof notebooks. Fay also learned other tricks, such as staying downwind of an elephant to get as close to the elephant as possible. He could then identify its size, its age, and the length of its tusks.

Social Studies ACTIVITY

WRITING SKILL Many organizations around the world are committed to helping preserve biodiversity. Conduct some Internet and library research to find out about an organization that works to keep species safe from extinction. Create a poster that describes the organization and some of the species that the organization protects.

go.hrw.com
To learn more about these Science in Action topics, visit go.hrw.com and type in the keyword HL5CLSF.

Current Science
Check out Current Science® articles related to this chapter by visiting go.hrw.com. Just type in the keyword HL5CS09.

12

Bacteria and Viruses

The Big Idea

Bacteria, archaea, and viruses can play important roles in the environment and human health.

About the Photo

Bacteria are everywhere. Some provide us with medicines, and some make foods we eat. Others, such as the one pictured here, can cause illness. This bacterium is a kind of *Salmonella,* and it can cause food poisoning. *Salmonella* can live inside chickens and other birds. Cooking eggs and chicken properly helps make sure that you don't get sick from *Salmonella.*

PRE-READING ACTIVITY

FOLDNOTES **Double Door** Before you read the chapter, create the FoldNote entitled "Double Door" described in the **Study Skills** section of the Appendix. Write "Bacteria" on one flap of the double door and "Viruses" on the other flap. As you read the chapter, compare the two topics, and write characteristics of each on the inside of the appropriate flap.

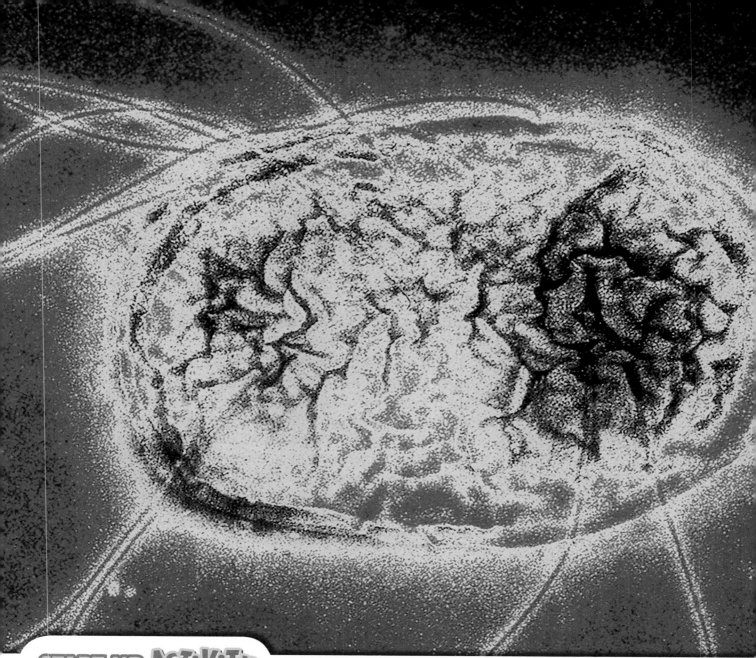

Our Constant Companions

Bacteria are in the soil, in the air, and even inside your body. When grown in a laboratory, microscopic bacteria form colonies that you can see. In this activity, you will observe some of the bacteria that share your world.

Procedure

1. Get **three plastic Petri dishes containing nutrient agar** from your teacher. Label one dish "Hand," another "Breath," and another "Soil."

2. Wipe your finger across the agar in the dish labeled "Hand." Breathe into the dish labeled "Breath." Place a **small amount of soil** in the dish labeled "Soil."

3. Secure the Petri dish lids with **transparent tape.** Wash your hands. Keep the dishes upside down in a warm, dark place for about one week. **Caution:** Do not open the Petri dishes after they are sealed.

4. Observe the Petri dishes each day. What do you see? Record your observations.

Analysis

1. How does the appearance of the colonies growing on the agar in each dish differ? What do bacterial colonies look like?

2. Which source caused the most bacterial growth— your hand, your breath, or the soil? Why do you think this source caused the most growth?

Bacteria and Archaea

How many bacteria are in a handful of soil? Would you believe that a single gram of soil—which is about the mass of a pencil eraser—may have more than 2.5 billion bacteria? A handful of soil may contain trillions of bacteria!

All living things fit into one of three domains: Bacteria, Archaea, or Eukarya. The domains Bacteria and Archaea consist of single-celled organisms that do not have a nucleus. Members of the domain Bacteria live in soil, water, and other organisms. The domain Archaea includes organisms that are found in extreme environments, such as hot springs. These two domains consist of the oldest forms of life on Earth.

What You Will Learn

- Describe the characteristics of prokaryotes.
- Explain how prokaryotes reproduce.
- Relate the characteristics of archaea.

Vocabulary

prokaryote
binary fission
endospore

READING STRATEGY

Prediction Guide Before reading this section, predict whether each of the following statements is true or false:
- There are only a few kinds of bacteria.
- Most bacteria are too small to see.

Some Characteristics of Bacteria and Archaea

There are more bacteria on Earth than there are all other living things combined. Most bacteria are too small to be seen without a microscope. But not all bacteria are the same size. In fact, the largest known bacteria are 1,000 times as large as the average bacterium. One of these types of giant bacteria was found inside a surgeonfish and is shown in **Figure 1.** Members of the domain Bacteria are usually one of three main shapes: rod shaped, spherical, and spiral shaped.

✔ **Reading Check** What are the three shapes of bacteria? (*See the Appendix for answers to Reading Checks.*)

Figure 1 *The giant bacteria inside this fish are 0.6 mm long, which is big enough to see without a microscope.*

Figure 2 The Most Common Shapes of Bacteria

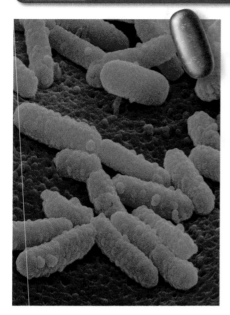

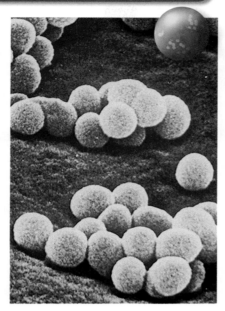

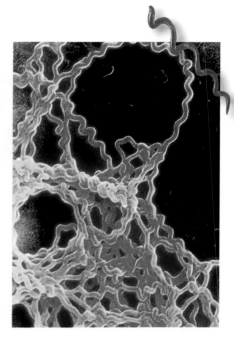

Bacilli (buh SIL ie) are rod shaped. They have a large surface area, which helps them take in nutrients. But a large surface area can cause them to dry out easily.

Cocci (KAHK sie) are spherical. They do not dry out as quickly as rod-shaped bacteria.

Spirilla (spie RIL uh) are long and spiral shaped. They use flagella at both ends to move like a corkscrew.

The Shape of Bacteria

Most bacteria have a rigid cell wall that gives them their shape. **Figure 2** shows the three most common shapes of bacteria. Bacilli (buh SIL ie) are rod shaped. Cocci (KAHK sie) are spherical. Spirilla (spie RIL uh) are long and spiral shaped. Each shape helps bacteria in a different way.

Some bacteria have hairlike parts called *flagella* (fluh JEL uh) that help them move around. Flagella spin to push a bacterium through water or other liquids.

No Nucleus!

All bacteria and archaea are single-celled organisms that do not have a nucleus. An organism that does not have a nucleus is called a **prokaryote** (proh KAR ee OHT). A prokaryote is able to move, get energy, and reproduce like cells that have a nucleus, which are called *eukaryotes* (yoo KAR ee OHTZ).

Prokaryotes function as independent organisms. Some bacteria stick together to form strands or films, but each bacterium is still functioning as a single organism. Most prokaryotes are much simpler and smaller than eukaryotes. Prokaryotes also reproduce differently than eukaryotes do.

prokaryote an organism that consists of a single cell that does not have a nucleus

Spying on Spirilla

1. Using a **microscope,** observe prepared **slides of bacteria.** Draw each type of bacteria you see.
2. What different shapes do you see? What are these shapes called?

Figure 3 **Binary Fission**

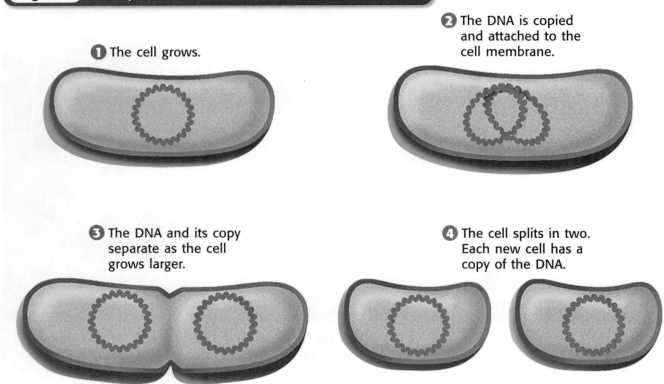

❶ The cell grows.

❷ The DNA is copied and attached to the cell membrane.

❸ The DNA and its copy separate as the cell grows larger.

❹ The cell splits in two. Each new cell has a copy of the DNA.

Prokaryote Reproduction

Prokaryotes reproduce by the process shown in **Figure 3.** This process is called binary fission (BIE nuh ree FISH uhn). **Binary fission** is reproduction in which one single-celled organism splits into two single-celled organisms.

Prokaryotes have no nucleus, so their DNA is not surrounded by a membrane. The DNA of prokaryotes is in circular loops. In the first step of binary fission, the cell's DNA is copied. The DNA and its copy then bind to different places on the inside of the cell membrane. As the cell and its membrane grow bigger, the loops of DNA separate. Finally, when the cell is about double its original size, the membrane pinches inward as shown in **Figure 4.** A new cell wall forms and separates the two new cells. Each new cell has one exact copy of the parent cell's DNA.

✓ **Reading Check** What is binary fission?

binary fission a form of asexual reproduction in single-celled organisms by which one cell divides into two cells of the same size

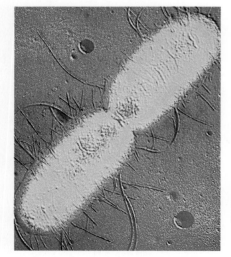

Figure 4 *This bacterium is about to complete binary fission.*

Endospores

Most species of bacteria do well in warm, moist places. In dry or cold surroundings, some species of bacteria will die. In these conditions, other bacteria become inactive and form endospores (EN doh SPAWRZ). An **endospore** contains genetic material and proteins and is covered by a thick, protective coat. Many endospores can survive in hot, cold, and very dry places. When conditions improve, the endospores break open, and the bacteria become active again. Scientists found endospores inside an insect that was preserved in amber for 30 million years. When the endospores were moistened in a laboratory, bacteria began to grow! A similar piece of amber can be seen in **Figure 5.**

Figure 5 *Endospores found in a preserved insect like this one showed scientists that bacteria can survive for millions of years.*

The Domain Bacteria

Most known prokaryotes are bacteria. The domain Bacteria has more individuals than all other domains combined do. Scientists think that bacteria have lived on Earth for more than 3.5 billion years.

Classification of Bacteria

Bacteria are classified in part by the way they get food. Most bacteria, such as those breaking down the leaf in **Figure 6,** are consumers. Consumers get their food by eating other organisms. Many bacteria are decomposers, which feed on dead organisms. Other bacterial consumers live in or on the body of another organism. Bacteria that make their own food are called *producers*. These bacteria use energy from sunlight to make food and are often green.

endospore a thick-walled protective spore that forms inside a bacterial cell and resists harsh conditions

Figure 6 *Decomposers, such as the ones helping to decay this leaf, return nutrients to the soil for other living things to use.*

Colorful Names *Cyanobacteria* means "blue bacteria." Many other names also refer to colors. You might not recognize these colors because the words for the colors are in another language. Look at the list of Greek color words below. Write down two English words that have one of the color roots in them. (Hint: Many words have the color as the first part of the word.)

> *melano* = black
> *chloro* = green
> *erythro* = red
> *leuko* = white

Cyanobacteria

Cyanobacteria (SIE uh noh bak TIR ee uh) are producers. Cyanobacteria usually live in water. These bacteria contain the green pigment chlorophyll. Chlorophyll is important to photosynthesis (the process of making food from the energy in sunlight). Many cyanobacteria have other pigments as well. Some have a blue pigment that helps in photosynthesis. This pigment gives those cyanobacteria a blue tint. Other cyanobacteria have red pigment. Flamingos get their pink color from eating red cyanobacteria.

Some scientists think that billions of years ago, bacteria similar to cyanobacteria began to live inside larger cells. According to this theory, the bacteria made food, and the cells provided protection. This combination may have given rise to the first plants on Earth.

The Domain Archaea

The three main types of archaea are *heat lovers*, *salt lovers*, and *methane makers*. Heat lovers live in ocean vents and hot springs. They live in very hot water, usually from 60°C to 80°C, but they can survive temperatures of more than 250°C. Salt lovers live in environments that have high levels of salt, such as the Dead Sea and Great Salt Lake. Methane makers give off methane gas and live in swamps and animal intestines. **Figure 7** shows one type of methane maker found in the mud of swamps.

Figure 7 *These archaea are methane makers. This micrograph shows two archaea sliced across their narrow side and a dividing archaean sliced lengthwise.*

Harsh Environments

Archaea often live where nothing else can. Most archaea prefer environments where there is little or no oxygen. Scientists have found them in the hot springs at Yellowstone National Park and beneath 430 m of ice in Antarctica. Archaea have even been found living 8 km below the Earth's surface! Even though they are often found in these harsh environments, many archaea can also be found in moderate environments in Earth's oceans.

Archaea are very different from bacteria. Not all archaea have cell walls. When they do have them, the cell walls are chemically different from those of bacteria.

INTERNET ACTIVITY

For another activity related to this chapter, go to **go.hrw.com** and type in the keyword **HL5VIRW**.

SECTION Review

Summary

- Bacteria and archaea are prokaryotes, which are single-celled organisms that lack a nucleus.

- Most bacteria have a cell wall. The main shapes of bacteria are rod shaped, spherical, and spiral shaped.

- Prokaryotes reproduce by binary fission. In binary fission, one cell divides into two cells.

- Bacteria are classified in part by the way that they get food. Consumers eat other organisms. Producers can make their own food.

- Archaea live in harsh environments. The three main types of archaea are heat lovers, salt lovers, and methane makers.

Using Key Terms

The statements below are false. For each statement, replace the underlined term to make a true statement.

1. Bacteria are <u>eukaryotes.</u>

2. Bacteria reproduce by <u>primary fission.</u>

Understanding Key Ideas

3. The structure that helps some bacteria survive harsh conditions is called a(n)
   a. endospore.   **c.** exospore.
   b. shell.   **d.** exoskeleton.

4. How are bacteria and archaea different?

5. Draw and label the four stages of binary fission.

6. Describe one advantage of each shape of bacteria.

7. What two things do producer bacteria and plants have in common?

Math Skills

8. An ounce (oz) is equal to about 28 g. If 1 g of soil contains 2.5 billion bacteria, how many bacteria are in 1 oz of soil?

Critical Thinking

9. **Applying Concepts** Many bacteria cannot reproduce in cooler temperatures and are destroyed at high temperatures. How do humans take advantage of this fact when preparing and storing food?

10. **Making Comparisons** Scientists are studying cold and dry environments on Earth that are like the environment on Mars. What kind of prokaryotes do you think they might find in these environments on Earth? Explain.

11. **Forming Hypotheses** You are studying a lake and the prokaryotes that live in it. What conditions of the lake would you measure to form a hypothesis about the kind of prokaryotes that live in the lake?

SCI LINKS

NSTA

Developed and maintained by the
National Science Teachers Association

For a variety of links related to this chapter, go to www.scilinks.org

Topic: Bacteria
SciLinks code: HSM0133

Bacteria's Role in the World

Have you ever had strep throat or a cavity in your tooth? Did you know that both are caused by bacteria?

Bacteria live in our water, our food, and our bodies. Much of what we know about bacteria was learned by scientists fighting bacterial diseases. But of the thousands of types of bacteria, only a few hundred cause disease. Many bacteria do things that are important and even helpful to us.

Good for the Environment

Life as we know it could not exist without bacteria. Bacteria are very important to the health of Earth. They help recycle dead animals and plants. Bacteria also play an important role in the nitrogen cycle.

Nitrogen Fixation

Most living things depend on plants. Plants need nitrogen to grow. Nitrogen gas makes up about 78% of the air, but most plants cannot use nitrogen directly from the air. They need to take in a different form of nitrogen. Nitrogen-fixing bacteria take in nitrogen from the air and change it to a form that plants can use. This process, called *nitrogen fixation,* is described in **Figure 1.**

✓ **Reading Check** What is nitrogen fixation? (*See the Appendix for answers to Reading Checks.*)

What You Will Learn

● Explain how life on Earth depends on bacteria.
● List three ways bacteria are useful to people.
● Describe two ways in which bacteria can be harmful to people.

Vocabulary
bioremediation
antibiotic
pathogenic bacteria

READING STRATEGY

Reading Organizer As you read this section, create an outline of the section. Use the headings from the section in your outline.

Figure 1 **Bacteria's Role in the Nitrogen Cycle**

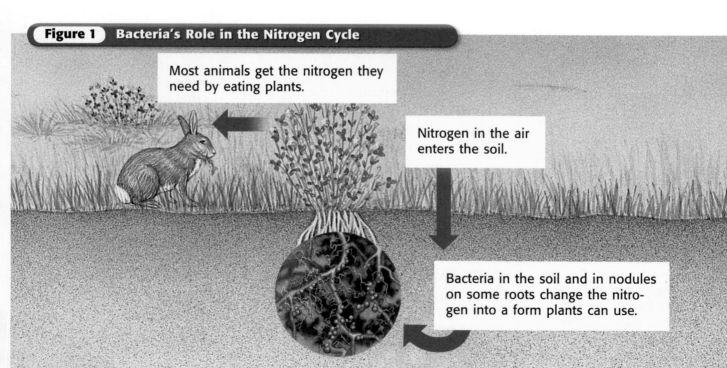

Most animals get the nitrogen they need by eating plants.

Nitrogen in the air enters the soil.

Bacteria in the soil and in nodules on some roots change the nitrogen into a form plants can use.

Recycling

Have you ever seen dead leaves and twigs on a forest floor? These leaves and twigs are recycled over time with the help of bacteria. Decomposer bacteria break down dead plant and animal matter. Breaking down dead matter makes nutrients available to other living things.

Cleaning Up

Bacteria and other microorganisms are also used to fight pollution. **Bioremediation** (BIE oh ri MEE dee AY shuhn) means using microorganisms to change harmful chemicals into harmless ones. Bioremediation is used to clean up hazardous waste from industries, farms, and cities. It is also used to clean up oil spills. The workers in **Figure 2** are using bacteria to remove pollutants from the soil.

Figure 2 *Bioremediating bacteria are added to soil to eat pollutants. The bacteria then release the pollutants as harmless waste.*

Good for People

Bacteria do much more than help keep our environment clean. Bacteria also help produce many of the foods we eat every day. They even help make important medicines.

bioremediation the biological treatment of hazardous waste by living organisms

Bacteria in Your Food

Believe it or not, people raise bacteria for food! Every time you eat cheese, yogurt, buttermilk, or sour cream, you are also eating bacteria. Lactic acid-producing bacteria break down the sugar in milk, which is called *lactose*. In the process, the bacteria change lactose into lactic acid. Lactic acid preserves and adds flavor to the food. All of the foods shown in **Figure 3** were made with the help of bacteria.

Make a Meal Plan

With an adult, create a week's meal plan without any foods made with bacteria. What would your diet be like without bacteria?

Figure 3 *Bacteria are used to make many kinds of foods.*

Figure 4 *Genes from the Xenopus frog were used to produce the first genetically engineered bacteria.*

antibiotic medicine used to kill bacteria and other microorganisms

pathogenic bacteria bacteria that cause disease

Figure 5 *Vaccines can protect you from bacterial diseases such as tetanus and diptheria.*

Making Medicines

What's the best way to fight disease-causing bacteria? Would you believe that the answer is to use other bacteria? **Antibiotics** are medicines used to kill bacteria and other microorganisms. Many antibiotics are made by bacteria.

Insulin

The human body needs insulin to break down and use sugar and carbohydrates. People who have diabetes do not make enough insulin. In the 1970s, scientists discovered how to put genes into bacteria so that the bacteria would make human insulin. The insulin can then be separated from the bacteria and given to people who have diabetes.

Genetic Engineering

When scientists change the genes of bacteria, or any other living thing, the process is called *genetic engineering.* Scientists have been genetically engineering bacteria since 1973. In that year, researchers put genes from a frog like the one in **Figure 4** into the bacterium *Escherichia coli* (ESH uh RIK ee uh KOH LIE). The bacterium then started making copies of the frog genes. Scientists can now engineer bacteria to make many products, such as insecticides, cleansers, and adhesives.

✓ Reading Check What is genetic engineering?

Harmful Bacteria

Humans couldn't live without bacteria, but bacteria can also cause harm. Scientists learned in the 1800s that some bacteria are pathogenic (PATH uh JEN ik). **Pathogenic bacteria** are bacteria that cause disease. Pathogenic bacteria get inside a host organism and take nutrients from the host's cells. In the process, they harm the host. Today, we are protected from many bacterial diseases by vaccination, as shown in **Figure 5.** Many bacterial diseases can also be treated with antibiotics.

Diseases in Other Organisms

Bacteria cause diseases in other organisms as well as in people. Have you ever seen a plant with odd-colored spots or soft rot? If so, you've seen bacterial damage to plants. Pathogenic bacteria attack plants, animals, protists, fungi, and even other bacteria. They can cause damage to grain, fruit, and vegetable crops. The branch of the pear tree in **Figure 6** shows the effects of pathogenic bacteria. Plants are sometimes treated with antibiotics. Scientists have also genetically engineered certain plants to be resistant to disease-causing bacteria.

Figure 6 *This branch of a pear tree has a bacterial disease called* fire blight.

SECTION Review

Summary

- Bacteria are important to life on Earth because they fix nitrogen and decompose dead matter.
- Bacteria are useful to people because they help make foods and medicines.
- Scientists have genetically engineered bacteria to make medicines.
- Pathogenic bacteria are harmful to people. Bacteria can also harm the crops we grow for food.

Using Key Terms

1. In your own words, write a definition for the term *bioremediation*.

2. Use the following terms in the same sentence: *pathogenic bacteria* and *antibiotic*.

Understanding Key Ideas

3. What are two ways that bacteria affect plants?

4. How can bacteria both cause and cure diseases?

5. Explain two ways in which bacteria are crucial to life on Earth.

6. Describe two ways your life was affected by bacteria today.

Math Skills

7. Nitrogen makes up about 78% of air. If you have 2 L of air, how many liters of nitrogen are in the air?

Critical Thinking

8. **Identifying Relationships** Legumes, which include peas and beans, are efficient nitrogen fixers. Legumes are also a good source of amino acids. What chemical element would you expect to find in amino acids?

9. **Applying Concepts** Design a bacterium that will be genetically engineered. What do you want it to do? How would it help people or the environment?

Viruses

One day, you discover red spots on your skin. More and more spots appear, and they begin turning into itchy blisters. What do you have?

The spots could be chickenpox. Chickenpox is a disease caused by a virus. A **virus** is a microscopic particle that gets inside a cell and often destroys the cell. Many viruses cause diseases, such as the common cold, flu, and acquired immune deficiency syndrome (AIDS).

It's a Small World

Viruses are tiny. They are smaller than the smallest bacteria. About 5 billion virus particles could fit in a single drop of blood. Viruses can change rapidly. So, a virus's effect on living things can also change. Because viruses are so small and change so often, scientists don't know exactly how many types exist. These properties also make them difficult to fight.

Are Viruses Living?

Like living things, viruses contain protein and genetic material. But viruses, such as the ones shown in **Figure 1,** don't act like living things. They can't eat, grow, break down food, or use oxygen. In fact, a virus cannot function on its own. A virus can reproduce only inside a living cell that serves as a host. A **host** is a living thing that a virus or parasite lives on or in. Using a host's cell as a tiny factory, the virus forces the host to make viruses rather than healthy new cells.

What You Will Learn

● Explain how viruses are similar to and different from living things.
● List the four major virus shapes.
● Describe the two kinds of viral reproduction.

Vocabulary

virus
host

READING STRATEGY

Discussion Read this section silently. Write down questions that you have about this section. Discuss your questions in a small group.

virus a microscopic particle that gets inside a cell and often destroys the cell

host an organism from which a parasite takes food or shelter

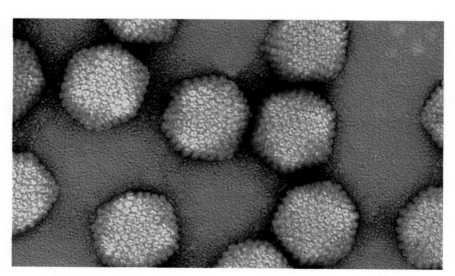

Figure 1 *Viruses are not cells. They do not have cytoplasm or organelles.*

Figure 2 The Basic Shapes of Viruses

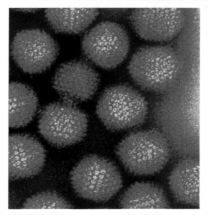

Crystals
The polio virus is shaped like the crystals shown here.

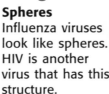

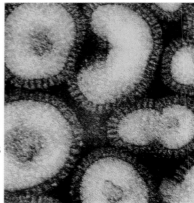

Spheres
Influenza viruses look like spheres. HIV is another virus that has this structure.

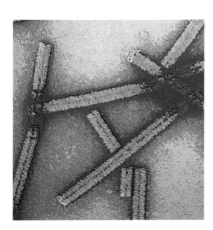

Cylinders
The tobacco mosaic virus is shaped like a cylinder and attacks tobacco plants.

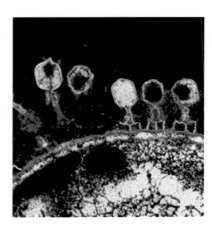

Spacecraft
One group of viruses attacks only bacteria. Many of these look almost like spacecraft.

Classifying Viruses

Viruses can be grouped by their shape, the type of disease they cause, their life cycle, or the kind of genetic material they contain. The four main shapes of viruses are shown in **Figure 2.** Every virus is made up of genetic material inside a protein coat. The protein coat protects the genetic material and helps a virus enter a host cell. Many viruses have a protein coat that matches characteristics of their specific host.

The genetic material in viruses is either DNA or RNA. Most RNA is made up of one strand of nucleotides. Most DNA is made up of two strands of nucleotides. Both DNA and RNA contain information for making proteins. The viruses that cause warts and chickenpox contain DNA. The viruses that cause colds and the flu contain RNA. The virus that causes AIDS, which is called the *human immunodeficiency virus* (HIV), also contains RNA.

✓ **Reading Check** What are two ways in which viruses can be classified? (*See the Appendix for answers to Reading Checks.*)

Sizing Up a Virus
If you enlarged an average virus 600,000 times, it would be about the size of a small pea. How tall would you be if you were enlarged 600,000 times?

Figure 3 The Lytic Cycle

1 The virus finds and joins itself to a host cell.

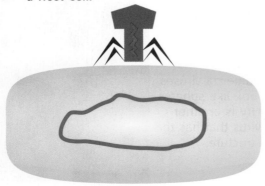

2 The virus enters the cell, or the virus's genetic material is injected into the cell.

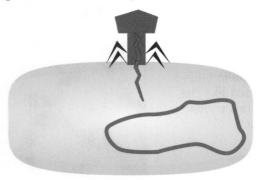

3 Once the virus's genes are inside, they take over the direction of the host cell and turn it into a virus factory.

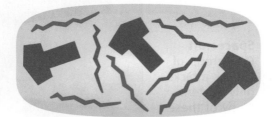

4 The new viruses break out of the host cell, which kills the host cell. The cycle begins again.

A Destructive House Guest

The one thing that viruses do that living things also do is make more of themselves. Viruses attack living cells and turn them into virus factories. This cycle is called the *lytic cycle* (LIT ik SIE kuhl), and it is shown in **Figure 3**.

✓ Reading Check What is the lytic cycle?

A Time Bomb

Some viruses don't go straight into the lytic cycle. These viruses also put their genetic material into the host cell. But new viruses are not made right away. In the lysogenic (LIE soh JEN ik) cycle, each new cell gets a copy of the virus's genes when the host cell divides. The genes can stay inactive for a long time. When the genes do become active, they begin the lytic cycle and make copies of the virus.

Treating a Virus

Antibiotics do not kill viruses. But scientists have recently developed antiviral (AN tie VIE ruhl) medications. Many of these medicines stop viruses from reproducing. Because many viral diseases do not have cures, it is best to prevent a viral infection from happening in the first place. Childhood vaccinations give your immune system a head start in fighting off viruses. Having current vaccinations can prevent you from getting a viral infection. It is also a good practice to wash your hands often and never to touch wild animals. If you do get sick from a virus, like the boy in **Figure 4,** it is often best to rest and drink extra fluids. As with any sickness, you should tell your parents or a doctor.

Figure 4 *The chickenpox virus resides inside your body even after the red spots are gone.*

SECTION Review

Summary

- Viruses have characteristics of living and nonliving things. They reproduce in living cells.
- Viruses may be classified by their shape, the kind of disease they cause, or their life cycle.
- To reproduce, a virus must enter a cell, reproduce itself, and then break open the cell. This is called the lytic cycle.
- In the lysogenic cycle, the genes of a virus are incorporated into the genes of the host cell.

Using Key Terms

1. Use the following terms in the same sentence: *virus* and *host*.

Understanding Key Ideas

2. One characteristic viruses have in common with living things is that they
   - **a.** eat.
   - **b.** reproduce.
   - **c.** sleep.
   - **d.** grow.

3. Describe the four steps in the lytic cycle.

4. Explain how the lytic cycle and the lysogenic cycle are different.

Math Skills

5. A bacterial cell infected by a virus divides every 20 min. After 10,000 divisions, the new viruses are released from their host cell. About how many weeks will this process take?

Critical Thinking

6. **Making Inferences** Do you think modern transportation has had an effect on the way viruses spread? Explain.

7. **Identifying Relationships** What characteristics of viruses do you think have made finding drugs to attack them difficult?

8. **Expressing Opinions** Do you think that vaccinations are important even in areas where a virus is not found?

SCILINKS®

NSTA
Developed and maintained by the
National Science Teachers Association

For a variety of links related to this chapter, go to www.scilinks.org

Topic: Viruses
SciLinks code: HSM1607

Inquiry Lab

OBJECTIVES

Design an experiment that will answer a specific question.

Investigate what kind of organisms make food spoil.

MATERIALS

- gloves, protective
- items, such as sealable plastic bags, food samples, a scale, or a thermometer, to be determined by the students and approved by the teacher as needed for each experiment

SAFETY

Aunt Flossie and the Intruder

Aunt Flossie is a really bad housekeeper! She never cleans the refrigerator, and things get really gross in there. Last week she pulled out a plastic bag that looked like it was going to explode! The bag was full of gas that she did not put there! Aunt Flossie remembered from her school days that gases are released from living things as waste products. Something had to be alive in the bag!

Aunt Flossie became very upset that there was an intruder in her refrigerator. She refuses to bake another cookie until you determine the nature of the intruder.

Ask a Question

1. How did gas get into Aunt Flossie's bag?

Form a Hypothesis

2. Write a hypothesis which answers the question above. Explain your reasoning.

Test the Hypothesis

3. Design an experiment that will determine how gas got into Aunt Flossie's bag. Make a list of the materials you will need, and prepare all the data tables you will need for recording your observations.

4. Get your teacher's approval of your experimental design and your list of materials before you begin.

5. Dispose of your materials according to your teacher's instructions at the end of your experiment. **Caution:** Do not open any bags of spoiled food or allow any of the contents to escape.

Ask a Question

Form a Hypothesis

Test the Hypothesis

Analyze the Results

1 **Organizing Data** What data did you collect from your experiment?

Draw Conclusions

2 **Drawing Conclusions** What conclusions can you draw from your investigation? Where did the gas come from?

3 **Evaluating Methods** If you were going to perform another investigation, what would you change in the experiment to give better results? Explain your answer.

Communicating Your Data

WRITING SKILL Write a letter to Aunt Flossie describing your experiment. Explain what produced the gas in the bag and your recommendations for preventing these intruders in her refrigerator in the future.

Analyze the Results

Draw Conclusions

No

Do they support your hypothesis?

Yes

Chapter Review

USING KEY TERMS

1 In your own words, write a definition for the term *pathogenic bacteria*.

Complete each of the following sentences by choosing the correct term from the word bank.

binary fission   endospore
antibiotic   bioremediation
virus   bacteria

2 Most prokaryotes reproduce by ___.

3 Bacterial infections can be treated with ___.

4 A(n) ___ needs a host to reproduce.

UNDERSTANDING KEY IDEAS

Multiple Choice

5 Bacteria are used for all of the following EXCEPT

  a. making certain foods.

  b. making antibiotics.

  c. cleaning up oil spills.

  d. preserving fruit.

6 In the lytic cycle, the host cell

  a. is destroyed.

  b. destroys the virus.

  c. becomes a virus.

  d. undergoes cell division.

7 A bacterial cell

  a. is an endospore.

  b. has a loop of DNA.

  c. has a distinct nucleus.

  d. is a eukaryote.

8 Bacteria

  a. include methane makers.

  b. include decomposers.

  c. all have chlorophyll.

  d. are rod-shaped.

9 Cyanobacteria

  a. are consumers.

  b. are parasites.

  c. contain chlorophyll.

  d. are decomposers.

10 Archaea

  a. are special types of bacteria.

  b. live only in places without oxygen.

  c. are lactic acid-producing bacteria.

  d. can live in hostile environments.

11 Viruses

  a. are about the same size as bacteria.

  b. have nuclei.

  c. can reproduce only within a host cell.

  d. do not infect plants.

12 Bacteria are important to the planet as

  a. decomposers of dead organic matter.

  b. processors of nitrogen.

  c. makers of medicine.

  d. All of the above

Short Answer

13 How are the functions of nitrogen-fixing bacteria and decomposers similar?

14 Which cycle takes more time, the lytic cycle or the lysogenic cycle?

15 Describe two ways in which viruses do not act like living things.

16 What is bioremediation?

17 Describe how doctors can treat a viral infection.

CRITICAL THINKING

18 **Concept Mapping** Use the following terms to create a concept map: *bacteria, bacilli, cocci, spirilla, consumers, producers,* and *cyanobacteria.*

19 **Predicting Consequences** Describe some of the problems you think bacteria might face if there were no humans.

20 **Applying Concepts** Many modern soaps contain chemicals that kill bacteria. Describe one good outcome and one bad outcome of the use of antibacterial soaps.

21 **Identifying Relationships** Some people have digestive problems after they take a course of antibiotics. Why do you think these problems happen?

INTERPRETING GRAPHICS

The diagram below illustrates the stages of binary fission. Match each statement with the correct stage.

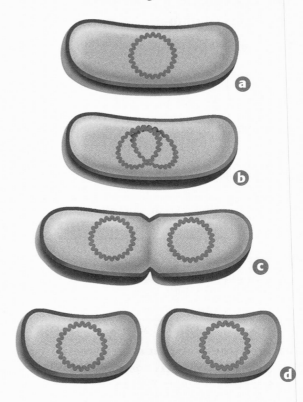

22 The DNA loops separate.

23 The DNA loop replicates.

24 The parent cell starts to expand.

25 The DNA attaches to the cell membrane.

Multiple Choice

1. **Domain Bacteria and domain Archaea include prokaryotes. Of the two domains, which of the following characteristics describes only organisms in domain Archaea?**

    A. They lack a nucleus.

    B. They are single-celled.

    C. They reproduce by binary fission.

    D. They live in extreme environments.

Use the table below to answer question 2.

Time (hrs)	Number of Bacteria
0	1,000
2	10,000
4	100,000
8	105,000
16	104,000

2. **Jeanne conducted an experiment to study the effectiveness of an antibacterial soap. Her experimental results are given in the table above. The antibacterial soap was not present when the experiment began. Based on the data, the antibacterial soap was added**

    A. at the 2-hour point in the experiment.

    B. at the 4-hour point in the experiment.

    C. at the 8-hour point in the experiment.

    D. at the 16-hour point in the experiment.

3. **How are bacteria classified?**

    A. by their size

    B. by how they get food

    C. by how they reproduce

    D. by whether they live in an extreme environment

4. **In which of the following bodies of water would a member of domain Archaea most likely be found?**

    A. geyser

    B. lake

    C. sea

    D. stream

5. **Xavier wants to grow plants in a small garden. The soil needs nitrogen. But Xavier doesn't want to use fertilizer on the soil. Which of the following is the best way to add nitrogen to the soil?**

    A. mix bacteria into the soil

    B. add nitrogen gas to the soil

    C. increase the temperature of the soil

    D. grow plants that have bacteria in their roots

6. **Some bacteria cause disease in humans. How can people protect themselves before they become infected by pathogenic bacteria?**

    A. insulin

    B. vaccines

    C. antibiotics

    D. antiviral medications

7. Cyanobacteria are in domain Bacteria. Which of the following traits is characteristic of cyanobacteria?

   A. They live in the soil.

   B. They live in very hot areas.

   C. They live in the human body.

   D. They can make their own food.

8. Viruses reproduce by inserting their DNA into the DNA of the host cell. How do viruses harm an organism?

   A. The lytic cycle results in burst cells.

   B. The lysogenic cycle damages the DNA.

   C. The injection of the viral DNA damages the cell.

   D. The insertion of viral DNA interferes with DNA replication.

9. Which of the following statements describes both bacteria and viruses?

   A. They do not eat.

   B. They have DNA.

   C. They do not grow.

   D. They reproduce by binary fission.

Use the illustration below to answer question 10.

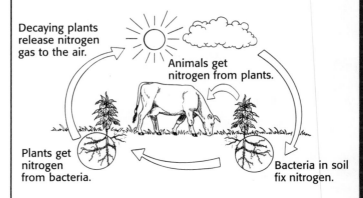

Decaying plants release nitrogen gas to the air.

Animals get nitrogen from plants.

Plants get nitrogen from bacteria.

Bacteria in soil fix nitrogen.

10. Isaac made the sketch above to summarize some of the key points from a field investigation of the nitrogen cycle. Based on the sketch, which of the following is a valid conclusion?

   A. Nitrogen is contained in water.

   B. Animals get nitrogen directly from the air.

   C. Bacteria play an important role in the nitrogen cycle.

   D. Plants give off nitrogen gas into the air during photosynthesis.

Open Response

11. Bacteria have one of three different shapes. Viruses have one of four shapes. Name the shapes of bacteria and viruses.

12. Scientists aren't sure if viruses are living things. Why is it so difficult for scientists to determine if viruses are living organisms?

Standardized Test Preparation

Science in Action

Science, Technology, and Society

Edible Vaccines

Vaccines protect you from life-threatening diseases. But vaccinations are expensive, and the people who give them must go through extensive training. These and other factors often prevent people in developing countries from getting vaccinations. But help may be on the way. Scientists are developing edible vaccines. Imagine eating a banana and getting the same protection you would from several painful injections. These vaccines are made from DNA that encodes a protein in the disease-causing particles. This DNA can then be inserted into the banana's genes. Researchers are still working on safe and effective edible vaccines.

Scientific Discoveries

Spanish Flu and the Flu Cycle

In 1918, a version of the influenza (the flu) virus killed millions of people worldwide. This disease, mistakenly called the Spanish Flu (it probably started in China), was one of the worst epidemics in history. Doctors and scientists realized that the large movement of people during the First World War probably made it easier for the Spanish Flu to spread. But the question of how this common disease could become so deadly remained unknown. One important factor is that the influenza virus is constantly changing. Many scientists now think that the influenza virus mutates into a more deadly form about every 30 years. There were flu epidemics in 1918, 1957, and 1968, which leads some scientists to believe that we are overdue for another flu epidemic.

Language Arts ACTiViTY

WRITING SKILL Write an advertisement for an edible vaccine. Be sure to describe the benefits of vaccinations.

Social Studies ACTiViTY

WRITING SKILL Conduct an interview with an older member of your family. Ask them how the flu, smallpox, tuberculosis, or polio has affected their lives. Write a report that includes information on how doctors deal with the disease today.

Laytonville Middle School

Composting Project In 1973, Mary Appelhof tried an experiment. She knew that bacteria can help break down dead organic matter. In her basement, she set up a bin with worms and dumped her food scraps in there. Her basement didn't smell like garbage because her worms were eating the food scraps! Composting uses heat, bacteria, and, sometimes, worms to break down food wastes. Composting turns these wastes into fertilizer.

Binet Payne, a teacher at the Laytonville Middle School in California, decided to try Appelhof's composting system. Ms. Payne asked her students to separate their school cafeteria's trash into different categories: veggie wastes (worm food), protein foods (meat, milk, and cheese), bottles, cans, bags (to be recycled), and "yucky trash" (napkins and other nonrecyclables). The veggie waste was placed into the worm bins, and the protein foods were used to feed a local farm's chickens and pigs. In the first year, the Garden Project saved the school $6,000, which otherwise would have been used to dump the garbage into a landfill.

Math ACTiViTY

If the school saved $6,000 the first year, how much money did the school save each day of the year?

Composting can help reduce the amount of waste that is sent to a landfill.

To learn more about these Science in Action topics, visit **go.hrw.com** and type in the keyword **HL5VIRF.**

Current Science

Check out Current Science® articles related to this chapter by visiting **go.hrw.com. Just** type in the keyword **HL5CS10.**

13

Protists and Fungi

The Big Idea
Protists and fungi are eukaryotes.

About the Photo

These glowing disks may look like spaceships, but they are mushrooms! Some fungi—and some protists—glow with bioluminescence (BIE oh LOO muh NES uhns), just as fireflies do. Bioluminescence is the production of light from chemical reactions in an organism. The function of bioluminescence in fungi is not known. Some scientists think that the glow attracts insects that help spread the fungi's spores. Other scientists think that the light is just a way to release energy.

PRE-READING ACTIVITY

FOLDNOTES **Booklet** Before you read the chapter, create the FoldNote entitled "Booklet" described in the **Study Skills** section of the Appendix. Label each page of the booklet with a main idea from the chapter. As you read the chapter, write what you learn about each main idea on the appropriate page of the booklet.

START-UP ACTIVITY

A Microscopic World

In this activity, you will find some common protists in pond water or in a solution called a *hay infusion*.

Procedure

1. Use a **plastic eyedropper** to place **one drop of pond water or hay infusion** onto a **microscope slide.**
2. Add a **drop of ProtoSlo™** to the slide.
3. Add a **plastic coverslip** by putting one edge on the slide and then slowly lowering the coverslip over the drop to prevent air bubbles.
4. Observe the slide under low power of a **microscope.**
5. Find an organism in the liquid on the slide.
6. Observe the organism under high power to get a closer look.
7. Sketch the organism as you see it under high power. Then, return the microscope to low power, and find other organisms to sketch. Return the microscope to high power, and sketch the new organisms.

Analysis

1. How many kinds of organisms do you see?
2. Are the organisms alive? Support your answer with evidence.
3. How many cells does each organism appear to have?

protist an organism that belongs to the kingdom Protista

Protists

Some are so tiny that they cannot be seen without a microscope. Others grow many meters long. Some are poisonous. And some provide food for people.

What are they? The organisms described above are protists. A **protist** is a member of the kingdom Protista. Protists differ from other living things in many ways. Look at **Figure 1** to see a variety of protists.

General Characteristics

Protists are very diverse and have few traits in common. Most protists are single-celled organisms, but some are made of many cells, and others live in colonies. Some protists produce their own food, and some eat other organisms or decaying matter. Some protists can control their own movement, and others cannot. However, protists do share a few characteristics. For example, all protists are *eukaryotic* (yoo KAR ee AHT ik), which means that their cells each have a nucleus.

Members of the kingdom Protista are related more by how they differ from members of other kingdoms than by how they are similar to other protists. Protists are less complex than other eukaryotic organisms are. For example, unlike fungi, plants, and animals, protists do not have specialized tissues. Because protists are so diverse, some scientists think that kingdom Protista should be broken up into several kingdoms. Scientists are still revising the classification of protists.

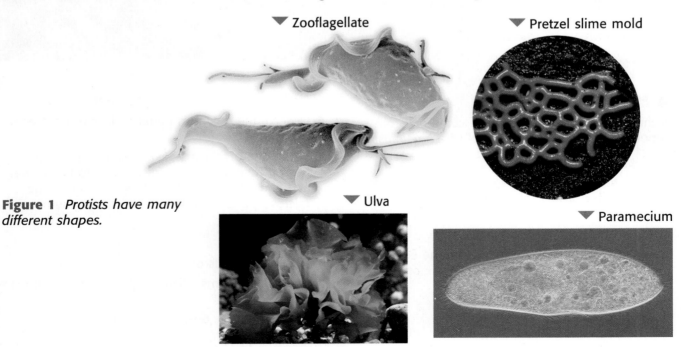

▼ Zooflagellate

▼ Pretzel slime mold

▼ Ulva

▼ Paramecium

Figure 1 *Protists have many different shapes.*

Protists and Food

Protists get food in many ways. Some protists can make their own food. Other protists eat other organisms, parts or products of other organisms, or the remains of other organisms. Some protists use more than one method of getting food.

Producing Food

Some protists are *producers*. Like green plants, these protists make their own food. Protist producers have special structures called *chloroplasts* (KLAWR uh PLASTS) in their cells. These structures capture energy from the sun. Protists use this energy to produce food in a process called *photosynthesis* (FOHT oh SIN thuh sis). Plants use this same process to make their own food.

✓ Reading Check How do protist producers get their food? (*See the Appendix for answers to Reading Checks.*)

Finding Food

Some protists must get food from their environment. These protists are heterotrophs (HET uhr oh TROHFS). **Heterotrophs** are organisms that cannot make their own food. These organisms eat other organisms, parts or products of other organisms, or the remains of other organisms.

Many protist heterotrophs eat small living organisms, such as bacteria, yeast, or other protists. The way that these heterotrophs get food is similar to how many animals get food. Some protist heterotrophs are decomposers. *Decomposers* get energy by breaking down dead organic matter. Some protists get energy in more than one way. For example, slime molds, such as the one in **Figure 2,** get energy by engulfing both small organisms and particles of organic matter.

Some protist heterotrophs are parasites. A **parasite** invades another organism to get the nutrients that it needs. An organism that a parasite invades is called a **host.** Parasites cause harm to their host. Parasitic protists may invade fungi, plants, or animals. During the mid-1800s, a parasitic protist wiped out most of the potatoes in Ireland. Without potatoes to eat, many people died of starvation. Today, people know how to protect crops from many such protists.

SCHOOL to HOME

Food for Thought

With your family, review how producers, consumers, decomposers, and parasites get energy. Think of organisms that live near your home and that get their food in these different ways. Then, make a poster to display your examples. Be sure that the poster describes each way of getting food.

ACTIVITY

heterotroph an organism that gets food by eating other organisms or their byproducts and that cannot make organic compounds from inorganic materials

parasite an organism that feeds on an organism of another species (the host) and that usually harms the host; the host never benefits from the presence of the parasite

host an organism from which a parasite takes food or shelter

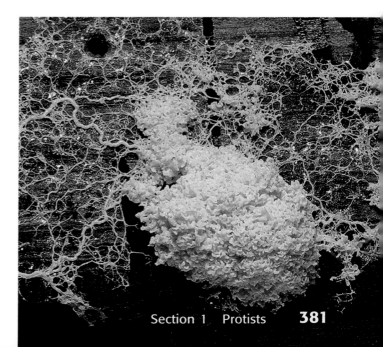

Figure 2 *Slime molds get energy from small organisms and particles of organic matter.*

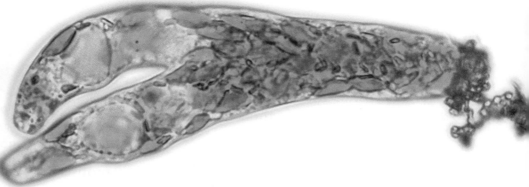

Figure 3 *Members of the genus* Euglena *reproduce by dividing lengthwise during fission.*

Producing More Protists

Like all living things, protists reproduce. Protists reproduce in several ways. Some protists reproduce asexually, and some reproduce sexually. Some protists even reproduce asexually at one stage in their life cycle and sexually at another stage.

Asexual Reproduction

Most protists reproduce asexually. In asexual reproduction, the offspring come from just one parent. These offspring are identical to the parent. **Figure 3** shows a member of the genus *Euglena* reproducing asexually by fission. In *binary fission,* a single-celled protist divides into two cells. In some cases, single-celled protists use *multiple fission* to make more than two offspring from one parent. Each new cell is a single-celled protist.

✓ **Reading Check** What are two ways that protists can reproduce asexually by fission?

Sexual Reproduction

Some protists can reproduce sexually. Sexual reproduction requires two parents. Members of the genus *Paramecium* (PAR uh MEE see uhm) sometimes reproduce sexually by a process called *conjugation.* During conjugation, two individuals join together and exchange genetic material by using a small, second nucleus. Then, they divide to produce four protists that have new combinations of genetic material. **Figure 4** shows two paramecia in the process of conjugation.

Many protists can reproduce asexually and sexually. In some protist producers, the kind of reproduction alternates by generation. For example, a parent will reproduce asexually, and its offspring will reproduce sexually. Other protists reproduce asexually until environmental conditions become stressful, such as when there is little food or water. When conditions are stressful, these protists will use sexual reproduction until conditions improve.

Figure 4 *Members of the genus* Paramecium *can reproduce by conjugation, a type of sexual reproduction.*

Reproductive Cycles

Some protists have complex reproductive cycles. These protists may change forms many times. **Figure 5** shows the life cycle of *Plasmodium vivax* (plaz MOH dee uhm VIE vaks), the protist that causes the disease malaria. *P. vivax* depends on both humans and mosquitoes to reproduce.

Figure 5 P. vivax *infects both humans and mosquitoes as it reproduces.*

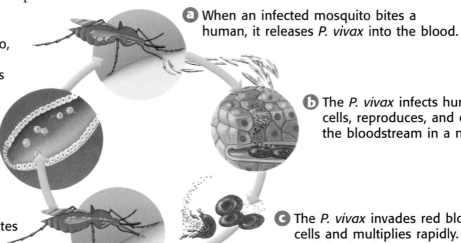

a When an infected mosquito bites a human, it releases *P. vivax* into the blood.

e In the mosquito, the *P. vivax* matures into its original form. The cycle then repeats.

b The *P. vivax* infects human liver cells, reproduces, and enters the bloodstream in a new form.

d A mosquito bites a human and picks up *P. vivax*.

c The *P. vivax* invades red blood cells and multiplies rapidly. The red blood cells burst open with *P. vivax* in another new form.

SECTION Review

Summary

- Protists are a diverse group of single-celled and many-celled organisms.
- Protists are grouped in their own kingdom because they differ from other organisms in many ways.
- Protists get food by producing it or by getting it from their environment.
- Some protists reproduce asexually, some reproduce sexually, and some reproduce both asexually and sexually.

Using Key Terms

1. Use the following terms in the same sentence: *parasite* and *host*.

2. In your own words, write a definition for each of the following terms: *protist* and *heterotroph*.

Understanding Key Ideas

3. What is one way that protists differ from plants and animals?
   a. Protists are eukaryotic.
   b. All protists have many cells.
   c. Protists do not have specialized tissues.
   d. Protists are not eukaryotic.

4. Name a characteristic shared by all protists.

5. Name three ways that protists can differ from each other.

6. Describe four ways that protists get food.

7. Describe three ways that protists reproduce.

Math Skills

8. If seven individuals of the genus *Euglena* reproduce at one time, how many individuals result?

Critical Thinking

9. **Identifying Relationships** How is conjugation similar to fission?

10. **Applying Concepts** The spread of malaria depends on both human and mosquito hosts. Use this fact to think of a way to stop the spread of malaria.

SCiLINKS.

Developed and maintained by the National Science Teachers Association

For a variety of links related to this chapter, go to www.scilinks.org

Topic: Protists
SciLinks code: HSM1245

Kinds of Protists

Would you believe that there is an organism that lives in the forest and looks like a pile of scrambled eggs? This organism exists, and it's a protist.

What You Will Learn

● Describe how protists can be organized into three groups based on their shared traits.
● List an example for each group of protists.

Vocabulary
algae
phytoplankton

READING STRATEGY

Reading Organizer As you read this section, make a table comparing protist producers, heterotrophs that can move, and heterotrophs that cannot move.

Slimy masses of protists can look like spilled food. Smears of protists on the walls of a fish tank may look like dirt. Few of the many kinds of protists look alike.

These unique organisms are hard to classify. Scientists are always learning more about protist relationships. So, organizing protists into groups is not easy. One way that protists are grouped is based on shared traits. Using this method, scientists can place protists into three groups: producers, heterotrophs that can move, and heterotrophs that can't move. These groups do not show how protists are related to each other. But these groups do help us understand how protists can differ.

Protist Producers

Many protists are producers. Like plants, protist producers use the sun's energy to make food through photosynthesis. These protist producers are known as **algae** (AL JEE). All algae (singular, *alga*) have the green pigment chlorophyll, which is used for making food. But most algae also have other pigments that give them a color. Almost all algae live in water.

Some algae are made of many cells, as shown in **Figure 1.** Many-celled algae generally live in shallow water along the shore. You may know these algae as *seaweeds*. Some of these algae can grow to many meters in length.

Free-floating single-celled algae are called **phytoplankton** (FIET oh PLANGK tuhn). These algae cannot be seen without a microscope. They usually float near the water's surface. Phytoplankton provide food for most other organisms in the water. They also produce much of the world's oxygen.

algae eukaryotic organisms that convert the sun's energy into food through photosynthesis but that do not have roots, stems, or leaves (singular, *alga*)

phytoplankton the microscopic, photosynthetic organisms that float near the surface of marine or fresh water

Figure 1 *Some kinds of algae, such as this giant kelp, can grow to be many meters in length.*

Figure 2 *This* Sebdenia *(seb DEE nee uh) is a red alga.*

Red Algae

Most of the world's seaweeds are red algae. Most red algae live in tropical oceans, attached to rocks or to other algae. Red algae are usually less than 1 m in length. Their cells contain chlorophyll, but a red pigment gives them their color. Their red pigment allows them to absorb the light that filters deep into the clear water of the Tropics. Red algae can grow as deep as 260 m below the surface of the water. An example of a red alga can be seen in **Figure 2.**

Reading Check **If red algae have chlorophyll in their cells, why aren't they green?** (*See the Appendix for answers to Reading Checks.*)

Green Algae

The green algae are the most diverse group of protist producers. They are green because chlorophyll is the main pigment in their cells. Most live in water or moist soil. But others live in melting snow, on tree trunks, and inside other organisms.

Many green algae are single-celled organisms. Others are made of many cells. These many-celled species may grow to be 8 m long. Individual cells of some species of green algae live in groups called *colonies*. **Figure 3** shows colonies of *Volvox.*

Figure 3 Volvox *is a green alga that grows in round colonies.*

Brown Algae

Most of the seaweeds found in cool climates are brown algae. They attach to rocks or form large floating beds in ocean waters. Brown algae have chlorophyll and a yellow-brown pigment. Many are very large. Some grow 60 m—as long as about 20 cars—in just one season! Only the tops of these gigantic algae are exposed to sunlight. These parts of the algae make food through photosynthesis. This food is transported to parts of the algae that are too deep in the water to receive sunlight.

Diatoms

Diatoms (DIE e TAHMZ) are single celled. They are found in both salt water and fresh water. Diatoms get their energy from photosynthesis. They make up a large percentage of phytoplankton. **Figure 4** shows some diatoms' many unusual shapes. The cell walls of diatoms contain a glasslike substance called *silica*. The cells of diatoms are enclosed in a two-part shell.

Dinoflagellates

Most dinoflagellates (DIE noh FLAJ uh lits) are single celled. Most live in salt water, but a few species live in fresh water. Some dinoflagellates even live in snow. Dinoflagellates have two whiplike strands called *flagella* (singular, *flagellum*). The beating of these flagella causes the cells to spin through the water. Most dinoflagellates get their energy from photosynthesis, but a few are consumers, decomposers, or parasites.

✓ **Reading Check** Name three places where dinoflagellates live.

Euglenoids

Euglenoids (yoo GLEE NOYDZ) are single-celled protists. Most euglenoids live in fresh water. They use their flagella to move through the water. Many euglenoids are producers and so make their own food. But when there is not enough light to make food, these euglenoids can get food as heterotrophs. Other euglenoids do not contain chlorophyll and cannot make food. These euglenoids are full-time consumers or decomposers. Because euglenoids can get food in several ways, they do not fit well into any one protist group. **Figure 5** shows the structure of a euglenoid.

Figure 4 *Although most diatoms are free floating, some cling to plants, shellfish, sea turtles, and whales.*

Figure 5 **The Structure of Euglenoids**

Photosynthesis takes place in **chloroplasts.** These structures contain the green pigment chlorophyll.

Most euglenoids have two **flagella,** one long and one short. Euglenoids use flagella to move through water.

Euglenoids can't see, but they have **eyespots** that sense light.

A special structure called a **contractile vacuole** holds excess water and removes it from the cell.

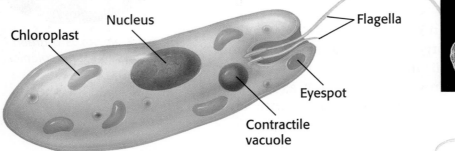

Chloroplast
Nucleus
Flagella
Eyespot
Contractile vacuole

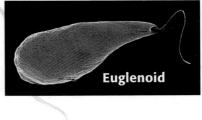

Euglenoid

Figure 6 Amoebic Movement

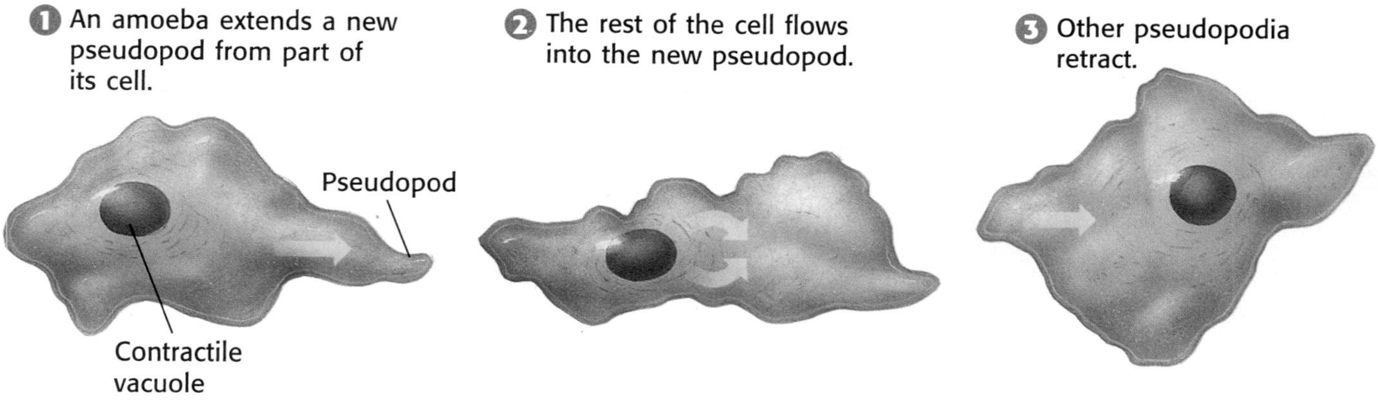

1 An amoeba extends a new pseudopod from part of its cell.

2 The rest of the cell flows into the new pseudopod.

3 Other pseudopodia retract.

Pseudopod

Contractile vacuole

Heterotrophs That Can Move

Some heterotrophic protists have special traits that allow them to move. Other heterotrophic protists cannot move on their own. Those that can move are usually single-celled consumers or parasites. These mobile protists are sometimes called *protozoans* (PROHT oh ZOH uhnz).

Amoebas

Amoebas (uh MEE buhs) and similar amoeba-like protists are soft, jellylike protozoans. They are found in both fresh and salt water, in soil, and as parasites in animals. Although amoebas look shapeless, they are highly structured cells. Amoebas have contractile vacuoles to get rid of excess water. Many amoebas eat bacteria and small protists. But some amoebas are parasites that get food by invading other organisms. Certain parasitic amoebas live in human intestines and cause amoebic dysentery (uh MEE bik DIS uhn TER ee). This painful disease causes internal bleeding.

Amoebic Movement

Amoebas and amoeba-like protists move with pseudopodia (soo doh POH dee uh). *Pseudopodia* means "false feet." To move, an amoeba stretches a pseudopod out from the cell. The cell then flows into the pseudopod. **Figure 6** shows how an amoeba uses pseudopodia to move.

Amoebas and amoeba-like protists use pseudopodia to catch food, too. When an amoeba senses a food source, it moves toward the food. The amoeba surrounds the food with its pseudopodia. This action forms a *food vacuole*. Enzymes move into the vacuole to digest the food, and the digested food passes into the amoeba. **Figure 7** shows an amoeba catching food. To get rid of wastes, an amoeba reverses the process. A waste-filled vacuole is moved to the edge of the cell and is released.

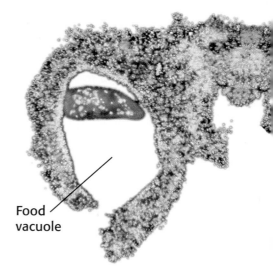

Food vacuole

Figure 7 *An amoeba engulfs its prey with its pseudopodia.*

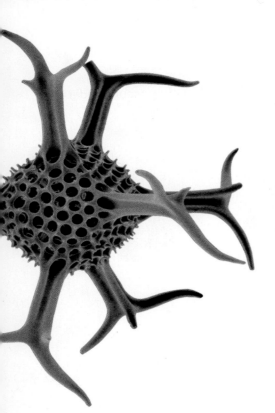

Figure 8 *Radiolarians are amoeba-like protists that have shells.*

Shelled Amoeba-Like Protists

Not all amoeba-like protists look shapeless. Some have an outer shell. *Radiolarian* (RAY dee oh LER ee uhn) shells look like glass ornaments, as shown in **Figure 8.** *Foraminiferans* (fuh RAM uh NIF uhr uhnz) have snail-like shells. These protists move by poking pseudopodia out of pores in the shells.

✓ Reading Check Name two shelled, amoeba-like protists.

Zooflagellates

Zooflagellates (ZOH uh FLAJ uh LAYTS) are protists that wave flagella back and forth to move. Some zooflagellates live in water. Others live in the bodies of other organisms.

Some zooflagellates are parasites that cause disease. The parasite *Giardia lamblia* (jee AWR dee uh LAM blee uh) can live in the digestive tract of many vertebrates. One form of *G. lamblia* lives part of its life in water. People who drink water infected with *G. lamblia* can get severe stomach cramps.

Some zooflagellates live in mutualism with other organisms. In *mutualism,* one organism lives closely with another organism. Each organism helps the other live. The zooflagellate in **Figure 9** lives in the gut of termites. This zooflagellate digests the cell walls of the wood that the termites eat. Both organisms benefit from the arrangement. The protist helps the termite digest wood. The termite gives the protist food and a place to live.

Figure 9 **The Structure of Flagellates**

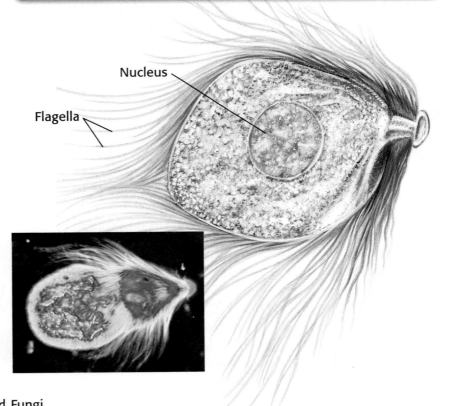

Nucleus

Flagella

Figure 10 The Structure of a Paramecium

Members of the genus *Paramecium* eat by using cilia to sweep food into a **food passageway.**

Food enters a **food vacuole,** where enzymes digest the food.

Food waste is removed from the cell through the **anal pore.**

A **contractile vacuole** pumps out excess water.

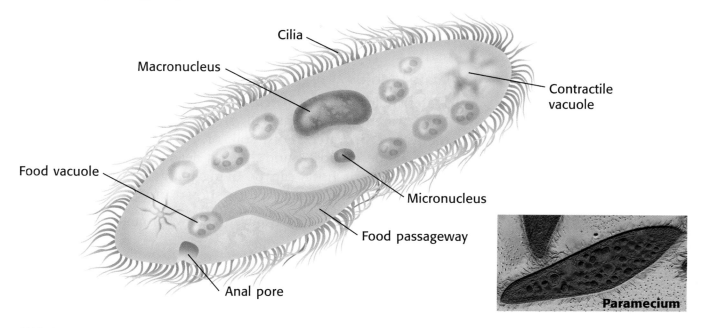

Cilia

Macronucleus

Contractile vacuole

Food vacuole

Micronucleus

Food passageway

Anal pore

Paramecium

Ciliates

Ciliates (SIL ee its) are complex protists. They have hundreds of tiny, hairlike structures known as *cilia*. The cilia move a protist forward by beating back and forth. Cilia can beat up to 60 times a second! Ciliates also use their cilia for feeding. The cilia sweep food toward the protist's food passageway. The best-known genus of ciliates is *Paramecium*, shown in **Figure 10.**

The cell of a paramecium has two kinds of nuclei. A large nucleus called a *macronucleus* controls the functions of the cell. A smaller nucleus, the *micronucleus,* passes genes to another paramecium during sexual reproduction.

Heterotrophs That Can't Move

Not all protist heterotrophs have features that help them move. Some of these protists are parasites that do not move about. Others can move only at certain phases in their life cycle.

Spore-Forming Protists

Many spore-forming protists are parasites. They absorb nutrients from their hosts. They have no cilia or flagella, and they cannot move on their own. Spore-forming protists have complicated life cycles that usually include two or more hosts. For example, the spore-forming protist that causes malaria uses both mosquitoes and humans as hosts.

CONNECTION TO Social Studies

Malaria *Plasmodium vivax* is a spore-forming protist that causes malaria. People get malaria in tropical areas when they are bitten by mosquitoes carrying *P. vivax*. Malaria can be treated with drugs, but many people do not have access to these drugs. Millions of people die from malaria each year. Research malaria rates in different parts of the world, and give a presentation of your findings to the class.

ACTIVITY

Figure 11 *Parasitic water molds attack various organisms, including fish.*

Water Molds

Water molds are also heterotrophic protists that can't move. Most water molds are small, single-celled organisms. Water molds live in water, moist soil, or other organisms. Some of them are decomposers and thus eat dead matter. But many are parasites. Their hosts can be living plants, animals, algae, or fungi. A parasitic water mold is shown in **Figure 11.**

✓ **Reading Check** Name two ways that water molds get food.

Slime Molds

Slime molds are heterotrophic protists that can move only at certain phases of their life cycle. They look like thin, colorful, shapeless globs of slime. Slime molds live in cool, moist places in the woods. They use pseudopodia to move and to eat bacteria and yeast. They also decompose small bits of rotting organic matter by surrounding small pieces of the matter and then digesting them.

Some slime molds live as a giant cell that has many nuclei and a single cytoplasm at one stage of life. As long as food and water are available, the cell will continue to grow. One cell may be more than 1 m across! Other slime molds live as single-celled individuals that can come together as a group when food or water is hard to find.

When environmental conditions are stressful, slime molds grow stalklike structures with rounded knobs at the top, as shown in **Figure 12.** The knobs contain spores. *Spores* are small reproductive cells covered by a thick cell wall. The spores can survive for a long time without water or nutrients. As spores, slime molds cannot move. When conditions improve, the spores will develop into new slime molds.

INTERNET ACTIVITY

For another activity related to this chapter, go to **go.hrw.com** and type in the keyword **HL5PROW.**

Figure 12 *The spore-containing knobs of a slime mold are called* sporangia *(spoh RAN jee uh).*

Summary

- Protists can be organized into the following groups: producers, heterotrophs that can move, and heterotrophs that cannot move.

- Protist producers make their own food through photosynthesis. They are known as *algae,* and most live in water. Free-floating single-celled algae are phytoplankton.

- Red algae, green algae, brown algae, diatoms, dinoflagellates, and some euglenoids are producers.

- Heterotrophic protists cannot make their own food. They are consumers, decomposers, or parasites. Those that can move are sometimes called *protozoans*.

- Amoeba-like protists, shelled amoeba-like protists, flagellates, and ciliates are heterotrophs that can move.

- Spore-forming protists, water molds, and slime molds are protists that cannot move or can move only in certain phases of their life cycle.

Using Key Terms

1. Use the following terms in the same sentence: *phytoplankton* and *algae.*

Understanding Key Ideas

2. Which of the following kinds of protists are producers?
   a. diatoms
   b. amoebas
   c. slime molds
   d. ciliates

3. How do many amoeba-like protists eat?
   a. They secrete digestive juices onto food.
   b. They produce food from sunlight.
   c. They engulf food with pseudopodia.
   d. They use cilia to sweep food toward them.

4. Give an example of one protist from each of the three groups of protists.

5. Explain why it makes sense to group protists based on shared traits rather than by how they are related to each other.

Critical Thinking

6. **Making Comparisons** How do protist producers, heterotrophs that can move, and heterotrophs that can't move differ?

7. **Making Inferences** You learned how shelled amoeba-like protists move. How do you think they get food into their shells in order to eat?

Interpreting Graphics

Use the photo below to answer the questions that follow.

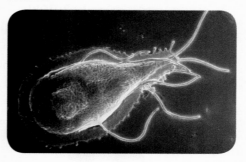

8. How does this protist move?

9. Identify what kind of protist is shown. To do so, first make a list of the kinds of protists that this organism could not be.

SCiLINKS.

NSTA
Developed and maintained by the
National Science Teachers Association

For a variety of links related to this chapter, go to www.scilinks.org

Topic: Algae; Protozoans
SciLinks code: HSM0042; HSM1247

Fungi

How are cheese, bread, and soy sauce related to fungi? A fungus can help make each of these foods.

Fungi (singular, *fungus*) are everywhere. The mushrooms on pizza are a type of fungus. The yeast used to make bread is a fungus. And if you've ever had athlete's foot, you can thank a fungus for that, too.

Characteristics of Fungi

Fungi are eukaryotic heterotrophs that have rigid cell walls and no chlorophyll. They are so different from other organisms that they are placed in their own kingdom. As you can see in **Figure 1,** fungi come in a variety of shapes, sizes, and colors.

Food for Fungi

Fungi are heterotrophs, but they cannot catch or surround food. Fungi must live on or near their food supply. Most fungi are consumers. These fungi get nutrients by secreting digestive juices onto a food source and then absorbing the dissolved food. Many fungi are decomposers, which feed on dead plant or animal matter. Other fungi are parasites.

Some fungi live in mutualism with other organisms. For example, many types of fungi grow on or in the roots of a plant. The plant provides nutrients to the fungus. The fungus helps the root absorb minerals and protects the plant from some disease-causing organisms. This relationship between a plant and a fungus is called a *mycorrhiza* (MIE koh RIE zuh).

Figure 1 *Fungi vary greatly in their appearance.*

▼ Straight coral fungus

▲ Bird's nest fungus

▼ Witch's hat fungus

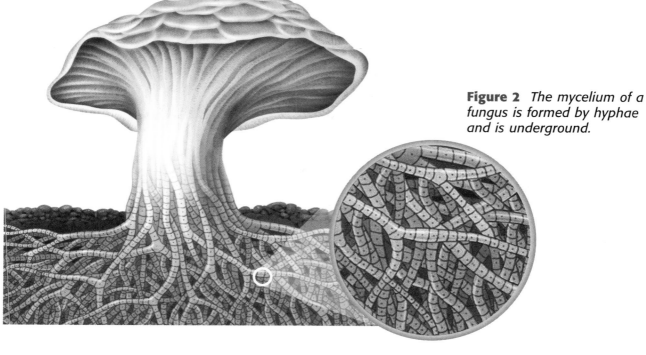

Figure 2 *The mycelium of a fungus is formed by hyphae and is underground.*

Hidden from View

All fungi are made of eukaryotic cells, which have nuclei. Some fungi are single celled, but most fungi are made of many cells. These many-celled fungi are made up of chains of cells called hyphae (HIE fee). **Hyphae** (singular, *hypha*) are threadlike fungal filaments. These filaments are made of cells that have openings in their cell walls. These openings allow cytoplasm to move freely between the cells.

Most of the hyphae that make up a fungus grow together to form a twisted mass called the **mycelium** (mie SEE lee uhm). The mycelium makes up the major part of the fungus. However, this mass is hidden from view underneath the ground. **Figure 2** shows the hyphae of a fungus.

Making More Fungi

Reproduction in fungi may be either asexual or sexual. Asexual reproduction in fungi occurs in two ways. In one type of asexual reproduction, the hyphae break apart, and each new piece becomes a new fungus. Asexual reproduction can also take place by the production of spores. **Spores** are small reproductive cells that are protected by a thick cell wall. Spores are light and easily spread by wind. When the growing conditions where a spore lands are right, the spore will grow into a new fungus.

Sexual reproduction in fungi happens when special structures form to make sex cells. The sex cells join to produce sexual spores that grow into a new fungus. **Figure 3** shows a fungus releasing sexual spores into the air.

✓ **Reading Check** What are two ways that fungi can reproduce asexually? (*See the Appendix for answers to Reading Checks.*)

fungus an organism whose cells have nuclei, rigid cell walls, and no chlorophyll and that belongs to the kingdom Fungi

hypha a nonreproductive filament of a fungus

mycelium the mass of fungal filaments, or hyphae, that forms the body of a fungus

spore a reproductive cell or multicellular structure that is resistant to stressful environmental conditions and that can develop into an adult without fusing with another cell

Figure 3 *This puffball is releasing sexual spores that can produce new fungi.*

Figure 4 *Black bread mold is a soft, cottony mass that grows on bread and fruit.*

mold a fungus that looks like wool or cotton

Kinds of Fungi

Fungi are classified based on their shape and the way that they reproduce. There are four main groups of fungi. Most species of fungi fit into one of these groups. These groups are threadlike fungi, sac fungi, club fungi, and imperfect fungi.

Threadlike Fungi

Have you ever seen fuzzy mold growing on bread? A **mold** is a shapeless, fuzzy fungus. **Figure 4** shows a black bread mold. This particular mold belongs to a group of fungi called *threadlike fungi*. Most of the fungi in this group live in the soil and are decomposers. However, some threadlike fungi are parasites.

Threadlike fungi can reproduce asexually. Parts of the hyphae grow into the air and form round spore cases at the tips. These spore cases are called *sporangia* (spoh RAN jee uh). **Figure 5** shows some magnified sporangia. When the sporangia break open, many tiny spores are released into the air. New fungi will develop from these spores if they land in an area with good growing conditions.

Threadlike fungi can also reproduce sexually. Threadlike fungi reproduce sexually when a hypha from one individual joins with a hypha from another individual. The hyphae grow into specialized sporangia that can survive times of cold or little water. When conditions improve, these specialized sporangia release spores that can grow into new fungi.

Reading Check Describe two ways that threadlike fungi can reproduce.

Figure 5 *Each of the round sporangia contains thousands of spores.*

Quick Lab

Moldy Bread

1. Dampen a **slice of bread** with a **few drops of water,** and then seal it in a **plastic bag** for 1 week.

2. Draw a picture of the bread in the plastic bag.

3. Predict what you think will happen during the week. Will the bread get moldy?

4. After the week has passed, check on the bread in the plastic bag. Compare it with your original drawing. What happened? Were your predictions correct?

5. With a partner, discuss where you think mold spores come from and how they grow.

Figure 6 *Morels are only part of a larger fungus. They are the sexual reproductive part of a fungus that lives under the soil.*

Sac Fungi

Sac fungi are the largest group of fungi. Sac fungi include yeasts, powdery mildews, truffles, and morels. Some morels are shown in **Figure 6.**

Sac fungi can reproduce both asexually and sexually during their life cycles. Most of the time, they use asexual reproduction. When they reproduce sexually, they form a sac called an *ascus*. This sac gives the sac fungi their name. Sexually produced spores develop within the ascus.

Most sac fungi are made of many cells. However, *yeasts* are single-celled sac fungi. When yeasts reproduce asexually, they use a process called *budding*. In budding, a new cell pinches off from an existing cell. **Figure 7** shows a yeast that is budding. Yeasts are the only fungi that reproduce by budding.

Figure 7 *Yeasts reproduce by budding. A round scar forms where a bud breaks off from a parent cell.*

Some sac fungi are very useful to humans. For example, yeasts are used in making bread and alcohol. Yeasts use sugar as food and produce carbon dioxide gas and alcohol as waste. Trapped bubbles of carbon dioxide cause bread dough to rise. This process is what makes bread light and fluffy. Other sac fungi are sources of antibiotics and vitamins. And some sac fungi, such as truffles and morels, are prized as human foods.

Not all sac fungi are helpful. In fact, many sac fungi are parasites. Some cause plant diseases, such as chestnut blight and Dutch elm disease. The effects of Dutch elm disease are shown in **Figure 8.**

Figure 8 *Dutch elm disease is a fungal disease that has killed millions of elm trees.*

Figure 9 *A ring of mushrooms can appear overnight. In European folk legends, these were known as "fairy rings."*

Observe a Mushroom

1. Identify the stalk, cap, and gills on a **mushroom** that your teacher has provided.

2. Carefully twist or cut off the cap, and cut it open with a **plastic knife.** Use a **magnifying lens** to observe the gills. Look for spores.

3. Use the magnifying lens to observe the other parts of the mushroom. The mycelium begins at the bottom of the stalk. Try to find individual hyphae.

4. Sketch the mushroom, and label the parts.

Club Fungi

The umbrella-shaped mushrooms are the most familiar fungi. Mushrooms belong to a group of fungi called *club fungi*. This group gets its name from structures that the fungi grow during reproduction. Club fungi reproduce sexually. During reproduction, they grow special hyphae that form clublike structures. These structures are called *basidia* (buh SID ee uh), the Greek word for "clubs." Sexual spores develop on the basidia.

When you think of a mushroom, you probably picture only the spore-producing, above-ground part of the organism. But most of the organism is underground. The mass of hyphae from which mushrooms are produced may grow 35 m across. That's about as long as 18 adults lying head to toe! Mushrooms usually grow at the edges of the mass of hyphae. As a result, mushrooms often appear in circles, as shown in **Figure 9.**

The most familiar mushrooms are known as *gill fungi*. The basidia of these mushrooms develop in structures called *gills,* under the mushroom cap. Some varieties are grown commercially and sold in supermarkets. However, not all gill fungi are edible. For example, the white destroying angel is a very poisonous fungus. Simply a taste of this mushroom can be fatal. See if you can pick out the poisonous fungus in **Figure 10.**

Reading Check What part of a club fungus grows above the ground?

Figure 10 *Many poisonous mushrooms look just like edible ones. Never eat a mushroom from the wild unless a professional identifies it in person.*

Figure 11 *Bracket fungi look like shelves on trees. The underside of the bracket contains spores.*

Nonmushroom Club Fungi

Mushrooms are not the only club fungi. Bracket fungi, puffballs, smuts, and rusts are also club fungi. Bracket fungi grow outward from wood and form small shelves or brackets, as shown in **Figure 11.** Smuts and rusts are common plant parasites. They often attack crops such as corn and wheat. The corn in **Figure 12** has been infected with a smut.

Imperfect Fungi

The *imperfect fungi* group includes all of the species of fungi that do not quite fit in the other groups. These fungi do not reproduce sexually. Most are parasites that cause diseases in plants and animals. One common human disease caused by these fungi is athlete's foot, a skin disease. Another fungus from this group produces a poison called *aflatoxin* (AF luh TAHKS in), which can cause cancer.

Some imperfect fungi are useful. *Penicillium,* shown in **Figure 13,** is the source of the antibiotic penicillin. Other imperfect fungi are also used to produce medicines. Some imperfect fungi are used to produce cheeses, soy sauce, and the citric acid used in cola drinks.

Figure 12 *This corn is infected with a club fungus called* smut.

Figure 13 *The fungus* Penicillium *produces a substance that kills certain bacteria.*

CONNECTION TO Language Arts

Beatrix Potter Beatrix Potter (1866–1943) is best known for writing children's stories, such as *The Tale of Peter Rabbit* and *The Tale of Two Bad Mice.* Potter lived and worked in England and had a scholarly interest in fungi. She was a shy person, and she was not taken seriously by fungi scholars of her time. But today, she is widely respected as a mycologist (a scientist who studies fungi). She wrote many valuable papers about fungi and made detailed drawings of more than 270 fungi. Research Potter's life, and present a report to your class.

ACTiViTY

▲ Wolf lichen

British soldier ▶
lichen

▼ Christmas lichen

Figure 14 *These are some of the many types of lichens.*

lichen a mass of fungal and algal cells that grow together in a symbiotic relationship and that are usually found on rocks or trees

Lichens

A **lichen** (LIE kuhn) is a combination of a fungus and an alga that grow together. The alga actually lives inside the protective walls of the fungus. The resulting organism is different from either organism growing alone. The lichen is a result of a mutualistic relationship. But the merging of the two organisms to form a lichen is so complete that scientists give lichens their own scientific names. **Figure 14** shows some examples of lichens.

Unlike fungi, lichens are producers. The algae in the lichens produce food through photosynthesis. And unlike algae, lichens can keep from drying out. The protective walls of the fungi keep water inside the lichens. Lichens are found in almost every type of land environment. They can even grow in dry environments, such as deserts, and cold environments, such as the Arctic.

Because lichens need only air, light, and minerals to grow, they can grow on rocks. As lichens grow, the changes that they make to their surroundings allow other organisms to live there, too. For example, lichens make acids that break down rocks and cause cracks. When bits of rock and dead lichens fill the cracks, soil is made. Other organisms then grow in this soil.

Lichens absorb water and minerals from the air. As a result, lichens are easily affected by air pollution. So, the presence or absence of lichens can be a good measure of air quality in an area.

✓ Reading Check How can lichens affect rocks?

Summary

- Fungi can be consumers, decomposers, or parasites, or they can live in mutualistic relationships with other organisms.

- Most fungi are made up of chains of cells called *hyphae*. Many hyphae join together to form a mycelium.

- The four main groups of fungi are thread-like fungi, sac fungi, club fungi, and imperfect fungi.

- Threadlike fungi are primarily decomposers that form sporangia containing spores.

- During sexual reproduction, sac fungi form little sacs in which sexual spores develop.

- Club fungi form structures called *basidia* during sexual reproduction.

- The imperfect fungi include all of the species that do not quite fit in the other groups. Many are parasites that reproduce only by asexual reproduction.

- A lichen is a combination of a specific fungus and a specific alga. The lichen is different from either organism growing alone.

Using Key Terms

1. In your own words, write a definition for each of the following terms: *spore* and *mold*.

For each pair of terms, explain how the meanings of the terms differ.

2. *fungus* and *lichen*

3. *hyphae* and *mycelium*

Understanding Key Ideas

4. Which of the following statements about fungi is true?
   a. All fungi are eukaryotic.
   b. All fungi are decomposers.
   c. All fungi reproduce by sexual reproduction.
   d. All fungi are producers.

5. What are the four main groups of fungi? Give a characteristic of each group.

6. How are fungi able to withstand periods of cold or drought?

Critical Thinking

7. **Analyzing Processes** Many fungi are decomposers. Imagine what would happen to the natural world if decomposers no longer existed. Write a description of how a lack of decomposers might affect the processes of nature.

8. **Identifying Relationships** Explain how two organisms make up a lichen.

Interpreting Graphics

Use the photo below to answer the questions that follow.

9. To which group of fungi does this organism belong? How can you be sure?

10. What part of the organism is shown in this photo? What part is not shown? Explain.

Developed and maintained by the National Science Teachers Association

For a variety of links related to this chapter, go to www.scilinks.org

Topics: Fungi; Lichens
SciLinks codes: HSM0628; HSM0871

Skills Practice Lab

There's a Fungus Among Us!

Fungi share many characteristics with plants. For example, most fungi live on land and cannot move from place to place. But fungi have several unique features that suggest that they are not closely related to any other kingdom of organisms. In this activity, you will observe some of the unique structures of a mushroom, a member of the kingdom Fungi.

OBJECTIVES

Examine the parts of a mushroom.

Describe your observations of the mushroom.

MATERIALS

- gloves, protective
- incubator
- microscope or magnifying lens
- mushroom
- paper, white (2 sheets)
- Petri dish with fruit-juice agar plate
- tape, masking
- tape, transparent
- tweezers

SAFETY

Procedure

1 Put on your safety goggles and gloves. Get a mushroom from your teacher. Carefully pull the cap of the mushroom from the stem.

2 Using tweezers, remove one of the gills from the underside of the cap. Place the gill on a sheet of white paper.

3 Place the mushroom cap gill-side down on the other sheet of paper. Use masking tape to keep the mushroom cap in place. Place the paper aside for at least 24 hours.

4 Use tweezers to take several 1 cm pieces from the stem, and place these pieces in your Petri dish. Record the appearance of the plate by drawing the plate in a notebook. Cover the Petri dish, and incubate it overnight.

5 Use tweezers to gently pull the remaining mushroom stem apart lengthwise. The individual fibers or strings that you see are the hyphae, which form the structure of the fungus. Place a thin strand on the same piece of paper on which you placed the gill that you removed from the cap.

6 Use a magnifying lens or microscope to observe the gill and the stem hyphae.

7 After at least 24 hours, record any changes that occurred in the Petri dish.

8 Carefully remove the mushroom cap from the paper. Place a piece of transparent tape over the print left behind on the paper. Record your observations.

Analyze the Results

1 Describing Events Describe the structures that you saw on the gill and hyphae.

2 Explaining Events What makes up the print that was left on the white paper?

3 Examining Data Describe the structures on the mushroom gill. Explain how these structures are connected to the print.

4 Analyzing Data Compare your original drawing of the Petri dish to your observations of the dish after leaving it for 24 hours.

Draw Conclusions

5 Evaluating Results Explain how the changes that occurred in your Petri dish are related to methods of fungal reproduction.

Applying Your Data

Fungi such as mushrooms and yeast are used in cooking and baking in many parts of the world. Bread is a staple food in many cultures. There are thousands of kinds of bread. Conduct library and Internet research on how yeast makes bread rise. Find a bread recipe, and show how the recipe involves the care and feeding of yeast. Ask an adult to help you bake a loaf of bread to share with your class during your presentation.

Chapter Review

1 In your own words, write a definition for each of the following terms: *mycelium, lichen,* and *heterotroph.*

2 Use the following terms in the same sentence: *protists, algae,* and *phytoplankton.*

3 Use the following terms in the same sentence: *spore* and *mold.*

For each pair of terms, explain how the meanings of the terms differ.

4 *fungus* and *hypha*

5 *parasite* and *host*

Multiple Choice

6 Protist producers include
  a. euglenoids and ciliates.
  b. lichens and zooflagellates.
  c. spore-forming protists and smuts.
  d. dinoflagellates and diatoms.

7 Protists can be
  a. parasites or decomposers.
  b. made of chains of cells called *hyphae.*
  c. divided into four major groups.
  d. only parasites.

8 A euglenoid has
  a. a micronucleus.
  b. pseudopodia.
  c. two flagella.
  d. cilia.

9 Which statement about fungi is true?
  a. Fungi are producers.
  b. Fungi cannot eat or engulf food.
  c. Fungi are found only in the soil.
  d. Fungi are primarily single celled.

10 A lichen is made up of
  a. a fungus and a funguslike protist that live together.
  b. an alga and a fungus that live together.
  c. two kinds of fungi that live together.
  d. an alga and a funguslike protist that live together.

11 Heterotrophic protists that can move
  a. are also known as *protozoans.*
  b. include amoebas and paramecia.
  c. may be either free living or parasitic.
  d. All of the above

Short Answer

12 How are fungi helpful to humans?

13 What is the function of cilia in a paramecium?

14 How are fungi different from protists that get food as decomposers?

15 How are slime molds and amoebas similar?

16 What is a contractile vacuole?

17 Compare how *Paramecium, Plasmodium vivax,* and *Euglena* reproduce.

18 Compare how phytoplankton, amoebas, and *Giardia lamblia* get food.

19 Explain how protists differ from other organisms.

20 Give an example of where you might find each of the following fungi: threadlike fungi, sac fungi, club fungi, and imperfect fungi.

CRITICAL THINKING

21 **Concept Mapping** Use the following terms to create a concept map: *yeast, basidia, threadlike fungi, mushrooms, fungi, bread mold, ascus,* and *club fungi.*

22 **Applying Concepts** Why do you think bread turns moldy less quickly when it is kept in a refrigerator than when it is kept at room temperature?

23 **Making Inferences** Some protozoans, such as radiolarians and foraminiferans, have shells around their bodies. How might these shells be helpful to the protists that live in them?

24 **Predicting Consequences** Suppose a forest where many threadlike fungi live goes through a very dry summer and fall and then a very cold winter. How could this extreme weather affect the reproductive patterns of these fungi?

INTERPRETING GRAPHICS

Use the pictures of fungi below to answer the questions that follow.

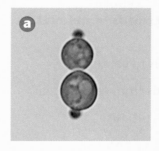
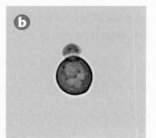
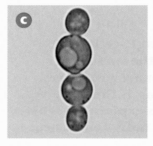
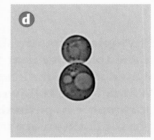

25 What kind of fungus is shown here?

26 What cellular process is shown in these pictures?

27 Which picture was taken first? Which was taken last? Arrange the pictures in order.

28 Which is the original parent cell? How do you know?

Standardized Test Preparation

Multiple Choice

1. **Some mushrooms are poisonous to animals. Which of the following is the most reasonable hypothesis explaining why this trait is beneficial to mushrooms?**

   A. It encourages animals to eat them.

   B. It discourages animals from eating them.

   C. It helps with photosynthesis.

   D. It helps them reproduce faster.

2. **Phytoplankton are single-celled algae that float near the surface of water. Phytoplankton are producers. Which of the following is the most reasonable hypothesis explaining why phytoplankton are usually found near the surface of water?**

   A. Phytoplankton need oxygen to breathe.

   B. Phytoplankton need sunlight for photosynthesis, and sunlight is more available near the water's surface.

   C. There are fewer predators near the water's surface.

   D. Phytoplankton need to be near the nitrogen contained in air.

3. **Which of the following hypotheses about fungi is NOT testable?**

   A. Fungi may reproduce sexually and asexually.

   B. Fungi cells have a nucleus.

   C. Fungi are consumers.

   D. Fungi are from another planet.

Use the diagram below to answer question 4.

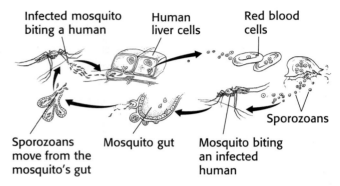

Infected mosquito biting a human · Human liver cells · Red blood cells · Sporozoans · Sporozoans move from the mosquito's gut · Mosquito gut · Mosquito biting an infected human

4. **During a field investigation, Thomas made the sketch above to show how *Plasmodium vivax* causes malaria. Analyze the sketch. Based on his sketch, which of the following statements about liver cells is FALSE?**

   A. They are the site from which sporozoans invade the bloodstream.

   B. They burst in response to the invasion by *Plasmodium vivax*.

   C. They are the sites where sporozoans form.

   D. They are the first cells to be affected by the *Plasmodium vivax*.

5. **If an amoeba can move at a speed of 10 microns/second, how many seconds will it take the amoeba to move 0.5 mm? (1 micron = 1/1000 mm)**

   A. 50 s

   B. 100 s

   C. 500 s

   D. 1000 s

6. During a field investigation, Juanita discovers a mushroom that looks like a type often used in cooking. Which of the following practices is safe for Juanita to perform?

A. tasting the mushroom

B. inhaling deeply to see if the mushroom has a smell

C. handling the mushroom with bare hands

D. using a tool to place the mushroom in a plastic bag

Use the table below to answer question 7.

Date	Total Length (m)
February 1	10.0
March 1	20.0
April 1	25.0
May 1	27.5

7. Nell studied a particular protist that grows in the ocean near Sea Island, Georgia. She collected the data above about the total length of the protist over time. What was the average growth rate from February 1 through April 1?

A. 5.0 m/month

B. 7.5 m/month

C. 11.6 m/month

D. 15.0 m/month

8. Which statement is true of all members of the kingdom Protista?

A. All protists are single-celled organisms.

B. All protists live in colonies.

C. All protists reproduce asexually.

D. All protists are eukaryotic.

9. Which word does NOT describe a heterotrophic protist?

A. producer

B. consumer

C. decomposer

D. parasite

Open Response

10. Marissa's class studied pond water under a microscope. They examined amoebas and other single-celled protists. How does an amoeba use a pseudopod to move?

11. Lichens are usually composed of a fungus and an alga. Some lichens are composed of a fungus and a kind of cyanobacterium. What can you infer from this information?

Standardized Test Preparation

Science in Action

Science, Technology, and Society

Algae Ice Cream

If someone offered you a bowl of algae ice cream, would you eat it? Would you eat algae pudding? These foods may not sound appetizing, but algae are a central ingredient in these foods. You eat many kinds of algae every day. Parts of brown algae help thicken ice cream and other dairy products. Red algae help keep breads and pastries from drying out. They are also used in chocolate, milk, eggnog, ice cream, sherbet, instant pudding, and frosting. Green algae contain a pigment that is used as yellow and orange food coloring. Algae are all around you!

Social Studies ACTiViTY

Food products are not the only products that use protist producers. In groups, research how people take advantage of the shiny shells of diatoms. Then, present your findings to the class.

Weird Science

Glowing Protists

As your kayak drifts silently through the night, it leaves a trail of swirling green light in the water behind it. You jump in the water to swim, and your hands turn into glowing underwater comets, which leave sparkling trails that slowly fade away. This may sound like a dream, but it happens every night for swimmers at Mosquito Bay on the island of Vieques in Puerto Rico. The source of this green glow is a protist. The waters of this bay contain millions of dinoflagellates that glow when the water around them is disturbed.

The species of dinoflagellates in Mosquito Bay is *Pyrodinium bahamense*, which means "whirling fire." These spherical single-celled protists are covered by armored plates. Each individual has two flagella that spin it through the water. The light is produced by a chemical reaction that is similar to the reaction in fireflies.

Math ACTiViTY

Living in every gallon of water in Mosquito Bay are 750,000 dinoflagellates. Suppose you took a gallon of water from this bay and dumped it into a bathtub full of 6 gal of fresh water that didn't contain any dinoflagellates. Then, you mixed up the water and turned out the lights to see if the bathtub would glow in the dark. How many dinoflagellates would be in each gallon of water in the bathtub after you mixed up the water?

Terrie Taylor

Fighting Malaria Malaria claims about 2 million victims each year. A person gets malaria when the blood is infected by protists from the genus *Plasmodium*. Dr. Terrie Taylor of Michigan State University's College of Osteopathic Medicine has devoted her life to malaria research. Since 1987, Dr. Taylor has spent six months of every year in Malawi, a small African country in which malaria is widespread.

When Dr. Taylor first traveled to Malawi, she did not have a particular interest in malaria. However, she quickly started to realize that the majority of her patients were infected with the deadly disease. The patients who were suffering the most were children. For every 100 children infected with malaria and treated by Dr. Taylor, between 20 and 25 would die from a malaria-induced coma. When a malaria coma starts, the patient becomes confused and sleepy. The patient then falls into a coma, which may lead to death. Dr. Taylor worked with other doctors at the hospital to develop a coma scale so that doctors could have a standardized way to assess patients moving toward coma. This scale is now used around the world.

Dr. Taylor wanted to find out why malaria victims fell into a coma. She took blood samples from malaria patients. She realized that severe malaria often led to a rapid fall in the patient's blood-sugar level. Dr. Taylor hypothesizes that the drop in blood sugar is related to the fact that the protists that cause malaria primarily infect a person's liver. The liver is the organ responsible for releasing sugar into the blood. Dr. Taylor has used this information to create a new treatment. Whenever she treats children who have a severe case of malaria, she gives them glucose, the type of sugar that is found in the bloodstream. This simple treatment has already saved hundreds of lives!

Language Arts ACTIVITY

The word *malaria* is a combination of two words. *Mala* means "bad," and *aria* means "air." Why do you think that people would use these words to describe the disease? Note that people did not realize that malaria was transmitted to people by mosquitoes until about 1899.

To learn more about these Science in Action topics, visit go.hrw.com and type in the keyword **HL5PROF.**

Current Science

Check out Current Science® articles related to this chapter by visiting go.hrw.com. Just type in the keyword HL5CS11.

14

Introduction to Plants

The Big Idea

Plants have several common characteristics and can be classified by their structures.

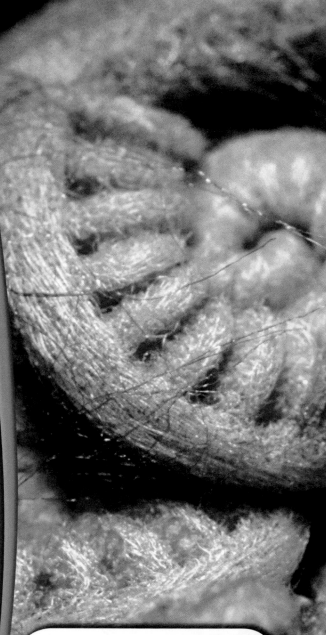

About the Photo

In Costa Rica's Monteverde Cloud Forest Preserve, a green coil begins to unfold. It is hidden from all but the most careful observer. The coil looks alien, but it is very much of this Earth. The coil is the leaf of a fern, a plant that grows in moist areas. Soon, the coil will unfold into a lacy, delicate frond.

PRE-READING ACTIVITY

FOLDNOTES **Pyramid** Before you read the chapter, create the FoldNote entitled "Pyramid" described in the **Study Skills** section of the Appendix. Label the sides of the pyramid with "Nonvascular plants," "Seedless vascular plants," and "Seed plants." As you read the chapter, define each kind of plant, and write characteristics of each kind of plant on the appropriate pyramid side.

Observing Plant Growth

When planting a garden, you bury seeds and water them. What happens to the seeds below the soil? How do seeds grow into plants?

Procedure

1. Fill a clear **2 L soda bottle** to within 8 cm of the top with **moist potting soil.** Your teacher will have already cut off the neck of the bottle.

2. Press **three or four bean seeds** into the soil and against the wall of the bottle. Add enough additional potting soil to increase the depth by 5 cm.

3. Cover the sides of the bottle with **aluminum foil** to keep out light. Leave the top of the bottle uncovered.

4. Water the seeds with about **60 mL of water,** or water them until the soil is moist. Add more water when the soil dries out.

5. Place the bottle in an area that receives sunshine. Check on your seeds each day, and record your observations.

Analysis

1. How many seeds grew?

2. How long did the seeds take to start growing?

3. From where did the seeds most likely get the energy to grow?

What You Will Learn

● Identify four characteristics that all plants share.
● Describe the four main groups of plants.
● Explain the origin of plants.

Vocabulary

nonvascular plant
vascular plant
gymnosperm
angiosperm

READING STRATEGY

Reading Organizer As you read this section, create an outline of the section. Use the headings from the section in your outline.

What Is a Plant?

Imagine spending a day without plants. What would you eat? It would be impossible to make chocolate chip cookies and many other foods.

Without plants, you couldn't eat much. Almost all food is made from plants or from animals that eat plants. Life would be very different without plants!

Plant Characteristics

Plants come in many different shapes and sizes. So, what do cactuses, water lilies, ferns, and all other plants have in common? One plant may seem very different from another. But most plants share certain characteristics.

Photosynthesis

Take a look at **Figure 1.** Do you know why this plant is green? Plant cells contain chlorophyll (KLAWR uh FIL). *Chlorophyll* is a green pigment that captures energy from sunlight. Chlorophyll is found in chloroplasts (KLAWR uh PLASTS). Chloroplasts are organelles found in many plant cells and some protists. Plants use energy from sunlight to make food from carbon dioxide and water. This process is called *photosynthesis* (FOHT oh SIN thuh sis). Because plants make their own food, they are called *producers*.

Cuticles

Most plants live on dry land and need sunlight to live. But why don't plants dry out? Plants are protected by a cuticle. A *cuticle* is a waxy layer that coats most of the surfaces of plants that are exposed to air. The cuticle keeps plants from drying out.

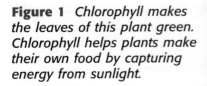

Figure 1 *Chlorophyll makes the leaves of this plant green. Chlorophyll helps plants make their own food by capturing energy from sunlight.*

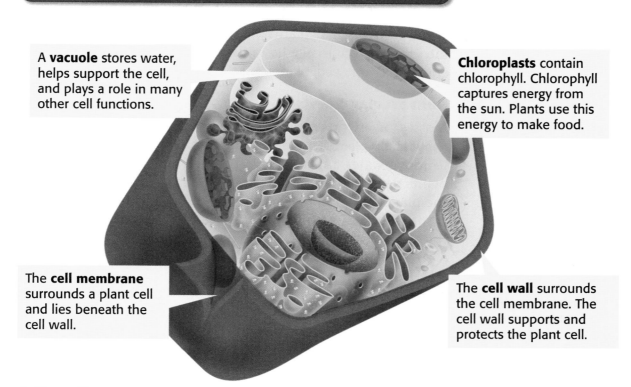

Figure 2 Some Structures of a Photosynthetic Plant Cell

A **vacuole** stores water, helps support the cell, and plays a role in many other cell functions.

Chloroplasts contain chlorophyll. Chlorophyll captures energy from the sun. Plants use this energy to make food.

The **cell membrane** surrounds a plant cell and lies beneath the cell wall.

The **cell wall** surrounds the cell membrane. The cell wall supports and protects the plant cell.

Cell Walls

How do plants stay upright? They do not have skeletons like many animals do. Instead, plant cells are surrounded by a rigid cell wall. The cell wall lies outside the cell membrane, as shown in **Figure 2.** Carbohydrates and proteins in the cell wall form a hard material. Cell walls support and protect the plant cell. Some plant cells also have a secondary cell wall that forms after the cell is mature. When this wall has formed, a plant cell cannot grow larger.

Reproduction

Plants have two stages in their life cycle—the sporophyte (SPAWR uh FIET) stage and the gametophyte (guh MEET uh FIET) stage. In the sporophyte stage, plants make spores. In a suitable environment, such as damp soil, the spores of some plants grow. These new plants are called *gametophytes*.

During the gametophyte stage, female gametophytes produce eggs. Male gametophytes produce sperm. Eggs and sperm are sex cells. Sex cells cannot grow directly into new plants. Instead, a sperm must fertilize an egg. The fertilized egg grows into a sporophyte. The sporophyte makes more spores. So, the cycle starts again.

Reading Check How do plants reproduce? (*See the Appendix for answers to Reading Checks.*)

Plant Classification

Although all plants share basic characteristics, they can be classified into four groups. First, they are classified as nonvascular plants and vascular plants. Vascular plants are further divided into three groups—seedless plants, nonflowering seed plants, and flowering seed plants.

Nonvascular Plants

Mosses, liverworts, and hornworts are nonvascular plants. A **nonvascular plant** is a plant that doesn't have specialized tissues to move water and nutrients through the plant. Nonvascular plants depend on diffusion to move materials from one part of the plant to another. Diffusion is possible because nonvascular plants are small. If nonvascular plants were large, the cells of the plants would not get enough water and nutrients.

Vascular Plants

In the same way that the human body has special tissues to move materials through the body, so do many plants. A plant that has tissues to deliver water and nutrients from one part of the plant to another is called a **vascular plant.** These tissues are called *vascular tissues*. Vascular tissues can move water to any part of a plant. So, vascular plants can be almost any size.

Vascular plants are divided into three groups—seedless plants and two types of seed plants. Seedless vascular plants include ferns, horsetails, and club mosses. Nonflowering seed plants are called **gymnosperms** (JIM noh SPUHRMZ). Flowering seed plants are called **angiosperms** (AN jee oh SPUHRMZ). The four main groups of plants are shown in **Figure 3.**

Reading Check What are the four main groups of plants?

---

nonvascular plant the three groups of plants (liverworts, hornworts, and mosses) that lack specialized conducting tissues and true roots, stems, and leaves

vascular plant a plant that has specialized tissues that conduct materials from one part of the plant to another

gymnosperm a woody, vascular seed plant whose seeds are not enclosed by an ovary or fruit

angiosperm a flowering plant that produces seeds within a fruit

---

Figure 3 The Main Groups of Plants

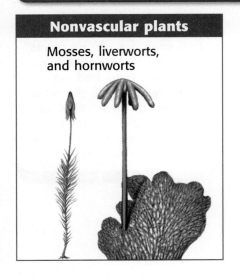

Nonvascular plants	Vascular plants		
Mosses, liverworts, and hornworts	Seedless plants	Seed plants	
	Ferns, horsetails, and club mosses	Nonflowering	Flowering
		Gymnosperms	Angiosperms

The Origin of Plants

Imagine that you traveled back in time about 440 million years. The Earth seems like a strange, bare, and unfriendly place. For one thing, no plants live on land. So, where did plants come from?

Take a look at **Figure 4.** The photo on the left shows a green alga. The photo on the right shows a fern. The green alga may look like a plant, such as a fern, but it isn't a plant. However, green algae and plants have many similarities. Green algae cells and plant cells have the same kind of chlorophyll. They have similar cell walls. Green algae and plants make their own food through photosynthesis. Both store energy in the form of starch. Like plants, green algae have a two-stage life cycle. Because of these similarities, some scientists think that green algae and plants share a common ancestor.

Figure 4 *The similarities between a modern green alga (left) and plants, such as ferns (right), suggest that both may have originated from an ancient species of green algae.*

✓ Reading Check What are some characteristics that green algae and plants have in common?

SECTION Review

Summary

- All plants make their own food and have cuticles, cells walls, and a two-stage life cycle.

- Plants are first classified into two groups: nonvascular plants and vascular plants. Vascular plants are further divided into seedless plants, gymnosperms, and angiosperms.

- Similarities between green algae and plants suggest they may have a common ancestor.

Using Key Terms

For each pair of terms, explain how the meanings of the terms differ.

1. *nonvascular plants* and *vascular plants*

2. *gymnosperms* and *angiosperms*

Understanding Key Ideas

3. Which of the following plants is nonvascular?
   a. ferns   c. gymnosperms
   b. mosses   d. club mosses

4. What are four characteristics that all plants share?

5. What do green algae and plants have in common?

6. Describe the plant life cycle.

Math Skills

7. A plant produced 200,000 spores and one-third as many eggs. How many eggs did the plant produce?

Critical Thinking

8. **Making Inferences** One difference between green algae and plants is that green algae do not have a cuticle. Why don't green algae have a cuticle?

9. **Applying Concepts** Imagine an environment that is very dry and receives a lot of sunlight. Water is found deep below the soil. Which of the four groups of plants could survive in this environment? Explain your answer.

SCiLINKS®

NSTA

Developed and maintained by the National Science Teachers Association

For a variety of links related to this chapter, go to www.scilinks.org

Topic: Plant Characteristics;
How Are Plants Classified?
SciLinks code: HSM1158; HSM0763

Seedless Plants

When you think of plants, you probably think of plants, such as trees and flowers, that make seeds. But two groups of plants don't make seeds.

One group of seedless plants is the nonvascular plants—mosses, liverworts, and hornworts. The other group is seedless vascular plants—ferns, horsetails, and club mosses.

Nonvascular Plants

Mosses, liverworts, and hornworts are small. They grow on soil, the bark of trees, and rocks. These plants don't have vascular tissue. So, nonvascular plants usually live in places that are damp. Each cell of the plant must get water from the environment or from a nearby cell.

Mosses, liverworts, and hornworts don't have true stems, roots, or leaves. They do, however, have structures that carry out the activities of stems, roots, and leaves.

Mosses

Mosses often live together in large groups. They cover soil or rocks with a mat of tiny green plants. Mosses have leafy stalks and rhizoids (RIE ZOYDZ). A **rhizoid** is a rootlike structure that holds nonvascular plants in place. Rhizoids help the plants get water and nutrients. As you can see in **Figure 1,** mosses have two stages in their life cycle.

What You Will Learn

- List three nonvascular plants and three seedless vascular plants.
- Explain how seedless plants are important to the environment.
- Describe the relationship between seedless vascular plants and coal.

Vocabulary
rhizoid
rhizome

READING STRATEGY

Paired Summarizing Read this section silently. In pairs, take turns summarizing the material. Stop to discuss ideas that seem confusing.

rhizoid a rootlike structure in nonvascular plants that holds the plants in place and helps plants get water and nutrients

Figure 1 Moss Life Cycle

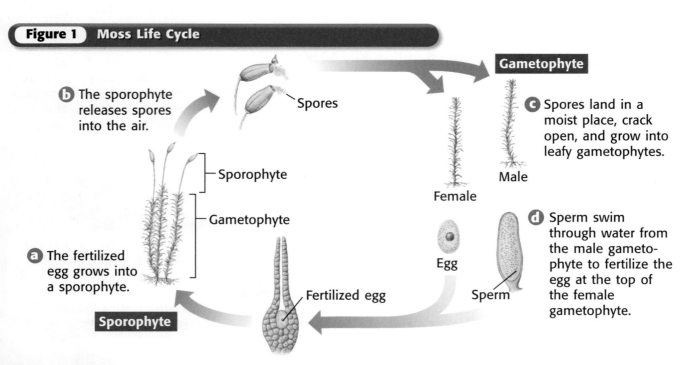

b The sporophyte releases spores into the air.

Spores

Sporophyte

Gametophyte

a The fertilized egg grows into a sporophyte.

Fertilized egg

Sporophyte

Gametophyte

Female

Male

c Spores land in a moist place, crack open, and grow into leafy gametophytes.

Egg

Sperm

d Sperm swim through water from the male gametophyte to fertilize the egg at the top of the female gametophyte.

Liverworts and Hornworts

Like mosses, liverworts and hornworts are small, nonvascular plants that usually live in damp places. The life cycles of liverworts and hornworts are similar to the life cycle of mosses. The gametophytes of liverworts can be leafy and mosslike or broad and flattened. Hornworts also have broad, flattened gametophytes. Both liverworts and hornworts have rhizoids.

The Importance of Nonvascular Plants

Nonvascular plants have an important role in the environment. They are usually the first plants to live in a new environment, such as newly exposed rock. When these nonvascular plants die, they form a thin layer of soil. New plants can grow in this soil. More nonvascular plants may grow and hold the soil in place. This reduces soil erosion. Some animals eat nonvascular plants. Other animals use these plants for nesting material.

Peat mosses are important to humans. Peat mosses grow in bogs and other wet places. In some places, dead peat mosses have built up over time. This peat can be dried and burned as a fuel. Peat mosses are also used in potting soil.

Reading Check How are nonvascular plants important to the environment? (*See the Appendix for answers to Reading Checks.*)

Seedless Vascular Plants

Ancient ferns, horsetails, and club mosses grew very tall. Club mosses grew to 40 m in ancient forests. Horsetails once grew to 18 m tall. Some ferns grew to 8 m tall. Today, ferns, horsetails, and club mosses are usually much smaller. But because they have vascular tissue, they are often larger than nonvascular plants. **Figure 2** shows club mosses and horsetails.

Moss Mass

1. Determine the mass of a small sample of **dry sphagnum moss.**

2. Observe what happens when you put a small piece of the moss in **water.** Predict what will happen if you put the entire sample in water.

3. Place the moss sample in a **large beaker of water** for 10 to 15 minutes.

4. Remove the wet moss from the beaker, and determine the mass of the moss.

5. How much mass did the moss gain? Compare your result with your prediction.

6. What could this plant be used for?

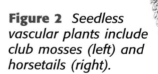

Figure 2 *Seedless vascular plants include club mosses (left) and horsetails (right).*

Ferns

Ferns grow in many places, from the cold Arctic to warm, humid tropical forests. Many ferns are small plants. But some tropical tree ferns grow as tall as 24 m. Most ferns have a rhizome. A **rhizome** is an underground stem from which new leaves and roots grow. At first, fern leaves, or fronds, are tightly coiled. These fronds look like the end of a violin, or fiddle. So, they are called *fiddleheads*. You are probably most familiar with the leafy fern sporophyte. The fern gametophyte is a tiny plant about half the size of one of your fingernails. The fern gametophyte is green and flat. It is usually shaped like a tiny heart. The life cycle of ferns is shown in **Figure 3.**

rhizome a horizontal, underground stem that produces new leaves, shoots, and roots

Horsetails and Club Mosses

Modern horsetails can be as tall as 8 m. But many horsetails are smaller. They usually grow in wet, marshy places. Their stems are hollow and contain silica. The silica gives horsetails a gritty texture. In fact, early American pioneers referred to horsetails as *scouring rushes*. They used horsetails to scrub pots and pans. Horsetails and ferns have similar life cycles.

Club mosses are often about 20 cm tall. They grow in woodlands. Club mosses are not actually mosses. Unlike mosses, club mosses have vascular tissue. The life cycle of club mosses is similar to the fern life cycle.

Figure 3 **Fern Life Cycle**

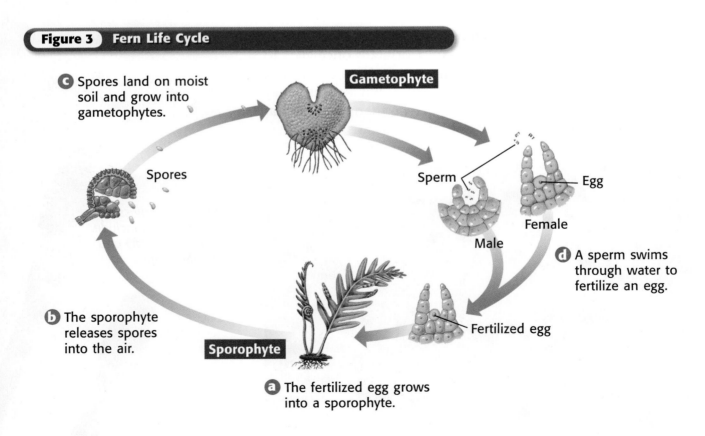

c Spores land on moist soil and grow into gametophytes.

Gametophyte

Spores

Sperm

Egg

Female

Male

d A sperm swims through water to fertilize an egg.

Fertilized egg

b The sporophyte releases spores into the air.

Sporophyte

a The fertilized egg grows into a sporophyte.

The Importance of Seedless Vascular Plants

Seedless vascular plants play important roles in the environment. Ferns, horsetails, and club mosses help form soil. They also help prevent soil erosion. In rocky areas, ferns can play a role in the formation of communities. After lichens and mosses create a layer of soil, ferns may take over. Ferns add to soil depth, which allows other plants to grow.

Ferns and some club mosses are popular houseplants. The fiddleheads of some ferns can be cooked and eaten. Young horsetail shoots and their roots are also edible. Horsetails are used in some dietary supplements, shampoos, and skin-care products.

Seedless vascular plants that lived and died about 300 million years ago are among the most important to humans. The remains of these ancient ferns, horsetails, and club mosses formed coal. Coal is a fossil fuel that humans mine from the Earth's crust. Humans rely on coal for energy.

✓ Reading Check How are seedless vascular plants important to the environment?

CONNECTION TO Language Arts

WRITING SKILL **Selling Plants** Imagine that you work for an advertising agency. Your next assignment is to promote seedless vascular plants. Write an advertisement describing seedless vascular plants and ways people benefit from them. Your advertisement should be exciting and persuasive.

SECTION Review

Summary

- Nonvascular plants include mosses, liverworts, and hornworts.
- Seedless vascular plants include ferns, horsetails, and club mosses.
- The rhizoids and rhizomes of seedless plants prevent erosion by holding soil in place.
- The remains of seedless vascular plants that lived and died about 300 million years ago formed coal. Humans rely on coal for energy.

Using Key Terms

1. Use each of the following terms in a separate sentence: *rhizoid* and *rhizome*.

Understanding Key Ideas

2. Seedless plants
   a. help form communities.
   b. reduce soil erosion.
   c. add to soil depth.
   d. All of the above

3. Describe six kinds of seedless plants.

4. What is the relationship between coal and seedless vascular plants?

Math Skills

5. Club mosses once grew as tall as 40 m. Now, they grow no taller than 20 cm. What is the difference in height between ancient and modern club mosses?

Critical Thinking

6. **Making Inferences** Imagine a very damp area. Mosses cover the rocks and trees in this area. Liverworts and hornworts are also very abundant. What might happen if the area dries out? Explain your answer.

7. **Applying Concepts** Modern ferns, horsetails, and club mosses are smaller than they were millions of years ago. Why might these plants be smaller?

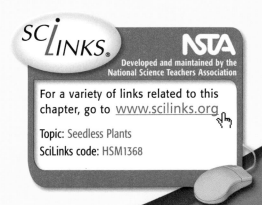

SCILINKS **NSTA** Developed and maintained by the National Science Teachers Association

For a variety of links related to this chapter, go to www.scilinks.org

Topic: Seedless Plants
SciLinks code: HSM1368

Seed Plants

Think about the seed plants that you use during the day. You likely use dozens of seed plants, from the food you eat to the paper you write on.

The two groups of vascular plants that produce seeds are gymnosperms and angiosperms. Gymnosperms are trees and shrubs that do not have flowers or fruit. Angiosperms have flowers and seeds that are protected by fruit.

Characteristics of Seed Plants

As with seedless plants, the life cycle of seed plants alternates between two stages. But seed plants, such as the plant in **Figure 1,** differ from seedless plants in the following ways:

- Seed plants produce seeds. Seeds nourish and protect young sporophytes.
- Unlike the gametophytes of seedless plants, the gametophytes of seed plants do not live independently of the sporophyte. The gametophytes of seed plants are tiny. The gametophytes form within the reproductive structures of the sporophyte.
- The sperm of seedless plants need water to swim to the eggs of female gametophytes. The sperm of seed plants do not need water to reach an egg. Sperm form inside tiny structures called **pollen.** Pollen can be transported by wind or by animals.

These three characteristics of seed plants allow them to live just about anywhere. For this reason, seed plants are the most common plants on Earth today.

✓ **Reading Check** List three characteristics of seed plants. (*See the Appendix for answers to Reading Checks.*)

What You Will Learn

- Describe three ways that seed plants differ from seedless plants.
- Describe the structure of seeds.
- Compare angiosperms and gymnosperms.
- Explain the economic and environmental importance of gymnosperms and angiosperms.

Vocabulary

pollen
pollination

READING STRATEGY

Reading Organizer As you read this section, make a table comparing angiosperms and gymnosperms.

pollen the tiny granules that contain the male gametophyte of seed plants

Figure 1 *Dandelion fruits, which each contain a seed, are spread by wind.*

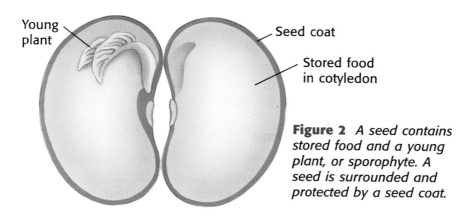

Young plant

Seed coat

Stored food in cotyledon

Figure 2 *A seed contains stored food and a young plant, or sporophyte. A seed is surrounded and protected by a seed coat.*

The Structure of Seeds

A seed forms after fertilization, when sperm and eggs are joined. A seed is made up of three parts, as shown in **Figure 2.** The first part is a young plant, or the sporophyte. The second part is stored food. It is often found in the cotyledons (KAHT uh LEED uhnz), or the seed leaves of the young plant. Finally, a seed coat surrounds and protects the young plant.

Seed plants have some advantages over seedless plants. For example, when a seed begins to grow, the young plant uses the food stored in the seed. The spores of seedless plants don't have stored food to help a new plant grow. Another advantage of seed plants is that seeds can be spread by animals. The spores of seedless plants are usually spread by wind. Animals spread seeds more efficiently than the wind spreads spores.

✓ Reading Check Describe two advantages that seed plants have over seedless plants.

CONNECTION TO Environmental Science

WRITING SKILL **Animals That Help Plants** Animals need plants to live, but some plants benefit from animals, too. These plants produce seeds with tough seed coats. An animal's digestive system can wear down these seed coats and speed the growth of a seed. Identify a plant that animals help in this way. Then, find out how being eaten by animals makes it possible for seeds to grow. Write about your findings in your **science journal.**

Dissecting Seeds

1. Soak a **lima bean seed** in **water** overnight. Draw the seed before placing it in the water.

2. Remove the seed from the water. Draw what you see.

3. The seed will likely look wrinkly. This is the seed coat. Use a **toothpick** to gently remove the seed coat from the lima bean seed.

4. Gently separate the halves of the lima bean seed. Draw what you see.

5. What did you see after you split the lima bean seed in half?

6. What part of the seed do you think provides the lima bean plant with the energy to grow?

Gymnosperms

Seed plants that do not have flowers or fruit are called *gymnosperms*. Gymnosperm seeds are usually protected by a cone. The four groups of gymnosperms are conifers, ginkgoes, cycads, and gnetophytes (NEE toh FIETS). You can see some gymnosperms in **Figure 3.**

The Importance of Gymnosperms

Conifers are the most economically important gymnosperms. People use conifer wood for building materials and paper products. Pine trees produce a sticky fluid called *resin*. Resin is used to make soap, turpentine, paint, and ink. Some conifers produce an important anticancer drug. Some gnetophytes produce anti-allergy drugs. Conifers, cycads, and ginkgoes are popular in gardens and parks.

Figure 3 Examples of Gymnosperms

Conifers The conifers, such as this ponderosa pine, are the largest group of gymnosperms. There are about 550 species of conifers. Most conifers are evergreens that keep their needle-shaped leaves all year. Conifer seeds develop in cones.

Ginkgoes Today, there is only one living species of ginkgo, the ginkgo tree. Ginkgo seeds are not produced in cones. The seeds have fleshy seed coats and are attached directly to the branches of the tree.

Cycads The cycads were more common millions of years ago. Today, there are only about 140 species of cycads. These plants grow in the Tropics. Like conifer seeds, cycad seeds develop in cones.

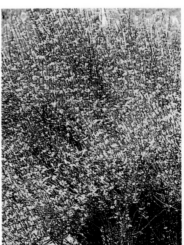

Gnetophytes About 70 species of gnetophytes, such as this joint fir, exist today. Many gnetophytes are shrubs that grow in dry areas. The seeds of most gnetophytes develop in cones.

Figure 4 Pine Life Cycle

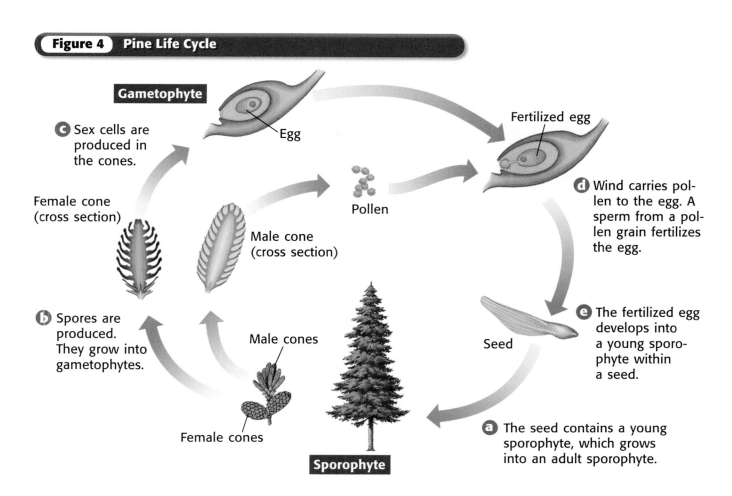

Gametophyte

c Sex cells are produced in the cones.

Egg

Fertilized egg

Female cone (cross section)

Pollen

Male cone (cross section)

d Wind carries pollen to the egg. A sperm from a pollen grain fertilizes the egg.

b Spores are produced. They grow into gametophytes.

Male cones

Seed

e The fertilized egg develops into a young sporophyte within a seed.

Female cones

Sporophyte

a The seed contains a young sporophyte, which grows into an adult sporophyte.

Gymnosperm Life Cycle

The gymnosperms that are most familiar to you are probably the conifers. The word *conifer* comes from two words that mean "cone-bearing." Conifers have two kinds of cones—male cones and female cones. The spores of each kind of cone become tiny gametophytes.

The male gametophytes of gymnosperms are found in pollen. Pollen contain sperm. The female gametophytes produce eggs. Wind carries pollen from the male cones to the female cones. This transfer of pollen from the male cones to the female cones is called **pollination.** The female cones can be on the same plant. Or, they can be on a different plant of the same species.

Sperm from pollen fertilize the eggs of the female cone. A fertilized egg develops into a young sporophyte within the female cone. The sporophyte is surrounded by a seed. Eventually, the seed is released. Some cones release seeds right away. Other cones release seeds under special circumstances, such as after forest fires. If conditions are right, the seed will grow. The life cycle of a pine tree is shown in **Figure 4.**

✓ Reading Check Describe the gymnosperm life cycle.

pollination the transfer of pollen from the male reproductive structures to the female structures of seed plants

Angiosperms

Vascular plants that produce flowers and fruits are called *angiosperms*. Angiosperms are the most abundant plants today. There are at least 235,000 species of angiosperms. Angiosperms can be found in almost every land ecosystem.

Angiosperm Reproduction

Flowers help angiosperms reproduce. Some angiosperms depend on the wind for pollination. But others have flowers that attract animals. As shown in **Figure 5,** when animals visit different flowers, the animals may carry pollen from flower to flower.

Fruits surround and protect seeds. Some fruits and seeds have structures that help the wind carry them short or long distances. Other fruits attract animals that eat the fruits. The animals discard the seeds away from the plant. Some fruits, such as burrs, are carried from place to place by sticking to the fur of animals.

✓ Reading Check Why do angiosperms have flowers and fruits?

Two Kinds of Angiosperms

Angiosperms are divided into two classes—monocots and dicots. The two classes differ in the number of cotyledons, or seed leaves, their seeds have. Monocot seeds have one cotyledon. Grasses, orchids, onions, lilies, and palms are monocots. Dicot seeds have two cotyledons. Dicots include roses, cactuses, sunflowers, peanuts, and peas. Other differences between monocots and dicots are shown in **Figure 6.**

Figure 5 *This bee is on its way to another squash flower, where it will leave some of the pollen it is carrying.*

Figure 6 Two Classes of Angiosperms

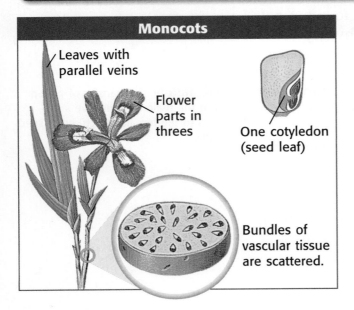

Monocots

Leaves with parallel veins

Flower parts in threes

One cotyledon (seed leaf)

Bundles of vascular tissue are scattered.

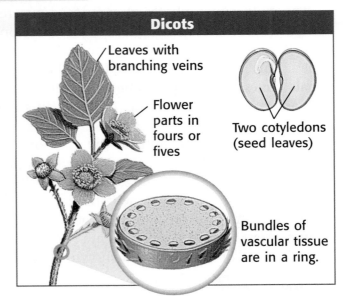

Dicots

Leaves with branching veins

Flower parts in fours or fives

Two cotyledons (seed leaves)

Bundles of vascular tissue are in a ring.

The Importance of Angiosperms

Flowering plants provide many land animals with the food they need to survive. A field mouse that eats seeds and berries is using flowering plants directly as food. An owl that eats a field mouse is using flowering plants indirectly as food.

People use flowering plants in many ways. Major food crops, such as corn, wheat, and rice, are flowering plants. Some flowering plants, such as oak trees, are used for building materials. Flowering plants, such as cotton and flax, are used to make clothing and rope. Flowering plants are also used to make medicines, rubber, and perfume oils.

Reading Check How are flowering plants important to humans?

INTERNET ACTIVITY

For another activity related to this chapter, go to **go.hrw.com** and type in the keyword **HL5PL1W**.

SECTION Review

Summary

- Seeds nourish the young sporophyte of seed plants. Seed plant gametophytes rely on the sporophyte. Also, they do not need water for fertilization.

- Seeds nourish a young plant until it can make food by photosynthesis.

- Gymnosperms do not have flowers or fruits. Gymnosperm seeds are usually protected by cones. Gymnosperms are used for building materials, paper, resin, and medicines.

- Angiosperms have flowers and fruits. Angiosperms are used for food, medicines, fibers for clothing, rubber, and building materials.

Using Key Terms

1. In your own words, write a definition for each of the following terms: *pollen* and *pollination*.

Understanding Key Ideas

2. One advantage of seed plants is that
   a. seed plants grow in few places.
   b. they can begin photosynthesis as soon as they begin to grow.
   c. they need water for fertilization.
   d. young plants are nourished by food stored in the seed.

3. The gametophytes of seed plants
   a. live independently of the sporophytes.
   b. are very large.
   c. are protected in the reproductive structures of the sporophyte.
   d. None of the above

4. Describe the structure of seeds.

5. Briefly describe the four groups of gymnosperms. Which group is the largest and most economically important?

6. Compare angiosperms and gymnosperms.

Math Skills

7. More than 265,000 species of plants have been discovered. Approximately 235,000 of those species are angiosperms. What percentage of plants are NOT angiosperms?

Critical Thinking

8. **Making Inferences** In what ways are flowers and fruits adaptations that help angiosperms reproduce?

9. **Applying Concepts** An angiosperm lives in a dense rainforest, close to the ground. It receives little wind. Several herbivores live in this area of the rainforest. What are some ways the plant can ensure its seeds are carried throughout the forest?

SCILINKS

Developed and maintained by the National Science Teachers Association

For a variety of links related to this chapter, go to www.scilinks.org

Topic: Plants with Seeds
SciLinks code: HSM1168

What You Will Learn

● List three functions of roots and three functions of stems.
● Describe the structure of a leaf.
● Identify the parts of a flower and their functions.

Vocabulary

xylem   stamen
phloem   pistil
sepal   ovary
petal

READING STRATEGY

Mnemonics As you read this section, create a mnemonic device to help you remember the parts of a plant.

Structures of Seed Plants

You have different body systems that carry out many functions. Plants have systems too—a root system, a shoot system, and a reproductive system.

A plant's root system and shoot system supply the plant with what it needs to survive. The root system is made up of roots. The shoot system includes stems and leaves.

The vascular tissues of the root and shoot systems are connected. There are two kinds of vascular tissue—xylem (ZIE luhm) and phloem (FLOH EM). **Xylem** is vascular tissue that transports water and minerals through the plant. Xylem moves materials from the roots to the shoots. **Phloem** is vascular tissue that transports food molecules to all parts of a plant. Xylem and phloem are found in all parts of vascular plants.

Roots

Most roots are underground, as shown in **Figure 1.** So, many people do not realize how extensive root systems can be. For example, a corn plant that is 2.5 m tall can have roots that grow 2.5 m deep and 1.2 m out and away from the stem!

Root Functions

The following are the three main functions of roots:

● Roots supply plants with water and dissolved minerals. These materials are absorbed from the soil. The water and minerals are transported to the shoots in the xylem.

● Roots hold plants securely in the soil.

● Roots store surplus food made during photosynthesis. The food is produced in the leaves. Then, it is transported in the phloem to the roots. In the roots, the surplus food is usually stored as sugar or starch.

xylem the type of tissue in vascular plants that provides support and conducts water and nutrients from the roots

phloem the tissue that conducts food in vascular plants

Onion   **Dandelion**   **Carrots**

Figure 1 *The roots of these plants provide the plants with water and minerals.*

Root Structure

The structures of a root are shown in **Figure 2.** The layer of cells that covers the surface of roots is called the *epidermis*. Some cells of the epidermis extend from the root. These cells, or root hairs, increase the surface area of the root. This surface area helps the root absorb water and minerals. After water and minerals are absorbed by the epidermis, they diffuse into the center of the root, where the vascular tissue is located.

Roots grow longer at their tips. A group of cells called the *root cap* protects the tip of a root. The root cap produces a slimy substance. This substance makes it easier for the root to push through soil as it grows.

Root Systems

There are two kinds of root systems—taproot systems and fibrous root systems. A taproot system has one main root, or a taproot. The taproot grows downward. Many smaller roots branch from the taproot. Taproots can reach water deep underground. Dicots and gymnosperms usually have taproot systems.

A fibrous root system has several roots that spread out from the base of a plant's stem. The roots are usually the same size. Fibrous roots usually get water from close to the soil surface. Monocots usually have fibrous roots.

Reading Check What are two types of root systems? (*See the Appendix for answers to Reading Checks.*)

Practice with Percentages

The following table gives an estimate of the number of species in each plant group.

Plant Species	
Plant group	Number of species
Mosses, liverworts, and hornworts	15,600
Ferns, horsetails, and club mosses	12,000
Gymnosperms	760
Angiosperms	235,000

What percentage of plants do not produce seeds?

Figure 2   **The Structures of a Root**

A root absorbs water and minerals, which move into the xylem. Growth occurs at the tip of a root. The root cap releases a slimy substance that helps the root grow through soil.

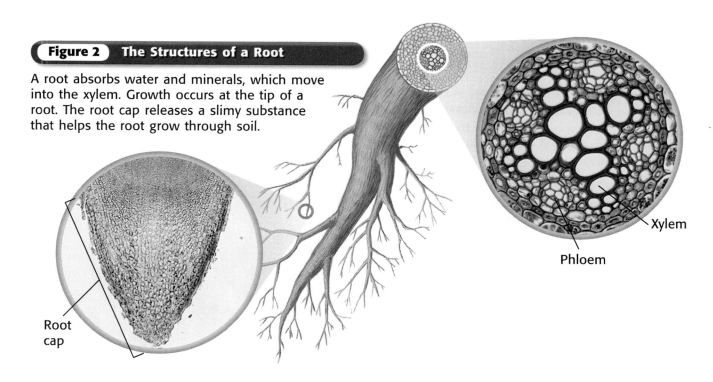

Root cap

Xylem

Phloem

Stems

Stems vary greatly in shape and size. Stems are usually located above ground. However, many plants have underground stems. The trunk of the valley oak in **Figure 3** is a stem.

Stem Functions

A stem connects a plant's roots to its leaves and flowers. A stem also has the following functions:

- Stems support the plant body. Leaves are arranged along stems or on the ends of stems. This arrangement helps leaves get sunlight for photosynthesis. Stems hold up flowers, which helps pollinators, such as bees, see the flowers.

- Stems transport materials between the root system and the shoot system. Xylem carries water and dissolved minerals from the roots to the leaves and other shoot parts. Phloem carries the food made during photosynthesis to roots and other parts of the plant.

- Some stems store materials. For example, the stems of cactuses and some trees are adapted for water storage.

Herbaceous Stems

Many plants have stems that are soft, thin, and flexible. These stems are called *herbaceous stems* (huhr BAY shuhs STEMZ). Examples of plants that have herbaceous stems include wildflowers, such as clovers and poppies. Many crops, such as beans, tomatoes, and corn, have herbaceous stems. A cross section of an herbaceous stem is shown in **Figure 4.**

✓ Reading Check What are herbaceous stems? Give an example of a plant that has an herbaceous stem.

Figure 3 *The stem, or trunk, of this valley oak keeps the tree upright, which helps leaves get sunlight for photosynthesis.*

Figure 4 **Cross Section of an Herbaceous Stem**

Buttercups are just one plant that has herbaceous stems. Wildflowers and many vegetables have soft, thin, and flexible stems.

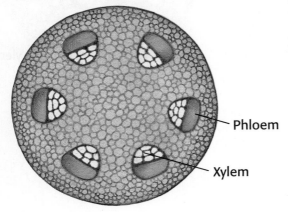

Phloem

Xylem

Figure 5 Cross Section of a Woody Stem

Some plants, such as these trees, have woody stems. Plants that have woody stems usually live for many years. People can use growth rings to estimate the age of a plant.

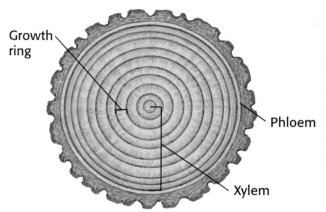

Woody Stems

Trees and shrubs have rigid stems made of wood and bark. These stems are called *woody stems*. **Figure 5** shows a cross section of a woody stem. Trees or shrubs that live in areas with cold winters have a growing period during the spring and summer. These plants have a dormant period during the winter. At the beginning of each growing period, large xylem cells are produced. As fall approaches, the plants produce smaller xylem cells, which appear darker. In the fall and winter, the plants stop producing new cells. The cycle begins again the next spring. A ring of dark cells surrounding a ring of light cells makes up a growth ring.

Leaves

Leaves vary greatly in shape. They may be round, narrow, heart-shaped, or fan-shaped. Leaves also vary in size. The raffia palm has leaves that may be six times longer than you are tall. The leaves of duckweed, a tiny aquatic plant, are so small that several of the leaves can fit on your fingernail. **Figure 6** shows a poison ivy leaf.

Leaf Functions

The main function of leaves is to make food for the plant. Chloroplasts in the cells of leaves capture energy from sunlight. The leaves also absorb carbon dioxide from the air. The leaves use the captured energy to make food, or sugar, from carbon dioxide and water.

Figure 6 *The leaves of poison ivy are very distinctive. They make food to help the plant survive.*

Figure 7 The Structure of a Leaf

Leaf cells are arranged in layers. These layers allow the leaf to work efficiently.

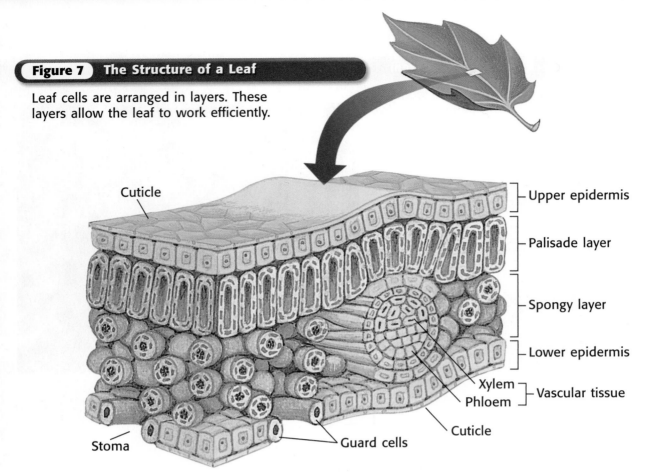

Cuticle

Upper epidermis

Palisade layer

Spongy layer

Lower epidermis

Xylem
Phloem

Vascular tissue

Cuticle

Guard cells

Stoma

Leaf Structure

The structure of leaves, shown in **Figure 7,** is related to their main function—photosynthesis. The outer surfaces of a leaf are covered by a cuticle. The cuticle prevents water loss from the leaf. A single layer of cells, the epidermis, lies beneath the cuticle. Light passes through the epidermis. Tiny openings in the epidermis, called *stomata* (singular, *stoma*), let carbon dioxide enter the leaf. Guard cells open and close the stomata.

Most photosynthesis takes place in the middle of a leaf. This part of a leaf often has two layers. Cells in the upper layer, the palisade layer, contain many chloroplasts. Photosynthesis takes place in the chloroplasts. Carbon dioxide moves freely in the space between the cells of the second layer, the spongy layer. Xylem and phloem are also found in the spongy layer.

✓ *Reading Check* What are the cell layers of a leaf?

Leaf Adaptations

Some leaves have functions other than photosynthesis. For example, the leaves of many cactuses are modified as spines. These spines keep animals from eating the cactuses. The leaves of another plant, the sundew, are modified to catch insects. Sundews grow in soil that does not contain enough nitrogen to meet the plants' needs. By catching and digesting insects, a sundew is able to get enough nitrogen.

Looking at Leaves

Leaves are many shapes and sizes. They are also arranged on a stem in many ways. Walk around your home. In your **science journal,** sketch the leaves of the plants you see. Notice how the leaves are arranged on the stem, the shapes of the leaves, and the veins in the leaves. Use a ruler to measure the size of the leaves.

ACTiViTY

Flowers

Most people admire the beauty of flowers, such as the wild-flowers in **Figure 8.** But why do plants have flowers? Flowers are adaptations for sexual reproduction.

Flowers come in many shapes, colors, and fragrances. Brightly colored and fragrant flowers usually rely on animals for pollination. For example, some flowers look and smell like rotting meat. These flowers attract flies. The flies pollinate the flowers. Plants that lack brightly colored flowers and fragrances, such as grasses, depend on the wind to spread pollen.

Many flowers also produce nectar. Nectar is a fluid that contains sugar. Nectar attracts birds and insects. These animals move from flower to flower and drink the nectar. As they do so, they often carry pollen to the flowers.

Sepals and Petals

Flowers usually have the following basic parts: sepals, petals, stamens, and one or more pistils. The flower parts are usually arranged in rings around the central pistil.

Sepals are modified leaves that make up the outermost ring of flower parts and protect the bud. Sepals are often green like other leaves. Sepals cover and protect the flower while it is a bud. As the blossom opens, the sepals fold back. Then, the petals can unfold and become visible. **Petals** are broad, flat, thin leaflike parts of a flower. Petals vary greatly in color and shape. Petals attract insects or other animals to the flower. These animals help plants reproduce by carrying pollen from flower to flower.

sepal in a flower, one of the outermost rings of modified leaves that protect the flower bud

petal one of the ring or rings of the usually brightly colored, leaf-shaped parts of a flower

Figure 8 *Many flowers help the plants reproduce by attracting pollinators with bright petals and strong fragrances.*

Figure 9 The Structure of a Flower

The stamens, which produce pollen, and the pistil, which produces eggs, are surrounded by the petals and the sepals.

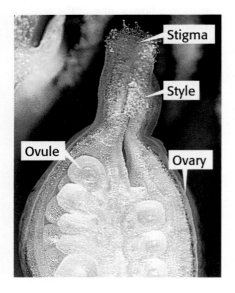

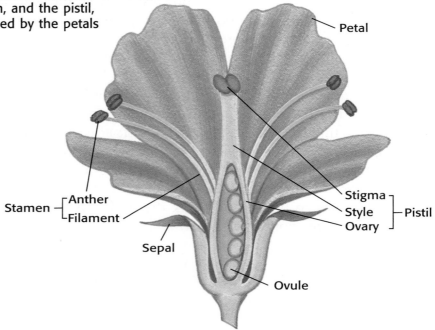

Stamens and Pistils

As you can see in **Figure 9,** the stamens of flowers are usually found just above the petals. A **stamen** is a male reproductive structure of flowers. Each stamen has a thin stalk called a *filament*. The filament is topped by an anther. Anthers are saclike structures that produce pollen.

Found in the center of most flowers is one or more pistils. A **pistil** is the female reproductive structure of flowers. The tip of the pistil is called the *stigma*. Pollen grains collect on stigmas, which are often sticky or feathery. The long, slender part of the pistil is the style. The rounded base of a pistil that contains one or more ovules is called the **ovary.** Each ovule contains an egg. When the egg is fertilized, the ovule develops into a seed. The ovary develops into a fruit.

✓ Reading Check Describe stamens and pistils. Which are the female parts of a flower? the male parts of a flower?

The Importance of Flowers

Flowers help plants reproduce. Humans also use flowers for many things. Roses and many other flowers are used for floral arrangements. Some flowers, such as artichokes, broccoli, and cauliflower, can be eaten. Other flowers, such as hibiscus and chamomile flowers, are used to make tea. Flowers used as spices include cloves and saffron. Flowers are also used in perfumes, lotions, and shampoos.

stamen the male reproductive structure of a flower that produces pollen and consists of an anther at the tip of a filament

pistil the female reproductive part of a flower that produces seeds and consists of an ovary, style, and stigma

ovary in flowering plants, the lower part of a pistil that produces eggs in ovules

Summary

- Roots supply plants with water and dissolved minerals. They support and anchor plants. Roots also store surplus food made during photosynthesis.

- Stems support the body of a plant. They allow transport of material between the root system and shoot system. Some stems store materials, such as water.

- A leaf has a thin epidermis on its upper and lower surfaces. The epidermis allows sunlight to pass through to the center of the leaf.

- Most photosynthesis takes place in the palisade layer of a leaf. The spongy layer of a leaf allows the movement of carbon dioxide and contains the xylem and phloem.

- The four main parts of a flower are the sepals, the petals, the stamens, and one or more pistils.

- Flowers are usually arranged around the pistil. The ovary of a pistil contains ovules. When the eggs are fertilized, ovules develop into seeds and the ovary becomes a fruit.

Using Key Terms

1. In your own words, write a definition for each of the following terms: *xylem, phloem, stamen,* and *pistil.*

2. Use each of the following terms in a separate sentence: *sepal, petal, pistil,* and *ovary.*

Understanding Key Ideas

3. Which of the following flower structures produces pollen?
   a. pistil
   b. filament
   c. anther
   d. stigma

4. The ___ of a leaf allows carbon dioxide to enter.
   a. stoma
   b. epidermis
   c. palisade layer
   d. spongy layer

5. Compare xylem and phloem.

6. Describe the internal structure of a leaf.

7. What are the functions of stems?

8. Identify the two types of stems, and briefly describe them.

9. How do people use flowers?

Critical Thinking

10. **Making Inferences** Describe two kinds of root systems. How does the structure of each system help the roots perform their three functions?

11. **Applying Concepts** Pampas grass flowers are found at the top of tall stems, are light-colored, and are unscented. Explain how pampas grass flowers are most likely pollinated.

Interpreting Graphics

Use the table below to answer the questions that follow.

Age of Trees in a Small Forest	
Number of trees	**Number of growth rings**
5	71
1	73
3	68

12. How many trees are older than 70 years?

13. What is the average age of these trees, in years?

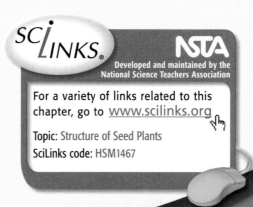

Model-Making Lab

Build a Flower

OBJECTIVES

Build a model of a flower.

Explain how the model represents an actual flower.

Describe the basic parts of a flower.

MATERIALS

- art materials such as colored paper, pipe cleaners, beads, and yarn
- card, index, 3 × 5 in.
- glue
- recycled items such as paper plates and cups, yogurt containers, wire, string, buttons, cardboard, and bottles
- scissors
- tape

SAFETY

Scientists often make models in the laboratory. Models help scientists understand processes and structures. Models are especially useful when scientists are trying to understand processes that are too small to be seen easily, such as pollination, or processes that are too large to be examined in a laboratory, such as the growth of a tree. Models also make it possible to examine the structures of objects, such as flowers.

In this activity, you will use your creativity and your understanding of the structure of a flower to make a model of a flower from recycled materials and art supplies.

Procedure

① Draw a flower similar to the one shown in the figure below. This flower has both male and female parts. Not all flowers have this structure. The flowers of many species of plants have only male parts or only female parts, not both.

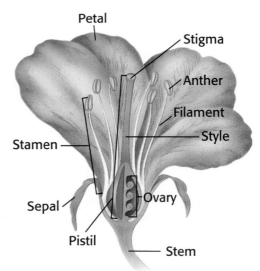

② Decide which materials you will use to represent each flower part. Then, build a three-dimensional model of a flower that looks like one of the flowers shown on the next page. The model you build should contain each of the following parts: stem, sepals, petals, stamens (anther and filament), and pistil (stigma, style, and ovary).

Lily

Tulip

Hibiscus

3 After you build your model, draw a key for your flower model on an index card. Label each of the structures represented on your flower.

Analyze the Results

1 Organizing Data List the structures of a flower, and explain the function of each part.

2 Identifying Patterns What is the outermost part of your flower? the innermost part of your flower?

3 Analyzing Data How are your flower model and an actual flower alike? How are they different?

Draw Conclusions

4 Drawing Conclusions How might your flower attract pollinators? What modifications could you make to your flower to attract a greater number of pollinators?

5 Evaluating Models Is your model an accurate representation of a flower? Why or why not?

6 Making Predictions If you based your flower model on a plant species that had flowers that did not have both male and female parts, how would that model be different from your current model?

Applying Your Data

Research flowering plants whose flowers do not have both male and female reproductive parts. Build models of the male flower and the female flower for one of these flowering plants. Then, compare the new models to your original model, which includes both male and female reproductive parts.

Chapter Review

USING KEY TERMS

Complete each of the following sentences by choosing the correct term from the word bank.

pistil
vascular plant
xylem
pollen
nonvascular plant

rhizoid
rhizome
phloem
stamen

1 A ___ is the male part of a flower.

2 ___ transports water and nutrients through a plant.

3 An underground stem that produces new leaves and roots is called a ___.

4 The male gametophytes of flowers are contained in structures called ___.

5 A ___ does not have specialized tissues for transporting water.

6 ___ transports food through a plant.

UNDERSTANDING KEY IDEAS

Multiple Choice

7 Which of the following statements about angiosperms is NOT true?

a. Their seeds are protected by cones.

b. They produce seeds.

c. They provide animals with food.

d. They have flowers.

8 Roots

a. supply water and nutrients.

b. anchor and support a plant.

c. store surplus food.

d. All of the above

9 Which of the following statements about plants and green algae is true?

a. Plants and green algae may have a common ancestor.

b. Green algae are plants.

c. Plants and green algae have cuticles.

d. None of the above

10 In which part of a leaf does most photosynthesis take place?

a. palisade layer   c. xylem

b. phloem   d. epidermis

Short Answer

11 List four characteristics that all plants share.

12 List the four main groups of plants.

13 Name three nonvascular plants and three seedless vascular plants.

14 Why do scientists think green algae and plants have a common ancestor?

15 How are seedless plants, gymnosperms, and angiosperms important to the environment?

16 What are two advantages that seeds have over spores?

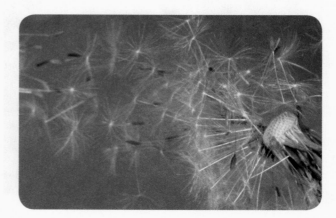

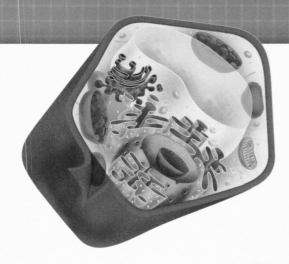

17 **Concept Mapping** Use the following terms to create a concept map: *flowers*, *pollen*, *stamens*, *ovaries*, *pistils*, *stigmas*, *filaments*, *anthers*, *ovules*, *petals*, and *sepals*.

18 **Making Comparisons** Imagine that a seed and a spore are beginning to grow in a deep, dark crack in a rock. Which of the two is more likely to grow into an adult plant? Explain your answer.

19 **Identifying Relationships** Grass flowers do not have strong fragrances or bright colors. How might these characteristics be related to the way by which grass flowers are pollinated?

20 **Analyzing Ideas** Plants that are pollinated by wind produce more pollen than plants pollinated by animals do. Why might wind-pollinated plants produce more pollen?

21 **Applying Concepts** A scientist discovered a new plant. The plant has vascular tissue and produces seeds. It has brightly colored and strongly scented flowers. It also has sweet fruits. Based on this information, which of the four main types of plants did the scientist discover? How is the plant most likely pollinated? How does the plant most likely spread its seeds?

INTERPRETING GRAPHICS

22 Look at the cross section of a woody stem below. Use the diagram to determine the age of the tree.

Use the diagram of the flower below to answer the questions that follow.

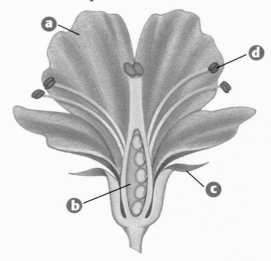

23 Which letter corresponds to the structure in which pollen is produced? What is the name of this structure?

24 Which letter corresponds to the structure that contains the ovules? What is the name of this structure?

25 Which letter corresponds to the structure that protects the flower bud? What is the name of this structure?

Standardized Test Preparation

Multiple Choice

Use the table below to answer question 1.

	Sporophyte
Specimen A	spore
Specimen B	cone
Specimen C	seed, one seed leaf
Specimen D	seed, two seed leaves

1. **Jessica is sorting specimens at the natural history museum. The only information on the specimen packets is listed in the table above. Which specimen can be placed in the bin marked "monocot"?**

   A. specimen A

   B. specimen B

   C. specimen C

   D. specimen D

2. **In which part of a plant cell does photosynthesis occur?**

   A. cell wall

   B. cell membrane

   C. vacuole

   D. chloroplast

3. **Where in a leaf will xylem and phloem be found?**

   A. cuticle

   B. vascular tissue

   C. guard cells

   D. stoma

4. **All plants have a life cycle that alternates between two stages. What are the two stages of a plant life cycle?**

   A. phloem and xylem

   B. vascular and nonvascular

   C. gametophyte and sporophyte

   D. angiosperm and gymnosperm

5. **Mosses, hornworts, and liverworts are nonvascular plants. What do these plants lack that vascular plants have?**

   A. special tissues for making food

   B. special tissues for reproduction

   C. special tissues for taking in water and nutrients

   D. special tissues for moving water through the plant

6. **Compared to plants without vascular tissue, plants with vascular tissue can survive better in**

   A. moist environments.

   B. the sporophyte stage.

   C. all environments.

   D. drier environments.

7. **Xylem is one of a plant's**

   A. systems.

   B. tissues.

   C. cells.

   D. organs.

8. Stems vary greatly in shape and size. Stems are usually located above the ground, but some plants have underwater stems. Which of the following best describes the function of stems?

   A. Stems make food for plants.

   B. Stems support the plant body and transport material between the root system and the shoot system.

   C. Stems supply plants with water and dissolved minerals from the soil.

   D. Stems are part of the female reproductive part of plants.

9. LeRoy lives near a river bed. During the summer, the river began to dry up and many large rocks were exposed. When LeRoy examined the river bed, he found some plants growing on the rocks. Which plants did LeRoy most likely find in the river bed?

   A. club mosses

   B. gingkoes

   C. hornworts

   D. monocots

10. Seeds are protected by a hard outer seed coat. What happens when a seed germinates?

   A. The force of the water pressure inside the seed pushes the seed coat open.

   B. The seed uses its stored food to force the seed coat open.

   C. The seed coat dissolves to allow the seedling to emerge.

   D. The seedling emerges through a small passageway in the seed coat.

Use the diagram below to answer question 11.

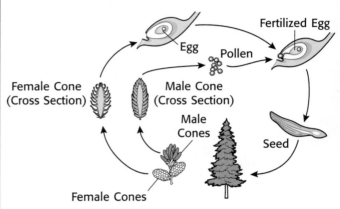

Pine Life Cycle

11. If a sporophyte contains two copies of each of the pine tree's chromosomes, which part of the pine life cycle is also a sporophyte?

   A. seed

   B. female cone

   C. sperm

   D. male cone

Open Response

12. What are three survival advantages that seed-producing plants have over non-seed-producing plants?

13. Explain how monocot and dicot angiosperms are the same, and list two ways in which they are different.

Standardized Test Preparation

Science in Action

Scientific Debate

Are Herbal Supplements Safe?

Humans have always used plants for food, for shelter, or for medicine. In fact, one of our most common medicines, aspirin, is similar to a chemical found in the bark of a willow tree. Today, many people still use natural plant products, such as pills or teas, as medicine. These products are often called *herbal supplements*. Echinacea, St. John's wort, and ma huang are just a few examples of the herbal supplements that people use to treat a variety of health problems. People spend billions of dollars on herbal supplements each year. But are herbal supplements safe to use?

Social Studies ACTIVITY

Make a poster illustrating a plant used for medicine by native cultures and the health problems the plant is used to treat.

Science, Technology, and Society

Plant Poachers

Imagine you're walking through a swamp. The swamp is full of life. You're surrounded by trees, vines, and water lilies. You can hear frogs singing and mosquitoes buzzing. Then, you notice a ghost orchid hanging from a tree branch. The flower of this orchid looks like a ghost or like a white frog leaping. For some people, this orchid is worth stealing. These people, called *plant poachers*, steal orchids and other plants from the wild. Many plant species and natural areas are threatened by plant theft.

Math ACTIVITY

A plant poacher stole 100 plants from a nature preserve. He planned on selling each plant for $50, but he was caught and was fined $300 for each plant he stole. What is the difference between the total fine and the total amount of money the plant poacher planned on selling the plants for?

Paul Cox

Ethnobotanist Paul Cox is an ethnobotanist. He travels to remote places to look for plants that can help treat diseases. He seeks the advice of native healers in his search. In Samoan cultures, the healer is one of the most valued members of the community. In 1984, Cox met a 78-year-old Samoan healer named Epenesa. Epenesa understood human anatomy, and she dispensed medicines with great accuracy.

After Cox spent months observing Epenesa, she gave him her treatment for yellow fever. Cox brought the yellow-fever remedy to the United States. In 1986, researchers at the National Cancer Institute found that the plant contains a virus-fighting chemical called *prostratin*, which may have potential as a treatment for AIDS.

When two of the Samoan healers that Cox observed died in 1993, generations of medical knowledge was lost with them. The healers' deaths show the urgency of recording this knowledge before all of the healers are gone. Cox and other ethnobotanists work hard to gather knowledge from healers before their knowledge is lost.

Language Arts ACTiViTY

WRITING SKILL Imagine that you are a healer. Write a letter to an ethnobotanist describing some of the plants you use to treat diseases.

To learn more about these Science in Action topics, visit go.hrw.com and type in the keyword **HL5PL1F**.

Current Science

Check out Current Science® articles related to this chapter by visiting go.hrw.com. Just type in the keyword **HL5CS12**.

UNIT 5

TIMELINE

Animals and Ecology

Have you ever been to a zoo or watched a wild-animal program on TV? If so, you have some idea of how many types of animals—from tiny insects to massive whales—are found on Earth.

Animals are fascinating, in part because of their variety in appearance and behavior. They also teach us about ourselves because humans are also classified as animals.

In this unit, you will learn about many types of animals and the way they interact with the environment.

1610
Galileo Galilei uses a compound microscope to study insect anatomy.

1681
The Mauritius Dodo, a flightless bird, becomes extinct.

1827
John James Audubon publishes the first edition of *Birds of America.*

1839
The first bicycle is constructed.

1983
The U.S. Space Shuttle *Challenger* is launched. Sally Ride, the first American woman in space, is on board.

1987
The last wild California condor is captured in an effort to save the species from extinction.

1995
Fourteen Canadian gray wolves are reintroduced into Yellowstone National Park.

1693
John Ray correctly identifies whales as mammals.

1761
The first veterinary school is founded in Lyons, France.

1775
J. C. Fabricius develops a system for the classification of insects.

1882
Research on the ship *The Albatross* helps increase our knowledge of marine life.

1935
Francis B. Sumner studies the protective coloration of fish.

1960
Jane Goodall, an English zoologist, begins her research on chimpanzees in Tanzania.

1998
Keiko, the killer-whale star of the movie *Free Willy,* is taught to catch fish so that he can be released from captivity.

2003
Researchers find that individual cloned pigs behave in very different ways. This finding shows that environmental conditions affect behavior.

15

Introduction to Animals

The Big Idea

Animals have many unique characteristics to perform their life functions.

About the Photo

Many marine bird species are found on the California coast, including the booby. This bird can spot a fish in the water from as high as 15 m (50 ft). With the fish in sight, the booby power dives beak first and closes its wings only just before it hits the water. It may not resurface for several seconds.

PRE-READING ACTIVITY

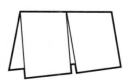

FOLDNOTES **Two-Panel Flip Chart**
Before you read this chapter, create the FoldNote entitled "Two-Panel Flip Chart" described in the **Study Skills** section of the Appendix. Write "Invertebrates" on one flap of the two-Panel Flip chart and "Vertebrates" on the other flap. As you read the chapter, write the characteristics of invertebrates and vertebrates under the appropriate flaps.

START-UP ACTIVITY

Observing Animal Characteristics

You don't have to travel far to see interesting animals. If you look closely, you can find many animals nearby. In this activity, you will observe the characteristics of two different animals. **Caution:** Always be careful around wild or unfamiliar animals, because they may bite or sting. Do not handle wild animals or any animals that are unfamiliar to you.

Procedure

1. Go outside, and find **two different kinds of animals** to observe.

2. Without disturbing the animals, watch them quietly for a few minutes from a distance. You may want to use **binoculars** or a **magnifying lens.**

3. Write down everything that you notice about each animal. Do you know what kind of animal each is? Where did you find them? What do they look like? What are they doing? You may want to draw a picture of them.

Analysis

4. Compare the two animals that you studied. Do they look alike? Identify their body parts.

5. How do the animals move? What structures are they using to help them move?

6. Can you tell what each animal eats? What characteristics of each animal help it find or catch food?

What Is an Animal?

What do you think of when you hear the word **animal?** You may think of your dog or cat. You may think about giraffes or grizzly bears. But would you think of a sponge?

The natural sponges that some people use for washing are the remains of an animal. Animals come in many shapes and sizes. Some have four legs and fur, but most do not. Some are too small to be seen without a microscope, and others are bigger than a school bus. They are all part of the animal kingdom.

Animal Characteristics

Sponges, worms, penguins, and lions are all animals. But until about 200 years ago, most people thought sponges were plants. And worms don't look like penguins or lions. Some different kinds of organisms are shown in **Figure 1.** The feather star has many flexible arms that it uses to trap food. The coral has a rigid skeleton that is attached to a hard surface. Fish move their bodies to swim from place to place. So, are all of these organisms animals? And what determines whether an organism is an animal, a plant, or something else? There is no simple answer. But all animals share characteristics that set them apart from all other organisms.

✓ Reading Check How are a feather star and a fish similar? (*See the Appendix for answers to Reading Checks.*)

What You Will Learn

● Animals are multicellular organisms.
● Animals have specialized cells, tissues, organs, and organ systems.
● Animals have seven basic characteristics.

Vocabulary

coelom
consumer
differentiation

READING STRATEGY

Brainstorming The main idea of this section is that all animals share certain characteristics. Brainstorm words and phrases related to the characteristics of animals.

Figure 1 *Most of the organisms in this picture are animals.*

Feather star

Fish

Coral

Multicellular Makeup

Like all organisms, animals are made up of cells. Unlike plant cells, animal cells do not have cell walls. Animal cells are surrounded by only cell membranes. All animals are made up of many cells and are therefore *multicellular* organisms. In animals, all of the cells work together to perform the life functions of the animal.

Organization in Animals

Animals have different levels of structural organization in their bodies. Each cell in a multicellular organism does not perform every life function of the organism. Instead, a specific kind of cell can specialize to perform a specific function. For example, muscle cells in an animal help the animal move. Groups of the same kinds of cells that work together form *tissues*. For example, muscle cells form muscle tissue.

When different kinds of tissues work together to perform a specific function for the organism, these tissues form an *organ.* The heart, lungs, and kidneys are organs. When a group of organs work together to perform a specific function, the organs form an *organ system.* Each organ system has a unique job that is important to the survival of the whole organism. The failure of any organ system may lead to the death of the organism. The shark shown in **Figure 2** has organ systems that allow the shark to digest food, pump blood, and sense the environment.

Reading Check What would happen to the shark if its heart failed?

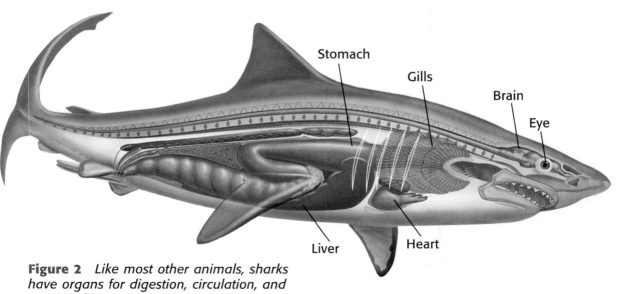

Figure 2 *Like most other animals, sharks have organs for digestion, circulation, and sensing the environment.*

Figure 3 Symmetry in Animal Body Plans

This tortoise has **bilateral symmetry.** The two sides of its body mirror each other. On each side of its body, the tortoise has one eye, one ear, and two legs.

This sea star has **radial symmetry.** Its body is organized around the center, like spokes on a wheel.

This sponge is **asymmetrical.** You cannot draw a straight line to divide its body into two or more equal parts. Its body is not organized around a center.

coelom (SEE luhm) a body cavity that contains the internal organs

consumer (kuhn SOOM uhr) an organism that eats other organisms or organic matter

Body Plans

Animal bodies have two basic types of *symmetry*. Symmetry can be bilateral (bievLAT uhr uhl) or radial (RAY dee uhl). Animals that have no symmetry are asymmetrical (AY suh ME tri kuhl). Most animals have bilateral symmetry. **Figure 3** shows an example of each type of symmetry.

Another basic characteristic of a body plan is whether or not it has a *coelom*. A **coelom** is a body cavity that surrounds and protects many organs, such as the heart. Many animals have coeloms.

Getting Energy

All organisms need energy to survive. Plants can make their own food to get the energy that they need to live. Unlike plants however, animals cannot make their own food. Animals get energy by consuming other organisms or parts and products of other organisms. Therefore, animals are *consumers*. A **consumer** is an organism that feeds on other organisms to meet its energy needs. One way in which animals differ from plants is that animals are consumers. Although there are a few exceptions, most plants do not feed on other organisms.

Animals eat many kinds of foods. As **Figure 4** shows, pandas eat bamboo. Spiders eat other animals. Mosquitoes drink blood. Butterflies drink nectar from flowers. Also, some animals eat more than one kind of food. For example, the black bear eats both fruits and other animals.

Figure 4 *Pandas eat about 13.6 kg of bamboo every day.*

Reproduction

Animals make more animals like themselves through reproduction. Some animals reproduce asexually. In *asexual reproduction,* a parent has offspring that are genetically identical to the parent. For example, hydras can reproduce by budding. In *budding,* part of an organism develops into a new organism. As the new organism develops, it breaks off from the parent. Another kind of asexual reproduction is called *fragmentation.* In fragmentation, parts of an organism break off and then develop into new individuals.

Most animals reproduce sexually. In *sexual reproduction,* offspring are formed when sex cells from two parent combine. The female parent produces sex cells called *eggs.* The male parent produces sex cells called *sperm.* When an egg's nucleus and a sperm's nucleus join in a process called *fertilization,* the first cell of a new organism is formed.

differentiation (DIF uhr EN shee AY shuhn) the process in which the structure and function of the parts of an organism change to enable specialization of those parts

Development

A fertilized egg cell divides into many cells to form an *embryo* (EM bree OH). An embryo is one of the early stages of development of an organism, such as the mouse embryo shown in **Figure 5.**

As a multicellular organism develops, its cells become specialized through *differentiation.* **Differentiation** is the process by which cells that will perform different functions develop different structures. For example, some nerve cells grow very long, to carry electrical signals from your spine to your feet.

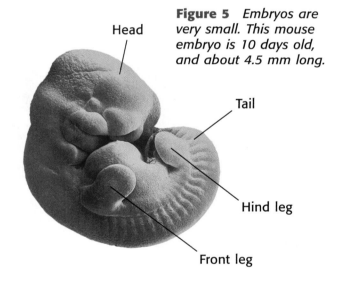

Head

Figure 5 *Embryos are very small. This mouse embryo is 10 days old, and about 4.5 mm long.*

Tail

Hind leg

Front leg

✓ **Reading Check** What happens during differentiation?

Differentiating Blood Cells

1. Examine the **slide of the red bone marrow smear.**
2. Notice the different kinds of blood cells in the smear. Sketch a red blood cell and a white blood cell.
3. All blood cells differentiate from the same kind of cell called a blood stem cell. Examine the sketch of a *blood stem cell* made by your teacher.
4. Make a **flip book animation** that shows how one of the blood cells that you sketched developed from the blood stem cell.

Movement

Nearly all animals move to search for food, shelter, or mates. **Figure 6** shows some of the different ways in which animals move. Some animals can move from place to place only at certain stages of their life. For example, a young sea anemone finds its food as it drifts in ocean currents. When a sea anemone is older, it will swim to the ocean floor and attach itself there. As an adult, a sea anemone cannot move around and must wait for food to come within reach of its tentacles, as **Figure 6** shows.

Most movement in animals is possible because of muscle cells. By contracting and relaxing, groups of muscle cells work together to help an animal move. For example, a parrot flies because the muscles that are attached to its breast bone and bones in its wings contract and relax.

✓ Reading Check How do muscle cells allow a parrot to fly?

Figure 6 **How Animals Move**

Anemone catching food

Nautilus swimming

Fish swimming

Caterpillar crawling

Moth flying

Parrot flying

Gibbon walking

Maintaining Body Temperature

To function well, all animals need to maintain their bodies within a specific range of temperatures. Birds and mammals maintain their own body temperatures by using some of the energy released by chemical reactions. These kinds of animals are called *endotherms* (EN doh THURMZ).

Animals that rely on their environment to maintain their body temperature are called *ectotherms* (EK toh THURMZ). Some ectotherms have developed different behaviors to control their body temperatures. For example, some lizards sit in the sun to warm themselves in the morning before they hunt. When the weather gets too hot, the lizard may burrow underground to stay cool.

SECTION Review

Summary

- All animals are multicellular organisms. Specialized cells in animals are organized into tissues, organs, and organ systems.
- Most animals have bilateral symmetry or radial symmetry. Some are asymmetrical.
- Animals consume other organisms to get energy.
- Animals reproduce asexually or sexually.
- As an embryo develops, its cells differentiate.
- Animals move in many ways.
- Animals that maintain their own body temperature are endotherms. Animals that rely on their environment to maintain their body temperature are ectotherms.

Using Vocabulary

1. Write an original definition for *embryo* and *consumer*.

Understanding Concepts

2. **Identifying** What is differentiation?

3. **Describing** Starting at the level of the cell, describe the levels of structural organization in animals.

Critical Thinking

4. **Making Comparisons** What are the two main kinds of reproduction in animals? How do the kinds of reproduction differ?

5. **Identifying Relationships** A fish tank contains water, chemicals, fish, snails, algae, and gravel. Which of these items are alive? Which of these items are animals? Why are some of the living organisms not classified as animals?

6. **Making Inferences** Could a parrot fly if it did not have muscle cells? Explain.

Interpreting Graphics

The graph shows body temperatures of organism A and organism B and shows the ground temperature. Use the graph below to answer the following question.

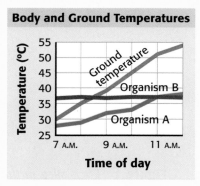

Body and Ground Temperatures

Temperature (°C): 25, 30, 35, 40, 45, 50, 55

Ground temperature

Organism B

Organism A

Time of day: 7 A.M., 9 A.M., 11 A.M.

7. **Evaluating Data** How do the body temperatures of the two organisms change as the ground temperature changes?

The Animal Kingdom

Both eagles and butterflies have wings. Are eagles and butterflies closely related because they both have wings? The answer is no. Butterflies are insects, and eagles are birds. Insects, birds, and other animals show great diversity in body structure and function, as well as in how and where they live.

What You Will Learn

- The animal kingdom is made up of many different kinds of animals.
- Animals can be divided into two main groups: invertebrates and vertebrates.
- Each group of animals has unique characteristics.

Vocabulary

invertebrate
exoskeleton
vertebrate
endoskeleton

READING STRATEGY

Reading Organizer In your Science Journal, make a concept map that relates the invertebrates discussed in this section by levels of complexity.

Animal Diversity

Scientists have named more than 1 million species of animals. Many species that exist have not yet been discovered and named. Some scientists estimate that more than 3 million species of animals live on Earth. Some of these animals are becoming extinct before they have been discovered or described.

Animals that have been discovered and described have been placed into groups. Placing animals into groups makes it easier to study all of the different kinds of animals. The pie graph in **Figure 1** shows the proportions of the main groups of animals in the animal kingdom.

✓ **Reading Check** What is one advantage to placing animals in groups? (*See the Appendix for answers to Reading Checks.*)

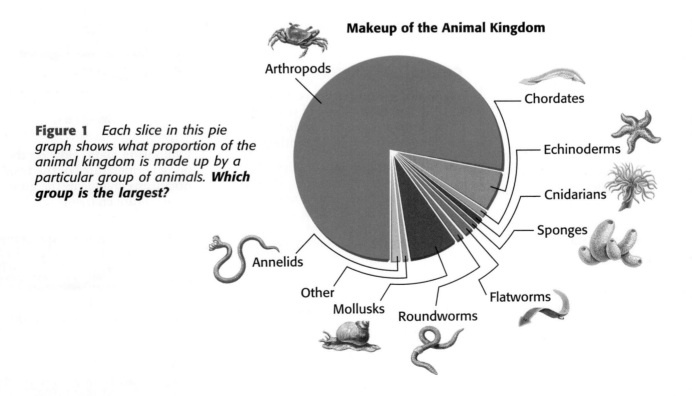

Makeup of the Animal Kingdom

Arthropods

Chordates

Echinoderms

Cnidarians

Sponges

Flatworms

Roundworms

Mollusks

Other

Annelids

Figure 1 *Each slice in this pie graph shows what proportion of the animal kingdom is made up by a particular group of animals.* **Which group is the largest?**

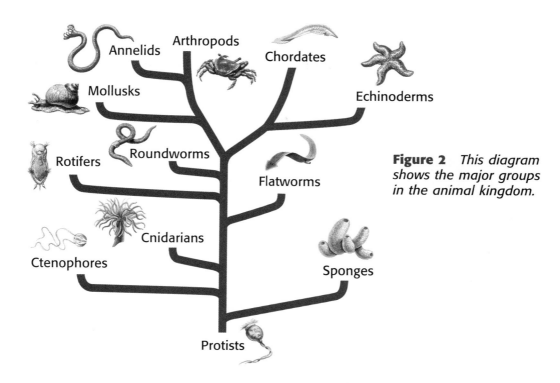

Annelids
Arthropods
Chordates
Mollusks
Echinoderms
Rotifers
Roundworms
Flatworms
Cnidarians
Ctenophores
Sponges
Protists

Figure 2 *This diagram shows the major groups in the animal kingdom.*

Classification

Scientists organize animals into groups based on the animals' characteristics and evolutionary relationships. In the past, scientists grouped animals based on only structural characteristics, such as symmetry. Today, scientists also use DNA to place animals into groups. **Figure 2** shows groups of animals and how they are related to each other. All animals, except for most of the members of chordates, are known as *invertebrates*.

Invertebrate Characteristics

Most of the animals on Earth are invertebrates. An **invertebrate** is an animal that does not have a backbone. In fact, invertebrates do not have any bones. Insects, snails, jellyfish, and worms are all examples of invertebrates. Invertebrates can be found living in every environment on Earth. Sponges are some of the simplest invertebrates.

Sponges

Most sponges live in the ocean. Sponges have an asymmetrical body plan. A sponge is a mass of specialized cells that is held together by a jelly-like material. Tiny, glassy structures in the sponge also provide support. The body of a sponge has many tubes and thousands of small holes or *pores*. A sponge sweeps water through the pores into the tubes. In the tubes, specialized cells filter and digest food particles from the water. Sponges reproduce asexually by fragmentation and sexually.

Reading Check Describe the body of a sponge.

invertebrate (in VUHR tuh brit) an animal that does not have a backbone

Grouping Organisms by Characteristics

1. On a **sheet of paper**, write a list of six organisms from this chapter.

2. Divide the organisms into two groups based on one characteristic. Record the animals in each group.

3. Divide each group into two new groups based on a different characteristic. Keep a record of the animals in each group.

4. Repeat step 3 until there is only one animal in a group.

5. Exchange your list with another student, and try to figure out the characteristics the student used to divide his or her list of organisms.

Figure 3 *This jellyfish has a medusa body form. It floats in ocean currents and traps prey with its tentacles.*

Cnidarians

Cnidarians are also invertebrates, but they are more complex than sponges. Most cnidarians (ni DER ee uhnz) live in the ocean. The three major classes of cnidarians are hydrozoans (HIE droh ZOH uhnz), jellyfish, and sea anemones and corals.

Cnidarians have one of two radially symmetrical body plans—the *medusa* or the *polyp* form. The medusa is a cup or bell-shaped body that has tentacles extending from it. The jellyfish **Figure 3** shows, has the medusa body form. Sea anemones and corals have medusa body forms when they are young, or *larvae*. As adults, sea anemones and corals have polyp body forms. Polyps attach to hard surfaces at the base of the cup. The tentacles of the animal then extend into the water. Specialized stinging cells, called *cnidocytes* (NEE doh siets), are located on the tentacles. Cnidocytes are used to stun and capture prey. Many cnidarians reproduce by sexual reproduction. Some cnidarians can also reproduce by budding or fragmentation.

Reading Check Describe two cnidarian body plans.

Flatworms

Flatworms are the simplest worms. Many flatworms live in water, while some live in damp soils. Other flatworms are parasites. A parasite is an organism that invades and feeds on the body of another organism. For example, tapeworms are parasites that live in the intestines of humans.

Flatworms have more-complex bodies than sponges or cnidarians do. Flatworms have flat bodies that are bilaterally symmetrical. The flatworm, as **Figure 4** shows, has a clearly defined head with eyespots, which are sensitive to light. Flatworms reproduce both sexually and by fragmentation.

Roundworms

Unlike flatworms, roundworms have a coelom and are cylindrical, like spaghetti. Roundworms also have bilateral symmetry. Most roundworms are little more than 2 cm long. They live in freshwater habitats, in damp soils, and as parasites in the tissues and body fluids of other animals. Some roundworms eat tiny organisms. Other roundworms break down dead organisms and make soils more fertile.

exoskeleton (EKS oh SKEL uh tuhn) a hard, external, supporting structure

Figure 4 *This flatworm has a head with eyespots and sensory lobes. This kind of flatworm is often about 15 mm long.*

Eyespot

Sensory lobe

Mollusks

Snails, slugs, clams, oysters, squids, and octopuses are mollusks. Although most mollusks live in the ocean, some live in fresh water. Others live on land. Mollusks have a specialized tissue called a *mantle.* The mantle secretes the shell of snails, clams, and oysters. Mollusks also have a muscular foot. Snails use the foot to move. In squids, such as the one in **Figure 5,** and in octopuses, the foot has evolved into tentacles. Squids and octopuses use their tentacles to capture prey, such as fish. Mollusks that do not have tentacles feed differently. Clams and oysters filter food from the water. Snails and slugs feed on plants and break down dead organisms. Mollusks reproduce sexually.

Figure 5 *The squid is a mollusk that moves by forcing water out of its mantle.*

Annelids

Annelids live in the ocean and on land. Annelids have round, bilaterally symmetrical bodies. Because annelids are made up of repeating compartments, or segments, annelids are also called *segmented worms.* Leeches are annelids that suck blood. Earthworms, such as the worm in **Figure 6,** break down dead organisms as they burrow through soil. Marine annelids eat mollusks and small animals. Each annelid has both male and female sex organs. But individuals cannot fertilize themselves. Individuals fertilize each other to reproduce sexually.

Arthropods

Arthropods are the most diverse group in the animal kingdom. Arthropods have bilaterally symmetry and a strong, external armor called an **exoskeleton.** The exoskeleton provides defense against predators. The exoskeleton also prevents the animal from drying out in the air and in the sun. Insects, such as the bumblebee in **Figure 7,** are a familiar group of arthropods that live on land. Insects' bodies are clearly divided into a head, thorax, and abdomen. Millipedes, centipedes, and arachnids, such as spiders, and scorpions are also arthropods. Arthropods that live in the water include crab and shrimp. Most arthropods are either males or females and reproduce sexually.

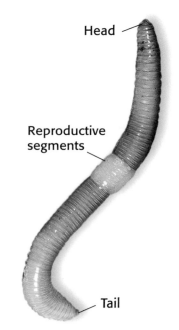

Head

Reproductive segments

Tail

Figure 6 *Except for the head, tail, and reproductive segments, all of the segments of this common garden earthworm are identical.*

Figure 7 *The bumblebee has two antennae, two wings, six legs, a head, a thorax, and an abdomen.*

Figure 8 *Sea urchins are common in kelp forests along the coast of California.*

Echinoderms

Echinoderms (ee KIE noh DUHRMZ) are invertebrates that live in the ocean and include sea stars, sea urchins, and sand dollars. The name *echinoderm* means "spiny skinned." Echinoderms, such as the sea urchins in **Figure 8,** have an exoskeleton covered in bumps and spines. Echinoderms have bilateral symmetry as larvae but have radial symmetry as adults. They also have a unique system of canals filled with water called the *water vascular system* (WAWT uhr VAS kuh luhr SIS tuhm). The water vascular system uses water pumps to help the animals move, eat, breathe, and sense the environment. Most echinoderms feed by scavenging and filtering food out of the water. However, many sea stars prey on mollusks, such as clams.

Echinoderms usually reproduce sexually. For fertilization to take place, males release sperm into the water and females release eggs into the water. Larvae are formed when the sperm fertilizes the eggs. Some sea stars can regenerate a whole individual from an arm that is cut off. This is a form of asexual reproduction.

vertebrate (VUHR tuh brit) an animal that has a backbone

endoskeleton (EN doh SKEL uh tuhn) an internal skeleton made of bone and cartilage

Vertebrate Characteristics

Vertebrates belong to the phylum Chordata. Members of this phylum are called *chordates* (KAWR DAYTS). Lancelets (LANS lits), such as the one shown in **Figure 9,** and tunicates (TOO ni kits) are also chordates. All chordates share some characteristics, such as a *notochord*, during their life cycle. The notochord is a stiff but flexible rod that supports the body of the animal.

As a vertebrate develops, the notochord is replaced by a backbone. **Vertebrates** are animals that have backbones. The backbone is a strong but flexible column of individual bony units called *vertebrae* (VUHR tuh BRAY). The backbone is a part of the endoskeleton of a vertebrate. An **endoskeleton** is an internal skeleton that supports the body of the animal and provides a place for muscles to attach. Muscles that are attached to the endoskeleton allow the animal to move.

Less than 5% of the known animal species are vertebrates. Vertebrates are divided into five main groups: fishes, amphibians, reptiles, birds, and mammals. Vertebrates can live in water and on land. Some vertebrates feed on only plants or on only animals. Some feed on both plants and animals. Vertebrates are either male or female and reproduce mainly by sexual reproduction.

Figure 9 *Lancelets are one of the few marine organisms grouped as chordates. A lancelet has a notochord but does not have a backbone.*

✓ *Reading Check* How do lancelets differ from vertebrates?

Fish

More than half of the species of vertebrates are fish. The oldest recognizable vertebrates that appeared nearly 500 million years ago were small, odd-looking fish without jaws. Today, there are two small groups of jawless fishes. All other fishes can be divided into two main groups: the *cartilaginous fish* and the *bony fish*. Cartilaginous fish have a skeleton made of a flexible tissue called *cartilage*. This group includes sharks and stingrays. All other fish have a bony skeleton. Bony fish, such as the Garibaldi in **Figure 10,** are found in marine and freshwater environments around the world.

Figure 10 *This Garibaldi, is a bony fish that is commonly found in the kelp forests along the coast of California.*

Amphibians

Most modern amphibians live near fresh water because their eggs and larvae need water to survive. Salamanders, frogs, toads, and caecilians are amphibians. Adult frogs, such as the frog shown in **Figure 11,** and toads do not have tails. Frogs and toads have long hind legs used for hopping and swimming. Adult salamanders have tails, and most have legs equal in size to the tail. Like frogs, some salamanders live completely in the water. However, others spend their lives on land and return to water only to reproduce. Caecilians are tropical amphibians that live under logs and in burrows. All amphibians have thin skins that must be moist. Most amphibians have an aquatic larval stage in their life cycle. In the larval stage, a frog is called a tadpole.

Figure 11 *The Pacific Tree frog can be found in western North America, including California.*

Reptiles

Reptiles live nearly anywhere on land because they do not need water to lay their eggs. Reptile eggs are protected from drying out by membranes and a shell. Some reptiles, such as turtles, alligators, and snakes can also live in water. Some reptiles feed on plants. Other reptiles feed on insects and other arthropods. Some reptiles, such as the snake in **Figure 12,** eat other vertebrates. Reptiles mainly reproduce sexually.

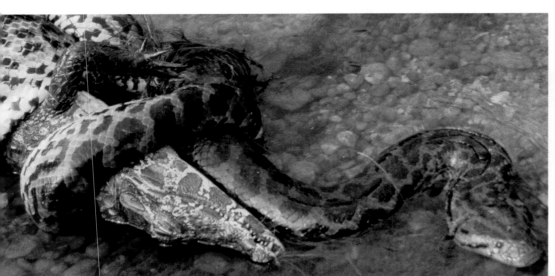

Figure 12 *Both the caiman and the snake are reptiles. The caiman and the snake share many characteristics, such as tails and scaly skins.*

Birds

Some birds live on land. Others live in the water. Birds such as the pelican in **Figure 13** live on land and on the water. Birds share many characteristics with reptiles, such as similar structures in their feet. But birds also have unique characteristics. For example, birds are the only living animals that have feathers. Feathers are important for maintaining body temperature. Feathers also help shape the body and the wings for flying. Some birds, such as the penguin, no longer use their wings to fly. The penguin uses its wings to swim. Birds such as the ostrich and emu do not fly but have unique characteristics that help them run. All birds reproduce by sexual reproduction.

✓ *Reading Check* List two reasons that feathers are important?

Mammals

All of the approximately 5,000 species of mammals share certain characteristics. For example, all mammals have hair, and all female mammals can produce milk for their young. Some members of the three main groups of mammals are shown in **Figure 14.** The echidna is a monotreme. Monotremes lay eggs that have shells. Kangaroos and opossums are marsupials or "pouched mammals." Marsupials give birth to embryos. The embryos continue to develop in their mother's pouch. The sea otter is a placental mammal, which means that is has placenta in its uterus. The *placenta* is an organ through which nutrients and wastes are exchanged between the mother and developing offspring. All mammals reproduce by sexual reproduction.

Figure 13 *The California brown pelican can live on land and on water. Pelicans feed on fish.*

Figure 14 Examples of Three Kinds of Mammals

Echidna (monotreme)

Kangaroo (marsupial)

Sea Otter (placental mammal)

Summary

- The animal kingdom can be divided into two main groups: invertebrates and vertebrates. Invertebrates do not have backbones. Vertebrates have backbones.

- Sponges, cnidarians, flatworms, roundworms, mollusks, annelids, arthropods, and echinoderms are groups of invertebrates.

- Fish, amphibians, reptiles, birds, and mammals are groups of vertebrates.

- Invertebrate bodies can be asymmetrical, radially symmetrical, or bilaterally symmetrical. Some invertebrates have different body symmetries at different stages in their life cycle.

- Most vertebrate bodies have bilateral symmetry.

- Many invertebrates reproduce by asexual reproduction and sexual reproduction. Most vertebrates reproduce only by sexual reproduction.

Using Vocabulary

1. Write an original definition for *exoskeleton*.

2. Use the following terms in the same sentence: *invertebrate and vertebrate,* and *placenta.*

Understanding Concepts

3. **Describing** Describe the kinds of cnidarian body forms and cnidarian stinging cells.

4. **Identifying** Name two characteristics that are found in mollusks.

5. **Comparing** What are two main differences between a sponge and a roundworm?

6. **Identifying** Identify one similarity and one difference between vertebrates and other chordates.

7. **Classifying** Into what group would you classify a female organism that is covered in fur and that provides milk for its young?

Math Skills

8. **Making Calculations** A bird that weighs 15 g eats 10 times its weight in food in a week. Calculate how much food the bird eats in a day.

Critical Thinking

9. **Applying Concepts** Explain why adult amphibians have to live near water or in a very wet habitat.

10. **Analyzing Relationships** What is the relationship between the kind of eggs reptiles produce and where reptiles can live?

Interpreting Graphics

Use the two diagrams below to answer the next question.

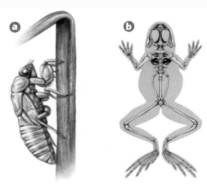

11. **Making Comparisons** What kind of skeleton does the organism in (a) have? What kind of skeleton does the organism in (b) have?

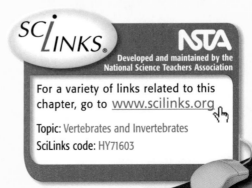

For a variety of links related to this chapter, go to www.scilinks.org

Topic: Vertebrates and Invertebrates
SciLinks code: HY71603

Invertebrates

Humans and snakes have them, but octopuses and butterflies don't. What are they? Backbones! Most animals do not have backbones. These animals are called *invertebrates*.

Invertebrate Characteristics

Invertebrates can be found in nearly every environment on Earth. Invertebrates also have many different shapes and sizes. For example, grasshoppers, clams, earthworms, and jellyfish are all invertebrates. Some invertebrates have heads, and others do not. Some invertebrates eat food through their mouths. Others absorb food particles through their tissues.

The structures of invertebrates show how well adapted invertebrates are to their environment. For example, insects have different kinds of wings that help them fly. Some invertebrates have legs that help them burrow through the ground. Others have strong bodies that help them swim. But all invertebrates are similar because they do not have backbones.

Body Symmetry

Invertebrate bodies have one of two kinds of symmetry or no symmetry at all. Sponges have irregular shapes and are therefore asymmetrical. Jellyfish have radial symmetry. In animals that have radial symmetry, many lines can be drawn through the center of the body. Each line divides the animal into opposite, or mirror images. Animals that have radial symmetry have only a top and a bottom.

Most invertebrates have "two sides," or bilateral symmetry. A body with bilateral symmetry can be divided into two parts by one vertical line. A line through the middle of the body divides the body into nearly equal right and left halves. Animals with bilateral symmetry have a top and bottom, as well as a front end and a back end. The development of a head is only seen in organisms with bilateral symmetry, such as in the sea hare seen in **Figure 1.**

Reading Check Would you expect an animal with radial symmetry to have a head? Explain. (*See the Appendix for answers to Reading Checks.*)

Figure 1 *The* Aplysia californica *is a species of sea hare. This mollusk has bilateral symmetry.*

Figure 2 Segmentation in Invertebrate Bodies

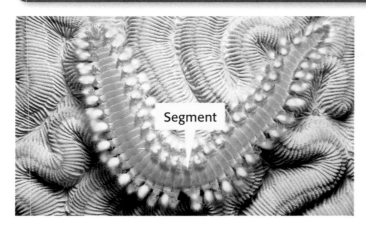

Abdomen

Thorax

Head

Segmentation

The bodies of many animals are divided into sections or **segments.** The body of the marine worm shown in **Figure 2** has many nearly equal segments. The body of the insect shown in **Figure 2** has three unequal segments. The insect has a head, a thorax, and an abdomen. Segmentation in the body has many advantages. For example, each segment in an earthworm has a set of muscles that help the earthworm push through soil.

segment (SEG muhnt) any part of a larger structure, such as the body of an organism, that is set off by natural or arbitrary boundaries

Support of the Body

Invertebrate bodies need support and protection. **Figure 3** shows three invertebrates that have different kinds of support. The body of a sponge is supported by a jelly-like material and tiny, glassy structures. Other invertebrates have tough outer coverings. For example, round worms have thick skins, and lobsters have exoskeletons. These coverings are also important because muscles that are attached to these coverings contract and relax to help invertebrates move.

✓ **Reading Check** Why are outer coverings important for movement in animals?

Figure 3 Support in Invertebrate Bodies

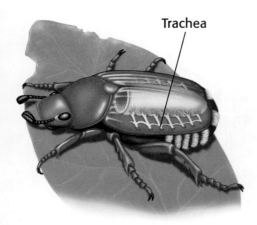

Trachea

Figure 4 *This beetle moves air into its body and out of its body through small holes along the sides of its body.*

Respiratory and Circulatory Systems

All animals need oxygen to live. Animals take oxygen into their bodies and release carbon dioxide from their bodies through respiration. Respiration is performed by the *respiratory system* (RES puhr uh TAWR ee SIS tuhm). In lobsters, gills are the main organs that perform respiration. In insects, such as the beetle in **Figure 4,** a network of tubes inside the body, called *tracheae* (TRAY kee EE), performs respiration.

Oxygen, carbon dioxide, and nutrients must be moved or circulated throughout the body. The *circulatory system* transports many substances in a fluid called *blood*. Most mollusks have an **open circulatory system.** In open circulatory systems, blood moves through open spaces in the body. Invertebrates, such as annelids, have a **closed circulatory system.** In closed circulatory systems, blood moves through tubes that form a closed loop.

 **Reading Check** What would happen to an insect if its tracheae became clogged?

Digestive and Excretory Systems

Animals obtain the energy they need by digesting food. Digestion is performed by the *digestive system*. Food is digested as it is consumed and broken down. Any remaining material is expelled from the body. Invertebrates have relatively simple digestive systems. The mouth and anus form two ends of a tube called a *digestive tract*. The snail shown in **Figure 5** has a stomach and other specialized areas along the digestive tract.

As cells in the body use up nutrients, wastes are formed. The *excretory system* (EKS kruh TAWR ee SIS tuhm) eliminates these wastes from cells with any excess water. In many invertebrates, the digestive tract also eliminates this kind of waste. Other invertebrates have separate excretory systems. These systems have specialized organs to eliminate excess water and waste from cells.

INTERNET ACTIVITY

For another activity related to this chapter, go to **go.hrw.com** and type in the keyword **HY7INVW.**

Figure 5 *The digestive system in the snail is made up of a digestive tract that has four parts: a mouth, a stomach, an intestine, and an anus.*

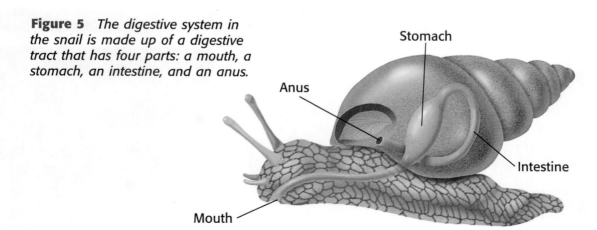

Stomach

Anus

Intestine

Mouth

Figure 6 Examples of Invertebrate Nervous Systems

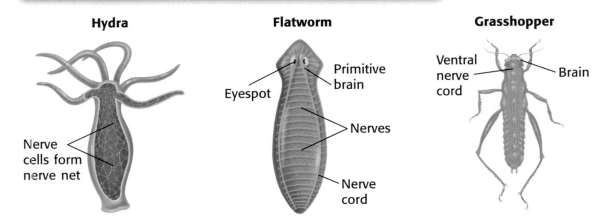

Hydra

Flatworm

Grasshopper

Nerve cells form nerve net

Eyespot

Primitive brain

Nerves

Nerve cord

Ventral nerve cord

Brain

Nervous Systems

The *nervous system* is specialized for receiving and sending electrical signals that control all of the functions of the body. **Figure 6** shows examples of the nervous systems of three invertebrates. Many nervous systems have a specialized area called the *brain*. The brain acts as the control center. Nervous systems also have specialized areas called *sense organs*. Sense organs collect information, such as sound and light, from outside and inside the body. For example, eyes are organs that sense light. When light enters the eye, signals are sent to the brain. The brain interprets the signals as an image.

open circulatory system
(OH puhn SUHR kyuh luh TAWR ee SIS tuhm) a circulatory system in which the circulatory fluid is not contained entirely within vessels

closed circulatory system
(KLOHZD SUHR kyuh luh TAWR ee SIS tuhm) a circulatory system in which the heart circulates blood through a network of vessels that form a closed loop

Seeing Like an Insect

Insects have a compound eye made up of repeating units. Each unit has its own lens.

1. Use a **ruler** to draw a grid with dimensions of about 10 cm × 10 cm on a **sheet of tracing paper.** The grid lines should be separated by 0.5 cm.
2. Place the **grid** over a **black-and-white image.** Secure the grid with **tape.**
3. Note the relative amount of black ink that shows through in each box.
4. Use a **black marker** to fill in the grid boxes that are on top of an area that is mostly black. Don't fill in the grid boxes that are above squares that are mostly white.
5. Remove your grid, and examine it from across the room. Describe what you see?
6. What part of the activity mimicked the repeating units in the eye of an insect?
7. How might the curve of the insect eye further change how an insect sees images?

Reproduction and Development

Many invertebrates reproduce asexually. One kind of asexual reproduction is called *budding*. Budding happens when a part of the parent organism develops into a new organism. The new organism then pinches off from the parent and lives independently. The hydra, shown in **Figure 7,** reproduces by budding. The new hydra is genetically identical to its parent. Fragmentation is a second kind of asexual reproduction. In fragmentation, parts of an organism break off and then develop into a new individual that is identical to the original organism. Certain organisms, such as flatworms called *planaria*, reproduce by fragmentation.

Complete Metamorphosis

Many insects reproduce sexually and lay eggs. As an insect hatches from an egg and develops, the insect changes form through a process called **metamorphosis.** Most insects go through a complex change called *complete metamorphosis*. As shown in **Figure 8,** complete metamorphosis has four main stages: egg, larva, pupa (PYOO puh), and adult. Butterflies, beetles, flies, bees, wasps, and ants go through this change.

✓ **Reading Check** Compare the life cycle of a hydra with the life cycle of a butterfly.

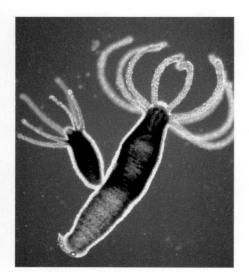

Figure 7 *Hydra reproduce by asexual reproduction. The offspring look similar to and are genetically identical to the parent.*

metamorphosis (met uh MAWR fuh sis) a process in the lifecycle of many animals during which a rapid change from the immature organism to the adult takes place

Figure 8 **The Stages of Complete Metamorphosis**

e The adult butterfly pumps blood-like fluid into its wings until they are full-sized. The butterfly is now ready to fly.

d Adult body parts replace the larval body parts. The **adult** splits its chrysalis and emerges.

c After its final molt, the caterpillar makes a chrysalis and becomes a **pupa.** The pupal stage may last a few days or several months. During this stage, the insect is inactive.

a An adult lays **eggs.** An embryo forms inside each egg.

b A **larva** hatches from the egg. Butterfly and moth larvae are called *caterpillars*. The caterpillar eats leaves and grows rapidly. As the caterpillar grows, it sheds its outer layer several times. This process is called *molting*.

Incomplete Metamorphosis

Grasshoppers and cockroaches are two kinds of insects that go through *incomplete metamorphosis*. Incomplete metamorphosis is less complicated than complete metamorphosis. As shown in **Figure 9,** incomplete metamorphosis has three main stages: egg, nymph, and adult. Some nymphs shed their exoskeleton several times in a process called *molting.* An insect in the nymph stage looks very much like an adult insect. But a nymph does not have wings and is smaller than an adult. Through molting, the nymph develops into an adult.

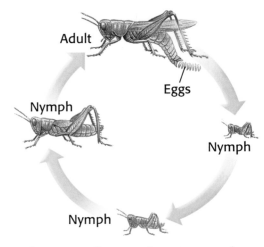

Figure 9 *The grasshopper nymphs look like smaller versions of the adult.*

SECTION Review

Summary

- Invertebrate bodies are asymmetrical, have radial symmetry, or bilateral symmetry.
- The bodies of many invertebrates are divided into segments.
- Invertebrates have protective outer coverings that provide support and serve as a place for muscles to attach.
- Invertebrates may have many basic organ systems, such as a respiratory system, a circulatory system, a digestive system, an excretory system, a nervous system, and a reproductive system.
- Invertebrates reproduce asexually and sexually. Invertebrates develop from embryos into larvae and from larvae into adults.

Understanding Concepts

1. **Describing** Explain why respiration is important. Be sure to include an example of an invertebrate respiratory system.

2. **Comparing** How is the support in the body of a sponge different from the support in the body of an insect?

3. **Identifying** How do invertebrates remove wastes that are produced by cells in their bodies?

4. **Comparing** In the life cycle of a grasshopper, what are two main differences between nymphs and adults?

5. **Inferring** If an animal has a head, which kind of body symmetry would you expect the animal to have?

Math Skills

6. **Making Calculations** A sea urchin lost 12 of its 178 spines in a storm. What percentage of its spines does the sea urchin still have?

Critical Thinking

7. **Analyzing Processes** Describe metamorphosis in the life cycle of a butterfly and in the life cycle of a grasshopper.

8. **Making Comparisons** Compare an open circulatory system and a closed circulatory system.

9. **Expressing Opinions** Why are earthworms in a different group than roundworms? Explain.

10. **Applying Concepts** Why can't insects see in complete darkness?

11. **Applying Concepts** If the head of an insect became stuck underwater, would the insect drown? Explain your answer.

12. **Making Inferences** What other body part do invertebrates that have ears or noses have?

For a variety of links related to this chapter, go to www.scilinks.org

Topic: Sponges; Echinoderms
SciLinks code: HY71443; HY70458

Vertebrates

You may have seen a dinosaur skeleton at a museum. You have probably also seen many fish. Have you ever thought about what these animals might have in common with each other? These animals have backbones, which makes them vertebrates.

Vertebrate Characteristics

Vertebrates live in the oceans, in freshwater, and on land. Vertebrates swim, crawl, burrow, hop, run, and fly. Like many invertebrates, vertebrates have organ systems to perform their life functions. However, vertebrates also have features that other organisms do not have. For example, only vertebrates have a backbone, which is part of a skeleton that is made of bone. Bone is a special type of very hard tissue that is found only in vertebrates.

Vertebrates also have a well-developed head that is protected by a skull. The skull is made of either cartilage or bone. **Cartilage** is a flexible material made of cells and proteins. The skeletons of all embryos are made of cartilage. But as most vertebrates grow, the cartilage is replaced by the much harder bone.

Body Symmetry

All vertebrates, such as the frog in **Figure 1,** are bilaterally symmetrical. In vertebrates, the head is distinct from the rest of the body. A bilaterally symmetrical body has at least four main parts. For example, the upper body surface, or back, is the *dorsal* side. The lower surface or belly is the *ventral* side. The head is in the front, or *anterior* of the body. The tail is in the back, or *posterior* of the body.

Figure 1 *This frog has bilateral symmetry.*

Figure 2 Body Coverings in Vertebrates

Scales	Feathers	Fur	Skin

Body Coverings

The body of a vertebrate is covered by skin. One function of skin is to protect the body from the external environment. The skin of vertebrates varies in structure. For example, reptiles, such as the chameleon in **Figure 2,** and most fish are covered in small, thin plates called *scales*. However, fish scales have a different structure than reptile scales do. The scales of fish are also covered in a slippery fluid called *mucus* (MYOO kuhs), while the scales of reptiles are dry. The skin of amphibians is also covered in mucus and functions in part as a respiratory organ. Feathers on birds and the hair and fur on mammals help keep the organisms' body temperatures stable. Some body coverings display colors and patterns that allow vertebrates to hide from predators.

cartilage (KAHRT uhl ij) a flexible and strong connective tissue

Support of the Body

The body of a vertebrate is supported by an endo-skeleton. **Figure 3** shows the endoskeleton of a bird. The three main parts of an endoskeleton are the skull, the backbone, and the limb bones. The skull surrounds and protects the brain of the vertebrate. The backbone is made up of many vertebrae. Vertebrae surround and protect the spinal cord. Limb bones, such as leg bones, are an important part of movement in vertebrates. Bones provide a place for muscles to attach. As muscles contract and relax, the bones move. For example, in arms and in legs, pairs of muscles work together to move the limb. Vertebrates need large bones and muscles for support and movement on land.

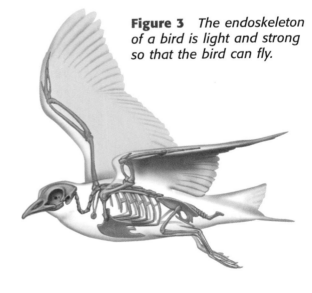

Figure 3 *The endoskeleton of a bird is light and strong so that the bird can fly.*

Reading Check Describe the three main parts of an endoskeleton. (*See the Appendix for answers to Reading Checks.*)

Figure 4 **Respiratory Systems in Vertebrates**

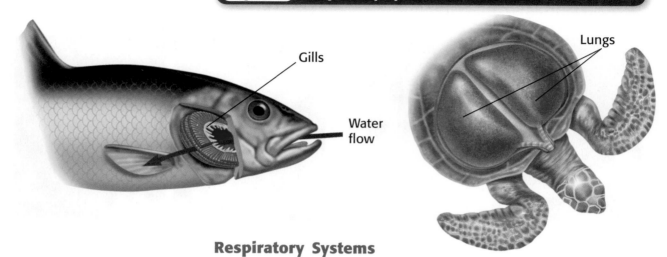

Gills

Water
flow

Lungs

Respiratory Systems

Like invertebrates, vertebrates have a respiratory system to perform respiration. **Figure 4** shows the two kinds of respiratory systems in vertebrates. The main respiratory organs in vertebrates are either lungs or gills. These organs have many blood vessels that provide the organs with a steady blood supply. In fish, water flows into the mouth and over the gills. Oxygen from the water moves across the gills and into the bloodstream. At the same time, carbon dioxide moves from the bloodstream, across the gills, and into the water.

In vertebrates that live on land, respiratory organs must be protected from drying out. Therefore, the main respiratory organs are inside the body. Lungs are sacs that are kept moist by the body's fluids. The internal surface of the lungs is made up of small pockets that increase the area available for the exchange of oxygen and carbon dioxide.

Circulatory Systems

Vertebrates have a closed circulatory system made up of blood, vessels, and a pump. Blood is pushed through the vessels by a pump, or *heart*. Vessels that carry blood away from the heart are called *arteries*. Vessels that carry blood to the heart are called *veins*. Arteries are connected to veins by a network of *capillaries*. Capillaries are the smallest blood vessels in the body. **Figure 5** shows the circulatory system of a frog.

In land vertebrates, the heart first pumps the blood to the lungs or gills. In lungs or gills, oxygen moves into the blood. At the same time, carbon dioxide moves out of the body from the blood. Then, the oxygen-rich blood returns to the heart and is pumped to the rest of the body. The circulatory system also transports nutrients and other substances around the body.

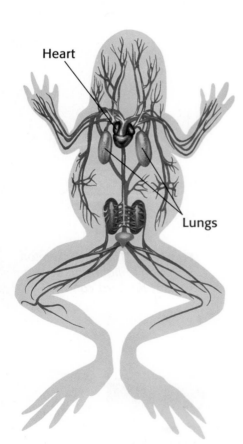

Heart

Lungs

Figure 5 *The frog has a closed circulatory system. The arteries are shown in red, and the veins are shown in blue.*

✓ **Reading Check** Describe how the circulatory system and the respiratory system in a vertebrate work together.

Digestive and Excretory Systems

Vertebrates have digestive systems to break down food. The digestive system is made up of a long tube called the *digestive tract*. Some vertebrates, such as fish and snakes, swallow their food whole. Other vertebrates crush or chew their food before swallowing. Food passes from the mouth to the stomach. Acids and other chemicals in the stomach turn the food into a kind of soup. This soup then moves into the next part of the digestive tract, an organ called the **small intestine.** Blood vessels in the small intestine absorb nutrients. Then, the materials move into an organ called the **large intestine.** The large intestine absorbs excess water and converts undigested material into feces.

Some cell activities result in the formation of nitrogen compounds, such as ammonia. Ammonia diffuses into the blood and is removed from the body by the excretory system. In mammals, the liver converts ammonia into urea. Then, the *kidneys* filter urea from the blood. Urea is then combined with excess water to form urine, which is expelled from the body.

Nervous Systems

In the nervous system of a vertebrate, the brain is part of the spinal cord. The brain is an organ that serves as the main control center of the body. Nerves from the spinal cord branch throughout the body. Nerves carry impulses between the brain and the body. For example, when a sound reaches the ear, the ear sends an impulse through *sensory nerves* and the spinal cord, to the brain. To make the body react, the brain interprets the impulses and sends command impulses throughout the body through *motor nerves*.

The brain of a fish is much smaller than the brain of a dog, as **Figure 6** shows. Animals that have larger brains depend more on learning than on instinct. Learning is a behavior that changes the reaction of an animal based on new experiences.

Reading Check Describe what happens when a sound reaches the ear.

Amplifying Sound

1. Roll a **sheet of paper** into a loose cone.
2. Wrap the smaller open end of the cone around the stem of a **funnel.** Use **tape** to secure the shape of the cone.
3. Place the funnel over an ear.
4. Move the cone towards a faint sound and then away from the sound. How does the sound change?
5. Make a new cone with several sheets of paper. Repeat step 4. How does the size of the cone affect what you hear?

small intestine
(SMAWL in TES tuhn) the organ between the stomach and the large intestine where most of the breakdown of food happens and most of the nutrients from food are absorbed

large intestine (LAHRJ in TES tuhn) the wider and shorter portion of the intestine that removes water from mostly digested food and that turns the waste into semisolid feces, or stool

Figure 6 Nervous Systems in Vertebrates

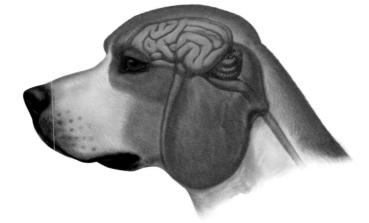
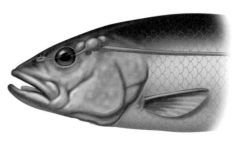

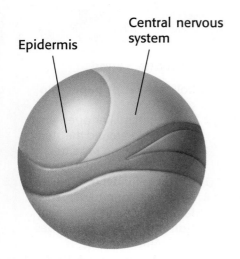

Epidermis

Central nervous system

Figure 7 *Parts of a frog embryo are beginning to differentiate into the kind of cells they will become.*

Reproduction and Development

Most vertebrates reproduce by sexual reproduction. Fertilization happens when the nucleus of a sperm cell fuses with the nucleus of an egg cell. A fertilized egg cell divides many times as it becomes a multicellular embryo. As the embryo develops, its cells differentiate. Differentiation is the process in which cells become specialized. For example, cells that will perform different functions, such as skin cells and blood cells, will develop different structures. **Figure 7** shows the differentiation of some tissues of a frog embryo.

In most fish and amphibians, larvae hatch in the water and live on their own. These larvae behave similarly to adults. However, larvae cannot reproduce. Eventually, the larvae metamorphose into adults.

Reptiles, birds, and mammals do not have a larval stage in their lifecycle. The eggs of reptiles, birds, and mammals are protected by special membranes. The eggs of reptiles, birds, and some mammals also have a shell. Eggs that have shells are laid on land. Most mammals do not lay eggs, and the embryo develops in the female until the offspring is born. **Figure 8** shows the embryos of vertebrates during early stages of their development. Embryos of different species are similar to each other at early stages of development. Embryos begin to look more like the adults of their own species as they develop. Offspring of reptiles, birds, and mammals look similar to adults when they are born. These offspring gradually develop into adults.

✓ **Reading Check** Why do cells in a developing embryo undergo differentiation?

Figure 8 The Embryos of Different Vertebrates

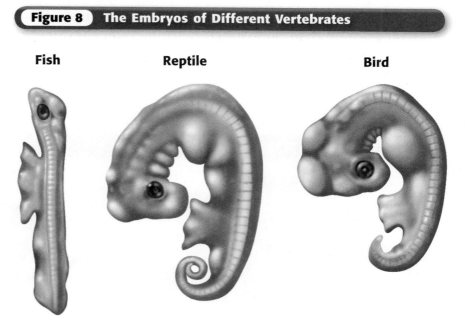

Fish   Reptile   Bird

Parental Care

Some vertebrates do not care for their young. The female simply lays the eggs and leaves. These animals lay hundreds of eggs, so at least a few offspring will survive. Many fish species and reptile species guard the nest until the eggs hatch. Afterward, the offspring are left on their own. Birds and mammals are very different. Birds and mammals have only a few offspring at a time. Therefore, birds and mammals spend a lot of time and energy feeding and protecting their offspring. The fish shown in **Figure 9** is unusual because it cares for its offspring after they hatch. The parent fish holds its offspring in its mouth to protect them as they develop. Parental care increases the chances of offspring surviving.

Figure 9 *This fish will hold its offspring in its mouth to protect them from predators.*

SECTION Review

Summary

- Skin protects the body from the environment. Skin of vertebrates may be covered in scales, feathers, or fur.

- Most vertebrates have an endoskeleton made of bone. The endoskeleton provides support, protection, and a place for muscles to attach.

- Major organs systems of vertebrates are the respiratory system, circulatory system, digestive system, excretory system, nervous system, and reproductive system.

- Cells of embryos differentiate and specialize as the embryo develops.

- The amount of parental care given to offspring varies among species of vertebrates.

Understanding Concepts

1. **Demonstrating** How do different kinds of cells develop in an embryo?

2. **Describing** Describe the structure of the backbone and what it provides the vertebrate body.

3. **Identifying** What kind of circulatory system do vertebrates have?

Interpreting Graphics

Use the graph below to answer the next two questions.

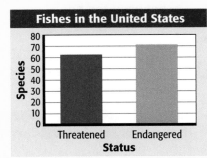

Fishes in the United States

4. **Evaluating** How many fish species in the United States are endangered?

5. **Calculating** What is the total number of endangered and threatened fish species in the United States?

Critical Thinking

6. **Making Comparisons** How does gas exchange in gills differ from gas exchange in lungs?

7. **Applying Concepts** What is an advantages and a disadvantage of depositing a large number of eggs?

8. **Applying Concepts** How does an egg become fertilized? Is this sexual or asexual reproduction? Explain your answer.

9. **Making Inferences** What factors might limit the maximum body size to which land vertebrates can grow?

10. **Applying Concepts** Why might large ears be better able to hear a sound than small ears?

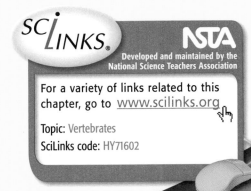

Developed and maintained by the National Science Teachers Association

For a variety of links related to this chapter, go to www.scilinks.org

Topic: Vertebrates
SciLinks code: HY71602

OBJECTIVES

Determine the density of three kinds of animal bones.

Compare the bone of a mammal, a fish, and a bird.

Identify the relationship between the structure of the bone and the function of the bone.

MATERIALS

- balance, laboratory
- beef bone
- chicken bone
- fish bone
- graduated cylinder, large
- string
- wire

SAFETY

Structure and Function of Bone

The structure of each body part of an organism is related to the function of that body part. For example, animals depend on specialized body parts for movement. Animals contract and relax muscles that are attached to bones in order to move. Some animals have legs, wings, or fins to move around. In vertebrates, most movement is the result of bones and muscles working together. Bones that support a lot of weight are thick and heavy, such as in elephants. Bones that do not support a lot of weight are light, such as in the wings of birds.

You have already learned that the bones of vertebrates have many similarities. In this activity, you will compare the bones of a mammal, a bird, and a fish. Through this activity, you will learn how differences in the structure of different bones relates to the function of these bones.

Ask a Question

1 Lets ask, "Are the bones of animals that walk more dense than the bones of animals that swim or of animals that fly?"

Form a Testable Hypothesis

2 To change the question into a testable hypothesis, you may come up with the following: "There are no differences in density between the bones of animals that walk, swim, or fly."

Procedure

3 Create a table like the one below to record the measurements for each kind of bone.

Bone Measurements			
Kind of bone	Mass of bone (g)	Volume of bone (cm³)	Density of bone (g/cm³)
Mammal bone			
Chicken bone			
Fish bone			

DO NOT WRITE IN BOOK

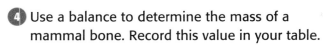

4. Use a balance to determine the mass of a mammal bone. Record this value in your table.

5. Fill a graduated cylinder about 3/4 full with water. Note the water level in the cylinder. (Note: 1 mL = 1 cm^3)

6. Tie a string around the beef bone. Gently lower it into the cylinder. When the bone is completely submerged, note the new water level.

7. Determine the volume of the bone, by subtracting the initial water level in the graduated cylinder from the water level when the bone was submerged. Record you finding in your table.

8. Calculate the density of this bone by dividing the bone's mass by its volume. Record this value in grams per centimeter cubed (g/cm^3) in you table.

9. Repeat steps 4–8 using a chicken bone and a fish bone. If a bone floats, you will need to hold it under the surface of the water by using a length of wire.

Analyze the Results

10. **Analyzing Results** Which bones sank? Which bones floated?

11. **Evaluating Results** Which bone was the most dense? Which bone was the least dense?

Draw Conclusions

12. **Drawing Conclusions** Did you prove or disprove the hypothesis?

13. **Applying Results** What can you assume about the muscles that are needed to move these bones?

14. **Making Inferences** What other factors may affect the characteristics of the muscles required to move these bones?

15. **Making Inferences** How is the density of the different bones related to how the organisms move? How is the density of the different bones related to where the organism lives?

16. **Applying Conclusions** If an organism that was the size of a whale lived on land, what kind of bones would the organism have? What kind of muscles would the animal need to move those bones?

17. **Identifying Relationships** Describe how the structure of a bone is related to a life function of the animal. Make sure to include examples in your answer.

Chapter Review

USING KEY TERMS

1 In your own words, write a definition for each of the following terms: *coelom*, *consumer*, and *differentiation*.

2 Use the following terms in the same sentence: *open circulatory system* and *invertebrate*.

For each pair of terms, explain how the meanings of the terms differ.

3 *endoskeleton* and *exoskeleton*

4 *invertebrate* and *vertebrate*

5 *asexual reproduction* and *sexual reproduction*

UNDERSTANDING KEY IDEAS

Multiple Choice

6 The sea urchin's body is organized around the organism's center, like the spokes on a wheel. What kind of symmetry does the sea urchin have?
- **a.** bilateral
- **b.** radial
- **c.** asymmetrical
- **d.** unilateral

7 Members of which of the following groups of invertebrates have segmented bodies?
- **a.** mollusks
- **b.** sea anemones
- **c.** roundworms
- **d.** arthropods

8 What would happen if the gills of a fish stopped working?
- **a.** The fish would probably die.
- **b.** The fish would make its own oxygen.
- **c.** The fish would make more carbon dioxide.
- **d.** The fish would not be able to maintain its body temperature.

9 Which of the following is NOT a function of the endoskeleton?
- **a.** The endoskeleton provides a place for muscles to attach.
- **b.** The endoskeleton supports the body from the outside of the body.
- **c.** The endoskeleton supports the body from the inside of the body.
- **d.** The endoskeleton protects the organs of the body.

Short Answer

10 **Listing** List the seven basic characteristics of animals.

11 **Inferring** Some insects develop from nymphs into adults. What kind of metamorphosis do these insects undergo? Explain.

12 **Comparing** How does fragmentation in sponges differ from reproduction in reptiles?

13 **Listing** What are the levels of structural organization in the body of a shark?

Math Skills

14 **Making Calculations** All of the females in a boar population produce exactly 10 offspring during their lifetime. What percentage of each female's offspring must survive so that the population remains constant?

15 Concept Mapping Use the following terms to create a concept map: *vertebrates, bilateral symmetry, fish, sponge, radial symmetry, sea urchin, sexual reproduction, asymmetrical, asexual reproduction*, and *invertebrates*.

16 Identifying Relationships Why are vertebrates classified as chordates?

17 Making Comparisons Describe three groups of mammals and how they differ.

18 Predicting Consequences If differentiation in an embryo is stopped, predict what is likely to happen to the embryo. Explain.

19 Analyzing Methods Could you identfy the entire life cycle of an animal by studying only the adult forms of that animal? Explain.

20 Analyzing Relationships How do the eyes of a dog help the dog fetch a ball?

21 Predicting Consequences Cats are endotherms, and geckos are ectotherms. Describe what would happen to a cat and a gecko if they were caught in a snowstorm.

22 Making Inferences A bird may have only two or three offspring at a time. A sea turtle may lay 100 eggs at a time. Which of these two organisms is more likely to provide its offspring with more parental care?

23 Making Comparisons Compare the circulatory system in an insect with a fish.

24 Analyzing Processes If you found a shark that lacks the muscles needed to pump water over its gills, what would that information tell you about how the shark lives?

25 Making Inferences On land, only animals that have endoskeletons become very large. Why are vertebrates on land larger than invertebrates on land?

The graph below shows the kinds of amphibians that are threatened or endangered in the United States. Use the graph to answer the next two questions.

Threatened and Endangered Amphibian Species in the United States

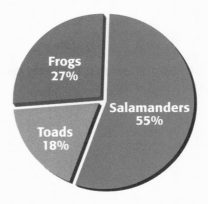

26 Making Conversions If the total number of threatened and endangered amphibian species in the United States is 22, how many more species of salamanders are threatened or endangered than species of frogs and toads?

27 Making Inferences What do you expect to happen to the percentage of toads in the pie graph as endangered toad species become extinct?

Multiple Choice

1. **What is the function of the coelom?**

   A. protection

   B. respiration

   C. digestion

   D. reproduction

2. **What characteristic distinguishes an invertebrate animal from a vertebrate animal?**

   A. the ability to reproduce

   B. the way it moves

   C. bilateral symmetry

   D. the presence of a backbone

3. **Which of the following is a method of asexual reproduction?**

   A. monotreme

   B. budding

   C. segmentation

   D. metamorphosis

Use the image below to answer question 4.

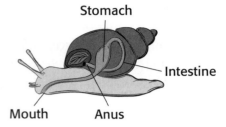

Stomach

Intestine

Mouth   Anus

4. **In the image of the snail above, which organ system is shown?**

   A. the respiratory system

   B. the nervous system

   C. the circulatory system

   D. the digestive system

5. **Which of the following is a difference between invertebrates and vertebrates?**

   A. Vertebrates have exoskeletons, and invertebrates have endoskeletons.

   B. Invertebrates reproduce only asexually, and vertebrates reproduce only sexually.

   C. Vertebrates have a backbone, while invertebrates do not.

   D. Invertebrates have bilateral symmetry, while vertebrates have radial symmetry.

6. **What type of body symmetry does an adult sea urchin have?**

   A. radial

   B. skeletal

   C. bilateral

   D. asymetrical

7. Which of the following statements about vertebrate embryos is true?

A. As embryos develop, their cells become specialized to perform different functions.

B. All vertebrate embryos develop fins before becoming adults.

C. Cell differentiation occurs after the birth of a vertebrate.

D. Even as embryos, vertebrates look much like the adults of the species.

8. Most vertebrates reproduce sexually. When does fertilization occur in sexual reproduction?

A. when a male animal releases sperm and a female animal releases eggs

B. when part of an organism breaks off and begins to grow independently

C. when the cells of the embryo begin to differentiate and become specialized

D. when the nucleus of a sperm cell fuses with the nucleus of an egg cell

Use the image below to answer question 9.

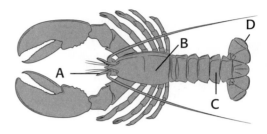

9. In the diagram of a lobster shown above, which segment of the lobster's body is labeled B?

A. the thorax

B. the abdomen

C. the head

D. the nerves

10. What role does an earthworm play in the transfer of energy in the food web of an ecosystem?

A. decomposer

B. annelid

C. producer

D. invertebrate

Open Response

11. How is the nervous system involved in the learning and behavior of a vertebrate animal?

12. Discuss the advantages and disadvantages of bilateral symmetry compared to radial symmetry.

Standardized Test Preparation

Science in Action

Science, Technology, and Society

Leeches to the Rescue

Bloodsucking leeches may sound scary, but they could save your toes! Leeches are used in operations to reattach lost limbs, fingers, or toes. During these operations, doctors can reconnect arteries, but not small veins, which are more delicate. As a result, blood flow in the limb, finger, or toe is impaired. The tissues may become swollen with blood. If this happens, the tissues of the reattached parts die. But if leeches suck the extra blood from the reattached part, the tissues can remain healthy until the veins grow back.

Math ACTIVITY

Measure the widest and narrowest parts of the leech in the photo. Calculate how many times larger the wide part is than the narrow part. Which end of the leech do you think is the head? Why do you think so? Record your work in your **Science Journal.**

Weird Science

Sounds of the Lyrebird

Imagine that you are hiking in an Australian forest. You hear many different bird calls, beaks snapping, and wings rustling. There must be many species of birds around, right? Not if a lyrebird is nearby—all of those sounds could be coming from just one bird! The lyrebird imitates the songs of other birds. In fact, lyrebirds can imitate almost any sound they hear. Many Australians have heard lyrebirds singing the sounds of chainsaws, car engines, and dog barks. According to stories, a lyrebird once confused timbermill workers when it sang the sound of the mill's whistle and caused the workers to quit for the day.

Language Arts ACTIVITY

A lyrebird's ability to imitate noises could lead to a lot of humorous confusion for people who hear its songs. Think about how lyrebirds could mimic human-made sounds and cause confusion for the people nearby. Then, write a short story in your **Science Journal** about the situation.

George Matsumoto

Marine Biologist Dr. George Matsumoto is a marine biologist at the Monterey Bay Aquarium in California. A seventh-grade snorkeling class first sparked his interest in ocean research. Since then, he has studied the oceans by snorkeling, scuba diving, using research vessels, using remotely operated vehicles (ROVs), and using deep-sea submersibles. On the Johnson Sea Link submersible, he traveled to 1,000 m (3,281 ft) below sea level!

Marine biology is a field in which there are many strange and wonderful creatures. Matsumoto focuses on marine invertebrates, particularly the delicate animals called comb jellies. Comb jellies are also called *ctenophores* (TEN uh FAWRZ), which means "comb-bearers." Ctenophores have eight rows of cilia that look like the rows of a comb. These cilia help ctenophores move through the water. Some ctenophores glow when they are disturbed. By studying ctenophores and similar marine invertebrates, Matsumoto and other marine scientists can learn about the ecology of ocean communities.

Social Studies ACTIVITY

One kind of ctenophore from the United States took over both the Black Sea and the Sea of Azov by eating small fish. This left little food for bigger fish and thus changed the ecosystem and ruined the fisheries. Write a paragraph in your **Science Journal** about how Matsumoto's work as a marine biologist could help solve problems like this one.

To learn more about these Science in Action topics, visit go.hrw.com and type in the keyword HY7AMLF.

Current Science

Check out Current Science® articles related to this chapter by visiting go.hrw.com. Just type in the keyword HY7AMLC.

16

Interactions of Living Things

The Big Idea

Organisms interact with each other and with the nonliving parts of their environment.

About the Photo

A chameleon is about to grab an insect using its long tongue. A chameleon's body can change color to match its surroundings. Blending in helps the chameleon sneak up on its prey and also keeps the chameleon safe from animals that would like to make a snack out of a chameleon.

PRE-READING ACTIVITY

FOLDNOTES **Tri-Fold** Before you read the chapter, create the FoldNote entitled "Tri-Fold" described in the **Study Skills** section of the Appendix. Write what you know about the interactions of living things in the column labeled "Know." Then, write what you want to know in the column labeled "Want." As you read the chapter, write what you learn about the interactions of living things in the column labeled "Learn."

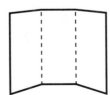

STARTUP ACTIVITY

Who Eats Whom?

In this activity, you will learn how organisms interact when finding (or becoming) the next meal.

Procedure

1. On each of **five index cards,** print the name of one of the following organisms: killer whale, cod fish, krill shrimp, algae, and leopard seal.

2. On your desk, arrange the cards in a chain to show who eats whom.

3. Record the order of your cards.

4. In nature, would you expect to see more killer whales or cod? Arrange the cards in order of most individuals in an organism group to fewest.

Analysis

1. What might happen to the other organisms if algae were removed from this group? What might happen if the killer whales were removed?

2. Are there any organisms in this group that eat more than one kind of food? (Hint: What else might a seal, a fish, or a killer whale eat?) How could you change the order of your cards to show this information? How could you use pieces of string to show these relationships?

Everything Is Connected

An alligator drifts in a weedy Florida river, watching a long, thin fish called a *gar.* The gar swims too close to the alligator. Then, in a rush of murky water, the alligator swallows the gar whole and slowly swims away.

It is clear that two organisms have interacted when one eats the other. But organisms have many interactions other than simply "who eats whom." For example, alligators dig underwater holes to escape from the heat. After the alligators abandon these holes, fish and other aquatic organisms live in the holes during the winter dry period.

Studying the Web of Life

All living things are connected in a web of life. Scientists who study the web of life specialize in the science of ecology. **Ecology** is the study of the interactions of organisms with one another and with their environment.

The Two Parts of an Environment

An organism's environment consists of all the things that affect the organism. These things can be divided into two groups. All of the organisms that live together and interact with one another make up the **biotic** part of the environment. The **abiotic** part of the environment consists of the nonliving factors, such as water, soil, light, and temperature. How many biotic parts and abiotic parts do you see in **Figure 1?**

What You Will Learn

● Distinguish between the biotic and abiotic parts of the environment.
● Explain how populations and communities are related.
● Describe how the abiotic parts of the environment affect ecosystems.

Vocabulary

ecology   community
biotic   ecosystem
abiotic   biosphere
population

READING STRATEGY

Reading Organizer As you read this section, create an outline of the section. Use the headings from the section in your outline.

Figure 1 *The alligator affects, and is affected by, many organisms in its environment.*

Organization in the Environment

At first glance, the environment may seem disorganized. However, the environment can be arranged into different levels, as shown in **Figure 2.** The first level is made of an individual organism. The second level is larger and is made of similar organisms, which form a population. The third level is made of different populations, which form a community. The fourth level is made of a community and its abiotic environment, which form an ecosystem. The fifth and final level contains all ecosystems, which form the biosphere.

ecology the study of the interactions of living organisms with one another and with their environment

biotic describes living factors in the environment

abiotic describes the nonliving part of the environment, including water, rocks, light, and temperature

Figure 2 **The Five Levels of Environmental Organization**

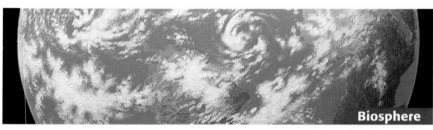

Biosphere

Ecosystem

Community

Population

Organism

Meeting the Neighbors

1. Explore two or three blocks of your neighborhood.

2. Draw a map of the area's biotic and abiotic features. For example, map the location of sidewalks, large rocks, trees, water features, and any animals you see. Remember to approach all plants and animals with caution. Use your map to answer the following questions.

3. How are the biotic factors affected by the abiotic factors?

4. How are the abiotic factors affected by the biotic factors?

Populations

A salt marsh, such as the one shown in **Figure 3,** is a coastal area where grasslike plants grow. Within the salt marsh are animals. Each animal is a part of a **population,** or a group of individuals of the same species that live together. For example, all of the seaside sparrows that live in the same salt marsh are members of a population. The individuals in the population often compete with one another for food, nesting space, and mates.

Communities

A **community** consists of all of the populations of species that live and interact in an area. The animals and plants you see in **Figure 3** form a salt-marsh community. The populations in a community depend on each other for food, shelter, and many other things.

population a group of organisms of the same species that live in a specific geographical area

community all the populations of species that live in the same habitat and interact with each other

Figure 3 *Examine the picture of a salt marsh. Try to find examples of each level of organization in this environment.*

Laughing gull

Egret

Cordgrass

Seaside sparrows eat insects, spiders, and small crabs. A male and his mate weave a nest out of cordgrass stalks.

Heron

Juvenile sea croaker

The little marsh crab eats cordgrass as well as tiny shrimp.

Some animals eat cordgrass, along with the microscopic algae that grow on the surface of its leaves and stems.

Jellyfish

The periwinkle snail eats the algae that grow on the cordgrass. The periwinkle snail also uses the cordgrass as a place to hide from predators.

Ecosystems

An **ecosystem** is made up of a community of organisms and the abiotic environment of the community. An ecologist studying the ecosystem could examine how organisms interact as well as how temperature, precipitation, and soil characteristics affect the organisms. For example, the rivers that empty into the salt marsh carry nutrients, such as nitrogen, from the land. These nutrients affect the growth of the cordgrass and algae.

The Biosphere

The **biosphere** is the part of Earth where life exists. It extends from the deepest parts of the ocean to high in the air where plant spores drift. Ecologists study the biosphere to learn how organisms interact with the abiotic environment—Earth's atmosphere, water, soil, and rock. The water in the abiotic environment includes fresh water and salt water as well as water that is frozen in polar icecaps and glaciers.

✓ **Reading Check** **What is the biosphere?** (*See the Appendix for answers to Reading Checks.*)

ecosystem a community of organisms and their abiotic environment

biosphere the part of Earth where life exists

For another activity related to this chapter, go to go.hrw.com and type in the keyword HL5INTW.

SECTION Review

Summary

- All living things are connected in a web of life.
- The biotic part of an environment is made up of all of the living things found within it.
- The abiotic part of an environment is made up of all of the nonliving things found within it, such as water and light.
- An ecosystem is made up of a community of organisms and its abiotic environment.

Using Key Terms

1. In your own words, write a definition for the term *ecology*.

2. Use the following terms in the same sentence: *biotic* and *abiotic*.

Understanding Key Ideas

3. Which one of the following is the highest level of environmental organization?

   a. ecosystem   **c.** population
   b. community   **d.** organism

4. What makes up a community?

5. Give two examples of how abiotic factors can affect an ecosystem.

Math Skills

6. From sea level, the biosphere goes up about 9 km and down about 19 km. What is the thickness of the biosphere in meters?

Critical Thinking

7. **Analyzing Relationships** What would happen to the other organisms in the salt-marsh ecosystem if the cordgrass suddenly died?

8. **Identifying Relationships** Explain in your own words what people mean when they say that everything is connected.

9. **Analyzing Ideas** Do ecosystems have borders? Explain your answer.

SCILINKS

Developed and maintained by the National Science Teachers Association

For a variety of links related to this chapter, go to www.scilinks.org

Topic: Biotic and Abiotic Factors; Organization in the Environment
SciLinks code: HSM0164; HSM1079

SECTION 2

Living Things Need Energy

Do you think you could survive on only water and vitamins? Eating food satisfies your hunger because it provides something you cannot live without—energy.

What You Will Learn

- Describe the functions of producers, consumers, and decomposers in an ecosystem.
- Distinguish between a food chain and a food web.
- Explain how energy flows through a food web.
- Describe how the removal of one species affects the entire food web.

Vocabulary

herbivore	food chain
carnivore	food web
omnivore	energy pyramid

READING STRATEGY

Reading Organizer As you read this section, make a table comparing producers, consumers, and decomposers.

Living things need energy to survive. For example, black-tailed prairie dogs, which live in the grasslands of North America, eat grass and seeds to get the energy they need. Everything a prairie dog does requires energy. The same is true for the plants that grow in the grasslands where the prairie dogs live.

The Energy Connection

Organisms, in a prairie or any community, can be divided into three groups based on how they get energy. These groups are producers, consumers, and decomposers. Examine **Figure 1** to see how energy passes through an ecosystem.

Producers

Organisms that use sunlight directly to make food are called *producers*. They do this by using a process called *photosynthesis*. Most producers are plants, but algae and some bacteria are also producers. Grasses are the main producers in a prairie ecosystem. Examples of producers in other ecosystems include cordgrass and algae in a salt marsh and trees in a forest. Algae are the main producers in the ocean.

Figure 1 *Living things get their energy either from the sun or from eating other organisms.*

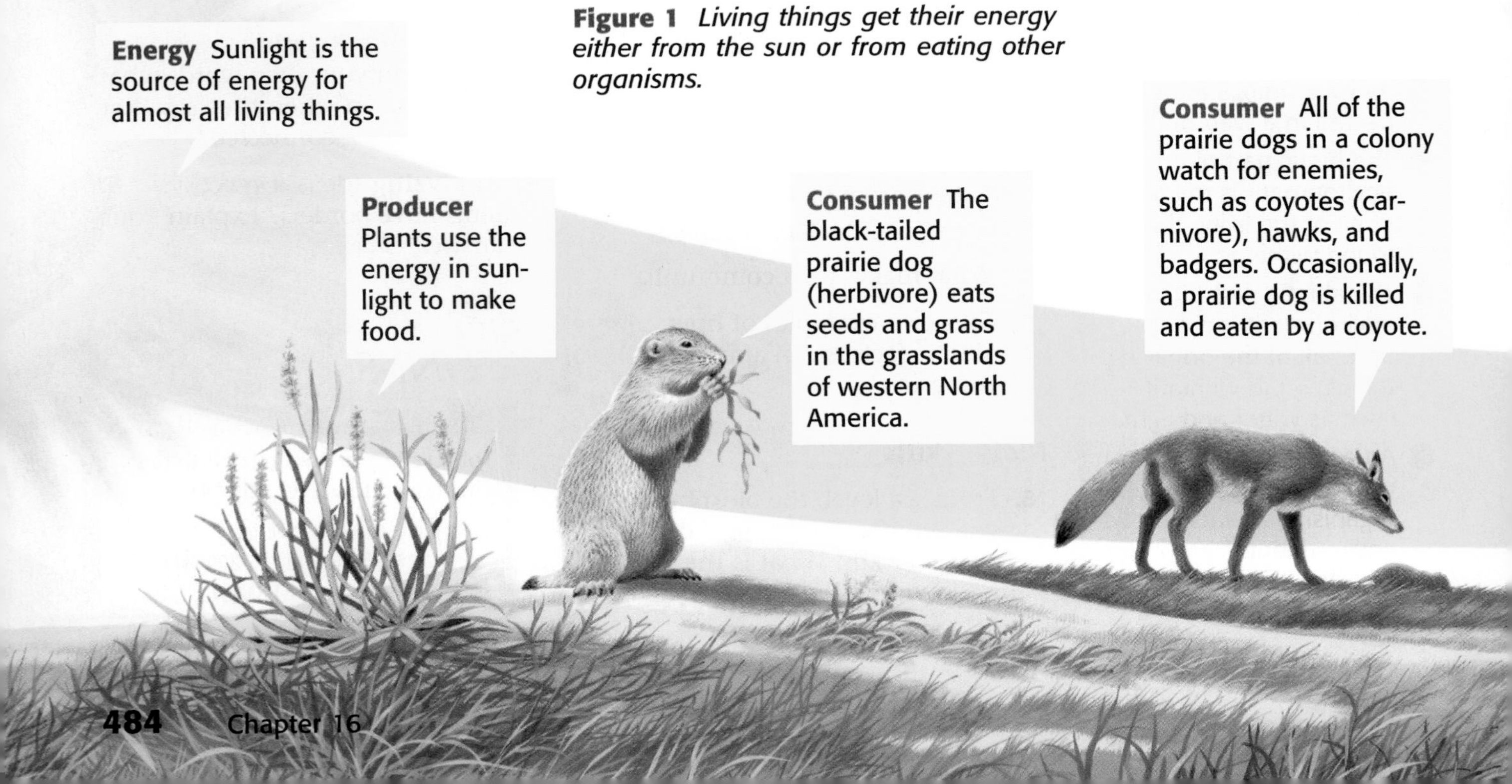
Energy Sunlight is the source of energy for almost all living things.
Producer Plants use the energy in sunlight to make food.
Consumer The black-tailed prairie dog (herbivore) eats seeds and grass in the grasslands of western North America.
Consumer All of the prairie dogs in a colony watch for enemies, such as coyotes (carnivore), hawks, and badgers. Occasionally, a prairie dog is killed and eaten by a coyote.

Consumers

Organisms that eat other organisms are called *consumers*. They cannot use the sun's energy to make food like producers can. Instead, consumers eat producers or other animals to obtain energy. There are several kinds of consumers. A consumer that eats only plants is called a **herbivore.** Herbivores found in the prairie include grasshoppers, prairie dogs, and bison. A **carnivore** is a consumer that eats animals. Carnivores in the prairie include coyotes, hawks, badgers, and owls. Consumers known as **omnivores** eat both plants and animals. The grasshopper mouse is an example of an omnivore. It eats insects, lizards, and grass seeds.

Scavengers are omnivores that eat dead plants and animals. The turkey vulture is a scavenger in the prairie. A vulture will eat what is left after a coyote has killed and eaten an animal. Scavengers also eat animals and plants that have died from natural causes.

✓Reading Check What are organisms that eat other organisms called? (*See the Appendix for answers to Reading Checks*.)

Decomposers

Organisms that get energy by breaking down dead organisms are called *decomposers*. Bacteria and fungi are decomposers. These organisms remove stored energy from dead organisms. They produce simple materials, such as water and carbon dioxide, which can be used by other living things. Decomposers are important because they are nature's recyclers.

herbivore an organism that eats only plants

carnivore an organism that eats animals

omnivore an organism that eats both plants and animals

A Chain Game

With the help of your parent, make a list of the foods you ate at your most recent meal. Trace the energy of each food back to the sun. Which foods on your list were consumers? How many were producers?

Consumer A turkey vulture (scavenger) may eat some of the coyote's leftovers. A scavenger can pick bones completely clean.

Decomposer Any prairie dog remains not eaten by the coyote or the turkey vulture are broken down by bacteria (decomposer) and fungi that live in the soil.

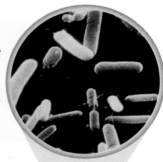

Food Chains and Food Webs

food chain the pathway of energy transfer through various stages as a result of the feeding patterns of a series of organisms

food web a diagram that shows the feeding relationships between organisms in an ecosystem

Figure 1 on the previous page, shows a food chain. A **food chain** is a diagram that shows how energy in food flows from one organism to another. Because few organisms eat just one kind of food, simple food chains are rare.

The energy connections in nature are more accurately shown by a food web than by a food chain. A **food web** is a diagram that shows the feeding relationships between organisms in an ecosystem. **Figure 2** shows a simple food web. Notice that an arrow goes from the prairie dog to the coyote, showing that the prairie dog is food for the coyote. The prairie dog is also food for the mountain lion. Energy moves from one organism to the next in a one-way direction, even in a food web. Any energy not immediately used by an organism is stored in its tissues. Only the energy stored in an organism's tissues can be used by the next consumer. There are two main food webs on Earth: a land food web and an aquatic food web.

Figure 2 *The green arrows show how energy moves when one organism eats another. Most consumers eat a variety of foods and can be eaten by a variety of other consumers.*

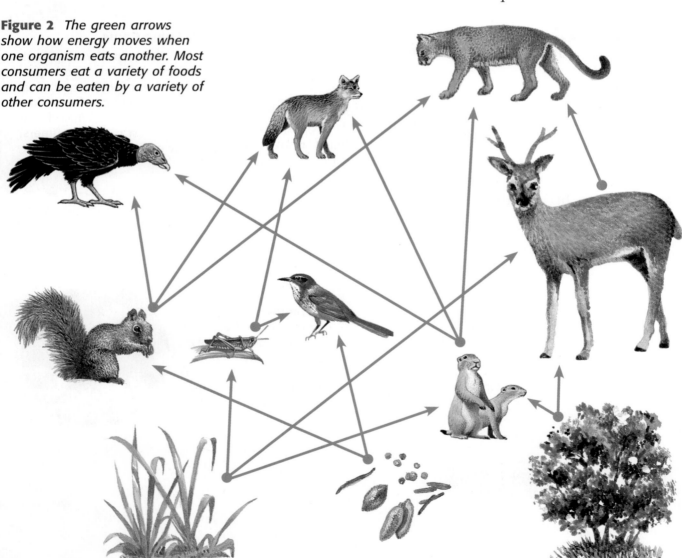

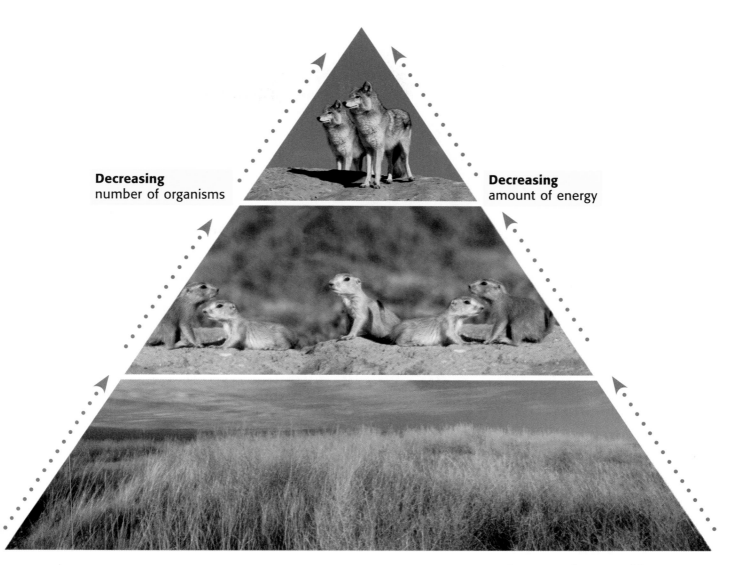

Decreasing number of organisms

Decreasing amount of energy

Figure 3 *The pyramid represents energy. As you can see, more energy is available at the base of the pyramid than at its top.*

Energy Pyramids

Grass uses most of the energy it gets from sunlight for its own life processes. But some of the energy is stored in the grass' tissues. This energy is used by the prairie dogs and other animals that eat the grass. Prairie dogs use most of the energy they get from eating grass and store only a little in their tissues. Therefore, a population of prairie dogs can support only a few coyotes. In the community, there must be more grass than prairie dogs and more prairie dogs than coyotes.

The energy at each level of the food chain can be seen in an energy pyramid. An **energy pyramid** is a diagram that shows an ecosystem's loss of energy. An example of an energy pyramid is shown in **Figure 3.** You can see that the energy pyramid has a large base and a small top. Less energy is available at higher levels because only energy stored in the tissues of an organism can be transferred to the next level.

☑ Reading Check What is an energy pyramid?

energy pyramid a triangular diagram that shows an ecosystem's loss of energy, which results as energy passes through the ecosystem's food chain

Figure 4 *As the wilderness was settled, the gray wolf population in the United States declined.*

Wolves and the Energy Pyramid

One species can be very important to the flow of energy in an environment. Gray wolves, which are shown in **Figure 4,** are consumers that control the populations of many other animals. The diet of gray wolves can include anything from a lizard to an elk. Because gray wolves are predators that prey on large animals, their place is at the top of the food pyramid.

Once common throughout much of the United States, gray wolves were almost wiped out as the wilderness was settled. Without wolves, some species, such as elk, were no longer controlled. The overpopulation of elk in some areas led to overgrazing. The overgrazing left too little grass to support the elk and other populations who depended on the grass for food. Soon, almost all of the populations in the area were affected by the loss of the gray wolves.

✔ **Reading Check** How were other animals affected by the disappearance of the gray wolf?

Gray Wolves and the Food Web

Gray wolves were brought back to Yellowstone National Park in 1995. The reintroduced wolves soon began to breed. **Figure 5** shows a wolf caring for pups. The U.S. Fish and Wildlife Service thinks the return of the wolves will restore the natural energy flow in the area, bring populations back into balance, and help restore the park's natural integrity.

Not everyone approves, however. Ranchers near Yellowstone are concerned about the safety of their livestock. Cows and sheep are not the natural prey of wolves. However, the wolves will eat cows and sheep if they are given the chance.

Figure 5 *In small wolf packs, only one female has pups. They are cared for by all of the males and females in the pack.*

Balance in Ecosystems

As wolves become reestablished in Yellowstone National Park, they kill the old, injured, and diseased elk. This process is reducing the number of elk. The smaller elk population is letting more plants grow. So, the numbers of animals that eat the plants, such as snowshoe hares, and the animals that eat the hares, such as foxes, are increasing.

All organisms in a food web are important for the health and balance of all other organisms in the food web. But the debate over the introduction of wolves to Yellowstone National Park will most likely continue for years to come.

Energy Pyramids

Draw an energy pyramid for a river ecosystem that contains four levels—aquatic plants, insect larvae, bluegill fish, and a largemouth bass. The plants obtain 10,000 units of energy from sunlight. If each level uses 90% of the energy it receives from the previous level, how many units of energy are available to the bass?

SECTION
Review

Summary

- Producers use the energy in sunlight to make their own food.
- Consumers eat producers and other organisms to gain energy.
- Food chains represent how energy flows from one organism to another.
- All organisms are important to maintain the balance of energy in the food web.
- Energy pyramids show how energy is lost at each food chain level.

Using Key Terms

1. Use each of the following terms in a separate sentence: *herbivores, carnivores,* and *omnivores.*

2. In your own words, write a definition for each of the following terms: *food chain, food web,* and *energy pyramid.*

Understanding Key Ideas

3. Herbivores, carnivores, and scavengers are all examples of
   a. producers.   c. consumers.
   b. decomposers.   d. omnivores.

4. Explain the importance of decomposers in an ecosystem.

5. Describe how producers, consumers, and decomposers are linked in a food chain.

6. Describe how energy flows through a food web.

Math Skills

7. The plants in each square meter of an ecosystem obtained 20,810 Calories of energy from sunlight per year. The herbivores in that ecosystem ate all the plants but obtained only 3,370 Calories of energy. How much energy did the plants use?

Critical Thinking

8. **Identifying Relationships** Draw two food chains, and depict how they link together to form a food web.

9. **Applying Concepts** Are consumers found at the top or bottom of an energy pyramid? Explain your answer.

10. **Predicting Consequences** What would happen if a species disappeared from an ecosystem?

Developed and maintained by the National Science Teachers Association

For a variety of links related to this chapter, go to www.scilinks.org

Topic: Food Chains and Food Webs
SciLinks code: HSM0594

Types of Interactions

What You Will Learn

● Explain the relationship between carrying capacity and limiting factors.
● Describe the two types of competition.
● Distinguish between mutualism, commensalism, and parasitism. Give an example of coevolution.

Vocabulary

carrying capacity   mutualism
prey   commensalism
predator   parasitism
symbiosis   coevolution

READING STRATEGY

Reading Organizer As you read this section, make a concept map by using the terms above.

Look at the seaweed forest shown in **Figure 1** below. How many fish do you see? How many seaweed plants do you count? Why do you think there are more members of the seaweed population than members of the fish population?

In natural communities, the sizes of populations of different organisms can vary greatly. This variation happens because everything in the environment affects every other thing. Populations also affect every other population.

Interactions with the Environment

Most living things produce more offspring than will survive. A female frog, for example, might lay hundreds of eggs in a small pond. In a few months, the population of frogs in that pond will be about the same as it was the year before. Why won't the pond become overrun with frogs? An organism, such as a frog, interacts with biotic and abiotic factors in its environment that can control the size of its population.

Limiting Factors

Populations cannot grow without stopping, because the environment contains a limited amount of food, water, living space, and other resources. A resource that is so scarce that it limits the size of a population is called a *limiting factor*. For example, food becomes a limiting factor when a population becomes too large for the amount of food available. Any single resource can be a limiting factor to a population's size.

Figure 1 *This seaweed forest is home to a large number of interacting species.*

Carrying Capacity

The largest population that an environment can support is known as the **carrying capacity.** When a population grows larger than its carrying capacity, limiting factors in the environment cause individuals to die off or leave. As individuals die or leave, the population decreases.

For example, after a rainy season, plants may produce a large crop of leaves and seeds. This large amount of food may cause an herbivore population to grow. If the next year has less rainfall, there won't be enough food to support the large herbivore population. In this way, a population may become larger than the carrying capacity, but only for a little while. A limiting factor will cause the population to die back. The population will return to a size that the environment can support.

carrying capacity the largest population that an environment can support at any given time

Interactions Between Organisms

Populations contain individuals of a single species that interact with one another, such as a group of rabbits feeding in the same area. Communities contain interacting populations, such as a coral reef with many species of corals trying to find living space. Ecologists have described four main ways that species and individuals affect each other: competition, predators and prey, symbiotic relationships, and coevolution.

✔ Reading Check **What are four main ways organisms affect one another?** (*See the Appendix for answers to Reading Checks.*)

Competition

When two or more individuals or populations try to use the same resource, such as food, water, shelter, space, or sunlight, it is called *competition.* Because resources are in limited supply in the environment, their use by one individual or population decreases the amount available to other organisms.

Competition happens between individuals *within* a population. The elks in Yellowstone National Park are herbivores that compete with each other for the same food plants in the park. This competition is a big problem in winter when many plants die.

Competition also happens *between* populations. The different species of trees in **Figure 2** are competing with each other for sunlight and space.

Figure 2 *Some of the trees in this forest grow tall to reach sunlight, which reduces the amount of sunlight available to shorter trees nearby.*

prey an organism that is killed and eaten by another organism

predator an organism that eats all or part of another organism

Predators and Prey

Many interactions between species consist of one organism eating another. The organism that is eaten is called the **prey.** The organism that eats the prey is called the **predator.** When a bird eats a worm, the worm is prey and the bird is the predator.

Predator Adaptations

To survive, predators must be able to catch their prey. Predators have a wide variety of methods and abilities for doing so. The cheetah, for example, is able to run very quickly to catch its prey. The cheetah's speed gives it an advantage over other predators competing for the same prey.

Other predators, such as the goldenrod spider, shown in **Figure 3,** ambush their prey. The goldenrod spider blends in so well with the goldenrod flower that all it has to do is wait for its next insect meal to arrive.

Prey Adaptations

Prey have their own methods and abilities to keep from being eaten. Prey are able to run away, stay in groups, or camouflage themselves. Some prey are poisonous. They may advertise their poison with bright colors to warn predators to stay away. The fire salamander, shown in **Figure 4,** sprays a poison that burns. Predators quickly learn to recognize its *warning coloration.*

Many animals run away from predators. Prairie dogs run to their underground burrows when a predator approaches. Many small fishes, such as anchovies, swim in groups called *schools.* Antelopes and buffaloes stay in herds. All the eyes, ears, and noses of the individuals in the group are watching, listening, and smelling for predators. This behavior increases the likelihood of spotting a potential predator.

Figure 3 *The goldenrod spider is difficult for its insect prey to see. Can you see it?*

Figure 4 *Many predators know better than to eat the fire salamander! This colorful animal will make a predator very sick.*

Camouflage

One way animals avoid being eaten is by being hard to see. A rabbit often freezes so that its natural color blends into a background of shrubs or grass. Blending in with the background is called *camouflage*. Many animals mimic twigs, leaves, stones, bark, or other materials in their environment. One insect, called a walking stick, looks just like a twig. Some walking sticks even sway a bit, as though a breeze were blowing.

✓ **Reading Check** What is camouflage, and how does it prevent an animal from being eaten?

Defensive Chemicals

The spines of a porcupine clearly signal trouble to a potential predator, but other defenses may not be as obvious. Some animals defend themselves with chemicals. The skunk and the bombardier beetle both spray predators with irritating chemicals. Bees, ants, and wasps inject a powerful acid into their attackers. The skin of both the poison arrow frog and a bird called the *hooded pitohui* contains a deadly toxin. Any predator that eats, or tries to eat, one of these animals will likely die.

Warning Coloration

Animals that have a chemical defense need a way to warn predators that they should look elsewhere for a meal. Their chemical weapons are often advertised by warning colors, as shown in **Figure 5.** Predators will avoid any animal that has the colors and patterns they associate with pain, illness, or unpleasant experiences. The most common warning colors are bright shades of red, yellow, orange, black, and white.

CONNECTION TO Environmental Science

Pretenders Some animals are pretenders. They don't have defensive chemicals. But they use warning coloration to their advantage. The Scarlet king snake has colored stripes that make it look like the poisonous coral snake. Even though the Scarlet king snake is harmless, predators see its bright colors and leave it alone. What might happen if there were more pretenders than there were animals with real defensive chemicals?

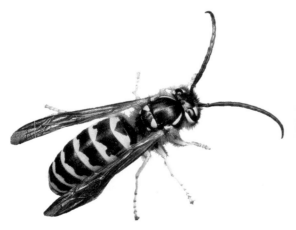

Figure 5 *The warning coloration of the yellow jacket (left) and the pitohui (above) warns predators that they are dangerous.*

Symbiosis

Some species have very close interactions with other species. **Symbiosis** is a close, long-term association between two or more species. The individuals in a symbiotic relationship can benefit from, be unaffected by, or be harmed by the relationship. Often, one species lives in or on the other species. The thousands of symbiotic relationships in nature are often classified into three groups: mutualism, commensalism, and parasitism.

symbiosis a relationship in which two different organisms live in close association with each other

mutualism a relationship between two species in which both species benefit

commensalism a relationship between two organisms in which one organism benefits and the other is unaffected

Mutualism

A symbiotic relationship in which both organisms benefit is called **mutualism** (MYOO choo uhl IZ uhm). For example, you and a species of bacteria that lives in your intestines benefit each other! The bacteria get food from you, and you get vitamins that the bacteria produce.

Mutualism also occurs between some corals and the algae living inside those corals. In this relationship, a coral receives the extra food that the algae make by photosynthesis. In turn, these algae also receive a place to live, as **Figure 6** shows. These algae also receive some nutrients from the coral. Both organisms benefit from this relationship.

Figure 6 *In the smaller photo above, you can see the gold-colored algae inside the coral.*

✓ **Reading Check** Which organism benefits in mutualism?

Commensalism

A symbiotic relationship in which one organism benefits and the other is unaffected is called **commensalism.** One example of commensalism is the relationship between sharks and smaller fish called *remoras*. **Figure 7** shows a shark with a remora attached to its body. Remoras "hitch a ride" and feed on scraps of food left by sharks. The remoras benefit from this relationship, while sharks are unaffected.

Figure 7 *The remora attached to the shark benefits from the relationship. The shark neither benefits from nor is harmed by the relationship.*

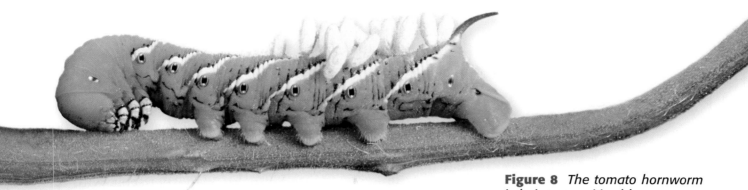

Figure 8 *The tomato hornworm is being parasitized by young wasps. Do you see their cocoons?*

Parasitism

A symbiotic association in which one organism benefits while the other is harmed is called **parasitism** (PAR uh SIT IZ uhm). The organism that benefits is called the *parasite*. The organism that is harmed is called the *host*. The parasite gets nourishment from its host while the host is weakened. Sometimes, a host dies. Parasites, such as ticks, live outside the host's body. Other parasites, such as tapeworms, live inside the host's body.

Figure 8 shows a bright green caterpillar called a *tomato hornworm*. A female wasp laid tiny eggs on the caterpillar. When the eggs hatch, each young wasp will burrow into the caterpillar's body. The young wasps will actually eat the caterpillar alive! In a short time, the caterpillar will be almost completely eaten and will die. When that happens, the adult wasps will fly away.

In this example of parasitism, the host dies. Most parasites, however, do not kill their hosts. Most parasites don't kill their hosts because parasites depend on their hosts. If a parasite were to kill its host, the parasite would have to find a new host.

parasitism a relationship between two species in which one species, the parasite, benefits from the other species, the host, which is harmed

coevolution the evolution of two species that is due to mutual influence, often in a way that makes the relationship more beneficial to both species

Coevolution

Relationships between organisms change over time. Interactions can also change the organisms themselves. When a long-term change takes place in two species because of their close interactions with one another, the change is called **coevolution.**

The ant and the acacia tree shown in **Figure 9** have a mutualistic relationship. The ants protect the tree by attacking other organisms that come near the tree. The tree has special structures that make food for the ants. The ants and the acacia tree may have coevolved through interactions between the two species. Coevolution can take place between any organisms that live close together. But changes happen over a very long period of time.

Figure 9 *Ants collect food made by the acacia tree and store the food in their shelter, which is also made by the tree.*

Rabbits in Australia In 1859, settlers released 12 rabbits in Australia. There was plenty of food and no natural predators for the rabbits. The rabbit population increased so fast that the country was soon overrun by rabbits. Then, the Australian government introduced a rabbit virus to control the population. The first time the virus was used, more than 99% of the rabbits died. The survivors reproduced, and the rabbit population grew large again. The second time the virus was used, about 90% of the rabbits died. Once again, the rabbit population increased. The third time the virus was used, only about 50% of the rabbits died. Suggest what changes might have occurred in the rabbits and the virus.

Coevolution and Flowers

A *pollinator* is an organism that carries pollen from one flower to another. Pollination is necessary for reproduction in most plants.

Flowers have changed over millions of years to attract pollinators. Pollinators such as bees, bats, and hummingbirds can be attracted to a flower because of its color, odor, or nectar. Flowers pollinated by hummingbirds make nectar with the right amount of sugar for the bird. Hummingbirds have long beaks, which help them drink the nectar.

Some bats, such as the one shown in **Figure 10,** changed over time to have long, thin tongues and noses to help them reach the nectar in flowers. As the bat feeds on the nectar, its nose becomes covered with pollen. The next flower it eats from will be pollinated with the pollen it is gathering from this flower. The long nose helps it to feed and also makes it a better pollinator.

Because flowers and their pollinators have interacted so closely over millions of years, there are many examples of coevolution between them.

Reading Check Why do flowers need to attract pollinators?

Figure 10 *This bat is drinking nectar with its long, skinny tongue. The bat has coevolved with the flower over millions of years.*

SECTION Review

Summary

- Limiting factors in the environment keep a population from growing without limit.
- Two or more individuals or populations trying to use the same resource is called *competition.*
- A predator is an organism that eats all or part of another organism. The organism that is eaten is called *prey.*
- Prey have developed features such as camouflage, chemical defenses, and warning coloration, to protect them from predators.
- Symbiosis occurs when two organisms form a very close relationship with one another over time.
- Close relationships over a very long time can result in coevolution. For example, flowers and their pollinators have evolved traits that benefit both.

Using Key Terms

1. In your own words, write a definition for the term *carrying capacity*.

2. Use each of the following terms in a separate sentence: *mutualism, commensalism,* and *parasitism*.

Understanding Key Ideas

3. Which of the following is NOT a prey adaptation?
   - **a.** camouflage
   - **b.** chemical defenses
   - **c.** warning coloration
   - **d.** parasitism

4. Identify two things organisms compete with one another for.

5. Briefly describe one example of a predator-prey relationship. Identify the predator and the prey.

Critical Thinking

6. **Making Comparisons** Compare coevolution with symbiosis.

7. **Identifying Relationships** Explain the probable relationship between the giant *Rafflesia* flower, which smells like rotting meat, and the carrion flies that buzz around it. (Hint: *Carrion* means "rotting flesh.")

8. **Predicting Consequences** Predict what might happen if all of the ants were removed from an acacia tree.

Interpreting Graphics

The population graph below shows the growth of a species of *Paramecium* (single-celled microorganism) over 18 days. Food was added to the test tube occasionally. Use this graph to answer the questions that follow.

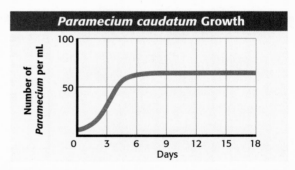

Paramecium caudatum Growth

Number of Paramecium per mL (y-axis: 0, 50, 100)

Days (x-axis: 0, 3, 6, 9, 12, 15, 18)

9. What is the carrying capacity of the test tube as long as food is added?

10. Predict what will happen if no more food is added?

11. What keeps the number of *Paramecium* at a steady level?

Skills Practice Lab

Capturing the Wild Bean

When wildlife biologists study a group of organisms in an area, they need to know how many organisms live there. Sometimes, biologists worry that a certain organism is outgrowing the environment's carrying capacity. Other times, scientists need to know if an organism is becoming rare so that steps can be taken to protect it. However, animals can be difficult to count because they can move around and hide. Because of this challenge, biologists have developed methods to estimate the number of animals in a specific area. One of these counting methods is called the *mark-recapture method*.

In this activity, you will enter the territory of the wild pinto bean to estimate the number of beans that live in the paper-bag habitat.

Procedure

1 Prepare a data table like the one below.

Mark-Recapture Data Table				
Number of animals in first capture	Total number of animals in recapture	Number of marked animals in recapture	Calculated estimate of population	Actual total population
	DO NOT WRITE IN BOOK			

2 Your teacher will provide you with a paper bag containing an unknown number of beans. Carefully reach into the bag, and remove a handful of beans.

3) Count the number of beans you have "captured." Record this number in your data table under "Number of animals in first capture."

4) Use the permanent marker to carefully mark each bean that you have just counted. Allow the marks to dry completely. When all the marks are dry, place the marked beans back into the bag.

5) Gently mix the beans in the bag so that the marks won't rub off. Once again, reach into the bag. "Capture" and remove a handful of beans.

6) Count the number of beans in your "recapture." Record this number in your data table under "Total number of animals in recapture."

7) Count the beans in your recapture that have marks from the first capture. Record this number in your data table under "Number of marked animals in recapture."

8) Calculate your estimation of the total number of beans in the bag by using the following equation:

$$\frac{\text{number of beans in recapture} \times \text{number of beans marked}}{\text{number of marked beans in recapture}} = \text{calculated estimate of population}$$

Enter this number in your data table under "Calculated estimate of population."

9) Place all the beans in the bag. Then empty the bag on your work table. Be careful that no beans escape! Count each bean as you place them one at a time back into the bag. Record the number in your data table under "Actual total population."

Analyze the Results

1) **Evaluating Results** How close was your estimate to the actual number of beans?

Draw Conclusions

2) **Evaluating Methods** If your estimate was not close to the actual number of beans, how might you change your mark-recapture procedure? If you did not recapture any marked beans, what might be the cause?

Applying Your Data

How could you use the mark-recapture method to estimate the population of turtles in a small pond? Explain your procedure.

Chapter Review

USING KEY TERMS

1 Use each of the following terms in a separate sentence: *symbiosis, mutualism, commensalism,* and *parasitism.*

Complete each of the following sentences by choosing the correct term from the word bank.

biotic   abiotic

ecosystem   community

2 The environment includes _____ factors including water, rocks, and light.

3 The environment also includes _____, or living, factors.

4 A community of organisms and their environment is called a(n) _____.

For each pair of terms, explain how the meanings of the terms differ.

5 *community* and *population*

6 *ecosystem* and *biosphere*

7 *producers* and *consumers*

UNDERSTANDING KEY IDEAS

Multiple Choice

8 A tick sucks blood from a dog. In this relationship, the tick is the _____ and the dog is the _____.

a. parasite, prey   **c.** parasite, host

b. predator, host   **d.** host, parasite

9 Resources such as water, food, or sunlight are likely to be limiting factors

a. when population size is decreasing.

b. when predators eat their prey.

c. when the population is small.

d. when a population is approaching the carrying capacity.

10 Nature's recyclers are

a. predators.   **c.** producers.

b. decomposers.   **d.** omnivores.

11 A beneficial association between coral and algae is an example of

a. commensalism.   **c.** mutualism.

b. parasitism.   **d.** predation.

12 The process by which energy moves through an ecosystem can be represented by

a. food chains.

b. energy pyramids.

c. food webs.

d. All of the above

13 Which organisms does the base of an energy pyramid represent?

a. producers   **c.** herbivores

b. carnivores   **d.** scavengers

14 Which of the following is the correct order in a food chain?

a. sun→producers→herbivores→scavengers→carnivores

b. sun→consumers→predators→parasites→hosts

c. sun→producers→decomposers→consumers→omnivores

d. sun→producers→herbivores→carnivores→scavengers

15 Remoras and sharks have a relationship that is best described as

a. mutualism.　　**c.** predator and prey.

b. commensalism. **d.** parasitism.

Short Answer

16 Describe how energy flows through a food web.

17 Explain how the food web changed when the gray wolf disappeared from Yellowstone National Park.

18 How are the competition between two trees of the same species and the competition between two different species of trees similiar?

19 How do limiting factors affect the carrying capacity of an environment?

20 What is coevolution?

CRITICAL THINKING

21 **Concept Mapping** Use the following terms to create a concept map: *herbivores, organisms, producers, populations, ecosystems, consumers, communities, carnivores,* and *biosphere.*

22 **Identifying Relationships** Could a balanced ecosystem contain producers and consumers but not decomposers? Why or why not?

23 **Predicting Consequences** Some biologists think that certain species, such as alligators and wolves, help maintain biological diversity in their ecosystems. Predict what might happen to other organisms, such as gar fish or herons, if alligators were to become extinct in the Florida Everglades.

24 **Expressing Opinions** Do you think there is a carrying capacity for humans? Why or why not?

INTERPRETING GRAPHICS

Use the energy pyramid below to answer the questions that follow.

25 According to the energy pyramid, are there more prairie dogs or plants?

26 What level has the most energy?

27 Would an energy pyramid such as this one exist in nature?

28 How could you change this pyramid to look like one representing a real ecosystem?

Standardized Test Preparation

Multiple Choice

1. **Population, community, biosphere, organism, and ecosystem are all terms that are related to the environment. Choose the set that has the terms arranged in order from simplest to most complex.**

   A. organism, population, community, biosphere, ecosystem

   B. organism, community, population, ecosystem, biosphere

   C. organism, population, community, ecosystem, biosphere

   D. biosphere, ecosystem, community, population, organism

2. **Which of the following can contain an ecosystem?**

   A. community

   B. population

   C. biosphere

   D. individual organism

3. **The characteristics of a praying mantis make it easy for it to be camouflaged by the green stems of plants. While camouflaged, a praying mantis can feed on other insects that inhabit or feed on a plant. If a praying mantis feeds on natural enemies of a plant, what type of relationship is occurring between the praying mantis and the plant?**

   A. camouflage

   B. competition

   C. mutualism

   D. parasitism

Use the picture below to answer question 4.

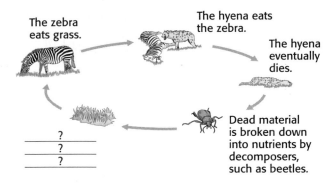

The zebra eats grass.

The hyena eats the zebra.

The hyena eventually dies.

Dead material is broken down into nutrients by decomposers, such as beetles.

?
?
?

4. **The diagram above shows a typical food chain in a grassland ecosystem. What description should go next to the drawing of grass to complete the food chain?**

   A. Grass grows by absorbing nutrients from the air and sun.

   B. Scavengers, such as vultures, eat grass.

   C. Grass is decomposed by sunlight and water.

   D. Grass grows by absorbing nutrients from the soil.

5. **Which of the following increases an animal's chance for survival?**

   A. Coloration on an insect makes it stand out from its physical surroundings.

   B. A wolf separates itself from the pack.

   C. A peacock's bright feathers make it easier to be spotted by predators.

   D. A frog's brightly colored skin alerts predators that it is poisonous.

6. Juanita finds an interesting lizard near a pond. Its tail is colored bright yellow and red. What type of defense against predators does this lizard most likely have?

   A. camouflage

   B. chemical

   C. grouping

   D. speed

7. Which of the following is NOT a limiting factor on a population in a land ecosystem?

   A. food

   B. water

   C. living space

   D. air

8. A pigeon finds its way home using landmarks such as mountain ranges and buildings. These landmarks are

   A. external stimuli.

   B. internal stimuli.

   C. known as body language.

   D. known as estivation.

Use the graph below to answer question 9.

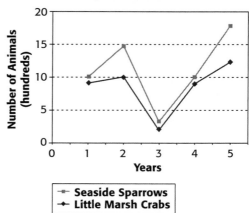

9. The graph above shows the number of seaside sparrows and little marsh crabs in a small salt marsh habitat over a five-year period. During this time, a disease killed off most of the cordgrass in the marsh. How many little marsh crabs were alive during the year that the disease occurred?

   A. 1

   B. 2

   C. 9

   D. 10

Open Response

10. Where would you expect to find the most stored energy in the ocean? Where would you find the least stored energy? Where would you expect to find producers and consumers? Explain.

11. What is the difference between a food chain and a food web? Explain why food chains are rare and food webs are common.

Science in Action

Scientific Debate

How Did Dogs Become Pets?

Did humans change dogs to be the social and helpful creatures they are today? Or were dogs naturally social? Did dogs start moving closer to our campfires long ago? Or did humans find dogs and bring them into our homes? The way in which dogs became our friends, companions, and helpers is still a question. Some scientists think humans and training are the reasons for many of our dogs' best features. Other scientists think dogs and humans have both changed over time to form their strong and unique bond.

Math ACTIVITY

Scientists have found fossils of dogs that are 15,000 years old. Generation time is the time between the birth of one generation and the next. If the generation time for dogs is 1.5 years, how many generations have there been in the last 15,000 years?

Weird Science

Follicle Mites

What has a tiny tubelike body and short stumpy legs and lives in your eyebrows and eyelashes? Would you believe a small animal lives there? It's called a follicle mite, and humans are its host. Studies show that more than 97% of adults have these mites. Except in rare cases, follicle mites are harmless.

Like all large animals, human beings are hosts to a variety of smaller creatures that live in or on our bodies and share our bodies' resources. Bacteria that live in our lower digestive tracks help to produce vitamins such as folic acid and vitamin K. Other bacteria may help maintain proper pH levels in our bodies.

Language Arts ACTIVITY

WRITING SKILL Imagine that you were shrunk to the size of a follicle mite. How would you get food? Where would you sleep? Write a short story describing one day in your new, tiny life.

Dalton Dockery

Horticulture Specialist Did you know that instead of using pesticides to get rid of insects that are eating the plants in your garden, you can use other insects? "It is a healthy way of growing vegetables without the use of chemicals and pesticides, and it reduces the harmful effects pesticides have on the environment," says Dalton Dockery, a horticulture specialist in North Carolina. Some insects, such as ladybugs and praying mantises, are natural predators of many insects that are harmful to plants. They will eat other bugs but leave your precious plants in peace. Using bugs to drive off pests is just one aspect of natural gardening. Natural gardening takes advantage of relationships that already exist in nature and uses these interactions to our benefit. For Dockery, the best parts about being a horticultural specialist are teaching people how to preserve the environment, getting to work outside regularly, and having the opportunity to help people on a daily basis.

Social Studies ACTiViTy

WRITING SKILL Research gardening or farming techniques in other cultures. Do other cultures use any of the same aspects of natural gardening as horticultural specialists? Write a short report describing your findings.

To learn more about these Science in Action topics, visit **go.hrw.com** and type in the keyword **HL5INTF.**

Current Science

Check out Current Science® articles related to this chapter by visiting go.hrw.com. Just type in the keyword HL5CS18.

Cycles in Nature

The Big Idea

Ecosystems change over time and depend on the cycling of matter.

About the Photo

These penguins have a unique playground on this iceberg off the coast of Antarctica. Icebergs break off from glaciers and float out to sea. A glacier is a giant "river" of ice that slides slowly downhill. Glaciers are formed from snow piling up in mountains. Eventually, glaciers and icebergs melt and become liquid water. Water in oceans and lakes rises into the air and then falls down again as rain or snow. There is a lot of water on Earth, and most of it is constantly moving and changing form.

PRE-READING ACTIVITY

FOLDNOTES **Pyramid** Before you read the chapter, create the FoldNote entitled "Pyramid" described in the **Study Skills** section of the Appendix. Label the sides of the pyramid with "Water cycle," "Carbon cycle," and "Nitrogen cycle." As you read the chapter, define each cycle, and write the steps of each cycle on the appropriate pyramid side.

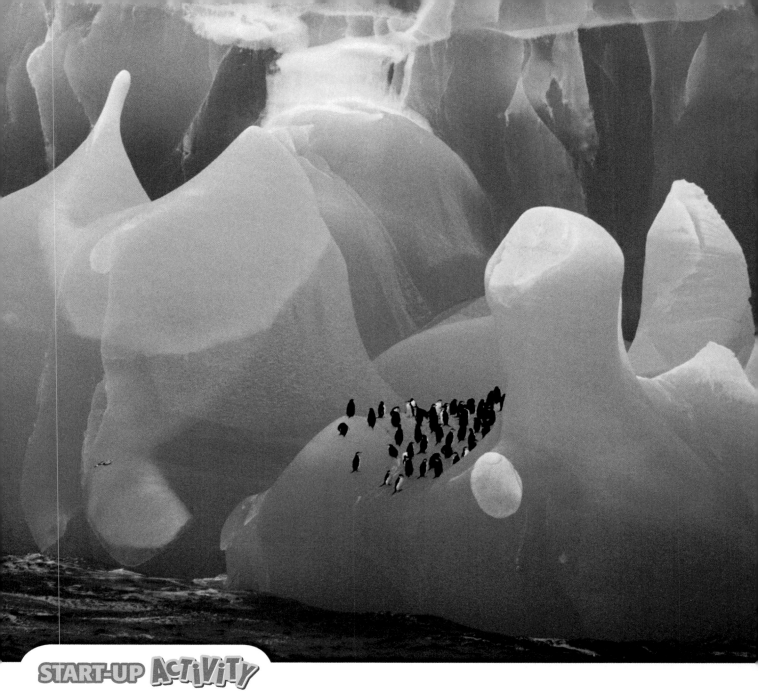

START-UP ACTIVITY

Making Rain

Do you have the power to make rain? Yes!—on a small scale. In this activity, you will cause water to change state in the same way that rain is formed. This process is one way that water is reused on Earth.

Procedure

1. Start with a **large, sealable, plastic freezer bag.** Be sure that the bag is clean and dry and has no leaks. Place a **small, dark-colored bowl** inside the bag. Position the bag with the opening at the top.

2. Fill the bowl halfway with water. Place a few drops of **red food coloring** in the water. Seal the bag.

3. Place the bowl and bag under a strong, warm **light source,** such as a lamp or direct sunlight.

4. Leave the bag in the light for as long as possible. Observe the bag at regular time intervals.

Analysis

1. Each time you observe the bag, describe what you see. Explain what you think is happening.

2. After observing the bag several times, carefully remove the bowl from the bag. Observe and describe any water that is now in the bag. Where did this water come from? How does it differ from the water in the bowl?

The Cycles of Matter

The matter in your body has been on Earth since the planet formed billions of years ago!

Matter on Earth is limited, so the matter is used over and over again. Each kind of matter has its own cycle. In these cycles, matter moves between the environment and living things.

The Water Cycle

The movement of water between the oceans, atmosphere, land, and living things is known as the *water cycle.* The parts of the water cycle are shown in **Figure 1.**

How Water Moves

During **evaporation,** the sun's heat causes water to change from liquid to vapor. In the process of **condensation,** the water vapor cools and returns to a liquid state. The water that falls from the atmosphere to the land and oceans is **precipitation.** Rain, snow, sleet, and hail are forms of precipitation. Most precipitation falls into the ocean. Some of the precipitation that falls on land flows into streams, rivers, and lakes and is called *runoff.* Some precipitation seeps into the ground and is stored in spaces between or within rocks. This water, known as *groundwater,* will slowly flow back into the soil, streams, rivers, and oceans.

What You Will Learn

- Diagram the water cycle, and explain its importance to living things.
- Diagram the carbon cycle, and explain its importance to living things.
- Diagram the nitrogen cycle, and explain its importance to living things.

Vocabulary

evaporation   decomposition
condensation   combustion
precipitation

evaporation the change of a substance from a liquid to a gas

condensation the change of state from a gas to a liquid

precipitation any form of water that falls to the Earth's surface from the clouds

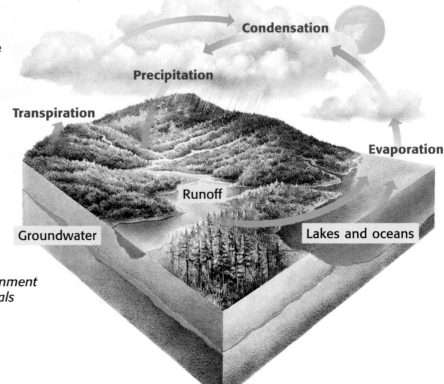

Figure 1 *Water from the environment moves through plants and animals and back to the environment.*

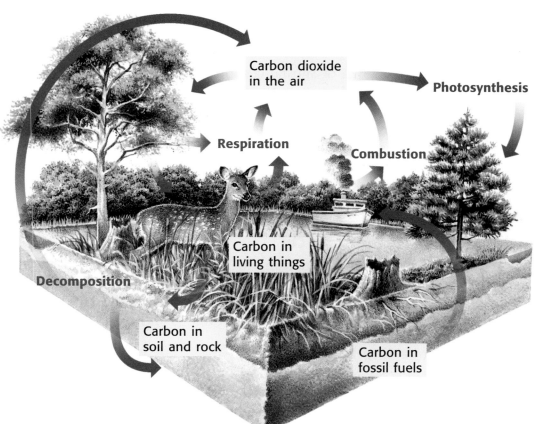

Figure 2 *Carbon may remain in the environment for millions of years before becoming available to living things.*

Water and Life

Without water, there would be no life on Earth. All organisms, from bacteria to animals and plants, are composed mostly of water. Water helps transport nutrients and wastes within an organism. Water also helps regulate temperature. For example, when you sweat, water evaporates from your skin and cools your body. Eventually, all the water taken in by organisms is returned to the environment. For example, plants release a large amount of water vapor in a process called *transpiration*.

✓ Reading Check Why is water important? (*See the Appendix for answers to Reading Checks.*)

The Carbon Cycle

Besides water, the most common molecules in living things are *organic* molecules, or molecules that contain carbon. The exchange of carbon between the environment and living things is known as the *carbon cycle*, as shown in **Figure 2.**

Photosynthesis and Respiration

Photosynthesis is the basis of the carbon cycle. During photosynthesis, plants use carbon dioxide from air to make sugars. Most animals get the carbon and energy they need by eating plants. How does carbon return to the environment? It returns when sugar molecules are broken down to release energy. This process, called *respiration*, uses oxygen. Carbon dioxide and water are released as byproducts of respiration.

MATH PRACTICE

Where's the Water?
There are about 37.5 million cubic kilometers of fresh water on Earth. Of this fresh water, about 8.3 million cubic kilometers is groundwater. What percentage of Earth's fresh water is groundwater?

decomposition the breakdown of substances into simpler molecular substances

combustion the burning of a substance

Combustion

1. Place a **candle** on a **jar lid,** and secure the candle with **modeling clay.** Have your teacher light the candle.

2. Hold the jar near the candle flame. Do not cover the flame with the jar. Describe the jar. Where did the substance on the jar come from?

3. Now, place the jar over the candle. What is deposited inside the jar? Where did this substance come from?

Decomposition and Combustion

The breakdown of substances into simpler molecules is called **decomposition.** For example, when fungi and bacteria decompose organic matter, carbon dioxide and water are returned to the environment. You may have witnessed another way to break down organic matter—using fire. **Combustion** is the process of burning a substance, such as wood or fossil fuels. Like decomposition, combustion of organic matter releases carbon dioxide into the atmosphere.

The Nitrogen Cycle

Nitrogen is also important to living things. Organisms need nitrogen to build proteins and DNA for new cells. The movement of nitrogen between the environment and living things is called the *nitrogen cycle.* This cycle is shown in **Figure 3.**

Converting Nitrogen Gas

About 78% of the Earth's atmosphere is nitrogen gas. Most organisms cannot use nitrogen gas directly. However, bacteria in the soil are able to change nitrogen gas into forms that plants can use. This process is called *nitrogen fixation.* Other organisms may then get the nitrogen they need by eating plants or eating organisms that eat plants.

Figure 3 *Without bacteria, nitrogen could not enter living things or be returned to the atmosphere.*

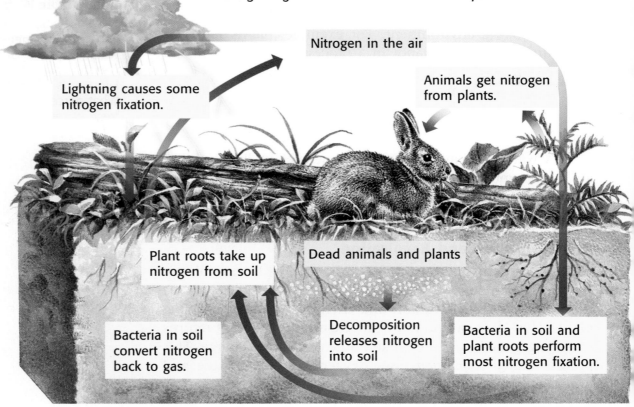

Nitrogen in the air

Lightning causes some nitrogen fixation.

Animals get nitrogen from plants.

Plant roots take up nitrogen from soil

Dead animals and plants

Bacteria in soil convert nitrogen back to gas.

Decomposition releases nitrogen into soil

Bacteria in soil and plant roots perform most nitrogen fixation.

Passing It On

When organisms die, decomposers break down the remains. Decomposition releases a form of nitrogen into the soil that plants can use. Finally, certain types of bacteria in the soil convert nitrogen to a gas, which is returned to the atmosphere.

Many Cycles

Other forms of matter on Earth also pass through cycles. Many of the minerals that living cells need, such as calcium and phosphorous, are cycled through the environment. When an organism dies, every substance in its body is likely to be recycled or reused.

Each of the cycles is connected in many ways. For example, some forms of nitrogen and carbon are carried through the environment by water. Many nutrients pass from soil to plants to animals and back. Living organisms play a part in each of the cycles.

✓ Reading Check Give an example of a form of matter—other than carbon, water, or nitrogen—that is cycled through the environment.

CONNECTION TO Environmental Science

Global Warming The quantity of carbon dioxide being released into the atmosphere is increasing. Carbon dioxide can cause the atmosphere to hold heat. A warmer atmosphere would cause the temperatures of the land and ocean to increase. Scientists think that this situation, known as *global warming,* may be happening. Research data on changes in average global temperature and carbon dioxide levels for the past 50 years, and summarize your findings.

SECTION Review

Summary

- Precipitation, evaporation, transpiration, and condensation are parts of the water cycle.
- Photosynthesis, respiration, decomposition, and combustion are parts of the carbon cycle.
- In the nitrogen cycle, nitrogen gas is converted into other forms and back to gas again.
- Many forms of matter on Earth pass through cycles. These cycles may be connected in many ways.

Using Key Terms

For each pair of terms, explain how the meanings of the terms differ.

1. *evaporation* and *condensatIion*

2. *decomposition* and *combustion*

Understanding Key Ideas

3. Nitrogen fixation
   a. is done only by plants.
   b. is done mostly by bacteria.
   c. is how animals make proteins.
   d. is a form of decomposition.

4. Describe the water cycle.

5. Describe the carbon cycle.

Math Skills

6. The average person in the United States uses about 78 gal of water each day. How many liters of water does this equal? How many liters of water will the average person use in a year?

Critical Thinking

7. **Analyzing Processes** Draw a simple diagram of each of the cycles discussed in this section. Draw lines between the cycles to show how parts of each cycle are related.

8. **Applying Concepts** Give an example of how the calcium in an animal's bones might be cycled back into the environment.

SCiLINKS **NSTA**

Developed and maintained by the National Science Teachers Association

For a variety of links related to this chapter, go to www.scilinks.org

Topic: Cycles of Matter
SciLinks code: HSM0373

Ecological Succession

Imagine you have a time machine that can take you back to the summer of 1988. If you had visited Yellowstone National Park during that year, you would have seen fires raging throughout the area.

By the end of that summer, large areas of the park were burned to the ground. When the fires were put out, a layer of gray ash blanketed the forest floor. Most of the trees were dead, although many of them were still standing.

Regrowth of a Forest

The following spring, the appearance of the "dead" forest began to change. **Figure 1** shows the changes after just one year. Some of the dead trees fell over, and small, green plants grew in large numbers. Within 10 years, scientists reported that many trees were growing and the forest community was coming back.

A gradual development of a community over time, such as the regrowth of the burned areas of Yellowstone National Park, is called **succession.** Succession takes place in all communities, not just those affected by disturbances such as forest fires.

✓ **Reading Check** What happened after the Yellowstone fires?
(*See the Appendix for answers to Reading Checks.*)

succession the replacement of one type of community by another at a single place over a period of time

Figure 1 *Huge areas of Yellowstone National Park were burned in 1988 (left). By the spring of 1989, regrowth was evident in the burned parts of the park (right).*

Primary Succession

Sometimes, a small community starts to grow in an area where other organisms had not previously lived. There is no soil in this area. And usually, there is just bare rock. Over a very long time, a series of organisms live and die on the rock. The rock is slowly transformed into soil. This process is called *primary succession,* as shown in **Figure 2.** The first organisms to live in an area are called **pioneer species.**

pioneer species a species that colonizes an uninhabited area and that starts a process of succession

Figure 2 An Example of Primary Succession

1 A slowly retreating glacier exposes bare rock where nothing lives, and primary succession begins.

2 Most primary succession begins with lichens. Acids from the lichens begin breaking the rocks into small particles. These particles mix with the remains of dead lichens to start forming soil. Lichens are an example of a pioneer species.

3 After many years, there is enough soil for mosses to grow. The mosses eventually replace the lichens. Insects and other tiny organisms begin to live there. When they die, their remains add to the soil.

4 Over time, the soil deepens, and the mosses are replaced by ferns. The ferns may slowly be replaced by grasses and wildflowers. If there is enough soil, shrubs and small trees may grow.

5 After hundreds or even thousands of years, the soil may be deep and stable enough to support a forest.

INTERNET ACTIVITY

For another activity related to this chapter, go to **go.hrw.com** and type in the keyword **HL5CYCW**.

Secondary Succession

Sometimes, an existing community is destroyed by a natural disaster, such as a fire or a flood. Sometimes, a community is affected by another type of disturbance. For example, a farmer might stop growing crops in an area that had been cleared. In either case, if soil is left intact, the original community may regrow through a series of stages called *secondary succession*. **Figure 3** shows an example of secondary succession.

✓ **Reading Check** How does secondary succession differ from primary succession?

Figure 3   An Example of Secondary Succession

❶ The first year after a farmer stops growing crops or the first year after some other major disturbance, weeds start to grow. In farming areas, crab grass is the weed that often grows first.

❷ By the second year, new weeds appear. Their seeds may have been blown into the field by the wind, or insects may have carried them. Horseweed is common during the second year.

❸ In 5 to 15 years, small conifer trees may start growing among the weeds. The trees continue to grow, and after about 100 years, a forest may form.

❹ As older conifers die, they may be replaced by hardwoods, such as oak or maple trees, if the climate can support them.

Mature Communities and Biodiversity

In the early stages of succession, only a few species grow in an area. These species grow quickly and make many seeds that scatter easily. But all species are vulnerable to disease, disturbances, and competition. As a community matures, it may be dominated by well-adapted, slow-growing *climax species*.

Furthermore, as succession proceeds, more species may become established. The variety of species that are present in an area is referred to as *biodiversity*. Biodiversity is important to communities of organisms. For example, a forest that has a high degree of biodiversity is less likely to be destroyed by an invasion of insects. Most plant-damaging insects prefer to attack only one species of plants. The presence of a variety of plants will lessen the impact and spread of invading insects.

Keep in mind that a mature community may not always be a forest. A mature community simply has organisms that are well adapted to live together in the same area over time. For example, the plants of the Sonoran Desert, shown in **Figure 4,** are well-adapted to the desert's conditions.

Figure 4 *This area of the Sonoran Desert in Arizona is a mature community.*

SECTION Review

Summary

- Ecological succession is the gradual development of communities over time. Often a series of stages is observed during succession.
- Primary succession occurs in an area that was not previously inhabited by living things; no soil is present.
- Secondary succession takes place in an area where an earlier community was disturbed by fire, landslides, floods, or plowing for crops and where soil is present.

Using Key Terms

1. In your own words, write a definition for the term *succession*.

Understanding Key Ideas

2. An area where a glacier has just melted away will begin the process of
   a. primary succession.
   b. secondary succession.
   c. stability.
   d. regrowth.

3. Describe succession that takes place in an abandoned field.

4. Describe a mature community. How does a mature community develop?

Math Skills

5. The fires in 1988 burned 739,000 of the 2.2 million acres that make up Yellowstone National Park. What percentage of the park was burned?

Critical Thinking

6. **Applying Concepts** Give an example of a community that has a high degree of biodiversity, and an example of one that has a low degree of biodiversity.

7. **Analyzing Ideas** Explain why soil formation is always the first stage of primary succession. Does soil formation ever stop? Explain your answer.

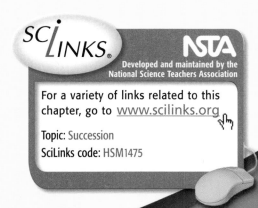

SCiLINKS®

NSTA
Developed and maintained by the National Science Teachers Association

For a variety of links related to this chapter, go to www.scilinks.org

Topic: Succession
SciLinks code: HSM1475

Skills Practice Lab

Nitrogen Needs

The nitrogen cycle is one of several cycles that are vital to living organisms. Without nitrogen, living organisms cannot make amino acids, the building blocks of proteins. Animals obtain nitrogen by eating plants that contain nitrogen and by eating animals that eat those plants. When animals die, decomposers return the nitrogen to the soil in the form of a nitrogen-containing chemical called *ammonia*.

In this activity, you will investigate the nitrogen cycle inside a closed system to discover how decomposers return nitrogen to the soil.

OBJECTIVES

Investigate the nitrogen cycle inside a closed system.

Discover how decomposers return nitrogen to the soil.

MATERIALS

- balance or scale
- beaker, 50 mL
- funnel
- gloves, protective
- graduated cylinder, 25 mL
- insects from home or schoolyard, large, dead (5)
- jar with lid, 1 pt (or 500 mL)
- paper, filter (2 pieces)
- pH paper
- soil, potting, commercially prepared without fertilizer
- water, distilled, 60 mL

SAFETY

Procedure

1. Fit a piece of filter paper into a funnel. Place the funnel inside a 50 mL beaker, and pour 5 g of soil into the funnel. Add 25 mL of distilled water to the soil.

2. Test the filtered water with pH paper, and record your observations.

3. Place some soil in a jar to cover the bottom with about 5 cm of soil. Add 10 mL of distilled water to the soil.

4. Place the dead insects in the jar, and seal the jar with the lid.

5. Check the jar each day for 5 days for an ammonia odor. (If you do not know what ammonia smells like, ask your teacher.) Record your observations. **Caution:** Your teacher will demonstrate how to check for a chemical odor by wafting. Notice how to gently wave the chemical fumes toward your nose with your hand. Do not put your nose in the jar and inhale!

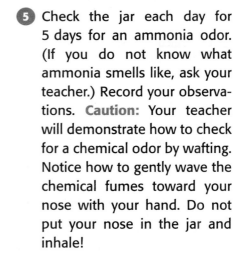

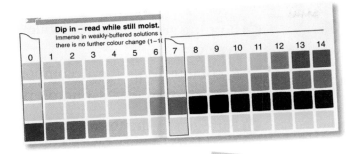

Dip in – read while still moist.

Immerse in weakly-buffered solutions there is no further colour change (1–1

0 1 2 3 4 5 6 7 8 9 10 11 12 13 14

6 On the fifth day, place a second piece of filter paper into the funnel, and place the funnel inside a 50 mL beaker. Remove about 5 g of soil from the jar, and place it in the funnel. Add 25 mL of distilled water to the soil.

7 Once again, test the filtered water with pH paper, and record your observations.

Analyze the Results

1 **Examining Data** What was the pH of the water in the beaker in the first trial? A pH of 7 indicates that the water is neutral. A pH below 7 indicates that the water is acidic, and a pH above 7 indicates that the water is basic. Was the water in the beaker neutral, acidic, or basic?

2 **Analyzing Data** What was the pH of the water in the beaker in the second trial? Explain the difference, if any, between the results of the first trial and the results of the second trial.

Draw Conclusions

3 **Drawing Conclusions** Based on the results of your pH tests, do you think ammonia is acidic or basic?

4 **Evaluating Results** On which days in your investigation were you able to detect an ammonia odor? Explain what caused the odor.

5 **Applying Conclusions** Describe the importance of decomposers in the nitrogen cycle.

Applying Your Data

Test the importance of nitrogen to plants. Fill two 12 cm flowerpots with commercially pre-pared potting soil and water. Be sure to use soil that has had no fertilizer added. Obtain a dozen tomato or radish seeds. Plant six seeds in each pot. Water your seeds so that the soil is constantly damp but not soaked. Keep your pots in a sunny window. Use a nitrogen-rich liquid plant fertilizer to fertilize one of the pots once a week. Dilute or mix the fertilizer with water according to the directions on the con-tainer. Water the other pot once a week with plain tap water.

1. After the seedlings appear, use a metric ruler to measure the growth of the plants in both pots. Measure the plants once a week, and record your results.

2. You may plant other seeds of your choice, but do not use legume (bean) seeds. Research to find out why!

Chapter Review

USING KEY TERMS

Complete each of the following sentences by choosing the correct term from the word bank.

evaporation   condensation
precipitation   decomposition
combustion   succession

1 The breakdown of dead materials into carbon dioxide and water is called ___.

2 The gradual development of a community over time is called ___.

3 During ___, the heat causes water to change from liquid to vapor.

4 ___ is the process of burning a substance.

5 Water that falls from the atmosphere to the land and oceans is ___.

6 In the process of ___, water vapor cools and returns to a liquid state.

UNDERSTANDING KEY IDEAS

Multiple Choice

7 Clouds form in the atmosphere through the process of

  a. precipitation.   **c.** condensation.
  b. respiration.   **d.** decomposition.

8 Which of the following statements about groundwater is true?

  a. It stays underground for a few days.
  b. It is stored in underground caverns or porous rock.
  c. It is salty like ocean water.
  d. It never reenters the water cycle.

9 Burning gas in an automobile is a type of

  a. combustion.   **c.** decomposition.
  b. respiration.   **d.** photosynthesis.

10 Nitrogen in the form of a gas can be used directly by some kinds of

  a. plants.   **c.** bacteria.
  b. animals.   **d.** fungi.

11 Bacteria are most important in the process of

  a. combustion.   **c.** nitrogen fixation.
  b. condensation. **d.** evaporation.

12 The pioneer species on bare rock are usually

  a. ferns.   **c.** mosses.
  b. pine trees. **d.** lichens.

13 Which of the following is an example of primary succession?

  a. the recovery of Yellowstone National Park following the fires of 1988
  b. the appearance of lichens and mosses in an area where a glacier has recently melted away
  c. the growth of weeds in a field after a farmer stops using the field
  d. the growth of weeds in an empty lot that is no longer being mowed

14 One of the most common plants in a recently abandoned farm field is

  a. oak or maple trees.
  b. pine trees.
  c. mosses.
  d. crabgrass.

Short Answer

15 List four places where water can go after it falls as precipitation.

16 In what forms can water on Earth be found?

17 What role do animals have in the carbon cycle?

18 What roles do humans have in the carbon cycle?

19 Earth's atmosphere is mostly made up of what substance?

20 Compare and contrast the two forms of succession.

CRITICAL THINKING

21 **Concept Mapping** Use the following terms to create a concept map: *abandoned farmland, lichens, bare rock, soil formation, horseweed, succession, forest fire, primary succession, secondary succession,* and *pioneer species*.

22 **Identifying Relationships** Is snow a part of the water cycle? Why or why not?

23 **Analyzing Processes** Make a list of several places where water might be found on Earth. For each item on your list, state how it is part of the water cycle.

24 **Forming Hypotheses** Predict what would happen if the water on Earth suddenly stopped evaporating.

25 **Forming Hypotheses** Predict what would happen if all of the bacteria on Earth suddenly disappeared.

26 **Making Inferences** Describe why a lawn usually doesn't go through succession.

27 **Making Inferences** Can one scientist observe all of the stages of secondary succession on an abandoned field? Explain your answer.

INTERPRETING GRAPHICS

The graph below shows how water is used each day by an average household in the United States. Use the graph to answer the questions that follow.

Average Household Daily Water Use

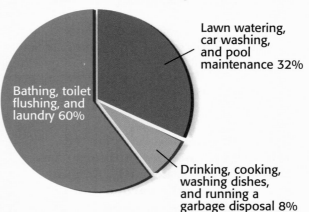

Lawn watering, car washing, and pool maintenance 32%

Bathing, toilet flushing, and laundry 60%

Drinking, cooking, washing dishes, and running a garbage disposal 8%

28 According to this graph, which of the following activities uses the greatest amount of water?

a. bathing

b. toilet flushing

c. washing laundry

d. There is not enough information to determine the answer.

29 An average family used 380 L of water per day, until they stopped washing their car, stopped watering their lawn, and stopped using their pool. Now, how much water per day do they use?

Multiple Choice

1. **Lichen begins to grow on cool lava in Hawaii. Lichen is an example of a**

    A. stable environment.

    B. weed.

    C. climax species.

    D. pioneer species.

2. **What is nitrogen fixation?**

    A. Bacteria in the soil change nitrogen gas into forms that plants can use.

    B. Bacteria in the soil release nitrogen gas into the atmosphere.

    C. Bacteria in the soil use nitrogen and water to form sugars, which animals eat.

    D. Bacteria in the atmosphere change nitrogen gas into forms animals can use.

3. **Adriana's father has not planted vegetables in their vegetable garden for several years. Recently, Adriana went to look at the garden and found that it was full of small pine trees. If Adriana lets the plot of land grow naturally, which of the following plants will begin to take root and grow next?**

    A. crabgrass

    B. horseweed

    C. mosses

    D. oaks

4. **What process converts carbon into food, making the carbon available for the carbon cycle on Earth?**

    A. respiration

    B. photosynthesis

    C. transpiration

    D. condensation

Use the table below to answer question 5.

Year	Plants Present
0	cotton, corn, beans
1	crabgrass and other very early weeds
2	horseweed and other weeds
5–15	conifers grow among the weeds
15–100	forest forms, hardwoods replace dead conifers

5. **The table above shows what happened on a farm in northern Kentucky that was abandoned in 1865. How would the former farm be described today?**

    A. nitrogen fixation

    B. secondary succession

    C. primary succession

    D. mature community

6. **Which part of the water cycle can cause runoff?**

    A. evaporation

    B. condensation

    C. precipitation

    D. transpiration

7. **Which of the following statements best describes the interactions of matter and energy in the decay of biomass?**

   A. Producers create energy from biomass in a process called decay.

   B. Consumers decay the matter in biomass to create the energy that the consumers need to live.

   C. Decomposers break biomass matter into simpler compounds. This process releases energy that the decomposers use to live.

   D. Consumers eat decomposers. The decomposers then create energy for the consumer from the biomass matter that makes up the consumer.

8. **In July 1994, tropical storm Alberto brought massive flooding to parts of Alabama, Georgia, and Florida. Around 10,000 square miles of land were under water. In some areas, mud wiped out all of the vegetation. By the next year, however, these areas were green again. What process was underway within a year of the floods?**

   A. primary succession

   B. biodiversity

   C. decomposition

   D. secondary succession

9. **What do decomposers do?**

   A. break down only plants

   B. rearrange matter in biomass to release energy

   C. produce their own food

   D. get energy from biomass without breaking it down

Use the illustration below to answer question 10.

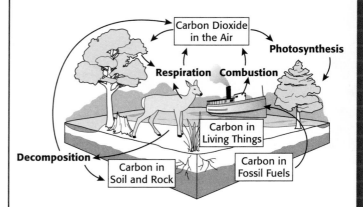

10. **The illustration above shows the carbon cycle. Which of the following processes is primarily involved in making carbon available to living things in the form of sugars?**

    A. combustion

    B. decomposition

    C. photosynthesis

    D. respiration

Open Response

11. **The movement of water between the oceans, atmosphere, land, and organisms is the water cycle. Without water, there would be no life on Earth. What are three ways in which water is important to life on Earth?**

12. **All organisms need nitrogen to build their body cells. Nitrogen exists in the atmosphere as a gas. Most organisms cannot use nitrogen in this form. At what stage in the nitrogen cycle is it turned into a form that plants can use? How do animals get nitrogen?**

Standardized Test Preparation

Science in Action

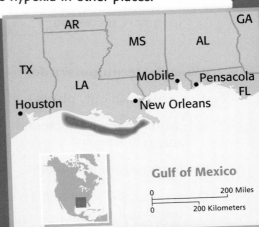

Science, Technology, and Society

Desalination

By the year 2025, it is estimated that almost a billion people on Earth will face water shortages. Only about 3% of the water on Earth is *fresh water*—the kind of water that we use for drinking and farming. And the human population is using and polluting Earth's fresh water too quickly. The other 97% of Earth's water is mostly in oceans and is much too salty for drinking or farming.

Until recently, it was very expensive and time-consuming to filter salt out of water, a process known as *desalination*. But new technologies are making desalination an affordable option for some areas.

Math ACTIVITY

You need to drink about 2 quarts of water each day. Imagine that you have a simple device that evaporates sea water and collects fresh, drinkable water at the rate of 6 mL/min. How long will it take your device to collect enough water each day?

Scientific Discoveries

The Dead Zone

Every summer, millions of fish are killed in an area in the Gulf of Mexico called a hypoxia region. *Hypoxia* (hy PAWK see UH) is a condition of water with unusually low levels of oxygen. The Gulf's hypoxia region is called a "dead zone" because a large number of organisms in the area die. Why does this happen? Scientists think that the region may be polluted with large amounts of nitrogen and phosphorus. These nutrients promote the growth of algae, which "bloom" and then die in huge numbers. When the algae is decomposed by bacteria, the bacteria use up oxygen in the water and hypoxia results. Scientists think that the polluting chemicals are washed into the Gulf by the Mississippi River. This river receives runoff from a large area that includes farms, housing, and cities. The scientists propose that adding wetlands to the Mississippi River watershed could reduce the chemicals reaching the Gulf.

Language Arts ACTIVITY

WRITING SKILL The Gulf of Mexico is not the only place where a hypoxia region exists. Research other bodies of water to find out how widespread the problem is. Write a short report telling what scientists are doing to reduce hypoxia in other places.

For several years after it was first noticed, the Gulf of Mexico hypoxia region became larger.

Michael Fan

Wastewater Manager If you are concerned about clean water and you like to work both in a laboratory and outdoors, you might like a career in wastewater management. The water cycle helps to keep water in nature pure enough for most organisms. But when humans use water in houses, factories, and farms, we create *wastewater*, often faster than natural processes can clean it up. To make the water safe again, we can imitate the ways water gets cleaned up in nature—and speed up the process.

Michael M. Fan is the Assistant Superintendent of wastewater operations at the Wastewater Treatment Plant at the University of California in Davis, California. This plant has one of the most advanced wastewater management systems in the country. Mr. Fan finds his job exciting. The plant operates 24 hours a day, and there are many tasks to manage. Running the plant requires skills in chemistry, physics, microbiology, and engineering. Many organisms in the Davis area are counting on Mr. Fan to make sure that the water used by the University campus is safely returned to nature.

Social Studies ACTIVITY

Research the ways that the ancient Romans managed their wastewater. Make a poster that illustrates some of their methods and technologies.

To learn more about these Science in Action topics, visit go.hrw.com and type in the keyword **HL5CYCF**

Current Science

Check out Current Science® articles related to this chapter by visiting go.hrw.com. Just type in the keyword **HL5CS19**.

UNIT 6

TIMELINE

Matter and Motion

It's hard to imagine a world where nothing ever moves. Without motion or forces to cause motion, life would be very dull! In this unit, you will learn how to describe the motion of objects, how forces affect motion, and how fluids exert force. This timeline shows some events and discoveries that have occurred as scientists have worked to understand the motion of objects here on Earth and in space.

Around 250 BCE

Archimedes, a Greek mathematician, develops the principle that bears his name. The principle relates the buoyant force on an object in a fluid to the amount of fluid displaced by the object.

1764

In London, Wolfgang Amadeus Mozart composes his first symphony—at the age of 8.

1846

After determining that the orbit of Uranus is different from what is predicted from the law of universal gravitation, scientists discover Neptune whose gravitational force is causing Uranus's unusual orbit.

1947

While flying a Bell X-1 rocket-powered airplane, American pilot Chuck Yeager becomes the first human to travel faster than the speed of sound.

Around 240 BCE

Chinese astronomers are the first to record a sighting of Halley's Comet.

1519

Portuguese explorer Ferdinand Magellan begins the first voyage around the world.

1687

Sir Isaac Newton, a British mathematician and scientist, publishes *Principia*, a book describing his laws of motion and the law of universal gravitation.

PHILOSOPHIÆ
NATURALIS
PRINCIPIA
MATHEMATICA.

Autore JS. NEWTON, Trin. Coll. Cantab. Soc. Matheseos Profeſſore Lucaſiano, & Societatis Regalis Sodali.

1905

While employed as a patent clerk, German physicist Albert Einstein publishes his special theory of relativity. The theory states that the speed of light is constant no matter what the reference frame is.

1921

Bessie Coleman becomes the first African American woman licensed to fly an airplane.

1971

American astronaut Alan Shepard takes a break from gathering lunar data to play golf on the moon during the *Apollo 14* mission.

1990

The *Magellan* spacecraft begins orbiting Venus for a four-year mission to map the planet. By using the sun's gravitational forces, it propels itself to Venus without burning much fuel.

2003

NASA launches *Spirit* and *Opportunity*, two Mars Exploration Rovers, to study Mars.

18

Properties and States of Matter

The Big Idea

Matter has properties that are observable and measurable.

About the Photo

An American alligator prepares to make a meal of a yellowbelly slider turtle in the Everglades. As the turtle becomes lunch and is digested, physical and chemical changes occur. These changes give the alligator energy to stay on the prowl. This process is an example of matter cycling through the environment. As matter cycles, the properties of matter and the identity of matter may change, but matter is never created or destroyed during normal physical and chemical changes.

PRE-READING ACTIVITY

Graphic Organizer

Concept Map Before you read the chapter, create the graphic organizer entitled "Concept Map" described in the **Study Skills** section of the Appendix. As you read the chapter, fill in the concept map with details about the properties and states of matter.

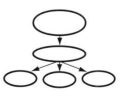

START-UP ACTIVITY

Mystery Mixture

In this activity, you will separate the various dyes that are found in an ink mixture.

Procedure

1. Place a **pencil** on top of a **clear plastic cup.** Tear a strip of paper from a **coffee filter.** Wrap one end of the strip around the pencil so that the other end just touches the bottom of the plastic cup. Use **tape** to attach the paper to the pencil.

2. Take the paper out of the cup. Using a **water-soluble black marker,** make a small dot in the center of the strip about 2 cm from the bottom of the strip.

3. Pour **water** in the cup to a depth of 1 cm. Lower the paper into the cup. Keep the dot above water.

4. Remove the paper when the water is 1 cm from the top. Record your observations.

Analysis

1. What happened as the paper soaked up the water?

2. Which colors make up the marker's black ink?

3. Compare your results with those of your classmates. Record your observations.

4. Before doing this activity, did you think of ink as a pure substance? Why is the ink called a *mixture*?

What You Will Learn

- Describe the two properties of all matter.
- Describe the difference between a pure substance and a mixture.
- Define physical properties
- Define chemical properties.
- Explain how matter is organized.

Vocabulary

matter
atom
pure substance
element
compound
mixture
physical property
chemical property

READING STRATEGY

Reading Organizer As you read this section, create an outline of the section. Use the headings from the section in your outline.

Properties of Matter

Your friend has a birthday coming up, and you are going to bake her a cake. What materials do you need to gather?

Like the cooks in **Figure 1,** you might gather ingredients such as flour, sugar, salt, milk, eggs, and butter. You would also need cake pans, utensils, and measuring cups. What do these items have in common? All are examples of matter.

What Is Matter?

The word *matter* may not seem like a technical term, but it does have a scientific meaning. **Matter** is anything that has mass and takes up space. Everything that you can see in the universe is matter. Even some things that you cannot see are matter. For example, the air that we breathe is matter.

How do we know that air is matter? Think about inflating a balloon. Using a sensitive balance, you could measure the mass of an empty balloon and then measure the mass of the inflated balloon. The inflated balloon would have more mass than the empty balloon did. So, air has mass. Air also takes up space. When you breathe in, air takes up space in your lungs. When you inflate the balloon, air takes up space in the balloon.

Atoms: Building Blocks of Matter

All types of matter are made up of particles called *atoms.* **Atoms** are the building blocks of matter because they combine with one another to make many different materials.

Figure 1 *Everything that you can see in this kitchen is matter. Atoms combine in different ways to form all matter on Earth.*

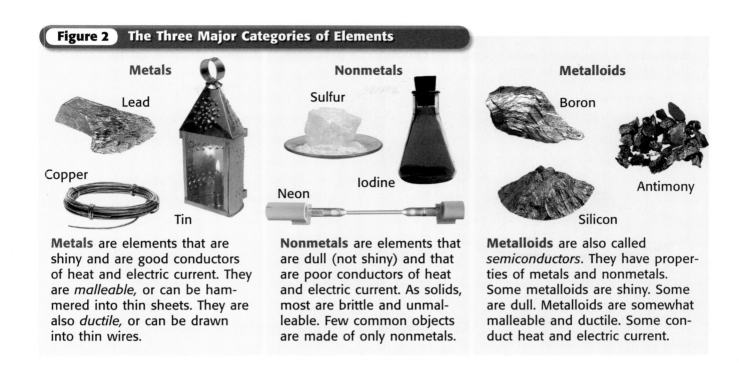

Figure 2 The Three Major Categories of Elements

Metals

Lead

Copper

Tin

Metals are elements that are shiny and are good conductors of heat and electric current. They are *malleable,* or can be hammered into thin sheets. They are also *ductile,* or can be drawn into thin wires.

Nonmetals

Sulfur

Iodine

Neon

Nonmetals are elements that are dull (not shiny) and that are poor conductors of heat and electric current. As solids, most are brittle and unmalleable. Few common objects are made of only nonmetals.

Metalloids

Boron

Antimony

Silicon

Metalloids are also called *semiconductors.* They have properties of metals and nonmetals. Some metalloids are shiny. Some are dull. Metalloids are somewhat malleable and ductile. Some conduct heat and electric current.

Pure Substances

There are several ways that atoms make up matter. Atoms often combine chemically to form *molecules.* Matter that consists of only one type of atom or one type of molecule is considered to be a **pure substance.** There are two types of pure substances: elements and compounds. Each is an example of matter that cannot be broken down into simpler substances by physical means.

✓ *Reading Check* What is a pure substance? (*See the Appendix for answers to Reading Checks.*)

Elements: A Single Type of Atom

The helium gas in a balloon is a pure substance called an *element.* **Elements** are substances that are composed of a single kind of atom. Elements cannot be broken down into simpler substances by physical or chemical means.

Elements can be composed of individual atoms or of molecules, all of which are much too small for us to see. Helium gas is composed of individual helium atoms. Nitrogen gas, the main part of air, is composed of nitrogen molecules. Each nitrogen molecule is composed of two nitrogen atoms that are joined to each other.

There are more than 100 elements. **Figure 2** shows one way of classifying them. For any element, all of the atoms of the element are alike regardless of the location of the atoms. For example, all atoms of gold are alike whether the atoms are in a ring, in a gold nugget, or in someone's dental work.

matter anything that has mass and takes up space

atom the smallest unit of an element that maintains the properties of that element

pure substance a sample of matter, either a single element or a single compound, that has definite chemical and physical properties

element a substance that cannot be separated or broken down into simpler substances by chemical means

Figure 3 Forming Sodium Chloride

Sodium is a soft, silvery white metal that reacts violently with water.

Chlorine is a poisonous, greenish yellow gas.

Sodium chloride, or table salt, is a white solid. It dissolves easily in water and is safe to eat.

compound a substance made up of atoms of two or more different elements joined by chemical bonds

mixture a combination of two or more substances that are not chemically combined

Figure 4 *You can see each topping on this mixture, which is better known as a pizza.*

Compounds: A Single Type of Molecule

A **compound** is a pure substance that is composed of molecules that form when two or more kinds of atoms bond. Water is a compound. A water molecule is composed of hydrogen and oxygen atoms. Like all compounds, water has a fixed composition. So, all water molecules are alike. Each water molecule is made of two hydrogen atoms and one oxygen atom.

Figure 3 shows that sodium reacts with chlorine to form a new pure substance, sodium chloride. The properties of the compound sodium chloride differ from the properties of the elements sodium and chlorine. Every compound has properties that differ from the properties of the elements that form it.

Mixtures

Matter that contains two or more pure substances is called a **mixture.** Apple juice, for example, is not a pure substance. It is a mixture that includes water, sugars, and acids. The apple juice mixture can be physically separated by evaporating the water. This process leaves the sugars, acids, and other dissolved compounds. A mixture can be physically separated into the pure substances that make up the mixture.

Mixtures are divided into two categories based on how completely the substances are mixed together. A *homogeneous* (HOH moh JEE nee uhs) *mixture* is the same throughout. Apple juice is a homogeneous mixture. The pizza in **Figure 4** is a *heterogeneous* (HET uhr OH JEE nee uhs) *mixture* because the substances in it are not uniformly mixed. For example, you can see that there is no cheese on the crust of the pizza.

✓ *Reading Check* Is a chocolate chip cookie a heterogeneous mixture or a homogeneous mixture? Why?

Solutions

A *solution* is a homogeneous mixture that appears to be a single substance. A solution is composed of two or more substances that are distributed evenly throughout the solution. Salt water is one example of a solution. In solutions, the particles are so small that they do not settle out and separate from the rest of the solution. They are also too small to see. Many solutions are liquids, but solutions can also form in a gas or a solid. Dry air is a gaseous solution of oxygen in nitrogen. Brass is an example of a solid solution—it is a solution of zinc in copper.

Suspensions

In some mixtures, the particles are much larger than the particles in a solution. You can stir or shake these mixtures to mix the particles, but the particles eventually separate and settle out. Such mixtures are called *suspensions,* and they are always heterogeneous mixtures. In suspensions, particles can be distributed in a liquid or in a gas. The mixture in the snow globe in **Figure 5** is an example of a suspension.

Colloids

Colloids are mixtures whose particles are smaller than the particles in suspensions but larger than the particles in solutions. The particles in a colloid do not settle out. Because the particles do not settle out, colloids are usually homogeneous mixtures. In colloids, particles can be dispersed in a solid, liquid, or gas. Clouds are colloids because they contain very small water droplets or ice crystals that are suspended in the air. The whipped cream and gelatin in **Figure 5** are colloids.

Make a Colloid!
Ask a family member to do this experiment with you. In a shallow dish or small cup, mix 2 tablespoons (Tbsp) of cornstarch and 1 Tbsp of water completely with a spoon. No dry cornstarch or liquid water should be left. This mixture is a colloid because the particles of cornstarch stay suspended in the water. Try pushing the spoon into the mixture quickly and then slowly. Try pouring some of the mixture out of the container. Discuss how the colloid behaves and whether you think that it is more like a solid or more like a liquid.

Figure 5　**Properties of Suspensions and Colloids**

Suspension This snow globe contains solid particles that will mix with the clear liquid when you shake the globe. But the particles soon sink when the globe is at rest.

Colloid This dessert includes two tasty examples of colloids—fruity gelatin and whipped cream.

Figure 6 *These two desserts have similar shapes. You can tell them apart by their physical properties.*

physical property a characteristic of a substance that does not involve a chemical change, such as density, color, or hardness

Identifying Matter with Physical Properties

The desserts in **Figure 6** have similar shapes but differ in color, odor, and texture. Shape, color, odor, and texture are examples of physical properties that help us tell things apart. A **physical property** is a characteristic of matter that can be observed or measured without the matter going through a chemical change, or a change in identity. For example, we can detect the desserts' color without changing their identity. If we cut the desserts—the matter—to test a physical property such as hardness, the identity of the matter would not change.

✔ **Reading Check** Name two physical properties.

Mass and Weight

All matter has mass. *Mass* is a physical property that is a measure of the amount of matter in an object. The mass of an object is constant anyplace in the universe because the amount of matter does not change. Mass can be expressed in grams (g). Weight is sometimes confused with mass, but they are different. *Weight* is a measure of the force of gravity on an object and is expressed in newtons (N). The force of gravity changes depending on where you are in the universe. So, the weight of an object varies depending on where the object is.

Volume

Matter also takes up space. The measure of the amount of space that matter occupies is a physical property called *volume*. In science, milliliters (mL) and cubic centimeters (cm^3) are often used to express volume. A milliliter is equal to a cubic centimeter (1 mL = 1 cm^3).

Density

Which would you rather have fall on your foot—a brick or a foam block that is the size of the brick? Even though both are the same size, the mass of the brick is much greater than the mass of the foam block! You can identify each block by its density. Density is the mass of an object per unit volume. Density equals mass divided by volume. Because 1.0 g of water has a volume of 1.0 mL, water has a density of 1 g/mL.

Other Important Physical Properties

There are many other physical properties that help scientists identify and classify matter. Aluminum can be beaten into thin sheets (foil) because it is *malleable*. Copper conducts electric current, but glass and rubber do not. So, the *conductivity* of copper is greater than that of glass or rubber. *Boiling point* is an important physical property of liquids. These properties can be determined without changing the identity of the matter.

Identifying Matter with Chemical Properties

Scientists can also identify and classify matter by understanding its chemical properties. **Chemical properties** describe matter based on its ability to participate in chemical reactions and form new substances. The reaction of baking soda and vinegar to form bubbles of carbon dioxide gas is shown in **Figure 7**. This reaction is evidence of *reactivity*, a chemical property of baking soda. Because wood burns, it has the chemical property of *flammability*. As wood and oxygen react, they change into ash, smoke, carbon dioxide, and water. These new substances have different properties from the original wood and oxygen.

Reading Check Name a chemical property of wood.

chemical property a property of matter that describes a substance's ability to participate in chemical reactions

Figure 7 *Sugar, on the left, shows no reaction when mixed with vinegar in the beaker. Baking soda, on the right, shows the chemical property reactivity when mixed with vinegar. Reactivity is the ability of substances to combine and form one or more new substances.*

Figure 8 The Classification of Matter

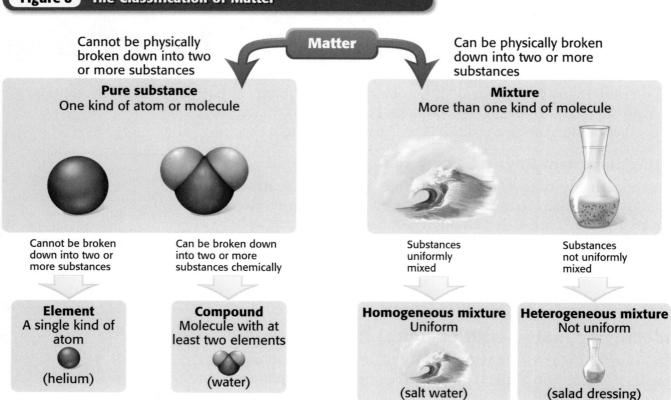

Cannot be physically broken down into two or more substances

Matter

Can be physically broken down into two or more substances

Pure substance
One kind of atom or molecule

Mixture
More than one kind of molecule

Cannot be broken down into two or more substances

Can be broken down into two or more substances chemically

Substances uniformly mixed

Substances not uniformly mixed

Element
A single kind of atom

(helium)

Compound
Molecule with at least two elements

(water)

Homogeneous mixture
Uniform

(salt water)

Heterogeneous mixture
Not uniform

(salad dressing)

Categories of Matter and Their Properties

You have learned that all matter can be classified into the categories shown in **Figure 8.** This classification is based on the chemical and physical properties of matter.

Properties of Pure Substances

All samples of a pure substance have exactly the same physical and chemical properties. The reason is that all samples of a pure substance have the same composition. They are composed of either the same atoms (an element) or the same molecules (a compound). Every sample of table salt, for example, has the same melting point and the same taste.

✓ Reading Check Why do all samples of a pure substance have the same chemical and physical properties?

Properties of Mixtures

The physical and chemical properties of a mixture can vary. The reason is that a mixture is a blend of pure substances in which each substance retains its own identity and properties. For example, a mixture of sugar and salt may be used to flavor popcorn. The popcorn will taste both sweet and salty. But the flavor will vary depending on the proportion of sugar and salt on each kernel.

Summary

- Matter has mass and occupies space.
- Matter is organized into two main categories: pure substances and mixtures.
- A pure substance cannot be physically broken down into simpler substances.
- Pure substances can be elements or compounds.
- A mixture contains pure substances that can be physically separated.

- Mixtures can be homogeneous or heterogeneous.
- Physical properties can be determined without changing the identity of matter.
- Chemical properties describe how matter can change into new substances.
- Matter is organized based on properties.

Understanding Key Ideas

1. Which of the following is a chemical property?
   a. color
   b. mass
   c. density
   d. flammability

2. In which state of matter would individual atoms be visible?
   a. gas
   b. liquid
   c. solid
   d. None of the above

3. Explain why a stick of chalk is a pure substance, but a stick of candy is not. Why are both classified as matter?

4. What is one chemical property that is different for sugar than it is for baking soda?

5. Explain how an element differs from a compound, and give an example of each.

6. Which type of matter is a radio? Use the properties of a radio to explain your choice.

Math Skills

7. There are eight elements that make up 98.5% of the Earth's crust: 46.6% oxygen, 8.1% aluminum, 5.0% iron, 3.6% calcium, 2.8% sodium, 2.6% potassium, and 2.1% magnesium. The rest is silicon. What percentage of Earth's crust is silicon?

Critical Thinking

8. Water has a density of 1.0 g/mL, and cooking oil has a density of 0.5 g/mL. If you mix them, they will form two layers. Which will form the top layer? Explain your answer.

9. List several physical properties that you could use to distinguish between copper, glass, and rubber.

10. The surface gravity on Earth's moon is 16% of the surface gravity on Earth. For a mineral specimen, what physical property would have a different measurement on Earth than on the moon?

11. A beaker containing 10 mL of alcohol is heated until all of the alcohol boils out of the beaker. The alcohol gas is captured in a balloon that has a volume of 120 mL. What properties of the alcohol have changed? Explain.

SCiLINKS®

NSTA

Developed and maintained by the
National Science Teachers Association

For a variety of links related to this chapter, go to www.scilinks.org

Topic: What Is Matter? Describing Matter
SciLinks code: HSM1662; HSM0391

Physical and Chemical Changes

Sand and sugar are similar in some ways, but you would not want to put sand in cookies! How are sand and sugar made? And what happens when you eat sugar in cookies?

Conservation of Mass

The **law of conservation of mass** says that mass is not created or destroyed in ordinary chemical and physical changes. Consider sand. The matter that makes up sand may have come from mountains where boulders were eroded into pebbles. These pebbles were washed toward the ocean and were broken into smaller pieces as they traveled. Eventually, many of the small pieces collected on the beach as sand. The amount of matter, or the *mass,* did not change. Only the form changed—from a few large boulders into many tiny grains of sand.

Conservation of Mass When New Chemicals Form

What happens when you eat a sugary cookie? Your body changes oxygen from your lungs and sugar from your cookie into carbon dioxide and water to release energy. But no matter is lost! The mass of oxygen and sugar that your body starts with equals the mass of carbon dioxide and water produced. The physical changes that happen as sand forms, the chemical changes that happen as your body uses sugar, and the changes in **Figure 1** all obey the law of conservation of mass.

law of conservation of mass
the law that states that mass cannot be created or destroyed in ordinary chemical and physical changes

Figure 1 *A physical change happens when sea water rearranges the sand. Chemical changes happen when wood is burned and marshmallows are digested.*

Figure 2 Physical Changes to Separate Sulfur and Salt

❶ In the first step, water is added, and the mixture is stirred. Salt dissolves in water. Sulfur does not.

❷ In the second step, the mixture is poured through a filter. The filter traps the solid sulfur.

❸ In the third step, the water is evaporated. The salt is left behind.

Physical Changes in Our World

You have learned that the formation of sand is a physical change. What else would be considered a physical change? A **physical change** is any change in which the physical properties of a substance change but the substance's identity does not.

For example, physical changes can be used to separate a mixture of the solids sulfur and sodium chloride (table salt), as **Figure 2** shows. In step 1, the white salt and yellow sulfur are mixed with water. The salt dissolves in the water, and the sulfur floats on top. The salt is in solution in the water and goes through the filter with the water in step 2. Because the sulfur does not dissolve, it is trapped in the filter. In step 3, the water is evaporated, which leaves the salt behind. The sulfur and salt have been separated by using only physical changes. During the separation process, the form of each substance changed, but the identity of each substance did not.

✓ **Reading Check** What is a physical change? (*See the Appendix for answers to Reading Checks.*)

physical change a change of matter from one form to another without a change in chemical properties

Figure 3 *Freezing—a physical change—does not change the identity of water molecules. But some physical properties of the water, such as density, change. Ice is less dense than liquid water, so ice floats on top of the lake.*

Physical Changes in Nature

Look around you. What evidence of physical changes in nature do you see? Movement of soil and rock can happen suddenly in a landslide or gradually as wind blows topsoil from one field to another. Water can move pebbles and sand in the current of a stream. But physical changes can also occur in nature without the movement of matter. The liquid water in **Figure 3** undergoes a physical change when it freezes into ice. All of these changes happen without the formation of new substances.

Figure 4 Bringing Sugar from the Field to the Table Through Physical Changes

1 **A Source of Sugar** Sugar cane is grown in large fields like the one shown here. The cane contains sugar dissolved in liquid inside the plant.

2 **Harvesting Sugar Cane** The sugar cane is cut. The cane pieces are washed and shredded. Then, they are squeezed to press out the juice containing dissolved sugar.

3 **Making Raw Sugar** The sweet liquid from the plants is processed to remove plant materials, such as wax and gums, from the juice. The water is then evaporated from the juice, and raw sugar crystals form.

4 **Making Refined Sugar** The raw sugar is dissolved in water. The solution is cleaned to get rid of impurities. Some of the water is evaporated, and the refined sugar crystallizes out of the solution. The sugar crystals are dried, packaged, and shipped to stores.

5 **Ready to Eat** The sugar molecules in the crystals on your table are the same sugar molecules that were stored in the sugar cane plants.

Physical Changes in Industry

All cultures have learned to use physical changes to modify and make use of the world around them. Wood products such as furniture, toothpicks, and musical instruments are made through a series of physical changes. Trees are harvested and cut into smaller sections. These sections are dried, and then the wood is ready to be cut into lumber. The lumber is used to make all kinds of products. Although the wood has changed form—from part of a tree to wood products—its identity has not changed. Another example of a product made through a series of physical changes is table sugar. **Figure 4** describes the physical changes that take place in the production of sugar.

Chemical Changes in Our World

How do chemical changes differ from physical changes? In a physical change, the identity of matter does not change. In a **chemical change,** new substances form and their identities and properties differ from the identities and properties of the original matter. Chemical changes happen when bonds between atoms are broken or new bonds are formed to make new substances. These changes are also called *chemical reactions*. A variety of clues indicate chemical changes. A change in color or the production of heat, sound, or light may indicate a chemical change. For example, fizzing and foaming signal that a chemical change happens when vinegar and baking soda are mixed. New substances, including carbon dioxide gas, form.

Reading Check What is a chemical change?

chemical change a change that occurs when one or more substances change into entirely new substances with different properties

Figure 5 *Pigments called* carotenoids *in the spoonbill's feathers and legs were released during the chemical changes of digestion.*

Chemical Changes in Nature

Chemical changes occur frequently in nature. One of the most important chemical changes in nature happens when green plants make food. In this process, called *photosynthesis,* plants use energy from sunlight to change water and carbon dioxide into oxygen and carbohydrates, such as sugar. In animals, chemical changes occur during digestion. Digestion frees nutrients from food to give an animal energy. Other chemical changes that can affect the appearance of an animal can also occur during digestion. For example, **Figure 5** shows a spoonbill eating. Eating is the process that begins digestion. Chemical changes during digestion will release pigments from the bodies of organisms that the spoonbill is eating, such as shrimp. These pigments give the spoonbill its distinctive color. Growing, aging, and decaying are other processes in which chemical changes occur.

Figure 6 *The refining of oil produces both chemical and physical changes. A chemical change occurs in the flame, where byproducts are being burned.*

Chemical Changes in Industry

Many things around you are products of industry. Think about how a bicycle is made. Making metal involves chemical changes. Ore is mined and then refined to make metal for the bike's frame. The paint and plastic parts of the bike are made by chemically changing raw materials into paint and plastic. These processes and other industrial processes usually require more than one step. During these steps, physical changes as well as chemical changes may occur. Some of these changes produce byproducts, or extra materials that differ from the desired product of the process. **Figure 6** shows an oil refinery and the burning of byproducts of gasoline production.

 **Reading Check** Give an example of a chemical change in industry.

INTERNET ACTIVITY

My New Material Create a new substance, and describe its properties. Go to **go.hrw.com**, and type in the keyword **HP5MATW.**

Changing Change

1. Place a folded **paper towel** in a small **pie plate.**

2. Pour **vinegar** into the pie plate to wet the entire paper towel.

3. Place **three shiny pennies** on top of the paper towel.

4. Put the pie plate in a safe place. Wait 24 hours.

5. Describe and explain the change that took place.

Are Physical and Chemical Changes Reversible?

If you freeze water to make ice, you can melt the ice to form water again. If you dissolve salt in water, you can evaporate the water to reclaim the salt. Most physical changes are reversible because they do not alter the identity of the matter. Physical changes affect only the form of the matter.

Some chemical changes are also reversible. If you pass an electric current through water, you will get hydrogen and oxygen gases. If you combine hydrogen and oxygen gases, you can produce water. However, most chemical changes are not reversible. You cannot un-burn paper, un-rot an apple, or un-eat a pizza! The products from most chemical changes cannot be recombined to form the original substance.

CONNECTION TO Environmental Science

Coal and Chemical Changes
Coal is a fossil fuel that is formed from plant material. Make a poster showing the chemical changes involved in the formation of coal and in the burning of coal for energy. Show the pros and cons of the chemical changes involved in burning coal.

ACTIVITY

SECTION Review

Summary

- According to the law of conservation of mass, mass is neither gained nor lost during chemical and physical changes.
- Physical changes affect the physical properties but not the identity of a substance.
- Chemical changes result in the production of new substances.
- Most physical changes are reversible.
- Most chemical changes are not reversible.

Understanding Key Ideas

1. Why is dissolving salt in water a physical change?

2. Why is photosynthesis a chemical change?

3. Is the freezing of water a chemical change or a physical change?

4. Sodium (Na) metal reacts with water (H_2O) to form sodium hydroxide (NaOH) and hydrogen (H_2) gas. Why is this change a chemical change?
    a. because water is involved in the reaction
    b. because new substances are formed
    c. because the metal disappears in the water
    d. because the amount of matter changes

5. The amount of matter present before a change is the same as the amount present after the change. This principle is called
    a. the law of conservation of energy.
    b. the law of conservation of mass.
    c. photosynthesis.
    d. a reversible change.

Math Skills

6. If 2 g of hydrogen is burned in the presence of 16 g of oxygen, what will be the mass of the resulting water vapor?

Critical Thinking

7. **Analyzing Processes** Describe a reversible physical change, and explain how it could be reversed.

8. **Applying Concepts** List three chemical changes that are NOT reversible.

9. **Making Comparisons** Explain why the *production* of sugar is a physical change while the *eating* of sugar is a chemical change.

SCiLINKS

NSTA
Developed and maintained by the National Science Teachers Association

For a variety of links related to this chapter, go to www.scilinks.org

Topic: Physical Changes; Chemical Changes
SciLinks code: HSM1142; HSM0266

What You Will Learn

- Explain why particles in matter are always in motion.
- Compare the properties of solids, liquids, and gases.
- Explain the behavior of gases.
- Describe plasma.

Vocabulary

solid
liquid
gas
pressure
plasma

READING STRATEGY

Reading Organizer As you read this section, make a table comparing the properties of the solid, liquid, gas, and plasma states of matter.

States of Matter

When you're walking to class, you come into contact with all kinds of matter. You feel wind on your face and cement under your feet. If it is raining, you will feel water, too.

You can tell that matter moves when you feel wind and rain. But within matter, there is movement that we cannot see or feel. All of the individual atoms and molecules that make up matter are always in motion.

Particles of Matter in Motion

The sand in the sand castle in **Figure 1** is not moving. But if you could see the particles within a single grain of sand, you would see molecules in constant motion. How can this be? The molecules maintain their positions in the sand grain, so the sand itself does not move. But the molecules are vibrating and rotating at their fixed positions. These are the movements in matter that are too small for you to see or feel.

The Energy of Particles and the States of Matter

Particles in matter are always in motion because particles have energy. The more energy a particle has, the faster the particle moves. This section will explore how particle energy and movement help determine the *states of matter,* or the physical forms of matter. The four states of matter that will be described are the solid, liquid, gaseous, and plasma states. Their physical differences are due in part to the different energies of particles.

Figure 1 *Sand is being moved to build this castle. A different kind of motion is also occurring as particles are in constant motion within each sand grain.*

Figure 2 Three States of Matter for the Element Bromine

Arrangement of particles in a solid

Arrangement of particles in a liquid

Arrangement of particles in a gas

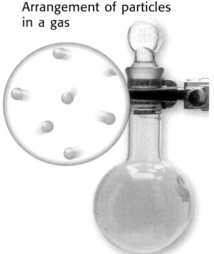

Physical Differences Between States of Matter

The solid, liquid, and gaseous states of the element bromine are shown in **Figure 2.** Each state is composed of bromine molecules. The physical properties of each state are different. For example, liquid bromine is denser than bromine gas. But the chemical properties of bromine are the same whether the bromine is a solid, liquid, or gas.

solid the state of matter in which the volume and shape of a substance are fixed

The Rigid Structure of Solids

The state of matter in which particles are fixed in a rigid structure that does not change shape or size is a **solid.** Particles in a solid are close together and do not move around easily. In fact, particles in a solid just vibrate and rotate in place. For example, ice is the solid state of water. Water molecules are strongly attracted to each other. Water molecules in ice do not move around, but they do vibrate and rotate in place. Heating ice transfers more energy to the molecules, which increases their motion. If the molecules gain enough energy to free themselves from their fixed positions, the ice *melts.*

Temperature is a measure of the energy of particles in matter. The temperature at which a solid melts is called the *melting point* of the solid. The melting point of ice is 0°C. Sodium chloride, shown in **Figure 3,** has a melting point of more than 800°C! Because the attraction between sodium chloride particles is stronger than the attraction between water molecules, sodium chloride requires more energy to melt than water does.

✓ Reading Check Describe how particles in a solid are arranged. (*See the Appendix for answers to Reading Checks.*)

Figure 3 *These crystals of salt (sodium chloride) have been magnified 840 times. The particles in the crystals are fixed in positions that form the cubic structure visible here.*

Figure 4 *Liquids take the shape of their container. If a liquid is poured from one container to another, its shape can change, but its volume cannot change.*

CONNECTION TO Language Arts

WRITING SKILL **Changes of State** Imagine that you are a molecule. The group of molecules you are with changes from a gas to a liquid and then from a liquid to a solid. In a one-page report, describe what happens to you.

liquid the state of matter that has a definite volume but not a definite shape

gas a form of matter that does not have a definite volume or shape

The Changing Shape of Liquids

A **liquid** is the state of matter that has a definite volume but no definite shape. In liquids, the attractions between particles are much weaker than they are in solids. As a result, particles tend to move farther apart in a liquid than they were in the solid. The particles in a liquid are in contact with each other but are not in fixed positions. As the molecules move around, the liquid can change shape. Liquids assume the shape of their container, as shown in **Figure 4.** But no matter what the shape is, the volume of the liquid does not change. You can observe this phenomenon when you pour lemonade from a pitcher into a glass. The shape of the lemonade changes, but the total volume does not change.

The Changing Shape and Volume of Gases

If molecules in a liquid gain enough energy, they can escape the attractions with other molecules and become a gas. A **gas** is the state of matter that has no definite shape and no definite volume. The change from liquid to gas is called *evaporation* or *boiling*. Because of their high energy and rapid motion, gas particles will spread out to fill whatever volume is available to them, such as a balloon or a room. The particles of a gas are the same size as the particles that are present when the matter is a solid or a liquid. But in a gas, the particles are quite far apart and move even more freely than they do in a liquid.

✓ Reading Check How are particles in a gas arranged?

Changes from One State to Another

You have learned that adding energy to a solid by heating the solid can cause the solid to melt and become a liquid. And if energy is added to a liquid, the liquid can boil or evaporate to become a gas. Changes from one state to another are called *changes of state*. These changes are physical because the physical form—and not the identity—of the substance changes.

Changes of state can also occur when energy is removed from a substance by cooling the substance. If a gas is cooled enough, attractions between particles overcome the motion of the particles and the particles clump together. The gas *condenses* into a liquid. In the liquid state, there is contact between particles, but the particles can slide past each other. If a liquid cools enough, it will *freeze* into a solid. What happens when a liquid freezes? As energy is removed, the particles slow down. At the freezing point, attractions become strong enough to lock the particles in fixed positions, and a solid forms.

Behavior of Gases

The volume of a gas is the amount of space in which gas particles move around within a container, such as a balloon. The volume can change if the space between the particles changes as the particles move closer together or farther apart.

Temperature

How much helium gas is needed to fill a parade balloon, such as the one in **Figure 5**? The answer depends on the temperature. On a hot day, the gas molecules have more energy, so they move faster and hit the inside walls of the balloon harder. The gas pushes on the balloon with greater force than it will on a colder day. Thus, less helium is needed to fill the balloon on a hot day. On a cold day, the helium molecules will have less energy, and they will not push as hard on the walls of the balloon. More helium will be needed to fill the balloon on a cold day.

Changes in Gas Volume

1. Inflate a balloon, and tie it closed. Measure around the widest part of the balloon, and record the measurement.

2. Put the balloon in places such as a freezer and a sunny window for at least 15 min. Each time you take the balloon from a location, measure around the widest part of the balloon.

3. Describe what is happening to the gas molecules as the balloon changes temperature.

4. How does the behavior of these molecules differ from the behavior of molecules in a liquid or solid?

Figure 5 *To properly inflate a helium balloon, you must consider the temperature outside the balloon.*

Figure 6 Gas and Pressure

High pressure: basketball cannot expand

Low pressure: beach ball would expand or burst if more air is added

The basketball has a higher pressure because it contains more particles of gas and the particles are closer together. The particles collide with the inside of the ball more frequently.

The beach ball has a lower pressure because it contains fewer particles of gas and the particles are farther apart. The particles in the beach ball collide with the inside of the ball less frequently.

Volume

Volume is the amount of space that an object takes up. Because gas molecules spread out, the volume of a gas depends on the container that holds the gas. For example, you can squeeze balloons filled with air into smaller shapes. This change is possible because gas can be compressed, or the gas molecules squeezed together, into a smaller volume. If you try to squeeze a water-filled balloon, it will probably burst. The balloon will burst because a liquid cannot be compressed as much as a gas can be.

Pressure

When particles of gas collide with a surface, they exert force on the surface. **Pressure** is a measure of the amount of force per unit area of a surface. The number and force of collisions affect the pressure. Look at **Figure 6.** The beach ball contains fewer particles of gas than the basketball does. There are fewer collisions of gas particles with the inside walls of the beach ball than there are with the inside walls of the basketball. As a result, the pressure in the beach ball is less than the pressure in the basketball. Increasing the temperature of a gas in a container that cannot expand, such as a basketball, also increases the pressure. The molecules speed up, so they collide harder and more often with the container, and the pressure increases.

pressure the amount of force exerted per unit area of a surface

plasma a state of matter that starts as a gas and then becomes ionized; it consists of free-moving ions and electrons, it takes on an electric charge, and its properties differ from those of a solid, liquid, or gas

✓ **Reading Check** What are two ways to increase the pressure of a gas in a container that cannot expand?

Plasma: A Fourth State of Matter

If enough energy is added to a gas, the gas particles will break apart. This process creates a **plasma,** the state of matter that is a blend of electrons and positively charged ions. Positive ions are particles that have lost one or more electrons. Like a gas, plasma does not have a fixed shape or volume. Unlike a gas, plasma conducts electric current and is affected by magnetic fields.

The sun is plasma, and more than 99% of the matter in the universe is plasma. As **Figure 7** shows, plasma sometimes forms during storms on Earth by the electrical energy in lightning. Plasma also forms in neon and fluorescent light bulbs and in plasma screens when energy from an electric current is passed through a gas in the device.

Figure 7 *Plasma is formed in the electric discharge of a lightning bolt.*

SECTION
Review

Summary

- Particles in matter are always in motion.
- Solids contain particles in close contact and at fixed positions. Solids have a fixed shape and volume.
- Liquids contain particles in close contact, but the particles move freely. Liquids have a fixed volume but do not have a fixed shape.
- Gases have particles that are far apart, and the particles move freely. Gases do not have a fixed shape or a fixed volume.
- Temperature and pressure affect the volume of gases.
- Plasma is a state of matter that forms when energy is added to a gas.

Using Key Terms

1. Use *gas* and *plasma* in the same sentence.

2. Use *gas* and *pressure* in the same sentence.

Understanding Key Ideas

3. In which type of matter do particles have the lowest energy?
   a. gas   **c.** plasma
   b. solid   **d.** liquid

4. Is there a state of matter in which particles do not move? Explain your answer.

Critical Thinking

5. **Applying Concepts** Which state of matter does each of the following represent: apple juice, bread, a book, and the helium in a balloon?

6. **Predicting Consequences** Why do bicycle tires go "flat" in cold weather?

7. **Making Inferences** In which material do molecules have a greater attraction for each other: solid butter or liquid butter?

Interpreting Graphics

Use the image below to answer the following two questions.

8. Identify the state of matter in the jar.

9. Discuss how the particles in the jar are attracted to each other.

For a variety of links related to this chapter, go to www.scilinks.org

Topic: Solids, Liquids, and Gases; Changes of State

SciLinks code: HSM1420; HSM0254

Skills Practice Lab

A Hot and Cool Lab

OBJECTIVES

Measure and record time and temperature accurately.

Graph the temperature change of water as the water changes state.

Analyze and interpret graphs of changes of state.

MATERIALS

- beaker, 250 mL or 400 mL
- coffee can, large
- gloves, heat-resistant
- graduated cylinder, 100 mL
- graph paper
- hot plate
- ice, crushed
- rock salt
- stopwatch
- thermometer
- water
- wire-loop stirring device

SAFETY

When you add energy to a substance through heating, does the substance's temperature always increase? When you remove energy from a substance through cooling, does the substance's temperature always decrease? In this lab, you will try to answer these questions by studying a common substance—water.

Procedure

1. Fill the beaker about one-third to one-half full with water.

2. Put on heat-resistant gloves. Turn on the hot plate, and put the beaker on it. Put the thermometer in the beaker. **Caution:** Be careful not to touch the hot plate.

3. Make a copy of Table 1. Record the temperature of the water every 30 s. Do this until about one-fourth of the water boils away. Note the first temperature reading at which the water steadily boils.

Table 1								
Time (s)	30	60	90	120	150	180	210	etc.
Temperature (°C)		DO NOT		WRITE	IN	BOOK		

4. Turn off the hot plate.

5. While the beaker is cooling, make a graph of temperature (y-axis) versus time (x-axis). Draw an arrow pointing to the first temperature at which the water was steadily boiling.

6 After you finish the graph, use heat-resistant gloves to pick up the beaker. Pour the warm water out, and rinse the warm beaker with cool water. **Caution:** Even after cooling, the beaker is still too warm to handle without gloves.

7 Put approximately 20 mL of water in the graduated cylinder.

8 Put the graduated cylinder in the coffee can, and fill in around the graduated cylinder with crushed ice. Pour rock salt on the ice around the graduated cylinder. Place the thermometer and the wire-loop stirring device in the graduated cylinder.

9 As the ice melts and mixes with the rock salt, the level of ice will decrease. Add ice and rock salt to the can as needed to maintain the starting level of ice and salt.

10 Make another copy of Table 1. Record the temperature of the water in the graduated cylinder every 30 s. Use the stirring device to stir the water. **Caution:** Do not use the thermometer to stir.

11 Once the water begins to freeze, stop stirring. Do not try to pull the thermometer out of the solid ice in the cylinder.

12 Note the temperature at which you first notice ice crystals forming in the water. Take readings until all of the water in the graduated cylinder is completely frozen.

13 Make a graph of temperature (*y*-axis) versus time (*x*-axis). Draw an arrow to the temperature reading at which the first ice crystals form in the water in the graduated cylinder.

Analyze the Results

1 **Describing Events** What happens to the temperature of boiling water when you continue to add energy to the water through heating?

2 **Describing Events** What happens to the temperature of freezing water when you continue to remove energy through cooling?

3 **Analyzing Data** What does the slope of each graph represent?

4 **Analyzing Results** How does the slope of the graph that shows water boiling compare with the slope of the graph before the water starts to boil? Why does the slope differ between the two periods?

5 **Analyzing Results** How does the slope of the graph showing water freezing compare with the slope of the graph before the water starts to freeze? Why does the slope differ between the two periods?

Draw Conclusions

6 **Evaluating Data** The particles that make up solids, liquids, and gases are in constant motion. Adding or removing energy causes changes in the movement of these particles. Using this idea, explain why the temperature graphs of the two experiments look the way that they do.

Chapter Review

USING KEY TERMS

Complete each of the following sentences by choosing the correct term from the word bank.

gas   solid
liquid   mixture
physical change   chemical change
pressure   compound

1 A ___ can be physically separated into two or more pure substances.

2 Molecules do not have much contact with each other in a ___.

3 The ___ of a gas in a closed container will increase if the temperature is increased.

4 In a ___, both the volume and shape of matter are fixed.

5 A ___ is a change in matter that does not involve a change in chemical properties.

UNDERSTANDING KEY IDEAS

Multiple Choice

6 Which of the following would cause a chemical change in a toothpick?

a. putting the toothpick in the freezer

b. breaking the toothpick in half

c. soaking the toothpick in water

d. burning the toothpick with a match

7 Which of the following properties is a chemical property?

a. flammability   **c.** hardness

b. malleability   **d.** color

8 Marta stirs potassium chloride crystals into a beaker of water. They dissolve in the clear liquid. She observes the beaker the next day and sees a clear liquid. What type of matter is in the beaker?

a. a suspension   **c.** a colloid

b. a solution   **d.** a pure substance

9 Enough energy is added to a liquid that the motion of the particles overcomes the attractions between the particles. What is likely to happen to the liquid?

a. It will change into a solid.

b. It will change into a plasma.

c. It will change into a gas.

d. It will change into a crystal.

10 Water is an unusual compound because it exists naturally on Earth in three states: solid, liquid, and gas. In which of the following are the water molecules farthest apart?

a. in an iceberg   **c.** in river water

b. in a raindrop   **d.** in vapor in the air

11 Josie determined the mass of 5 cm³ of each of the following substances and got these values:

Aluminum   13.5 g
Diamond   17.5 g
Water   5.0 g
Wax   4.5 g

Which substance has the highest density?

a. aluminum

b. diamond

c. water

d. wax

Short Answer

12 What is matter?

13 List four physical properties of matter.

14 What happens to matter during a chemical change?

15 Describe a reversible physical change that a spoonful of sugar could undergo.

16 List the four states of matter in order from the highest to the lowest energy that the particles would have in each state.

17 Is it possible to tell whether a chemical change has occurred by watching atoms form new substances?

CRITICAL THINKING

18 **Concept Mapping** Use the following terms to create a concept map: *solid, liquid, gas, melt, evaporate, boil,* and *states of matter.*

19 **Evaluating Assumptions** Your friend does not believe in the law of conservation of mass because the charcoal left in your campfire is much lighter than the wood that was burned. Explain how the law of conservation of mass applies in this situation.

20 **Applying Concepts** Describe the process that you would use to classify chocolate-covered raisins as one of the following: an element, a compound, a homogeneous mixture, or a heterogeneous mixture.

21 **Making Comparisons** You have been asked to compare the physical and chemical properties of sand, a candle, and aluminum foil. You have water, matches, and any other tools that you need. Describe your experiments, and predict their results. Make a list of the properties that you might discover about each of your solids.

INTERPRETING GRAPHICS

The photo below shows the reaction of baking soda and vinegar. Use the photo to answer the questions that follow.

22 For which states of matter do you see evidence in the beaker? Describe the motion and spacing of the particles in each state.

23 Would you classify the matter in the beaker as an element, a compound, a heterogeneous mixture, or a homogeneous mixture? Why?

Standardized Test Preparation

Multiple Choice

Use the table below to answer question 1.

Properties of Some Substances*		
Substance	State	Density (g/cm³)
Helium	Gas	0.0001663
Pyrite	Solid	5.02
Mercury	Liquid	13.55
Gold	Solid	19.32

* at room temperature and pressure

1. **If a nugget of pyrite and a nugget of gold each have a mass of 50 g, what can you conclude about the volume of each nugget? (D=$\frac{m}{v}$)**

   A. The volume of pyrite is greater than the volume of gold.

   B. The volume of pyrite is less than the volume of gold.

   C. The volumes of the substances are equal.

   D. There is not enough information to determine the answer.

2. **Rust forms when oxygen in the air reacts with iron to form iron oxide. Which statement is correct?**

   A. This is a physical change.

   B. This is a chemical change.

   C. Iron and iron oxide have the same properties.

   D. Oxygen and iron have similar properties.

3. **Which is a chemical change?**

   A. clear water turning red after a dye is added

   B. ice melting into liquid water

   C. salt dissolving in water when the water is stirred rapidly

   D. vinegar and baking soda combining to form carbon dioxide gas

4. **Which is true of chemical properties?**

   A. They can be observed when the identity of a substance changes.

   B. They can always be observed without changing the identity of a substance.

   C. They are easier to observe than physical properties.

   D. They are the properties that are most useful in identifying a substance.

5. **Which physical property could be used to classify oxygen, helium, and propane in the same group?**

   A. flammability

   B. state

   C. reactivity

   D. malleability

6. **Which of the following could describe oxygen at room temperature?**

   A. It has a definite shape and a strong odor.

   B. It has a constant volume and takes the shape of its container.

   C. Its particles move fast enough to overcome the attraction between them.

   D. Its particles can be crystalline.

7. All matter is made up of atoms. Each atom has mass, most of which is in the nucleus of the atom. How is matter visible to the unaided human eye?

A. If a single atom is large enough, it is visible.

B. Two atoms become visible when they combine to form a molecule.

C. The nucleus of a single atom is visible, but the rest of the atom is not.

D. Ordinary objects are visible because they are made of billions of atoms.

8. Jorge transferred a substance into a beaker and observed that the substance took the shape of the beaker but did not change in volume. The substance is a

A. liquid.

B. gas.

C. solid.

D. plasma.

9. An ad for a brand of dry ice claims that it keeps food cold without getting it wet. Which of the following is a valid explanation for this claim?

A. Dry ice keeps food from freezing.

B. Dry ice is not frozen.

C. Dry ice is colder than regular ice.

D. Dry ice undergoes sublimation.

Use the diagram below to answer question 10.

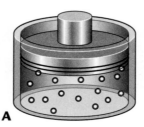

A   B

10. The figure above shows gas particles in a car engine cylinder. Figure B shows that the volume of the cylinder has been reduced. What is happening in Figure B?

A. The gas particles are moving apart.

B. The gas particles are moving closer together.

C. The gas particles are being held in place.

D. Less pressure is being exerted on the gas particles.

Open Response

11. Magnesium burns with a hot flame in the presence of oxygen. How do you know that a chemical change is taking place?

12. The change of state from a liquid to a solid is exothermic. Describe a lab experiment that could test this.

Standardized Test Preparation

Science in Action

Weird Science

A Safer "Water" for Fighting Fires

If water is used to fight fire near electronic equipment, the equipment is usually ruined. Water shorts out electronics and may damage equipment. The SAPPHIRE Fire Suppression System, made in Florida, uses a chemical to put out fires without damaging electronics. The new liquid, Novec 1230, is nonconductive. That is, it does not conduct electric current easily, so equipment will not short out. Novec 1230 also evaporates quickly, so it does not damage machinery by soaking into machinery the way that water can. Other chemicals have been used to fight electrical fires, but many are harmful to the environment. Novec 1230 is a breakthrough because it puts out electrical fires without harming equipment or the environment!

Scientific Discoveries

A Fifth State of Matter

Deborah Jin, a scientist at the National Institute of Standards and Technology, works on an apparatus used to create a fifth state of matter. Years ago, scientists wondered, Is there a very cold state of matter that differs from the solid state? Properties of this state were predicted by Satyendra Nath Bose and Albert Einstein in the 1920s. It was not until 1995 that scientists were able to make and observe the Bose-Einstein Condensate. They made this new state of matter by cooling about 2,000 rubidium atoms to a temperature close to 0 K (absolute zero). At this temperature, the atoms merged into a single blob of matter. Some scientists call this state of matter a *superatom*, because in this state, all of the atoms exist in the same space.

Math ACTIVITY

The Bose-Einstein Condensate could not exist in deep space because deep space is too warm—about 3 K! Determine the temperature of deep space in degrees Celsius and in degrees Fahrenheit.

Social Studies ACTIVITY

WRITING SKILL Research the history of firefighting in the United States. Write a short report that focuses on either the technology of fighting fires or the ways in which communities organize to fight fires.

Andy Goldsworthy

Nature Artist Most of the art that Andy Goldsworthy creates will melt, decay, evaporate, or just blow away. He uses leaves, water, sticks, rocks, ice, and snow to create art. Goldsworthy observes how nature works and how it changes over time, and he uses what he learns to create his art. For example, on cold, sunny mornings, Goldsworthy makes frost shadows. He stands with his back to the sun, which creates a shadow on the ground. The rising sun warms the ground and melts the frost around his shadow. When he steps away, he can see the shape of his body in the frost that is left on the ground.

In his art, Goldsworthy sometimes shows water in the process of changing states. For example, he made huge snowballs filled with branches, pebbles, and flowers. He then stored these snowballs in a freezer until summer, when they were displayed in a museum. As they melted, the snowballs slowly revealed their contents. Goldsworthy says his art reflects nature, because nature is constantly changing. Fortunately, he takes pictures of his art so that we can enjoy it even after it disappears!

Language Arts ACTIVITY

WRITING SKILL Research Andy Goldsworthy's art. Write a one-page review of one of his creations. Be sure to include what you like or don't like about the art.

To learn more about these Science in Action topics, visit **go.hrw.com** and type in the keyword **HT6FMF8F.**

Current Science

Check out Current Science® articles related to this chapter by visiting go.hrw.com. Just type in the keyword HP5CS03.

19

Matter in Motion

The Big Idea

Forces act on objects and can produce motion.

About the Photo

Speed skaters are fast. In fact, some skaters can skate at a rate of 12 m/s! That's equal to a speed of 27 mi/h. To reach such a speed, skaters must exert large forces. They must also use friction to turn corners on the slippery surface of the ice.

PRE-READING ACTIVITY

FOLDNOTES **Four-Corner Fold**
Before you read the chapter, create the FoldNote entitled "Four-Corner Fold" described in the **Study Skills** section of the Appendix. Label the flaps of the four-corner fold with "Motion," "Forces," "Friction," and "Gravity." Write what you know about each topic under the appropriate flap. As you read the chapter, add other information that you learn.

The Domino Derby

Speed is the distance traveled by an object in a certain amount of time. In this activity, you will observe one factor that affects the speed of falling dominoes.

Procedure

1. Set up **25 dominoes** in a straight line. Try to keep equal spacing between the dominoes.

2. Use a **meterstick** to measure the total length of your row of dominoes, and record the length.

3. Use a **stopwatch** to time how long it takes for the dominoes to fall. Record this measurement.

4. Predict what would happen to that amount of time if you changed the distance between the dominoes. Write your predictions.

5. Repeat steps 2 and 3 several times using distances between the dominoes that are smaller and larger than the distance used in your first setup. Use the same number of dominoes in each trial.

Analysis

1. Calculate the average speed for each trial by dividing the total distance (the length of the domino row) by the time the dominoes take to fall.

2. How did the spacing between dominoes affect the average speed? Is this result what you expected? If not, explain.

Measuring Motion

Look around you—you are likely to see something in motion. Your teacher may be walking across the room, or perhaps your friend is writing with a pencil.

Even if you don't see anything moving, motion is still occurring all around you. Air particles are moving, the Earth is circling the sun, and blood is traveling through your blood vessels!

Observing Motion by Using a Reference Point

You might think that the motion of an object is easy to detect—you just watch the object. But you are actually watching the object in relation to another object that appears to stay in place. The object that appears to stay in place is a *reference point.* When an object changes position over time relative to a reference point, the object is in **motion.** You can describe the direction of the object's motion with a reference direction, such as north, south, east, west, up, or down.

✓ **Reading Check** What is a reference point? (*See the Appendix for answers to Reading Checks.*)

Common Reference Points

The Earth's surface is a common reference point for determining motion, as shown in **Figure 1.** Nonmoving objects, such as trees and buildings, are also useful reference points.

A moving object can also be used as a reference point. For example, if you were on the hot-air balloon shown in **Figure 1,** you could watch a bird fly by and see that the bird was changing position in relation to your moving balloon.

What You Will Learn

● Describe the motion of an object by the position of the object in relation to a reference point.
● Identify the two factors that determine speed.
● Explain the difference between speed and velocity.
● Analyze the relationship between velocity and acceleration.
● Demonstrate that changes in motion can be measured and represented on a graph.

Vocabulary

motion   velocity
speed   acceleration

Figure 1 *During the interval between the times that these pictures were taken, the hot-air balloon changed position relative to a reference point—the mountain.*

Speed Depends on Distance and Time

Speed is the distance traveled by an object divided by the time taken to travel that distance. Look again at **Figure 1.** Suppose the time interval between the pictures was 10 s and that the balloon traveled 50 m in that time. The speed of the balloon is (50 m)/(10 s), or 5 m/s.

The SI unit for speed is meters per second (m/s). Kilometers per hour (km/h), feet per second (ft/s), and miles per hour (mi/h) are other units commonly used to express speed.

Determining Average Speed

Most of the time, objects do not travel at a constant speed. For example, you probably do not walk at a constant speed from one class to the next. So, it is very useful to calculate *average speed* using the following equation:

$$average\ speed = \frac{total\ distance}{total\ time}$$

Recognizing Speed on a Graph

Suppose a person drives from one city to another. The blue line in the graph in **Figure 2** shows the total distance traveled during a 4 h period. Notice that the distance traveled during each hour is different. The distance varies because the speed is not constant. The driver may change speed because of weather, traffic, or varying speed limits. The average speed for the entire trip can be calculated as follows:

$$average\ speed = \frac{360\ km}{4\ h} = 90\ km/h$$

The red line on the graph shows how far the driver must travel each hour to reach the same city if he or she moved at a constant speed. The slope of this line is the average speed.

motion an object's change in position relative to a reference point

speed the distance traveled divided by the time interval during which the motion occurred

What's Your Speed?

Measure a distance of 5 m or a distance of 25 ft inside or outside. Ask a family member to use a stopwatch or a watch with a second hand to time you as you travel the distance you measured. Then, find your average speed. Find the average speed of other members of your family in the same way.

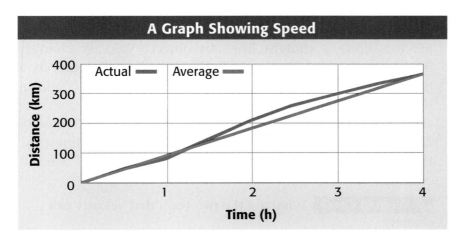

Figure 2 *Speed can be shown on a graph of distance versus time.*

Calculating Average Speed An athlete swims a distance from one end of a 50 m pool to the other end in a time of 25 s. What is the athlete's average speed?

Step 1: Write the equation for average speed.

$$average\ speed = \frac{total\ distance}{total\ time}$$

Step 2: Replace the total distance and total time with the values given, and solve.

$$average\ speed = \frac{50\ m}{25\ s} = 2\ m/s$$

Now It's Your Turn

1. Kira jogs to a store 72 m away in a time of 36 s. What is Kira's average speed?
2. If you travel 7.5 km and walk for 1.5 h, what is your average speed?
3. An airplane traveling from San Francisco to Chicago travels 1,260 km in 3.5 h. What is the airplane's average speed?

Velocity: Direction Matters

Imagine that two birds leave the same tree at the same time. They both fly at 10 km/h for 5 min, 12 km/h for 8 min, and 5 km/h for 10 min. Why don't they end up at the same place?

Have you figured out the answer? The birds went in different directions. Their speeds were the same, but they had different velocities. **Velocity** (vuh LAHS uh tee) is the speed of an object in a particular direction.

Be careful not to confuse the terms *speed* and *velocity*. They do not have the same meaning. Velocity must include a reference direction. If you say that an airplane's velocity is 600 km/h, you would not be correct. But you could say the plane's velocity is 600 km/h south. **Figure 3** shows an example of the difference between speed and velocity.

Changing Velocity

You can think of velocity as the rate of change of an object's position. An object's velocity is constant only if its speed and direction don't change. Therefore, constant velocity is always motion along a straight line. An object's velocity changes if either its speed or direction changes. For example, as a bus traveling at 15 m/s south speeds up to 20 m/s south, its velocity changes. If the bus continues to travel at the same speed but changes direction to travel east, its velocity changes again. And if the bus slows down at the same time that it swerves north to avoid a cat, the velocity of the bus changes, too.

Reading Check What are the two ways that velocity can change?

Figure 3 *The speeds of these cars may be similar, but the velocities of the cars differ because the cars are going in different directions.*

Figure 4 Finding Resultant Velocity

Person's resultant velocity
15 m/s east + 1 m/s east = 16 m/s east

When you combine two velocities that are **in the same direction,** add them together to find the resultant velocity.

Person's resultant velocity
15 m/s east − 1 m/s west = 14 m/s east

When you combine two velocities that are **in opposite directions,** subtract the smaller velocity from the larger velocity to find the resultant velocity. The resultant velocity is in the direction of the larger velocity.

Combining Velocities

Imagine that you are riding in a bus that is traveling east at 15 m/s. You and the other passengers are also traveling at a velocity of 15 m/s east. But suppose you stand up and walk down the bus's aisle while the bus is moving. Are you still moving at the same velocity as the bus? No! **Figure 4** shows how you can combine velocities to find the *resultant velocity.*

Acceleration

Although the word *accelerate* is commonly used to mean "speed up," the word means something else in science. **Acceleration** (ak SEL uhr AY shuhn) is the rate at which velocity changes. Velocity changes if speed changes, if direction changes, or if both change. So, an object accelerates if its speed, its direction, or both change.

An increase in velocity is commonly called *positive acceleration.* A decrease in velocity is commonly called *negative acceleration,* or *deceleration.* Keep in mind that acceleration is not only how much velocity changes but also how fast velocity changes. The faster the velocity changes, the greater the acceleration is.

velocity the speed of an object in a particular direction

acceleration the rate at which velocity changes over time; an object accelerates if its speed, direction, or both change

1 m/s   2 m/s   3 m/s   4 m/s   5 m/s

South

Figure 5 *This cyclist is accelerating at 1 m/s² south.*

Calculating Acceleration

Use the equation for average acceleration to do the following problem.

A plane passes over point A at a velocity of 240 m/s north. Forty seconds later, it passes over point B at a velocity of 260 m/s north. What is the plane's average acceleration?

Calculating Average Acceleration

You can find average acceleration by using the equation:

$$average\ acceleration = \frac{final\ velocity - starting\ velocity}{time\ it\ takes\ to\ change\ velocity}$$

Velocity is expressed in meters per second (m/s), and time is expressed in seconds (s). So acceleration is expressed in meters per second per second, or (m/s)/s, which equals m/s². For example, look at **Figure 5.** Every second, the cyclist's southward velocity increases by 1 m/s. His average acceleration can be calculated as follows:

$$average\ acceleration = \frac{5\ m/s - 1\ m/s}{4\ s} = 1\ m/s^2\ south$$

✓ Reading Check What are the units of acceleration?

Recognizing Acceleration on a Graph

Suppose that you are riding a roller coaster. The roller-coaster car moves up a hill until it stops at the top. Then, you are off! The graph in **Figure 6** shows your acceleration for the next 10 s. During the first 8 s, you move down the hill. You can tell from the graph that your acceleration is positive for the first 8 s because your velocity increases as time passes. During the last 2 s, your car starts climbing the next hill. Your acceleration is negative because your velocity decreases as time passes.

Figure 6 *Acceleration can be shown on a graph of velocity versus time.*

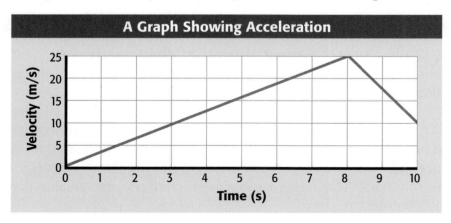

A Graph Showing Acceleration

Circular Motion: Continuous Acceleration

You may be surprised to know that even when you are completely still, you are experiencing acceleration. You may not seem to be changing speed or direction, but you are! You are traveling in a circle as the Earth rotates. An object traveling in a circular motion is always changing its direction. Therefore, its velocity is always changing, so it is accelerating. The acceleration that occurs in circular motion is known as *centripetal acceleration* (sen TRIP uht uhl ak SEL uhr AY shuhn). Centripetal acceleration occurs on a Ferris wheel at an amusement park or as the moon orbits Earth. Another example of centripetal acceleration is shown in **Figure 7.**

Figure 7 *The blades of these windmills are constantly changing direction. Thus, centripetal acceleration is occurring.*

SECTION Review

Summary

- An object is in motion if it changes position over time in relation to a reference point.
- Speed is the distance traveled by an object divided by the time the object takes to travel that distance.
- Velocity is speed in a given direction.
- Acceleration is the rate at which velocity changes.
- An object can accelerate by changing speed, direction, or both.
- Speed can be represented on a graph of distance versus time.
- Acceleration can be represented by graphing velocity versus time.

Using Key Terms

1. In your own words, write definitions for each of the following terms: *motion* and *acceleration*.

2. Use each of the following terms in a separate sentence: *speed* and *velocity*.

Understanding Key Ideas

3. Which of the following is NOT an example of acceleration?
   a. a person jogging at 3 m/s along a winding path
   b. a car stopping at a stop sign
   c. a cheetah running 27 m/s east
   d. a plane taking off

4. Which of the following would be a good reference point to describe the motion of a dog?
   a. the ground
   b. another dog running
   c. a tree
   d. All of the above

5. Explain the difference between speed and velocity.

6. What two things must you know to determine speed?

7. How are velocity and acceleration related?

Math Skills

8. Find the average speed of a person who swims 105 m in 70 s.

9. What is the average acceleration of a subway train that speeds up from 9.6 m/s to 12 m/s in 0.8 s on a straight section of track?

Critical Thinking

10. **Applying Concepts** Why is it more helpful to know a tornado's velocity rather than its speed?

11. **Evaluating Data** A wolf is chasing a rabbit. Graph the wolf's motion using the following data: 15 m/s at 0 s, 10 m/s at 1 s, 5 m/s at 2 s, 2.5 m/s at 3 s, 1 m/s at 4 s, and 0 m/s at 5 s. What does the graph tell you?

SCI**LINKS**®

NSTA

Developed and maintained by the National Science Teachers Association

For a variety of links related to this chapter, go to www.scilinks.org

Topic: Measuring Motion
SciLinks code: HSM0927

READING STRATEGY

Reading Organizer As you read this section, make a table comparing balanced forces and unbalanced forces.

What Is a Force?

You have probably heard the word **force** in everyday conversation. People say things such as "That storm had a lot of force" or "Our football team is a force to be reckoned with." But what, exactly, is a force?

In science, a **force** is simply a push or a pull. All forces have both size and direction. A force can change the acceleration of an object. This acceleration can be a change in the speed or direction of the object. In fact, any time you see a change in an object's motion, you can be sure that the change in motion was created by a force. Scientists express force using a unit called the **newton** (N).

Forces Acting on Objects

All forces act on objects. For any push to occur, something has to receive the push. You can't push nothing! The same is true for any pull. When doing schoolwork, you use your fingers to pull open books or to push the buttons on a computer keyboard. In these examples, your fingers are exerting forces on the books and the keys. So, the forces act on the books and keys. Another example of a force acting on an object is shown in **Figure 1.**

However, just because a force acts on an object doesn't mean that motion will occur. For example, you are probably sitting on a chair. But the force you are exerting on the chair does not cause the chair to move. The chair doesn't move because the floor is also exerting a force on the chair.

Figure 1 *The bulldozer is exerting a force on the pile of soil. But the pile of soil also exerts a force by just sitting on the ground!*

Unseen Sources and Receivers of Forces

It is not always easy to tell what is exerting a force or what is receiving a force, as shown in **Figure 2.** You cannot see what exerts the force that pulls magnets to refrigerators. And you cannot see that the air around you is held near Earth's surface by a force called *gravity.*

Determining Net Force

Usually, more than one force is acting on an object. The **net force** is the combination all of the forces acting on an object. So, how do you determine the net force? The answer depends on the directions of the forces.

Forces in the Same Direction

Suppose the music teacher asks you and a friend to move a piano. You pull on one end and your friend pushes on the other end, as shown in **Figure 3.** The forces you and your friend exert on the piano act in the same direction. The two forces are added to determine the net force because the forces act in the same direction. In this case, the net force is 45 N. This net force is large enough to move the piano—if it is on wheels, that is!

✓Reading Check How do you determine the net force on an object if all forces act in the same direction? (*See the Appendix for answers to Reading Checks.*)

Figure 2 *Something that you cannot see exerts a force that makes this cat's fur stand up.*

force a push or a pull exerted on an object in order to change the motion of the object; force has size and direction

newton the SI unit for force (symbol, N)

net force the combination of all of the forces acting on an object

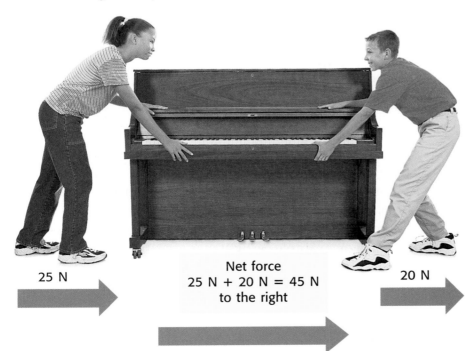

25 N

Net force
25 N + 20 N = 45 N
to the right

20 N

Figure 3 *When forces act in the same direction, you add the forces to determine the net force. The net force will be in the same direction as the individual forces.*

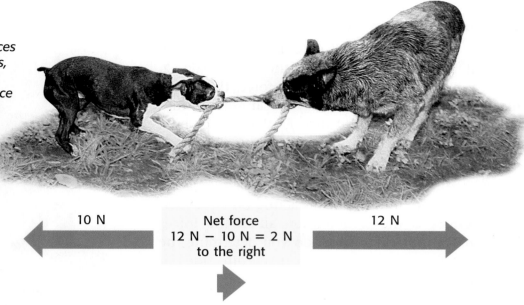

Figure 4 *When two forces act in opposite directions, you subtract the smaller force from the larger force to determine the net force. The net force will be in the same direction as the larger force.*

10 N

Net force
12 N − 10 N = 2 N
to the right

12 N

Forces in Different Directions

Look at the two dogs playing tug of war in **Figure 4.** Each dog is exerting a force on the rope. But the forces are in opposite directions. Which dog will win the tug of war?

Because the forces are in opposite directions, the net force on the rope is found by subtracting the smaller force from the larger one. In this case, the net force is 2 N in the direction of the dog on the right. Give that dog a dog biscuit!

✓ **Reading Check** What is the net force on an object when you combine a force of 7 N north with a force of 5 N south?

Balanced and Unbalanced Forces

If you know the net force on an object, you can determine the effect of the net force on the object's motion. Why? The net force tells you whether the forces on the object are balanced or unbalanced.

Balanced Forces

When the forces on an object produce a net force of 0 N, the forces are *balanced*. Balanced forces will not cause a change in the motion of a moving object. And balanced forces do not cause a nonmoving object to start moving.

Many objects around you have only balanced forces acting on them. For example, a light hanging from the ceiling does not move because the force of gravity pulling down on the light is balanced by the force of the cord pulling upward. A bird's nest in a tree and a hat resting on your head are also examples of objects that have only balanced forces acting on them. **Figure 5** shows another example of balanced forces.

Figure 5 *Because all the forces on this house of cards are balanced, none of the cards move.*

Unbalanced Forces

When the net force on an object is not 0 N, the forces on the object are *unbalanced*. Unbalanced forces produce a change in motion, such as a change in speed or a change in direction. Unbalanced forces are necessary to cause a nonmoving object to start moving.

Unbalanced forces are also necessary to change the motion of moving objects. For example, consider the soccer game shown in **Figure 6.** The soccer ball is already moving when it is passed from one player to another. When the ball reaches another player, that player exerts an unbalanced force—a kick—on the ball. After the kick, the ball moves in a new direction and has a new speed.

An object can continue to move when the unbalanced forces are removed. For example, when it is kicked, a soccer ball receives an unbalanced force. The ball continues to roll on the ground long after the force of the kick has ended.

Figure 6 *The soccer ball moves because the players exert an unbalanced force on the ball each time they kick it.*

SECTION Review

Summary

- A force is a push or a pull. Forces have size and direction and are expressed in newtons.

- Force is always exerted by one object on another object.

- Net force is determined by combining forces. Forces in the same direction are added. Forces in opposite directions are subtracted.

- Balanced forces produce no change in motion. Unbalanced forces produce a change in motion.

Using Key Terms

1. In your own words, write a definition for each of the following terms: *force* and *net force*.

Understanding Key Ideas

2. Which of the following may happen when an object receives unbalanced forces?
   a. The object changes direction.
   b. The object changes speed.
   c. The object starts to move.
   d. All of the above

3. Explain the difference between balanced and unbalanced forces.

4. Give an example of an unbalanced force causing a change in motion.

5. Give an example of an object that has balanced forces acting on it.

6. Explain the meaning of the phrase "Forces act on objects."

Math Skills

7. A boy pulls a wagon with a force of 6 N east as another boy pushes it with a force of 4 N east. What is the net force?

Critical Thinking

8. **Making Inferences** When finding net force, why must you know the directions of the forces acting on an object?

9. **Applying Concepts** List three forces that you exert when riding a bicycle.

SCiLINKS.

NSTA
Developed and maintained by the
National Science Teachers Association

For a variety of links related to this chapter, go to www.scilinks.org

Topic: Forces
SciLinks code: HSM0604

Friction: A Force That Opposes Motion

What You Will Learn

- Explain why friction occurs.
- List the two types of friction, and give examples of each type.
- Explain how friction can be both harmful and helpful.

Vocabulary

friction

READING STRATEGY

Brainstorming The key idea of this section is friction. Brainstorm words and phrases related to friction.

friction a force that opposes motion between two surfaces that are in contact

While playing ball, your friend throws the ball out of your reach. Rather than running for the ball, you walk after it. You know that the ball will stop. But do you know why?

You know that the ball is slowing down. An unbalanced force is needed to change the speed of a moving object. So, what force is stopping the ball? The force is called friction. **Friction** is a force that opposes motion between two surfaces that are in contact. Friction can cause a moving object, such as a ball, to slow down and eventually stop.

The Source of Friction

Friction occurs because the surface of any object is rough. Even surfaces that feel smooth are covered with microscopic hills and valleys. When two surfaces are in contact, the hills and valleys of one surface stick to the hills and valleys of the other surface, as shown in **Figure 1.** This contact causes friction.

The amount of friction between two surfaces depends on many factors. Two factors include the force pushing the surfaces together and the roughness of the surfaces.

The Effect of Force on Friction

The amount of friction depends on the force pushing the surfaces together. If this force increases, the hills and valleys of the surfaces can come into closer contact. The close contact increases the friction between the surfaces. Objects that weigh less exert less downward force than objects that weigh more do, as shown in **Figure 2.** But changing how much of the surfaces come in contact does not change the amount of friction.

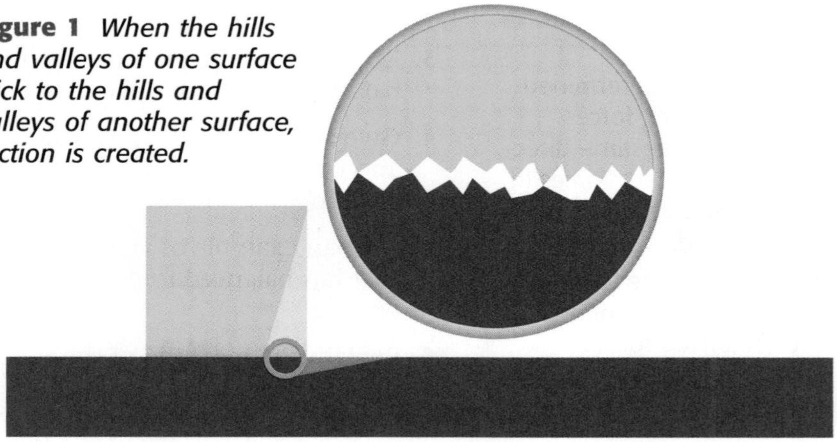

Figure 1 *When the hills and valleys of one surface stick to the hills and valleys of another surface, friction is created.*

Figure 2 Force and Friction

ⓐ There is more friction between the book with more weight and the table than there is between the book with less weight and the table. A harder push is needed to move the heavier book.

ⓑ Turning a book on its edge does not change the amount of friction between the table and the book.

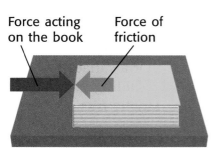

Force acting on the book   Force of friction

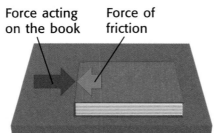

Force acting on the book   Force of friction

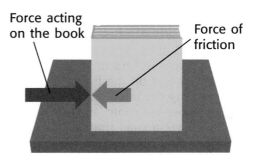

Force acting on the book   Force of friction

The Effect of Rougher Surfaces on Friction

Rough surfaces have more microscopic hills and valleys than smooth surfaces do. So, the rougher the surface is, the greater the friction is. For example, a ball rolling on the ground slows down because of the friction between the ball and the ground. A large amount of friction is produced because the ground has a rough surface. But imagine that you were playing ice hockey. If the puck passed out of your reach, it would slide across the ice for a long while before stopping. The reason the puck would continue to slide is that the ice is a smooth surface that has very little friction.

✓ **Reading Check** Why is friction greater between surfaces that are rough? (*See the Appendix for answers to Reading Checks.*)

The Friction 500

1. Make a short ramp out of **a piece of cardboard** and **one or two books** on a table.

2. Put a **toy car** at the top of the ramp, and let go of the car. If necessary, adjust the ramp height so that your car does not roll off the table.

3. Put the car at the top of the ramp again, and let go of the car. Record the distance the car travels after leaving the ramp.

4. Repeat step 3 two more times, and calculate the average for your results.

5. Change the surface of the table by covering the table with **sandpaper.** Repeat steps 3 and 4.

6. Change the surface of the table one more time by covering the table with **cloth.** Repeat steps 3 and 4 again.

7. Which surface had the most friction? Why? What do you predict would happen if the car were heavier?

Types of Friction

There are two types of friction. The friction you observe when sliding books across a tabletop is called *kinetic friction*. The other type of friction is *static friction*. You observe static friction when you push on a piece of furniture and it does not move.

Kinetic Friction

The word *kinetic* means "moving." So, kinetic friction is friction between moving surfaces. The amount of kinetic friction between two surfaces depends in part on how the surfaces move. Surfaces can slide past each other. Or a surface can roll over another surface. Usually, the force of sliding kinetic friction is greater than the force of rolling kinetic friction. Thus, it is usually easier to move objects on wheels than to slide the objects along the floor, as shown in **Figure 3**.

Kinetic friction is very useful in everyday life. You use sliding kinetic friction when you apply the brakes on a bicycle and when you write with a pencil or a piece of chalk. You also use sliding kinetic friction when you scratch a part of your body that is itchy!

Rolling kinetic friction is an important part of almost all means of transportation. Anything that has wheels—bicycles, in-line skates, cars, trains, and planes—uses rolling kinetic friction.

Figure 3 Comparing Kinetic Friction

ⓐ Moving a heavy piece of furniture in your room can be hard work because **the force of sliding kinetic friction is large.**

ⓑ Moving a heavy piece of furniture is easier if you put it on wheels. **The force of rolling kinetic friction is smaller** and easier to overcome.

Figure 4 Static Friction

Block		
Table		

a There is no friction between the block and the table when no force is applied to the block.

	Force applied	Static friction

b If a small force (purple arrow) is exerted on the block, the block does not move. The force of static friction (green arrow) balances the force applied.

	Force applied	Kinetic friction

c When the force exerted on the block is greater than the force of static friction, the block starts moving. When the block starts moving, all static friction is gone, and only kinetic friction (green arrow) opposes the force applied.

Static Friction

When a force is applied to an object but does not cause the object to move, *static friction* occurs. The word *static* means "not moving." The object does not move because the force of static friction balances the force applied. Static friction can be overcome by applying a large enough force. Static friction disappears as soon as an object starts moving, and then kinetic friction immediately occurs. Look at **Figure 4** to understand under what conditions static friction affects an object.

✓ Reading Check What does the word *static* mean?

Friction: Harmful and Helpful

Think about how friction affects a car. Without friction, the tires could not push against the ground to move the car forward, and the brakes could not stop the car. Without friction, a car is useless. However, friction can also cause problems in a car. Friction between moving engine parts increases their temperature and causes the parts to wear down. A liquid coolant is added to the engine to keep the engine from overheating. And engine parts need to be changed as they wear out.

Friction is both harmful and helpful to you and the world around you. Friction can cause holes in your socks and in the knees of your jeans. Friction by wind and water can cause erosion of the topsoil that nourishes plants. On the other hand, friction between your pencil and your paper is necessary to allow the pencil to leave a mark. Without friction, you would just slip and fall when you tried to walk. Because friction can be both harmful and helpful, it is sometimes necessary to decrease or increase friction.

For another activity related to this chapter, go to **go.hrw.com** and type in the keyword **HP5MOTW**.

CONNECTION TO Social Studies

WRITING SKILL **Invention of the Wheel** Archeologists have found evidence that the first vehicles with wheels were used in ancient Mesopotamia sometime between 3500 and 3000 BCE. Before wheels were invented, people used planks or sleds to carry loads. In your **science journal**, write a paragraph about how your life would be different if wheels did not exist.

Some Ways to Reduce Friction

One way to reduce friction is to use lubricants (LOO bri kuhnts). *Lubricants* are substances that are applied to surfaces to reduce the friction between the surfaces. Some examples of common lubricants are motor oil, wax, and grease. Lubricants are usually liquids, but they can be solids or gases. An example of a gas lubricant is the air that comes out of the tiny holes of an air-hockey table. **Figure 5** shows one use of a lubricant.

Friction can also be reduced by switching from sliding kinetic friction to rolling kinetic friction. Ball bearings placed between the wheels and axles of in-line skates and bicycles make it easier for the wheels to turn by reducing friction.

Another way to reduce friction is to make surfaces that rub against each other smoother. For example, rough wood on a park bench is painful to slide across because there is a large amount of friction between your leg and the bench. Rubbing the bench with sandpaper makes the bench smoother and more comfortable to sit on. The reason the bench is more comfortable is that the friction between your leg and the bench is reduced.

Reading Check List three common lubricants.

Figure 5 *When you work on a bicycle, watch out for the chain! You might get dirty from the grease or oil that keeps the chain moving freely. Without this lubricant, friction between the sections of the chain would quickly wear the chain out.*

Some Ways to Increase Friction

One way to increase friction is to make surfaces rougher. For example, sand scattered on icy roads keeps cars from skidding. Baseball players sometimes wear textured batting gloves to increase the friction between their hands and the bat so that the bat does not fly out of their hands.

Another way to increase friction is to increase the force pushing the surfaces together. For example, if you are sanding a piece of wood, you can sand the wood faster by pressing harder on the sandpaper. Pressing harder increases the force pushing the sandpaper and wood together. So, the friction between the sandpaper and wood increases. **Figure 6** shows another example of friction increased by pushing on an object.

Figure 6 *No one likes cleaning dirty pans. To get this chore done quickly, press down with the scrubber to increase friction.*

SECTION Review

Summary

- Friction is a force that opposes motion.
- Friction is caused by hills and valleys on the surfaces of two objects touching each other.
- The amount of friction depends on factors such as the roughness of the surfaces and the force pushing the surfaces together.
- Two kinds of friction are kinetic friction and static friction.
- Friction can be helpful or harmful.

Using Key Terms

1. In your own words, write a definition for the term *friction*.

Understanding Key Ideas

2. Why is it easy to slip when there is water on the floor?
   a. The water is a lubricant and reduces the friction between your feet and the floor.
   b. The friction between your feet and the floor changes from kinetic to static friction.
   c. The water increases the friction between your feet and the floor.
   d. The friction between your feet and the floor changes from sliding kinetic friction to rolling kinetic friction.

3. Explain why friction occurs.

4. How does the roughness of surfaces that are touching affect the friction between the surfaces?

5. Describe how the amount of force pushing two surfaces together affects friction.

6. Name two ways in which friction can be increased.

7. List the two types of friction, and give an example of each.

Interpreting Graphics

8. Why do you think the sponge shown below has a layer of plastic bristles attached to it?

Critical Thinking

9. **Applying Concepts** Name two ways that friction is harmful and two ways that friction is helpful to you when riding a bicycle.

10. **Making Inferences** Describe a situation in which static friction is useful.

Developed and maintained by the National Science Teachers Association

For a variety of links related to this chapter, go to www.scilinks.org

Topic: Force and Friction
SciLinks code: HSM0601

Gravity: A Force of Attraction

What You Will Learn

● Describe gravity and its effect on matter.
● Explain the law of universal gravitation.
● Describe the difference between mass and weight.

Vocabulary

gravity
weight
mass

READING STRATEGY

Paired Summarizing Read this section silently. In pairs, take turns summarizing the material. Stop to discuss ideas that seem confusing.

gravity a force of attraction between objects that is due to their masses

Have you ever seen a video of astronauts on the moon? They bounce around like beach balls even though they wear big, bulky spacesuits. Why is leaping on the moon easier than leaping on Earth?

The answer is gravity. **Gravity** is a force of attraction between objects that is due to their masses. The force of gravity can change the motion of an object by changing its speed, direction, or both. In this section, you will learn about gravity and its effects on objects, such as the astronaut in **Figure 1.**

The Effects of Gravity on Matter

All matter has mass. Gravity is a result of mass. Therefore, all matter is affected by gravity. That is, all objects experience an attraction toward all other objects. This gravitational force pulls objects toward each other. Right now, because of gravity, you are being pulled toward this book, your pencil, and every other object around you.

These objects are also being pulled toward you and toward each other because of gravity. So why don't you see the effects of this attraction? In other words, why don't you notice objects moving toward each other? The reason is that the mass of most objects is too small to cause a force large enough to move objects toward each other. However, you are familiar with one object that is massive enough to cause a noticeable attraction—the Earth.

Figure 1 *Because the moon has less gravity than the Earth does, walking on the moon's surface was a very bouncy experience for the Apollo astronauts.*

The Size of Earth's Gravitational Force

Compared with all objects around you, Earth has a huge mass. Therefore, Earth's gravitational force is very large. You must apply forces to overcome Earth's gravitational force any time you lift objects or even parts of your body.

Earth's gravitational force pulls everything toward the center of Earth. Because of this force, the books, tables, and chairs in the room stay in place, and dropped objects fall to Earth rather than moving together or toward you.

Reading Check Why must you exert a force to pick up an object? (*See the Appendix for answers to Reading Checks.*)

Newton and the Study of Gravity

For thousands of years, people asked two very puzzling questions: Why do objects fall toward Earth, and what keeps the planets moving in the sky? The two questions were treated separately until 1665 when a British scientist named Sir Isaac Newton realized that they were two parts of the same question.

The Core of an Idea

The legend is that Newton made the connection between the two questions when he watched a falling apple, as shown in **Figure 2.** He knew that unbalanced forces are needed to change the motion of objects. He concluded that an unbalanced force on the apple made the apple fall. And he reasoned that an unbalanced force on the moon kept the moon moving circularly around Earth. He proposed that these two forces are actually the same force—a force of attraction called *gravity.*

The Birth of a Law

Newton summarized his ideas about gravity in a law now known as the *law of universal gravitation.* This law describes the relationships between gravitational force, mass, and distance. The law is called *universal* because it applies to all objects in the universe.

CONNECTION TO Biology

Seeds and Gravity Seeds respond to gravity. The ability to respond to gravity causes seeds to send roots down and the green shoot up. But scientists do not understand how seeds can sense gravity. Plan an experiment to study how seedlings respond to gravity. After getting your teacher's approval, do your experiment and report your observations in a poster.

ACTIVITY

Figure 2 *Sir Isaac Newton realized that the same unbalanced force affected the motions of the apple and the moon.*

The Law of Universal Gravitation

The law of universal gravitation is the following: All objects in the universe attract each other through gravitational force. The size of the force depends on the masses of the objects and the distance between the objects. Understanding the law is easier if you consider it in two parts.

Part 1: Gravitational Force Increases as Mass Increases

Imagine an elephant and a cat. Because an elephant has a larger mass than a cat does, the amount of gravity between an elephant and Earth is greater than the amount of gravity between a cat and Earth. So, a cat is much easier to pick up than an elephant! There is also gravity between the cat and the elephant, but that force is very small because the cat's mass and the elephant's mass are so much smaller than Earth's mass. **Figure 3** shows the relationship between mass and gravitational force.

This part of the law of universal gravitation also explains why the astronauts on the moon bounce when they walk. The moon has less mass than Earth does. Therefore, the moon's gravitational force is less than Earth's. The astronauts bounced around on the moon because they were not being pulled down with as much force as they would have been on Earth.

✓ **Reading Check** How does mass affect gravitational force?

Figure 3 **How Mass Affects Gravitational Force**

The gravitational force between objects increases as the masses of the objects increase. The arrows indicate the gravitational force between two objects. The length of the arrows indicates the strength of the force.

ⓐ Gravitational force is small between objects that have small masses.

ⓑ Gravitational force is large when the mass of one or both objects is large.

Part 2: Gravitational Force Decreases as Distance Increases

The gravitational force between you and Earth is large. Whenever you jump up, you are pulled back down by Earth's gravitational force. On the other hand, the sun is more than 300,000 times more massive than Earth. So why doesn't the sun's gravitational force affect you more than Earth's does? The reason is that the sun is so far away.

You are about 150 million kilometers (93 million miles) away from the sun. At this distance, the gravitational force between you and the sun is very small. If there were some way you could stand on the sun, you would find it impossible to move. The gravitational force acting on you would be so great that you could not move any part of your body!

Although the sun's gravitational force on your body is very small, the force is very large on Earth and the other planets, as shown in **Figure 4.** The gravity between the sun and the planets is large because the objects have large masses. If the sun's gravitational force did not have such an effect on the planets, the planets would not stay in orbit around the sun. **Figure 5** will help you understand the relationship between gravitational force and distance.

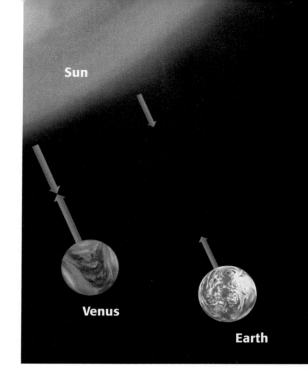

Figure 4 *Venus and Earth have approximately the same mass. But because Venus is closer to the sun, the gravitational force between Venus and the sun is greater than the gravitational force between Earth and the sun.*

Figure 5 **How Distance Affects Gravitational Force**

The gravitational force between objects decreases as the distance between the objects increases. The length of the arrows indicates the strength of the gravitational force between two objects.

ⓐ Gravitational force is strong when the distance between two objects is small.

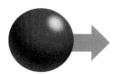

ⓑ If the distance between two objects increases, the gravitational force pulling them together decreases rapidly.

Weight as a Measure of Gravitational Force

Gravity is a force of attraction between objects. **Weight** is a measure of the gravitational force on an object. When you see or hear the word *weight,* it usually refers to Earth's gravitational force on an object. But weight can also be a measure of the gravitational force exerted on objects by the moon or other planets.

The Differences Between Weight and Mass

Weight is related to mass, but they are not the same. Weight changes when gravitational force changes. **Mass** is the amount of matter in an object. An object's mass does not change. Imagine that an object is moved to a place that has a greater gravitational force—such as the planet Jupiter. The object's weight will increase, but its mass will remain the same. **Figure 6** shows the weight and mass of an astronaut on Earth and on the moon. The moon's gravitational force is about one-sixth of Earth's gravitational force.

Gravitational force is about the same everywhere on Earth. So, the weight of any object is about the same everywhere. Because mass and weight are constant on Earth, the terms *weight* and *mass* are often used to mean the same thing. This can be confusing. Be sure you understand the difference!

✓ **Reading Check** How is gravitational force related to the weight of an object?

CONNECTION TO Language Arts

WRITING SKILL **Gravity Story** Suppose you had a device that could increase or decrease the gravitational force of Earth. In your **science journal,** write a short story describing what you might do with the device, what you would expect to see, and what effect the device would have on the weight of objects.

weight a measure of the gravitational force exerted on an object; its value can change with the location of the object in the universe

mass a measure of the amount of matter in an object

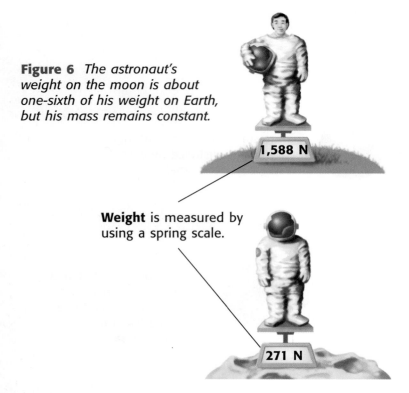
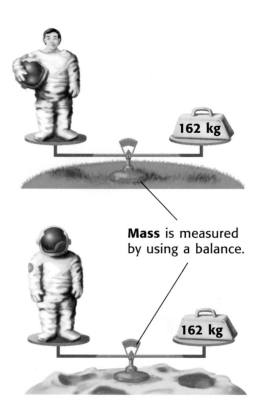

Figure 6 *The astronaut's weight on the moon is about one-sixth of his weight on Earth, but his mass remains constant.*

1,588 N

162 kg

Weight is measured by using a spring scale.

271 N

Mass is measured by using a balance.

162 kg

Units of Weight and Mass

You have learned that the SI unit of force is a newton (N). Gravity is a force, and weight is a measure of gravity. So, weight is also measured in newtons. The SI unit of mass is the kilogram (kg). Mass is often measured in grams (g) and milligrams (mg) as well. On Earth, a 100 g object, such as the apple shown in **Figure 7,** weighs about 1 N.

When you use a bathroom scale, you are measuring the gravitational force between your body and Earth. So, you are measuring your weight, which should be given in newtons. However, many bathroom scales have units of pounds and kilograms instead of newtons. Thus, people sometimes mistakenly think that the kilogram (like the pound) is a unit of weight.

Figure 7 *A small apple weighs approximately 1 N.*

SECTION Review

Summary

- Gravity is a force of attraction between objects that is due to their masses.
- The law of universal gravitation states that all objects in the universe attract each other through gravitational force.
- Gravitational force increases as mass increases.
- Gravitational force decreases as distance increases.
- Weight and mass are not the same. Mass is the amount of matter in an object. Weight is a measure of the gravitational force on an object.

Using Key Terms

1. In your own words, write a definition for the term *gravity*.

2. Use each of the following terms in a separate sentence: *mass* and *weight*.

Understanding Key Ideas

3. If Earth's mass doubled without changing its size, your weight would
   a. increase because gravitational force increases.
   b. decrease because gravitational force increases.
   c. increase because gravitational force decreases.
   d. not change because you are still on Earth.

4. What is the law of universal gravitation?

5. How does the mass of an object relate to the gravitational force that the object exerts on other objects?

6. How does the distance between objects affect the gravitational force between them?

7. Why are mass and weight often confused?

Math Skills

8. The gravitational force on Jupiter is approximately 2.3 times the gravitational force on Earth. If an object has a mass of 70 kg and a weight of 686 N on Earth, what would the object's mass and weight on Jupiter be?

Critical Thinking

9. **Applying Concepts** Your friend thinks that there is no gravity in space. How could you explain to your friend that there must be gravity in space?

10. **Making Comparisons** Explain why it is your weight and not your mass that would change if you landed on Mars.

For a variety of links related to this chapter, go to www.scilinks.org

Topic: Matter and Gravity
SciLinks code: HSM0922

Skills Practice Lab

Detecting Acceleration

Have you ever noticed that you can "feel" acceleration? In a car or in an elevator, you may notice changes in speed or direction—even with your eyes closed! You are able to sense these changes because of tiny hair cells in your ears. These cells detect the movement of fluid in your inner ear. The fluid accelerates when you do, and the hair cells send a message about the acceleration to your brain. This message allows you to sense the acceleration. In this activity, you will build a device that detects acceleration. This device is called an *accelerometer* (ak SEL uhr AHM uht uhr).

Procedure

1. Cut a piece of string that reaches three-quarters of the way into the container.

2. Use a pushpin to attach one end of the string to the cork or plastic-foam ball.

3. Use modeling clay to attach the other end of the string to the center of the inside of the container lid. The cork or ball should hang no farther than three-quarters of the way into the container.

4. Fill the container with water.

5. Put the lid tightly on the container. The string and cork or ball should be inside the container.

6. Turn the container upside down. The cork should float about three-quarters of the way up inside the container, as shown at left. You are now ready to detect acceleration by using your accelerometer and completing the following steps.

7. Put the accelerometer on a tabletop. The container lid should touch the tabletop. Notice that the cork floats straight up in the water.

8. Now, gently push the accelerometer across the table at a constant speed. Notice that the cork quickly moves in the direction you are pushing and then swings backward. If you did not see this motion, repeat this step until you are sure you can see the first movement of the cork.

9. After you are familiar with how to use your accelerometer, try the following changes in motion. For each change, record your observations of the cork's first motion.

   a. As you move the accelerometer across the table, gradually increase its speed.

   b. As you move the accelerometer across the table, gradually decrease its speed.

   c. While moving the accelerometer across the table, change the direction in which you are pushing.

   d. Make any other changes in motion you can think of. You should make only one change to the motion for each trial.

Analyze the Results

1. **Analyzing Results** When you move the bottle at a constant speed, why does the cork quickly swing backward after it moves in the direction of acceleration?

2. **Explaining Events** The cork moves forward (in the direction you were moving the bottle) when you speed up but moves backward when you slow down. Explain why the cork moves this way. (Hint: Think about the direction of acceleration.)

Draw Conclusions

3. **Making Predictions** Imagine you are standing on a corner and watching a car that is waiting at a stoplight. A passenger inside the car is holding some helium balloons. Based on what you observed with your accelerometer, what do you think will happen to the balloons when the car begins moving?

Applying Your Data

If you move the bottle in a circle at a constant speed, what do you predict the cork will do? Try it, and check your answer.

Chapter Review

USING KEY TERMS

Complete each of the following sentences by choosing the correct term from the word bank.

mass	gravity
friction	weight
speed	velocity
net force	newton

1 ___ opposes motion between surfaces that are touching.

2 The ___ is the unit of force.

3 ___ is determined by combining forces.

4 Acceleration is the rate at which ___ changes.

5 ___ is a measure of the gravitational force on an object.

UNDERSTANDING KEY IDEAS

Multiple Choice

6 If a student rides her bicycle on a straight road and does not speed up or slow down, she is traveling with a

a. constant acceleration.

b. constant velocity.

c. positive acceleration.

d. negative acceleration.

7 A force

a. is expressed in newtons.

b. can cause an object to speed up, slow down, or change direction.

c. is a push or a pull.

d. All of the above

8 If you are in a spacecraft that has been launched into space, your weight would

a. increase because gravitational force is increasing.

b. increase because gravitational force is decreasing.

c. decrease because gravitational force is decreasing.

d. decrease because gravitational force is increasing.

9 The gravitational force between 1 kg of lead and Earth is ___ the gravitational force between 1 kg of marshmallows and Earth.

a. greater than   **c.** the same as

b. less than   **d.** None of the above

10 Which of the following is a measurement of velocity?

a. 16 m east   **c.** 55 m/h south

b. 25 m/s^2 **d.** 60 km/h

Short Answer

11 Describe the relationship between motion and a reference point.

12 How is it possible to be accelerating and traveling at a constant speed?

13 Explain the difference between mass and weight.

Math Skills

14 A kangaroo hops 60 m to the east in 5 s. Use this information to answer the following questions.

   a. What is the kangaroo's average speed?

   b. What is the kangaroo's average velocity?

   c. The kangaroo stops at a lake for a drink of water and then starts hopping again to the south. Each second, the kangaroo's velocity increases 2.5 m/s. What is the kangaroo's acceleration after 5 s?

15 Concept Mapping Use the following terms to create a concept map: *speed, velocity, acceleration, force, direction,* and *motion.*

16 Applying Concepts Your family is moving, and you are asked to help move some boxes. One box is so heavy that you must push it across the room rather than lift it. What are some ways you could reduce friction to make moving the box easier?

17 Analyzing Ideas Considering the scientific meaning of the word *acceleration,* how could using the term *accelerator* when talking about a car's gas pedal lead to confusion?

18 Identifying Relationships Explain why it is important for airplane pilots to know wind velocity and not just wind speed during a flight.

Use the figures below to answer the questions that follow.

19 Is the graph below showing positive acceleration or negative acceleration? How can you tell?

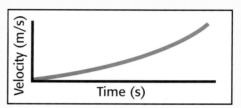

20 You know how to combine two forces that act in one or two directions. The same method can be used to combine several forces acting in several directions. Look at the diagrams, and calculate the net force in each diagram. Predict the direction each object will move.

a.

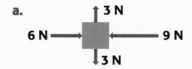

b.

c.

Standardized Test Preparation

Multiple Choice

Use the table below to answer questions 1–3.

Time (seconds)	Distance (meters)
0	0
1	96
2	192
3	288
4	384

1. **During a field experiment about speed, a scientist created the chart above, which shows distance and time measurements for a racing car in motion on the straight section of a racing track. What is the racing car's speed?**

   A. 0 m/s

   B. 96 m/s

   C. 192 m/s

   D. 384 m/s

2. **What is the racing car's acceleration?**

   A. 0 m/s²

   B. 96 m/s²

   C. 192 m/s²

   D. 384 m/s²

3. **Theodore plots the data in the table at left. He plots distance on the *y*-axis and time on the *x*-axis. How will the movement of the racing car be represented on a graph?**

   A. a curved line

   B. a straight line

   C. a series of connected straight lines

   D. a single point

4. **A downhill skier has her skis sharpened and waxed before every race. What effect would this have on her performance?**

   A. The force of friction between the skis and snow would increase, and her speed would decrease.

   B. The force of friction between the skis and snow would decrease, and her speed would decrease.

   C. The force of friction between the skis and snow would increase, and her speed would increase.

   D. The force of friction between the skis and snow would decrease, and her speed would increase.

5. **Which of the following pairs of forces is balanced?**

   A. 16 N north and 16 N south

   B. 16 N north and 16 N east

   C. 16 N north and 16 N west

   D. 16 N north and 16 N north

Use the graph below to answer questions 6–7.

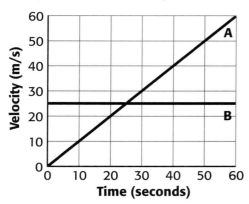

6. **The graph above describes the motion of two different balls—ball A and ball B. According to the graph, which of the following statements is true?**

   A. The velocity of ball A is increasing over time at a constant acceleration.

   B. The velocity of ball B is increasing over time at a constant acceleration.

   C. The velocity of ball A is decreasing over time at a constant acceleration.

   D. The velocity of ball B is decreasing over time at a constant acceleration.

7. **Which of the following is a valid conclusion about ball B according to the data in the graph?**

   A. The ball is moving, but not accelerating.

   B. The ball's acceleration is positive and not constant.

   C. The ball's acceleration is negative and not constant.

   D. The ball is moving with constant deceleration.

8. **How will the motion of a ball rolling on the ground change if the ball encounters a frictional force that opposes its motion?**

   A. The ball will speed up.

   B. The ball will slow down.

   C. The ball's speed will not change.

   D. The ball will change direction.

Open Response

9. **Two balls are on a billiards table. Ball B is at rest. Then, Ball A hits Ball B and both balls bounce around until each eventually rolls to a stop. What force acts on the billiard balls to bring them to a stop? Explain.**

10. **At a picnic, Sheila and three of her friends challenge four other girls to a tug-of-war. On Sheila's team, each girl except Sheila is able to pull with a force of 140 N. Sheila can pull with a force of 160 N. On the other team, one girl can pull with a force of 120 N, one can pull with a force of 130 N, and two can each pull with a force of 140 N. Calculate the net force on the tug-of-war rope in newtons and state which team wins the tug-of-war. Show your work.**

Science in Action

Science, Technology, and Society

GPS Watch System

Some athletes are concerned about knowing their speed during training. To calculate speed, they need to know distance and time. Finding time by using a watch is easy to do. But determining distance is more difficult. However, a GPS watch system is now available to help with this problem. *GPS* stands for *global positioning system*. A GPS unit, which is worn on an athlete's upper arm, monitors the athlete's position by using signals from satellites. As the athlete moves, the GPS unit calculates the distance traveled. The GPS unit sends a signal to the watch, which keeps the athlete's time, and the watch displays the athlete's speed.

Math ACTIVITY

Suppose an athlete wishes to finish a 5 K race in under 25 min. The distance of a 5 K is 5 km. (Remember that 1 km = 1,000 m.) If the athlete runs the race at a constant speed of 3.4 m/s, will she meet her goal?

Weird Science

The Segway™ Human Transporter

In November 2002, a new people-moving machine was introduced, and people have been fascinated by the odd-looking device ever since. The device is called the *Segway Human Transporter*. The Segway is a two-wheeled device that is powered by a rechargeable battery. To move forward, the rider simply leans forward. Sensors detect this motion and send signals to the on-board computer. The computer, in turn, tells the motor to start going. To slow down, the rider leans backward, and to stop, the rider stands straight up. The Segway has a top speed of 20 km/h (about 12.5 mi/h) and can travel up to 28 km (about 17.4 mi) on a single battery charge.

Language Arts ACTIVITY

WRITING SKILL The inventor of the Segway thinks that the machine will make a good alternative to walking and bicycle riding. Write a one-page essay explaining whether you think using a Segway is better or worse than riding a bicycle.

Victor Petrenko

Snowboard and Ski Brakes Have you ever wished for emergency brakes on your snowboard or skis? Thanks to Victor Petrenko and the Ice Research Lab of Dartmouth College, snowboards and skis that have braking systems may soon be available.

Not many people know more about the properties of ice and ice-related technologies than Victor Petrenko does. He has spent most of his career researching the electrical and mechanical properties of ice. Through his research, Petrenko learned that ice can hold an electric charge. He used this property to design a braking system for snowboards. The system is a form of electric friction control.

The power source for the brakes is a battery. The battery is connected to a network of wires embedded on the bottom surface of a snowboard. When the battery is activated, the bottom of the snowboard gains a negative charge. This negative charge creates a positive charge on the surface of the snow. Because opposite charges attract, the snowboard and the snow are pulled together. The force that pulls the surfaces together increases friction, and the snowboard slows down.

Social Studies ACTIVITY

Research the history of skiing. Make a poster that includes a timeline of significant dates in the history of skiing. Illustrate your poster with photos or drawings.

To learn more about these Science in Action topics, visit go.hrw.com and type in the keyword **HP5MOTF.**

Current Science

Check out Current Science® articles related to this chapter by visiting go.hrw.com. Just type in the keyword **HP5CS05.**

20

Forces and Motion

The Big Idea

Unbalanced forces cause changes in motion that can be predicted and described.

About the Photo

To train for space flight, astronauts fly in a modified KC-135 cargo airplane. The airplane first flies upward at a steep angle. Then, it flies downward at a 45° angle, which causes the feeling of reduced gravity inside. Under these conditions, the astronauts in the plane can float and can practice carrying out tasks that they will need to perform when they are in orbit. Because the floating makes people queasy, this KC-135 is nicknamed the "Vomit Comet."

PRE-READING ACTIVITY

Graphic Organizer

Spider Map Before you read the chapter, create the graphic organizer entitled "Spider Map" described in the **Study Skills** section of the Appendix. Label the circle "Motion." Create a leg for each law of motion, a leg for gravity, and a leg for momentum. As you read the chapter, fill in the map with details about how motion is related to the laws of motion, gravity, and momentum.

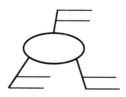

STARTUP ACTIVITY

Falling Water

Gravity is one of the most important forces in your life. In this activity, you will observe the effect of gravity on a falling object.

Procedure

1. Place a **wide plastic tub** on the floor. Punch a small hole in the side of a **paper cup,** near the bottom.

2. Hold your finger over the hole, and fill the cup with **water.** Keep your finger over the hole, and hold the cup waist-high above the tub.

3. Uncover the hole. Record your observations as Trial 1.

4. Predict what will happen to the water if you drop the cup at the same time you uncover the hole.

5. Cover the hole, and refill the cup with water.

6. Uncover the hole, and drop the cup at the same time. Record your observations as Trial 2.

7. Clean up any spilled water with **paper towels.**

Analysis

1. What differences did you observe in the behavior of the water during the two trials?

2. In Trial 2, how fast did the cup fall compared with how fast the water fell?

3. How did the results of Trial 2 compare with your prediction?

Forces and Motion **589**

Gravity and Motion

Suppose you dropped a baseball and a marble at the same time from the top of a tall building. Which do you think would land on the ground first?

In ancient Greece around 400 BCE, a philosopher named Aristotle (AR is TAWT uhl) thought that the rate at which an object falls depended on the object's mass. If you asked Aristotle whether the baseball or the marble would land first, he would have said the baseball. But Aristotle never tried dropping objects with different masses to test his idea about falling objects.

Gravity and Falling Objects

In the late 1500s, a young Italian scientist named Galileo Galilei (GAL uh LAY oh GAL uh LAY) questioned Aristotle's idea about falling objects. Galileo argued that the mass of an object does not affect the time the object takes to fall to the ground. According to one story, Galileo proved his argument by dropping two cannonballs of different masses from the top of the Leaning Tower of Pisa in Italy. The people watching from the ground below were amazed to see the two cannonballs land at the same time. Whether or not this story is true, Galileo's work changed people's understanding of gravity and falling objects.

Gravity and Acceleration

Objects fall to the ground at the same rate because the acceleration due to gravity is the same for all objects. Why is this true? Acceleration depends on both force and mass. A heavier object experiences a greater gravitational force than a lighter object does. But a heavier object is also harder to accelerate because it has more mass. The extra mass of the heavy object exactly balances the additional gravitational force. **Figure 1** shows objects that have different masses falling with the same acceleration.

What You Will Learn

● Explain the effect of gravity and air resistance on falling objects.
● Explain why objects in orbit are in free fall and appear to be weightless.
● Describe how projectile motion is affected by gravity.

Vocabulary

terminal velocity
free fall
projectile motion

READING STRATEGY

Reading Organizer As you read this section, create an outline of the section. Use the headings from the section in your outline.

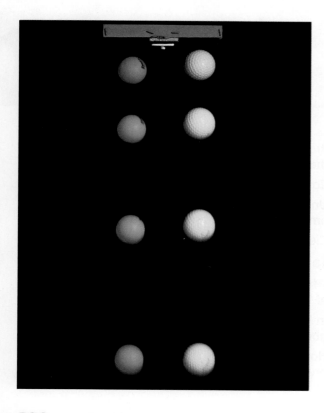

Figure 1 *This stop-action photo shows that a table-tennis ball and a golf ball fall at the same rate even though they have different masses.*

Acceleration Due to Gravity

Acceleration is the rate at which velocity changes over time. So, the acceleration of an object is the object's change in velocity divided by the amount of time during which the change occurs. All objects accelerate toward Earth at a rate of 9.8 meters per second per second. This rate is written as 9.8 m/s/s, or 9.8 m/s^2. So, for every second that an object falls, the object's downward velocity increases by 9.8 m/s, as shown in **Figure 2.**

Reading Check What is the acceleration due to gravity? (*See the Appendix for answers to Reading Checks.*)

Velocity of Falling Objects

You can calculate the change in velocity (Δv) of a falling object by using the following equation:

$$\Delta v = g \times t$$

In this equation, g is the acceleration due to gravity on Earth (9.8 m/s^2), and t is the time the object takes to fall (in seconds). The change in velocity is the difference between the final velocity and the starting velocity. If the object starts at rest, this equation yields the velocity of the object after a certain time period.

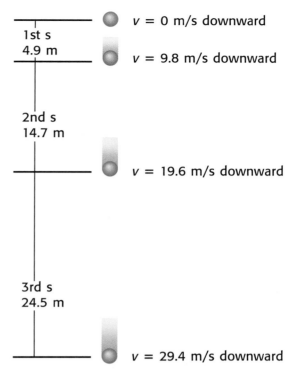

1st s
4.9 m

2nd s
14.7 m

3rd s
24.5 m

v = 0 m/s downward

v = 9.8 m/s downward

v = 19.6 m/s downward

v = 29.4 m/s downward

Figure 2 *A falling object accelerates at a constant rate. The object falls faster and farther each second than it did the second before.*

Calculating the Velocity of Falling Objects A stone at rest is dropped from a cliff, and the stone hits the ground after a time of 3 s. What is the stone's velocity when it hits the ground?

Step 1: Write the equation for change in velocity.

$$\Delta v = g \times t$$

Step 2: Replace g with its value and t with the time given in the problem, and solve.

$$\Delta v = 9.8 \, \frac{\text{m/s}}{\cancel{s}} \times 3 \, \cancel{s}$$
$$= 29.4 \text{ m/s}$$

To rearrange the equation to find time, divide by the acceleration due to gravity:

$$t = \frac{\Delta v}{g}$$

Now It's Your Turn

1. A penny at rest is dropped from the top of a tall stairwell. What is the penny's velocity after it has fallen for 2 s?
2. The same penny hits the ground in 4.5 s. What is the penny's velocity as it hits the ground?
3. A marble at rest is dropped from a tall building. The marble hits the ground with a velocity of 98 m/s. How long was the marble in the air?
4. An acorn at rest falls from an oak tree. The acorn hits the ground with a velocity of 14.7 m/s. How long did it take the acorn to land?

Figure 3 Effect of Air Resistance on a Falling Object

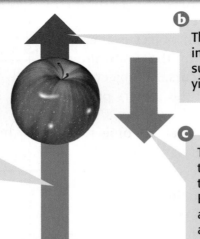

a The **force of gravity** is pulling down on the apple. If gravity were the only force acting on the apple, the apple would accelerate at a rate of 9.8 m/s².

b The **force of air resistance** is pushing up on the apple. This force is subtracted from the force of gravity to yield the net force.

c The **net force** on the apple is equal to the force of air resistance subtracted from the force of gravity. Because the net force is not 0 N, the apple accelerates downward. But the apple does not accelerate as fast as it would without air resistance.

Figure 4 *The parachute increases the air resistance of this sky diver and slows him to a safe terminal velocity.*

terminal velocity the constant velocity of a falling object when the force of air resistance is equal in magnitude and opposite in direction to the force of gravity

Air Resistance and Falling Objects

Try dropping two sheets of paper—one crumpled in a tight ball and the other kept flat. What happened? Does this simple experiment seem to contradict what you just learned about falling objects? The flat paper falls more slowly than the crumpled paper because of *air resistance*. Air resistance is the force that opposes the motion of objects through air.

The amount of air resistance acting on an object depends on the size, shape, and speed of the object. Air resistance affects the flat sheet of paper more than the crumpled one. The larger surface area of the flat sheet causes the flat sheet to fall slower than the crumpled one. **Figure 3** shows the effect of air resistance on the downward acceleration of a falling object.

✓ *Reading Check* Will air resistance have more effect on the acceleration of a falling leaf or the acceleration of a falling acorn?

Acceleration Stops at the Terminal Velocity

As the speed of a falling object increases, air resistance increases. The upward force of air resistance continues to increase until it is equal to the downward force of gravity. At this point, the net force is 0 N and the object stops accelerating. The object then falls at a constant velocity called the **terminal velocity.**

Terminal velocity can be a good thing. Every year, cars, buildings, and vegetation are severely damaged in hailstorms. The terminal velocity of hailstones is between 5 and 40 m/s, depending on their size. If there were no air resistance, hailstones would hit the ground at velocities near 350 m/s! **Figure 4** shows another situation in which terminal velocity is helpful.

Free Fall Occurs When There Is No Air Resistance

Sky divers are often described as being in free fall before they open their parachutes. However, that is an incorrect description, because air resistance is always acting on the sky diver.

An object is in **free fall** only if gravity is pulling it down and no other forces are acting on it. Because air resistance is a force, free fall can occur only where there is no air. Two places that have no air are in space and in a vacuum. A vacuum is a place in which there is no matter. **Figure 5** shows objects falling in a vacuum. Because there is no air resistance in a vacuum, the two objects are in free fall.

Orbiting Objects Are in Free Fall

Look at the astronaut in **Figure 6.** Why is the astronaut floating inside the space shuttle? You may be tempted to say that she is weightless in space. However, it is impossible for any object to be weightless anywhere in the universe.

Weight is a measure of gravitational force. The size of the force depends on the masses of objects and the distances between them. Suppose you traveled in space far away from all the stars and planets. The gravitational force acting on you would be very small because the distance between you and other objects would be very large. But you and all the other objects in the universe would still have mass. Therefore, gravity would attract you to other objects—even if just slightly—so you would still have weight.

Astronauts float in orbiting spacecrafts because of free fall. To better understand why astronauts float, you need to know what *orbiting* means.

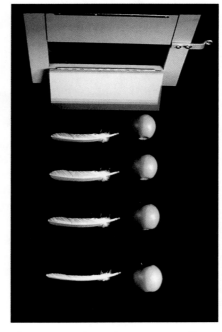

Figure 5 *Air resistance usually causes a feather to fall more slowly than an apple falls. But in a vacuum, a feather and an apple fall with the same acceleration because both are in free fall.*

free fall the motion of a body when only the force of gravity is acting on the body

Figure 6 *Astronauts appear to be weightless while they are floating inside the space shuttle— but they are not weightless!*

Figure 7 How an Orbit Is Formed

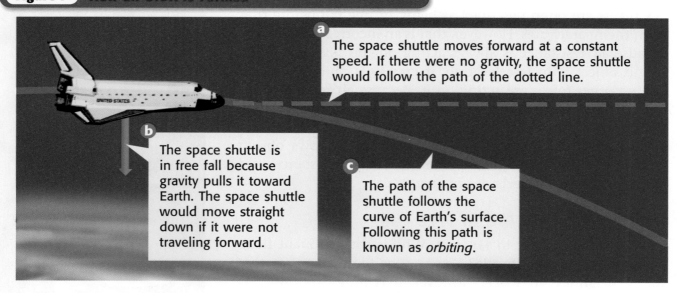

a The space shuttle moves forward at a constant speed. If there were no gravity, the space shuttle would follow the path of the dotted line.

b The space shuttle is in free fall because gravity pulls it toward Earth. The space shuttle would move straight down if it were not traveling forward.

c The path of the space shuttle follows the curve of Earth's surface. Following this path is known as *orbiting*.

Two Motions Combine to Cause Orbiting

An object is orbiting when it is traveling around another object in space. When a spacecraft orbits Earth, it is moving forward. But the spacecraft is also in free fall toward Earth. **Figure 7** shows how these two motions combine to cause orbiting.

As you can see in **Figure 7,** the space shuttle is always falling while it is in orbit. So why don't astronauts hit their heads on the ceiling of the falling shuttle? Because they are also in free fall—they are always falling, too. Because astronauts are in free fall, they float.

Orbiting and Centripetal Force

Besides spacecrafts and satellites, many other objects in the universe are in orbit. The moon orbits the Earth. Earth and the other planets orbit the sun. In addition, many stars orbit large masses in the center of galaxies. Many of these objects are traveling in a circular or nearly circular path. Any object in circular motion is constantly changing direction. Because an unbalanced force is necessary to change the motion of any object, there must be an unbalanced force working on any object in circular motion.

The unbalanced force that causes objects to move in a circular path is called a *centripetal force* (sen TRIP uht uhl FOHRS). Gravity provides the centripetal force that keeps objects in orbit. The word *centripetal* means "toward the center." As you can see in **Figure 8,** the centripetal force on the moon points toward the center of the moon's circular orbit.

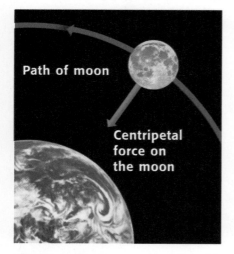

Path of moon

Centripetal force on the moon

Figure 8 *The moon stays in orbit around Earth because Earth's gravitational force provides a centripetal force on the moon.*

✓ **Reading Check** What does the word *centripetal* mean?

Projectile Motion and Gravity

The motion of a hopping grasshopper is an example of projectile motion (proh JEK tuhl MOH shuhn). **Projectile motion** is the curved path an object follows when it is thrown or propelled near the surface of the Earth. Projectile motion has two components—horizontal motion and vertical motion. The two components are independent, so they have no effect on each other. When the two motions are combined, they form a curved path, as shown in **Figure 9.** Some examples of projectile motion include the following:

- a frog leaping
- water sprayed by a sprinkler
- a swimmer diving into water
- balls being juggled
- an arrow shot by an archer

Horizontal Motion

When you throw a ball, your hand exerts a force on the ball that makes the ball move forward. This force gives the ball its horizontal motion, which is motion parallel to the ground.

After you release the ball, no horizontal forces are acting on the ball (if you ignore air resistance). Even gravity does not affect the horizontal component of projectile motion. So, there are no forces to change the ball's horizontal motion. Thus, the horizontal velocity of the ball is constant after the ball leaves your hand, as shown in **Figure 9.**

projectile motion the curved path that an object follows when thrown, launched, or otherwise projected near the surface of Earth

---

Figure 9 Projectile Motion

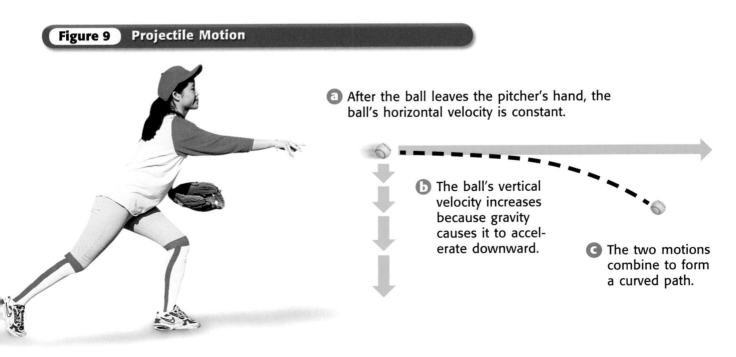

ⓐ After the ball leaves the pitcher's hand, the ball's horizontal velocity is constant.

ⓑ The ball's vertical velocity increases because gravity causes it to accelerate downward.

ⓒ The two motions combine to form a curved path.

INTERNET ACTIVITY

For another activity related to this chapter, go to **go.hrw.com** and type in the keyword **HP5FORW**.

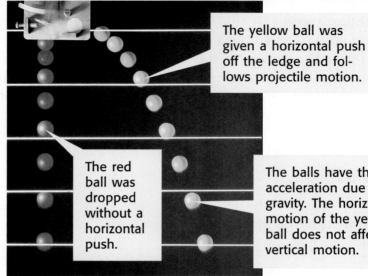

Figure 10 Projectile Motion and Acceleration Due to Gravity

The yellow ball was given a horizontal push off the ledge and follows projectile motion.

The red ball was dropped without a horizontal push.

The balls have the same acceleration due to gravity. The horizontal motion of the yellow ball does not affect its vertical motion.

Vertical Motion

Gravity pulls everything on Earth downward toward the center of Earth. A ball in your hand is prevented from falling by your hand. After you throw the ball, gravity pulls it downward and gives the ball vertical motion. Vertical motion is motion that is perpendicular to the ground. Gravity pulls objects in projectile motion down at an acceleration of 9.8 m/s² (if air resistance is ignored). This rate is the same for all falling objects. **Figure 10** shows that the downward acceleration of a thrown object and a falling object are the same.

Because objects in projectile motion accelerate downward, you always have to aim above a target if you want to hit it with a thrown or propelled object. That's why when you aim an arrow directly at a bull's-eye, your arrow strikes the bottom of the target rather than the middle of the target.

✓ **Reading Check** What gives an object in projectile motion its vertical motion?

Penny Projectile Motion

1. Position a **flat ruler** and **two pennies** on a **desk or table** as shown below.

2. Hold the ruler by the end that is on the desk. Move the ruler quickly in the direction shown so that the ruler knocks the penny off the table and so that the other penny also drops. Repeat this step several times.

3. Which penny travels with projectile motion? In what order do the pennies hit the ground? Record and explain your answers.

SECTION
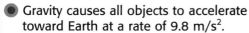
Review

Summary

- Gravity causes all objects to accelerate toward Earth at a rate of 9.8 m/s^2.

- Air resistance slows the acceleration of falling objects. An object falls at its terminal velocity when the upward force of air resistance equals the downward force of gravity.

- An object is in free fall if gravity is the only force acting on it.

- Objects in orbit appear to be weightless because they are in free fall.

- A centripetal force is needed to keep objects in circular motion. Gravity acts as a centripetal force to keep objects in orbit.

- Projectile motion is the curved path an object follows when thrown or propelled near the surface of Earth.

- Projectile motion has two components—horizontal motion and vertical motion. Gravity affects only the vertical motion of projectile motion.

Using Key Terms

1. Use each of the following terms in a separate sentence: *terminal velocity* and *free fall*.

Understanding Key Ideas

2. Which of the following is in projectile motion?
   a. a feather falling in a vacuum
   b. a cat leaping on a toy
   c. a car driving up a hill
   d. a book laying on a desk

3. How does air resistance affect the acceleration of falling objects?

4. How does gravity affect the two components of projectile motion?

5. How is the acceleration of falling objects affected by gravity?

6. Why is the acceleration due to gravity the same for all objects?

Math Skills

7. A rock at rest falls off a tall cliff and hits the valley below after 3.5 s. What is the rock's velocity as it hits the ground?

Critical Thinking

8. **Applying Concepts** Think about a sport that uses a ball. Identify four examples from that sport in which an object is in projectile motion.

9. **Making Inferences** The moon has no atmosphere. Predict what would happen if an astronaut on the moon dropped a hammer and a feather at the same time from the same height.

Interpreting Graphics

10. Whenever Jon delivers a newspaper to the Zapanta house, the newspaper lands in the bushes, as shown below. What should Jon do to make sure the newspaper lands on the porch?

For a variety of links related to this chapter, go to www.scilinks.org

Topic: Gravity and Orbiting Objects; Projectile Motion

SciLinks code: HSM0692; HSM1223

What You Will Learn

- Describe Newton's first law of motion, and explain how it relates to objects at rest and objects in motion.
- State Newton's second law of motion, and explain the relationship between force, mass, and acceleration.
- State Newton's third law of motion, and give examples of force pairs.

Vocabulary

inertia

READING STRATEGY

Paired Summarizing Read this section silently. In pairs, take turns summarizing the material. Stop to discuss ideas that seem confusing.

Newton's Laws of Motion

Imagine that you are playing baseball. The pitch comes in, and—crack—you hit the ball hard! But instead of flying off the bat, the ball just drops to the ground. Is that normal?

You would probably say no. You know that force and motion are related. When you exert a force on a baseball by hitting it with a bat, the baseball should move. In 1686, Sir Isaac Newton explained this relationship between force and the motion of an object with his three laws of motion.

Newton's First Law of Motion

An object at rest remains at rest, and an object in motion remains in motion at constant speed and in a straight line unless acted on by an unbalanced force.

Newton's first law of motion describes the motion of an object that has a net force of 0 N acting on it. This law may seem complicated when you first read it. But, it is easy to understand when you consider its two parts separately.

Part 1: Objects at Rest

An object that is not moving is said to be at rest. A chair on the floor and a golf ball balanced on a tee are examples of objects at rest. Newton's first law says that objects at rest will stay at rest unless they are acted on by an unbalanced force. For example, objects will not start moving until a push or a pull is exerted on them. So, a chair won't slide across the room unless you push the chair. And, a golf ball won't move off the tee unless the ball is struck by a golf club, as shown in **Figure 1.**

Figure 1 *A golf ball will remain at rest on a tee until it is acted on by the unbalanced force of a moving club.*

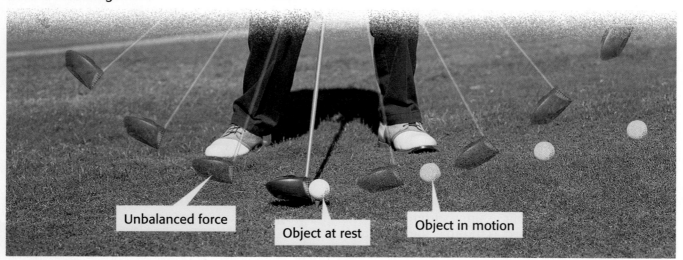

Unbalanced force

Object at rest

Object in motion

Part 2: Objects in Motion

The second part of Newton's first law is about objects moving with a certain velocity. Such objects will continue to move forever with the same velocity unless an unbalanced force acts on them.

Think about driving a bumper car at an amusement park. Your ride is pleasant as long as you are driving in an open space. But the name of the game is bumper cars! Sooner or later you are likely to run into another car, as shown in **Figure 2.** Your bumper car stops when it hits another car. But, you continue to move forward until the force from your seat belt stops you.

Friction and Newton's First Law

An object in motion will stay in motion forever unless it is acted on by an unbalanced force. So, you should be able to give your desk a push and send it sliding across the floor. If you push your desk, the desk quickly stops. Why?

There must be an unbalanced force that acts on the desk to stop its motion. That unbalanced force is friction. The friction between the desk and the floor works against the motion of the desk. Because of friction, observing the effects of Newton's first law is often difficult. For example, friction will cause a rolling ball to slow down and stop. Friction will also make a car slow down if the driver lets up on the gas pedal. Because of friction, the motion of objects changes.

 **Reading Check** When you ride a bus, why do you fall forward when the bus stops moving? (*See the Appendix for answers to Reading Checks.*)

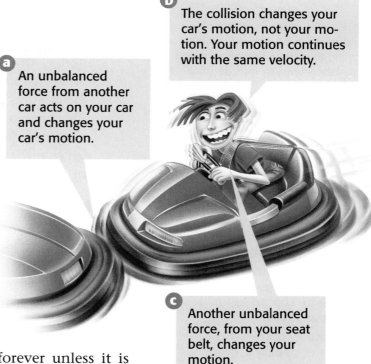

b The collision changes your car's motion, not your motion. Your motion continues with the same velocity.

a An unbalanced force from another car acts on your car and changes your car's motion.

c Another unbalanced force, from your seat belt, changes your motion.

Figure 2 *Bumper cars let you have fun with Newton's first law.*

First Law Skateboard

1. Place an **empty soda can** on top of a **skateboard.**

2. Ask a friend to catch the skateboard after you push it. Now, give the skateboard a quick, firm push. What happened to the soda can?

3. Put the can on the skateboard again. Push the skateboard gently so that the skateboard moves quickly but so that the can does not fall.

4. Ask your friend to stop the skateboard after he or she allows it to travel a short distance. What happened to the can?

5. Explain how Newton's first law applies to what happened.

inertia the tendency of an object to resist being moved or, if the object is moving, to resist a change in speed or direction until an outside force acts on the object

First-Law Magic

1. On a **table or desk**, place a **large, empty plastic cup** on top of a **paper towel.**

2. Without touching the cup or tipping it over, remove the paper towel from under the cup. How did you accomplish this? Repeat this step.

3. Fill the cup half full with **water,** and place the cup on the paper towel.

4. Once again, remove the paper towel from under the cup. Was it easier or harder to do this time?

5. Explain your observations in terms of mass, inertia, and Newton's first law of motion.

Inertia and Newton's First Law

Newton's first law of motion is sometimes called the *law of inertia*. **Inertia** (in UHR shuh) is the tendency of all objects to resist any change in motion. Because of inertia, an object at rest will remain at rest until a force makes it move. Likewise, inertia is the reason a moving object stays in motion with the same velocity unless a force changes its speed or direction. For example, because of inertia, you slide toward the side of a car when the driver turns a corner. Inertia is also why it is impossible for a plane, car, or bicycle to stop immediately.

Mass and Inertia

Mass is a measure of inertia. An object that has a small mass has less inertia than an object that has a large mass. So, changing the motion of an object that has a small mass is easier than changing the motion of an object that has a large mass. For example, a softball has less mass and therefore less inertia than a bowling ball. Because the softball has a small amount of inertia, it is easy to pitch a softball and to change its motion by hitting it with a bat. Imagine how difficult it would be to play softball with a bowling ball! **Figure 3** further shows the relationship between mass and inertia.

Figure 3 *Inertia makes it harder to accelerate a car than to accelerate a bicycle. Inertia also makes it easier to stop a moving bicycle than a car moving at the same speed.*

Newton's Second Law of Motion

The acceleration of an object depends on the mass of the object and the amount of force applied.

Newton's second law describes the motion of an object when an unbalanced force acts on the object. As with Newton's first law, you should consider the second law in two parts.

Part 1: Acceleration Depends on Mass

Suppose you are pushing an empty cart. You have to exert only a small force on the cart to accelerate it. But, the same amount of force will not accelerate the full cart as much as the empty cart. Look at the first two photos in **Figure 4.** They show that the acceleration of an object decreases as its mass increases and that its acceleration increases as its mass decreases.

Part 2: Acceleration Depends on Force

Suppose you give the cart a hard push, as shown in the third photo in **Figure 4.** The cart will start moving faster than if you gave it only a soft push. So, an object's acceleration increases as the force on the object increases. On the other hand, an object's acceleration decreases as the force on the object decreases.

The acceleration of an object is always in the same direction as the force applied. The cart in **Figure 4** moved forward because the push was in the forward direction.

✓ Reading Check What is the relationship between the force on an object and the object's acceleration?

CONNECTION TO Environmental Science

Car Sizes and Pollution

On average, newer cars pollute the air less than older cars do. One reason for this is that newer cars have less mass than older cars have. An object that has less mass requires less force to achieve the same acceleration as an object that has more mass. So, a small car can have a small engine and still have good acceleration. Because small engines use less fuel than large engines use, small engines create less pollution. Research three models of cars from the same year, and make a chart to compare the mass of the cars with the amount of fuel they use.

ACTIVITY

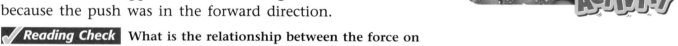

Figure 4 Mass, Force, and Acceleration

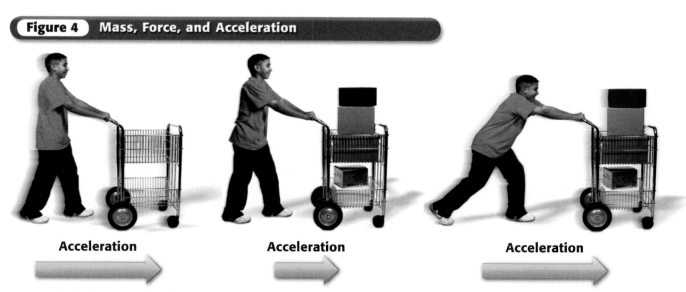

Acceleration

Acceleration

Acceleration

If the force applied to the carts is the same, the acceleration of the empty cart is greater than the acceleration of the loaded cart.

Acceleration will increase when a larger force is exerted.

Figure 5 Newton's Second Law and Acceleration Due to Gravity

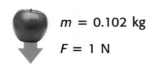

$m = 0.102$ kg

$F = 1$ N

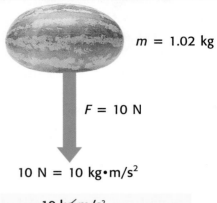

$m = 1.02$ kg

$F = 10$ N

1 N $= 1$ kg•m/s^2

$$a = \frac{1 \text{ kg•m/s}^2}{0.102 \text{ kg}} = 9.8 \text{ m/s}^2$$

10 N $= 10$ kg•m/s^2

$$a = \frac{10 \text{ kg•m/s}^2}{1.02 \text{ kg}} = 9.8 \text{ m/s}^2$$

The apple has less mass than the watermelon does. So, less force is needed to give the apple the same acceleration that the watermelon has.

Expressing Newton's Second Law Mathematically

The relationship of acceleration (a) to mass (m) and force (F) can be expressed mathematically with the following equation:

$$a = \frac{F}{m}, \text{ or } F = m \times a$$

Notice that the equation can be rearranged to find the force applied. Both forms of the equation can be used to solve problems.

Newton's second law explains why objects fall to Earth with the same acceleration. In **Figure 5,** you can see how the large force of gravity on the watermelon is offset by its large mass. Thus, you find that the accelerations of the watermelon and the apple are the same when you solve for acceleration.

Second-Law Problems What is the acceleration of a 3 kg mass if a force of 14.4 N is used to move the mass? (Note: 1 N is equal to 1 kg•m/s^2)

Step 1: Write the equation for acceleration.

$$a = \frac{F}{m}$$

Step 2: Replace F and m with the values given in the problem, and solve.

$$a = \frac{14.4 \text{ kg•m/s}^2}{3 \text{ kg}} = 4.8 \text{ m/s}^2$$

Now It's Your Turn

1. What is the acceleration of a 7 kg mass if a force of 68.6 N is used to move it toward Earth?

2. What force is necessary to accelerate a 1,250 kg car at a rate of 40 m/s^2?

3. Zookeepers carry a stretcher that holds a sleeping lion. The total mass of the lion and the stretcher is 175 kg. The lion's forward acceleration is 2 m/s^2. What is the force necessary to produce this acceleration?

Newton's Third Law of Motion

> *Whenever one object exerts a force on a second object, the second object exerts an equal and opposite force on the first.*

Newton's third law can be simply stated as follows: All forces act in pairs. If a force is exerted, another force occurs that is equal in size and opposite in direction. The law itself addresses only forces. But the way that force pairs interact affects the motion of objects.

How do forces act in pairs? Study **Figure 6** to learn how one force pair helps propel a swimmer through water. Action and reaction force pairs are present even when there is no motion. For example, you exert a force on a chair when you sit on it. Your weight pushing down on the chair is the action force. The reaction force is the force exerted by the chair that pushes up on your body. The force is equal to your weight.

✓ **Reading Check** How are the forces in each force pair related?

Force Pairs Do Not Act on the Same Object

A force is always exerted by one object on another object. This rule is true for all forces, including action and reaction forces. However, action and reaction forces in a pair do not act on the same object. If they did, the net force would always be 0 N and nothing would ever move! To understand how action and reaction forces act on objects, look at **Figure 6** again. The action force was exerted on the water by the swimmer's hands. But the reaction force was exerted on the swimmer's hands by the water. The forces did not act on the same object.

SCHOOL to HOME

Newton Ball
Play catch with an adult. As you play, discuss how Newton's laws of motion are involved in the game. After you finish your game, make a list in your **science journal** of what you discussed.

ACTIVITY

Figure 6 *The action force and reaction force are a pair. The two forces are equal in size but opposite in direction.*

The action force is the swimmer's hands pushing on the water.

The reaction force is the water pushing on the hands. The reaction force moves the swimmer forward.

Figure 7 Examples of Action and Reaction Force Pairs

The rabbit's legs exert a force on Earth. Earth exerts an equal force on the rabbit's legs and causes the rabbit to accelerate upward.

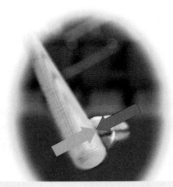

The space shuttle's thrusters push the exhaust gases downward as the gases push the shuttle upward with an equal force.

The bat exerts a force on the ball and sends the ball flying. The ball exerts an equal force on the bat, but the bat does not move backward because the batter is exerting another force on the bat.

All Forces Act in Pairs—Action and Reaction

Newton's third law says that all forces act in pairs. When a force is exerted, there is always a reaction force. A force never acts by itself. **Figure 7** shows some examples of action and reaction force pairs. In each example, the action force is shown in yellow and the reaction force is shown in red.

The Effect of a Reaction Can Be Difficult to See

Another example of a force pair is shown in **Figure 8.** Gravity is a force of attraction between objects that is due to their masses. If you drop a ball, gravity pulls the ball toward Earth. This force is the action force exerted by Earth on the ball. But gravity also pulls Earth toward the ball. The force is the reaction force exerted by the ball on Earth.

It's easy to see the effect of the action force—the ball falls to Earth. Why don't you notice the effect of the reaction force—Earth being pulled upward? To find the answer to this question, think about Newton's second law. It states that the acceleration of an object depends on the force applied to it and on the mass of the object. The force on Earth is equal to the force on the ball. But the mass of Earth is much larger than the mass of the ball. Thus, the acceleration of Earth is much smaller than the acceleration of the ball. The acceleration of the Earth is so small that you can't see or feel the acceleration. So, it is difficult to observe the effect of Newton's third law on falling objects.

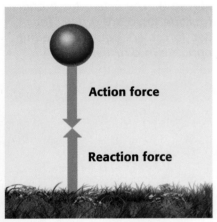

Figure 8 *The force of gravity between Earth and a falling object is a force pair.*

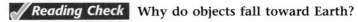
Reading Check Why do objects fall toward Earth?

Summary

- Newton's first law of motion states that the motion of an object will not change if no unbalanced forces act on it.
- Objects at rest will not move unless acted upon by an unbalanced force.
- Objects in motion will continue to move at a constant speed and in a straight line unless acted upon by an unbalanced force.
- Inertia is the tendency of matter to resist a change in motion. Mass is a measure of inertia.

- Newton's second law of motion states that the acceleration of an object depends on its mass and on the force exerted on it.
- Newton's second law is represented by the following equation: $F = m \times a$.
- Newton's third law of motion states that whenever one object exerts a force on a second object, the second object exerts an equal and opposite force on the first object.

Using Key Terms

1. In your own words, write a definition for the term *inertia*.

Understanding Key Ideas

2. Which of the following will increase the acceleration of an object that is pushed by a force?
   a. decreasing the mass of the object
   b. increasing the mass of the object
   c. increasing the force pushing the object
   d. Both (a) and (c)

3. Give three examples of force pairs that occur when you do your homework.

4. What does Newton's first law of motion say about objects at rest and objects in motion?

5. Use Newton's second law to describe the relationship between force, mass, and acceleration.

Math Skills

6. What force is necessary to accelerate a 70 kg object at a rate of 4.2 m/s²?

Critical Thinking

7. **Applying Concepts** When a truck pulls a trailer, the trailer and truck accelerate forward even though the action and reaction forces are the same size but are in opposite directions. Why don't these forces balance each other?

8. **Making Inferences** Use Newton's first law of motion to explain why airbags in cars are important during head-on collisions.

Interpreting Graphics

9. Imagine you accidentally bumped your hand against a table, as shown in the photo below. Your hand hurts after it happens. Use Newton's third law of motion to explain what caused your hand to hurt.

For a variety of links related to this chapter, go to www.scilinks.org

Topic: Newton's Laws of Motion
SciLinks code: HSM1028

What You Will Learn

● Calculate the momentum of moving objects.
● Explain the law of conservation of momentum.

Vocabulary
momentum

READING STRATEGY

Prediction Guide Before reading this section, write the title of each heading in this section. Next, under each heading, write what you think you will learn.

momentum a quantity defined as the product of the mass and velocity of an object

Momentum

Imagine a compact car and a large truck traveling with the same velocity. The drivers of both vehicles put on the brakes at the same time. Which vehicle will stop first?

You would probably say that the compact car will stop first. You know that smaller objects are easier to stop than larger objects. But why? The answer is momentum (moh MEN tuhm).

Momentum, Mass, and Velocity

The **momentum** of an object depends on the object's mass and velocity. The more momentum an object has, the harder it is to stop the object or change its direction. In the example above, the truck has more mass and more momentum than the car has. So, a larger force is needed to stop the truck. Similarly, a fast-moving car has a greater velocity and thus more momentum than a slow-moving car of the same mass. So, a fast-moving car is harder to stop than a slow-moving car. **Figure 1** shows another example of an object that has momentum.

Calculating Momentum

Momentum (*p*) can be calculated with the equation below:

$$p = m \times v$$

In this equation, *m* is the mass of an object in kilograms and *v* is the object's velocity in meters per second. The units of momentum are kilograms multiplied by meters per second, or kg•m/s. Like velocity, momentum has a direction. Its direction is always the same as the direction of the object's velocity.

Figure 1 *The teen on the right has less mass than the teen on the left. But, the teen on the right can have a large momentum by moving quickly when she kicks.*

Momentum Calculations What is the momentum of an ostrich with a mass of 120 kg that runs with a velocity of 16 m/s north?

Step 1: Write the equation for momentum.

$$p = m \times v$$

Step 2: Replace m and v with the values given in the problem, and solve.

$$p = 120 \text{ kg} \times 16 \text{ m/s north}$$
$$p = 19{,}200 \text{ kg•m/s north}$$

Now It's Your Turn
1. What is the momentum of a 6 kg bowling ball that is moving at 10 m/s down the alley toward the pins?
2. An 85 kg man is jogging with a velocity of 2.6 m/s to the north. Nearby, a 65 kg person is skateboarding and is traveling with a velocity of 3 m/s north. Which person has greater momentum? Show your calculations.

The Law of Conservation of Momentum

When a moving object hits another object, some or all of the momentum of the first object is transferred to the object that is hit. If only some of the momentum is transferred, the rest of the momentum stays with the first object.

Imagine that a cue ball hits a billiard ball so that the billiard ball starts moving and the cue ball stops, as shown in **Figure 2.** The white cue ball had a certain amount of momentum before the collision. During the collision, all of the cue ball's momentum was transferred to the red billiard ball. After the collision, the billiard ball moved away with the same amount of momentum the cue ball had. This example shows the *law of conservation of momentum.* The law of conservation of momentum states that any time objects collide, the total amount of momentum stays the same. The law of conservation of momentum is true for any collision if no other forces act on the colliding objects. This law applies whether the objects stick together or bounce off each other after they collide.

✓ Reading Check What can happen to momentum when two objects collide? (*See the Appendix for answers to Reading Checks.*)

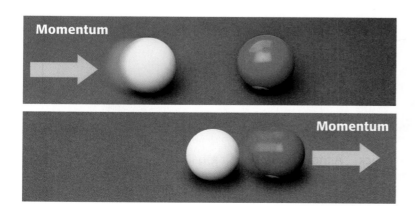

Figure 2 *The momentum before a collision is equal to the momentum after the collision.*

Objects Sticking Together

Sometimes, objects stick together after a collision. The football players shown in **Figure 3** are an example of such a collision. A dog leaping and catching a ball and a teen jumping on a skateboard are also examples. After two objects stick together, they move as one object. The mass of the combined objects is equal to the masses of the two objects added together. In a head-on collision, the combined objects move in the direction of the object that had the greater momentum before the collision. But together, the objects have a velocity that differs from the velocity of either object before the collision. The objects have a different velocity because momentum is conserved and depends on mass and velocity. So, when mass changes, the velocity must change, too.

Objects Bouncing Off Each Other

In some collisions, the objects bounce off each other. The bowling ball and bowling pins shown in **Figure 3** are examples of objects that bounce off each other after they collide. Billiard balls and bumper cars are other examples. During these types of collisions, momentum is usually transferred from one object to another object. The transfer of momentum causes the objects to move in different directions at different speeds. However, the total momentum of all the objects will remain the same before and after the collision.

Reading Check What are two ways that objects may interact after a collision?

Figure 3 Examples of Conservation of Momentum

When football players tackle another player, they stick together. The velocity of each player changes after the collision because of conservation of momentum.

Although the bowling ball and bowling pins bounce off each other and move in different directions after a collision, momentum is neither gained nor lost.

Conservation of Momentum and Newton's Third Law

Conservation of momentum can be explained by Newton's third law of motion. In the example of the billiard ball, the cue ball hit the billiard ball with a certain amount of force. This force was the action force. The reaction force was the equal but opposite force exerted by the billiard ball on the cue ball. The action force made the billiard ball start moving, and the reaction force made the cue ball stop moving, as shown in **Figure 4.** Because the action and reaction forces are equal and opposite, momentum is neither gained nor lost.

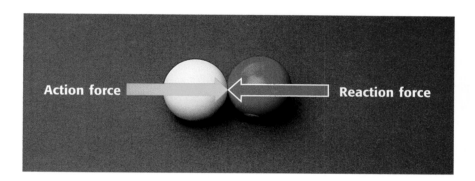

Action force   Reaction force

Figure 4 *The action force makes the billiard ball begin moving, and the reaction force stops the cue ball's motion.*

SECTION Review

Summary

● Momentum is a property of moving objects.

● Momentum is calculated by multiplying the mass of an object by the object's velocity.

● When two or more objects collide, momentum may be transferred, but the total amount of momentum does not change. This is the law of conservation of momentum.

Using Key Terms

1. Use the following term in a sentence: *momentum*.

Understanding Key Ideas

2. Which of the following has the smallest amount of momentum?
   a. a loaded truck driven at highway speeds
   b. a track athlete running a race
   c. a baby crawling on the floor
   d. a jet airplane being towed toward an airport

3. Explain the law of conservation of momentum.

4. How is Newton's third law of motion related to the law of conservation of momentum?

Math Skills

5. Calculate the momentum of a 2.5 kg puppy that is running with a velocity of 4.8 m/s south.

Critical Thinking

6. **Applying Concepts** A car and a train are traveling with the same velocity. Do the two objects have the same momentum? Explain your answer.

7. **Analyzing Ideas** When you catch a softball, your hand and glove move in the same direction that the ball is moving. Analyze the motion of your hand and glove in terms of momentum.

SCLINKS®

NSTA
Developed and maintained by the
National Science Teachers Association

For a variety of links related to this chapter, go to www.scilinks.org

Topic: Momentum
SciLinks code: HSM0988

Skills Practice Lab

Inertia-Rama!

Inertia is a property of all matter, from small particles of dust to enormous planets and stars. In this lab, you will investigate the inertia of various shapes and kinds of matter. Keep in mind that each investigation requires you to either overcome or use the object's inertia.

Station 1: Magic Eggs

Procedure

1. There are two eggs at this station—one is hard-boiled (solid all the way through) and the other is raw (liquid inside). The masses of the two eggs are about the same. The eggs are not marked. You should not be able to tell them apart by their appearance. Without breaking them open, how can you tell which egg is raw and which egg is hard-boiled?

2. Before you do anything to either egg, make some predictions. Will there be any difference in the way the two eggs spin? Which egg will be the easier to stop?

3. First, spin one egg. Then, place your finger on it gently to make it stop spinning. Record your observations.

4. Repeat step 3 with the second egg.

5. Compare your predictions with your observations. (Repeat steps 3 and 4 if necessary.)

6. Which egg is hard-boiled and which one is raw? Explain.

Analyze the Results

1. **Explaining Events** Explain why the eggs behave differently when you spin them even though they should have the same inertia. (Hint: Think about what happens to the liquid inside the raw egg.)

Draw Conclusions

2. **Drawing Conclusions** Explain why the eggs react differently when you try to stop them.

Station 2: Coin in a Cup

Procedure

1. At this station, you will find a coin, an index card, and a cup. Place the card over the cup. Then, place the coin on the card over the center of the cup, as shown below.

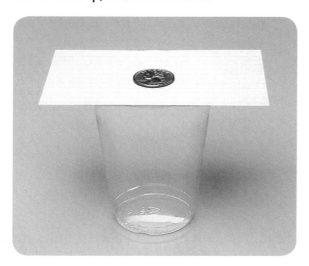

2. Write down a method for getting the coin into the cup without touching the coin and without lifting the card.

3. Try your method. If it doesn't work, try again until you find a method that does work.

Analyze the Results

1. **Describing Events** Use Newton's first law of motion to explain why the coin falls into the cup if you remove the card quickly.

Draw Conclusions

2. **Defending Conclusions** Explain why pulling on the card slowly will not work even though the coin has inertia. (Hint: Friction is a force.)

Station 3: The Magic Thread

Procedure

1. At this station, you will find a spool of thread and a mass hanging from a strong string. Cut a piece of thread about 40 cm long. Tie the thread around the bottom of the mass, as shown at right.

2. Pull gently on the end of the thread. Observe what happens, and record your observations.

3. Stop the mass from moving. Now hold the end of the thread so that there is a lot of slack between your fingers and the mass.

4. Give the thread a quick, hard pull. You should observe a very different event. Record your observations. Throw away the thread.

Analyze the Results

1. **Analyzing Results** Use Newton's first law of motion to explain why the result of a gentle pull is different from the result of a hard pull.

Draw Conclusions

2. **Applying Conclusions** Both moving and non-moving objects have inertia. Explain why throwing a bowling ball and catching a thrown bowling ball are hard.

3. **Drawing Conclusions** Why is it harder to run with a backpack full of books than to run with an empty backpack?

Chapter Review

USING KEY TERMS

Complete each of the following sentences by choosing the correct term from the word bank.

free fall	projectile motion
inertia	terminal velocity
momentum	

1 An object in motion has ___, so it tends to stay in motion.

2 An object is falling at its ___ if it falls at a constant velocity.

3 ___ is the path that a thrown object follows.

4 ___ is a property of moving objects that depends on mass and velocity.

5 ___ occurs only when air resistance does not affect the motion of a falling object.

UNDERSTANDING KEY IDEAS

Multiple Choice

6 When a soccer ball is kicked, the action and reaction forces do not cancel each other out because

a. the forces are not equal in size.

b. the forces act on different objects.

c. the forces act at different times.

d. All of the above

7 An object is in projectile motion if it

a. is thrown with a horizontal push.

b. is accelerated downward by gravity.

c. does not accelerate horizontally.

d. All of the above

8 Newton's first law of motion applies to

a. moving objects.

b. objects that are not moving.

c. objects that are accelerating.

d. Both (a) and (b)

9 To accelerate two objects at the same rate, the force used to push the object that has more mass should be

a. smaller than the force used to push the object that has less mass.

b. larger than the force used to push the object that has less mass.

c. the same as the force used to push the object that has less mass.

d. equal to the object's weight.

10 A golf ball and a bowling ball are moving at the same velocity. Which of the two has more momentum?

a. The golf ball has more momentum because it has less mass.

b. The bowling ball has more momentum because it has more mass.

c. They have the same momentum because they have the same velocity.

d. There is not enough information to determine the answer.

Short Answer

11 Give an example of an object that is in free fall.

12 Describe how gravity and air resistance are related to an object's terminal velocity.

13 Why can friction make observing Newton's first law of motion difficult?

Math Skills

14 A 12 kg rock falls from rest off a cliff and hits the ground in 1.5 s.

a. Without considering air resistance, what is the rock's velocity just before it hits the ground?

b. What is the rock's momentum just before it hits the ground?

CRITICAL THINKING

15 **Concept Mapping** Use the following terms to create a concept map: *gravity, free fall, terminal velocity, projectile motion,* and *air resistance.*

16 **Identifying Relationships** During a space shuttle launch, about 830,000 kg of fuel is burned in 8 min. The fuel provides the shuttle with a constant thrust, or forward force. How does Newton's second law of motion explain why the shuttle's acceleration increases as the fuel is burned?

17 **Analyzing Processes** When using a hammer to drive a nail into wood, you have to swing the hammer through the air with a certain velocity. Because the hammer has both mass and velocity, it has momentum. Describe what happens to the hammer's momentum after the hammer hits the nail.

18 **Applying Concepts** Suppose you are standing on a skateboard or on in-line skates and you toss a backpack full of heavy books toward your friend. What do you think will happen to you? Explain your answer in terms of Newton's third law of motion.

INTERPRETING GRAPHICS

19 The picture below shows a common desk toy. If you pull one ball up and release it, it hits the balls at the bottom and comes to a stop. In the same instant, the ball on the other side swings up and repeats the cycle. How does conservation of momentum explain how this toy works?

Standardized Test Preparation

Multiple Choice

Use the table below to answer question 1.

Force	Acceleration
25 N	5 m/s^2
50 N	10 m/s^2
75 N	15 m/s^2

1. **The table above shows the accelerations produced by different forces on a 5-kilogram mass. Assuming that the pattern continues, use this data to predict what acceleration would be produced by a 100-newton force.**

   A. 10 m/s^2

   B. 20 m/s^2

   C. 30 m/s^2

   D. 100 m/s^2

2. **Friction acting on a rolling ball that eventually brings it to a stop is an example of which of the following?**

   A. gravity

   B. momentum

   C. a balanced force

   D. an unbalanced force

3. **A picture is hanging on a nail in the wall. Which forces are interacting most with the picture?**

   A. compression and tension

   B. gravity and friction

   C. tension and gravity

   D. friction and compression

4. **A short time after jumping from an airplane, a skydiver reaches a constant speed. Which of the following statements about the skydiver is true?**

   A. The skydiver is accelerating toward the ground at 9.8 m/s^2.

   B. An unbalanced force acts on the skydiver.

   C. No unbalanced forces act on the skydiver.

   D. Air resistance does not affect the skydiver's speed.

5. **If two objects in motion have different masses, how does this difference affect the force needed to achieve the same acceleration?**

   A. The object with less mass will require more force to achieve the same rate of change.

   B. Force does not affect the rate of change of an object.

   C. It will take the same amount of force to achieve the same rate of change for the two objects.

   D. The object with greater mass will require more force to achieve the same rate of change.

6. **The equation *a = F/m* represents Newton's second law of motion. Based on this equation, if balanced forces act on an object, which of the following outcomes can be expected?**

   A. The object's acceleration will be negative.

   B. The object's acceleration will be zero.

   C. The object's mass will decrease.

   D. The object's mass will increase.

Use the diagram below to answer question 7.

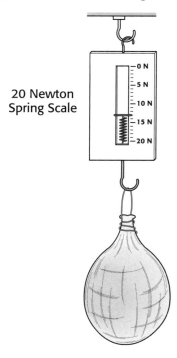

20 Newton
Spring Scale

- 0 N
- 5 N
- 10 N
- 15 N
- 20 N

7. If none of the objects in the diagram above is in motion, what force(s) must be being exerted?

A. Only that of the spring scale exerting an upward force of 17 N on the water balloon.

B. Only that of the water balloon exerting a downward force of 13 N on the spring scale.

C. The weight of the water balloon pulls the spring scale downward with a force of 13 N, and the spring scale exerts an upward force of 13 N on the water balloon.

D. The weight of the water balloon pulls the spring scale downward with a force of 7 N, and the spring scale exerts an upward force of 13 N on the water balloon.

8. Analyze the equation *a* = *F/m*. If the mass of an object decreases while a constant force is applied to it, what happens to the object's acceleration?

A. The object's acceleration increases.

B. The object's acceleration decreases.

C. The object's acceleration remains unchanged.

D. The object's acceleration is zero.

9. What does the magnitude of the gravitational attraction of two bodies depend upon?

A. the velocity of the bodies and the friction between them

B. the size of the bodies and their position relative to the ground

C. the weight of the bodies and how quickly they are moving

D. the mass of the bodies and the distance between them

Open Response

10. In archery, you use a bow to shoot an arrow at a target. Why must an archer point the arrow a little above the target in order to hit the target in the center? What forces are involved?

11. Luging is a sport in which a racer rides a sled down a long, curved, ice-covered track that runs down a slope. Identify the three main forces acting on the racer and describe whether each one acts to increase or to decrease the racer's speed.

Science in Action

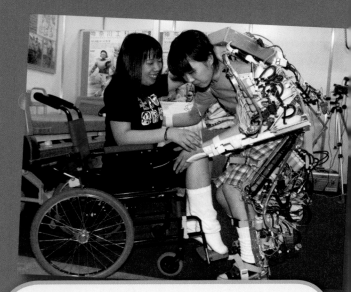

Scientific Discoveries

The Millennium Bridge

You may have heard the children's song, "London Bridge is falling down . . .". London Bridge never fell. But some people who walked on the Millennium Bridge thought that it might fall instead! The Millennium Bridge is a pedestrian bridge in London, England. The bridge opened on June 10, 2000, and more than 80,000 people crossed it that day. Immediately, people noticed something wrong—the bridge was swaying! The bridge was closed after two days so that engineers could determine what was wrong. After much research, the engineers learned that the force of the footsteps of the people crossing the bridge caused the bridge to sway.

Science, Technology, and Society

Power Suit for Lifting Patients

Imagine visiting a hospital and seeing someone who looked half human and half robot. No, it isn't a scene from a science fiction movie—it is a new invention that may some day help nurses lift patients easily. The invention, called a power suit, is a metal framework that a nurse would wear on his or her back. The suit calculates how much force a nurse needs to lift a patient, and then the robotic joints on the suit help the nurse exert the right amount of force. The suit will also help nurses avoid injuring their backs.

Math ACTiViTY

The pound (symbol £) is the currency in England. The inventor of the suit thinks that it will be sold for £1200. How much will the suit cost in dollars if $1 is equal to £0.60?

Language Arts ACTiViTY

WRITING SKILL Imagine that you were in London on June 10, 2000 and walked across the Millennium Bridge. Write a one-page story about what you think it was like on the bridge that day.

Careers

Steve Okamoto

Roller Coaster Designer Roller coasters have fascinated Steve Okamoto ever since his first ride on one. "I remember going to Disneyland as a kid. My mother was always upset with me because I kept looking over the sides of the rides, trying to figure out how they worked," he says. To satisfy his curiosity, Okamoto became a mechanical engineer. Today he uses his scientific knowledge to design and build machines, systems, and buildings. But his specialty is roller coasters.

Roller coasters really do coast along the track. A motor pulls the cars up a high hill to start the ride. After that, the cars are powered by only gravity. Designing a successful roller coaster is not a simple task. Okamoto has to calculate the cars' speed and acceleration on each part of the track. He must also consider the safety of the ride and the strength of the structure that supports the track.

Social Studies ACTIVITY

Research the history of roller coasters to learn how roller coaster design has changed over time. Make a poster to summarize your research.

To learn more about these Science in Action topics, visit go.hrw.com and type in the keyword **HP5FORF**.

Current Science

Check out Current Science® articles related to this chapter by visiting go.hrw.com. Just type in the keyword **HP5CS06**.

21

Forces in Fluids

The Big Idea
Forces in fluids are related to pressure and density and can affect the motion of objects in the fluid.

About the Photo

As you race downhill on your bicycle, the air around you pushes on your body and slows you down. "What a drag!" you say. Well, actually, it is a drag. When designing bicycle gear and clothing, manufacturers consider more than just looks and comfort. They also try to decrease drag, a fluid force that opposes motion. This photo shows cyclists riding their bikes in a wind tunnel in a study of how a fluid—air—affects their ride.

PRE-READING ACTIVITY

FOLDNOTES **Booklet** Before you read the chapter, create the FoldNote entitled "Booklet" described in the **Study Skills** section of the Appendix. Label each page of the booklet with a main idea from the chapter. As you read the chapter, write what you learn about each main idea on the appropriate page of the booklet.

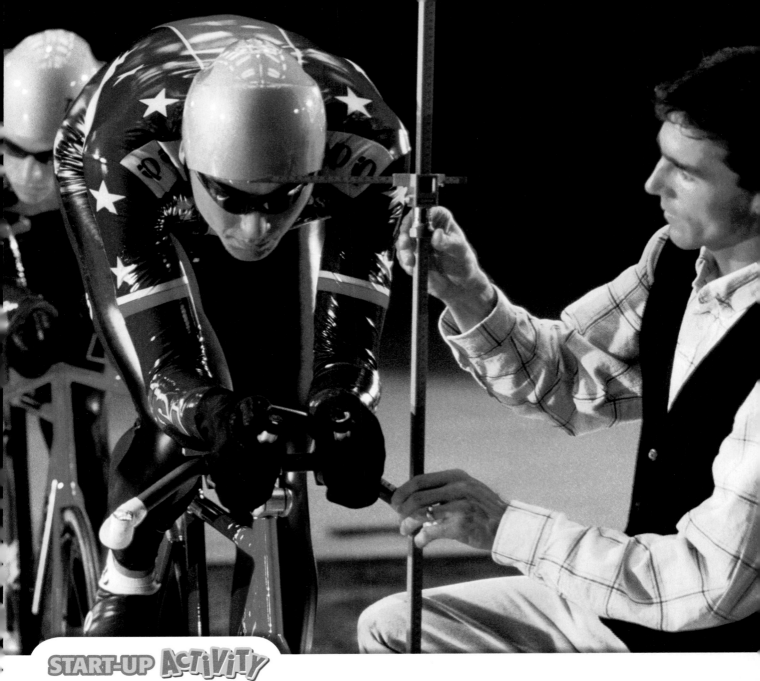

Taking Flight

In this activity, you will build a model airplane to learn how wing size affects flight.

Procedure

1. Fold a **sheet of paper** in half lengthwise. Then, open it. Fold the top corners toward the center crease. Keep the corners folded down, and fold the entire sheet in half along the center crease.

2. With the plane on its side, fold the top front edge down so that it meets the bottom edge. Fold the top edge down again so that it meets the bottom edge. Turn the plane over, and repeat.

3. Raise the wings so that they are perpendicular to the body.

4. Point the plane slightly upward, and gently throw it. Repeat several times. Describe what you see.

5. Make the wings smaller by folding them one more time. Gently throw the plane. Repeat several times. Describe what you see.

6. Using the smaller wings, try to achieve the same flight path you saw when the wings were bigger.

Analysis

1. What happened to the plane's flight when you reduced the size of its wings? What did you have to do to achieve the same flight path as when the wings were bigger?

2. What gave your plane its forward motion?

Forces in Fluids   **619**

What You Will Learn

● Describe how fluids exert pressure.
● Analyze how atmospheric pressure varies with depth.
● Explain how depth and density affect water pressure.
● Give examples of fluids flowing from high to low pressure.

Vocabulary

fluid
pressure
pascal
atmospheric pressure

READING STRATEGY

Brainstorming The key idea of this section is pressure. Brainstorm words and phrases related to pressure.

fluid a nonsolid state of matter in which the atoms or molecules are free to move past each other, as in a gas or liquid

pressure the amount of force exerted per unit area of a surface

pascal the SI unit of pressure (symbol, Pa)

atmospheric pressure the pressure caused by the weight of the atmosphere

Fluids and Pressure

What does a dolphin have in common with a sea gull? What does a dog have in common with a fly? What do you have in common with all these living things?

One answer to these questions is that you and all these other living things spend a lifetime moving through fluids. A **fluid** is any material that can flow and that takes the shape of its container. Fluids include liquids and gases. Fluids can flow because the particles in fluids move easily past each other.

Fluids Exert Pressure

You probably have heard the terms *air pressure* and *water pressure*. Air and water are fluids. All fluids exert pressure. So, what is pressure? Think about this example. When you pump up a bicycle tire, you push air into the tire. And like all matter, air is made of tiny particles that are constantly moving.

Look at **Figure 1.** Inside the tire, the air particles collide with each other and with the walls of the tire. Together, these collisions create a force on the tire. The amount of force exerted on a given area is **pressure.**

Calculating Pressure

Pressure can be calculated by using the following equation:

$$pressure = \frac{force}{area}$$

The SI unit for pressure is the **pascal.** One pascal (1 Pa) is the force of one newton exerted over an area of one square meter (1 N/m^2).

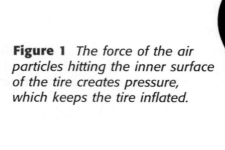

Figure 1 *The force of the air particles hitting the inner surface of the tire creates pressure, which keeps the tire inflated.*

Pressure, Force, and Area What is the pressure exerted by a book that has an area of 0.2 m² and a weight of 10 N?

Step 1: Write the equation for pressure.

$$pressure = \frac{force}{area}$$

Step 2: Replace *force* and *area* with the values given, and solve. (Hint: Weight is a measure of gravitational force.)

$$pressure = \frac{10 \text{ N}}{0.2 \text{ m}^2} = 50 \text{ N/m}^2 = 50 \text{ Pa}$$

The equation for pressure can be rearranged to find force or area, as shown below.

force = pressure × area (Rearrange by multiplying by area.)

$$area = \frac{force}{pressure}$$ (Rearrange by multiplying by area and then dividing by pressure.)

Now It's Your Turn

1. Find the pressure exerted by a 3,000 N crate that has an area of 2 m².
2. Find the weight of a rock that has an area of 10 m² and that exerts a pressure of 250 Pa.

Pressure and Bubbles

When you blow a soap bubble, you blow in only one direction. So, why does the bubble get rounder instead of longer as you blow? The shape of the bubble partly depends on an important property of fluids: Fluids exert pressure evenly in all directions. The air you blow into the bubble exerts pressure evenly in all directions. So, the bubble expands in all directions to create a sphere.

Atmospheric Pressure

The *atmosphere* is the layer of nitrogen, oxygen, and other gases that surrounds Earth. Earth's atmosphere is held in place by gravity, which pulls the gases toward Earth. The pressure caused by the weight of the atmosphere is called **atmospheric pressure.**

Atmospheric pressure is exerted on everything on Earth, including you. At sea level, the atmosphere exerts a pressure of about 101,300 N on every square meter, or 101,300 Pa. So, there is a weight of about 10 N (about 2 lbs) on every square centimeter of your body. Why don't you feel this crushing pressure? Like the air inside a balloon, the fluids inside your body exert pressure. **Figure 2** can help you understand why you don't feel the pressure.

✓ **Reading Check** Name two gases in the atmosphere.
(*See the Appendix for answers to Reading Checks.*)

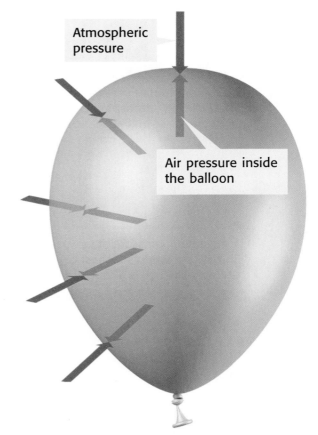

Figure 2 *The air inside a balloon exerts pressure that keeps the balloon inflated against atmospheric pressure. Similarly, fluid inside your body exerts pressure that works against atmospheric pressure.*

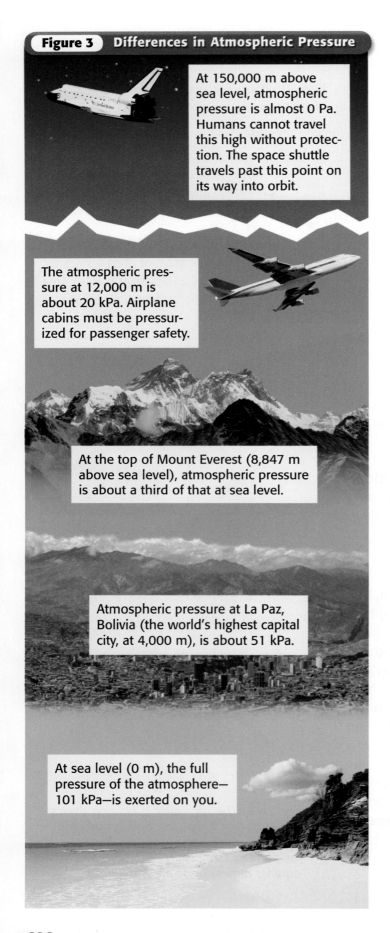

Figure 3 Differences in Atmospheric Pressure

At 150,000 m above sea level, atmospheric pressure is almost 0 Pa. Humans cannot travel this high without protection. The space shuttle travels past this point on its way into orbit.

The atmospheric pressure at 12,000 m is about 20 kPa. Airplane cabins must be pressurized for passenger safety.

At the top of Mount Everest (8,847 m above sea level), atmospheric pressure is about a third of that at sea level.

Atmospheric pressure at La Paz, Bolivia (the world's highest capital city, at 4,000 m), is about 51 kPa.

At sea level (0 m), the full pressure of the atmosphere—101 kPa—is exerted on you.

Variation of Atmospheric Pressure

The atmosphere stretches about 150 km above Earth's surface. However, about 80% of the atmosphere's gases are found within 10 km of Earth's surface. At the top of the atmosphere, pressure is almost nonexistent. The pressure is close to 0 Pa because the gas particles are far apart and rarely collide. Mount Everest in south-central Asia is the highest point on Earth. At the top of Mount Everest, atmospheric pressure is about 33,000 Pa, or 33 kilo-pascals (33 kPa). (Remember that the prefix *kilo-* means 1,000. So, 1 kPa is equal to 1,000 Pa.) At sea level, atmospheric pressure is about 101 kPa.

Atmospheric Pressure and Depth

Take a look at **Figure 3.** Notice how atmospheric pressure changes as you travel through the atmosphere. The further down through the atmosphere you go, the greater the pressure is. In other words, the pressure increases as the atmosphere gets "deeper." An important point to remember about fluids is that pressure varies depending on depth. At lower levels of the atmosphere, there is more fluid above that is being pulled by Earth's gravitational force. So, there is more pressure at lower levels of the atmosphere.

Reading Check Describe how pressure changes with depth.

Pressure Changes and Your Body

So, what happens to your body when atmospheric pressure changes? If you travel to higher or lower points in the atmosphere, the fluids in your body have to adjust to maintain equal pressure. You may have experienced this adjustment if your ears have "popped" when you were in a plane taking off or in a car traveling down a steep mountain road. The "pop" happens because of pressure changes in pockets of air behind your eardrums.

Water Pressure

Water is a fluid. So, it exerts pressure like the atmosphere does. Water pressure also increases as depth increases, as shown in **Figure 4.** The deeper a diver goes in the water, the greater the pressure is. The pressure increases because more water above the diver is being pulled by Earth's gravitational force. In addition, the atmosphere presses down on the water, so the total pressure on the diver includes water pressure and atmospheric pressure.

Water Pressure and Depth

Like atmospheric pressure, water pressure depends on depth. Water pressure does not depend on the total amount of fluid present. A swimmer would feel the same pressure swimming at 3 m below the surface of a small pond and at 3 m below the surface of an ocean. Even though there is more water in the ocean than in the pond, the pressure on the swimmer in the pond would be the same as the pressure on the swimmer in the ocean.

Density Making a Difference

Water is about 1,000 times more dense than air. *Density* is the amount of matter in a given volume, or mass per unit volume. Because water is more dense than air, a certain volume of water has more mass—and weighs more—than the same volume of air. So, water exerts more pressure than air.

For example, if you climb a 10 m tree, the decrease in atmospheric pressure is too small to notice. But if you dive 10 m underwater, the pressure on you increases to 201 kPa, which is almost twice the atmospheric pressure at the surface!

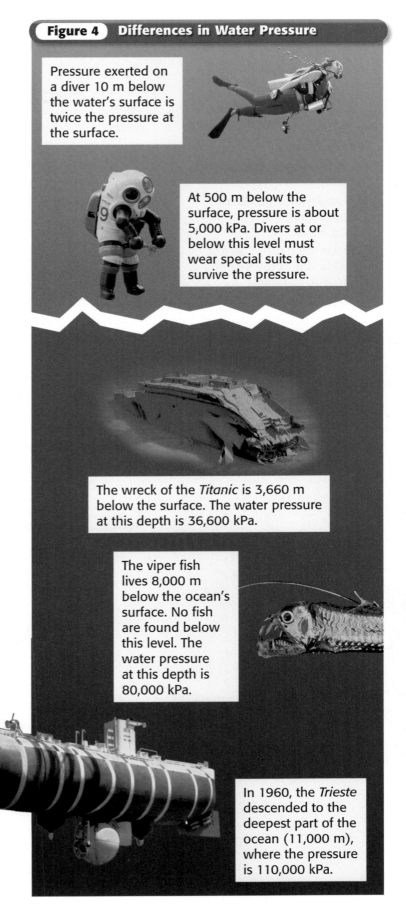

Figure 4 Differences in Water Pressure

Pressure exerted on a diver 10 m below the water's surface is twice the pressure at the surface.

At 500 m below the surface, pressure is about 5,000 kPa. Divers at or below this level must wear special suits to survive the pressure.

The wreck of the *Titanic* is 3,660 m below the surface. The water pressure at this depth is 36,600 kPa.

The viper fish lives 8,000 m below the ocean's surface. No fish are found below this level. The water pressure at this depth is 80,000 kPa.

In 1960, the *Trieste* descended to the deepest part of the ocean (11,000 m), where the pressure is 110,000 kPa.

Pressure Differences and Fluid Flow

When you drink through a straw, you remove some of the air in the straw. Because there is less air inside the straw, the pressure in the straw is reduced. But the atmospheric pressure on the surface of the liquid remains the same. Thus, there is a difference between the pressure inside the straw and the pressure outside the straw. The outside pressure forces the liquid up the straw and into your mouth. So, just by drinking through a straw, you can observe an important property of fluids: Fluids flow from areas of high pressure to areas of low pressure.

Reading Check When drinking through a straw, how do you decrease the pressure inside the straw?

Pressure Differences and Breathing

Take a deep breath—fluid is flowing from high to low pressure! When you inhale, a muscle increases the space in your chest and gives your lungs room to expand. This expansion decreases the pressure in your lungs. The pressure in your lungs becomes lower than the air pressure outside your lungs. Air then flows into your lungs—from high to low pressure. This air carries oxygen that you need to live. **Figure 5** shows how exhaling also causes fluids to flow from high to low pressure. You can see a similar flow of fluid when you open a carbonated beverage or squeeze toothpaste onto your toothbrush.

Figure 5 Exhaling, Pressure, and Fluid Flow

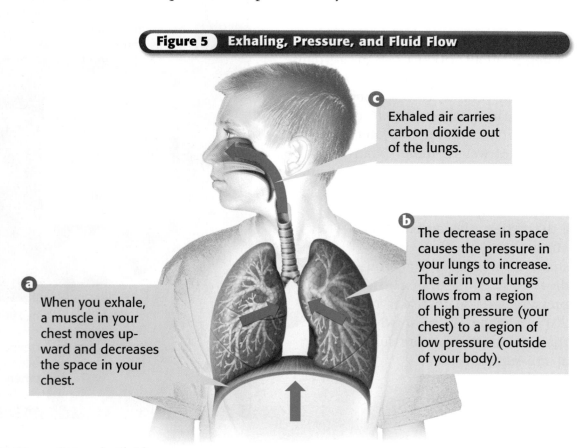

a When you exhale, a muscle in your chest moves upward and decreases the space in your chest.

b The decrease in space causes the pressure in your lungs to increase. The air in your lungs flows from a region of high pressure (your chest) to a region of low pressure (outside of your body).

c Exhaled air carries carbon dioxide out of the lungs.

Pressure Differences and Tornadoes

Look at the tornado in **Figure 6.** Some of the damaging winds caused by tornadoes are the result of pressure differences. The air pressure inside a tornado is very low. Because the air pressure outside of the tornado is higher than the pressure inside, air rushes into the tornado. The rushing air causes the tornado to be like a giant vacuum cleaner—objects are pushed into the tornado. The winds created are usually very strong and affect the area around the tornado. So, objects, such as trees and buildings, can be severely damaged by wind even if they are not in the direct path of a tornado.

Figure 6 *Tornadoes are like giant vacuum cleaners because of pressure differences.*

SECTION Review

Summary

- A fluid is any material that flows and takes the shape of its container.
- Pressure is force exerted on a given area.
- Moving particles of matter create pressure by colliding with one another and with the walls of their container.
- The pressure caused by the weight of the atmosphere is called *atmospheric pressure.*
- Fluid pressure increases as depth increases.
- As depth increases, water pressure increases faster than atmospheric pressure does because water is denser than air.
- Fluids flow from areas of high pressure to areas of low pressure.

Using Key Terms

1. In your own words, write a definition for each of the following terms: *fluid* and *atmospheric pressure.*

2. Use the following terms in the same sentence: *pressure* and *pascal.*

Understanding Key Ideas

3. Which of the following statements about fluids is true?
   a. Fluids rarely take the shape of their container.
   b. Fluids include liquids and gases.
   c. Fluids flow from low pressure to high pressure.
   d. Fluids exert the most pressure in the downward direction.

4. How do fluids exert pressure on a container?

5. Why are you not crushed by atmospheric pressure?

6. Explain why atmospheric pressure changes as depth changes.

7. Give three examples of fluids flowing from high pressure to low pressure in everyday life.

Math Skills

8. The water in a glass has a weight of 2.4 N. The bottom of the glass has an area of 0.012 m². What is the pressure exerted by the water on the bottom of the glass?

Critical Thinking

9. **Identifying Relationships** Mercury is a liquid that has a density of 13.5 g/mL. Water has a density of 1.0 g/mL. Equal volumes of mercury and water are in identical containers. Explain why the pressures exerted on the bottoms of the containers are different.

10. **Making Inferences** Why do airplanes need to be pressurized for passenger safety when flying high in the atmosphere?

SECTION 2

Buoyant Force

Why does an ice cube float on water? Why doesn't it sink to the bottom of your glass?

Imagine that you use a straw to push an ice cube under water. Then, you release the cube. A force pushes the ice back to the water's surface. The force, called **buoyant force** (BOY uhnt FAWRS), is the upward force that fluids exert on all matter.

What You Will Learn

● Explain the relationship between fluid pressure and buoyant force.
● Predict whether an object will float or sink in a fluid.
● Analyze the role of density in an object's ability to float.
● Explain how the overall density of an object can be changed.

Vocabulary

buoyant force
Archimedes' principle

READING STRATEGY

Discussion Read this section silently. Write down questions that you have about this section. Discuss your questions in a small group.

Buoyant Force and Fluid Pressure

Look at **Figure 1.** Water exerts fluid pressure on all sides of an object. The pressure exerted horizontally on one side of the object is equal to the pressure exerted on the opposite side. These equal pressures cancel one another. So, the only fluid pressures affecting the net force on the object are at the top and at the bottom. Pressure increases as depth increases. So, the pressure at the bottom of the object is greater than the pressure at the top. The water exerts a net upward force on the object. This upward force is buoyant force.

Determining Buoyant Force

Archimedes (AHR kuh MEE DEEZ), a Greek mathematician who lived in the third century BCE, discovered how to determine buoyant force. **Archimedes' principle** states that the buoyant force on an object in a fluid is an upward force equal to the weight of the fluid that the object takes the place of, or displaces. Suppose the object in **Figure 1** displaces 250 mL of water. The weight of that volume of displaced water is about 2.5 N. So, the buoyant force on the object is 2.5 N. Notice that only the weight of the displaced fluid determines the buoyant force on an object. The weight of the object does not affect buoyant force.

buoyant force the upward force that keeps an object immersed in or floating on a liquid

Archimedes' principle the principle that states that the buoyant force on an object in a fluid is an upward force equal to the weight of the volume of fluid that the object displaces

Figure 1 *There is more pressure at the bottom of an object because pressure increases with depth. This results in an upward buoyant force on the object.*

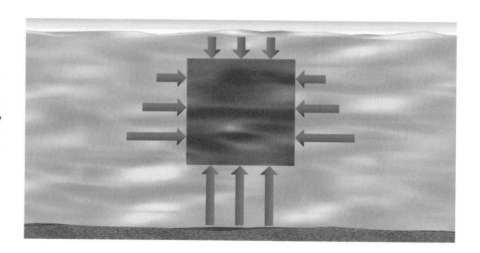

Weight Versus Buoyant Force

An object in a fluid will sink if its weight is greater than the buoyant force (the weight of the fluid it displaces). An object floats only when the buoyant force on the object is equal to the object's weight.

Sinking

The rock in **Figure 2** weighs 75 N. It displaces 5 L of water. Archimedes' principle says that the buoyant force is equal to the weight of the displaced water—about 50 N. The rock's weight is greater than the buoyant force. So, the rock sinks.

Floating

The fish in **Figure 2** weighs 12 N. It displaces a volume of water that weighs 12 N. Because the fish's weight is equal to the buoyant force, the fish floats in the water. In fact, the fish is suspended in the water as it floats. Now, look at the duck. The duck does not sink. So, the buoyant force on the duck must be equal to the duck's weight. But the duck isn't all the way underwater! Only the duck's feet, legs, and stomach have to be underwater to displace 9 N of water, which is equal to the duck's weight. So, the duck floats on the surface of the water.

Buoying Up

If the duck dove underwater, it would displace more than 9 N of water. So, the buoyant force on the duck would be greater than the duck's weight. When the buoyant force on an object is greater than the object's weight, the object is *buoyed up* (pushed up) in water. An object is buoyed up until the part of the object underwater displaces an amount of water that equals the object's entire weight. Thus, an ice cube pops to the surface when it is pushed to the bottom of a glass of water.

✓ Reading Check What causes an object to buoy up? (*See the Appendix for answers to Reading Checks.*)

Floating Fun

Fill a sink with water. Ask an adult to help you find five things that float in water and five things that sink in water. Discuss what the floating objects have in common and what the sinking objects have in common. In your **science journal,** list the objects, and summarize your discussion.

Figure 2 *Will an object sink or float? That depends on whether the buoyant force is less than or equal to the object's weight.*

Weight = 12 N
Buoyant force = 12 N
Fish floats and is suspended in the water.

Weight = 9 N
Buoyant force = 9 N
Duck floats on the surface.

Weight = 75 N
Buoyant force = 50 N
Rock sinks.

Floating, Sinking, and Density

Think again about the rock in the lake. The rock displaces 5 L of water. But volumes of solids are measured in cubic centimeters (cm^3). Because 1 mL is equal to 1 cm^3, the volume of the rock is 5,000 cm^3. But 5,000 cm^3 of rock weighs more than an equal volume of water. So, the rock sinks.

Because mass is proportional to weight, you can say that the rock has more mass per volume than water has. Mass per unit volume is density. The rock sinks because it is more dense than water is. The duck floats because it is less dense than water is. The density of the fish is equal to the density of the water.

More Dense Than Air

Why does an ice cube float on water but not in air? An ice cube floats on water because it is less dense than water. But most substances are *more* dense than air. So, there are few substances that float in air. The ice cube is more dense than air, so the ice cube doesn't float in air.

Less Dense Than Air

One substance that is less dense than air is helium, a gas. In fact, helium has one-seventh the density of air under normal conditions. A given volume of helium displaces an equal volume of air that is much heavier than itself. So, helium floats in air. Because helium floats in air, it is used in parade balloons, such as the one shown in **Figure 3**.

Figure 3 *Helium in a balloon floats in air for the same reason an ice cube floats on water—helium is less dense than the surrounding fluid.*

✔️ **Reading Check** Name a substance that is less dense than air.

Finding Density Find the density of a rock that has a mass of 10 g and a volume of 2 cm^3.

Step 1: Write the equation for density. Density is calculated by using this equation:

$$density = \frac{mass}{volume}$$

Step 2: Replace *mass* and *volume* with the values in the problem, and solve.

$$density = \frac{10 \text{ g}}{2 \text{ cm}^3} = 5 \text{ g/cm}^3$$

Now It's Your Turn

1. What is the density of a 20 cm^3 object that has a mass of 25 g?
2. A 546 g fish displaces 420 mL of water. What is the density of the fish? (Note: 1 mL = 1 cm^3)
3. A beaker holds 50 mL of a slimy green liquid. The mass of the liquid is 163 g. What is the density of the liquid?

---

628   Chapter 21   Forces in Fluids

Changing Overall Density

Steel is almost 8 times denser than water. And yet huge steel ships cruise the oceans with ease. But hold on! You just learned that substances that are more dense than water will sink in water. So, how does a steel ship float?

Changing Shape

The secret of how a ship floats is in the shape of the ship. What if a ship were just a big block of steel, as shown in **Figure 4**? If you put that block into water, the block would sink because it is more dense than water. So, ships are built with a hollow shape. The amount of steel in the ship is the same as in the block. But the hollow shape increases the volume of the ship. Remember that density is mass per unit volume. So, an increase in the ship's volume leads to a decrease in its density. Thus, ships made of steel float because their *overall density* is less than the density of water.

Most ships are built to displace more water than is necessary for the ship to float. Ships are made this way so that they won't sink when people and cargo are loaded on the ship.

CONNECTION TO Geology

Floating Rocks The rock that makes up Earth's continents is about 15% less dense than the molten (melted) mantle rock below it. Because of this difference in density, the continents are floating on the mantle. Research the structure of Earth, and make a poster that shows Earth's interior layers.

ACTIVITY

Figure 4 Shape and Overall Density

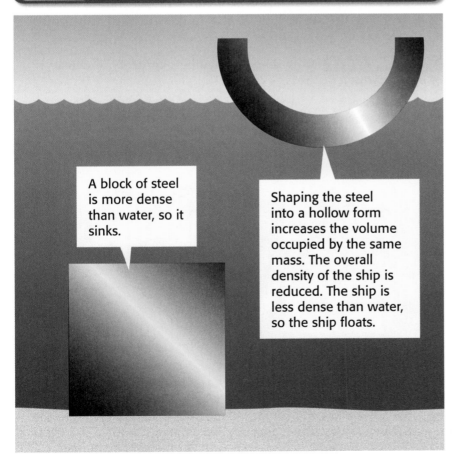

A block of steel is more dense than water, so it sinks.

Shaping the steel into a hollow form increases the volume occupied by the same mass. The overall density of the ship is reduced. The ship is less dense than water, so the ship floats.

INTERNET ACTIVITY

For another activity related to this chapter, go to **go.hrw.com** and type in the keyword **HP5FLUW**.

Quick Lab

Ship Shape

1. Roll a **piece of clay** into a ball the size of a golf ball, and drop it into a **container of water.** Record your observations.

2. With your hands, flatten the ball of clay until it is a bit thinner than your little finger, and press it into the shape of a bowl or canoe.

3. Place the clay boat gently in the water. How does the change of shape affect the buoyant force on the clay? How is that change related to the overall density of the clay boat? Record your answers.

Changing Mass

A submarine is a special kind of ship that can travel both on the surface of the water and underwater. Submarines have *ballast tanks* that can be opened to allow sea water to flow in. As water is added, the submarine's mass increases, but its volume stays the same. The submarine's overall density increases so that it can dive under the surface. Crew members control the amount of water taken in. In this way, they control how dense the submarine is and how deep it dives. Compressed air is used to blow the water out of the tanks so that the submarine can rise. Study **Figure 5** to learn how ballast tanks work.

✓ **Reading Check** How do crew members control the density of a submarine?

Figure 5 **Controlling Density Using Ballast Tanks**

When a submarine is floating on the ocean's surface, its ballast tanks are filled mostly with air.

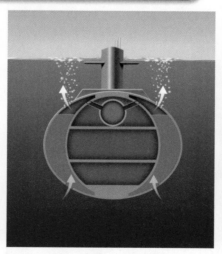

Vent holes on the ballast tanks are opened to allow the submarine to dive. Air escapes as the tanks fill with water.

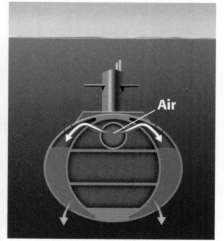

Vent holes are closed, and compressed air is pumped into the ballast tanks to force the water out, so the submarine rises.

Changing Volume

Like a submarine, some fish adjust their overall density to stay at a certain depth in the water. Most bony fishes have an organ called a *swim bladder,* shown in **Figure 6.** This swim bladder is filled with gases produced in a fish's blood. The inflated swim bladder increases the fish's volume and thereby decreases the fish's overall density, which keeps the fish from sinking in the water. The fish's nervous system controls the amount of gas in the bladder. Some fish, such as sharks, do not have a swim bladder. These fish must swim constantly to keep from sinking.

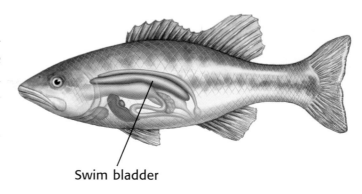
Swim bladder

Figure 6 *Most bony fishes have an organ called a* swim bladder *that allows them to adjust their overall density.*

SECTION Review

Summary

- All fluids exert an upward force called *buoyant force.*
- Buoyant force is caused by differences in fluid pressure.
- Archimedes' principle states that the buoyant force on an object is equal to the weight of the fluid displaced by the object.
- Any object that is more dense than the surrounding fluid will sink. An object that is less dense than the surrounding fluid will float.
- The overall density of an object can be changed by changing the object's shape, mass, or volume.

Using Key Terms

1. Use the following terms in the same sentence: *buoyant force* and *Archimedes' principle*.

Understanding Key Ideas

2. Which of the following changes increases the overall density of the object?
   a. A block of iron is formed into a hollow shape.
   b. A submarine fills its ballast tanks with water.
   c. A submarine fills its ballast tanks with air.
   d. A fish increases the amount of gas in its swim bladder.

3. Explain how differences in fluid pressure create buoyant force on an object.

4. How does an object's density determine whether the object will sink or float in water?

5. Name three methods that can be used to change the overall density of an object.

Math Skills

6. What is the density of an object that has a mass of 184 g and a volume of 50 cm³?

Critical Thinking

7. **Applying Concepts** An object weighs 20 N. It displaces a volume of water that weighs 15 N.
   a. What is the buoyant force on the object?
   b. Will this object float or sink? Explain your answer.

8. **Predicting Consequences** Iron has a density of 7.9 g/cm³. Mercury is a liquid that has a density of 13.5 g/cm³. Will iron float or sink in mercury? Explain your answer.

9. **Evaluating Hypotheses** Imagine that your brother tells you that all heavy objects sink in water. Explain why you agree or disagree with his statement.

SC*i*LINKS®

NSTA
Developed and maintained by the
National Science Teachers Association

For a variety of links related to this chapter, go to www.scilinks.org

Topic: Buoyant Force
SciLinks code: HSM0202

What You Will Learn

● Describe the relationship between pressure and fluid speed.
● Analyze the roles of lift, thrust, and wing size in flight.
● Describe drag, and explain how it affects lift.
● Explain Pascal's principle.

Vocabulary

Bernoulli's principle
lift
thrust
drag
Pascal's principle

READING STRATEGY

Reading Organizer As you read this section, create an outline of the section. Use the headings from the section in your outline.

Bernoulli's principle the principle that states that the pressure in a fluid decreases as the fluid's velocity increases

Fluids and Motion

Hold two sheets of paper so that the edges are hanging in front of your face about 4 cm apart. The flat faces of the paper should be parallel to each other. Now, blow as hard as you can between the two sheets of paper.

What's going on? You can't separate the sheets by blowing between them. In fact, the sheets move closer together the harder you blow. You may be surprised that the explanation for this unusual occurrence also includes how wings help birds and planes fly and how pitchers throw screwballs.

Fluid Speed and Pressure

The strange reaction of the paper is caused by a property of moving fluids. This property was first described in the 18th century by Daniel Bernoulli (ber NOO lee), a Swiss mathematician. **Bernoulli's principle** states that as the speed of a moving fluid increases, the fluid's pressure decreases. In the case of the paper, air speed between the two sheets increased when you blew air between them. Because air speed increased, the pressure between the sheets decreased. Thus, the higher pressure on the outside of the sheets pushed them together.

Science in a Sink

Bernoulli's principle is at work in **Figure 1.** A table-tennis ball is attached to a string and swung into a stream of water. Instead of being pushed out of the water, the ball is held in the water. Why? The water is moving faster than the air around it, so the water has a lower pressure than the surrounding air. The higher air pressure pushes the ball into the area of lower pressure—the water stream. Try this at home to see for yourself!

Figure 1 *This ball is pushed by the higher pressure of the air into an area of reduced pressure—the water stream.*

Figure 2 Wing Design and Lift

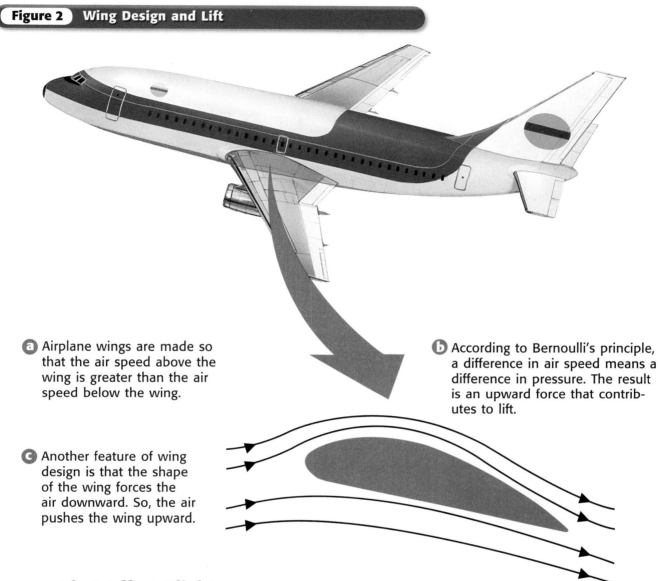

a Airplane wings are made so that the air speed above the wing is greater than the air speed below the wing.

b According to Bernoulli's principle, a difference in air speed means a difference in pressure. The result is an upward force that contributes to lift.

c Another feature of wing design is that the shape of the wing forces the air downward. So, the air pushes the wing upward.

Factors That Affect Flight

A common commercial airplane in the skies today is the Boeing 737 jet. Even without passengers, the plane weighs 350,000 N. How can something so big and heavy get off the ground and fly? Wing shape plays a role in helping these big planes—as well as smaller planes and birds—achieve flight, as shown in **Figure 2.**

According to Bernoulli's principle, the fast-moving air above the wing exerts less pressure than the slow-moving air below the wing. The greater pressure below the wing exerts an upward force. This upward force, known as **lift,** pushes the wings (and the rest of the airplane or bird) upward against the downward pull of gravity.

lift an upward force on an object that moves in a fluid

✔ **Reading Check** What is lift? (*See the Appendix for answers to Reading Checks.*)

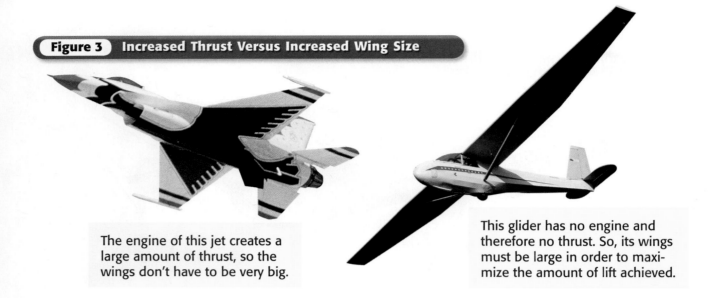

Figure 3 Increased Thrust Versus Increased Wing Size

The engine of this jet creates a large amount of thrust, so the wings don't have to be very big.

This glider has no engine and therefore no thrust. So, its wings must be large in order to maximize the amount of lift achieved.

thrust the pushing or pulling force exerted by the engine of an aircraft or rocket

CONNECTION TO Social Studies

The First Flight The first successful flight of an engine-driven machine that was heavier than air happened in Kitty Hawk, North Carolina, in 1903. Orville Wright was the pilot. The plane flew only 37 m (about the length of a 737 jet) before landing, and the entire flight lasted only 12 s. Research another famous pilot in the history of flight. Make a poster that includes information about the pilot as well as pictures of the pilot and his or her airplane.

ACTIVITY

Thrust and Lift

The amount of lift created by a plane's wing is determined partly by the speed at which air travels around the wing. The speed of a plane is determined mostly by its thrust. **Thrust** is the forward force produced by the plane's engine. In general, a plane with a large amount of thrust moves faster than a plane that has less thrust does. This faster speed means air travels around the wing at a higher speed, which increases lift.

Wing Size, Speed, and Lift

The amount of lift also depends partly on the size of a plane's wings. Look at the jet plane in **Figure 3.** This plane can fly with a relatively small wing size because its engine gives a large amount of thrust. This thrust pushes the plane through the sky at great speeds. So, the jet creates a large amount of lift with small wings by moving quickly through the air. Smaller wings keep a plane's weight low, which also helps it move faster.

Compared with the jet, the glider in **Figure 3** has a large wing area. A glider is an engineless plane. It rides rising air currents to stay in flight. Without engines, gliders produce no thrust and move more slowly than many other kinds of planes. Thus, a glider must have large wings to create the lift it needs to stay in the air.

Bernoulli and Birds

Birds don't have engines, so birds must flap their wings to push themselves through the air. A small bird must flap its wings at a fast pace to stay in the air. But a hawk flaps its wings only occasionally because it has larger wings than the small bird has. A hawk uses its large wings to fly with very little effort. Fully extended, a hawk's wings allow the hawk to glide on wind currents and still have enough lift to stay in the air.

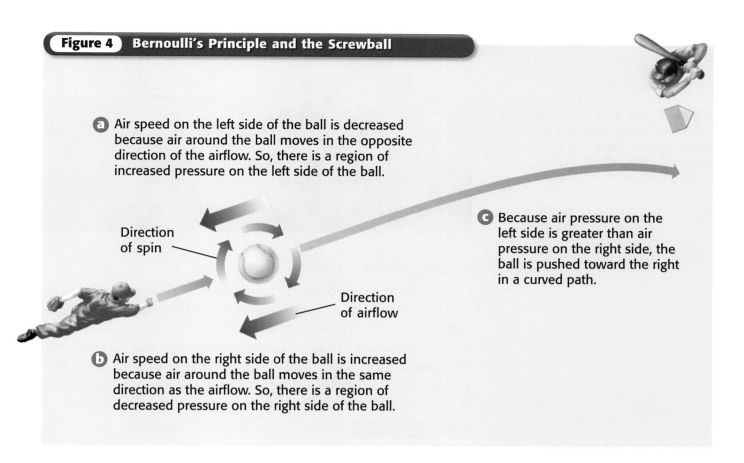

Figure 4 Bernoulli's Principle and the Screwball

a Air speed on the left side of the ball is decreased because air around the ball moves in the opposite direction of the airflow. So, there is a region of increased pressure on the left side of the ball.

Direction of spin

Direction of airflow

c Because air pressure on the left side is greater than air pressure on the right side, the ball is pushed toward the right in a curved path.

b Air speed on the right side of the ball is increased because air around the ball moves in the same direction as the airflow. So, there is a region of decreased pressure on the right side of the ball.

Bernoulli and Baseball

You don't have to look up at a bird or a plane flying through the sky to see Bernoulli's principle in your world. Any time fluids are moving, Bernoulli's principle is at work. **Figure 4** shows how a baseball pitcher can take advantage of Bernoulli's principle to throw a confusing screwball that is difficult for a batter to hit.

Drag and Motion in Fluids

Have you ever walked into a strong wind and noticed that the wind seemed to slow you down? It may have felt like the wind was pushing you backward. Fluids exert a force that opposes the motion of objects moving through the fluids. The force that opposes or restricts motion in a fluid is called **drag.**

In a strong wind, air "drags" on your body and makes it difficult for you to move forward. Drag also works against the forward motion of a plane or bird in flight. Drag is usually caused by an irregular flow of air. An irregular or unpredictable flow of fluids is known as *turbulence.*

drag a force parallel to the velocity of the flow; it opposes the direction of an aircraft and, in combination with thrust, determines the speed of the aircraft

✓ Reading Check What is turbulence?

Figure 5 *The pilot of this airplane can move these flaps to adjust the amount of lift when the airplane lands or takes off.*

Turbulence and Lift

Lift is often reduced when turbulence causes drag. Drag can be a serious problem for airplanes moving at high speeds. So, airplanes are equipped with ways to reduce turbulence as much as possible when in flight. For example, flaps like those shown in **Figure 5** can be used to change the shape or area of a wing. This change can reduce drag and increase lift. Similarly, birds can adjust their wing feathers in response to turbulence.

✓ *Reading Check* **How do airplanes reduce turbulence?**

Pascal's Principle

Imagine that the water-pumping station in your town increases the water pressure by 20 Pa. Will the water pressure be increased more at a store two blocks away or at a home 2 km away?

Believe it or not, the increase in water pressure will be the same at both locations. This equal change in water pressure is explained by Pascal's principle. **Pascal's principle** states that a change in pressure at any point in an enclosed fluid will be transmitted equally to all parts of that fluid. This principle was discovered by the 17th-century French scientist Blaise Pascal.

Pascal's principle the principle that states that a fluid in equilibrium contained in a vessel exerts a pressure of equal intensity in all directions

Pascal's Principle and Motion

Hydraulic (hie DRAW lik) devices use Pascal's principle to move or lift objects. Liquids are used in hydraulic devices because liquids cannot be easily compressed, or squeezed, into a smaller space. Cranes, forklifts, and bulldozers have hydraulic devices that help them lift heavy objects.

Hydraulic devices can multiply forces. Car brakes are a good example. In **Figure 6,** a driver's foot exerts pressure on a cylinder of liquid. This pressure is transmitted to all parts of the liquid-filled brake system. The liquid moves the brake pads. The pads press against the wheels, and friction stops the car. The force is multiplied because the pistons that push the brake pads are larger than the piston that is pushed by the brake pedal.

Figure 6 *Because of Pascal's principle, the touch of a foot can stop tons of moving metal.*

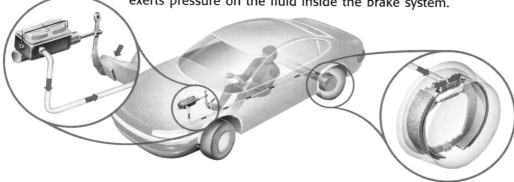

1 When the driver pushes the brake pedal, a small piston exerts pressure on the fluid inside the brake system.

2 The change in pressure is transmitted to the large pistons that push on the brake pads.

SECTION Review

Summary

- Bernoulli's principle states that fluid pressure decreases as the speed of the fluid increases.

- Wing shape allows airplanes to take advantage of Bernoulli's principle to achieve flight.

- Lift on an airplane is determined by wing size and thrust.

- Drag opposes motion through fluids.

- Pascal's principle states that a change in pressure in an enclosed fluid is transmitted equally to all parts of the fluid.

Using Key Terms

For each pair of terms, explain how the meanings of the terms differ.

1. *Bernoulli's principle* and *Pascal's principle*

2. *thrust* and *drag*

Understanding Key Ideas

3. The shape of an airplane's wing helps it gain
   - **a.** drag.
   - **b.** lift.
   - **c.** thrust.
   - **d.** turbulence.

4. What is the relationship between pressure and fluid speed?

5. What is Pascal's principle?

6. What force opposes motion through a fluid? How does this force affect lift?

7. How do thrust and lift help an airplane achieve flight?

Critical Thinking

8. **Applying Concepts** Air moving around a speeding race car can create lift. Upside-down wings, or spoilers, are mounted on the rear of race cars. Use Bernoulli's principle to explain how spoilers reduce the danger of accidents.

9. **Making Inferences** When you squeeze a balloon, where is the pressure inside the balloon increased the most? Explain.

Interpreting Graphics

10. Look at the image below. When the space through which a fluid flows becomes narrow, fluid speed increases. Using this information, explain how the two boats could collide.

SCiLINKS®

NSTA
Developed and maintained by the
National Science Teachers Association

For a variety of links related to this chapter, go to www.scilinks.org

Topic: Bernoulli's Principle
SciLinks code: HSM0143

Skills Practice Lab

Fluids, Force, and Floating

Why do some objects sink in fluids but others float? In this lab, you'll get a sinking feeling as you determine that an object floats when its weight equals the buoyant force exerted by the surrounding fluid.

OBJECTIVES

Calculate the buoyant force on an object.

Compare the buoyant force on an object with its weight.

MATERIALS

- balance
- mass set
- pan, rectangular baking
- paper towels
- ruler, metric
- tub, plastic, large rectangular
- water

SAFETY

Procedure

1. Copy the table shown below.

Measurement	Trial 1	Trial 2
Length (l), cm		
Width (w), cm		
Initial height (h_1), cm		
Initial volume (V_1), cm³ $V_1 = l \times w \times h_1$		
New height (h_2), cm		
New total volume (V_2), cm³ $V_2 = l \times w \times h_2$	*DO NOT WRITE IN BOOK*	
Displaced volume (ΔV), cm³ $\Delta V = V_2 - V_1$		
Mass of displaced water, g $m = \Delta V \times 1$ g/cm³		
Weight of displaced water, N (buoyant force)		
Weight of pan and masses, N		

2. Fill the tub half full with water. Measure (in centimeters) the length, width, and initial height of the water. Record your measurements in the table.

3. Using the equation given in the table, determine the initial volume of water in the tub. Record your results in the table.

4. Place the pan in the water, and place masses in the pan, as shown on the next page. Keep adding masses until the pan sinks to about three-quarters of its height. Record the new height of the water in the table. Then, use this value to determine and record the new total volume of water plus the volume of water displaced by the pan.

5 Determine the volume of the water that was displaced by the pan and masses, and record this value in the table. The displaced volume is equal to the new total volume minus the initial volume.

6 Determine the mass of the displaced water by multiplying the displaced volume by its density (1 g/cm³). Record the mass in the table.

7 Divide the mass by 100. The value you get is the weight of the displaced water in newtons (N). This is equal to the buoyant force. Record the weight of the displaced water in the table.

8 Remove the pan and masses, and determine their total mass (in grams) using the balance. Convert the mass to weight (N), as you did in step 7. Record the weight of the masses and pan in the table.

9 Place the empty pan back in the tub. Perform a second trial by repeating steps 4–8. This time, add masses until the pan is just about to sink.

Analyze the Results

1 **Identifying Patterns** Compare the buoyant force (the weight of the displaced water) with the weight of the pan and masses for both trials.

2 **Examining Data** How did the buoyant force differ between the two trials? Explain.

Draw Conclusions

3 **Drawing Conclusions** Based on your observations, what would happen if you were to add even more mass to the pan than you did in the second trial? Explain your answer in terms of the buoyant force.

4 **Making Predictions** What would happen if you put the masses in the water without the pan? What difference does the pan's shape make?

Chapter Review

USING KEY TERMS

In each of the following sentences, replace the incorrect term with the correct term from the word bank.

thrust   pressure
drag   lift
buoyant force   fluid
Pascal's principle
Bernoulli's principle

1 Lift increases with the depth of a fluid.

2 A plane's engines produce drag to push the plane forward.

3 A pascal can be a liquid or a gas.

4 A hydraulic device uses Archimedes' principle to lift or move objects.

5 Atmospheric pressure is the upward force exerted on objects by fluids.

UNDERSTANDING KEY IDEAS

Multiple Choice

6 The design of a wing

  a. causes the air above the wing to travel faster than the air below the wing.

  b. helps create lift.

  c. creates a low-pressure zone above the wing.

  d. All of the above

7 Fluid pressure is always directed

  a. up.   **c.** sideways.

  b. down.   **d.** in all directions.

8 An object surrounded by a fluid will displace a volume of fluid that is

  a. equal to its own volume.

  b. less than its own volume.

  c. greater than its own volume.

  d. denser than itself.

9 If an object weighing 50 N displaces a volume of water that weighs 10 N, what is the buoyant force on the object?

  a. 60 N   **c.** 40 N

  b. 50 N   **d.** 10 N

10 A helium-filled balloon will float in air because

  a. there is more air than helium.

  b. helium is less dense than air.

  c. helium is as dense as air.

  d. helium is more dense than air.

11 Materials that can flow to fit their containers include

  a. gases.

  b. liquids.

  c. both gases and liquids.

  d. gases, liquids, and solids.

Short Answer

12 Where is water pressure greater, at a depth of 1 m in a large lake or at a depth of 2 m in a small pond? Explain your answer.

13 Why are bubbles round?

14 Why are tornadoes like giant vacuum cleaners?

Math Skills

15 Calculate the area of a 1,500 N object that exerts a pressure of 500 Pa (500 N/m^2). Then, calculate the pressure exerted by the same object over twice that area.

CRITICAL THINKING

16 **Concept Mapping** Use the following terms to create a concept map: *fluid, pressure, depth, density,* and *buoyant force.*

17 **Forming Hypotheses** Gases can be easily compressed into smaller spaces. Why would this property of gases make gases less useful than liquids in hydraulic brakes?

18 **Making Comparisons** Will a ship loaded with beach balls float higher or lower in the water than an empty ship? Explain your reasoning.

19 **Applying Concepts** Inside all vacuum cleaners is a high-speed fan. Explain how this fan causes the vacuum cleaner to pick up dirt.

20 **Evaluating Hypotheses** A 600 N girl on stilts says to two 600 N boys sitting on the ground, "I am exerting over twice as much pressure as the two of you are exerting together!" Could this statement be true? Explain your reasoning.

INTERPRETING GRAPHICS

Use the diagram of an iceberg below to answer the questions that follow.

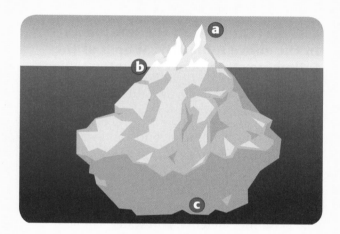

21 At what point (a, b, or c) is water pressure greatest on the iceberg?

22 How much of the iceberg has a weight equal to the buoyant force?

   a. all of it

   b. the section from a to b

   c. the section from b to c

   d. None of the above

23 How does the density of ice compare with the density of water?

24 Why do you think icebergs are dangerous to passing ships?

Multiple Choice

Use the table below to answer question 1.

Properties of Four Substances*			
Substance	Viscosity (mPa·s)	Density (g/cm³)	Surface Tension (mN/m)
Gasoline	0.508	0.70	21.14
Mercury	1.526	13.53	485.48
Rubbing alcohol	2.038	0.78	20.93
Water	0.890	1.00	71.99

* at room temperature and pressure

1. **Assume that none of the substances in the above table mix. Which of the following statements is true?**

   A. Gasoline, mercury, and rubbing alcohol will float on water.

   B. Gasoline, rubbing alcohol, and water will float on mercury.

   C. Mercury, rubbing alcohol, and water will float on gasoline.

   D. Gasoline, mercury, and water will float on rubbing alcohol.

2. **A lotion advertised in your favorite magazine claims to have a special ingredient that will reduce drag and enable you to run faster. How could you test that claim?**

   A. by conducting a molecular study of the lotion

   B. by researching the ingredients in the lotion

   C. by comparing the results of running after using that lotion and your regular lotion

   D. by researching the number of advertising claims that are actually true

3. **Which of the following materials can flow and take the shape of their containers?**

   A. solids and liquids

   B. plasmas and solids

   C. gases and solids

   D. liquids and gases

4. **Which statement best explains why a balloon stays inflated?**

   A. The air particles hitting the inner surface of the balloon and the air particles hitting the outer surface of the balloon create neutral buoyancy.

   B. The air particles spread apart and take up more space when they are under pressure.

   C. The force of the air particles hitting the inner surface of the balloon creates pressure.

   D. The air pressure outside the balloon is greater than the air pressure inside the balloon.

5. **Which of the following accurately describes the forces acting on a beach ball that is at rest on the surface of the water in a swimming pool?**

   A. The forces are unbalanced.

   B. The forces are balanced.

   C. There are no forces acting on the ball.

   D. The forces are all acting in the same direction.

6. In which of the following situations are the forces unbalanced?

A. A submarine rises to the surface as crewmembers empty the ballast tanks.

B. A shipwreck lies undisturbed on the bottom of the ocean.

C. Two children paddle a canoe in opposite directions, but the canoe does not move.

D. A fish floats just below the surface, suspended in the water.

7. Which of the following statements best explains why a steel boat can float in water?

A. Steel is denser than water.

B. Steel is less dense than water.

C. The boat displaces a volume of water that weighs less than the boat itself.

D. The buoyant force acting on the boat is equal to the weight of the boat.

8. Leah holds objects under water in the center of a tank and then releases them. She does this with an inflated balloon and with a steel washer. Then she attaches various numbers of steel washers to the balloon. In which of the following instances are the forces acting on the objects balanced?

A. The balloon rises, and the steel washer sinks.

B. The balloon with one steel washer attached to it rises.

C. The balloon with two steel washers attached to it is suspended in the water.

D. The balloon with three steel washers attached to it sinks.

Use the illustration below to answer question 9.

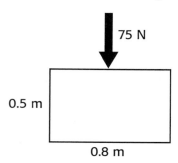

9. A piece of underwater equipment is made of a material that can withstand up to 150 kPA before cracking. If a force of 75 N is applied to a piece of the material (shown above), what will happen to the material? (P=F/A)

A. The material will crack because the pressure is 33.3 Pa.

B. The material will crack because the pressure is 187.5 kPa.

C. The material will withstand the pressure because it is only 187.5 Pa.

D. The material will withstand the pressure because it is only 33.3 kPa.

Open Response

10. Many power tools and power lifts have pneumatic parts, which use high-pressure air to move things. Like hydraulic devices, these pneumatic devices use an enclosed fluid to transmit force. While a hydraulic device uses a liquid (often water), a pneumatic device uses a gas (usually air). How does Pascal's principle apply to pneumatic devices?

11. A ship's hollow shape allows it to float in water. Why does the same ship sink when filled with water?

Standardized Test Preparation

Science in Action

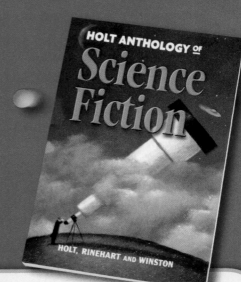

Science, Technology, and Society

Stayin' Aloft—The Story of the Frisbee®

In the late 1800s, a few fun-loving college students invented a game that involved tossing an empty tin pie plate. The pie plate was stamped with the name of a bakery: Frisbie's Pies. So, the game of Frisbie was created. Unfortunately, the metal pie plates tended to develop sharp edges that caused injuries. In 1947, plastic disks were made to replace the metal pie plates. These plastic disks were called Frisbees. How do Frisbees stay in the air? When you throw a Frisbee, you give it thrust. And as it moves through the air, lift is created because of Bernoulli's principle. But you don't have to think about the science behind Frisbees to have fun with them!

Math ACTIVITY

A Frisbee landed 10 m away from where it is thrown. The Frisbee was in the air for 2.5 s. What was the average speed of the Frisbee?

Science Fiction

"Wet Behind the Ears" by Jack C. Haldeman II

Willie Joe Thomas cheated to get a swimming scholarship. Now, he is faced with a major swim meet, and his coach told him that he has to swim or be kicked off the team. Willie Joe could lose his scholarship.

One day, Willie Joe's roommate, Frank, announces that he has developed a new "sliding compound." And Frank also said something about using the compound to make ships go faster. So, Willie Joe thought, if it works for ships, it might work for swimming.

See what happens when Willie Joe tries to save his scholarship by using Frank's compound at the swim meet. Read "Wet Behind the Ears," by Jack C. Haldeman II in the *Holt Anthology of Science Fiction*.

Language Arts ACTIVITY

Analyze the story structure of "Wet Behind the Ears." In your analysis, identify the introduction, the rising action, the climax, and the denouement. Summarize your analysis in a chart.

Alisha Bracken

Scuba Instructor Alisha Bracken first started scuba diving in her freshman year of college. Her first dives were in a saltwater hot spring near Salt Lake City, Utah. "It was awesome," Bracken says. "There were nurse sharks, angelfish, puffer fish and brine shrimp!" Bracken enjoyed her experience so much that she wanted to share it with other people. The best way to do that was to become an instructor and teach other people to dive.

Bracken says one of the biggest challenges of being a scuba instructor is teaching people to adapt and function in a foreign environment. She believes that learning to dive properly is important not only for the safety of the diver but also for the protection of the underwater environment. She relies on science principles to help teach people how to control their movements and protect the natural environment. "Buoyancy is the foundation of teaching people to dive comfortably," she explains. "Without it, we cannot float on the surface or stay off the bottom. Underwater life can be damaged if students do not learn and apply the concepts of buoyancy."

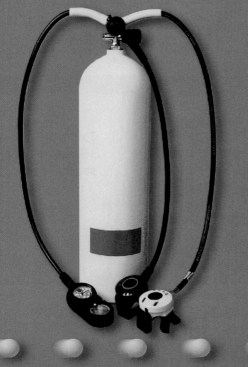

Social Studies ACTiViTY

Scuba divers and other underwater explorers sometimes investigate shipwrecks on the bottom of the ocean. Research the exploration of a specific shipwreck. Make a poster showing what artifacts were retrieved from the shipwreck and what was learned from the exploration.

To learn more about these Science in Action topics, visit go.hrw.com and type in the keyword **HP5FLUF.**

Current Science

Check out Current Science® articles related to this chapter by visiting go.hrw.com. Just type in the keyword **HP5CS07.**

Work, Machines, and Energy

Can you imagine living in a world with no machines? In this unit, you will explore the scientific meaning of *work* and learn how machines make work easier. You will find out how energy allows you to do work and how different forms of energy can be converted into other forms of energy. You will also learn about heat and how heating and cooling systems work. This timeline shows some of the inventions and discoveries made throughout history as people have advanced their understanding of work, machines, and energy.

Around 3000 BCE

The sail is used in Egypt. Sails use the wind rather than human power to move boats through the water.

1818

German inventor Baron Karl von Drais de Sauerbrun exhibits the first two-wheeled, rider-propelled machine. Made of wood, this early machine paves the way for the invention of the bicycle.

1948

Maria Telkes, a Hungarian-born physicist, designs the heating system for the first solar-heated house.

1972

The first American self-service gas station opens.

Around 200 BCE

Under the Han dynasty, the Chinese become one of the first civilizations to use coal as fuel.

1656

Dutch scientist Christiaan Huygens invents the pendulum clock.

1776

The American colonies declare their independence from Great Britain.

1893

The "Clasp Locker," an early zipper, is patented.

1908

The automobile age begins with the mass production of the Ford Model T.

1926

American scientist Robert Goddard launches the first rocket powered by liquid fuel. The rocket reaches a height of 12.5 m and a speed of 97 km/h.

1988

A wind-powered generator begins generating electrical energy in Scotland's Orkney Islands.

2000

The 2000 Olympic Summer Games are held in Sydney, Australia.

2001

A two-wheeled, battery-powered "people mover" is introduced. Gyroscopes and tilt sensors allow riders to guide the scooter-like transporter by leaning.

22

Work and Machines

The Big Idea

Work is the transfer of energy to an object, and power is the rate at which work is done. Machines are devices that help make work easier.

About the Photo

"One, two, stroke!" shouts the coach as the team races to the finish line. This paddling team is competing in Hong Kong's annual Dragon Boat Races. The Dragon Boat Festival is a 2,000-year-old Chinese tradition that commemorates Qu Yuan, a national hero. The paddlers that you see here are using the paddles to move the boat forward. Even though they are celebrating by racing their dragon boat, in scientific terms, this team is doing work.

PRE-READING ACTIVITY

FOLDNOTES **Booklet** Before you read the chapter, create the FoldNote entitled "Booklet" described in the **Study Skills** section of the Appendix. Label each page of the booklet with a main idea from the chapter. As you read the chapter, write what you learn about each main idea on the appropriate page of the booklet.

C'mon, Lever a Little!

In this activity, you will use a simple machine, a lever, to make your task a little easier.

Procedure

1. Stack **two books,** one on top of the other, on a **table.**

2. Slide your index finger underneath the edge of the bottom book. Using only the force of your finger, try to lift one side of the books 2 or 3 cm off the table. Is it hard to do so? Write your observations.

3. Slide the end of a **wooden ruler** underneath the edge of the bottom book. Then, slip a **large pencil eraser** or similar object under the ruler.

4. Again, using only your index finger, push down on the edge of the ruler and try to lift the books. Record your observations. **Caution:** Push down slowly to keep the ruler and eraser from flipping.

Analysis

1. Which was easier: lifting the books with your finger or lifting the books with the ruler? Explain your answer.

2. In what way did the direction of the force that your finger applied on the books differ from the direction of the force that your finger applied on the ruler?

Work and Machines   **649**

Work and Power

Your science teacher has just given you tonight's homework assignment. You have to read an entire chapter by tomorrow! That sounds like a lot of work!

Actually, in the scientific sense, you won't be doing much work at all! How can that be? In science, **work** is done when a force causes an object to move in the direction of the force. In the example above, you may have to put a lot of mental effort into doing your homework, but you won't be using force to move anything. So, in the scientific sense, you will not be doing work—except the work to turn the pages of your book!

What Is Work?

The student in **Figure 1** is having a lot of fun, isn't she? But she is doing work, even though she is having fun. She is doing work because she is applying a force to the bowling ball and making the ball move through a distance. However, she is doing work on the ball only as long as she is touching it. The ball will keep moving away from her after she releases it. But she will no longer be doing work on the ball because she will no longer be applying a force to it.

Figure 1
You might be surprised to find out that bowling is work!

Transfer of Energy

One way you can tell that the bowler in **Figure 1** has done work on the bowling ball is that the ball now has *kinetic energy*. This means that the ball is now moving. The bowler has transferred energy to the ball.

Differences Between Force and Work

Applying a force doesn't always result in work being done. Suppose that you help push a stalled car. You push and push, but the car doesn't budge. The pushing may have made you tired. But you haven't done any work on the car, because the car hasn't moved.

You do work on the car as soon as the car moves. Whenever you apply a force to an object and the object moves in the direction of the force, you have done work on the object.

✓ **Reading Check** Is work done every time a force is applied to an object? Explain. (*See the Appendix for answers to Reading Checks.*)

Force and Motion in the Same Direction

Suppose you are in the airport and late for a flight. You have to run through the airport carrying a heavy suitcase. Because you are making the suitcase move, you are doing work on it, right? Wrong! For work to be done on an object, the object must move in the *same direction* as the force. You are applying a force to hold the suitcase up, but the suitcase is moving forward. So, no work is done on the suitcase. But work *is* done on the suitcase when you lift it off the ground.

Work is done on an object if two things happen: (1) the object moves as a force is applied and (2) the direction of the object's motion is the same as the direction of the force. The pictures and arrows in **Figure 2** will help you understand when work is being done on an object.

work the transfer of energy to an object by using a force that causes the object to move in the direction of the force

Figure 2 Work or Not Work?

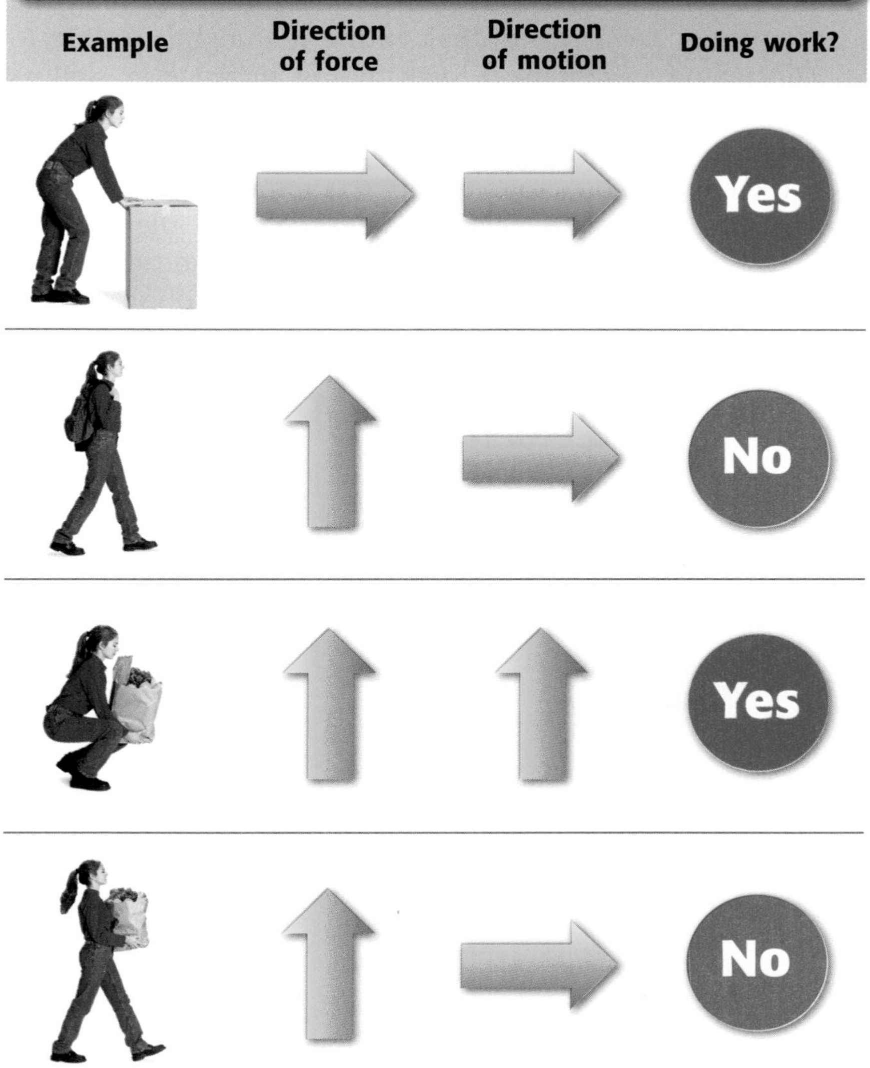

Example	Direction of force	Direction of motion	Doing work?
	→	→	Yes
	↑	→	No
	↑	↑	Yes
	↑	→	No

CONNECTION TO Biology

WRITING SKILL **Work in the Human Body**

You may not be doing any work on a suitcase if you are just holding it in your hands, but your body will still get tired from the effort because you are doing work on the muscles inside your body. Your muscles can contract thousands of times in just a few seconds while you try to keep the suitcase from falling. What other situations can you think of that might involve work being done somewhere inside your body? Describe these situations in your **science journal.**

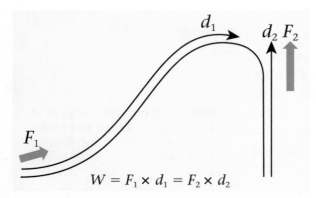

$$W = F_1 \times d_1 = F_2 \times d_2$$

Figure 3 *For each path, the same work is done to move the car to the top of the hill, although distance and force along the two paths differ.*

How Much Work?

Would you do more work on a car by pushing it up a long road to reach the top of a hill or by using a cable to raise the car up the side of a cliff to the top of the same hill? You would certainly need a different amount of force. Common use of the word *work* may make it seem that there would be a difference in the amount of work done in the two cases as well.

Same Work, Different Forces

You may be surprised to learn that the same amount of work is being done to push the car up a road as to raise it up the cliff. Look at **Figure 3.** A certain amount of energy is needed to move the car from the bottom to the top of the hill. Because the car ends up at the same place either way, the work done on the car is the same. However, pushing the car along the road up a hill seems easier than lifting it straight up. Why?

The reason is that work depends on distance as well as force. Consider a mountain climber who reaches the top of a mountain by climbing straight up a cliff, as in **Figure 4.** She must use enough force to overcome her entire weight. But the distance she travels up the cliff is shorter than the distance traveled by hikers who reach the top of the same mountain by walking up a slope. Either way, the same amount of work is done. But the hikers going up a slope don't need to use as much force as if they were going straight up the side of the cliff. This shows how you can use less force to do the same amount of work.

Figure 4 *Climbers going to the top of a mountain do the same amount of work whether they hike up a slope or go straight up a cliff.*

Calculating Work

The amount of work (*W*) done in moving an object, such as the barbell in **Figure 5,** can be calculated by multiplying the force (*F*) applied to the object by the distance (*d*) through which the force is applied, as shown in the following equation:

$$W = F \times d$$

Force is expressed in newtons, and the meter is the basic SI unit for length or distance. Therefore, the unit used to express work is the newton-meter (N × m), which is more simply called the **joule.** Because work is the transfer of energy to an object, the joule (J) is also the unit used to measure energy.

joule the unit used to express energy; equivalent to the amount of work done by a force of 1 N acting through a distance of 1 m in the direction of the force (symbol, J)

✓ **Reading Check** How is work calculated?

Figure 5 **Force Times Distance**

W = 80 N × 1 m = 80 J

The force needed to lift an object is equal to the gravitational force on the object—in other words, the object's weight.

W = 160 N × 1 m = 160 J

If you increase the weight, an increased force is needed to lift the object. This increases the amount of work done.

W = 80 N × 2 m = 160 J

Increasing the distance also increases the amount of work done.

Get to Work!

1. Use a **loop of string** to attach a **spring scale** to a **weight.**

2. Slowly pull the weight across a **table** by dragging the spring scale. Record the amount of force that you exerted on the weight.

3. Use a **metric ruler** to measure the distance that you pulled the weight.

4. Now, use the spring scale to slowly pull the weight up a **ramp.** Pull the weight the same distance that you pulled it across the table.

5. Calculate the work you did on the weight for both trials.

6. How were the amounts of work and force affected by the way you pulled the weight? What other ways of pulling the weight could you test?

Power: How Fast Work Is Done

Like the term *work*, the term *power* is used a lot in everyday language but has a very specific meaning in science. **Power** is the rate at which energy is transferred.

power the rate at which work is done or energy is transformed

watt the unit used to express power; equivalent to joules per second (symbol, W)

Calculating Power

To calculate power (*P*), you divide the amount of work done (*W*) by the time (*t*) it takes to do that work, as shown in the following equation:

$$P = \frac{W}{t}$$

The unit used to express power is joules per second (J/s), also called the **watt.** One watt (W) is equal to 1 J/s. So if you do 50 J of work in 5 s, your power is 10 J/s, or 10 W.

Power measures how fast work happens, or how quickly energy is transferred. When more work is done in a given amount of time, the power output is greater. Power output is also greater when the time it takes to do a certain amount of work is decreased, as shown in **Figure 6.**

Reading Check How is power calculated?

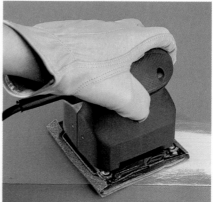

Figure 6 *No matter how fast you can sand by hand, an electric sander can do the same amount of work faster. Therefore, the electric sander has more power.*

MATH FOCUS

More Power to You A stage manager at a play raises the curtain by doing 5,976 J of work on the curtain in 12 s. What is the power output of the stage manager?

Step 1: Write the equation for power.

$$P = \frac{W}{t}$$

Step 2: Replace *W* and *t* with work and time.

$$P = \frac{5,976 \, \text{J}}{12 \, \text{s}} = 498 \, \text{W}$$

Now It's Your Turn
1. If it takes you 10 s to do 150 J of work on a box to move it up a ramp, what is your power output?
2. A light bulb is on for 12 s, and during that time it uses 1,200 J of electrical energy. What is the wattage (power) of the light bulb?

Increasing Power

It may take you longer to sand a wooden shelf by hand than by using an electric sander, but the amount of energy needed is the same either way. Only the power output is lower when you sand the shelf by hand (although your hand may get more tired). You could also dry your hair with a fan, but it would take a long time! A hair dryer is more powerful. It can give off energy more quickly than a fan does, so your hair dries faster.

Car engines are usually rated with a certain power output. The more powerful the engine is, the more quickly the engine can move a car. And for a given speed, a more powerful engine can move a heavier car than a less powerful engine can.

CONNECTION TO Language Arts

WRITING SKILL **Horsepower** The unit of power most commonly used to rate car engines is the *horsepower* (hp). Look up the word *horsepower* in a dictionary. How many watts is equal to 1 hp? Do you think all horses output exactly 1 hp? Why or why not? Write your answers in your **science journal.**

SECTION Review

Summary

- In scientific terms, *work* is done when a force causes an object to move in the direction of the force.
- Work is calculated as force times distance. The unit of work is the newton-meter, or joule.
- *Power* is a measure of how fast work is done.
- Power is calculated as work divided by time. The unit of power is the joule per second, or watt.

Using Key Terms

For each pair of terms, explain how the meanings of the terms differ.

1. *work* and *joule*
2. *power* and *watt*

Understanding Key Ideas

3. How is work calculated?
   a. force times distance
   b. force divided by distance
   c. power times distance
   d. power divided by distance

4. What is the difference between work and power?

Math Skills

5. Using a force of 10 N, you push a shopping cart 10 m. How much work did you do?

6. If you did 100 J of work in 5 s, what was your power output?

Critical Thinking

7. **Analyzing Processes** Work is done on a ball when a pitcher throws it. Is the pitcher still doing work on the ball as it flies through the air? Explain.

8. **Applying Concepts** You lift a chair that weighs 50 N to a height of 0.5 m and carry it 10 m across the room. How much work do you do on the chair?

Interpreting Graphics

9. What idea about work and force does the following diagram describe? Explain your answer.

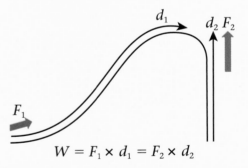

$$W = F_1 \times d_1 = F_2 \times d_2$$

For a variety of links related to this chapter, go to www.scilinks.org

Topic: Work and Power
SciLinks code: HSM1675

What You Will Learn

- Explain how a machine makes work easier.
- Describe and give examples of the force-distance trade-off that occurs when a machine is used.
- Calculate mechanical advantage.
- Explain why machines are not 100% efficient.

Vocabulary

machine
work input
work output
mechanical advantage
mechanical efficiency

READING STRATEGY

Prediction Guide Before reading this section, write the title of each heading in this section. Next, under each heading, write what you think you will learn.

What Is a Machine?

You are in the car with your mom on the way to a party when suddenly—KABLOOM hisssss—a tire blows out. "Now I'm going to be late!" you think as your mom pulls over to the side of the road.

You watch as she opens the trunk and gets out a jack and a tire iron. Using the tire iron, she pries the hubcap off and begins to unscrew the lug nuts from the wheel. She then puts the jack under the car and turns the jack's handle several times until the flat tire no longer touches the ground. After exchanging the flat tire with the spare, she lowers the jack and puts the lug nuts and hubcap back on the wheel.

"Wow!" you think, "That wasn't as hard as I thought it would be." As your mom drops you off at the party, you think how lucky it was that she had the right equipment to change the tire.

Machines: Making Work Easier

Now, imagine changing a tire without the jack and the tire iron. Would it have been easy? No, you would have needed several people just to hold up the car! Sometimes, you need the help of machines to do work. A **machine** is a device that makes work easier by changing the size or direction of a force.

When you think of machines, you might think of things such as cars, big construction equipment, or even computers. But not all machines are complicated. In fact, you use many simple machines in your everyday life. **Figure 1** shows some examples of machines.

Figure 1 **Some Everyday Machines**

Chopsticks

Wheelchair

Scissors

Work In, Work Out

Suppose that you need to get the lid off a can of paint. What do you do? One way to pry the lid off is to use a common machine known as a *lever*. **Figure 2** shows a screwdriver being used as a lever. You place the tip of the screwdriver under the edge of the lid and then push down on the screwdriver's handle. The tip of the screwdriver lifts the lid as you push down. In other words, you do work on the screwdriver, and the screwdriver does work on the lid.

Work is done when a force is applied through a distance. Look again at **Figure 2.** The work that you do on a machine is called **work input.** You apply a force, called the *input force,* to the machine through a distance. The work done by the machine on an object is called **work output.** The machine applies a force, called the *output force,* through a distance.

How Machines Help

You might think that machines help you because they increase the amount of work done. But that's not true. If you multiplied the forces by the distances through which the forces are applied in **Figure 2** (remember that $W = F \times d$), you would find that the screwdriver does not do more work on the lid than you do on the screwdriver. Work output can never be greater than work input. Machines allow force to be applied over a greater distance, which means that less force will be needed for the same amount of work.

✓ **Reading Check** How do machines make work easier? (*See the Appendix for answers to Reading Checks*.)

machine a device that helps do work by either overcoming a force or changing the direction of the applied force

work input the work done on a machine; the product of the input force and the distance through which the force is exerted

work output the work done by a machine; the product of the output force and the distance through which the force is exerted

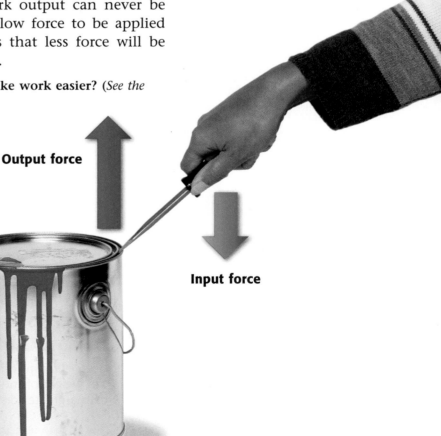

Output force

Input force

Figure 2 *When you use a machine, you do work on the machine, and the machine does work on something else.*

Same Work, Different Force

Machines make work easier by changing the size or direction (or both) of the input force. When a screwdriver is used as a lever to open a paint can, both the size and direction of the input force change. Remember that using a machine does not change the amount of work you will do. As **Figure 3** shows, the same amount of work is done with or without the ramp. The ramp decreases the size of the input force needed to lift the box but increases the distance over which the force is exerted. So, the machine allows a smaller force to be applied over a longer distance.

The Force-Distance Trade-Off

When a machine changes the size of the force, the distance through which the force is exerted must also change. Force or distance can increase, but both cannot increase. When one increases, the other must decrease.

Figure 4 shows how machines change force and distance. Whenever a machine changes the size of a force, the machine also changes the distance through which the force is applied. **Figure 4** also shows that some machines change only the direction of the force, not the size of the force or the distance through which the force is exerted.

✓ Reading Check What are the two things that a machine can change about how work is done?

Figure 3 Input Force and Distance

Lifting this box straight up requires an input force equal to the weight of the box.

$$W = 450 \text{ N} \times 1 \text{ m} = 450 \text{ J}$$

Using a ramp to lift the box requires an input force less than the weight of the box, but the input force must be exerted over a greater distance than if you didn't use a ramp.

$$W = 150 \text{ N} \times 3 \text{ m} = 450 \text{ J}$$

Figure 4 Machines Change the Size and/or Direction of a Force

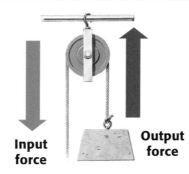

Input force

A nutcracker *increases* the force but applies it over a *shorter* distance.

A hammer *decreases* the force, but applies it over a *greater* distance.

Output force

Input force

Output force

A simple pulley changes the *direction* of the input force, but the size of the output force is the same as the input force.

When a screw-driver is used as a lever, it *increases* the force and *decreases* the distance over which the force is applied.

Input force

Output force

Output force

Input force

Mechanical Advantage

Some machines make work easier than others do because they can increase force more than other machines can. A machine's **mechanical advantage** is the number of times the machine multiplies force. In other words, the mechanical advantage compares the input force with the output force.

mechanical advantage a number that tells how many times a machine multiplies force

Calculating Mechanical Advantage

You can find mechanical advantage by using the following equation:

$$mechanical\ advantage\ (MA) = \frac{output\ force}{input\ force}$$

For example, imagine that you had to push a 500 N weight up a ramp and only needed to push with 50 N of force the entire time. The mechanical advantage of the ramp would be calculated as follows:

$$MA = \frac{500\ N}{50\ N} = 10$$

A machine that has a mechanical advantage that is greater than 1 can help move or lift heavy objects because the output force is greater than the input force. A machine that has a mechanical advantage that is less than 1 will reduce the output force but can increase the distance an object moves. **Figure 4** shows an example of such a machine—a hammer.

Finding the Advantage

A grocer uses a handcart to lift a heavy stack of canned food. Suppose that he applies an input force of 40 N to the handcart. The cart applies an output force of 320 N to the stack of canned food. What is the mechanical advantage of the handcart?

Mechanical Efficiency

The work output of a machine can never be greater than the work input. In fact, the work output of a machine is always less than the work input. Why? Some of the work done by the machine is used to overcome the friction created by the use of the machine. But keep in mind that no work is lost. The work output plus the work done to overcome friction is equal to the work input.

The less work a machine has to do to overcome friction, the more efficient the machine is. **Mechanical efficiency** (muh KAN i kuhl e FISH uhn see) is a comparison of a machine's work output with the work input.

mechanical efficiency a quantity, usually expressed as a percentage, that measures the ratio of work output to work input; it can be calculated by dividing work output by work input

Calculating Efficiency

A machine's mechanical efficiency is calculated using the following equation:

$$mechanical\ efficiency = \frac{work\ output}{work\ input} \times 100$$

The 100 in this equation means that mechanical efficiency is expressed as a percentage. Mechanical efficiency tells you what percentage of the work input gets converted into work output.

Figure 5 shows a machine that is used to drill holes in metal. Some of the work input is used to overcome the friction between the metal and the drill. This energy cannot be used to do work on the steel block. Instead, it heats up the steel and the machine itself.

✓ **Reading Check** How is mechanical efficiency calculated?

Useful Friction

Friction is always present when two objects touch or rub together, and friction usually slows down moving parts in a machine and heats them up. In some cases, parts in a machine are designed to increase friction. While at home, observe three situations in which friction is useful. Describe them in your **science journal.**

Figure 5 *In this machine, some of the work input is converted into sound and heat energy.*

Perfect Efficiency?

An *ideal machine* would be a machine that had 100% mechanical efficiency. An ideal machine's useful work output would equal the work done on the machine. Ideal machines are impossible to build, because every machine has moving parts. Moving parts always use some of the work input to overcome friction. But new technologies help increase efficiency so that more energy is available to do useful work. The train in **Figure 6** is floating on magnets, so there is almost no friction between the train and the tracks. Other machines use lubricants, such as oil or grease, to lower the friction between their moving parts, which makes the machines more efficient.

Figure 6 *There is very little friction between this magnetic levitation train and its tracks, so it is highly efficient.*

SECTION Review

Summary

- A machine makes work easier by changing the size or direction (or both) of a force.
- A machine can increase force or distance, but not both.
- Mechanical advantage tells how many times a machine multiplies force.
- Mechanical efficiency is a comparison of a machine's work output with work input.
- Machines are not 100% efficient because some of the work done is used to overcome friction.

Using Key Terms

For each pair of terms, explain how the meanings of the terms differ.

1. *work input* and *work output*

2. *mechanical advantage* and *mechanical efficiency*

Understanding Key Ideas

3. Which of the following is the correct way to calculate mechanical advantage?

   a. input force ÷ output force

   b. output force ÷ input force

   c. work input ÷ work output

   d. work output ÷ work input

4. Explain how using a ramp makes work easier.

5. Give a specific example of a machine, and describe how its mechanical efficiency might be calculated.

6. Why can't a machine be 100% efficient?

Math Skills

7. Suppose that you exert 60 N on a machine and the machine exerts 300 N on another object. What is the machine's mechanical advantage?

8. What is the mechanical efficiency of a machine whose work input is 100 J and work output is 30 J?

Critical Thinking

9. **Making Inferences** For a machine with a mechanical advantage of 3, how does the distance through which the output force is exerted differ from the distance through which the input force is exerted?

10. **Analyzing Processes** Describe the effect that friction has on a machine's mechanical efficiency. How do lubricants increase a machine's mechanical efficiency?

What You Will Learn

● Identify and give examples of the six types of simple machines.
● Analyze the mechanical advantage provided by each simple machine.
● Identify the simple machines that make up a compound machine.

Vocabulary

lever
pulley
wheel and
  axle
inclined plane

wedge
screw
compound
  machine

READING STRATEGY

Mnemonics As you read this section, create a mnemonic device to help you remember the different types of levers.

Types of Machines

Imagine that it's a hot summer day. You have a whole ice-cold watermelon in front of you. It would taste cool and delicious—if only you had a machine that could cut it!

The machine you need is a knife. But how is a knife a machine? A knife is actually a very sharp wedge, which is one of the six simple machines. The six simple machines are the lever, the inclined plane, the wedge, the screw, the pulley, and the wheel and axle. All machines are made from one or more of these simple machines.

Levers

Have you ever used the claw end of a hammer to remove a nail from a piece of wood? If so, you were using the hammer as a lever. A **lever** is a simple machine that has a bar that pivots at a fixed point, called a *fulcrum*. Levers are used to apply a force to a load. There are three classes of levers, which are based on the placements of the fulcrum, the load, and the input force.

First-Class Levers

With a first-class lever, the fulcrum is between the input force and the load, as shown in **Figure 1.** First-class levers always change the direction of the input force. And depending on the location of the fulcrum, first-class levers can be used to increase force or to increase distance.

Figure 1 **Examples of First-Class Levers**

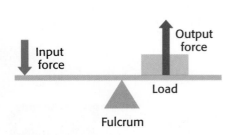
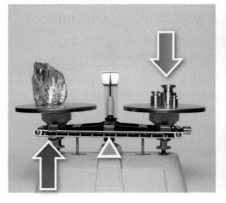
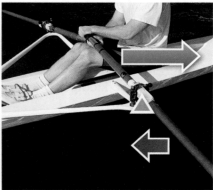

When the fulcrum is closer to the load than to the input force, the lever has a **mechanical advantage of greater than 1.** The output force is increased because it is exerted over a shorter distance.

When the fulcrum is exactly in the middle, the lever has a **mechanical advantage of 1.** The output force is not increased because the input force's distance is not increased.

When the fulcrum is closer to the input force than to the load, the lever has a **mechanical advantage of less than 1.** Although the output force is less than the input force, distance increases.

Figure 2 Examples of Second-Class Levers

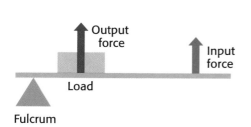

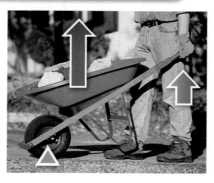

In a **second-class lever,** the output force, or load, is between the input force and the fulcrum.

Using a second-class lever results in a **mechanical advantage of greater than 1.** The closer the load is to the fulcrum, the more the force is increased and the greater the mechanical advantage is.

Second-Class Levers

The load of a second-class lever is between the fulcrum and the input force, as shown in **Figure 2.** Second-class levers do not change the direction of the input force. But they allow you to apply less force than the force exerted by the load. Because the output force is greater than the input force, you must exert the input force over a greater distance.

lever a simple machine that consists of a bar that pivots at a fixed point called a *fulcrum*

Third-Class Levers

The input force in a third-class lever is between the fulcrum and the load, as shown in **Figure 3.** Third-class levers do not change the direction of the input force. In addition, they do not increase the input force. Therefore, the output force is always less than the input force.

✓**Reading Check** How do the three types of levers differ from one another? (*See the Appendix for answers to Reading Checks.*)

Figure 3 Examples of Third-Class Levers

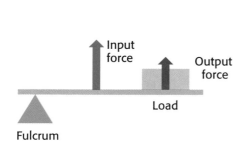

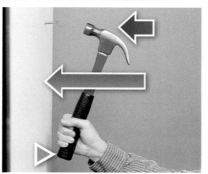

In a **third-class lever,** the input force is between the fulcrum and the load.

Using a third-class lever results in a **mechanical advantage of less than 1** because force is decreased. But third-class levers increase the distance through which the output force is exerted.

Pulleys

When you open window blinds by pulling on a cord, you're using a pulley. A **pulley** is a simple machine that has a grooved wheel that holds a rope or a cable. A load is attached to one end of the rope, and an input force is applied to the other end. Types of pulleys are shown in **Figure 4.**

pulley a simple machine that consists of a wheel over which a rope, chain, or wire passes

Fixed Pulleys

A fixed pulley is attached to something that does not move. By using a fixed pulley, you can pull down on the rope to lift the load up. The pulley changes the direction of the force. Elevators make use of fixed pulleys.

Movable Pulleys

Unlike fixed pulleys, movable pulleys are attached to the object being moved. A movable pulley does not change a force's direction. Movable pulleys do increase force, but they also increase the distance over which the input force must be exerted.

Block and Tackles

When a fixed pulley and a movable pulley are used together, the pulley system is called a *block and tackle*. The mechanical advantage of a block and tackle depends on the number of rope segments.

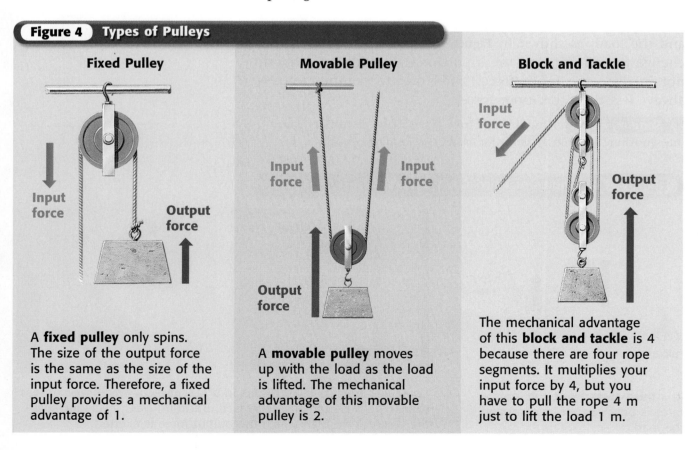

Figure 4   Types of Pulleys

Fixed Pulley

Input force

Output force

A **fixed pulley** only spins. The size of the output force is the same as the size of the input force. Therefore, a fixed pulley provides a mechanical advantage of 1.

Movable Pulley

Input force

Input force

Output force

A **movable pulley** moves up with the load as the load is lifted. The mechanical advantage of this movable pulley is 2.

Block and Tackle

Input force

Output force

The mechanical advantage of this **block and tackle** is 4 because there are four rope segments. It multiplies your input force by 4, but you have to pull the rope 4 m just to lift the load 1 m.

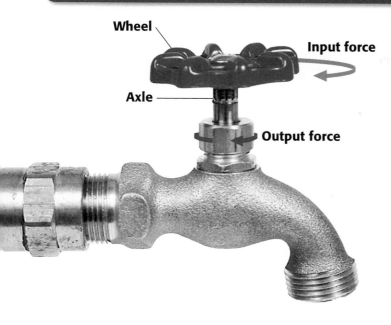

Figure 5 **How a Wheel and Axle Works**

Wheel

Axle

Input force

Output force

ⓐ When a small input force is applied to the wheel, the wheel rotates through a circular distance.

ⓑ As the wheel turns, so does the axle. But because the axle is smaller than the wheel, it rotates through a smaller distance, which makes the output force larger than the input force

Wheel and Axle

Did you know that a faucet is a machine? The faucet shown in **Figure 5** is an example of a **wheel and axle,** a simple machine consisting of two circular objects of different sizes. Doorknobs, wrenches, and steering wheels all use a wheel and axle. **Figure 5** shows how a wheel and axle works.

wheel and axle a simple machine consisting of two circular objects of different sizes; the wheel is the larger of the two circular objects

Mechanical Advantage of a Wheel and Axle

The mechanical advantage of a wheel and axle can be found by dividing the *radius* (the distance from the center to the edge) of the wheel by the radius of the axle, as shown in **Figure 6.** Turning the wheel results in a mechanical advantage of greater than 1 because the radius of the wheel is larger than the radius of the axle.

✓ **Reading Check** How is the mechanical advantage of a wheel and axle calculated?

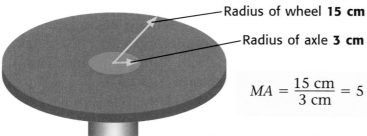

Radius of wheel **15 cm**

Radius of axle **3 cm**

$$MA = \frac{15 \text{ cm}}{3 \text{ cm}} = 5$$

Figure 6 *The mechanical advantage of a wheel and axle is the radius of the wheel divided by the radius of the axle.*

Section 3 Types of Machines **665**

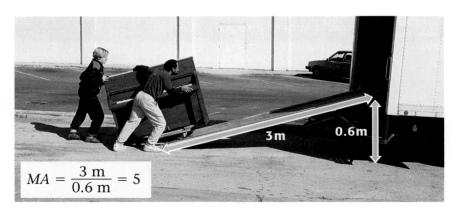

Figure 7 *The work you do on the piano to roll it up the ramp is the same as the work you would do to lift it straight up. An inclined plane simply allows you to apply a smaller force over a greater distance.*

$$MA = \frac{3\text{ m}}{0.6\text{ m}} = 5$$

Inclined Planes

Do you remember the story about how the Egyptians built the Great Pyramid? One of the machines they used was the **inclined plane.** An *inclined plane* is a simple machine that is a straight, slanted surface. A ramp is an inclined plane.

Using an inclined plane to load a piano into a truck, as **Figure 7** shows, is easier than lifting the piano into the truck. Rolling the piano along an inclined plane requires a smaller input force than is needed to lift the piano into the truck. The same work is done on the piano, just over a longer distance.

inclined plane a simple machine that is a straight, slanted surface, which facilitates the raising of loads; a ramp

✓ **Reading Check** What is an inclined plane?

Mechanical Advantage of Inclined Planes

The greater the ratio of an inclined plane's length to its height is, the greater the mechanical advantage is. The mechanical advantage (*MA*) of an inclined plane can be calculated by dividing the *length* of the inclined plane by the *height* to which the load is lifted. The inclined plane in **Figure 7** has a mechanical advantage of 3 m/0.6 m = 5.

Mechanical Advantage of an Inclined Plane A heavy box is pushed up a ramp that has an incline of 4.8 m long and 1.2 m high. What is the mechanical advantage of the ramp?

Step 1: Write the equation for the mechanical advantage of an inclined plane.

$$MA = \frac{l}{h}$$

Step 2: Replace *l* and *h* with length and height.

$$MA = \frac{4.8\text{ m}}{1.2\text{ m}} = 4$$

Now It's Your Turn

1. A wheelchair ramp is 9 m long and 1.5 m high. What is the mechanical advantage of the ramp?
2. As a pyramid is built, a stone block is dragged up a ramp that is 120 m long and 20 m high. What is the mechanical advantage of the ramp?
3. If an inclined plane were 2 m long and 8 m high, what would be its mechanical advantage?

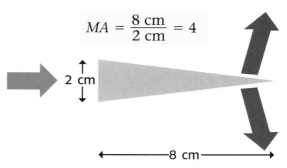

$$MA = \frac{8\ cm}{2\ cm} = 4$$

2 cm

8 cm

Figure 8 *A knife is a common example of a wedge, a simple machine consisting of two inclined planes back to back.*

Wedges

Imagine trying to cut a melon in half with a spoon. It wouldn't be easy, would it? A knife is much more useful for cutting because it is a **wedge.** A *wedge* is a pair of inclined planes that move. A wedge applies an output force that is greater than your input force, but you apply the input force over a greater distance. For example, a knife is a common wedge that can easily cut into a melon and push apart its two halves, as shown in **Figure 8.** Other useful wedges include doorstops, plows, ax heads, and chisels.

Mechanical Advantage of Wedges

The longer and thinner the wedge is, the greater its mechanical advantage is. That's why axes and knives cut better when you sharpen them—you are making the wedge thinner. Therefore, less input force is required. The mechanical advantage of a wedge can be found by dividing the length of the wedge by its greatest thickness, as shown in **Figure 8.**

Screws

A **screw** is an inclined plane that is wrapped in a spiral around a cylinder, as you can see in **Figure 9.** When a screw is turned, a small force is applied over the long distance along the inclined plane of the screw. Meanwhile, the screw applies a large force through the short distance it is pushed. Screws are used most commonly as fasteners.

Mechanical Advantage of Screws

If you could unwind the inclined plane of a screw, you would see that the plane is very long and has a gentle slope. Recall that the longer an inclined plane is compared with its height, the greater its mechanical advantage. Similarly, the longer the spiral on a screw is and the closer together the threads are, the greater the screw's mechanical advantage is. A jar lid is a screw that has a large mechanical advantage.

wedge a simple machine that is made up of two inclined planes and that moves; often used for cutting

screw a simple machine that consists of an inclined plane wrapped around a cylinder

Figure 9 *If you could unwind a screw, you would see that it is actually a very long inclined plane.*

Compound Machines

You are surrounded by machines. You even have machines in your body! But most of the machines in your world are **compound machines,** machines that are made of two or more simple machines. You have already seen one example of a compound machine: a block and tackle. A block and tackle consists of two or more pulleys.

Figure 10 shows a common example of a compound machine. A can opener may seem simple, but it is actually three machines combined. It consists of a second-class lever, a wheel and axle, and a wedge. When you squeeze the handle, you are making use of a second-class lever. The blade of the can opener acts as a wedge as it cuts into the can's top. The knob that you turn to open the can is a wheel and axle.

Mechanical Efficiency of Compound Machines

The mechanical efficiency of most compound machines is low. The efficiency is low because compound machines have more moving parts than simple machines do, thus there is more friction to overcome. Compound machines, such as automobiles and airplanes, can involve many simple machines. It is very important to reduce friction as much as possible, because too much friction can damage the simple machines that make up the compound machine. Friction can be lowered by using lubrication and other techniques.

✔ Reading Check What special disadvantage do compound machines have?

Everyday Machines

With an adult, think of five simple or compound machines that you encounter each day. List them in your **science journal,** and indicate what type of machine each is. Include at least one compound machine and one machine that is part of your body.

ACTIVITY

Figure 10 *A can opener is a compound machine. The handle is a second-class lever, the knob is a wheel and axle, and a wedge is used to open the can.*

Wheel and axle

Wedge

Second class lever

Summary

- In a first-class lever, the fulcrum is between the force and the load. In a second-class lever, the load is between the force and the fulcrum. In a third-class lever, the force is between the fulcrum and the load.

- The mechanical advantage of an inclined plane is length divided by height. Wedges and screws are types of inclined planes.

- A wedge is a type of inclined plane. Its mechanical advantage is its length divided by its greatest thickness.

- The mechanical advantage of a wheel and axle is the radius of the wheel divided by the radius of the axle.

- Types of pulleys include fixed pulleys, movable pulleys, and block and tackles.

- Compound machines consist of two or more simple machines.

- Compound machines have low mechanical efficiencies because they have more moving parts and therefore more friction to overcome.

Using Key Terms

1. In your own words, write a definition for the term *lever*.

2. Use the following terms in the same sentence: *inclined plane*, *wedge*, and *screw*.

Understanding Key Ideas

3. Which class of lever always has a mechanical advantage of greater than 1?
   a. first-class
   b. second-class
   c. third-class
   d. None of the above

4. Give an example of each of the following simple machines: first-class lever, second-class lever, third-class lever, inclined plane, wedge, and screw.

Math Skills

5. A ramp is 0.5 m high and has a slope that is 4 m long. What is its mechanical advantage?

6. The radius of the wheel of a wheel and axle is 4 times the radius of the axle. What is the mechanical advantage of the wheel and axle?

Critical Thinking

7. **Applying Concepts** A third-class lever has a mechanical advantage of less than 1. Explain why it is useful for some tasks.

8. **Making Inferences** Which compound machine would you expect to have the lowest mechanical efficiency: a can opener or a pair of scissors? Explain your answer.

Interpreting Graphics

9. Indicate two simple machines being used in the picture below.

For a variety of links related to this chapter, go to www.scilinks.org

Topic: Simple Machines; Compound Machines

SciLinks code: HSM1395; HSM0331

Skills Practice Lab

OBJECTIVES

Calculate the work and power used to climb a flight of stairs.

Compare your work and power with that of a 100 W light bulb.

MATERIALS

- flight of stairs
- ruler, metric
- stopwatch

A Powerful Workout

Does the amount of work that you do depend on how fast you do it? No! But the amount of time in which you do work does affect your power—the rate of work done. In this lab, you'll calculate your work and power for climbing a flight of stairs at different speeds. Then you'll compare your power with that of an ordinary household object—a 100 W light bulb.

Ask a Question

1. How does your power in climbing a flight of stairs compare with the power of a 100 W light bulb?

Form a Hypothesis

2. Write a hypothesis that answers the question in step 1. Explain your reasoning.

Data Collection Table				
Height of step (cm)	Number of steps	Height of stairs (m)	Time for slow walk (s)	Time for quick walk (s)
		DO NOT WRITE IN BOOK		

Test the Hypothesis

3. Copy the Data Collection Table onto a separate sheet of paper.

4. Use a metric ruler to measure the height of one stair step. Record the measurement in your Data Collection Table. Be sure to include units for all measurements.

5. Count the number of stairs, including the top step, and record this number in your Data Collection Table.

6. Calculate the height of the climb by multiplying the number of steps by the height of one step. Record your answer in meters. (You will need to convert your answer from centimeters to meters.)

7. Use a stopwatch to measure how many seconds it takes you to walk slowly up a flight of stairs. Record your measurement in your Data Collection Table.

8. Now measure how many seconds it takes you to walk quickly up a flight of stairs. Be careful not to overexert yourself. This is not a race to see who can get the fastest time!

Analyze the Results

1. **Constructing Tables** Copy the Calculations Table below onto a separate sheet of paper.

Calculations Table			
Weight (N)	Work (J)	Power for slow walk (W)	Power for quick walk (W)

DO NOT WRITE IN BOOK

2. **Examining Data** Determine your weight in newtons, and record it in your Calculations Table. Your weight in newtons is your weight in pounds (lb) multiplied by 4.45 N/lb.

3. **Examining Data** Calculate and record your work done in climbing the stairs by using the following equation:

$$work = force \times distance$$

(Hint: If you are having trouble determining the force exerted, remember that force is measured in newtons.)

4. **Examining Data** Calculate and record your power output by using the following equation:

$$power = \frac{work}{time}$$

The unit for power is the watt (1 watt = 1 joule/second).

Draw Conclusions

5. **Evaluating Methods** In step 3 of "Analyze the Results," you were asked to calculate your work done in climbing the stairs. Why weren't you asked to calculate your work for each trial (slow walk and quick walk)?

6. **Drawing Conclusions** Look at your hypothesis. Was your hypothesis correct? Now that you have measured your power, write a statement that describes how your power compares with that of a 100 W light bulb.

7. **Applying Conclusions** The work done to move one electron in a light bulb is very small. Write down two reasons why the power used is large. (Hint: How many electrons are in the filament of a light bulb? How did you use more power in trial 2?)

Communicating Your Data

Your teacher will provide a class data table on the board. Add your average power to the table. Then calculate the average power from the class data. How many students would it take to create power equal to the power of a 100 W bulb?

Chapter Review

1 *work* and *power*

2 *lever* and *inclined plane*

3 *wheel and axle* and *pulley*

UNDERSTANDING KEY IDEAS

Multiple Choice

4 Work is being done when

  a. you apply a force to an object.

  b. an object is moving after you applied a force to it.

  c. you exert a force that moves an object in the direction of the force.

  d. you do something that is difficult.

5 What is the unit for work?

  a. joule

  b. joule per second

  c. newton

  d. watt

6 Which of the following is a simple machine?

  a. a bicycle

  b. a jar lid

  c. a pair of scissors

  d. a can opener

7 A machine can increase

  a. distance by decreasing force.

  b. force by decreasing distance.

  c. neither distance nor force.

  d. Either (a) or (b)

8 What is power?

  a. the strength of someone or something

  b. the force that is used

  c. the work that is done

  d. the rate at which work is done

9 What is the unit for power?

  a. newton

  b. kilogram

  c. watt

  d. joule

Short Answer

10 Identify the two simple machines that make up a pair of scissors.

11 Explain why you do work on a bag of groceries when you pick it up but not when you carry it.

12 Why is the work output of a machine always less than the work input?

13 What does the mechanical advantage of a first-class lever depend upon? Describe how it can be changed.

Math Skills

14 You and a friend together apply a force of 1,000 N to a car, which makes the car roll 10 m in 1 min and 40 s.

  a. How much work did you and your friend do together?

  b. What was the power output?

15 A lever allows a 35 N load to be lifted with a force of 7 N. What is the mechanical advantage of the lever?

CRITICAL THINKING

16 Concept Mapping Use the following terms to create a concept map: *work, force, distance, machine,* and *mechanical advantage.*

17 Analyzing Ideas Explain why levers usually have a greater mechanical efficiency than other simple machines do.

18 Making Inferences The amount of work done on a machine is 300 J, and the machine does 50 J of work. What can you say about the amount of friction that the machine has while operating?

19 Applying Concepts The winding road shown below is a series of inclined planes. Describe how a winding road makes it easier for vehicles to travel up a hill.

20 Predicting Consequences Why wouldn't you want to reduce the friction involved in using a winding road?

21 Making Comparisons How does the way that a wedge's mechanical advantage is determined differ from the way that a screw's mechanical advantage is determined?

22 Identifying Relationships If the mechanical advantage of a certain machine is greater than 1, what does that tell you about the relationship between the input force and distance and output force and distance?

INTERPRETING GRAPHICS

For each of the images below, identify the class of lever used and calculate the mechanical advantage of the lever.

23

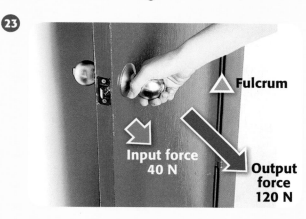

Fulcrum

Input force
40 N

Output force
120 N

24

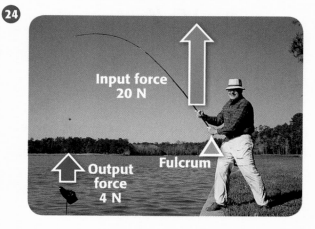

Input force
20 N

Output force
4 N

Fulcrum

Multiple Choice

1. If a simple machine decreases the input force required, it does so by

    A. changing the direction of the input force.

    B. increasing the amount of energy used to accomplish the work.

    C. increasing the distance over which the input force is exerted.

    D. decreasing the amount of work that is required.

2. A wheelchair ramp is 5.2 m long and 0.8 m high. What is the ramp's mechanical advantage?

    A. 4.16

    B. 4.40

    C. 5.20

    D. 6.50

Use the diagram below to answer question 3.

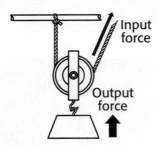

3. In this movable pulley, the input force is 20 N. What is the output force?

    A. 10 N

    B. 20 N

    C. 40 N

    D. 80 N

4. Which of the following is true for the way a screw works?

    A. A small input force is applied over a short distance.

    B. A large input force is applied over a short distance.

    C. A small input force is applied over a long distance.

    D. A large input force is applied over a long distance.

5. An inclined plane can be used to raise a heavy object. The object is pushed up the plane instead of lifted straight up. How does an inclined plane make work easier?

    A. It decreases the amount of work needed to raise the object.

    B. It decreases the force that must be applied to raise the object.

    C. It decreases the distance over which the force must be applied.

    D. It decreases the amount of energy needed to raise the object.

6. For all simple machines, when the output force is greater than the input force,

    A. a mechanical advantage of less than 1 results.

    B. the directions of input and output forces must be the same.

    C. the amount of work that is done is decreased.

    D. the input force is exerted over a larger distance than the output force.

Use the table below to answer question 7.

Industrial Rotary Saw	Work Input	Work Output
Saw A	1500 J	1342 J
Saw B	1350 J	1279 J
Saw C	1425 J	1200 J
Saw D	1610 J	1500 J

7. Patricia is evaluating saws to buy for her lumber mill. She calculates work inputs and outputs for each saw. Which saw has the highest mechanical efficiency?

   A. Saw A

   B. Saw B

   C. Saw C

   D. Saw D

8. A wheelbarrow is a second-class lever. Its wheel is the fulcrum, and its load is carried in a tray. What could be done to a wheelbarrow in order to make lifting and moving rocks easier?

   A. The handles could be shortened.

   B. The wheel could be made larger and wider.

   C. The distance between wheel and tray could be increased.

   D. The tray could be moved to the wheel.

9. Which of these common objects is a third-class lever?

   A. stapler

   B. chisel

   C. seesaw

   D. bottle opener

Open Response

10. What is the relation between work and machines? In your description, be sure to distinguish between simple and compound machines.

11. Francine is opening a tap to get water to drink. What kind of simple machines is she using and how do they work?

Science in Action

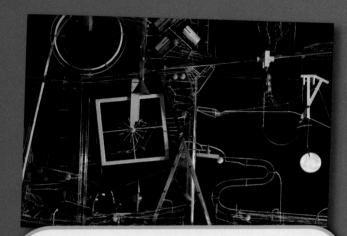

Science, Technology, and Society

Kinetic Sculpture

The collection of tubes, tracks, balls, and blocks of wood shown in the photo is an audio-kinetic sculpture. A conveyor belt lifts the balls to a point high on the track, and the balls wind their way down as they are pulled by the force of gravity and pushed by various other forces. They twist through spirals, drop straight down tubes, and sometimes go up and around loops as if on a roller coaster. All this is made possible by the artist's applications of principles of kinetic energy, the energy of motion.

Math ACTiViTY

A conveyor belt on a kinetic sculpture lifts a ball to a point 0.8 m high. It exerts 0.05 N of force as it does so. How much work does the conveyor belt do on the ball?

Weird Science

Nanomachines

The technology of making things smaller and smaller keeps growing and growing. Powerful computers can now be held in the palm of your hand. But what can motors that are smaller than grains of pepper do? How can gnat-sized robots that can swim through the bloodstream be used? One possible field in which very small machines, *nanomachines,* can be used is in medicine.

Some scientists are looking into the possibility of creating cell-sized machines called *nanobots.* These tiny robots may have many uses in medicine if they can be injected into a person's bloodstream.

Language Arts ACTiViTY

WRITING SKILL Write a short story in which nanobots are used to save someone's life. Describe the machines the nanobots use in destroying deadly bacteria, clearing blood clots, or delivering medicine.

Mike Hensler

The Surf Chair Mike Hensler was a lifeguard at Daytona Beach, Florida, when he realized that it was next to impossible for someone in a wheelchair to come onto the beach. Although he had never invented a machine before, Hensler decided to build a wheelchair that could be driven across sand without getting stuck. He began spending many evenings in his driveway with a pile of lawn-chair parts, designing the chair by trial and error.

The result of Hensler's efforts looks very different from a conventional wheelchair. With huge rubber wheels and a thick frame of white PVC pipe, the Surf Chair not only moves easily over sandy terrain but also is weather resistant and easy to clean. The newest models of the Surf Chair come with optional attachments, such as a variety of umbrellas, detachable armrests and footrests, and even places to attach fishing rods.

Social Studies ACTIVITY

List some simple and compound machines that are used as access devices for people who are disabled. Research how these machines came to be in common use.

To learn more about these Science in Action topics, visit go.hrw.com and type in the keyword HP5WRKF.

Current Science

Check out Current Science® articles related to this chapter by visiting go.hrw.com. Just type in the keyword HP5CS08.

23

Energy and Energy Resources

The Big Idea

Energy can be changed from one form into another form, but energy cannot be created or destroyed.

About the Photo

Imagine that you're a driver in this race. Your car needs a lot of energy to finish. So, it probably needs a lot of gasoline, right? No, it just needs a lot of sunshine! This car runs on solar energy. Solar energy is one of the many forms of energy. Energy is needed to drive a car, turn on a light bulb, play sports, and walk to school. Energy is always being changed into different forms for different uses.

PRE-READING ACTIVITY

FOLDNOTES **Layered Book** Before you read the chapter, create the FoldNote entitled "Layered Book" described in the **Study Skills** section of the Appendix. Label the tabs of the layered book with "Types of energy," "Energy conversions," "Conservation of energy," and "Energy resources." As you read the chapter, write information you learn about each category under the appropriate tab.

START-UP ACTIVITY

Energy Swings!

In this activity, you'll observe a moving pendulum to learn about energy.

Procedure

1. Make a pendulum by tying a **50 cm long string** around the hook of a **100 g hooked mass.**

2. Hold the string with one hand. Pull the mass slightly to the side, and let go of the mass without pushing it. Watch it swing at least 10 times.

3. Record your observations. Note how fast and how high the pendulum swings.

4. Repeat step 2, but pull the mass farther to the side.

5. Record your observations. Note how fast and how high the pendulum swings.

Analysis

1. Does the pendulum have energy? Explain your answer.

2. What causes the pendulum to move?

3. Do you think the pendulum had energy before you let go of the mass? Explain your answer.

What Is Energy?

What You Will Learn

● Explain the relationship between energy and work.
● Compare kinetic and potential energy.
● Describe the different forms of energy.

Vocabulary

energy
kinetic energy
potential energy
mechanical energy

READING STRATEGY

Discussion Read this section silently. Write down questions that you have about this section. Discuss your questions in a small group.

It's match point. The crowd is silent. The tennis player tosses the ball into the air and then slams it with her racket. The ball flies toward her opponent, who swings her racket at the ball. THWOOSH!! The ball goes into the net, causing it to shake. Game, set, and match!!

The tennis player needs energy to slam the ball with her racket. The ball also must have energy in order to cause the net to shake. Energy is around you all of the time. But what, exactly, is energy?

Energy and Work: Working Together

In science, **energy** is the ability to do work. Work is done when a force causes an object to move in the direction of the force. How do energy and work help you play tennis? The tennis player in **Figure 1** does work on her racket by exerting a force on it. The racket does work on the ball, and the ball does work on the net. When one object does work on another, energy is transferred from the first object to the second object. This energy allows the second object to do work. So, work is a transfer of energy. Like work, energy is expressed in units of joules (J).

☑ **Reading Check** What is energy? (*See the Appendix for answers to Reading Checks.*)

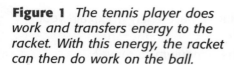

energy the capacity to do work

Figure 1 *The tennis player does work and transfers energy to the racket. With this energy, the racket can then do work on the ball.*

Kinetic Energy

In tennis, energy is transferred from the racket to the ball. As it flies over the net, the ball has kinetic (ki NET ik) energy. **Kinetic energy** is the energy of motion. All moving objects have kinetic energy. Like all forms of energy, kinetic energy can be used to do work. For example, kinetic energy allows a hammer to do work on a nail, as shown in **Figure 2.**

kinetic energy the energy of an object that is due to the object's motion

Kinetic Energy Depends on Mass and Speed

An object's kinetic energy can be found by the following equation:

$$kinetic\ energy = \frac{mv^2}{2}$$

The *m* stands for the object's mass in kilograms. The *v* stands for the object's speed. The faster something is moving, the more kinetic energy it has. Also, the greater the mass of a moving object, the greater its kinetic energy is.

A large car has more kinetic energy than a car that has less mass and that is moving at the same speed does. But as you can see from the equation, speed is squared. So speed has a greater effect on kinetic energy than mass does. For this reason, car crashes are much more dangerous at higher speeds than at lower speeds. A moving car has *4 times* the kinetic energy of the same car going half the speed! This is because it's going twice the speed of the slower car, and 2 squared is 4.

Figure 2 *When you swing a hammer, you give it kinetic energy, which does work on the nail.*

MATH FOCUS

Kinetic Energy What is the kinetic energy of a car that has a mass of 1,200 kg and is moving at a speed of 20 m/s?

Step 1: Write the equation for kinetic energy.

$$KE = \frac{mv^2}{2}$$

Step 2: Replace *m* and *v* with the measurements given, and solve.

$$KE = \frac{1,200\ kg \times (20\ m/s)^2}{2}$$

$$KE = \frac{1,200\ kg \times 400\ m^2/s^2}{2}$$

$$KE = \frac{480,000\ kg{\bullet}m^2/s^2}{2}$$

$$KE = 240,000\ kg{\bullet}m^2/s^2 = 240,000\ J$$

Now It's Your Turn

1. What is the kinetic energy of a car that has a mass of 2,400 kg and is moving at 20 m/s? How does this kinetic energy compare to the kinetic energy of the car in the example given at left?
2. What is the kinetic energy of a 4,000 kg elephant that is running at 2 m/s? at 4 m/s? How do the two kinetic energies compare with one another?
3. What is the kinetic energy of a 2,000 kg bus that is moving at 30 m/s?
4. What is the kinetic energy of a 3,000 kg bus that is moving at 20 m/s?

Figure 3 *The stored potential energy of the bow and string allows them to do work on the arrow when the string is released.*

Potential Energy

Not all energy has to do with motion. **Potential energy** is the energy an object has because of its position. For example, the stretched bow shown in **Figure 3** has potential energy. The bow has energy because work has been done to change its shape. The energy of that work is turned into potential energy.

Gravitational Potential Energy

When you lift an object, you do work on it. You use a force that is against the force of gravity. When you do this, you transfer energy to the object and give the object *gravitational potential energy*. Books on a shelf have gravitational potential energy. So does your backpack after you lift it on to your back. The amount of gravitational potential energy that an object has depends on its weight and its height.

Calculating Gravitational Potential Energy

You can find gravitational potential energy by using the following equation:

gravitational potential energy = weight × height

Because weight is expressed in newtons and height in meters, gravitational potential energy is expressed in newton-meters (N•m), or joules (J).

Recall that *work = force × distance*. Weight is the amount of force that you must use on an object to lift it, and height is a distance. So, gravitational potential energy is equal to the amount of work done on the object to lift it to a certain height. Or, you can think of gravitational potential energy as being equal to the work that would be done by the object if it were dropped from that height.

MATH FOCUS

Gravitational Potential Energy What is the gravitational potential energy of a book with a weight of 13 N at a height of 1.5 m off the ground?

Step 1: Write the equation for gravitational potential energy (GPE).

GPE = weight × height

Step 2: Replace the weight and height with the measurements given in the problem, and solve.

GPE = 13 N × 1.5 m

GPE = 19.5 N•m = 19.5 J

Now It's Your Turn

1. What is the gravitational potential energy of a cat that weighs 40 N standing on a table that is 0.8 m above the ground?
2. What is the gravitational potential energy of a diver who weighs 500 N standing on a platform that is 10 m off the ground?
3. What is the gravitational potential energy of a diver who weighs 600 N standing on a platform that is 8 m off the ground?

Height Above What?

When you want to find out an object's gravitational potential energy, the "ground" that you measure the object's height from depends on where it is. For example, what if you want to measure the gravitational potential energy of an egg sitting on the kitchen counter? In this case, you would measure the egg's height from the floor. But if you were holding the egg over a balcony several stories from the ground, you would measure the egg's height from the ground! You can see that gravitational potential energy depends on your point of view. So, the height you use in calculating gravitational potential energy is a measure of how far an object has to fall.

Mechanical Energy

How would you describe the energy of the juggler's pins in **Figure 4**? To describe their total energy, you would state their mechanical energy. **Mechanical energy** is the total energy of motion and position of an object. Both potential energy and kinetic energy are kinds of mechanical energy. Mechanical energy can be all potential energy, all kinetic energy, or some of each. You can use the following equation to find mechanical energy:

mechanical energy = potential energy + kinetic energy

✓ Reading Check What two kinds of energy can make up the mechanical energy of an object?

Mechanical Energy in a Juggler's Pin

The mechanical energy of an object remains the same unless it transfers some of its energy to another object. But even if the mechanical energy of an object stays the same, the potential energy or kinetic energy it has can increase or decrease.

Look at **Figure 4.** While the juggler is moving the pin with his hand, he is doing work on the pin to give it kinetic energy. But as soon as the pin leaves his hand, the pin's kinetic energy starts changing into potential energy. How can you tell that the kinetic energy is decreasing? The pin slows down as it moves upwards. Eventually, all of the pin's kinetic energy turns into potential energy, and it stops moving upward.

As the pin starts to fall back down again, its potential energy starts changing back into kinetic energy. More and more of its potential energy turns into kinetic energy. You can tell because the pin speeds up as it falls towards the ground.

potential energy the energy that an object has because of the position, shape, or condition of the object

mechanical energy the amount of work an object can do because of the object's kinetic and potential energies

Figure 4 *As a pin is juggled, its mechanical energy is the sum of its potential energy and its kinetic energy at any point.*

Figure 5 Thermal Energy in Water

The particles in an ice cube vibrate in fixed positions and do not have a lot of kinetic energy.

The particles of water in a lake can move more freely and have more kinetic energy than water particles in ice do.

The particles of water in steam move rapidly, so they have more energy than the particles in liquid water do.

Other Forms of Energy

Energy can come in a number of forms besides mechanical energy. These forms of energy include thermal, chemical, electrical, sound, light, and nuclear energy. As you read the next few pages, you will learn what these different forms of energy have to do with kinetic and potential energy.

Thermal Energy

All matter is made of particles that are always in random motion. Because the particles are in motion, they have kinetic energy. *Thermal energy* is all of the kinetic energy due to random motion of the particles that make up an object.

As you can see in **Figure 5,** particles move faster at higher temperatures than at lower temperatures. The faster the particles move, the greater their kinetic energy and the greater the object's thermal energy. Thermal energy also depends on the number of particles. Water in the form of steam has a higher temperature than water in a lake does. But the lake has more thermal energy because the lake has more water particles.

Chemical Energy

Where does the energy in food come from? Food is made of chemical compounds. When compounds such as sugar form, work is done to join the different atoms together. *Chemical energy* is the energy of a compound that changes as its atoms are rearranged. Chemical energy is a form of potential energy because it depends on the position and arrangement of the atoms in a compound.

For another activity related to this chapter, go to **go.hrw.com** and type in the keyword **HP5ENGW.**

Quick Lab

Hear That Energy!

1. Make a simple drum by covering the open end of an **empty coffee can** with **wax paper.** Secure the wax paper with a **rubber band.**

2. Using the eraser end of a **pencil,** tap lightly on the wax paper. Describe how the paper responds. What do you hear?

3. Repeat step 2, but tap the paper a bit harder. Compare your results with those of step 2.

4. Cover half of the wax paper with one hand. Now, tap the paper. What happened? How can you describe sound energy as a form of mechanical energy?

Electrical Energy

The electrical outlets in your home allow you to use electrical energy. *Electrical energy* is the energy of moving electrons. Electrons are the negatively charged particles of atoms.

Suppose you plug an electrical device, such as the amplifier shown in **Figure 6,** into an outlet and turn it on. The electrons in the wires will transfer energy to different parts inside the amplifier. The electrical energy of moving electrons is used to do work that makes the sound that you hear from the amplifier.

The electrical energy used in your home comes from power plants. Huge generators turn magnets inside loops of wire. The changing position of a magnet makes electrical energy run through the wire. This electrical energy can be thought of as potential energy that is used when you plug in an electrical appliance and use it.

Figure 6 *The movement of electrons produces the electrical energy that an amplifier and a microphone use to produce sound.*

Sound Energy

Figure 7 shows how a vibrating object transmits energy through the air around it. Sound energy is caused by an object's vibrations. When you stretch a guitar string, the string stores potential energy. When you let the string go, this potential energy is turned into kinetic energy, which makes the string vibrate. The string also transmits some of this kinetic energy to the air around it. The air particles also vibrate, and transmit this energy to your ear. When the sound energy reaches your ear, you hear the sound of the guitar.

✓ Reading Check What does sound energy consist of?

Figure 7 *As the guitar strings vibrate, they cause particles in the air to vibrate. These vibrations transmit sound energy.*

Figure 8 *The energy used to cook food in a microwave is a form of light energy.*

Light Energy

Light allows you to see, but did you know that not all light can be seen? **Figure 8** shows a type of light that we use but can't see. *Light energy* is produced by the vibrations of electrically charged particles. Like sound vibrations, light vibrations cause energy to be transmitted. But the vibrations that transmit light energy don't need to be carried through matter. In fact, light energy can move through a vacuum (an area where there is no matter).

Nuclear Energy

There is a form of energy that comes from a tiny amount of matter. It is used to generate electrical energy, and it gives the sun its energy. It is *nuclear* (NOO klee uhr) *energy,* the energy that comes from changes in the nucleus (NOO klee uhs) of an atom.

Atoms store a lot of potential energy because of the positions of the particles in the nucleus of the atoms. When two or more small nuclei (NOO klee ie) join together, or when the nucleus of a large atom splits apart, energy is given off.

The energy given off by the sun comes from nuclear energy. In the sun, shown in **Figure 9,** hydrogen nuclei join together to make a larger helium nucleus. This reaction, known as *fusion,* gives off a huge amount of energy. The sun's light and heat come from these reactions.

When a nucleus of a heavy element such as uranium is split apart, the potential energy in the nucleus is given off. This kind of nuclear energy is called *fission*. Fission is used to generate electrical energy at nuclear power plants.

Figure 9 *Without the nuclear energy from the sun, life on Earth would not be possible.*

Reading Check Where does nuclear energy come from?

Summary

- Energy is the ability to do work, and work equals the transfer of energy. Energy and work are expressed in units of joules (J).
- Kinetic energy is energy of motion and depends on speed and mass.
- Potential energy is energy of position. Gravitational potential energy depends on weight and height.

- Mechanical energy is the sum of kinetic energy and potential energy.
- Thermal energy and sound energy can be considered forms of kinetic energy.
- Chemical energy, electrical energy, and nuclear energy can be considered forms of potential energy.

Using Key Terms

1. In your own words, write a definition for the term *energy*.

2. Use the following terms in the same sentence: *kinetic energy, potential energy,* and *mechanical energy.*

Understanding Key Ideas

3. What determines an object's thermal energy?
   a. the motion of its particles
   b. its size
   c. its potential energy
   d. its mechanical energy

4. How are energy and work related?

5. What two factors determine gravitational potential energy?

6. Describe why chemical energy is a form of potential energy.

Critical Thinking

7. **Identifying Relationships** When you hit a nail into a board by using a hammer, the head of the nail gets warm. In terms of kinetic and thermal energy, describe why you think the nail head gets warm.

8. **Applying Concepts** Explain why a high-speed collision may cause more damage to vehicles than a low-speed collision does.

Interpreting Graphics

9. Which part of mechanical energy does the girl in the picture below have the most of?

For a variety of links related to this chapter, go to www.scilinks.org

Topic: What Is Energy? ; Forms of Energy
SciLinks code: HSM1660; HSM0612

Energy Conversions

Imagine you're finishing a clay mug in art class. You turn around, and your elbow knocks the mug off the table. Luckily, you catch the mug before it hits the ground.

The mug has gravitational potential energy while it is on the table. As the mug falls, its potential energy changes into kinetic energy. This change is an example of an energy conversion. An **energy conversion** is a change from one form of energy to another. Any form of energy can change into any other form of energy. Often, one form of energy changes into more than one other form.

What You Will Learn

● Describe an energy conversion.
● Give examples of energy conversions for the different forms of energy.
● Explain how energy conversions make energy useful.
● Explain the role of machines in energy conversions.

Vocabulary

energy conversion

READING STRATEGY

Brainstorming The key idea of this section is energy conversion. Brainstorm words and phrases related to energy conversion.

Kinetic Energy and Potential Energy

Look at **Figure 1.** At the instant this picture was taken, the skateboarder on the left side of the picture was hardly moving. How did he get up so high in the air? As you might guess, he was moving at a high speed on his way up the half-pipe. So, he had a lot of kinetic energy. What happened to that energy? His kinetic energy changed into potential energy. Imagine that the picture below is a freeze-frame of a video. What happens once the video starts running again? The skateboarder's potential energy will become kinetic energy once again as he speeds down the side of the half-pipe.

energy conversion a change from one form of energy to another

Figure 1 Potential Energy and Kinetic Energy

When the skateboarder reaches the top of the half-pipe, his potential energy is at a maximum.

As he speeds down through the bottom of the half-pipe, the skateboarder's kinetic energy is at a maximum.

Elastic Potential Energy

A rubber band can be used to show another example of an energy conversion. Did you know that energy can be stored in a rubber band? Look at **Figure 2.** The wound-up rubber band in the toy airplane has a kind of potential energy called *elastic potential energy.* When the rubber band is let go, the stored energy becomes kinetic energy, spins the propeller, and makes the airplane fly.

You can change the shape of a rubber band by stretching it. Stretching the rubber band takes a little effort. The energy you put into stretching it becomes elastic potential energy. Like the skateboarder at the top of the half-pipe, the stretched rubber band stores potential energy. When you let the rubber band go, it goes back to its original shape. It releases its stored-up potential energy as it does so, as you know if you have ever snapped a rubber band against your skin!

✓ Reading Check How is elastic potential energy stored and released? (*See the Appendix for answers to Reading Checks.*)

Figure 2 *The wound-up rubber band in this model airplane has potential energy because its shape has been changed.*

Conversions Involving Chemical Energy

You may have heard someone say, "Breakfast is the most important meal of the day." Why is eating breakfast so important? As shown in **Figure 3,** chemical energy comes from the food you eat. Your body uses chemical energy to function. Eating breakfast gives your body the energy needed to help you start the day.

Figure 3 Chemical energy of food is converted into kinetic energy when you are active. It is converted into thermal energy to maintain body temperature.

Figure 4 From Light Energy to Chemical Energy

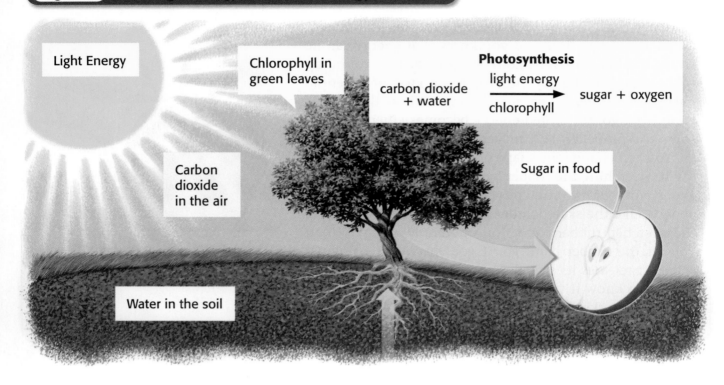

Light Energy

Chlorophyll in green leaves

Photosynthesis

carbon dioxide + water $\xrightarrow[\text{chlorophyll}]{\text{light energy}}$ sugar + oxygen

Carbon dioxide in the air

Sugar in food

Water in the soil

Energy Conversions in Plants

Did you know that the chemical energy in the food you eat comes from the sun's energy? When you eat fruits, vegetables, or grains, you are taking in chemical energy. This energy comes from a chemical change that was made possible by the sun's energy. When you eat meat from animals that ate plants, you are also taking in energy that first came from the sun.

As shown in **Figure 4,** photosynthesis (FOHT oh SIN thuh sis) uses light energy to make new substances that have chemical energy. In this way, light energy is changed into chemical energy. The chemical energy from a tree can be changed into thermal energy when you burn the tree's wood. So, if you follow the conversion of energy back far enough, the energy from a wood fire actually comes from the sun!

✓ **Reading Check** Where does the energy that plants use to grow come from?

The Process Continues

Let's trace where the energy goes. Plants change light energy into chemical energy. The chemical energy in the food you eat is changed into another kind of chemical energy that your body can use. Your body then uses that energy to give you the kinetic energy that you use in everything you do. It's an endless process—energy is always going somewhere!

Figure 5 Energy Conversions in a Hair Dryer

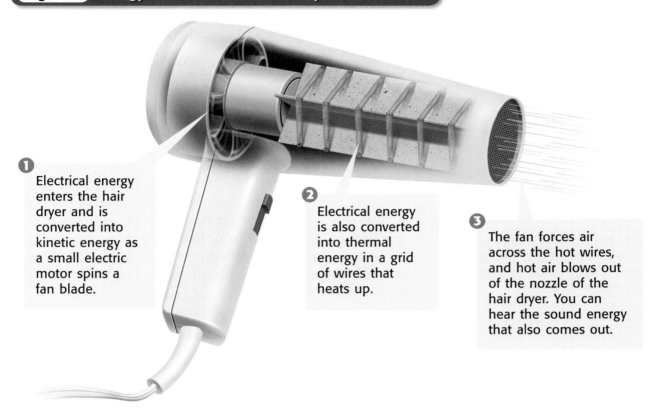

1 Electrical energy enters the hair dryer and is converted into kinetic energy as a small electric motor spins a fan blade.

2 Electrical energy is also converted into thermal energy in a grid of wires that heats up.

3 The fan forces air across the hot wires, and hot air blows out of the nozzle of the hair dryer. You can hear the sound energy that also comes out.

Why Energy Conversions Are Important

Energy conversions are needed for everything we do. Heating our homes, getting energy from a meal, and many other things use energy conversions. Machines, such as the hair dryer shown in **Figure 5,** help harness energy and make that energy work for you. Electrical energy by itself won't dry your hair. But you can use a hair dryer to change electrical energy into the thermal energy that will help you dry your hair.

Conversions Involving Electrical Energy

You use electrical energy all of the time. When you listen to the radio, when you make toast, and when you take a picture with a camera, you use electrical energy. Electrical energy can easily be changed into other forms of energy. **Table 1** lists some common energy conversions that involve electrical energy.

Table 1 Some Conversions of Electrical Energy	
Alarm clock	electrical energy ⟶ light energy and sound energy
Battery	chemical energy ⟶ electrical energy
Light bulb	electrical energy ⟶ light energy and thermal energy
Blender	electrical energy ⟶ kinetic energy and sound energy

Figure 6 *Some of the energy you transfer to a nutcracker is converted into sound energy as the nutcracker transfers energy to the nut.*

Energy and Machines

You've been learning about energy, its different forms, and the ways that it can change between forms. Another way to learn about energy is to look at how machines use energy. A machine can make work easier by changing the size or direction (or both) of the force needed to do the work.

Suppose you want to crack open a walnut. Using a nutcracker, such as the one shown in **Figure 6,** would be much easier (and less painful) than using your fingers. You transfer energy to the nutcracker, and it transfers energy to the nut. The nutcracker allows you to use less force over a greater distance to do the same amount of work as if you had used your bare hands. Another example of how energy is used by a machine is shown in **Figure 7.** Some machines change the energy put into them into other forms of energy.

✓ Reading Check What are two things that machines can do to force that is put into them?

Figure 7 **Energy Conversions in a Bicycle**

For your bike to start and keep moving, energy must be transferred and converted.

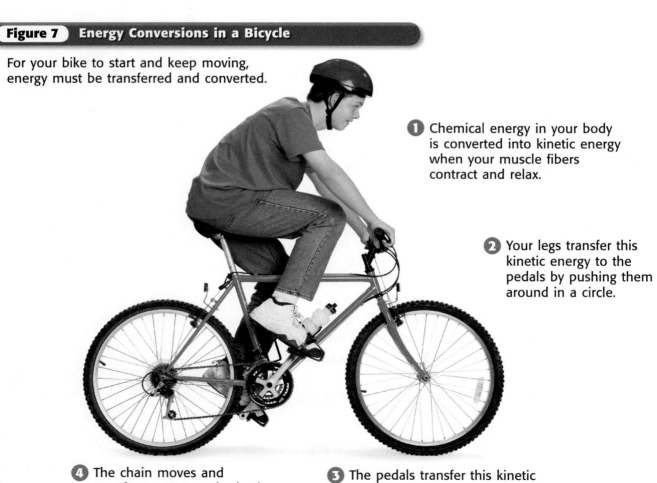

❶ Chemical energy in your body is converted into kinetic energy when your muscle fibers contract and relax.

❷ Your legs transfer this kinetic energy to the pedals by pushing them around in a circle.

❹ The chain moves and transfers energy to the back wheel, which gets you moving!

❸ The pedals transfer this kinetic energy to the gear wheel, which transfers kinetic energy to the chain.

Machines as Energy Converters

Machines help you use energy by converting it into the form that you need. **Figure 8** shows a device called a *radiometer*. It was invented to measure energy from the sun. Inside the glass bulb are four small vanes that absorb light energy. The vanes are dark on one side and light on the other. The dark sides absorb light energy better than the light sides do. As gases next to the dark sides of the vanes heat up, the gas molecules move faster, which causes the vanes to turn. The radiometer shows how a machine can convert energy from one form into another. It changes light energy into heat energy into kinetic energy.

Figure 8 *Machines can change energy into different forms. This radiometer converts light energy into kinetic energy.*

SECTION Review

Summary

- An energy conversion is a change from one form of energy to another. Any form of energy can be converted into any other form of energy.
- Kinetic energy is converted to potential energy when an object is moved against gravity.
- Elastic potential energy is another example of potential energy.
- Your body uses the food you eat to convert chemical energy into kinetic energy.
- Plants convert light energy into chemical energy.
- Machines can transfer energy and can convert energy into a more useful form.

Using Key Terms

1. In your own words, write a definition for the term *energy conversion*.

Understanding Key Ideas

2. In plants, energy is transformed from
   a. kinetic to potential.
   b. light to chemical.
   c. chemical to electrical.
   d. chemical to light.

3. Describe a case in which electrical energy is converted into thermal energy.

4. How does your body get the energy that it needs?

5. What is the role of machines in energy conversions?

Critical Thinking

6. **Applying Concepts** Describe the kinetic-potential energy conversions that occur when a basketball bounces.

7. **Applying Concepts** A car that brakes suddenly comes to a screeching halt. Is the sound energy produced in this conversion a useful form of energy? Explain your answer.

Interpreting Graphics

Look at the diagram below, and answer the following questions.

8. What kind of energy does the skier have at the top of the slope?

9. What happens to that energy after the skier races down the slope of the mountain?

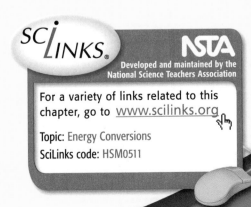

For a variety of links related to this chapter, go to www.scilinks.org

Topic: Energy Conversions
SciLinks code: HSM0511

Conservation of Energy

Many roller coasters have a mechanism that pulls the cars up to the top of the first hill. But the cars are on their own for the rest of the ride.

As the cars go up and down the hills on the track, their potential energy is converted into kinetic energy and back again. But the cars never return to the same height at which they started. Does energy get lost somewhere along the way? No, it is just converted into other forms of energy.

Where Does the Energy Go?

To find out where a roller coaster's original potential energy goes, you have to think about more than just the hills of the roller coaster. Friction plays a part too. **Friction** is a force that opposes motion between two surfaces that are touching. For the roller coaster to move, energy must be used to overcome friction. There is friction between the cars' wheels and the track and between the cars and the air around them. As a result, not all of the potential energy of the cars changes into kinetic energy as the cars go down the first hill. Likewise, as you can see in **Figure 1,** not all of the kinetic energy of the cars changes back into potential energy.

What You Will Learn

- Explain how energy is conserved within a closed system.
- Explain the law of conservation of energy.
- Give examples of how thermal energy is always a result of energy conversion.
- Explain why perpetual motion is impossible.

Vocabulary

friction
law of conservation of energy

READING STRATEGY

Paired Summarizing Read this section silently. In pairs, take turns summarizing the material. Stop to discuss ideas that seem confusing.

| **Figure 1** | **Energy Conversions in a Roller Coaster** |

Not all of the cars' potential energy (*PE*) is converted into kinetic energy (*KE*) as the cars go down the first hill. In addition, not all of the cars' kinetic energy is converted into potential energy as the cars go up the second hill. Some of it is changed into thermal energy because of friction.

ⓐ *PE* is greatest at the top of the first hill.

ⓒ *PE* at the top of the second hill is less than *KE* and *PE* from the first hill.

ⓑ *KE* at the bottom of the first hill is less than the *PE* at the top was.

Energy Is Conserved Within a Closed System

A *closed system* is a group of objects that transfer energy only to each other. For example, a closed system that involves a roller coaster consists of the track, the cars, and the air around them. On a roller coaster, some mechanical energy (the sum of kinetic and potential energy) is always converted into thermal energy because of friction. Sound energy also comes from the energy conversions in a roller coaster. If you add together the cars' kinetic energy at the bottom of the first hill, the thermal energy due to overcoming friction, and the sound energy made, you end up with the same total amount of energy as the original amount of potential energy. In other words, energy is conserved and not lost.

friction a force that opposes motion between two surfaces that are in contact

law of conservation of energy the law that states that energy cannot be created or destroyed but can be changed from one form to another

Law of Conservation of Energy

Energy is conserved in all cases. Because no exception to this rule has been found, this rule is described as a law. According to the **law of conservation of energy,** energy cannot be created or destroyed. The total amount of energy in a closed system is always the same. As **Figure 2** shows, energy can change from one form to another. But all of the different forms of energy in a system always add up to the same total amount of energy. It does not matter how many energy conversions take place.

✓ Reading Check Why is the conservation of energy considered a scientific law? (*See the Appendix for answers to Reading Checks.*)

Figure 2 **Energy Conservation in a Light Bulb**

Some energy is converted into thermal energy, which makes the bulb feel warm.

Some electrical energy is converted into light energy.

As electrical energy is carried through the wire, some of it is converted into thermal energy.

Energy Conversions

With an adult, find three examples of energy conversions that take place in your home. In your **science journal,** write down the kinds of energy that go into each conversion and the kinds of energy that result. For each type of energy that is output, indicate whether the energy is useful.

ACTIVITY

No Conversion Without Thermal Energy

Any time one form of energy is converted into another form, some of the original energy always gets converted into thermal energy. The thermal energy due to friction that results from energy conversions is not useful energy. That is, this thermal energy is not used to do work. Think about a car. You put gas into a car. But not all of the gasoline's chemical energy makes the car move. Some wasted thermal energy will always result from the energy conversions. Much of this energy leaves through the radiator and the exhaust pipe.

Perpetual Motion? No Way!

People have sometimes tried to make a machine that would run forever without any additional energy. This perpetual (puhr PECH oo uhl) motion machine would put out exactly as much energy as it takes in. But that's impossible, because some waste thermal energy always results from energy conversions. The only way a machine can keep moving is to have a constant supply of energy. For example, the "drinking bird" shown in **Figure 3** uses thermal energy from the air to evaporate the water from its head. So, it is not a perpetual motion machine.

✓ **Reading Check** Why is "perpetual motion" impossible?

Figure 3 The "Drinking Bird"

❶ When the bird "drinks," the felt covering its head gets wet.

❷ When the bird is upright, water evaporates from the felt, which decreases the temperature and pressure in the head. Fluid is drawn up from the tail, where pressure is higher, and the bird tips downward.

❸ After the bird "drinks," fluid returns to the tail, the bird flips upright, and the cycle repeats.

Making Conversions Efficient

You may have heard that a car is energy efficient if it gets good gas mileage, and that your home may be energy efficient if it is well insulated. In terms of energy conversions, *energy efficiency* (e FISH uhn see) is a comparison of the amount of energy before a conversion with the amount of useful energy after a conversion. A car with high energy efficiency can go farther than other cars with the same amount of gas.

Energy conversions that are more efficient end up wasting less energy. Look at **Figure 4.** Newer cars tend to be more energy efficient than older cars. One reason is the smooth, aerodynamic (ER oh die NAM ik) shape of newer cars. The smooth shape reduces friction between the car and the surrounding air. Because these cars move through air more easily, they use less energy to over-come friction. So, they are more efficient. Improving the efficiency of machines, such as cars, is important because greater efficiency results in less waste. If less energy is wasted, less energy is needed to operate a machine.

Figure 4 *The shape of newer cars reduces friction between the body of the car and the air.*

More aerodynamic car

Less aerodynamic car

SECTION Review

Summary

- Because of friction, some energy is always converted into thermal energy during an energy conversion.

- Energy is conserved within a closed system. According to the law of conservation of energy, energy cannot be created or destroyed.

- Perpetual motion is impossible because some of the energy put into a machine is converted into thermal energy because of friction.

Using Key Terms

1. Use the following terms in the same sentence: *friction* and *the law of conservation of energy.*

Understanding Key Ideas

2. Perpetual motion is impossible because
   a. things tend to slow down.
   b. energy is lost.
   c. machines are very inefficient.
   d. machines have friction.

3. Describe the energy conversions that take place on a roller coaster, and explain how energy is conserved.

Math Skills

4. A bike is pedaled with 80 J of energy and then coasts. It does 60 J of work in moving forward until it stops. How much of the energy that was put into the bike became thermal energy?

Critical Thinking

5. **Evaluating Conclusions** Imagine that you drop a ball. It bounces a few times and then it stops. Your friend says that the energy that the ball had is gone. Where did the energy go? Evaluate your friend's statement based on energy conservation.

6. **Evaluating Assumptions** If someone says that a car has high energy output, can you conclude that the car is efficient? Explain.

Developed and maintained by the National Science Teachers Association

For a variety of links related to this chapter, go to www.scilinks.org

Topic: Law of Conservation of Energy
SciLinks code: HSM0856

Energy Resources

Energy is used to light and warm our homes. It is used to make food, clothing, and other things. It is also used to transport people and products from place to place. Where does all of this energy come from?

An *energy resource* is a natural resource that can be converted into other forms of energy in order to do useful work. In this section, you will learn about several energy resources, including the one that most other energy resources come from—the sun.

Nonrenewable Resources

Some energy resources, called **nonrenewable resources,** cannot be replaced or are replaced much more slowly than they are used. Fossil fuels are the most important nonrenewable resources.

Oil and natural gas, shown in **Figure 1,** as well as coal, are the most common fossil fuels. **Fossil fuels** are energy resources that formed from the buried remains of plants and animals that lived millions of years ago. These plants stored energy from the sun by photosynthesis. Animals used and stored this energy by eating the plants. So, fossil fuels are concentrated forms of the sun's energy. Now, millions of years later, energy from the sun is released when these fossil fuels are burned.

✔ *Reading Check* **Why are fossil fuels considered nonrenewable resources?** *(See the Appendix for answers to Reading Checks.)*

What You Will Learn

● Name several energy resources.
● Explain how the sun is the source of most energy on Earth.
● Evaluate the advantages and disadvantages of using various energy resources.

Vocabulary

nonrenewable resource
fossil fuel
renewable resource

READING STRATEGY

Reading Organizer As you read this section, make a table comparing nonrenewable resources and renewable resources.

nonrenewable resource a resource that forms at a rate that is much slower than the rate at which it is consumed

fossil fuel a nonrenewable energy resource formed from the remains of organisms that lived long ago

Figure 1 Formation of Fossil Fuels

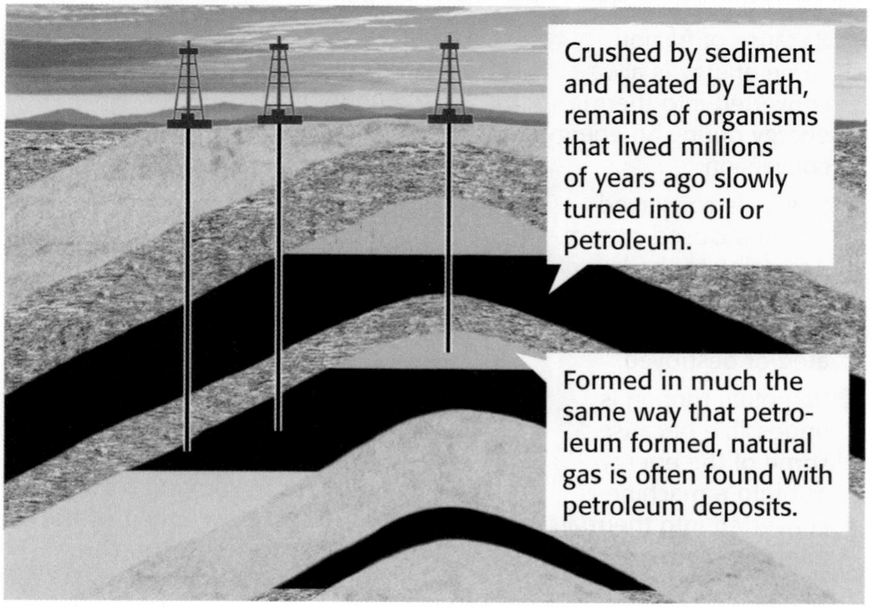

Crushed by sediment and heated by Earth, remains of organisms that lived millions of years ago slowly turned into oil or petroleum.

Formed in much the same way that petroleum formed, natural gas is often found with petroleum deposits.

Uses of Fossil Fuels

All fossil fuels contain stored energy from the sun, which can be converted into other kinds of energy. **Figure 2** shows some different ways that fossil fuels are used in our society.

People have been getting energy from the burning of coal, a fossil fuel, for hundreds of years. Today, burning coal is still a very common way to generate electrical energy. Many products, such as gasoline, wax, and plastics, are made from petroleum, another fossil fuel. A third kind of fossil fuel, natural gas, is often used in home heating.

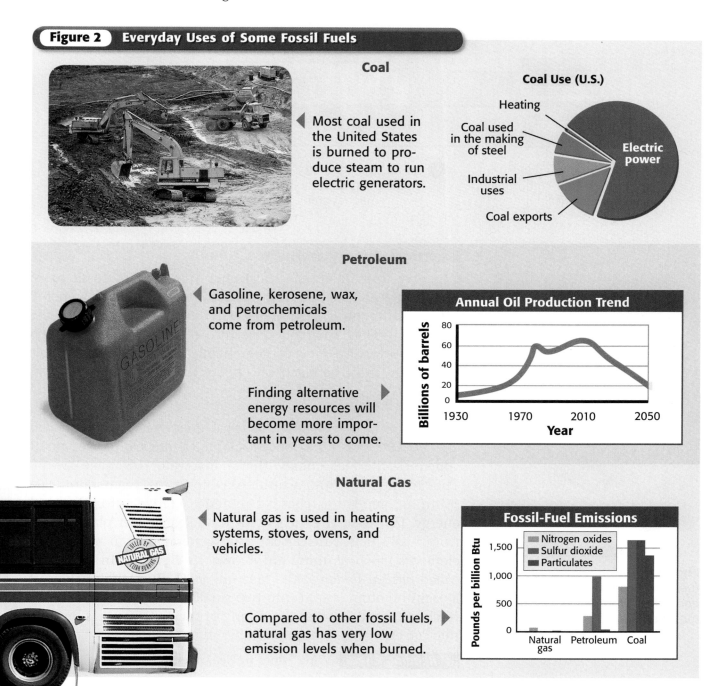

Figure 2 Everyday Uses of Some Fossil Fuels

Coal

Most coal used in the United States is burned to produce steam to run electric generators.

Coal Use (U.S.)

- Heating
- Coal used in the making of steel
- Industrial uses
- Coal exports
- Electric power

Petroleum

Gasoline, kerosene, wax, and petrochemicals come from petroleum.

Finding alternative energy resources will become more important in years to come.

Annual Oil Production Trend

Billions of barrels (0, 20, 40, 60, 80) vs. Year (1930, 1970, 2010, 2050)

Natural Gas

Natural gas is used in heating systems, stoves, ovens, and vehicles.

Compared to other fossil fuels, natural gas has very low emission levels when burned.

Fossil-Fuel Emissions

Pounds per billion Btu (0, 500, 1,000, 1,500)
- Nitrogen oxides
- Sulfur dioxide
- Particulates

Natural gas / Petroleum / Coal

Figure 3 **Converting Fossil Fuels into Electrical Energy**

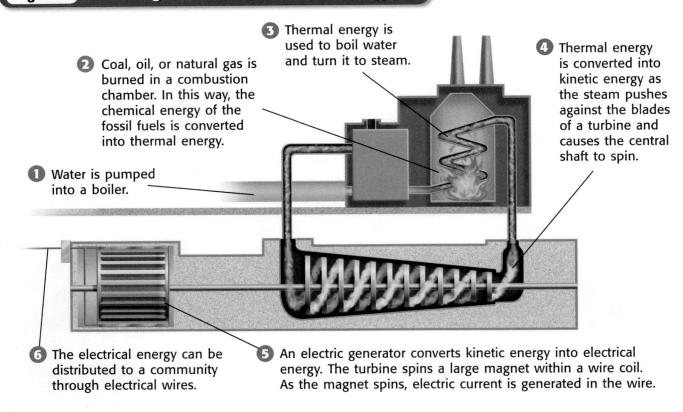

3 Thermal energy is used to boil water and turn it to steam.

2 Coal, oil, or natural gas is burned in a combustion chamber. In this way, the chemical energy of the fossil fuels is converted into thermal energy.

4 Thermal energy is converted into kinetic energy as the steam pushes against the blades of a turbine and causes the central shaft to spin.

1 Water is pumped into a boiler.

6 The electrical energy can be distributed to a community through electrical wires.

5 An electric generator converts kinetic energy into electrical energy. The turbine spins a large magnet within a wire coil. As the magnet spins, electric current is generated in the wire.

Electrical Energy from Fossil Fuels

One way to generate electrical energy is to burn fossil fuels. In fact, fossil fuels are the main source of electrical energy generated in the United States. *Electric generators* convert the chemical energy in fossil fuels into electrical energy by the process shown in **Figure 3.** The chemical energy in fossil fuels is changed into the electrical energy that you use every day.

Nuclear Energy

Another way to generate electrical energy is to use nuclear energy. Like fossil-fuel power plants, a nuclear power plant generates thermal energy that boils water to make steam. The steam then turns a turbine, which runs a generator. The spinning generator changes kinetic energy into electrical energy. However, the fuels used in nuclear power plants differ from fossil fuels. Nuclear energy is generated from radioactive elements, such as uranium, shown in **Figure 4.** In a process called *nuclear fission* (NOO klee uhr FISH uhn), the nucleus of a uranium atom is split into two smaller nuclei, which releases nuclear energy. Because the supply of these elements is limited, nuclear energy is a nonrenewable resource.

✓ *Reading Check* Where does nuclear energy come from?

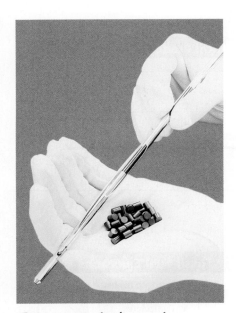

Figure 4 *A single uranium fuel pellet contains the energy equivalent of about 1 metric ton of coal.*

Renewable Resources

Some energy resources, called **renewable resources,** are naturally replaced more quickly than they are used. Some renewable resources, such as solar energy and wind energy, are considered practically limitless.

Solar Energy

Sunlight can be changed into electrical energy through solar cells. These cells can be used in devices such as calculators. Solar cells can also be placed on the roof of a house to provide electrical energy. Some houses can use solar energy by allowing sunlight into the house through large windows. The sun's energy can then be used to heat the house.

Energy from Water

The sun causes water to evaporate and fall again as rain that flows through rivers. The potential energy of water in a reservoir can be changed into kinetic energy as the water flows through a dam. **Figure 5** shows a hydroelectric dam. Falling water turns turbines in a dam. The turbines are connected to a generator that changes kinetic energy into electrical energy.

Wind Energy

Wind is caused by the sun's heating of Earth's surface. Because Earth's surface is not heated evenly, wind is created. The kinetic energy of wind can turn the blades of a windmill. Wind turbines are shown in **Figure 6.** A wind turbine changes the kinetic energy of the air into electrical energy by turning a generator.

renewable resource a natural resource that can be replaced at the same rate at which the resource is consumed

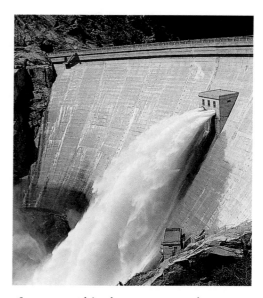

Figure 5 *This dam converts the energy from water going downstream into electrical energy.*

Figure 6 *These wind turbines are converting wind energy into electrical energy.*

Geothermal Energy

Thermal energy caused by the heating of Earth's crust is called *geothermal energy*. Some geothermal power plants pump water underground next to hot rock. The water returns to the surface as steam, which can then turn the turbine of a generator.

✓ Reading Check Where does geothermal energy come from?

Biomass

Plants use and store energy from the sun. Organic matter, such as plants, wood, and waste, that can be burned to release energy is called *biomass*. **Figure 7** shows an example. Some countries depend on biomass for energy.

Figure 7 *Plants capture the sun's energy. When wood is burned, it releases the energy it got from the sun, which can be used to generate electrical energy.*

The Two Sides to Energy Resources

All energy resources have advantages and disadvantages. How can you decide which energy resource to use? **Table 1** compares several energy resources. Depending on where you live, what you need energy for, and how much energy you need, one energy resource may be a better choice than another.

Table 1 Advantages and Disadvantages of Energy Resources		
Energy Resource	**Advantages**	**Disadvantages**
Fossil fuels	• provide a large amount of thermal energy per unit of mass • are easy to get and transport • can be used to generate electricity and to make products such as plastic	• are nonrenewable • produce smog • release substances that can cause acid precipitation • create a risk of oil spills
Nuclear	• is a very concentrated form of energy • does not produce air pollution	• produces radioactive waste • is nonrenewable
Solar	• is an almost limitless source of energy • does not produce pollution	• is expensive to use for large-scale energy production • is practical only in sunny areas
Water	• is renewable • does not produce air pollution	• requires dams, which disrupt a river's ecosystem • is available only where there are rivers
Wind	• is renewable • is relatively inexpensive to generate • does not produce air pollution	• is practical only in windy areas
Geothermal	• is an almost limitless source of energy • power plants require little land	• is practical only in areas near hot spots • produces wastewater, which can damage soil
Biomass	• is renewable • is inexpensive	• requires large areas of farmland • produces smoke

Choosing the Right Energy Resource

As **Table 1** shows, each source of energy that we know about on Earth has advantages and disadvantages. For example, you have probably heard that fossil fuels pollute the air. They will also run out after they are used up. Even renewable resources have their drawbacks. Generating lots of energy from solar energy is difficult. So it cannot be used to meet the energy needs of large cities. Geothermal energy is limited to the "hot spots" in the world where it is available. Hydroelectric energy requires large dams, which can affect the ecology of river life. Energy planning in all parts of the world requires careful consideration of energy needs and the availability and responsible use of resources.

CONNECTION TO Social Studies

WRITING SKILL **Earth's Energy Resources** Find examples of places in the world where the various energy resources mentioned in this chapter are used. List them in your **science journal.** Discuss any patterns that you notice, such as which regions of the world use certain energy resources.

SECTION Review

Summary

- An energy resource is a natural resource that can be converted into other forms of energy in order to do useful work.

- Nonrenewable resources cannot be replaced after they are used or can be replaced only after long periods of time. They include fossil fuels and nuclear energy.

- Renewable resources can be replaced in nature over a relatively short period of time. They include energy from the sun, wind, and water; geothermal energy; and biomass.

- The sun is the source of most energy on Earth.

- Choices about energy resources depend on where you live and what you need energy for.

Using Key Terms

1. In your own words, write a definition for the term *fossil fuel.*

Complete each of the following sentences by choosing the correct term from the word bank.

nonrenewable resources
renewable resources

2. There is a practically limitless supply of ___.

3. ___ are used up more quickly than they are being replaced.

Understanding Key Ideas

4. Which of the following is a renewable resource?
   a. wind
   b. coal
   c. nuclear energy
   d. petroleum

5. Compare fossil fuels and biomass as energy resources.

6. Trace electrical energy back to the sun.

Critical Thinking

7. **Making Comparisons** Describe the similarities and differences between transforming energy in a hydroelectric dam and a wind turbine.

8. **Analyzing Ideas** Name an energy resource that does NOT depend on the sun.

Interpreting Graphics

9. Use the pie chart below to explain why renewable resources are becoming more important to the United States.

U.S. Energy Sources

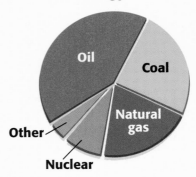

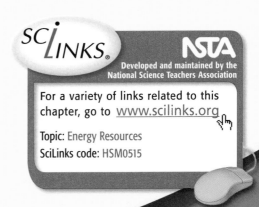

For a variety of links related to this chapter, go to www.scilinks.org

Topic: Energy Resources
SciLinks code: HSM0515

Skills Practice Lab

OBJECTIVES

Form a hypothesis about where kinetic energy comes from.

Test your hypothesis by collecting and analyzing data.

MATERIALS

- books (2 or 3)
- masking tape
- meterstick
- metric balance
- rolling cart
- stopwatch
- wooden board

Finding Energy

When you coast down a hill on a bike or skateboard, you may notice that you pick up speed, or go faster and faster. Because you are moving, you have kinetic energy—the energy of motion. Where does that energy come from? When you pedal the bike or push the skateboard, you are the source of the kinetic energy. But where does the kinetic energy come from when you roll down a hill without making any effort? In this lab, you will find out where such kinetic energy comes from.

Ask a Question

1 Where does the kinetic energy come from when you roll down a hill?

Form a Hypothesis

2 Write a hypothesis that is a possible answer to the question above. Explain your reasoning.

Test the Hypothesis

3 Copy the Data Collection Table below.

Data Collection Table							
Height of ramp (m)	Length of ramp (m)	Mass of cart (kg)	Weight of cart (N)	Time of trial (s)			Average time (s)
				1	2	3	
		DO NOT WRITE IN BOOK					

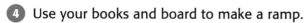

4. Use your books and board to make a ramp.

5. Use masking tape to mark a starting line at the top of the ramp. Be sure the starting line is far enough down from the top of the ramp to allow the cart to be placed behind the line.

6. Use masking tape to mark a finish line at the bottom of the ramp.

7. Find the height of the ramp by measuring the height of the starting line and subtracting the height of the finish line. Record the height of the ramp in your Data Collection Table.

8. Measure the distance in meters between the starting line and the finish line. In the Data Collection Table, record this distance as the length of the ramp.

9. Use the balance to find the mass of the cart in grams. Convert this measurement to kilograms by dividing it by 1,000. In your Data Collection Table, record the mass in kilograms.

10. Multiply the mass by 10 to get the weight of the cart in newtons. Record this weight in your Data Collection Table.

11. Set the cart behind the starting line, and release it. Use a stopwatch to time how long the cart takes to reach the finish line. Record the time in your Data Collection Table.

12. Repeat step 11 twice more, and average the results. Record the average time in your Data Collection Table.

Analyze the Results

1. **Organizing Data** Copy the Calculations Table shown at right onto a separate sheet of paper.

2. **Analyzing Data** Calculate and record the quantities for the cart in the Calculations Table by using your data and the four equations that follow.

Calculations Table			
Average speed (m/s)	Final speed (m/s)	Kinetic energy at bottom (J)	Gravitational potential energy at top (J)
DO NOT WRITE IN BOOK			

$$average\ speed = \frac{length\ of\ ramp}{average\ time}$$

Final speed = 2 × average speed
(This equation works because the cart accelerates smoothly from 0 m/s.)

$$kinetic\ energy = \frac{mass \times (final\ speed)^2}{2}$$

(Remember that 1 kg • m²/s² = 1 J, the unit used to express energy.)

Gravitational potential energy = weight × height
(Remember that 1 N = 1 kg • m/s², so 1 N × 1 m = 1 kg • m²/s² = 1 J)

Draw Conclusions

3. **Drawing Conclusions** How does the cart's gravitational potential energy at the top of the ramp compare with its kinetic energy at the bottom? Does this support your hypothesis? Explain your answer.

4. **Evaluating Data** You probably found that the gravitational potential energy of the cart at the top of the ramp was almost, but not exactly, equal to the kinetic energy of the cart at the bottom of the ramp. Explain this finding.

5. **Applying Conclusions** Suppose that while riding your bike, you coast down both a small hill and a large hill. Compare your final speed at the bottom of the small hill with your final speed at the bottom of the large hill. Explain your answer.

Chapter Review

USING KEY TERMS

For each pair of terms, explain how the meanings of the terms differ.

1 *potential energy* and *kinetic energy*

2 *mechanical energy* and *energy conversion*

3 *friction* and *the law of conservation of energy*

4 *renewable resources* and *nonrenewable resources*

5 *energy resources* and *fossil fuels*

UNDERSTANDING KEY IDEAS

Multiple Choice

6 Kinetic energy depends on
  a. mass and volume.
  b. velocity and weight.
  c. weight and height.
  d. velocity and mass.

7 Gravitational potential energy depends on
  a. mass and velocity.
  b. weight and height.
  c. mass and weight.
  d. height and distance.

8 Which of the following types of energy is not a renewable resource?
  a. wind energy
  b. nuclear energy
  c. solar energy
  d. geothermal energy

9 Which of the following sentences describes a conversion from chemical energy to thermal energy?
  a. Food is digested and used to regulate body temperature.
  b. Charcoal is burned in a barbecue pit.
  c. Coal is burned to produce steam.
  d. All of the above

10 When energy changes from one form to another, some of the energy always changes into
  a. kinetic energy.
  b. potential energy.
  c. thermal energy.
  d. mechanical energy.

Short Answer

11 Name two forms of energy, and relate them to kinetic or potential energy.

12 Give three examples of one form of energy being converted into another form.

13 Explain what a closed system is, and how energy is conserved within it.

14 How are fossil fuels formed?

Math Skills

15 A box has 400 J of gravitational potential energy.
  a. How much work had to be done to give the box that energy?
  b. If the box weighs 100 N, how far above the ground is it?

16 Concept Mapping Use the following terms to create a concept map: *energy, machines, sound energy, hair dryer, electrical energy, energy conversions, thermal energy,* and *kinetic energy.*

17 Applying Concepts Describe what happens in terms of energy when you blow up a balloon and release it.

18 Identifying Relationships After you coast down a hill on your bike, you will eventually come to a complete stop. Use this fact to explain why perpetual motion is impossible.

19 Predicting Consequences Imagine that the sun ran out of energy. What would happen to our energy resources on Earth?

20 Analyzing Processes Look at the photo below. Beginning with the pole vaulter's breakfast, trace the energy conversions necessary for the event shown to take place.

21 Forming Hypotheses Imagine two cars, one of which is more efficient than the other. Suggest two possible reasons one car is more efficient.

22 Evaluating Hypotheses Describe how you would test the two hypotheses you proposed in item 21. How would you determine whether one, both, or neither hypothesis is a factor in the car's efficiency?

Use the graphic below to answer the questions that follow.

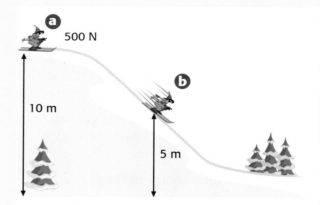

23 What is the skier's gravitational potential energy at point *a*?

24 What is the skier's gravitational potential energy at point *b*?

25 What is the skier's kinetic energy at point *b*? (Hint: mechanical energy = potential energy + kinetic energy)

Standardized Test Preparation

Multiple Choice

1. **At what point on a roller coaster ride is kinetic energy being converted to potential energy?**

   A. at the top of the first hill

   B. at the bottom of the first hill

   C. coming down a hill

   D. going up a hill

2. **Indira ate a peach. Which of the following is the best description of the energy transformation(s) that took place?**

   A. Photosynthesis transformed the sun's light energy into chemical energy, which was transferred to Indira.

   B. Chemical energy in the peach was transformed by chlorophyll into thermal energy to heat Indira's body.

   C. The sun gave off electrical energy that was transformed into chemical energy in the peach that Indira ate.

   D. The mechanical energy of the peach was converted to chemical energy when Indira ate the peach.

3. **The universe is considered a closed system. Which of the following is true about this system?**

   A. Energy is lost from the system as heat.

   B. The total amount of energy in the system stays the same.

   C. Thermal energy is added to the system.

   D. The system's kinetic energy equals its potential energy.

Use the picture below to answer question 4.

1   2   3

4. **The sketches above record everyday examples of types of energy. Which sketches show kinetic energy?**

   A. 1 only

   B. 2 only

   C. 3 only

   D. 1 and 2 only

5. **A hydroelectric power plant converts the energy from falling water into energy that is used by a light bulb. Which of the following shows the sequence in which energy was converted?**

   A. kinetic to mechanical to electrical to light

   B. mechanical to electrical to light to kinetic

   C. electrical to light to kinetic to mechanical

   D. mechanical to light to electrical to kinetic

6. **Two cars traveling at the same speed have a head-on collision. Which of the following is a reasonable description of the collision?**

   A. The larger car has more potential energy than the smaller car does.

   B. Mass has a greater effect on kinetic energy than speed does.

   C. The larger car experiences more friction than the smaller car does.

   D. The larger car has more kinetic energy than the smaller car does.

Use the table below to answer question 7.

Object	Weight	Gravitational Potential Energy
Book	20 N	10.00 J
Decorative Plate	5 N	7.50 J
Framed Picture	7 N	8.75 J
Statue	25 N	18.75 J

7. **The objects in the table above are all on shelves in a bookcase. Which of the objects is located on the highest shelf?**

   A. the book

   B. the decorative plate

   C. the framed picture

   D. the statue

8. **Which situation describes a conversion from kinetic energy to potential energy?**

   A. A storm develops, and it starts to rain and hail.

   B. A duck eats plants that are floating in the water.

   C. A rubber band is being wrapped around stalks of broccoli.

   D. A can rolls along a counter and then falls to the floor.

9. **What is the kinetic energy of a greyhound that has a mass of 30 kg and is running at a speed of 17 m/s?**

   A. 255 J

   B. 510 J

   C. 4335 J

   D. 8670 J

10. **How is energy affected when a cat knocks a plant off of a counter?**

    A. The cat transfers gravitational potential energy to the plant.

    B. The kinetic energy of the cat converts to gravitational potential energy.

    C. The cat loses potential energy and the plant loses potential energy.

    D. The gravitational potential energy of the plant converts to kinetic energy.

Open Response

11. **Early one morning, while camping at Barren Lake State Park in Lucas, Kentucky, Tyrone went out on a bicycle ride. His bike's headlight turned on as he pedaled. Describe three ways energy was converted from one form to another as Tyrone rode his bike.**

12. **Meredith fills a teapot and puts it on the stove. She turns the gas burner on and waits for the water to boil. When the water is boiling, Meredith pours it into a cup with a teabag in it. She drinks the tea after it has cooled slightly. Describe all the transfers of thermal energy in this example.**

Science in Action

Science, Technology, and Society

Underwater Jet Engines

Almost all boats that have engines use propellers. But in 2002, a British company announced that it had developed an underwater jet engine.

The underwater jet engine works by producing steam in a gasoline-powered boiler. When the steam hits the water, it condenses to a very small volume, which creates a vacuum. This vacuum causes thrust by sucking in water from the front of the tube. The underwater jet engine is extremely energy-efficient, produces a great amount of thrust, and creates very little pollution.

Social Studies ACTiViTY

Research the kinds of water propulsion people have used throughout history. Note which kinds were improvements on previous technology and which were completely new.

Scientific Discoveries

$E = mc^2$

The famous 20th-century scientist Albert Einstein discovered an equation that is almost as famous as he is. That equation is $E = mc^2$. You may have heard of it before. But what does it mean?

The equation represents a relationship between mass and energy. E represents energy, m represents mass, and c represents the speed of light. So, $E = mc^2$ means that a small amount of mass has a very large amount of energy! Nuclear reactors harness this energy, which is given off when radioactive atoms split.

Math ACTiViTY

The speed of light is approximately 300,000,000 m/s. How much energy is equivalent to the mass of 0.00000002 g of hydrogen?

Careers

Cheryl Mele

Power-Plant Manager Cheryl Mele is the manager of the Decker Power Plant in Austin, Texas, where she is in charge of almost 1 billion watts of electric power generation. Most of the electric power is generated by a steam-driven turbine system that uses natural gas fuel. Gas turbines are also used. Together, the systems make enough electrical energy for many homes and businesses.

Cheryl Mele says her job as plant manager is to do "anything that needs doing." Her training as a mechanical engineer allows her to run tests and to find problems in the plant. Previously, Mele had a job helping to design more-efficient gas turbines. That job helped prepare her for the job of plant manager.

Mele believes that engineering and power-plant management are interesting jobs because they allow you to work with many new technologies. Mele thinks young people should pursue what interests them. "Be sure to connect the math you learn to the science you are doing," she says. "This will help you to understand both."

Language Arts ACTIVITY

Look up the word *energy* in a dictionary. Compare the different definitions you find to the definition given in this chapter.

go.hrw.com

To learn more about these Science in Action topics, visit go.hrw.com and type in the keyword HP5ENGF.

Current Science

Check out Current Science® articles related to this chapter by visiting go.hrw.com. Just type in the keyword HP5CS09.

24

Heat and Heat Technology

The Big Idea

Heat is energy that moves from an object at a higher temperature to an object at a lower temperature.

About the Photo

This ice climber is using a lot of special equipment. This equipment includes a rope, a safety helmet, an ice pick, and warm clothing. The climber's clothing, which includes insulating layers inside a protective outer layer, keeps his body heat from escaping into the cold air. If he weren't wearing enough protective clothing, he would be feeling very cold, because thermal energy always moves into areas of lower temperature.

PRE-READING ACTIVITY

FOLDNOTES **Two-Panel Flip Chart**
Before you read the chapter, create the FoldNote entitled "Two-Panel Flip Chart" described in the **Study Skills** section of the Appendix. Label the flaps of the two-panel flip chart with "Heat" and "Temperature." As you read the chapter, write information you learn about each category under the appropriate flap.

Some Like It Hot

Sometimes, you can estimate an object's temperature by touching the object. In this activity, you will find out how well your hand works as a thermometer!

Procedure

1. Gather small pieces of the following materials: **metal, wood, plastic foam, rock, plastic,** and **cardboard.** Allow the materials to sit untouched on a table for a few minutes.

2. Put the palms of your hands on each of the materials. List the materials in order from coolest to warmest.

3. Place a **thermometer strip** on the surface of each material. Record the temperature of each material.

Analysis

1. Which material felt the warmest to your hands?

2. Which material had the highest temperature? Was it the same material that felt the warmest?

3. Why do you think some materials felt warmer than others?

4. Was your hand a good thermometer? Explain why or why not.

Temperature

You probably put on a sweater or a jacket when it's cold. Likewise, you probably wear shorts in the summer when it gets hot. But how hot is hot, and how cold is cold?

Think about the knobs on a water faucet: they are labeled "H" for hot and "C" for cold. But does only hot water come out when the hot-water knob is on? You may have noticed that when you first turn on the hot water, the water is warm or even cool. Is the label on the knob wrong? The terms *hot* and *cold* are not scientific terms. If you really want to specify how hot or cold something is, you must use temperature.

What Is Temperature?

You probably think of temperature as a measure of how hot or cold something is. But using the terms *hot* and *cold* can be confusing. Imagine that you are outside on a hot day. You step onto a shady porch where a fan is blowing. You think it feels cool there. Then, your friend comes out onto the porch from an air-conditioned house. She thinks it feels warm! Using the word *temperature* instead of words such as *cool* or *warm* avoids confusion. Scientifically, **temperature** is a measure of the average kinetic energy of the particles in an object.

Temperature and Kinetic Energy

All matter is made of atoms or molecules that are always moving, even if it doesn't look like they are. Because the particles are in motion, they have kinetic energy. The faster the particles are moving, the more kinetic energy they have. Look at **Figure 1.** The more kinetic energy the particles of an object have, the higher the temperature of the object is.

What You Will Learn

● Describe how temperature relates to kinetic energy.
● Compare temperatures on different temperature scales.
● Give examples of thermal expansion.

Vocabulary
temperature
thermal expansion
absolute zero

READING STRATEGY

Prediction Guide Before reading this section, write the title of each heading in this section. Next, under each heading, write what you think you will learn.

temperature a measure of how hot (or cold) something is; specifically, a measure of the average kinetic energy of the particles in an object

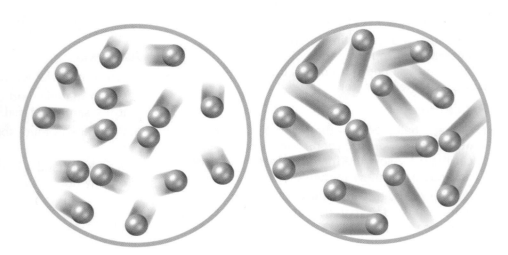

Figure 1 *The gas particles on the right have a higher average kinetic energy than those on the left. So, the gas on the right is at a higher temperature.*

Hot or Cold?

1. Put both your hands into a **bucket of warm water,** and note how the water feels.

2. Now, put one hand into a **bucket of cold water** and the other into a **bucket of hot water.**

3. After a minute, take your hands out of the hot and cold water and put them back in the warm water. Note how the water feels to each hand.

4. Can you rely on your hands to determine temperature? Explain your observations.

Average Kinetic Energy of Particles

Particles of matter are always moving. But they move in different directions and at different speeds. The motion of particles is random. Because particles are moving at different speeds, individual particles have different amounts of kinetic energy. But the *average* kinetic energy of all the particles in an object can be measured. When you measure an object's temperature, you measure the average kinetic energy of all the particles in the object.

The temperature of a substance depends on the average kinetic energy of all its particles. Its temperature does not depend on how much of it you have. Look at **Figure 2.** A pot of tea and a cup of tea each have a different amount of tea. But their atoms have the same average kinetic energy. So, the pot of tea and the cup of tea are at the same temperature.

✓ Reading Check How is temperature related to kinetic energy? (*See the Appendix for answers to Reading Checks.*)

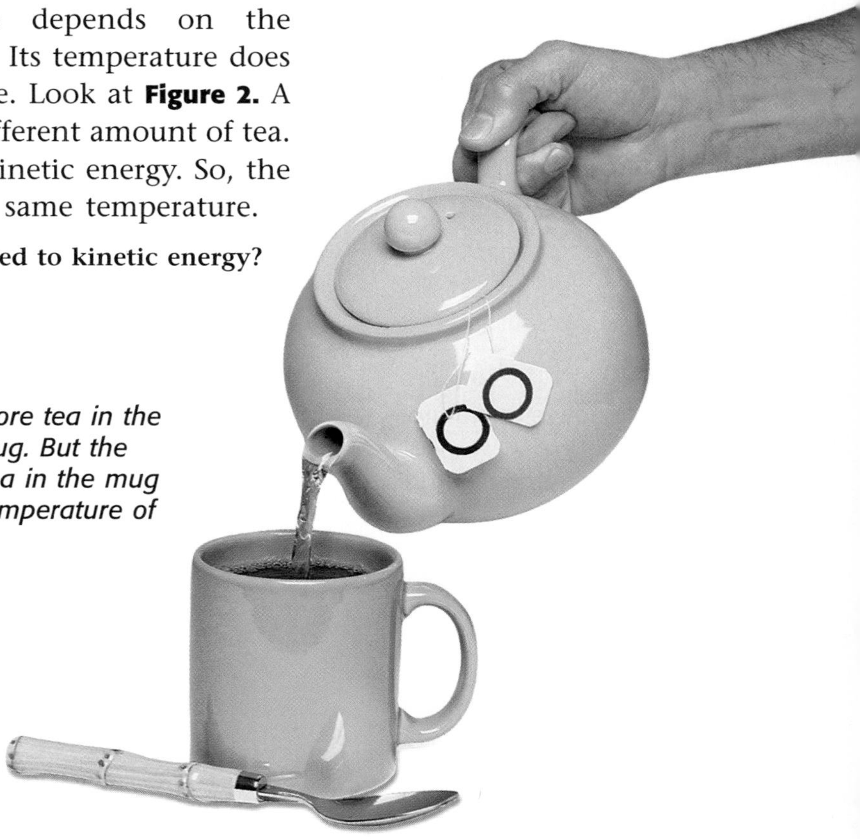

For another activity related to this chapter, go to **go.hrw.com** and type in the keyword **HP5HOTW.**

Figure 2 *There is more tea in the teapot than in the mug. But the temperature of the tea in the mug is the same as the temperature of the tea in the teapot.*

Measuring Temperature

How would you measure the temperature of a steaming cup of hot chocolate? Would you take a sip of it or stick your finger in it? You probably would not. You would use a thermometer.

Using a Thermometer

Many thermometers are thin glass tubes filled with a liquid. Mercury and alcohol are often used in thermometers because they remain in liquid form over a large temperature range.

Thermometers can measure temperature because of a property called thermal expansion. **Thermal expansion** is the increase in volume of a substance because of an increase in temperature. As a substance's temperature increases, its particles move faster and spread out. So, there is more space between them, and the substance expands. Mercury and alcohol expand by constant amounts for a given change in temperature.

Look at the thermometers in **Figure 3.** They are all at the same temperature. So, the alcohol in each thermometer has expanded the same amount. But the number for each thermometer is different because a different temperature scale is marked on each one.

Reading Check What property makes thermometers work?

thermal expansion an increase in the size of a substance in response to an increase in the temperature of the substance

absolute zero the temperature at which molecular energy is at a minimum (0 K on the Kelvin scale or −273.16°C on the Celsius scale)

Figure 3 Three Temperature Scales

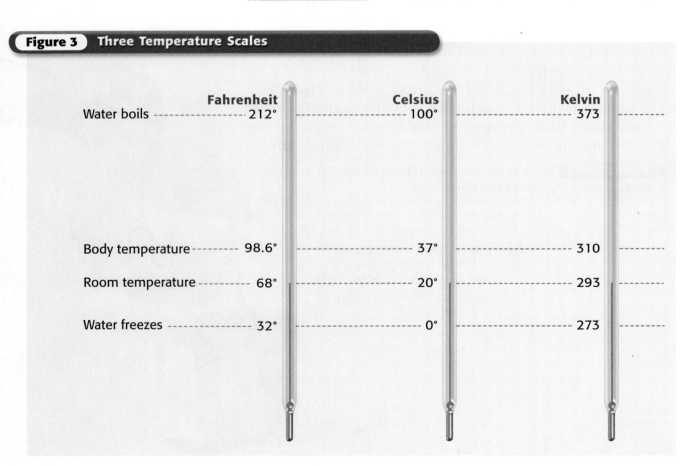

	Fahrenheit	Celsius	Kelvin
Water boils	212°	100°	373
Body temperature	98.6°	37°	310
Room temperature	68°	20°	293
Water freezes	32°	0°	273

Temperature Scales

Look at **Figure 4.** When a weather report is given, you will probably hear the temperature given in degrees Fahrenheit (°F). Scientists, however, often use the Celsius scale. In the Celsius scale, the temperature range between the freezing point and boiling point of water is divided into 100 equal parts, called degrees Celsius (°C). A third scale, the Kelvin (or absolute) scale, is the official SI temperature scale. The Kelvin scale is divided into units called kelvins (K)—not degrees kelvin.

The lowest temperature on the Kelvin scale is 0 K, which is called **absolute zero.** Absolute zero (about −459°F) is the temperature at which all molecular motion stops. It is not possible to actually reach absolute zero, although temperatures very close to 0 K have been reached in laboratories.

Temperature Conversion

As shown by the thermometers on the previous page, a given temperature is represented by different numbers on the three temperature scales. For example, the freezing point of water is 32°F, 0°C, or 273 K.

The temperature 0°C is actually much higher than 0 K. But a *change* of one kelvin is equal to a change of one Celsius degree. The temperature 0°C is higher than 0°F, but a change of one Fahrenheit degree is *not* equal to a change of one Celsius degree. You can convert from one scale to another using the equations shown in **Table 1** below.

Converting Temperatures

Use the equations in **Table 1** to answer the following questions:

1. What temperature on the Celsius scale is equivalent to 373 K?
2. Absolute zero is 0 K. What is the equivalent temperature on the Celsius scale? on the Fahrenheit scale?
3. Which temperature is colder, 0°F or 200 K?

Table 1 Converting Between Temperature Units		
To convert	**Use the equation**	**Example**
Celsius to Fahrenheit °C ⟶ °F	$°F = \left(\dfrac{9}{5} \times °C\right) + 32$	Convert 45°C to degrees Fahrenheit. $°F = \left(\dfrac{9}{5} \times 45°C\right) + 32 = 113°F$
Fahrenheit to Celsius °F ⟶ °C	$°C = \dfrac{5}{9} \times (°F - 32)$	Convert 68°F to degrees Celsius. $°C = \dfrac{5}{9} \times (68°F - 32) = 20°C$
Celsius to Kelvin °C ⟶ K	$K = °C + 273$	Convert 45°C to Kelvins. $K = 45°C + 273 = 318 K$
Kelvin to Celsius K ⟶ °C	$°C = K - 273$	Convert 32 K to degrees Celsius. $°C = 32 K - 273 = -241°C$

Figure 4 *Weather reports that you see on the news usually give temperatures in degrees Fahrenheit (°F).*

More About Thermal Expansion

You have learned about how thermal expansion works in the liquids that fill thermometers. Thermal expansion has many other applications. Below, you will read about a case in which thermal expansion can be dangerous, one in which it can be useful, and one in which it can carry you into the air!

Expansion Joints on Highways

Have you ever gone across a highway bridge in a car? You probably heard and felt a "thuh-thunk" every couple of seconds as you went over the bridge. That sound is made when the car goes over small gaps called *expansion joints,* shown in **Figure 5.**

If the weather is very hot, the bridge can heat up enough to expand. As it expands, there is a danger of the bridge breaking. Expansion joints keep segments of the bridge apart so that they have room to expand without the bridge breaking.

Reading Check What is the purpose of expansion joints in a bridge?

Bimetallic Strips in Thermostats

Thermal expansion also occurs in a thermostat, the device that controls the heater in your home. Some thermostats have a bimetallic strip inside. A *bimetallic strip* is made of two different metals stacked in a thin strip. Because different materials expand at different rates, one of the metals expands more than the other when the strip gets hot. This makes the strip coil and uncoil in response to changes in temperature. This coiling and uncoiling closes and opens an electric circuit that turns the heater on and off in your home, as shown in **Figure 6.**

Figure 5 *This gap in the bridge allows the concrete to expand and contract without breaking.*

Figure 6 How a Thermostat Works

Electrical contacts   **Bimetallic strip**

a As the room temperature drops below the desired level, the bimetallic strip coils more tightly, and the glass tube tilts. A drop of mercury closes an electric circuit that turns the heater on.

b As the room temperature rises above the desired level, the bimetallic strip uncoils slightly, becoming larger. The drop of mercury rolls back in the tube, opening the electric circuit, and the heater turns off.

Thermal Expansion in Hot-Air Balloons

You may have heard the expression "Hot air rises." If you have ever seen hot-air balloons peacefully gliding through the sky, you have seen this principle at work. But why does hot air rise?

When a gas is heated, as shown in **Figure 7,** its particles have more kinetic energy. They move around more quickly, so there is more space between them. The gas is then able to expand if it is not kept at the same volume by its container. When air (which is a mixture of gases) inside a hot-air balloon is heated, the air expands. As it expands, it becomes less dense than the air outside the balloon. So, the balloon goes up, up, and away!

Figure 7 *Thermal expansion helps get these hot-air balloons off the ground.*

SECTION Review

Summary

- Temperature is a measure of the average kinetic energy of the particles of a substance.
- Fahrenheit, Celsius, and Kelvin are three temperature scales.
- Thermal expansion is the increase in volume of a substance due to an increase in temperature.
- Absolute zero (0 K, or −273°C) is the lowest possible temperature.
- A thermostat works because of the thermal expansion of a bimetallic strip.

Using Key Terms

1. In your own words, write a definition for the term *temperature*.

2. Use each of the following terms in a separate sentence: *thermal expansion* and *absolute zero*.

Understanding Key Ideas

3. Which of the following is the coldest temperature possible?
   a. 0 K
   b. 0°C
   c. 0°F
   d. −273°F

4. Does temperature depend on the amount of the substance? Explain.

5. Describe the process of thermal expansion.

Math Skills

6. Convert 35°C to degrees Fahrenheit.

7. Convert 34°F to degrees Celsius.

8. Convert 0°C to kelvins.

9. Convert 100 K to degrees Celsius.

Critical Thinking

10. **Predicting Consequences** Why do you think heating a full pot of soup on the stove could cause the soup to overflow?

11. **Analyzing Processes** During thermal expansion, what happens to the density of a substance?

12. **Forming Hypotheses** A glass of cold water whose particles had a low average kinetic energy was placed on a table. The average kinetic energy in the cold water increased, while the average kinetic energy of the part of the table under the glass decreased. What do you think happened?

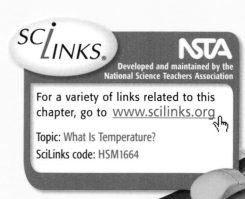

What Is Heat?

It's time for your annual physical. The doctor comes in and begins her exam by placing a metal stethoscope on your back. You jump a little and say, "Whoa! That's cold!"

What is it about the stethoscope that made it feel cold? The answer has to do with how energy moves between the metal and your skin. In this section, you'll learn about this kind of energy transfer.

Transferred Thermal Energy

You might think of the word *heat* as having to do with things that feel hot. But heat also has to do with things that feel cold—such as the stethoscope. In fact, heat is what causes objects to feel hot or cold or to get hot or cold under the right conditions. You probably use the word *heat* every day to mean different things. However, in this chapter, you will use only one specific meaning for *heat*. **Heat** is the energy transferred between objects that are at different temperatures.

Why do some things feel hot, while others feel cold? When two objects at different temperatures come into contact, energy is always transferred from the object that has the higher temperature to the object that has the lower temperature. Look at **Figure 1.** The doctor's stethoscope touches your back. Energy is transferred from your back to the stethoscope because your back has a higher temperature (about 37°C) than the stethoscope (probably room temperature, about 20°C) has. This energy is transferred quickly, so the stethoscope feels cold to you.

heat the energy transferred between objects that are at different temperatures

Figure 1 *The metal stethoscope feels cold because of heat!*

Heat and Thermal Energy

If heat is transferred energy, what form of energy is being transferred? The answer is thermal energy. **Thermal energy** is the total kinetic energy of the particles that make up a substance. Thermal energy, which is measured in joules (J), depends partly on temperature. Something at a high temperature has more thermal energy than it would have at a lower temperature. Thermal energy also depends on how much of a substance there is. Look at **Figure 2.** The more particles there are in a substance at a given temperature, the greater the thermal energy of the substance is.

Figure 2 *Although both soups are at the same temperature, there is more soup in the pan. So, the soup in the pan has more thermal energy than the soup in the bowl.*

Reaching the Same Temperature

Look at **Figure 3.** When objects that have different temperatures come into contact, energy will always be transferred. Energy will pass from the warmer object to the cooler object until both have the same temperature. When objects that are touching each other have the same temperature, there is no net change in the thermal energy of either one. Although one object may have more thermal energy than the other object, both objects will be at the same temperature.

thermal energy the kinetic energy of a substance's atoms

✓ Reading Check What will happen if two objects at different temperatures come into contact? (*See the Appendix for answers to Reading Checks.*)

Figure 3 **Transfer of Thermal Energy**

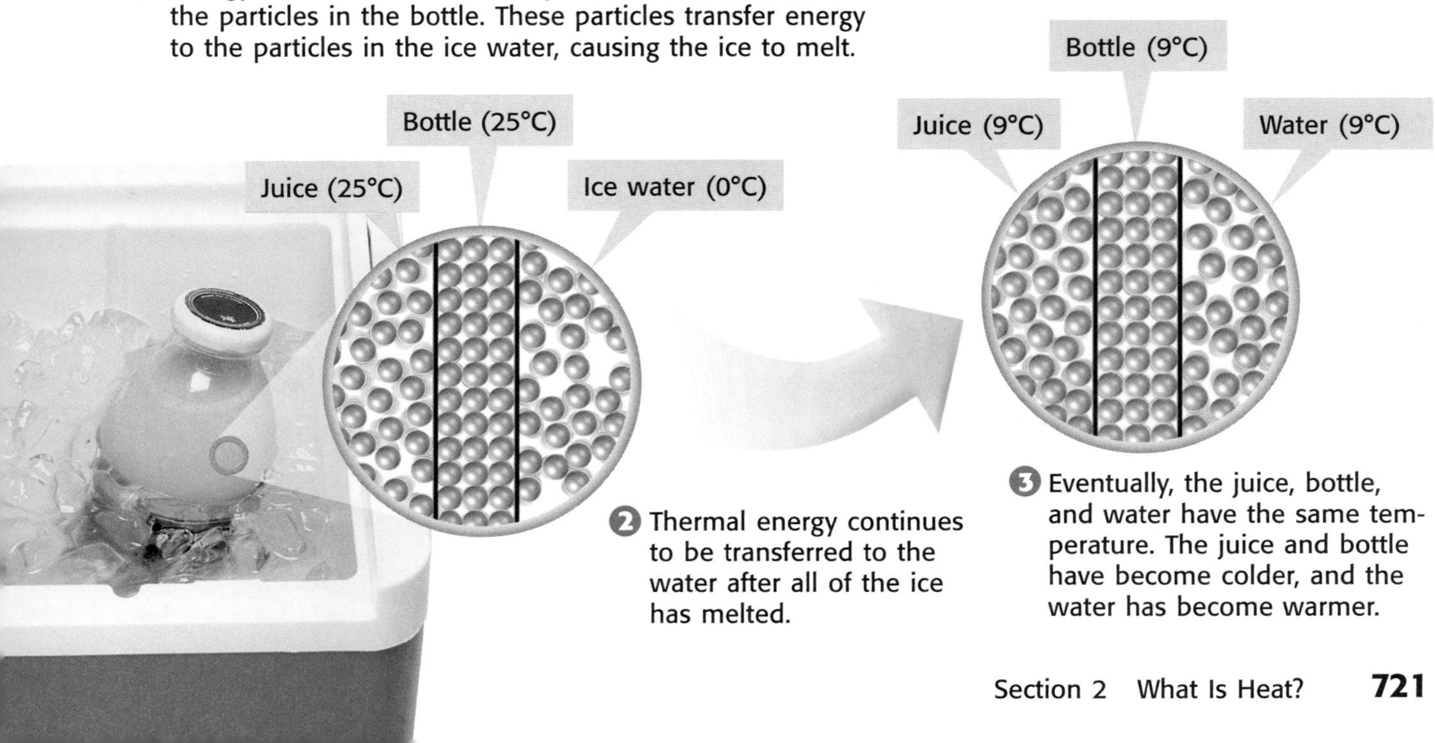

❶ Energy is transferred from the particles in the juice to the particles in the bottle. These particles transfer energy to the particles in the ice water, causing the ice to melt.

Juice (25°C)   Bottle (25°C)   Ice water (0°C)

Bottle (9°C)

Juice (9°C)   Water (9°C)

❷ Thermal energy continues to be transferred to the water after all of the ice has melted.

❸ Eventually, the juice, bottle, and water have the same temperature. The juice and bottle have become colder, and the water has become warmer.

Conduction, Convection, and Radiation

You already know several examples of energy transfer. You know that stoves transfer energy to soup in a pot. You adjust the temperature of your bath water by adding cold or hot water to the tub. And the sun warms your skin. In the next few pages, you'll learn about three ways to transfer thermal energy: *conduction, convection,* and *radiation.*

Conduction

Imagine that you have put a cold metal spoon in a bowl of hot soup, as shown in **Figure 4.** Soon, the handle of the spoon warms up—even though it is not in the soup! The entire spoon gets warm because of conduction. **Thermal conduction** is the transfer of thermal energy from one substance to another through direct contact. Conduction can also occur within a substance, such as the spoon in **Figure 4.**

How does conduction work? When objects touch each other, their particles collide. Thermal energy is transferred from the higher-temperature substance to the lower-temperature substance. Remember that particles of substances at different temperatures have different average kinetic energies. So, when particles collide, particles with higher kinetic energy transfer energy to those with lower kinetic energy. This transfer makes some particles slow down and other particles speed up until all particles have the same average kinetic energy. As a result, the substances have the same temperature.

thermal conduction the transfer of energy as heat through a material

Figure 4 *The end of this spoon will warm up because conduction, the transfer of energy through direct contact, occurs all the way up the handle.*

Conductors and Insulators

Substances that conduct thermal energy very well are called **thermal conductors.** For example, the metal in a doctor's stethoscope is a conductor. Energy is transferred rapidly from your warm skin to the cool stethoscope. That's why the stethoscope feels cold. Substances that do not conduct thermal energy very well are called **thermal insulators.** For example, a doctor's wooden tongue depressor is an insulator. It is at the same temperature as the stethoscope. But the tongue depressor doesn't feel cold. The reason is that thermal energy is transferred very slowly from your tongue to the wood. Some typical conductors and insulators are shown in **Table 1** at right.

Reading Check How can two objects that are the same temperature feel as if they are at different temperatures?

Table 1 Conductors and Insulators	
Conductors	**Insulators**
Curling iron	Flannel shirt
Cookie sheet	Oven mitt
Iron skillet	Plastic spatula
Copper pipe	Fiberglass insulation
Stove coil	Ceramic bowl

Convection

A second way thermal energy is transferred is **convection,** the transfer of thermal energy by the movement of a liquid or a gas. Look at **Figure 5.** When you boil water in a pot, the water moves in roughly circular patterns because of convection. The water at the bottom of a pot on a stove burner gets hot because it is touching the pot (conduction). As it heats, the water becomes less dense because its higher-energy particles spread apart. The warmer water rises through the denser, cooler water above it. At the surface, the warm water begins to cool. The particles move closer together, making the water denser. The cooler water then sinks back to the bottom. It is heated again, and the cycle begins again. This circular motion of liquids or gases due to density differences that result from temperature differences is called a *convection current.*

thermal conductor a material through which energy can be transferred as heat

thermal insulator a material that reduces or prevents the transfer of heat

convection the transfer of thermal energy by the circulation or movement of a liquid or gas

Figure 5 *The repeated rising and sinking of water during boiling are due to convection.*

Radiation

radiation the transfer of energy as electromagnetic waves

A third way thermal energy is transferred is **radiation,** the transfer of energy by electromagnetic waves, such as visible light and infrared waves. Unlike conduction and convection, radiation can involve either an energy transfer between particles of matter or an energy transfer across empty space.

All objects, including the heater in **Figure 6,** radiate electromagnetic waves. The sun emits visible light, which you can see, and waves of other frequencies, such as infrared and ultraviolet waves, which you cannot see. When your body absorbs infrared waves, you feel warmer.

Radiation and the Greenhouse Effect

Earth's atmosphere acts like the windows of a greenhouse. It allows the sun's visible light to pass through it. A greenhouse also traps heat energy, keeping the inside warm. The atmosphere traps some energy, too. This process, called the *greenhouse effect,* is illustrated in **Figure 7.** If our atmosphere did not trap the sun's energy in this way, most of the sun's energy that reached Earth would be radiated immediately back into space. Earth would be a cold, lifeless planet.

The atmosphere traps the sun's energy because of *greenhouse gases,* such as water vapor, carbon dioxide, and methane, which trap energy especially well. Some scientists are concerned that high levels of greenhouse gases in the atmosphere may trap too much energy and make Earth too warm.

Figure 6 *The coils of this portable heater warm a room partly by radiating visible light and infrared waves.*

✓ **Reading Check** What is the greenhouse effect?

Figure 7 **The Greenhouse Effect**

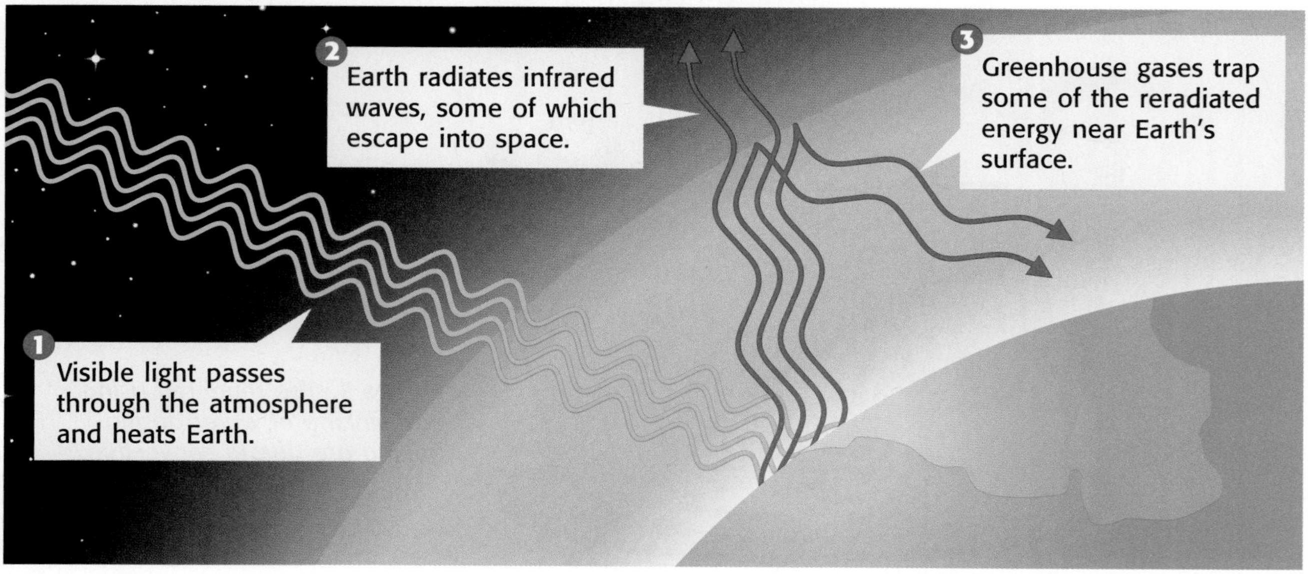

2 Earth radiates infrared waves, some of which escape into space.

3 Greenhouse gases trap some of the reradiated energy near Earth's surface.

1 Visible light passes through the atmosphere and heats Earth.

Heat and Temperature Change

Have you ever fastened your seat belt on a hot summer day? If so, you may have noticed that the metal buckle felt hotter than the cloth belt did. Why?

Thermal Conductivity

Different substances have different thermal conductivities. *Thermal conductivity* is the rate at which a substance conducts thermal energy. The metal buckle of a seat belt, such as the one shown in **Figure 8,** has a higher thermal conductivity than the cloth belt has. Because of its higher thermal conductivity, the metal transfers energy more rapidly to your hand when you touch it than the cloth does. So, even if the cloth and metal are at the same temperature, the metal feels hotter.

Figure 8 *The cloth part of a seat belt does not feel as hot as the metal part.*

Specific Heat

Another difference between the metal and the cloth is how easily each changes temperature when it absorbs or loses energy. When equal amounts of energy are transferred to or from equal masses of different substances, the change in temperature for each substance will differ. **Specific heat** is the amount of energy needed to change the temperature of 1 kg of a substance by 1°C.

Look at **Table 2.** The specific heat of the cloth of a seat belt is more than twice that of the metal buckle. So, for equal masses of metal and cloth, the same thermal energy will increase the temperature of the metal twice as much as the cloth. The higher the specific heat of something is, the more energy it takes to increase its temperature. **Table 2** shows that most metals have very low specific heats. On the other hand, the specific heat of water is very high. This is why swimming-pool water usually feels cool, even on a hot day. The same energy heats up the air more than it heats up the water.

specific heat the quantity of heat required to raise a unit mass of homogeneous material 1 K or 1°C in a specified way given constant pressure and volume

CONNECTION TO Social Studies

WRITING SKILL **Living near Coastlines** Water has a higher specific heat than land does. Because of water's high specific heat, the ocean has a moderating effect on the weather of coastal areas. The mild weather of coastal areas is one reason they tend to be heavily populated. Find out what the weather is like in various coastal areas in the world. Research the various reasons why coastal areas tend to be heavily populated, and write a brief report in your **science journal.**

Table 2 Specific Heat of Some Common Substances			
Substance	**Specific heat (J/kg•°C)**	**Substance**	**Specific heat (J/kg•°C)**
Lead	128	Glass	837
Gold	129	Aluminum	899
Copper	387	Cloth of seat belt	1,340
Iron	448	Ice	2,090
Metal of seat belt	500	Water	4,184

Mass of water = 0.2 kg
Temperature (before) = 25°C
Temperature (after) = 80°C
Specific heat of
    water = 4,184 J/kg•°C

Figure 9 *Information used to calculate heat, the amount of energy transferred to the water, is shown above.*

Heat, Temperature, and Amount

Unlike temperature, energy transferred between objects can not be measured directly. Instead, it must be calculated. When calculating energy transferred between objects, you can use the definition of *heat* as the amount of energy that is transferred between two objects that are at different temperatures. Heat can then be expressed in joules (J).

How much energy is needed to heat a cup of water to make tea? To answer this question, you have to consider the water's mass, its change in temperature, and its specific heat. These are all listed in **Figure 9.** In general, if you know an object's mass, its change in temperature, and its specific heat, you can use the equation below to calculate heat.

$$heat\ (J) = specific\ heat\ (J/kg{\bullet}°C) \times mass\ (kg)$$
$$\times change\ in\ temperature\ (°C)$$

Calculating Heat

Using the equation above, you can calculate the heat transferred to the water. Because the water's temperature increases, the value of heat is positive. You can also use this equation to calculate the heat transferred from an object when it cools down. The value for heat would then be negative because the temperature decreases.

✓ Reading Check What are the three pieces of information needed to calculate heat?

Calculating Heat Calculate the heat transferred to a mass of 0.2 kg of water to change the temperature of the water from 25°C to 80°C. (The specific heat of water is 4,184 J/kg•°C.)

Step 1: Write the equation for calculating heat.

$$heat = specific\ heat \times mass \times change\ in\ temperature$$

Step 2: Replace the specific heat, mass, and temperature change with the values given in the problem, and solve.

$$heat = 4{,}184\ J/kg{\bullet}°C \times 0.2\ kg \times (80°C - 25°C)$$
$$heat = 46{,}024\ J$$

Now It's Your Turn

1. Imagine that you heat 2.0 kg of water to make pasta. The temperature of the water before you heat it is 40°C, and the temperature after is 100°C. How much heat was transferred to the water?

Summary

- Heat is energy transferred between objects that are at different temperatures.
- Thermal energy is the total kinetic energy of the particles that make up a substance.
- Thermal energy will always be transferred from higher to lower temperature.
- Transfer of thermal energy ends when two objects that are in contact are at the same temperature.
- Conduction, convection, and radiation are three ways thermal energy is transferred.

- Specific heat is the amount of energy needed to change the temperature of 1 kg of a substance by 1°C.
- Energy transferred by heat cannot be measured directly. It must be calculated using specific heat, mass, and change in temperature.
- Energy transferred by heat is expressed in joules (J) and is calculated as follows: *heat* (J) = *specific heat* (J/kg•°C) × *mass* (kg) × *change in temperature* (°C).

Using Key Terms

For each pair of terms, explain how the meanings of the terms differ.

1. *thermal conductor* and *thermal insulator*
2. *convection* and *radiation*

Understanding Key Ideas

3. Two objects at different temperatures are in contact. Which of the following happens to their thermal energy?
   a. Their thermal energies remain the same.
   b. Thermal energy passes from the cooler object to the warmer object.
   c. Thermal energy passes from the warmer object to the cooler object.
   d. Thermal energy passes back and forth equally between the two objects.
4. What is heat?

Math Skills

5. The specific heat of lead is 128 J/kg•°C. How much heat is needed to raise the temperature of a 0.015 kg sample of lead by 10°C?

Critical Thinking

6. **Making Inferences** Two objects have the same total thermal energy. They are different sizes. Are they at the same temperature? Explain.

7. **Applying Concepts** Why do many metal cooking utensils have wooden handles?

Interpreting Graphics

8. Look at the photo below. It shows examples of heat transfer by conduction, convection, and radiation. Indicate which type of heat transfer is happening next to each letter.

For a variety of links related to this chapter, go to www.scilinks.org

Topic: What Is Heat?
SciLinks code: HSM1661

Matter and Heat

Have you ever eaten a frozen juice bar outside on a hot summer day? It's pretty hard to finish the entire thing before it starts to drip and make a big mess!

The juice bar melts because the sun radiates energy to the frozen juice bar. The energy absorbed by the juice bar increases the kinetic energy of the molecules in the juice bar, which starts to change to a liquid.

States of Matter

The matter that makes up a frozen juice bar has the same identity whether the juice bar is frozen or has melted. The matter is just in a different form, or state. The **states of matter** are the physical forms in which a substance can exist. Matter consists of particles that can move around at different speeds. The state a substance is in depends on the speed of its particles, the attraction between them, and the pressure around them. Three familiar states of matter are solid, liquid, and gas, shown in **Figure 1.**

Thermal energy is the total energy of all the particles that make up a substance. Suppose that you have equal masses of a substance in its three states, each at a different temperature. The substance will have the most thermal energy as a gas and the least thermal energy as a solid. The reason is that the particles of a gas move around fastest.

What You Will Learn

- Identify three states of matter.
- Explain how heat affects matter during a change of state.
- Describe how heat affects matter during a chemical change.
- Explain what a *calorimeter* is used for.

Vocabulary

states of matter
change of state

READING STRATEGY

Brainstorming The key idea of this section is the relationship between matter and heat. Brainstorm words and phrases related to matter and heat.

Figure 1 Particles of a Solid, a Liquid, and a Gas

Particles of a gas, such as carbon dioxide, move fast enough to overcome nearly all of the attraction between them. The particles move independently of one another.

Particles of a liquid move fast enough to overcome some of the attraction between them. The particles are able to slide past one another.

Particles of a solid, such as ice, do not move fast enough to overcome the strong attraction between them, so they are held tightly together. The particles vibrate in place.

Changes of State

When you melt cheese to make a cheese dip, such as that shown in **Figure 2,** the cheese changes from a solid to a thick, gooey liquid. A **change of state** is a change of a substance from one state of matter to another. A change of state is a *physical change* that affects one or more physical properties of a substance without changing the identity of the substance. Changes of state include *freezing* (liquid to solid), *melting* (solid to liquid), *boiling* (liquid to gas), and *condensing* (gas to liquid).

Energy and Changes of State

Suppose that you put an ice cube in a pan and set the pan on a stove burner. Soon, the ice will turn to water and then to steam. If you made a graph of the temperature of the ice versus the energy involved during this process, it would look something like the graph in **Figure 3.**

As the ice is heated, its temperature increases from –25°C to 0°C. As the ice melts, its temperature remains at 0°C even as more energy is added. This added energy changes the arrangement of the molecules in the ice. The temperature of the ice remains the same until all of the ice has become liquid water. At that point, the water's temperature starts to increase from 0°C to 100°C. At 100°C, the water begins to change to steam. Even as more energy is added, the water's temperature stays at 100°C as long as there is liquid water present. When all of the water has become steam, the temperature again increases.

Figure 2 *When you melt cheese, you change the state of the cheese but not its identity.*

states of matter the physical forms of matter, which include solid, liquid, and gas

change of state the change of a substance from one physical state to another

✓ **Reading Check** What happens to the temperature of a substance while it is undergoing a change of state? (*See the Appendix for answers to Reading Checks.*)

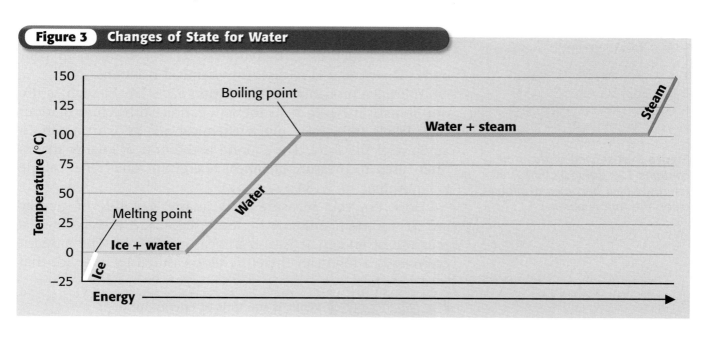

Figure 3 Changes of State for Water

Boiling point

Water + steam

Steam

Temperature (°C)

Water

Melting point

Ice + water

Ice

Energy

Figure 4 *In a natural-gas fireplace, the methane in natural gas and the oxygen in air change into carbon dioxide and water. As a result of the change, energy is given off, making a room feel warmer.*

Figure 5 *A serving of this fruit contains 120 Cal (502,080 J) of energy, which becomes available when the fruit is eaten.*

Heat and Chemical Changes

Heat is involved not only in changes of state, which are physical changes, but also in *chemical changes*—changes that occur when one or more substances are changed into entirely new substances that have different properties. During a chemical change, new substances are formed.

For a new substance to form, old bonds between particles must be broken, and new bonds must be formed. The breaking and creating of bonds between particles involves energy. Sometimes, a chemical change requires that thermal energy be put into substances for a reaction to occur. Other times, a chemical change, such as the one shown in **Figure 4,** will result in a release of energy.

Food and Chemical Energy

Food contains substances from which your body gets energy. Energy that your body can use is released when chemical compounds such as carbohydrates are broken down in your body. The energy is released in chemical reactions.

You have probably seen Nutrition Facts labels, such as the one shown in **Figure 5** on the left. Among other information, such labels show how much chemical energy is in a certain amount of the food. The Calorie is the unit of energy that is often used to measure chemical energy in food. One Calorie is equivalent to 4,184 J.

How do you measure how many Calories of energy are in a certain amount of food? Because the Calorie is a measure of energy, it is also a measure of heat. The amount of energy in food can therefore be measured by a device that measures heat.

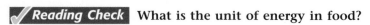 **Reading Check** What is the unit of energy in food?

Calorimeters

A *calorimeter* (KAL uh RIM uht uhr) is a device that measures heat. When one object transfers thermal energy to another object, the energy lost by one object is gained by the other object. This is the key to how a calorimeter works. Inside a calorimeter, shown in **Figure 6,** thermal energy is transferred from a known mass of a test substance to a known mass of another substance, usually water.

The energy of food, in Calories, is found in this way. In a special kind of calorimeter called a *bomb calorimeter,* a food sample is burned. The energy that is released is transferred to the water. By measuring the temperature change of the water and using water's specific heat, you can determine the exact amount of energy transferred by the food sample to the water. This amount of energy (heat) equals the energy content of the food.

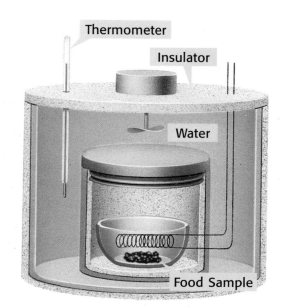

Figure 6 *A bomb calorimeter can measure energy content in food by measuring how much heat is given off by a food sample when it is burned.*

SECTION Review

Summary

- States of matter include solid, liquid, and gas.
- Thermal energy transferred during a change of state does not change a substance's temperature. Rather, it causes a substance's particles to be rearranged.
- Chemical changes can cause thermal energy to be released or absorbed.
- A calorimeter can measure energy changes by measuring heat.

Using Key Terms

1. Use each of the following terms in a separate sentence: *states of matter* and *change of state.*

Understanding Key Ideas

2. What determines a substance's state?
   a. the size of its particles
   b. the amount of the substance
   c. the speed of its particles and the attraction between them
   d. the chemical energy that the substance has

3. During a change of state, why doesn't the temperature of the substance change?

Math Skills

4. When burned in a calorimeter, a sample of popcorn released 627,600 J. How much energy, in Calories, did the popcorn have?

Critical Thinking

5. **Applying Concepts** Many cold packs used for sports injuries are activated by bending the package, causing the substances inside to chemically react. How is heat involved in this process?

6. **Analyzing Processes** When water evaporates (changes from a liquid to a gas), the air near the water's surface becomes cooler. Explain why.

SCLINKS®

NSTA

Developed and maintained by the National Science Teachers Association

For a variety of links related to this chapter, go to www.scilinks.org

Topic: Heat Energy
SciLinks code: HSM0727

Heat Technology

You probably wouldn't be surprised to learn that the heater in your home is an example of heat technology. But did you know that automobiles, refrigerators, and air conditioners are also examples of heat technology?

It's true! You can travel long distances, you can keep your food cold, and you can feel comfortable indoors during the summer—all because of heat technology.

Heating Systems

Many homes and buildings have a central heating system that controls the temperature in every room. On the next few pages, you will see some different central heating systems.

Hot-Water Heating

The high specific heat of water makes it useful for heating systems. A hot-water heating system is shown in **Figure 1.** A hot-water heater raises the temperature of water, which is pumped through pipes that lead to radiators in each room. The radiators then heat the colder air surrounding them. The water returns to the hot-water heater to be heated again.

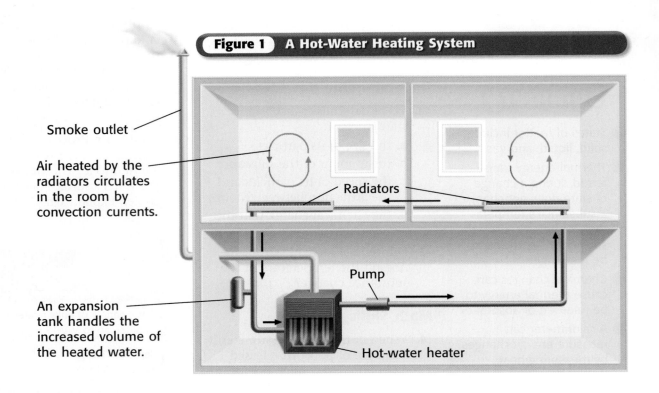

Figure 1 A Hot-Water Heating System

Smoke outlet

Air heated by the radiators circulates in the room by convection currents.

Radiators

Pump

An expansion tank handles the increased volume of the heated water.

Hot-water heater

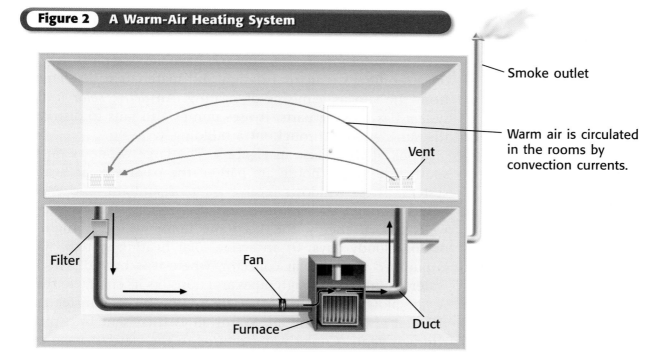

Figure 2 A Warm-Air Heating System

Smoke outlet

Warm air is circulated in the rooms by convection currents.

Vent

Filter

Fan

Furnace

Duct

Warm-Air Heating

Air cannot hold as much thermal energy as water can. But warm-air heating systems are used in many homes and offices in the United States. In a warm-air heating system, shown in **Figure 2,** air is heated by burning fuel (usually natural gas) in a furnace. The warm air travels through ducts to different rooms. The warm air heats air in the rooms. Cooler air sinks below the warm air and enters a vent near the floor. Then, a fan forces the cooler air into the furnace. The air is heated and returned to the ducts. An air filter cleans the air as it moves through the system.

insulation a substance that reduces the transfer of electricity, heat, or sound

Heating and Insulation

Heat may quickly escape out of a house during cold weather, and during hot weather a house may heat up. To keep the house comfortable, a heating system must run much of the time during the winter. Air conditioners often must run most of the time in the summer to keep a house cool. This can be wasteful. Insulation can help reduce the energy needed to heat and cool buildings. Fiberglass insulation is shown in **Figure 3.** **Insulation** is a material that reduces the transfer of thermal energy. When insulation is used in walls, ceilings, and floors, less heat passes into or out of the building. Insulation helps a house stay warm in the winter and cool in the summer.

Figure 3 Millions of tiny air pockets in this insulation help prevent thermal energy from flowing into or out of a building.

Reading Check How does insulation help reduce energy costs? (*See the Appendix for answers to Reading Checks.*)

Figure 4 *Passive and active solar heating systems work together to use the sun's energy to heat an entire house.*

Solar Heating

The sun gives off a huge amount of energy. Solar heating systems use this energy to heat houses and buildings. A *passive solar heating system* does not have moving parts. It relies on a building's structural design and materials to use energy from the sun as a means of heating. An *active solar heating system* has moving parts. It uses pumps and fans to distribute the sun's energy throughout a building.

Look at the house in **Figure 4.** The large windows on the south side of the house are part of the passive solar heating system. These windows receive a lot of sunlight, and energy enters through the windows into the rooms. Thick concrete walls absorb energy and keep the house warm at night or during cloudy days. In an active solar heating system, water is pumped to the solar collector, where it is heated. The hot water is pumped through pipes and transfers its energy to them. A fan blowing over the pipes helps the pipes transfer their thermal energy to the air. Warm air is then sent into rooms through vents. Cooler water returns to the water storage tank to be pumped back through the solar collector.

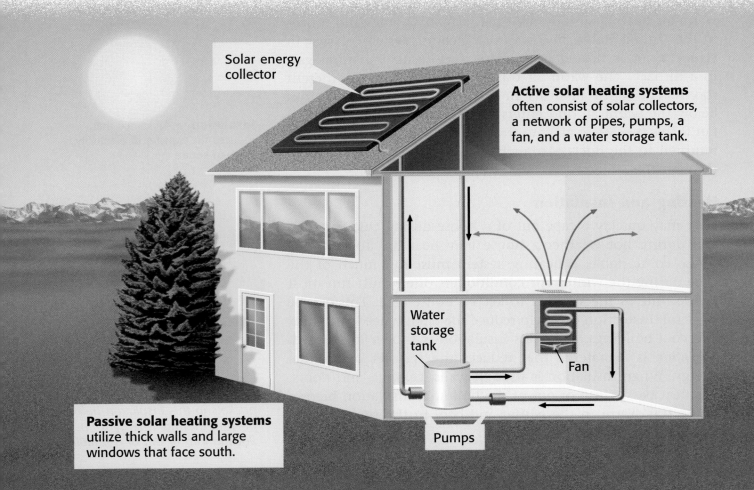

Solar energy collector

Active solar heating systems often consist of solar collectors, a network of pipes, pumps, a fan, and a water storage tank.

Water storage tank

Fan

Pumps

Passive solar heating systems utilize thick walls and large windows that face south.

Heat Engines

Did you know that automobiles work because of heat? A car has a **heat engine,** a machine that uses heat to do work. In a heat engine, fuel combines with oxygen in a chemical change that releases thermal energy. Heat engines burn fuel through this process, called *combustion*. Heat engines that burn fuel outside the engine are called *external combustion engines*. Heat engines that burn fuel inside the engine are called *internal combustion engines*. In both types of engines, fuel is burned to release thermal energy that can be used to do work.

✓ **Reading Check** What kind of energy do combustion engines use?

External Combustion Engines

A simple steam engine, shown in **Figure 5,** is an example of an external combustion engine. Coal is burned to heat water in a boiler and change the water to steam. The steam expands, which pushes a piston. The piston can be attached to other parts of the machine that do work.

Modern steam engines, such as those used to generate electrical energy at a power plant, drive turbines instead of pistons. In the case of generators that use steam to do work, thermal energy is converted into electrical energy.

heat engine a machine that transforms heat into mechanical energy, or work

CONNECTION TO Oceanography

Energy from the Ocean
Ocean engineers are developing a new technology called *Ocean Thermal Energy Conversion,* or OTEC. OTEC uses temperature differences between surface water and deep water in the ocean to generate electrical energy. Research more information about OTEC, and make a model or a poster demonstrating how it works.

ACTiViTY

Figure 5 An External Combustion Engine

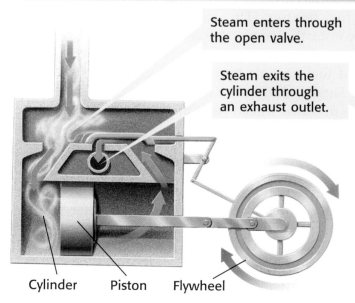

Steam enters through the open valve.

Steam exits the cylinder through an exhaust outlet.

Cylinder   Piston   Flywheel

❶ The expanding steam enters the cylinder from one side. The steam does work on the piston, forcing the piston to move.

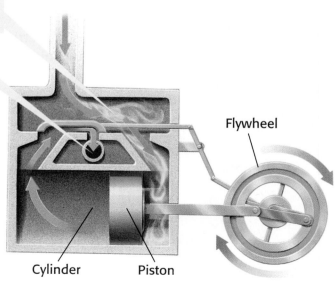

Flywheel

Cylinder   Piston

❷ As the piston moves to the other side, a second valve opens, and steam enters. The steam does work on the piston and moves it back. The motion of the piston turns a flywheel.

Wire to spark plug

Cylinder

Piston

Crankshaft

Figure 6 *The continuous cycling of the four strokes in the cylinders converts thermal energy into the kinetic energy needed to make a car move.*

Figure 7 *This air-conditioning unit keeps a building cool by moving thermal energy from inside the building to the outside.*

Internal Combustion Engines

The six-cylinder car engine shown in **Figure 6** is an internal combustion engine. Fuel is burned inside the engine. The fuel used is gasoline, which is burned inside the cylinders. The cylinders go through a series of steps in burning the fuel.

First, a mixture of gasoline and air enters each cylinder as the piston moves down. This step is called the *intake stroke.* Next, the crankshaft turns and pushes the piston up, compressing the fuel mixture. This step is called the *compression stroke.* Next comes the *power stroke,* in which the spark plug uses electrical energy to ignite the compressed fuel mixture. As the mixture of fuel and air burns, it expands and forces the piston down. Finally, during the *exhaust stroke,* the crankshaft turns, and the piston is forced back up, pushing exhaust gases out of the cylinder.

Cooling Systems

When the summer gets hot, an air-conditioned room can feel very refreshing. Cooling systems are used to transfer thermal energy out of a particular area so that it feels cooler. An air conditioner, shown in **Figure 7,** is a cooling system that transfers thermal energy from a warm area inside a building or car to an area outside. Thermal energy naturally tends to go from areas of higher temperature to areas of lower temperature. So, to transfer thermal energy outside where it is warmer, the air-conditioning system must do work. It's like walking uphill: if you are going against gravity, you must do work.

Figure 8 How a Refrigerator Works

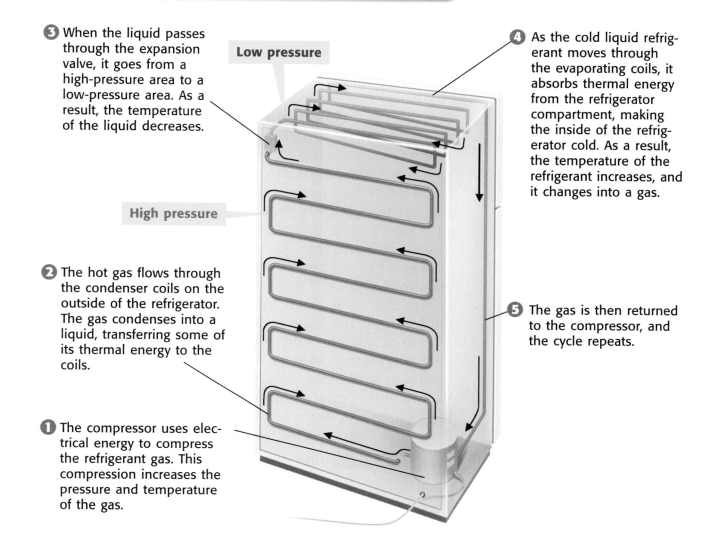

❸ When the liquid passes through the expansion valve, it goes from a high-pressure area to a low-pressure area. As a result, the temperature of the liquid decreases.

Low pressure

High pressure

❷ The hot gas flows through the condenser coils on the outside of the refrigerator. The gas condenses into a liquid, transferring some of its thermal energy to the coils.

❶ The compressor uses electrical energy to compress the refrigerant gas. This compression increases the pressure and temperature of the gas.

❹ As the cold liquid refrigerant moves through the evaporating coils, it absorbs thermal energy from the refrigerator compartment, making the inside of the refrigerator cold. As a result, the temperature of the refrigerant increases, and it changes into a gas.

❺ The gas is then returned to the compressor, and the cycle repeats.

Cooling and Energy

Most cooling systems require electrical energy to do the work of cooling. The electrical energy is used by a device called a compressor. The *compressor* does the work of compressing the refrigerant. The *refrigerant* is a gas that has a boiling point below room temperature, which allows it to condense easily.

To keep many foods fresh, you store them in a refrigerator. A refrigerator is another example of a cooling system. **Figure 8** shows how a refrigerator continuously transfers thermal energy from inside the refrigerator to the condenser coils on the outside of the refrigerator. That's why the area near the back of a refrigerator feels warm.

✓ Reading Check How does the inside of a refrigerator stay at a temperature that is cooler than the temperature outside the refrigerator?

Heat Technology and Thermal Pollution

Heating systems, car engines, and cooling systems all transfer thermal energy to the environment. Unfortunately, too much thermal energy released to the environment can have a negative effect.

Thermal Pollution

One of the negative effects of excess thermal energy is **thermal pollution,** the excessive heating of a body of water. Thermal pollution can happen near large power plants, which are often located near a body of water. Many electric-power plants burn fuel to release thermal energy that is used to generate electrical energy. Unfortunately, it is not possible for all of that thermal energy to do work. So, some thermal energy waste results and must be released to the environment.

Figure 9 shows how cool water is circulated through a power plant to absorb waste thermal energy. As the cool water absorbs energy, the water heats up. Sometimes the heated water is dumped into the same body of water that it came from. As a result, the temperature of the water can increase. Increased water temperature in lakes and streams can harm animals that live there. In extreme cases, the increase in temperature downstream from a power plant can adversely affect the ecosystem of the river or lake. Some power plants reduce thermal pollution by cooling the water before it is returned to the river.

✔ Reading Check Give an example of thermal pollution.

thermal pollution a temperature increase in a body of water that is caused by human activity and that has a harmful effect on water quality and on the ability of that body of water to support life

Figure 9 *Thermal pollution from power plants can result if the plant raises the water temperature of lakes and streams.*

Cool water

Warm water

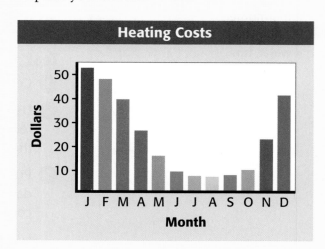

Summary

- Central heating systems include hot-water heating systems and warm-air heating systems.
- Solar heating systems can be passive or active. In passive solar heating, a building takes advantage of the sun's energy without the use of moving parts. Active solar heating uses moving parts to aid the flow of solar energy throughout a building.
- Heat engines use heat to do work.

- The two kinds of heat engines are external combustion engines, which burn fuel outside the engine, and internal combustion engines, which burn fuel inside the engine.
- A cooling system transfers thermal energy from cooler temperatures to warmer temperatures by doing work.
- Transferring excess thermal energy to lakes and rivers can result in thermal pollution.

Using Key Terms

1. Use each of the following terms in a separate sentence: *insulation, heat engine,* and *thermal pollution.*

Understanding Key Ideas

2. Which of the following describes how cooling systems transfer thermal energy?
   a. Thermal energy naturally flows from cooler areas to warmer areas.
   b. Thermal energy naturally flows from warmer areas to cooler areas.
   c. Work is done to transfer thermal energy from warmer areas to cooler areas.
   d. Work is done to transfer thermal energy from cooler areas to warmer areas.

3. Compare a hot-water heating system with a warm-air heating system.

4. What is the difference between an external combustion engine and an internal combustion engine?

Critical Thinking

5. **Identifying Relationships** How are changes of state important in how a refrigerator works?

6. **Expressing Opinions** Compare the advantages and disadvantages of solar heating systems. What do you think their overall benefits are, compared with those of other heating systems?

Interpreting Graphics

7. Look at the graph below. It shows the cost of heating a certain house month by month over the course of a year. During which times of the year is the most energy used for heating? Explain your answer.

Heating Costs

[Bar graph with vertical axis labeled "Dollars" showing values 10, 20, 30, 40, 50; horizontal axis labeled "Month" showing J F M A M J J A S O N D]

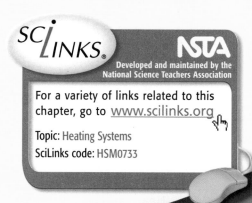

Skills Practice Lab

OBJECTIVES

Measure the temperature change when hot and cold objects come into contact.

Compare materials for their ability to hold thermal energy.

MATERIALS

- balance, metric
- cups, plastic-foam, 9 oz (2)
- cylinder, graduated, 100 mL
- nails (10 to 12)
- string, 30 cm length
- paper towels
- rubber band
- thermometer
- water, cold
- water, hot

SAFETY

Feel the Heat

Heat is the energy transferred between objects at different temperatures. Energy moves from objects at higher temperatures to objects at lower temperatures. If two objects are left in contact for a while, the warmer object will cool down and the cooler object will warm up until they eventually reach the same temperature. In this activity, you will combine equal masses of water and nails at different temperatures to determine which has a greater effect on the final temperature.

Ask a Question

1. When you combine substances at two different temperatures, will the final temperature be closer to the initial temperature of the warmer substance or of the colder substance, or halfway in between?

Form a Hypothesis

2. Write a prediction that answers the question in item 1.

Test the Hypothesis

3. Copy the table below onto a separate sheet of paper.

4. Use the rubber band to bundle the nails together. Find and record the mass of the bundle. Tie a length of string around the bundle, leaving one end of the string 15 cm long.

5. Put the bundle of nails into one of the cups, letting the string dangle outside the cup. Fill the cup with enough hot water to cover the nails, and set it aside for at least 5 min.

		Data Collection Table			
Trial	Mass of nails (g)	Volume of water that equals mass of nails (mL)	Initial temp. of water and nails (°C)	Initial temp. of water to which nails will be transferred (°C)	Final temp. of water and nails combined (°C)
1					
2					

DO NOT WRITE IN BOOK

6 Use the graduated cylinder to measure enough cold water to exactly equal the mass of the nails (1 mL of water = 1 g). Record this volume in the table.

7 Measure and record the temperature of the hot water with the nails and the temperature of the cold water.

8 Use the string to transfer the bundle of nails to the cup of cold water. Use the thermometer to monitor the temperature of the water-nail mixture. When the temperature stops changing, record this final temperature in the table.

9 Empty the cups, and dry the nails.

10 For Trial 2, repeat steps 4 through 9, but switch the hot and cold water. Record all of your measurements.

Analyze the Results

1 **Analyzing Results** In Trial 1, you used equal masses of cold water and nails. Did the final temperature support your initial prediction? Explain.

2 **Analyzing Results** In Trial 2, you used equal masses of hot water and nails. Did the final temperature support your initial prediction? Explain.

3 **Explaining Events** In Trial 1, which material—the water or the nails—changed temperature the most after you transferred the nails? What about in Trial 2? Explain your answers.

Draw Conclusions

4 **Drawing Conclusions** The cold water in Trial 1 gained energy. Where did the energy come from?

5 **Evaluating Results** How does the energy gained by the nails in Trial 2 compare with the energy lost by the hot water in Trial 2? Explain.

6 **Applying Conclusions** Which material seems to be able to hold energy better? Explain your answer.

7 **Interpreting Information** Specific heat is a property of matter that indicates how much energy is required to change the temperature of 1 kg of a material by 1°C. Which material in this activity has a higher specific heat (changes temperature less for the same amount of energy)?

8 **Making Predictions** Would it be better to have pots and pans made from a material with a high specific heat or a low specific heat? Explain your answer.

Communicating Your Data

Share your results with your classmates. Discuss how you would change your prediction to include your knowledge of specific heat.

Chapter Review

For each pair of terms, explain how the meanings of the terms differ.

1 *temperature* and *thermal energy*

2 *conduction* and *heat*

3 *conductor* and *insulator*

4 *states of matter* and *change of state*

5 *heat engine* and *thermal pollution*

UNDERSTANDING KEY IDEAS

Multiple Choice

6 Which of the following temperatures is the lowest?

  a. 100°C

  b. 100°F

  c. 100 K

  d. They are all the same.

7 Which of the following materials would NOT be a good insulator?

  a. wood

  b. cloth

  c. metal

  d. rubber

8 In an air conditioner, thermal energy is

  a. transferred from areas of higher temperatures to areas of lower temperatures.

  b. transferred from areas of lower temperatures to areas of higher temperatures.

  c. used to do work.

  d. transferred into the building.

9 The units of energy that you read on a food label are

  a. Newtons.

  b. Calories.

  c. Joules.

  d. Both (b) and (c)

10 Compared wih the Pacific Ocean, a cup of hot chocolate has

  a. more thermal energy and a higher temperature.

  b. less thermal energy and a higher temperature.

  c. more thermal energy and a lower temperature.

  d. less thermal energy and a lower temperature.

Short Answer

11 How does temperature relate to kinetic energy?

12 What are the differences between conduction, convection, and radiation?

13 Explain how heat affects matter during a change of state.

Math Skills

14 The weather forecast calls for a temperature of 84°F. What is the corresponding temperature in degrees Celsius? in kelvins?

15 Suppose 1.3 kg of water is heated from 20°C to 100°C. How much energy was transferred to the water? (Water's specific heat is 4,184 J/kg•°C.)

16 Concept Mapping Create a concept map using the following terms: *thermal energy, temperature, radiation, heat, conduction,* and *convection.*

17 Applying Concepts The metal lid is stuck on a glass jar of jelly. Explain why running hot water over the lid will help you get the lid off.

18 Applying Concepts How does a down jacket keep you warm? (Hint: Think about what insulation does.)

19 Predicting Consequences Would opening the refrigerator cool a room in a house? Explain your answer.

20 Evaluating Assumptions Someone claims that a large bowl of soup has more thermal energy than a small bowl of soup. Is this always true? Explain.

21 Analyzing Processes In a hot-air balloon, air is heated by a flame. Explain how this enables the balloon to float in the air.

22 Analyzing Processes What is different about the two kinds of metal on the bimetallic strip of a thermostat coil?

23 Making Comparisons How is radiation different from both conduction and convection?

INTERPRETING GRAPHICS

Examine the graph below, and then answer the questions that follow.

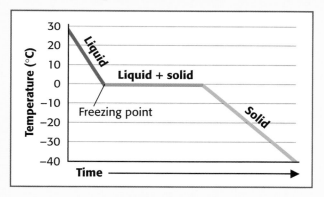

24 What physical change does this graph illustrate?

25 What is the freezing point of this liquid?

26 What is happening at the point where the line is horizontal?

Standardized Test Preparation

Multiple Choice

1. **Which of the following describes a chemical change that releases thermal energy?**

   A. Ice cream melts in an ice cream cone.

   B. Water freezes on a sidewalk in winter.

   C. A boy eats a tuna salad sandwich.

   D. A plant performs photosynthesis.

2. **How does thermal energy flow when a student holds a piece of ice in her hand?**

   A. Thermal energy flows from her hand to the ice cube.

   B. Thermal energy flows back and forth between her hand and the ice cube.

   C. Thermal energy flows from the ice cube to her hand.

   D. Thermal energy does not flow between her hand and the ice cube.

3. **Which of the following sentences best describes the process that occurs when liquid water becomes ice?**

   A. Energy is added to the water, so its molecules move apart.

   B. Energy is removed from the water, so its molecules lock in place.

   C. Energy is added to the water, so its molecules move more quickly.

   D. Energy is removed from the water, so its molecules move apart.

Use the figure below to answer question 4.

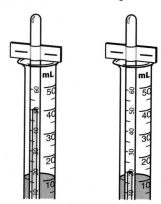

4. **If the water in the graduated cylinders is mixed together, which of the following will most likely be the temperature of the mixture?**

   A. 25°C

   B. 35°C

   C. 50°C

   D. 70°C

5. **On a sunny day, exposed rock on the top of a mountain gradually heats up. What causes the rock to become warm?**

   A. Thermal energy from the ground warms the rock through conduction.

   B. The hot air above the rock warms the rock through convection.

   C. Light waves from the sun transfer energy to the rock through radiation.

   D. Warm winds caused by convection warm the rock through conduction.

Use the table below to answer question 6.

Specific Heat Capacities of Some Common Substances

Substance	Specific heat capacity (J/kg·°C)	Substance	Specific heat capacity (J/kg·°C)
Lead	128	Glass	837
Gold	129	Aluminum	899
Mercury	138	Wood	1760
Silver	234	Steam	2010
Copper	387	Ice	2090
Iron	448	Water	4184

6. If samples, with the same mass, were made of each substance in the table above and placed in boiling water, which sample would reach 100°C most quickly?

   A. aluminum

   B. iron

   C. glass

   D. silver

7. Which statement best explains how a refrigerator works?

   A. Thermal energy is transferred from the room to the refrigerator compartment and refrigerant in the coils. This cools the compartment.

   B. Thermal energy from the liquid refrigerant in the coils is transferred to the refrigerator compartment, cooling the compartment in the process.

   C. Thermal energy from the refrigerator compartment is transferred to the liquid refrigerant in the coils, cooling the compartment in the process.

   D. Thermal energy is transferred between the refrigerator compartment and the refrigerant in the coils. This cools both the compartment and the refrigerant.

8. How are light energy and thermal energy related?

   A. Light energy can transfer thermal energy.

   B. Both types of energy move in waves.

   C. Thermal energy produces light energy in power plants.

   D. Both decrease the kinetic energy of particles.

9. Which of the following is an example of thermal expansion?

   A. water gaining volume as it freezes in an ice cube tray

   B. a jar lid loosening when it is placed under running hot water

   C. ice melting in a glass of tea and becoming the same temperature as the liquid

   D. a cup of tea and a pot of tea cooling to the same temperature

Open Response

10. As Jackie walks on the beach, the hot sand burns her feet. When she lies on a blanket in the sand, Jackie gradually becomes warm. To cool off, Jackie goes swimming in the ocean. Describe how energy and heat are being transferred in this situation.

11. Gordon pours 0.6 kg of 30°C water into a pan sitting on an electric stove. He boils the water to prepare oatmeal. How much heat is transferred to the water to get it to boil? (The specific heat of water is 4,184 J/kg • °C.) Describe how this heat was transferred from the stove to the water. (Heat (J) = specific heat × mass × change in temperature)

Standardized Test Preparation

Science in Action

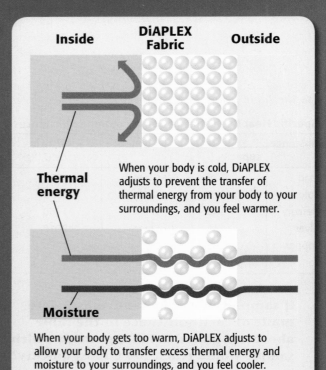

Inside · DiAPLEX Fabric · Outside

Thermal energy

When your body is cold, DiAPLEX adjusts to prevent the transfer of thermal energy from your body to your surroundings, and you feel warmer.

Moisture

When your body gets too warm, DiAPLEX adjusts to allow your body to transfer excess thermal energy and moisture to your surroundings, and you feel cooler.

Scientific Discoveries

The Deep Freeze

All matter is made up of tiny, constantly vibrating particles. Temperature is a measure of the average kinetic energy of particles. The colder a substance gets, the slower its particles move. Scientists are interested in how matter behaves when it is cooled to almost absolute zero, the absence of all thermal energy, which is about −273°C. In one method, scientists aim lasers at gas particles, holding them so still that their temperature is less than one-millionth of a degree from absolute zero. It's like turning on several garden hoses and pointing each from a different angle at a soccer ball so that the ball won't move in any direction.

Math ACTIVITY

Think of the coldest weather you have ever been in. What was the temperature? Convert this temperature to kelvins. Compare this temperature with absolute zero.

Science, Technology, and Society

DiAPLEX®: The Intelligent Fabric

Wouldn't it be great if you had a winter coat that could automatically adjust to keep you cozy regardless of the outside temperature? Well, scientists have developed a new fabric called DiAPLEX that can be used to make such a coat!

Like most winter coats, DiAPLEX is made from nylon. But whereas most nylon fabrics have thousands of tiny pores, or openings, DiAPLEX doesn't have pores. It is a solid film. This film makes DiAPLEX even more waterproof than other nylon fabrics.

Language Arts ACTIVITY

WRITING SKILL Think of two different items of clothing that you wear when the weather is cool or cold. Write a paragraph explaining how you think each of them works in keeping you warm when it is cold outside. Does one keep you warmer than the other? How does it do so?

Michael Reynolds

Earthship Architect Would you want to live in a house without a heating system? You could if you lived in an Earthship! Earthships are the brainchild of Michael Reynolds, an architect in Taos, New Mexico. These houses are designed to make the most of our planet's most abundant source of energy, the sun.

Each Earthship takes full advantage of passive solar heating. For example, large windows face south in order to maximize the amount of energy the house receives from the sun. Each home is partially buried in the ground. The soil helps keep the energy that comes in through the windows inside the house.

To absorb the sun's energy, the outer walls of Earthships are massive and thick. The walls may be made with crushed aluminum cans or stacks of old automobile tires filled with dirt. These materials absorb the sun's energy and naturally heat the house. Because an Earthship maintains a temperature around 15°C (about 60°F), it can keep its occupants comfortable through all but the coldest winter nights.

Social Studies ACTiViTY

Find out more about Michael Reynolds and other architects who have invented unique ways of building houses that are energy-efficient. Present your findings.

go.hrw.com

To learn more about these Science in Action topics, visit go.hrw.com and type in the keyword **HP5HOTF**.

Current Science

Check out Current Science® articles related to this chapter by visiting go.hrw.com. Just type in the keyword **HP5CS10**.

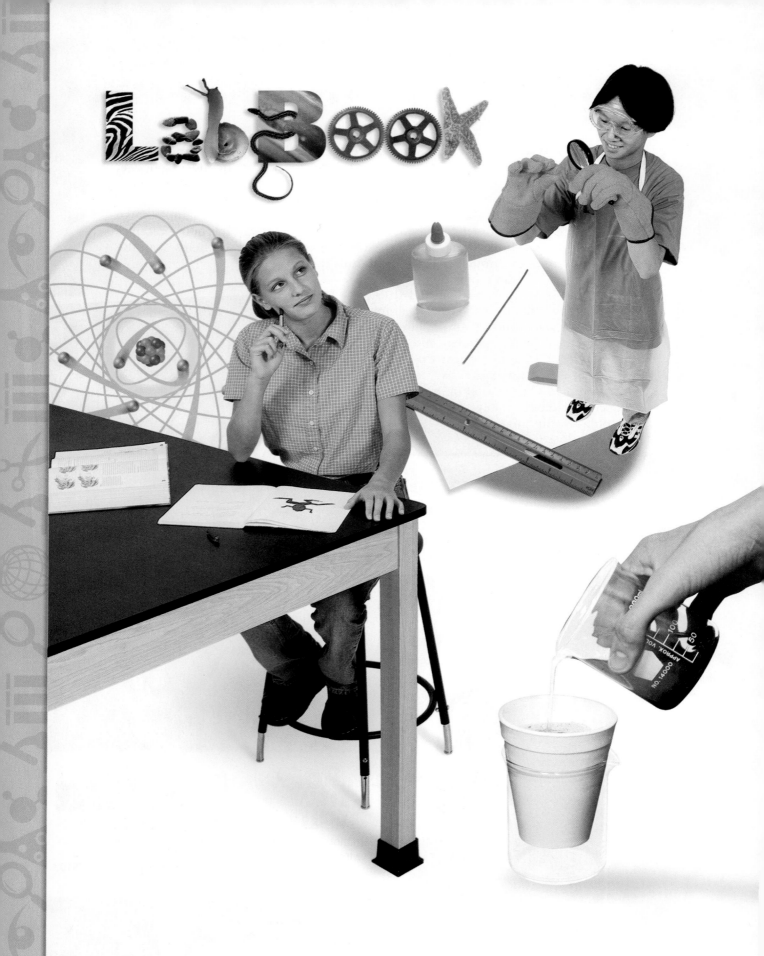

Contents

Skills Practice Lab

Great Ice Escape

Did you know that ice acts as a natural wrecking ball? Even rocks don't stand a chance against the power of ice. When water trapped in rock freezes, a process called *ice wedging* occurs. The water volume increases, and the rock cracks to "get out of the way." This expansion can fragment a rock into several pieces. In this exercise, you will see how this natural wrecker works, and you will try to stop the great ice escape.

Ask a Question

1 If a plastic jar is filled with water, is there a way to prevent the jar from breaking when the water freezes?

Form a Hypothesis

2 Write a hypothesis that is a possible answer to the question above. Explain your reasoning.

Test the Hypothesis

3 Fill three identical jars to overflowing with water, and close two of them securely.

4 Measure the height of the water in the unsealed container. Record the height.

5 Tightly wrap one of the closed jars with tape, string, or other items to reinforce the jar. These items must be removable.

6 Place all three jars in resealable sandwich bags, and leave them in the freezer overnight. (Make sure the open jar does not spill.)

7 Remove the jars from the freezer, and carefully remove the wrapping from the reinforced jar.

8 Did your reinforced jar crack? Why or why not?

9 What does each jar look like? Record your observations.

10 Record the height of the ice in the unsealed jar. How does the new height compare with the height you measured in step 4?

Analyze the Results

1 Do you think it is possible to stop the ice from breaking the sealed jars? Why or why not?

2 How could ice wedging affect soil formation?

MATERIALS

- bags, sandwich resealable (3)
- freezer
- jars, hard plastic with screw-on lids, such as spice containers (3)
- ruler, metric
- tape, strings, rubber bands, and other items to bind or reinforce the jars
- water

SAFETY

Skills Practice Lab

Clean Up Your Act

When you wash dishes, the family car, the bathroom sink, or your clothes, you wash them with water. But have you ever wondered how water gets clean? Two major methods of purifying water are filtration and evaporation. In this activity, you will use both of these methods to test how well they remove pollutants from water. You will test detritus (decaying plant matter), soil, vinegar, and detergent. Your teacher may also ask you to test other pollutants.

Form a Hypothesis

1. Form a hypothesis about whether filtration and evaporation will clean each of the four pollutants from the water and how well they might do it. Then, use the procedures below to test your hypothesis.

Part A: Filtration

Filtration is a common method of removing various pollutants from water. Filtration requires very little energy—gravity pulls water down through the layers of filter material. See how well this energy-efficient method works to clean your sample of polluted water.

Test the Hypothesis

2. Put on your gloves and goggles. Use scissors to carefully cut the bottom out of the empty soda bottle.

3. Using a small nail and hammer, carefully punch four or five small holes through the plastic cap of the bottle. Screw the plastic cap onto the bottle.

4. Turn the bottle upside down, and set its neck in a ring on a ring stand, as shown on the next page. Put a handful of gravel into the inverted bottle. Add a layer of activated charcoal, followed by thick layers of sand and gravel. Place a 400 mL beaker under the neck of the bottle.

5. Fill each of the large beakers with 1,000 mL of clean water. Set one beaker aside to serve as the control. Add three or four spoonfuls of each of the following pollutants to the other beaker: detritus, soil, household vinegar, and dishwashing detergent.

6. Copy the table on the next page, and record your observations for each beaker in the columns labeled "Before cleaning."

7. Observe the color of the water in each beaker.

8. Use a hand lens to examine the water for visible particles.

MATERIALS

Part A
- charcoal, activated
- goggles
- gravel
- hammer and small nail
- sand
- scissors
- soda bottle, plastic, with cap, 2 L

Part B
- bag, plastic sandwich, sealable
- flask, Erlenmeyer
- gloves, heat-resistant
- hot plate
- ice
- stopper, rubber, one-hole, with a glass tube
- tubing, plastic, 1.5 m

Parts A and B
- beaker, 400 mL
- beaker, 1,000 mL (2)
- detergent, dishwashing
- detritus (grass and leaf clippings)
- hand lens
- pH test strips
- ring stand with ring
- soil
- spoons, plastic (2)
- vinegar, household
- water, 2,000 mL

SAFETY

9 Smell the water, and note any unusual odors.

10 Stir the water in each beaker rapidly with a plastic spoon, and check for suds. Use a different spoon for each sample.

11 Use a pH test strip to find the pH of the water.

12 Gently stir the clean water, and then pour half of it through the filtration device.

13 Observe the water in the collection beaker for color, particles, odors, suds, and pH. Be patient. It may take several minutes for the water to travel through the filtration device.

14 Record your observations in the appropriate "After filtration" column in your table.

15 Repeat steps 12–14 using the polluted water.

Analyze the Results

1 How did the color of the polluted water change after the filtration? Did the color of the clean water change?

2 Did the filtration method remove all of the particles from the polluted water? Explain.

3 How much did the pH of the polluted water change? Did the pH of the clean water change? Was the final pH of the polluted water the same as the pH of the clean water before cleaning? Explain.

Results Table						
	Before cleaning (clean water)	Before cleaning (polluted water)	After filtration (clean water)	After filtration (polluted water)	After evaporation (clean water)	After evaporation (polluted water)
Color						
Particles						
Odor			DO NOT WRITE IN BOOK			
Suds						
pH						

Part B: Evaporation

Cleaning water by evaporation is more expensive than cleaning water by filtration. Evaporation requires more energy, which can come from a variety of sources. In this activity, you will use an electric hot plate as the energy source. See how well this method works to clean your sample of polluted water.

Form a Hypothesis

1 Write a hypothesis about which method you think will work better for water purification. Explain your reasoning.

Test the Hypothesis

2 Fill an Erlenmeyer flask with about 250 mL of the clean water, and insert the rubber stopper and glass tube into the flask.

3 Wearing goggles and gloves, connect about 1.5 m of plastic tubing to the glass tube.

4 Set the flask on the hot plate, and run the plastic tubing up and around the ring and down into a clean, empty 400 mL collection beaker.

5 Fill the sandwich bag with ice, seal the bag, and place the bag on the ring stand. Be sure the plastic bag and the tubing touch, as shown below.

6 Bring the water in the flask to a slow boil. As the water vapor passes by the bag of ice, the vapor will condense and drip into the collection beaker.

7 Observe the water in the collection beaker for color, particles, odor, suds, and pH. Record your observations in the "After evaporation" column in your data table.

8 Repeat steps 2–7 using the polluted water.

Analyze the Results

1 How did the color of the polluted water change after evaporation? Did the color of the clean water change after evaporation?

2 Did the evaporation method remove all of the particles from the polluted water? Explain.

3 How much did the pH of the polluted water change? Did the pH of the final clean water change? Was the final pH of the polluted water the same as the pH of the clean water before it was cleaned? Explain.

Draw Conclusions: Parts A and B

4 Which method—filtration or evaporation—removed the most pollutants from the water? Explain your reasoning.

5 Describe any changes that occurred in the clean water during this experiment.

6 What do you think are the advantages and disadvantages of each method?

7 Explain how you think each material (sand, gravel, and charcoal) used in the filtration system helped clean the water.

8 List areas of the country where you think each method of purification would be the most and the least beneficial. Explain your reasoning.

Applying Your Data

Do you think either purification method would remove oil from water? If time permits, repeat your experiment using several spoonfuls of cooking oil as the pollutant.

Filtration is only one step in the purification of water at water treatment plants. Research other methods used to purify public water supplies.

Model-Making Lab

Dune Movement

Wind moves the sand by a process called *saltation*. The sand skips and bounces along the ground in the same direction as the wind is blowing. As sand is blown across a beach, the dunes change. In this activity, you will investigate the effect wind has on a model sand dune.

MATERIALS

- bag, paper, large enough to hold half the box
- box, cardboard, shallow
- hair dryer
- marker
- mask, filter
- ruler, metric
- sand, fine

SAFETY

Procedure

1. Use the marker to draw and label vertical lines 5 cm apart along one side of the box.

2. Fill the box about halfway with sand. Brush the sand into a dune shape about 10 cm from the end of the box.

3. Use the lines you drew along the edge of the box to measure the location of the dune's peak to the nearest centimeter.

4. Slide the box into the paper bag until only about half the box is exposed, as shown below.

5. Put on your safety goggles and filter mask. Hold the hair dryer so that it is level with the peak of the dune and about 10–20 cm from the open end of the box.

6. Turn on the hair dryer at the lowest speed, and direct the air toward the model sand dune for 1 min.

7. Record the new location of the model dune.

8. Repeat steps 5 and 6 three times. After each trial, measure and record the location of the dune's peak.

Analyze the Results

1. How far did the dune move during each trial?

2. How far did the dune move overall?

Draw Conclusions

3. How might the dune's movement be affected if you were to turn the hair dryer to the highest speed?

Applying Your Data

Flatten the sand. Place a barrier, such as a rock, in the sand. Position the hair dryer level with the top of the sand's surface. How does the rock affect the dune's movement?

Skills Practice Lab

Go Fly a Bike!

Your friend Daniel just invented a bicycle that can fly! Trouble is, the bike can fly only when the wind speed is between 3 m/s and 10 m/s. If the wind is not blowing hard enough, the bike won't get enough lift to rise into the air, and if the wind is blowing too hard, the bike is difficult to control. Daniel needs to know if he can fly his bike today. Can you build a device that can estimate how fast the wind is blowing?

MATERIALS

- clay, modeling
- cups, paper, small (5)
- hole punch
- marker, colored
- pencil, sharp, with an eraser
- ruler, metric
- scissors
- stapler, small
- straws, straight plastic (2)
- tape, masking
- thumbtack
- watch (or clock) that indicates seconds

SAFETY

Ask a Question

1 How can I construct a device to measure wind speed?

Form a Hypothesis

2 Write a possible answer for the question above. Explain your reasoning.

Test the Hypothesis

3 Cut off the rolled edges of all five paper cups. They will then be lighter so that they can spin more easily.

4 Measure and place four equally spaced markings 1 cm below the rim of one of the paper cups.

5 Use the hole punch to punch a hole at each mark so that the cup has four equally spaced holes. Use the sharp pencil to carefully punch a hole in the center of the bottom of the cup.

6 Push a straw through two opposite holes in the side of the cup.

7 Repeat step 5 for the other two holes. The straws should form an X.

8 Measure 3 cm from the bottom of the remaining paper cups, and mark each spot with a dot.

9 At each dot, punch a hole in the paper cups with the hole punch.

10 Color the outside of one of the four cups.

11. Slide a cup on one of the straws by pushing the straw through the punched hole. Rotate the cup so that the bottom faces to the right.

12. Fold the end of the straw, and staple it to the inside of the cup directly across from the hole.

13. Repeat steps 11–12 for each of the remaining cups.

14. Push the tack through the intersection of the two straws.

15. Push the eraser end of a pencil through the bottom hole in the center cup. Push the tack as far as it will go into the end of the eraser.

16. Push the sharpened end of the pencil into some modeling clay to form a base. The device will then be able to stand up without being knocked over, as shown at right.

17. Blow into the cups so that they spin. Adjust the tack so that the cups can freely spin without wobbling or falling apart. Congratulations! You have just constructed an anemometer.

18. Find a suitable area outside to place the anemometer vertically on a surface away from objects that would obstruct the wind, such as buildings and trees.

19. Mark the surface at the base of the anemometer with masking tape. Label the tape "starting point."

20. Hold the colored cup over the starting point while your partner holds the watch.

21. Release the colored cup. At the same time, your partner should look at the watch or clock. As the cups spin, count the number of times the colored cup crosses the starting point in 10 s.

Analyze the Results

1. How many times did the colored cup cross the starting point in 10 s?

2. Divide your answer in step 21 by 10 to get the number of revolutions in 1 s.

3. Measure the diameter of your anemometer (the distance between the outside edges of two opposite cups) in centimeters. Multiply this number by 3.14 to get the circumference of the circle made by the cups of your anemometer.

4. Multiply your answer from step 3 by the number of revolutions per second (step 2). Divide that answer by 100 to get wind speed in meters per second.

5. Compare your results with those of your classmates. Did you get the same results? What could account for any slight differences in your results?

Draw Conclusions

6. Could Daniel fly his bicycle today? Why or why not?

Skills Practice Lab

Watching the Weather

Imagine that you own a private consulting firm that helps people plan for big occasions, such as weddings, parties, and celebrity events. One of your duties is making sure the weather doesn't put a damper on your clients' plans. In order to provide the best service possible, you have taken a crash course in reading weather maps. Will the celebrity golf match have to be delayed on account of rain? Will the wedding ceremony have to be moved inside so the blushing bride doesn't get soaked? It is your job to say yea or nay.

MATERIALS

• pencil

Procedure

1. Study the station model and legend shown on the next page. You will use the legend to interpret the weather map on the final page of this activity.

2. Weather data is represented on a weather map by a station model. A station model is a small circle that shows the location of the weather station along with a set of symbols and numbers around the circle that represent the data collected at the weather station. Study the table below.

Weather-Map Symbols					
Weather conditions		**Cloud cover**		**Wind speed (mph)**	
••	Light rain	○	No clouds	◎	Calm
∴•	Moderate rain	◑	One-eighth	╱	3–8
∴•	Heavy rain	◔	Scattered	╱	9–14
,	Drizzle	◐	Broken	╱╱	15–20
✲ ✲	Light snow	◕	Seven-eighths	╱╱	21–25
✲✲✲	Moderate snow	●	Overcast	╱╱╱	32–37
�R	Thunderstorm	⊗	Sky obscured	╱╱╱╱	44–48
∿	Freezing rain	**Special Symbols**		◢	55–60
∞	Haze	▲▲▲▲	Cold front	◢	66–71
≡	Fog	●●●●	Warm front		
		H	High pressure		
		L	Low pressure		
		ς	Hurricane		

Station Model

Wind speed is represented by whole and half tails.

A line indicates the direction the wind is coming from.

Air temperature

A symbol represents the current weather conditions. If there is no symbol, there is no precipitation.

Dew point temperature

Shading indicates the cloud coverage.

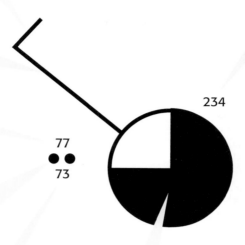

77
73
234

Atmospheric pressure in millibars (mbar). This number has been shortened on the station model. To read the number properly you must follow a few simple rules.

- If the first number is greater than 5, place a 9 in front of the number and a decimal point between the last two digits.

- If the first number is less than or equal to 5, place a 10 in front of the number and a decimal point between the last two digits.

Interpreting Station Models

The station model below is for Boston, Massachusetts. The current temperature in Boston is 42°F, and the dew point is 39°F. The barometric pressure is 1011.0 mbar. The sky is overcast, and there is moderate rainfall. The wind is coming from the southwest at 15–20 mph.

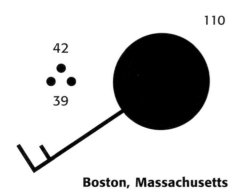

42
39
110

Boston, Massachusetts

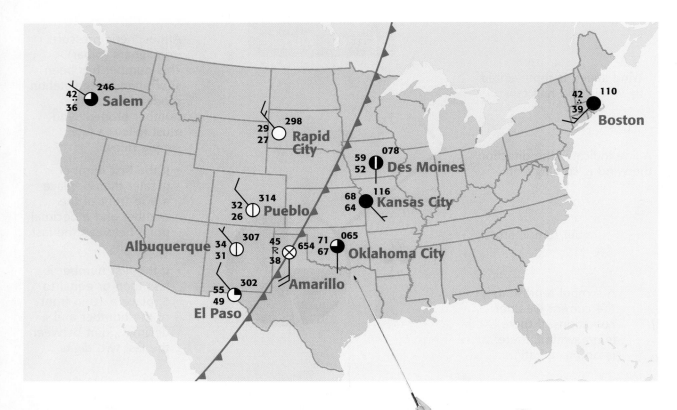

Analyze the Results

1 Based on the weather for the entire United States, what time of year is it? Explain your answer.

2 Interpret the station model for Salem, Oregon. What is the temperature, dew point, cloud coverage, wind direction, wind speed, and atmospheric pressure? Is there any precipitation? If so, what kind?

3 What is happening to wind direction, temperature, and pressure as the cold front approaches? as it passes?

Draw Conclusions

4 Interpret the station model for Amarillo, Texas.

Skills Practice Lab

For the Birds

You and a partner have a new business building birdhouses. But your first clients have told you that birds do not want to live in the birdhouses you have made. The clients want their money back unless you can solve the problem. You need to come up with a solution right away!

You remember reading an article about microclimates in a science magazine. Cities often heat up because the pavement and buildings absorb so much solar radiation. Maybe the houses are too warm! How can the houses be kept cooler?

You decide to investigate the roofs; after all, changing the roofs would be a lot easier than building new houses. In order to help your clients and the birds, you decide to test different roof colors and materials to see how these variables affect a roof's ability to absorb the sun's rays.

One partner will test the color, and the other partner will test the materials. You will then share your results and make a recommendation together.

MATERIALS

- cardboard (4 pieces)
- paint, black, white, and light blue tempera
- rubber, beige or tan
- thermometers, Celsius (4)
- watch (or clock)
- wood, beige or tan

SAFETY

Part A: Color Test

Ask a Question

1 What color would be the best choice for the roof of a birdhouse?

Form a Hypothesis

2 Write down the color you think will keep a birdhouse coolest.

Test the Hypothesis

3 Paint one piece of cardboard black, another piece white, and a third light blue.

4 After the paint has dried, take the three pieces of cardboard outside, and place a thermometer on each piece.

5 In an area where there is no shade, place each piece at the same height so that all three receive the same amount of sunlight. Leave the pieces in the sunlight for 15 min.

6 Leave a fourth thermometer outside in the shade to measure the temperature of the air.

7 Record the reading of the thermometer on each piece of cardboard. Also, record the outside temperature.

Analyze the Results

1 Did each of the three thermometers record the same temperature after 15 min? Explain.

2 Were the temperature readings on each of the three pieces of cardboard the same as the reading for the outside temperature? Explain.

Draw Conclusions

3 How do your observations compare with your hypothesis?

Part B: Material Test

Ask a Question

1 Which material would be the best choice for the roof of a birdhouse?

Form a Hypothesis

2 Write down the material you think will keep a birdhouse coolest.

Test the Hypothesis

3 Take the rubber, wood, and the fourth piece of cardboard outside, and place a thermometer on each.

4 In an area where there is no shade, place each material at the same height so that they all receive the same amount of sunlight. Leave the materials in the sunlight for 15 min.

5 Leave a fourth thermometer outside in the shade to measure the temperature of the air.

6 Record the temperature of each material. Also, record the outside temperature. After you and your partner have finished your investigations, take a few minutes to share your results.

Analyze the Results

1. Did each of the thermometers on the three materials record the same temperature after 15 min? Explain.

2. Were the temperature readings on the rubber, wood, and cardboard the same as the reading for the outside temperature? Explain.

Draw Conclusions

3. How do your observations compare with your hypothesis?

4. Which material would you use to build the roofs for your birdhouses? Why?

5. Which color would you use to paint the new roofs? Why?

Applying Your Data

Make three different-colored samples for each of the three materials. When you measure the temperatures for each sample, how do the colors compare for each material? Is the same color best for all three materials? How do your results compare with what you concluded in steps 4 and 5 under Draw Conclusions of this activity? What's more important, color or material?

Model-Making Lab

Why Do They Wander?

Before the discoveries of Nicholas Copernicus in the early 1500s, most people thought that the planets and the sun revolved around the Earth and that the Earth was the center of the solar system. But Copernicus observed that the sun is the center of the solar system and that all the planets, including Earth, revolve around the sun. He also explained a puzzling aspect of the movement of planets across the night sky.

If you watch a planet every night for several months, you'll notice that it appears to "wander" among the stars. While the stars remain in fixed positions relative to each other, the planets appear to move independently of the stars. Mars first travels to the left, then back to the right, and then again to the left.

In this lab, you will make your own model of part of the solar system to find out how Copernicus's model of the solar system explained this zigzag motion of the planets.

MATERIALS

- compass, drawing
- paper, white
- pencils, colored
- ruler, metric

SAFETY

Ask a Question

1 Why do the planets appear to move back and forth in the Earth's night sky?

Form a Hypothesis

2 Write a possible answer to the question above.

Test the Hypothesis

3 Use the compass to draw a circle with a diameter of 9 cm on the paper. This circle will represent the orbit of the Earth around the sun. (Note: The orbits of the planets are actually slightly elliptical, but circles will work for this activity.)

4 Using the same center point, draw a circle with a diameter of 12 cm. This circle will represent the orbit of Mars.

5 Using a blue pencil, draw three parallel lines diagonally across one end of your paper, as shown at right. These lines will help you plot the path Mars appears to travel in Earth's night sky. Turn your paper so the diagonal lines are at the top of the page.

6 Place 11 dots 2.5 cm apart from each other on your Earth orbit. Number the dots 1 through 11. These dots will represent Earth's position from month to month.

7 Now, place 11 dots along the top of your Mars orbit 0.5 cm apart from each other. Number the dots as shown. These dots will represent the position of Mars at the same time intervals. Notice that Mars travels slower than Earth.

8 Draw a green line to connect the first dot on Earth's orbit to the first dot on Mars's orbit. Extend this line to the first diagonal line at the top of your paper. Place a green dot where the green line meets the first blue diagonal line. Label the green dot "1."

9 Now, connect the second dot on Earth's orbit to the second dot on Mars's orbit, and extend the line all the way to the first diagonal at the top of your paper. Place a green dot where this line meets the first blue diagonal line, and label this dot "2."

10 Continue drawing green lines from Earth's orbit through Mars's orbit and finally to the blue diagonal lines. Pay attention to the pattern of dots you are adding to the diagonal lines. When the direction of the dots changes, extend the green line to the next diagonal line, and add the dots to that line instead.

11 When you are finished adding green lines, draw a red line to connect all the green dots on the blue diagonal lines in the order you drew them.

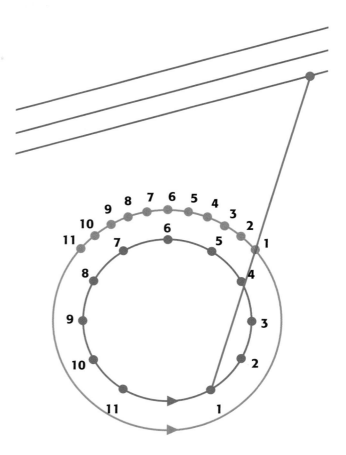

Analyze the Results

1 What do the green lines connecting points along Earth's orbit and Mars's orbit represent?

2 What does the red line connecting the dots along the diagonal lines look like? How can you explain this?

Draw Conclusions

3 What does this demonstration show about the motion of Mars?

4 Why do planets appear to move back and forth across the sky?

5 Were the Greeks justified in calling the planets *wanderers*? Explain.

Skills Practice Lab

The Best-Bread Bakery Dilemma

The chief baker at the Best-Bread Bakery thinks that the yeast the bakery received may be dead. Yeast is a central ingredient in bread. Yeast is a living organism, a member of the kingdom Fungi, and it undergoes the same life processes as other living organisms. When yeast grows in the presence of oxygen and other nutrients, yeast produces carbon dioxide. The gas forms bubbles that cause bread dough to rise. Thousands of dollars may be lost if the yeast is dead.

The Best-Bread Bakery has requested that you test the yeast. The bakery has furnished samples of live yeast and some samples of the yeast in question.

Procedure

1. Make a data table similar to the one below. Leave plenty of room to write your observations.

2. Examine each yeast sample with a magnifying lens. You may want to sniff the samples to determine the presence of an odor. (Your teacher will demonstrate the appropriate way to detect odors in this lab.) Record your observations in the data table.

3. Label three test tubes or plastic cups "Live Yeast," "Sample A Yeast," and "Sample B Yeast."

4. Fill a beaker with 125 mL of water, and place the beaker on a hot plate. Use a thermometer to be sure the water does not get warmer than 32°C. Attach the thermometer to the side of the beaker with a clip so the thermometer doesn't touch the bottom of the beaker. Turn off the hot plate when the water temperature reaches 32°C.

- beaker, 250 mL
- flour
- gloves, heat-resistant
- graduated cylinder
- hot plate
- magnifying lens
- scoopula (or small spoon)
- stirring sticks, wooden (3)
- sugar
- test-tube rack
- test tubes (3) (or clear plastic cups)
- thermometer, Celsius, with clip
- water, 125 mL
- yeast samples (live, A, and B)

SAFETY

Yeast sample	Observations	0 min	5 min	10 min	15 min	20 min	25 min	Dead or alive?
Live								
Sample A				*DO NOT WRITE IN BOOK*				
Sample B								

5. Add a small scoop (about 1/2 tsp) of each yeast sample to the correctly labeled container. Add a small scoop of sugar to each container.

6. Add 10 mL of the warm water to each container, and stir.

7. Add a small scoop of flour to each container, and stir again. The flour will help make the process more visible but is not necessary as food for the yeast.

8. Observe the samples carefully. Look for bubbles. Make observations at 5 min intervals. Write your observations in the data table.

9. In the last column of the data table, write "alive" or "dead" based on your observations during the experiment.

Analyze the Results

1. Describe any differences in the yeast samples before the experiment.

2. Describe the appearance of the yeast samples at the conclusion of the experiment.

3. Why was a sample of live yeast included in the experiment?

4. Why was sugar added to the samples?

5. Based on your observations, is either Sample A or Sample B alive?

Draw Conclusions

6. Write a letter to the Best-Bread Bakery stating your recommendation to use or not use the yeast samples. Give reasons for your recommendation.

Applying Your Data

Based on your observations of the nutrient requirements of yeast, design an experiment to determine the ideal combination of nutrients. Vary the amount of nutrients, or examine different energy sources.

Skills Practice Lab

Cells Alive!

You have probably used a microscope to look at single-celled organisms such as those shown below. They can be found in pond water. In the following exercise, you will look at *Protococcus*—algae that form a greenish stain on tree trunks, wooden fences, flowerpots, and buildings.

Euglena

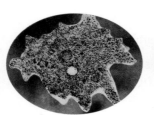
Amoeba

Paramecium

Procedure

1. Locate some *Protococcus*. Scrape a small sample into a container. Bring the sample to the classroom, and make a wet mount of it as directed by your teacher. If you can't find *Protococcus* outdoors, look for algae on the glass in an aquarium. Such algae may not be *Protococcus*, but it will be a very good substitute.

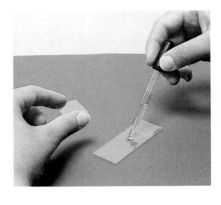

2. Set the microscope on low power to examine the algae. On a separate sheet of paper, draw the cells that you see.

3. Switch to high power to examine a single cell. Draw the cell.

4. You will probably notice that each cell contains several chloroplasts. Label a chloroplast on your drawing. What is the function of the chloroplast?

5. Another structure that should be clearly visible in all the algae cells is the nucleus. Find the nucleus in one of your cells, and label it on your drawing. What is the function of the nucleus?

6. What does the cytoplasm look like? Describe any movement you see inside the cells.

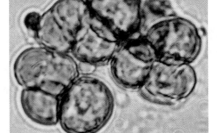
Protococcus

Analyze the Results

1. Are *Protococcus* single-celled organisms or multicellular organisms?

2. How are *Protococcus* different from amoebas?

Skills Practice Lab

Voyage of the USS *Adventure*

You are a crew member on the USS *Adventure*. The *Adventure* has been on a 5-year mission to collect life-forms from outside the solar system. On the voyage back to Earth, your ship went through a meteor shower, which ruined several of the compartments containing the extraterrestrial life-forms. Now it is necessary to put more than one life-form in the same compartment.

Life-form 1

You have only three undamaged compartments in your starship. You and your crewmates must stay in one compartment, and that compartment should be used for extraterrestrial life-forms only if absolutely necessary. You and your crewmates must decide which of the life-forms could be placed together. It is thought that similar life-forms will have similar needs. You can use only observable characteristics to group the life-forms.

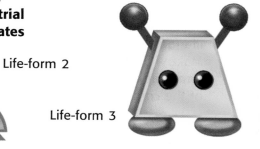

Life-form 2

Life-form 3

Procedure

1. Make a data table similar to the one below. Label each column with as many characteristics of the various life-forms as possible. Leave enough space in each square to write your observations. The life-forms are pictured on this page.

Life-form 4

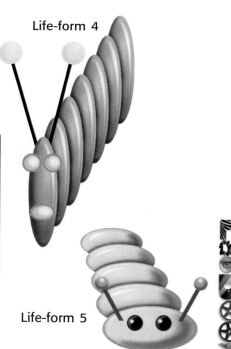

Life-form Characteristics				
	Color	Shape	Legs	Eyes
Life-form 1				
Life-form 2		DO NOT WRITE IN BOOK		
Life-form 3				
Life-form 4				

2. Describe each characteristic as completely as you can. Based on your observations, determine which of the life-forms are most alike.

Life-form 5

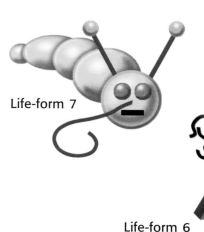

Life-form 7

Life-form 6

3 Make a data table like the one below. Fill in the table according to the decisions you made in step 2. State your reasons for the way you have grouped your life-forms.

Life-form Room Assignments		
Compartment	Life-forms	Reasons
1		
2		DO NOT WRITE IN BOOK
3		

4 The USS *Adventure* has to make one more stop before returning home. On planet X437 you discover the most interesting life-form ever found outside of Earth—the CC9, shown at right. Make a decision, based on your previous grouping of life-forms, about whether you can safely include CC9 in one of the compartments for the trip to Earth.

Analyze the Results

1 Describe the life-forms in compartment 1. How are they similar? How are they different?

2 Describe the life-forms in compartment 2. How are they similar? How do they differ from the life-forms in compartment 1?

3 Are there any life-forms in compartment 3? If so, describe their similarities. In which compartment will you and your crewmates remain for the journey home?

CC9

Draw Conclusions

4 Are you able to transport life-form CC9 safely back to Earth? If so, in which compartment will it be placed? How did you decide?

Applying Your Data

In 1831, Charles Darwin sailed from England on a ship called the HMS *Beagle*. You have studied the finches that Darwin observed on the Galápagos Islands. What were some of the other unusual organisms he found there? For example, find out about the Galápagos tortoise.

Model-Making Lab

Viral Decorations

Although viruses are made of only protein and nucleic acids, their structures have many different shapes that help them attach to and invade living cells. One viral shape can be constructed from the template provided by your teacher. In this activity, you will construct and modify a model of a virus.

Procedure

1 Obtain a virus model template from your teacher. Carefully copy the template on a piece of construction paper. You may make the virus model as large as your teacher allows.

2 Plan how you will modify your virus. For example, you might want to add the tail and tail fibers of a bacteriophage or wrap the model in plastic to represent the envelope that surrounds the protein coat in HIV.

3 Color your virus model, and cut it out by cutting on the solid black lines. Then, fold the virus model along the dotted lines.

4 Glue or tape each lettered tab under the corresponding lettered triangle. For example, glue or tape the large *Z* tab under the *Z*-shaded triangle. When you are finished, you should have a closed box with 20 sides.

5 Apply the modifications that you planned. Give your virus a name, and write it on the model. Decorate your classroom with your virus and those of your classmates.

Analyze the Results

1 Describe the modifications you made to your virus model, and explain how the virus might use them.

2 If your virus causes disease, explain what disease it causes, how it reproduces, and how the virus is spread.

MATERIALS

- glue (or tape)
- markers, colored
- paper, construction
- pipe cleaners, twist ties, buttons, string, plastic wrap, and other scrap materials for making variations of the virus
- scissors
- virus model template

SAFETY

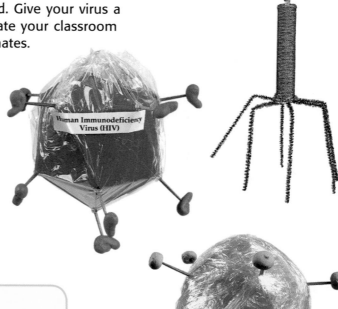

Communicating Your Data

Research in the library or on the Internet an unusual virus that causes an illness, such as the influenza virus, HIV, or Ebola virus. Write a paragraph explaining what is unusual about the virus, what illness it causes, and how it might be avoided.

Model-Making Lab

Making a Protist Mobile

You have studied many of the diverse species of organisms within the kingdom Protista. This may be the first time you have ever seen many of these single-celled eukaryotes. In this activity, you will have an opportunity to express a bit of creativity by using what you have learned about these interesting organisms.

Procedure

1 Research the different kinds of protists you have studied. You may cut out pictures of them from magazines, or you may find examples of protists on the Internet. You may want to investigate *Plasmodium, Euglena,* amoebas, slime molds, *Radiolaria, Paramecium, Foraminifera,* various other protozoans, or even algae.

2 Using the paper and recycled materials, make a model of each protist you want to include on your mobile. Be sure to include the special features of each protist, such as vacuoles, pseudopods, shells, cilia, or flagella.

3 Use tape or glue to attach special features to give your protists a three-dimensional look.

4 Provide labels for your protist models. For each protist, provide its name, classification, method of movement (if any), method for obtaining food, and any other interesting facts you have learned about it.

5 Attach your protist models to the wire hanger with wire or string. Use tape or glue to attach your labels to each model.

Analyze the Results

1 What have you learned about the diversity of protists? Include at least three habitats where protists may be found.

Communicating Your Data

Choose a disease-causing protist. Write a report describing the disease, its effect on people or the environment, and the efforts being made to control it.

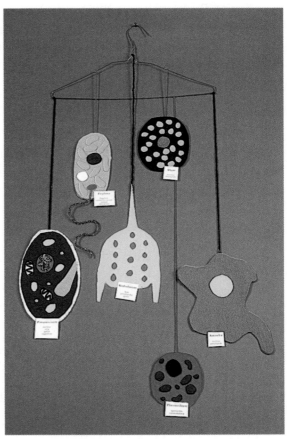

Skills Practice Lab

Leaf Me Alone!

Imagine you are a naturalist all alone on an expedition in a rain forest. You have found several plants that you think have never been seen before. You must contact a botanist, a scientist who studies plants, to confirm your suspicion. Because there is no mail service in the rain forest, you must describe these species completely and accurately by radio. The botanist must be able to draw the leaves of the plants from your description. In this activity, you will carefully describe five plant specimens by using the examples and vocabulary lists in this lab.

Procedure

1. Examine the leaf characteristics illustrated on the next page. These examples can be found on the following page. You will notice that more than one term is needed to completely describe a leaf. The leaf shown at right has been labeled for you using the examples and vocabulary lists found in this lab.

2. On a sheet of paper, draw a diagram of a leaf from each plant specimen.

3. Next to each drawing, carefully describe the leaf. Include general characteristics, such as relative size and color. For each plant, identify the following: leaf shape, stem type, leaf arrangement, leaf edge, vein arrangement, and leaf-base shape. Use the terms and vocabulary lists provided to describe each leaf as accurately as possible and to label your drawings.

Analyze the Results

1. What is the difference between a simple leaf and a compound leaf?

2. Describe two different vein arrangements in leaves.

3. Based on what you know about adaptation, explain why there are so many different leaf variations.

MATERIALS

- gloves, protective
- leaf specimens (5)
- plant guidebook (optional)

SAFETY

Compound Leaf

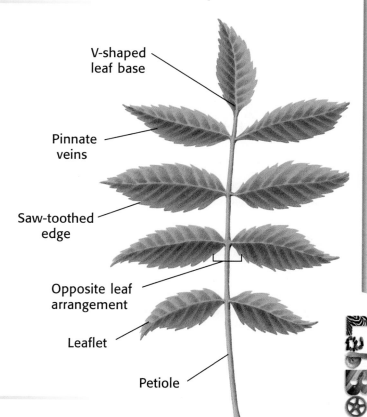

- V-shaped leaf base
- Pinnate veins
- Saw-toothed edge
- Opposite leaf arrangement
- Leaflet
- Petiole

Communicating Your Data

Choose a partner. Using the keys and vocabulary in this lab, describe a leaf, and see if your partner can draw the leaf from your description. Switch roles, and see if you can draw a leaf from your partner's description.

Leaf Shapes Vocabulary List

cordate—heart shaped
lanceolate—sword shaped
lobate—lobed
oblong—rounded at the tip
orbicular—disk shaped
ovate—oval shaped, widest at base of leaf
peltate—shield shaped
reniform—kidney shaped
sagittate—arrow shaped

Stems Vocabulary List

herbaceous—green, nonwoody stems
woody—bark or barklike covering on stem

Leaf Arrangements Vocabulary List

alternate—alternating leaves or leaflets along stem or petiole
compound—leaf divided into segments, or several leaflets on a petiole
opposite—compound leaf with several leaflets arranged oppositely along a petiole
palmate—single leaf with veins arranged around a center point
palmate compound—several leaflets arranged around a center point
petiole—leaf stalk
pinnate—single leaf with veins arranged along a center vein
pinnate compound—several leaflets on either side of a petiole
simple—single leaf attached to stem by a petiole

Leaf Veins

Parallel · Palmate · Pinnate

Leaf Arrangement on the Stem

Opposite

Alternate

Leaf Division

Simple · Palmate compound · Pinnate compound

Shape of the Leaf Base

V-shaped
Rounded
Flat
Heart
Uneven

Variations in Leaf Edges

Smooth
Saw-toothed
Double saw-toothed
Lobed

Skills Practice Lab

The Cricket Caper

Insects are a special class of invertebrates with more than 750,000 known species. Insects may be the most successful group of animals on Earth. In this activity you will observe a cricket's structure and the simple adaptive behaviors that help make it so successful. Remember, you will be handling a living animal that deserves to be treated with care.

MATERIALS

- aluminum foil
- apple
- bags, plastic, sealable (2)
- beaker, 600 mL (2)
- cricket (2)
- hand lens (optional)
- ice, crushed
- lamp
- plastic wrap
- tape, masking
- water, tap, hot

SAFETY

Procedure

1. Place a cricket in a clean 600 mL beaker, and quickly cover the beaker with plastic wrap. The supply of oxygen in the container is enough for the cricket to breathe while you complete your work.

2. While the cricket is getting used to the container, make a data table similar to the one below. Be sure to allow enough space to write your descriptions.

Cricket Body Structures	
Number	**Description**
Body segments	
Antennae	*DO NOT WRITE IN BOOK*
Eyes	
Wings	

3. Without making much movement, begin to examine the cricket. Fill in your data table with your observations of the cricket's structure.

4. Place a small piece of apple in the beaker. Set the beaker on a table. Sit quietly for several minutes and observe the cricket. Any movement may cause the cricket to stop what it is doing. Record your observations.

5. Remove the plastic wrap from the beaker, remove the apple, and quickly attach a second beaker. Join the two beakers together at the mouths with masking tape. Handle the beakers carefully. Remember, there is a living animal inside.

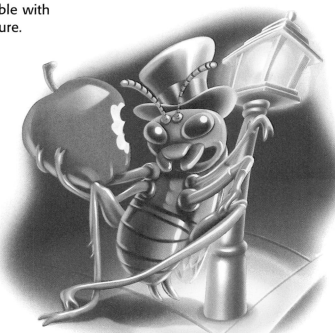

6 Wrap one of the joined beakers with aluminum foil.

7 If the cricket is hiding under the aluminum foil, gently tap the sides of the beaker until the cricket is exposed. Lay the joined beakers on their sides, and shine a lamp on the uncovered side. Record the cricket's location.

8 Record the cricket's location after 5 min. Without disturbing the cricket, carefully move the aluminum foil to the other beaker. After 5 min, record the cricket's location. Repeat this process one more time to see if you get the same result.

9 Fill a sealable plastic bag halfway with crushed ice. Fill another bag halfway with hot tap water. Seal each bag, and arrange them side by side on the table.

10 Remove the aluminum foil from the beakers. Gently rock the joined beakers from side to side until the cricket is in the center. Place the beakers on the plastic bags, as shown below.

11 Observe the cricket's behavior for 5 min. Record your observations.

12 Set the beakers on one end for several minutes to allow them to return to room temperature. Repeat steps 10–12 three times. (Why do you think it is necessary to allow the beakers to return to room temperature each time?)

13 Set the beakers on one end. Carefully remove the masking tape, and separate the beakers. Quickly replace the plastic wrap over the beaker containing the cricket. Allow your cricket to rest while you make two data tables similar to those at right.

14 Observe the cricket's movement in the beaker every 15 seconds for 3 min. Fill in the Cricket (alone) data table using the following codes: 0 = no movement, 1 = slight movement, and 2 = rapid movement.

15 Obtain a second cricket from your teacher, and place this cricket in the container with the first cricket. Every 15 seconds, record the movement of each cricket in the Cricket A and Cricket B data table using the codes given in step 14.

Analyze the Results

1 Describe crickets' feeding behavior. Are they lappers, suckers, or chewers?

2 Do crickets prefer light or darkness? Explain.

3 From your observations, what can you infer about a cricket's temperature preferences?

Draw Conclusions

4 Based on your observations of Cricket A and Cricket B, what general statements can you make about the social behavior of crickets?

Applying Your Data

Make a third data table titled "Cricket and Another Species of Insect." Introduce another insect, such as a grasshopper, into the beaker. Record your observations for 3 min. Write a short summary of the cricket's reaction to another species.

Cricket (alone)	
15 s	
30 s	
45 s	
60 s	
75 s	
90 s	DO NOT WRITE
105 s	IN BOOK
120 s	
135 s	
150 s	
165 s	
180 s	

Cricket A and Cricket B		
	A	B
15 s		
30 s		
45 s		
60 s		
75 s		
90 s	DO NOT WRITE	
105 s	IN BOOK	
120 s		
135 s		
150 s		
165 s		
180 s		

Skills Practice Lab

A Prince of a Frog

Imagine that you are a scientist interested in amphibians. You have heard in the news about amphibians disappearing all over the world. What a great loss it will be to the environment if all amphibians become extinct! Your job is to learn as much as possible about how frogs normally behave so that you can act as a resource for other scientists who are studying the problem. In this activity, you will observe a normal frog in a dry container and in water.

Procedure

1. Make a table similar to the one below to note all of your observations of the frog in this investigation.

Observations of a Live Frog	
Characteristic	**Observation**
Breathing	
Eyes	
Legs	
Response to food	DO NOT WRITE IN BOOK
Skin texture	
Swimming behavior	
Skin coloration	

2. Observe a live frog in a dry container. Draw a picture of the frog. Label the eyes, nostrils, front legs, and hind legs.

3. Watch the frog's movements as it breathes air with its lungs. Write a description of the frog's breathing.

4. Look closely at the frog's eyes, and note their location. Examine the upper and lower eyelids as well as the transparent third eyelid. Which of these three eyelids actually moves over the eye?

5. Study the frog's legs. Note in your data table the difference between the front and hind legs.

6. Place a live insect, such as a cricket, in the container. Observe and record how the frog reacts.

7. Carefully pick up the frog, and examine its skin. How does it feel?
Caution: Remember that a frog is a living thing and deserves to be handled gently and with respect.

8. Place a 600 mL beaker in the container. Place the frog in the beaker. Cover the beaker with your hand, and carry it to a container of dechlorinated water. Tilt the beaker and gently submerge it in the water until the frog swims out of the beaker.

9. Watch the frog float and swim in the water. How does the frog use its legs to swim? Notice the position of the frog's head.

10. As the frog swims, bend down and look up into the water so that you can see the underside of the frog. Then look down on the frog from above. Compare the color on the top and the underneath sides of the frog. Record your observations in your data table.

Analyze the Results

1. From the position of the frog's eyes, what can you infer about the frog's field of vision? How might the position of the frog's eyes benefit the frog while it is swimming?

2. How can a frog "breathe" while it is swimming in water?

3. How are the hind legs of a frog adapted for life on land and in water?

4. What differences did you notice in coloration on the frog's top side and its underneath side? What advantage might these color differences provide?

5. How does the frog eat? What senses are involved in helping the frog catch its prey?

Applying Your Data

Observe another type of amphibian, such as a salamander. How do the adaptations of other types of amphibians compare with those of the frog you observed in this investigation?

Model-Making Lab

Adaptation: It's a Way of Life

Since the beginning of life on Earth, species have had special characteristics called *adaptations* that have helped them survive changes in environmental conditions. Changes in a species' environment include climate changes, habitat destruction, or the extinction of prey. These things can cause a species to die out unless the species has a characteristic that helps it survive. For example, a species of bird may have an adaptation for eating sunflower seeds and ants. If the ant population dies out, the bird can still eat seeds and can therefore survive.

In this activity, you will explore several adaptations and design an organism with adaptations you choose. Then, you will describe how these adaptations help the organism survive.

MATERIALS

- arts-and-crafts materials, various
- markers, colored
- magazines for cutouts
- poster board
- scissors

SAFETY

Procedure

1. Study the chart below. Choose one adaptation from each column. For example, an organism might be a scavenger that burrows underground and has spikes on its tail!

Adaptations		
Diet	**Type of transportation**	**Special adaptation**
carnivore	flies	uses sensors to detect heat
herbivore	glides through the air	is active only at night and has excellent night vision
omnivore	burrows underground	changes colors to match its surroundings
scavenger	runs fast	has armor
decomposer	swims	has horns
	hops	can withstand extreme temperature changes
	walks	secretes a terrible and sickening scent
	climbs	has poison glands
	floats	has specialized front teeth
	slithers	has tail spikes
		stores oxygen in its cells so it does not have to breathe continuously
		one of your own invention

2 Design an organism that has the three adaptations you have chosen. Use poster board, colored markers, picture cutouts, or craft materials of your choosing to create your organism.

3 Write a caption on your poster describing your organism. Describe its appearance, its habitat, its niche, and the way its adaptations help it survive. Give your organism a two-part "scientific" name that is based on its characteristics.

4 Display your creation in your classroom. Share with classmates how you chose the adaptations for your organism.

Analyze the Results

1 What does your imaginary organism eat?

2 In what environment or habitat would your organism be most likely to survive—in the desert, tropical rain forest, plains, icecaps, mountains, or ocean? Explain your answer.

3 Is your creature a mammal, a reptile, an amphibian, a bird, or a fish? What modern organism (on Earth today) or ancient organism (extinct) is your imaginary organism most like? Explain the similarities between the two organisms. Do some research outside the lab, if necessary, to find out about a real organism that may be similar to your imaginary organism.

Draw Conclusions

4 If there were a sudden climate change, such as daily downpours of rain in a desert, would your imaginary organism survive? What adaptations for surviving such a change does it have?

Applying Your Data

Call or write to an agency such as the U.S. Fish and Wildlife Service to get a list of endangered species in your area. Choose an organism on that list. Describe the organism's niche and any special adaptations it has that help it survive. Find out why it is endangered and what is being done to protect it. Examine the illustration of the animal at right. Based on its physical characteristics, describe its habitat and niche. Is this a real animal?

Model-Making Lab

A Passel o' Pioneers

Succession is the natural process of the introduction and development of living things in an area. The area could be one that has never supported life before and has no soil, such as a recently cooled lava flow from a volcano. In an area where there is no soil, the process is called *primary succession.* In an area where soil already exists, such as an abandoned field or a forest after a fire, the process is called *secondary succession.*

In this investigation, you will build a model of secondary succession using natural soil.

Procedure

1 Place the natural soil you brought from home or the schoolyard into the fishbowl, and dampen the soil with 250 mL of water. Cover the top of the fishbowl with plastic wrap, and place the fishbowl in a sunny window.
Caution: Do not touch your face, eyes, or mouth during this activity. Wash your hands thoroughly when you are finished.

2 For 2 weeks, observe the fishbowl for any new growth. Describe and draw any new organisms you observe. Record these and all other observations.

3 Identify and record the names of as many of these new organisms as you can.

MATERIALS

- balance
- graduated cylinder, 250 mL
- large fishbowl
- plastic wrap
- protective gloves
- soil from home or schoolyard, 500 g
- water, 250 mL

SAFETY

Analyze the Results

1 What kinds of plants sprouted in your model of secondary succession? Were they tree seedlings, grasses, or weeds?

2 Were the plants that sprouted in the fishbowl unusual or common for your area?

Draw Conclusions

3 Explain how the plants that grew in your model of secondary succession can be called pioneer species.

Applying Your Data

Examine each of the photographs on this page. Determine whether each area, if abandoned forever, would undergo primary or secondary succession. You may decide that an area will not undergo succession at all. Explain your reasoning.

Bulldozed land

Eutrophic pond

Mount St. Helens volcano

Shipping port
parking lot

Skills Practice Lab

Determining Density

The density of an object is its mass divided by its volume. But how does the density of a small amount of a substance relate to the density of a larger amount of the same substance? In this lab, you will calculate the density of one marble and of a group of marbles. Then, you will confirm the relationship between the mass and volume of a substance.

MATERIALS

- balance, metric
- graduated cylinder, 100 mL
- marbles, glass (8–10)
- paper, graph
- paper towels
- water

SAFETY

Procedure

1. Copy the table below. Include one row for each marble.

Mass of marble (g)	Total mass of marbles (g)	Total volume (mL)	Volume of marbles (mL) (total volume minus 50.0 mL)	Density of marbles (g/mL) (total mass divided by volume)
		DO NOT WRITE IN BOOK		

2. Fill the graduated cylinder with 50 mL of water. If you put in too much water, twist one of the paper towels, and use it to absorb excess water.

3. Measure the mass of a marble as accurately as you can (to at least .01 g). Record the mass in the table.

4. Carefully drop the marble in the tilted cylinder, and measure the total volume. Record the volume in the third column.

5. Measure and record the mass of another marble. Add the masses of the marbles together, and record this value in the second column of the table.

6. Carefully drop the second marble in the graduated cylinder. Complete the row of information in the table.

7. Repeat steps 5 and 6. Add one marble at a time. Stop when you run out of marbles, the water no longer completely covers the marbles, or the graduated cylinder is full.

Analyze the Results

1. Examine the data in your table. As the number of marbles increases, what happens to the total mass of the marbles? What happens to the volume of the marbles? What happens to the density of the marbles?

2. Graph the total mass of the marbles (y-axis) versus the volume of the marbles (x-axis). Is the graph a straight line?

Draw Conclusions

3. Does the density of a substance depend on the amount of substance present? Explain how your results support your answer.

Applying Your Data

Calculate the slope of the graph. How does the slope compare with the values in the column entitled "Density of marbles"? Explain.

Skills Practice Lab

Science Friction

In this experiment, you will investigate three types of friction—static, sliding, and rolling—to determine which is the largest force and which is the smallest force.

Ask a Question

1 Which type of friction is the largest force—static, sliding, or rolling? Which is the smallest?

Form a Hypothesis

2 Write a statement or statements that answer the questions above. Explain your reasoning.

Test the Hypothesis

3 Cut a piece of string, and tie it in a loop that fits in the textbook, as shown on the next page. Hook the string to the spring scale.

4 Practice the next three steps several times before you collect data.

5 To measure the static friction between the book and the table, pull the spring scale very slowly. Record the largest force on the scale before the book starts to move.

6 After the book begins to move, you can determine the sliding friction. Record the force required to keep the book sliding at a slow, constant speed.

7 Place two or three rods under the book to act as rollers. Make sure the rollers are evenly spaced. Place another roller in front of the book so that the book will roll onto it. Pull the force meter slowly. Measure the force needed to keep the book rolling at a constant speed.

MATERIALS

- rods, wood or metal (3–4)
- scissors
- spring scale (force meter)
- string
- textbook (covered)

SAFETY

Analyze the Results

1 Which type of friction was the largest? Which was the smallest?

2 Do the results support your hypothesis? If not, how would you revise or retest your hypothesis?

Draw Conclusions

3 Compare your results with those of another group. Are there any differences? Working together, design a way to improve the experiment and resolve possible differences.

Skills Practice Lab

A Marshmallow Catapult

Catapults use projectile motion to launch objects. In this lab, you will build a simple catapult and determine the angle at which the catapult will launch an object the farthest.

MATERIALS

- marshmallows, miniature (2)
- meterstick
- protractor
- spoon, plastic
- tape, duct
- wood block, 3.5 cm × 3.5 cm × 1 cm

SAFETY

Ask a Question

1 At what angle, from 10° to 90°, will a catapult launch a marshmallow the farthest?

Form a Hypothesis

2 Write a hypothesis that is a possible answer to your question.

Angle	Distance 1 (cm)	Distance 2 (cm)	Average distance	Data Collection
10°	DO NOT WRITE IN BOOK			

Test the Hypothesis

3 Copy the table above. In your table, add one row each for 20°, 30°, 40°, 50°, 60°, 70°, 80°, and 90° angles.

4 Using duct tape, attach the plastic spoon to the 1 cm side of the block. Use enough tape to attach the spoon securely.

5 Place one marshmallow in the center of the spoon, and tape it to the spoon. This marshmallow serves as a ledge to hold the marshmallow that will be launched.

6 Line up the bottom corner of the block with the bottom center of the protractor, as shown in the photograph. Start with the block at 10°.

7 Place a marshmallow in the spoon, on top of the taped marshmallow. Pull the spoon back lightly, and let go. Measure and record the distance from the catapult that the marshmallow lands. Repeat the measurement, and calculate an average.

8 Repeat step 7 for each angle up to 90°.

Analyze the Results

1 At what angle did the catapult launch the marshmallow the farthest? Explain any differences from your hypothesis.

Draw Conclusions

2 At what angle should you throw a ball or shoot an arrow so that it will fly the farthest? Why? Support your answer with your data.

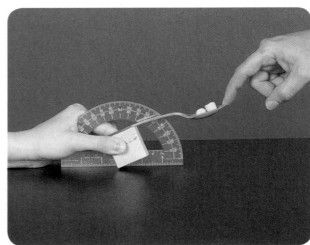

Model-Making Lab

Blast Off!

You have been hired as a rocket scientist for NASA. Your job is to design a rocket that will have a controlled flight while carrying a payload. Keep in mind that Newton's laws will have a powerful influence on your rocket.

Procedure

1. When you begin your experiment, your teacher will tape one end of the fishing line to the ceiling.

2. Use a pencil to poke a small hole in each side of the cup near the top. Place a 15 cm piece of string through each hole, and tape down the ends inside.

3. Inflate the balloon, and use the twist tie to hold it closed.

4. Tape the free ends of the strings to the sides of the balloon near the bottom. The cup should hang below the balloon. Your model rocket should look like a hot-air balloon.

5. Thread the fishing line that is hanging from the ceiling through the straw. Tape the balloon securely to the straw. Tape the loose end of the fishing line to the floor.

6. Untie the twist tie while holding the end of the balloon closed. When you are ready, release the end of the balloon. Mark and record the maximum height of the rocket.

7. Repeat the procedure, adding a penny to the cup each time until your rocket cannot lift any more pennies.

Analyze the Results

1. In a paragraph, describe how all three of Newton's laws influenced the flight of your rocket.

Draw Conclusions

2. Draw a diagram of your rocket. Label the action and reaction forces.

Applying Your Data

Brainstorm ways to modify your rocket so that it will carry the most pennies to the maximum height. Select the best design. When your teacher has approved all the designs, build and launch your rocket. Which variable did you modify? How did this variable affect your rocket's flight?

MATERIALS

- balloon, long, thin
- cup, paper, small
- fishing line, 3 m
- meterstick
- pencil
- pennies
- straw, straight plastic
- string, 15 cm (2)
- tape, masking
- twist tie

SAFETY

Skills Practice Lab

Quite a Reaction

Catapults have been used for centuries to throw objects great distances. According to Newton's third law of motion (whenever one object exerts a force on a second object, the second object exerts an equal and opposite force on the first), when an object is launched, something must also happen to the catapult. In this activity, you will build a kind of catapult that will allow you to observe the effects of Newton's third law of motion and the law of conservation of momentum.

Procedure

1. Glue the cardboard rectangles together to make a stack of three.

2. Push two of the pushpins into the cardboard stack near the corners at one end, as shown below. These pushpins will be the anchors for the rubber band.

3. Make a small loop of string.

4. Put the rubber band through the loop of string, and then place the rubber band over the two pushpin anchors. The rubber band should be stretched between the two anchors with the string loop in the middle.

5. Pull the string loop toward the end of the cardboard stack opposite the end with the anchors, and fasten the loop in place with the third pushpin.

6. Place the six straws about 1 cm apart on a tabletop or on the floor. Then, carefully center the catapult on top of the straws.

7. Put the marble in the closed end of the V formed by the rubber band.

8. Use scissors to cut the string holding the rubber band, and observe what happens. (Be careful not to let the scissors touch the cardboard catapult when you cut the string.)

⑨ Reset the catapult with a new piece of string. Try launching the marble several times to be sure that you have observed everything that happens during a launch. Record all your observations.

Analyze the Results

① Which has more mass, the marble or the catapult?

② What happened to the catapult when the marble was launched?

③ How far did the marble fly before it landed?

④ Did the catapult move as far as the marble did?

Draw Conclusions

⑤ Explain why the catapult moved backward.

⑥ If the forces that made the marble and the catapult move apart are equal, why didn't the marble and the catapult move apart the same distance? (Hint: The fact that the marble can roll after it lands is not the answer.)

⑦ The momentum of an object depends on the mass and velocity of the object. What is the momentum of the marble before it is launched? What is the momentum of the catapult? Explain your answers.

⑧ Using the law of conservation of momentum, explain why the marble and the catapult move in opposite directions after the launch.

Applying Your Data

How would you modify the catapult if you wanted to keep it from moving backward as far as it did? (It still has to rest on the straws.) Using items that you can find in the classroom, design a catapult that will move backward less than the one originally designed.

Skills Practice Lab

Density Diver

Crew members of a submarine can control the submarine's density underwater by allowing water to flow into and out of special tanks. These changes in density affect the submarine's position in the water. In this lab, you'll control a "density diver" to learn for yourself how the density of an object affects its position in a fluid.

MATERIALS

- bottle, plastic, with screw-on cap, 2 L
- dropper, medicine
- water

SAFETY

Ask a Question

1 How does the density of an object determine whether the object floats, sinks, or maintains its position in a fluid?

Form a Hypothesis

2 Write a possible answer to the question above.

Test the Hypothesis

3 Completely fill the 2 L plastic bottle with water.

4 Fill the diver (medicine dropper) approximately halfway with water, and place it in the bottle. The diver should float with only part of the rubber bulb above the surface of the water. If the diver floats too high, carefully remove it from the bottle, and add a small amount of water to the diver. Place the diver back in the bottle. If you add too much water and the diver sinks, empty out the bottle and diver, and go back to step 3.

5 Put the cap on the bottle tightly so that no water leaks out.

6 Apply various pressures to the bottle. Carefully watch the water level inside the diver as you squeeze and release the bottle. Record what happens.

7 Try to make the diver rise, sink, or stop at any level. Record your technique and your results.

Analyze the Results

1 How do the changes inside the diver affect its position in the surrounding fluid?

2 What relationship did you observe between the diver's density and the diver's position in the fluid?

Draw Conclusions

3 Explain how your density diver is like a submarine.

4 Explain how pressure on the bottle is related to the diver's density. Be sure to include Pascal's principle in your explanation.

Skills Practice Lab

Wheeling and Dealing

A crank handle, such as that used in pencil sharpeners, ice-cream makers, and water wells, is one kind of wheel and axle. In this lab, you will use a crank handle to find out how a wheel and axle helps you do work. You will also determine what effect the length of the handle has on the operation of the machine.

MATERIALS

- C-clamps (2)
- handles(4)
- mass, large
- meterstick
- spring scale
- string, 0.5 m
- wheel-and-axle assembly

SAFETY

Ask a Question

1 What effect does the length of a handle have on the operation of a crank?

Form a Hypothesis

2 Write a possible answer to the question above.

Test the Hypothesis

3 Copy Table 1.

4 Measure the radius (in meters) of the large dowel in the wheel-and-axle assembly. Record this in Table 1 as the axle radius, which remains constant throughout the lab. (Hint: Measure the diameter, and divide by 2.)

5 Using the spring scale, measure the weight of the large mass. Record this in Table 1 as the output force, which remains constant throughout the lab.

6 Use two C-clamps to secure the wheel-and-axle assembly to the table, as shown.

7 Measure the length (in meters) of handle 1. Record this length as a wheel radius in Table 1.

8 Insert the handle into the hole in the axle. Attach one end of the string to the large mass and the other end to the screw in the axle. The mass should hang down, and the handle should turn freely.

9 Turn the handle to lift the mass off the floor. Hold the spring scale upside down, and attach it to the end of the handle. Measure the force (in newtons) as the handle pulls up on the spring scale. Record this as the input force.

Table 1	Data Collection			
Handle	Axle radius (m)	Output force (N)	Wheel radius (m)	Input force (N)
1				
2				
3	DO NOT WRITE IN BOOK			
4				

10 Remove the spring scale, and lower the mass to the floor. Remove the handle.

11 Repeat steps 7 through 10 with the other three handles. Record all data in Table 1.

Analyze the Results

1 Copy Table 2.

Table 2 Calculations						
Handle	**Axle distance (m)**	**Wheel distance (m)**	**Work input (J)**	**Work output (J)**	**Mechanical efficiency (%)**	**Mechanical advantage**
1						
2						
3						
4						

DO NOT WRITE IN BOOK

2 Calculate the following for each handle, using the equations given. Record your answers in Table 2.

  a. *Distance axle rotates =* $2 \times \pi \times$ *axle radius*

   Distance wheel rotates = $2 \times \pi \times$ *wheel radius*

   (Use 3.14 for the value of π.)

  b. *Work input =* *input force × wheel distance*

   Work output = *output force × axle distance*

  c. *Mechanical efficiency =* $\dfrac{work\ output}{work\ input} \times 100$

  d. *Mechanical advantage =* $\dfrac{wheel\ radius}{axle\ radius}$

Draw Conclusions

3 What happens to work output and work input as the handle length increases? Why?

4 What happens to mechanical efficiency as the handle length increases? Why?

5 What happens to mechanical advantage as the handle length increases? Why?

6 What will happen to mechanical advantage if the handle length is kept constant and the axle radius gets larger?

7 What factors were controlled in this experiment? What was the variable?

Skills Practice Lab

Energy of a Pendulum

A pendulum clock is a compound machine that uses stored energy to do work. A spring stores energy, and with each swing of the pendulum, some of that stored energy is used to move the hands of the clock. In this lab, you will take a close look at the energy conversions that occur as a pendulum swings.

Procedure

1. Make a pendulum by tying the string around the hook of the mass. Use the marker and the meterstick to mark points on the string that are 50 cm, 70 cm, and 90 cm away from the mass.

2. Hold the string at the 50 cm mark. Gently pull the mass to the side, and release it without pushing it. Observe at least 10 swings of the pendulum.

3. Record your observations. Be sure to note how fast and how high the pendulum swings.

4. Repeat steps 2 and 3 while holding the string at the 70 cm mark and again while holding the string at the 90 cm mark.

Analyze the Results

1. List similarities and differences in the motion of the pendulum during all three trials.

2. At which point (or points) of the swing was the pendulum moving the slowest? the fastest?

Draw Conclusions

3. In each trial, at which point (or points) of the swing did the pendulum have the greatest potential energy? the least potential energy? (Hint: Think about your answers to question 2.)

4. At which point (or points) of the swing did the pendulum have the greatest kinetic energy? the least kinetic energy? Explain your answers.

5. Describe the relationship between the pendulum's potential energy and its kinetic energy on its way down. Explain.

6. What improvements might reduce the amount of energy used to overcome friction so that the pendulum would swing for a longer period of time?

Inquiry Lab

Save the Cube!

The biggest enemy of an ice cube is the transfer of thermal energy—heat. Energy can be transferred to an ice cube in three ways: conduction (the transfer of energy through direct contact), convection (the transfer of energy by the movement of a liquid or gas), and radiation (the transfer of energy through matter or space). Your challenge in this activity is to design a way to protect an ice cube as much as possible from all three types of energy transfer.

MATERIALS

- bag, plastic, small
- balance, metric
- cup, plastic or paper, small
- ice cube
- milk carton, empty, half-pint
- assorted materials provided by your teacher

Ask a Question

1. What materials prevent energy transfer most efficiently?

Form a Hypothesis

2. Design a system that protects an ice cube against each type of energy transfer. Describe your proposed design.

Test the Hypothesis

3. Use a plastic bag to hold the ice cube and any water if the ice cube melts. You may use any of the materials to protect the ice cube. The whole system must fit inside a milk carton.

4. Find the mass of the empty cup, and record it. Then, find and record the mass of an empty plastic bag.

5. Find and record the mass of the ice cube and cup together.

6. Quickly wrap the bag (and the ice cube inside) in its protection. Remember that the package must fit in the milk carton.

7. Place your ice cube in the "thermal zone" set up by your teacher. After 10 min, remove the ice cube from the zone.

8. Open the bag. Pour any water into the cup. Find and record the mass of the cup and water together.

9. Find and record the mass of the water by subtracting the mass of the empty cup from the mass of the cup and water.

10. Use the same method to determine the mass of the ice cube.

11. Using the following equation, find and record the percentage of the ice cube that melted:

$$\% \ melted = \frac{mass \ of \ water}{mass \ of \ ice \ cube} \times 100$$

Analyze the Results

1. Compared with other designs in your class, how well did your design protect against each type of energy transfer? How could you improve your design?

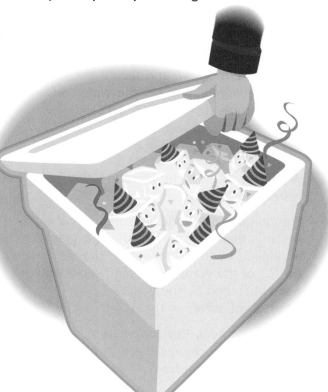

Model-Making Lab

Counting Calories

Energy transferred by heat is often expressed in units called *calories*. In this lab, you will build a model of a device called a *calorimeter*. Scientists often use calorimeters to measure the amount of energy that can be transferred by a substance. In this experiment, you will construct your own calorimeter and test it by measuring the energy released by a hot penny.

MATERIALS

- cup, plastic-foam, large
- cup, plastic-foam, small, with lid
- graduated cylinder, 100 mL
- heat source
- penny
- stopwatch
- thermometer
- tongs
- water

SAFETY

Procedure

1. Copy the table below.

Data Collection Table									
Seconds	0	15	30	45	60	75	90	105	120
Water temperature (°C)									

DO NOT WRITE IN BOOK

2. Place the lid on the small plastic-foam cup, and insert a thermometer through the hole in the top of the lid. (The thermometer should not touch the bottom of the cup.) Place the small cup inside the large cup to complete the calorimeter.

3. Remove the lid from the small cup, and add 50 mL of room-temperature water to the cup. Measure the water's temperature, and record the value in the first column (0 s) of the table.

4. Using tongs, heat the penny carefully. Add the penny to the water in the small cup, and replace the lid. Start your stopwatch.

5. Every 15 s, measure and record the temperature. Gently swirl the large cup to stir the water, and continue recording temperatures for 2 min (120 s).

Analyze the Results

1. What was the total temperature change of the water after 2 min?

2. The number of calories absorbed by the water is the mass of the water (in grams) multiplied by the temperature change (in °C) of the water. How many calories were absorbed by the water? (Hint: 1 mL water = 1 g water)

3. In terms of heat, explain where the calories to change the water temperature came from.

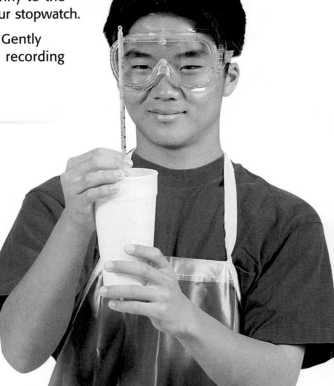

Contents

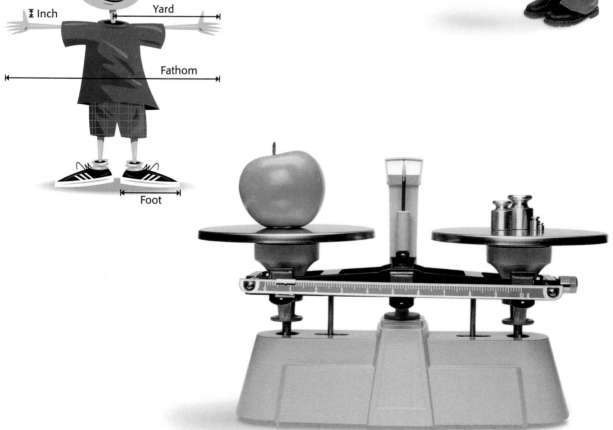

Inch   Yard

Fathom

Foot

Appendix

✓ *Reading Check* Answers

Chapter 1 Science in Our World

Section 1
Page 4: the knowledge gained by observing the natural world

Page 6: Recycling paper protects forests and saves fuel and chemicals from being used to make paper from trees.

Page 9: Science educators work in schools, zoos, aquariums, and national parks.

Section 2
Page 11: Scientific methods help scientists get reliable answers.

Page 13: A variable is the only factor that is changed in a controlled experiment.

Page 14: Scientists can make tables or graphs to organize their data.

Page 16: Scientists can write reports for scientific journals, give talks on their results, or put their results on the Internet.

Section 3
Page 19: Three kinds of models are physical, mathematical, and conceptual models.

Page 20: Models can represent both very large and very small objects at a size that you can easily see.

Section 4
Page 22: a tube that has lenses at each end, a stage, and a light

Page 25: Area measures how much surface area an object has.

Page 27: When you don't understand a safety symbol, you should ask your teacher for help.

Chapter 2 Weathering and Soil Formation

Section 1
Page 41: Wind, water, and gravity can cause abrasion.

Page 42: Answers may vary. Sample answer: ants, worms, mice, coyotes, and rabbits.

Page 45: Oxidation occurs when oxygen combines with an element to form an oxide.

Section 2
Page 47: As the surface area increases, the rate of weathering also increases.

Page 48: Warm, humid climates have higher rates of weathering because oxidation happens faster when temperatures are higher and when water is present.

Page 49: Mountains weather faster because they are exposed to more wind, rain, and ice, which are agents of weathering.

Section 3
Page 50: Soil is formed from parent rock, organic material, water, and air.

Page 53: Heavy rains leach precious nutrients into deeper layers of soil, resulting in a very thin layer of topsoil.

Page 54: Temperate climates have the most productive soil.

Section 4
Page 56: Soil provides nutrients to plants, houses for animals, and stores water.

Page 59: They restore important nutrients to the soil and provide cover to prevent erosion.

Chapter 3 The Flow of Fresh Water

Section 1
Page 70: The Colorado River eroded the rock over millions of years.

Page 72: A divide is the boundary that separates drainage areas, whereas a watershed is the area of land that is drained by a water system.

Page 73: An increase in a stream's gradient and discharge can cause the stream to flow faster.

Page 75: A mature river erodes its channel wider rather than deeper. It is not steep and has fewer falls and rapids. It also has good drainage and more discharge than a youthful river does.

Page 76: Rejuvenated rivers form when the land is raised by tectonic forces.

Section 2
Page 79: Deltas are made of the deposited load of the river, which is mostly mud.

Page 81: The flow of water can be controlled by dams and levees.

Section 3
Page 82: The zone of aeration is located underground. It is the area above the water table.

Page 84: The size of the recharge zone depends on how permeable rock is at the surface.

Page 85: A well must be deeper than the water table for it to be able to reach water.

Page 86: Deposition is the process that causes the formation of stalactites and stalagmites.

Section 4
Page 88: Nonpoint-source pollution is the hardest to control.

Page 91: Less than 8% of water in our homes is used for drinking.

Page 92: Drip irrigation systems deliver small amounts of water directly to the roots of the plant so that the plant absorbs the water before it can evaporate or runoff.

Page 93: Answers may vary. Sample answer: taking shorter showers, avoiding running water while brushing your teeth, and using the dishwasher only when it is full.

Chapter 4 Agents of Erosion and Deposition

Section 1

Page 105: The amount of energy released from breaking waves causes rock to break down, eventually forming sand.

Page 107: Large waves are more capable of moving large rocks on a shoreline because they have more energy than normal waves do.

Page 108: Beach material is material deposited by waves.

Section 2

Page 111: Deflation hollows form in areas where there is little vegetation.

Page 113: Dunes move in the direction of strong winds.

Section 3

Page 114: Alpine glaciers form in mountainous areas.

Page 119: A till deposit is made up of unsorted material, while stratified drift is made up of sorted material.

Section 4

Page 121: A slump is the result of a landslide in which a block of material moves downslope over a curved surface.

Page 122: A lahar is caused by the eruption of an ice-covered volcano, which melts ice and causes a hot mudflow.

Chapter 5 The Atmosphere

Section 1

Page 136: Water can be liquid (rain), solid (snow or ice), or gas (water vapor).

Page 138: The troposphere is the layer of turning or change. The stratosphere is the layer in which gases are layered and do not mix vertically. The mesosphere is the middle layer. The thermosphere is the layer in which temperatures are highest.

Page 140: The thermosphere does not feel hot because air molecules are spaced far apart and cannot collide to transfer much thermal energy.

Section 2

Page 143: Cold air is more dense than warm air, so cold air sinks and warm air rises. This produces convection currents.

Page 145: A greenhouse gas is a gas that absorbs thermal energy in the atmosphere.

Section 3

Page 147: Sinking air causes areas of high pressure because sinking air presses down on the air beneath it.

Page 148: the westerlies

Page 151: At night, the air along the mountain slopes cools. This cool air moves down the slopes into the valley and produces a mountain breeze.

Section 4

Page 152: Sample answer: smoke, dust and sea salt

Page 155: Answers may vary. Acid precipitation may decrease the soil nutrients that are available to plants.

Page 156: Powdered lime is used to counteract the effects of acidic snowmelt from snow that accumulated during the winter.

Page 158: Allowance trading establishes allowances for a certain type of pollutant. Companies are permitted to release their allowance of the pollutant, but if they exceed the allowance, they must buy additional allowances or pay a fine.

Chapter 6 Understanding Weather

Section 1

Page 170: The water cycle is the continuous movement of water from Earth's oceans and rivers into the atmosphere, into the ground, and back into the oceans and rivers.

Page 172: A psychrometer is used to measure relative humidity.

Page 173: The bulb of a wet-bulb thermometer is covered with moistened material. The bulb cools as water evaporates from the material. If the air is dry, more water will evaporate from the material, and the temperature recorded by the thermometer will be low. If the air is humid, less water will evaporate from the material, and the temperature recorded by the thermometer will be higher.

Page 175: Altostratus clouds form at middle altitudes.

Section 2

Page 179: A maritime tropical air mass causes hot and humid summer weather in the midwestern United States.

Page 181: An occluded front produces cool temperatures and large amounts of rain.

Page 183: An anticyclone can produce dry, clear weather.

Section 3

Page 185: A severe thunderstorm is a thunderstorm that produces high winds, hail, flash floods, or tornadoes.

Page 187: Hurricanes are also called *typhoons* or *cyclones.*

Page 188: Hurricanes get their energy from the condensation of water vapor.

Section 4

Page 192: Meteorologists use weather balloons to collect atmospheric data above Earth's surface.

Chapter 7 Climate

Section 1

Page 206: Climate is the average weather condition in an area over a long period of time. Weather is the condition of the atmosphere at a particular time.

Page 208: Locations near the equator have less seasonal variation because the tilt of the Earth does not change the amount of energy these locations receive from the sun.

Page 210: The atmosphere becomes less dense and loses its ability to absorb and hold thermal energy, at higher elevations.

Page 211: The Gulf Stream current carries warm water past Iceland, which heats the air and causes milder temperatures.

Page 212: Each biome has a different climate and different plant and animals communities.

Section 2

Page 214: You would find the tropical zone from 23.5° north latitude to 23.5° south latitude.

Page 217: Answers may vary. Sample answer: rats, lizards, snakes, and scorpions.

Section 3

Page 218: The temperate zone is located between the Tropics and the polar zone.

Page 220: Temperate deserts are cold at night because low humidity and cloudless skies allow energy to escape.

Page 223: Cities have higher temperatures than the surrounding rural areas because buildings and pavement absorb solar radiation instead of reflecting it.

Section 4

Page 225: Changes in the Earth's orbit and the tilt of the Earth's axis are the two things that Milankovitch says cause ice ages.

Page 226: Dust, ash, and smoke from volcanic eruptions block the sun's rays, which causes the Earth to cool.

Page 229: The deserts would receive less rainfall, making it harder for plants and animals in the desert to survive.

Chapter 8   A Family of Planets

Section 1

Page 241: Light travels about 300,000 km/s.

Page 243: Jupiter, Saturn, Uranus, and Neptune are in the outer solar system.

Section 2

Page 245: Radar technology was used to map the surface of Venus.

Page 246: Earth Science Enterprise is a NASA program that uses satellites to study Earth's atmosphere, land, oceans, life, and ice. This program will help scientists understand how humans affect the environment and how different parts of the global system interact.

Page 248: Mars' crust is chemically different from Earth's crust, so the Martian crust does not move. As a result, volcanoes build up in the same spots on Mars.

Section 3

Page 251: Saturn's rings are made of icy particles ranging in size from a few cm to several m wide.

Page 253: Neptune's interior releases energy to its outer layers, which creates belts of clouds in Neptune's atmosphere.

Section 4

Page 257: The moon formed from a piece of Earth's mantle, which broke off during a collision between Earth and a large object.

Page 259: During a solar eclipse, the moon blocks out the sun and casts a shadow on Earth.

Page 260: We don't see solar and lunar eclipses every month because the moon's orbit around Earth is tilted.

Page 261: Because Titan's atmosphere is similar to the atmosphere on Earth before life evolved, scientists can study Titan's atmosphere to learn how life began.

Page 262: Charon's period of revolution is the same as Pluto's period of rotation.

Section 5

Page 265: Comets come from the Oort cloud and the Kuiper belt.

Page 267: The major types of meteorites are stony, metallic, and stony-iron meteorites.

Page 268: Large objects strike Earth every few thousand years.

Chapter 9   It's Alive!! Or Is It?

Section 1

Page 283: Sample answer: They control their body temperature by moving from one environment to another. If they get too warm, they move to the shade. If they get too cool, they move out into the sunlight.

Page 284: making food, breaking down food, moving materials into and out of cells, and building cells

Section 2

Page 286: photosynthesis

Page 289: Simple carbohydrates are made of one sugar molecule. Complex carbohydrates are made of many sugar molecules linked together.

Page 290: Most fats are solid, and most oils are liquid.

Chapter 10   Cells: The Basic Units of Life

Section 1

Page 303: Sample answer: All organisms are made of one or more cells, the cell is the basic unit of all living things, and all cells come from existing cells.

Page 304: If a cell's volume gets too large, the cell's surface area will not be able to take in enough nutrients or get rid of wastes fast enough to keep the cell alive.

Page 305: Organelles are structures within a cell that perform specific functions for the cell.

Page 307: One difference between bacteria and archaea is that bacterial ribosomes differ from archaeal ribosomes.

Page 308: The main difference between prokaryotes and eukaryotes is that eukaryotic cells have a nucleus and membrane-bound organelles and prokaryotic cells do not.

Section 2

Page 311: A cell membrane encloses the cell and separates and protects the cell's contents from the cell's environment. The cell wall also controls the movement of materials into and out of the cell.

Page 312: The cytoskeleton is a web of proteins in the cytoplasm. This web gives the cell support and structure.

Page 314: Most of a cell's ATP is made in the cell's mitochondria.

Page 316: Lysosomes destroy worn-out organelles, attack foreign invaders, and get rid of waste material from inside the cell.

Section 3

Page 318: Sample answer: larger size, longer life, and cell specialization

Page 319: An organ is a structure of two or more tissues working together to perform a specific function in the body.

Page 320: cell, tissue, organ, organ system

Chapter 11   Classification

Section 1

Page 334: Sample answer: How many known species are there? What are the defining characteristics of each species? and What are the relationships between these species?

Page 337: genus name and specific name

Page 338: A dichotomous key is an identification aid that uses a series of descriptive statements.

Section 2

Page 341: One characteristic of organisms in the Domain Archaea is that they are commonly found in extreme environments.

Page 343: Sample answer: Plants make energy through photosynthesis. Some members of the kingdoms Fungi, Protista, and Animalia consume plants. When these organisms digest the plant material, they get energy and nutrients made by the plants.

Page 345: Sponges don't have sense organs, and they usually can't move around.

Chapter 12   Bacteria and Viruses

Section 1

Page 356: Bacteria are usually one of three main shapes   bacilli, cocci, or spirilla.

Page 358: Binary fission is a process of cell division in which one cell splits into two. All prokarytes reproduce by binary fission.

Section 2

Page 362: Nitrogen fixing is the process by which nitrogen gas in the air is transformed into a form that plants can use.

Page 364: In genetic engineering, scientists change the genes of bacteria or other living things.

Section 3

Page 367: Viruses can be classified by shape or by the type of genetic material that they contain. Other possible answers are that viruses can be classified by life cycle or by the kind of disease that they cause.

Page 368: when a virus attacks living cells and turns them into virus factories

Chapter 13   Protists and Fungi

Section 1

Page 381: Protist producers make their own food through photosynthesis.

Page 382: binary fission and multiple fission

Section 2

Page 385: Red algae also have a red pigment in their cells that gives the algae a red color.

Page 386: salt water, fresh water, and snow

Page 388: radiolarians and foraminiferans

Page 388: as decomposers or as parasites

Section 3

Page 393: hyphae breaking apart so that each piece becomes a new fungus or fungi producing spores

Page 394: asexually by releasing spores from sporangia or sexually by different individuals growing together into specialized sporangia

Page 396: the spore-forming structures, called *basidia*

Page 388: Lichens make acids that break down rocks, which causes cracks.

Chapter 14   Introduction to Plants

Section 1

Page 411: In the sporophyte stage, plants make spores, which grow into gametophytes. The gametophytes produce eggs and sperm. A sperm fertilizes an egg. The fertilized egg grows into a sporophyte.

Page 412: nonvascular plants, seedless vascular plants, gymnosperms, and angiosperms

Page 413: Sample answer: Green algae and plant cells have the same kind of chlorophyll, have similar cell walls, and make their own food through photosynthesis. Both store energy in the form of starch and have a two-stage life cycle.

Section 2

Page 415: Sample answer: Nonvascular plants are usually the first plants to live in a new environment. They form a thin layer of soil, where new plants can grow. Nonvascular plants also prevent erosion.

Page 417: Sample answer: Seedless vascular plants prevent erosion. They can grow in new soil and add to the soil's depth.

Section 3

Page 418: Sample answer: Seed plants produce seeds. The gametophytes of seed plants do not live independently of the sporophyte. The sperm of seed plants don't need water to fertilize eggs.

Page 419: Sample answer: Seeds have stored food to nourish a young plant, while spores do not. Seeds can be spread by animals, while spores are spread by wind. Animals spread seeds more efficiently than the wind does.

Page 421: Sample answer: Sperm from the male cone fertilize the eggs of the female cone. A fertilized egg develops into a young sporophyte surrounded by a seed within the female cone. Eventually, seeds are released from the cone.

Page 422: Sample answer: Flowers help angiosperms reproduce. Fruits surround and protect the seeds. Some fruits attract animals, which spread the seeds.

Page 423: Sample answer: Major food crops are flowering plants. Flowering plants provide building material, are used to make clothing and rope, and are used to make medicines, rubber, and perfume oils.

Section 4

Page 425: taproot systems and fibrous root systems

Page 426: Sample answer: Herbaceous stems are soft, thin, and flexible. Poppies have herbaceous stems.

Page 428: epidermis, palisade layer, and spongy layer

Page 430: Sample answer: Stamens, which have filaments topped by anthers, are the male reproductive parts of flowers. A pistil is the female part of a flower. A pistil has a stigma, style, and ovary.

Chapter 15   Introduction to Animals

Section 1

Page 445: If the shark's heart failed, its ability to pump blood through its body would also fail. As a result, the shark would die.

Page 447: Cells that will perform different functions develop different structures.

Page 448: The parrot can fly because the muscles that are attached to its breast bone and to the bones in its wings contract and relax. These muscles are made up of muscle cells that work together.

Section 2

Page 451: Sponges have asymmetrical body plans. Sponges are a mass of specialized cells that are held together by a jelly-like material. Tiny, glassy structures also provide the sponge with support.

Page 452: Cnidarians have two kinds of body forms, a medusa form and a polyp form. The medusa has a cup or bell-shaped body with tentacles hanging down from it. The cup of the polyp attaches to a hard surface and allows the tentacles to stick up into the water.

Page 454: Lancelets differ from vertebrates because lancelets do not have backbones as vertebrates do.

Page 456: Feathers are important in maintaining the bird's body temperature and in helping to shape the body and wings for flying.

Section 3

Page 458: no; I would not expect an animal with radial symmetry to have a head because it only has a top and a bottom, whereas animals that have a head have bilateral symmetry and therefore have a top, bottom, front, and a back.

Page 459: Outer coverings are important for the movement of animals because the muscles that are attached to these outer coverings contract and relax to allow movement.

Page 460: If an insect's tracheae became clogged, the insect would die because it would not be able to take in oxygen and expel carbon dioxide.

Page 461: A hydra reproduces by budding, which is a form of asexual reproduction. A part of the parent hydra develops into a new individual and pinches off from the parent. A butterfly reproduces by sexual reproduction and undergoes complete metamorphosis during its life cycle. A caterpillar hatches from an egg and develops into a pupa. The pupa metamorphoses into an adult.

Section 4

Page 465: The three main parts of an endoskeleton are the skull, the backbone, and the limb bones.

Page 466: The heart is part of the circulatory system. The heart pumps blood to the lungs, which are part of the respiratory system. Oxygen moves through the lungs and into the blood. At the same time, carbon dioxide moves from the blood, through the lungs and out of the body. The oxygen-rich blood travels back to the heart and is then pumped to the rest of the body.

Page 467: When a sound reaches the ear, the ear sends an impulse through sensory nerves and the spinal cord to the brain.

Page 468: Cells in an embryo undergo differentiation as they specialize, developing different structures to perform different functions.

Chapter 16   Interactions of Living Things

Section 1

Page 483: The biosphere is the part of Earth where life exists.

Section 2

Page 485: Organisms that eat other organisms are called *consumers*.

Page 487: An energy pyramid is a diagram that shows an ecosystem's loss of energy.

Page 488: Other animals in Yellowstone National Park were affected by the disappearance of the gray wolf because the food web was interrupted. The animals that would normally be prey for the gray wolf were more plentiful. These larger populations ate more vegetation.

Section 3

Page 491: The main ways that organisms affect each other are through competition, predator and prey relationships, symbiotic relationships, and coevolution.

Page 493: Camouflage helps an organism blend in with its surroundings because of its coloring. It is harder for a predator to find a camouflaged prey.

Page 494: In a mutualistic relationship, both organisms benefit from the relationship.

Page 496: Flowers need to attract pollinators to help the flowers reproduce with other members of their species.

Chapter 17   Cycles in Nature

Section 1

Page 509: Without water, there would be no life on Earth.

Page 511: Sample answer: calcium

Section 2

Page 512: Plants grew back, and the area is recovering.

Page 514: Primary succession happens in an area where organisms did not previously exist; secondary succession happens where organisms already exist.

Chapter 18   Properties and States of Matter

Section 1

Page 529: A pure substance is a sample of matter that has definite chemical and physical properties and is made of either one type of atom or one type of molecule.

Page 530: A chocolate chip cookie is a heterogeneous mixture because the substances in the cookie are not uniformly mixed. For example, the chocolate chips are different from the surrounding dough.

Page 532: Sample answer: Two physical properties are color and odor. (Other possibilities include hardness, melting point, boiling point, density, mass, and volume.)

Page 533: Sample answer: A chemical property of wood is flammability.

Page 534: Each sample of a pure substance has the same chemical and physical properties because each sample is composed of the same atoms or the same molecules.

Section 2

Page 537: A physical change is a change in which the physical properties of matter change but the identity of the matter does not.

Page 539: A chemical change is a change that happens when one or more substances change into new substances that have different chemical and physical properties than the original substances did.

Page 540: Accept all reasonable responses. Sample answer: Making metal from ore is a chemical change used in industry. (Other possibilities include making paints or plastics.)

Section 3

Page 543: In a solid, particles are close together and are in fixed positions.

Page 544: Particles in a gas are much farther apart than particles in a solid or a liquid are. They can move around easily and have no fixed positions.

Page 546: Two ways to increase the pressure of a gas in a container that cannot expand are to increase the temperature and to add more of the gas to the container.

Chapter 19   Matter in Motion

Section 1

Page 558: A reference point is an object that appears to stay in place.

Page 560: Velocity can change by changing speed or changing direction.

Page 562: The unit for acceleration is meters per second per second (m/s^2).

Section 2

Page 565: If all of the forces act in the same direction, you must add the forces to determine the net force.

Page 566: 2 N north

Section 3

Page 569: Friction is greater between rough surfaces because rough surfaces have more microscopic hills and valleys.

Page 571: *Static* means "not moving."

Page 572: Three common lubricants are oil, grease, and wax.

Section 4

Page 575: You must exert a force to overcome the gravitational force between the object and Earth.

Page 576: Gravitational force increases as mass increases.

Page 578: The weight of an object is a measure of the gravitational force on the object.

Chapter 20   Forces and Motion

Section 1

Page 591: The acceleration due to gravity is 9.8 m/s^2.

Page 592: Air resistance will have more of an effect on the acceleration of a falling leaf.

Page 594: The word *centripetal* means "toward the center."

Page 596: Gravity gives vertical motion to an object in projectile motion.

Section 2

Page 599: When the bus is moving, both you and the bus are in motion. When the bus stops moving, no unbalanced force acts on your body, so your body continues to move forward.

Page 601: The acceleration of an object increases as the force exerted on the object increases.

Page 603: The forces in a force pair are equal in size and opposite in direction.

Page 604: Objects accelerate toward Earth because the force of gravity pulls them toward Earth.

Section 3

Page 607: When two objects collide, some or all of the momentum of each object can be transferred to the other object.

Page 608: After a collision, objects can stick together or can bounce off each other.

Chapter 21   Forces in Fluids

Section 1

Page 621: Two gases in the atmosphere are nitrogen and oxygen.

Page 622: Pressure increases as depth increases.

Page 624: You decrease pressure inside a straw by removing some of the air inside the straw.

Section 2

Page 627: An object is buoyed up if the buoyant force on the object is greater than the object's weight.

Page 628: Helium is less dense than air.

Page 630: Crew members control the density of a submarine by controlling the amount of water in the ballast tanks.

Section 3

Page 633: Lift is an upward force on an object that is moving in a fluid.

Page 635: An irregular or unpredictable flow of fluids is known as *turbulence.*

Page 636: Airplanes can reduce turbulence by changing the shape or area of the wings.

Chapter 22   Work and Machines

Section 1

Page 650: No, work is done on an object only if force causes the object to move in a direction that is parallel to the force.

Page 653: Work is calculated as force times distance.

Page 654: Power is calculated as work done (in joules) divided by the time (in seconds) in which the work was done.

Section 2

Page 657: Machines make work easier by allowing a decreased force to be applied over a greater distance.

Page 658: Machines can change the force or the distance through which force is applied.

Page 660: *mechanical efficiency* = (work output ÷ work input) × 100

Section 3

Page 663: Each class of lever has a different set of mechanical advantage possibilities.

Page 665: The mechanical advantage of a wheel and axle is calculated by dividing the radius of the wheel by the radius of the axle.

Page 666: A slanted surface that makes the raising of loads easier, such as a ramp.

Page 668: They have more moving parts than simple machines do, so they tend to be less efficient than simple machines are.

Chapter 23   Energy and Energy Resources

Section 1

Page 680: Energy is the ability to do work.

Page 683: kinetic energy and potential energy

Page 685: Sound energy consists of vibrations carried through the air.

Page 686: Nuclear energy comes from changes in the nucleus of an atom.

Section 2

Page 689: Elastic potential energy can be stored by stretching a rubber band. Elastic potential energy is released when the rubber band goes back to its original shape.

Page 690: Plants get their energy from the sun.

Page 692: Machines can change the size or direction of the input force.

Section 3

Page 695: Conservation of energy is considered a scientific law because no exception to it has ever been observed.

Page 696: Perpetual motion is impossible because energy conversions always result in the production of waste thermal energy.

Section 4

Page 698: Fossil fuels are nonrenewable resources because they are used up more quickly than they are replaced.

Page 700: Nuclear energy comes from radioactive elements that give off energy during nuclear fission.

Page 702: Geothermal energy comes from the thermal energy given off by underground areas of hot rock.

Chapter 24   Heat and Heat Technology

Section 1

Page 715:   Temperature is a measure of the average kinetic energy of the particles of a substance.

Page 716:   Thermal expansion makes thermometers work.

Page 719:   Expansion joints on a bridge allow the bridge to undergo thermal expansion without breaking.

Section 2

Page 721:   If two objects at different temperatures come into contact, thermal energy will be transferred from the higher-temperature object to the lower-temperature object until both objects are at the same temperature.

Page 723:   Two objects that are at the same temperature can feel as though they are at different temperatures if one object is a better thermal conductor than the other is. The better conductor will feel colder because it will draw thermal energy away from your hand faster.

Page 724:   The greenhouse effect is the trapping of thermal energy from the sun in Earth's atmosphere.

Page 726:   Specific heat, mass, and the change in temperature are needed to calculate heat.

Section 3

Page 729:   While a substance is undergoing a change of state, the temperature of the substance remains the same.

Page 731:   The Calorie is the unit of food energy.

Section 4

Page 733:   Insulation helps save energy costs by keeping thermal energy from passing into or escaping from a building.

Page 735:   Combustion engines use thermal energy.

Page 737:   The inside of a refrigerator is able to stay cooler than the outside because thermal energy inside the refrigerator is continuously being transferred outside of the refrigerator.

Page 738:   Sample answer: Thermal pollution can take place when heated water from an electrical generating plant is returned to the river from which the water came. The heated water that is returned to the river raises the temperature of the river water.

Study Skills

FoldNote Instructions

Have you ever tried to study for a test or quiz but didn't know where to start? Or have you read a chapter and found that you can remember only a few ideas? Well, FoldNotes are a fun and exciting way to help you learn and remember the ideas you encounter as you learn science!

FoldNotes are tools that you can use to organize concepts. By focusing on a few main concepts, FoldNotes help you learn and remember how the concepts fit together. They can help you see the "big picture." Below you will find instructions for building 10 different FoldNotes.

Pyramid

1. Place a sheet of paper in front of you. Fold the lower left-hand corner of the paper diagonally to the opposite edge of the paper.

2. Cut off the tab of paper created by the fold (at the top).

3. Open the paper so that it is a square. Fold the lower right-hand corner of the paper diagonally to the opposite corner to form a triangle.

4. Open the paper. The creases of the two folds will have created an X.

5. Using scissors, cut along one of the creases. Start from any corner, and stop at the center point to create two flaps. Use tape or glue to attach one of the flaps on top of the other flap.

Double Door

1. Fold a sheet of paper in half from the top to the bottom. Then, unfold the paper.

2. Fold the top and bottom edges of the paper to the crease.

Appendix

Booklet

1. Fold a sheet of paper in half from left to right. Then, unfold the paper.

2. Fold the sheet of paper in half again from the top to the bottom. Then, unfold the paper.

3. Refold the sheet of paper in half from left to right.

4. Fold the top and bottom edges to the center crease.

5. Completely unfold the paper.

6. Refold the paper from top to bottom.

7. Using scissors, cut a slit along the center crease of the sheet from the folded edge to the creases made in step 4. Do not cut the entire sheet in half.

8. Fold the sheet of paper in half from left to right. While holding the bottom and top edges of the paper, push the bottom and top edges together so that the center collapses at the center slit. Fold the four flaps to form a four-page book.

Layered Book

1. Lay one sheet of paper on top of another sheet. Slide the top sheet up so that 2 cm of the bottom sheet is showing.

2. Hold the two sheets together, fold down the top of the two sheets so that you see four 2 cm tabs along the bottom.

3. Using a stapler, staple the top of the FoldNote.

Key-Term Fold

1. Fold a sheet of lined notebook paper in half from left to right.

2. Using scissors, cut along every third line from the right edge of the paper to the center fold to make tabs.

Four-Corner Fold

1. Fold a sheet of paper in half from left to right. Then, unfold the paper.

2. Fold each side of the paper to the crease in the center of the paper.

3. Fold the paper in half from the top to the bottom. Then, unfold the paper.

4. Using scissors, cut the top flap creases made in step 3 to form four flaps.

Three-Panel Flip Chart

1. Fold a piece of paper in half from the top to the bottom.

2. Fold the paper in thirds from side to side. Then, unfold the paper so that you can see the three sections.

3. From the top of the paper, cut along each of the vertical fold lines to the fold in the middle of the paper. You will now have three flaps.

Table Fold

1. Fold a piece of paper in half from the top to the bottom. Then, fold the paper in half again.

2. Fold the paper in thirds from side to side.

3. Unfold the paper completely. Carefully trace the fold lines by using a pen or pencil.

Two-Panel Flip Chart

1. Fold a piece of paper in half from the top to the bottom.

2. Fold the paper in half from side to side. Then, unfold the paper so that you can see the two sections.

3. From the top of the paper, cut along the vertical fold line to the fold in the middle of the paper. You will now have two flaps.

Tri-Fold

1. Fold a piece a paper in thirds from the top to the bottom.

2. Unfold the paper so that you can see the three sections. Then, turn the paper sideways so that the three sections form vertical columns.

3. Trace the fold lines by using a pen or pencil. Label the columns "Know," "Want," and "Learn."

Appendix

Graphic Organizer Instructions

 Have you ever wished that you could "draw out" the many concepts you learn in your science class? Sometimes, being able to *see* how concepts are related really helps you remember what you've learned. Graphic Organizers do just that! They give you a way to draw or map out concepts.

All you need to make a Graphic Organizer is a piece of paper and a pencil. Below you will find instructions for four different Graphic Organizers designed to help you organize the concepts you'll learn in this book.

Spider Map

1. Draw a diagram like the one shown. In the circle, write the main topic.

2. From the circle, draw legs to represent different categories of the main topic. You can have as many categories as you want.

3. From the category legs, draw horizontal lines. As you read the chapter, write details about each category on the horizontal lines.

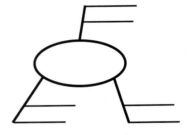

Comparison Table

1. Draw a chart like the one shown. Your chart can have as many columns and rows as you want.

2. In the top row, write the topics that you want to compare.

3. In the left column, write characteristics of the topics that you want to compare. As you read the chapter, fill in the characteristics for each topic in the appropriate boxes.

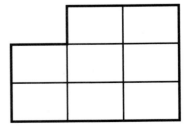

Chain-of-Events-Chart

1. Draw a box. In the box, write the first step of a process or the first event of a timeline.

2. Under the box, draw another box, and use an arrow to connect the two boxes. In the second box, write the next step of the process or the next event in the timeline.

3. Continue adding boxes until the process or timeline is finished.

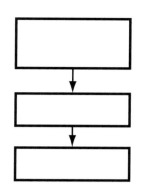

Concept Map

1. Draw a circle in the center of a piece of paper. Write the main idea of the chapter in the center of the circle.

2. From the circle, draw other circles. In those circles, write characteristics of the main idea. Draw arrows from the center circle to the circles that contain the characteristics.

3. From each circle that contains a characteristic, draw other circles. In those circles, write specific details about the characteristic. Draw arrows from each circle that contains a characteristic to the circles that contain specific details. You may draw as many circles as you want.

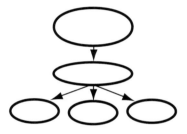

Appendix

Physical Science Laws and Principles

Law of Conservation of Mass

Mass cannot be created or destroyed during ordinary chemical or physical changes.

The total mass in a closed system is always the same no matter how many physical changes or chemical reactions occur.

Law of Conservation of Energy

Energy can be neither created nor destroyed.

The total amount of energy in a closed system is always the same. Energy can be changed from one form to another, but all of the different forms of energy in a system always add up to the same total amount of energy no matter how many energy conversions occur.

Law of Universal Gravitation

All objects in the universe attract each other by a force called *gravity*. The size of the force depends on the masses of the objects and the distance between the objects.

The first part of the law explains why lifting a bowling ball is much harder than lifting a marble. Because the bowling ball has a much larger mass than the marble does, the amount of gravity between the Earth and the bowling ball is greater than the amount of gravity between the Earth and the marble.

The second part of the law explains why a satellite can remain in orbit around the Earth. The satellite is carefully placed at a distance great enough to prevent the Earth's gravity from immediately pulling the satellite down but small enough to prevent the satellite from completely escaping the Earth's gravity and wandering off into space.

Newton's Laws of Motion

Newton's first law of motion states that an object at rest remains at rest and an object in motion remains in motion at constant speed and in a straight line unless acted on by an unbalanced force.

The first part of the law explains why a football will remain on a tee until it is kicked off or until a gust of wind blows it off.

The second part of the law explains why a bike rider will continue moving forward after the bike comes to an abrupt stop. Gravity and the friction of the sidewalk will eventually stop the rider.

Newton's second law of motion states that the acceleration of an object depends on the mass of the object and the amount of force applied.

The first part of the law explains why the acceleration of a 4 kg bowling ball will be greater than the acceleration of a 6 kg bowling ball if the same force is applied to both balls.

The second part of the law explains why the acceleration of a bowling ball will be larger if a larger force is applied to the bowling ball.

The relationship of acceleration (a) to mass (m) and force (F) can be expressed mathematically by the following equation:

$$acceleration = \frac{force}{mass}, \text{ or } a = \frac{F}{m}$$

This equation is often rearranged to the form

$$force = mass \times acceleration, \text{ or } F = m \times a$$

Newton's third law of motion states that whenever one object exerts a force on a second object, the second object exerts an equal and opposite force on the first.

This law explains that a runner is able to move forward because of the equal and opposite force that the ground exerts on the runner's foot after each step.

Law of Reflection

The **law of reflection** states that the angle of incidence is equal to the angle of reflection. This law explains why light reflects off a surface at the same angle that the light strikes the surface.

A line perpendicular to the mirror's surface is called the *normal*.

The beam of light reflected off the mirror is called the *reflected beam*.

The beam of light traveling toward the mirror is called the *incident beam*.

The angle between the incident beam and the normal is called the *angle of incidence*.

The angle between the reflected beam and the normal is called the *angle of reflection*.

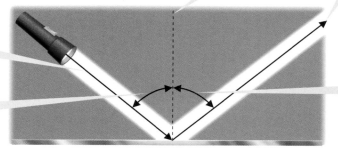

Charles's Law

Charles's law states that for a fixed amount of gas at a constant pressure, the volume of the gas increases as the temperature of the gas increases. Likewise, the volume of the gas decreases as the temperature of the gas decreases.

If a basketball that was inflated indoors is left outside on a cold winter day, the air particles inside the ball will move more slowly. They will hit the sides of the basketball less often and with less force. The ball will get smaller as the volume of the air decreases.

Boyle's Law

Boyle's law states that for a fixed amount of gas at a constant temperature, the volume of a gas increases as the pressure of the gas decreases. Likewise, the volume of a gas decreases as its pressure increases.

If an inflated balloon is pulled down to the bottom of a swimming pool, the pressure of the water on the balloon increases. The pressure of the air particles inside the balloon must increase to match that of the water outside, so the volume of the air inside the balloon decreases.

Pascal's Principle

Pascal's principle states that a change in pressure at any point in an enclosed fluid will be transmitted equally to all parts of that fluid.

When a mechanic uses a hydraulic jack to raise an automobile off the ground, he or she increases the pressure on the fluid in the jack by pushing on the jack handle. The pressure is transmitted equally to all parts of the fluid-filled jacking system. As fluid presses the jack plate against the frame of the car, the car is lifed off the ground.

Archimedes' Principle

Archimedes' principle states that the buoyant force on an object in a fluid is equal to the weight of the volume of fluid that the object displaces.

A person floating in a swimming pool displaces 20 L of water. The weight of that volume of water is about 200 N. Therefore, the buoyant force on the person is 200 N.

Bernoulli's Principle

> **Bernoulli's principle states that as the speed of a moving fluid increases, the fluid's pressure decreases.**

The lift on an airplane wing or on a Frisbee® can be explained in part by using Bernoulli's principle. Because of the shape of the Frisbee, the air moving over the top of the Frisbee must travel farther than the air below the Frisbee in the same amount of time. In other words, the air above the Frisbee is moving faster than the air below it. This faster-moving air above the Frisbee exerts less pressure than the slower-moving air below it does. The resulting increased pressure below exerts an upward force and pushes the Frisbee up.

Useful Equations

Average speed

$$\text{average speed} = \frac{\text{total distance}}{\text{total time}}$$

Example: A bicycle messenger traveled a distance of 136 km in 8 h. What was the messenger's average speed?

$$\frac{136 \text{ km}}{8 \text{ h}} = 17 \text{ km/h}$$

The messenger's average speed was **17 km/h.**

Average acceleration

$$\text{average acceleration} = \frac{\text{final velocity} - \text{starting velocity}}{\text{time it takes to change velocity}}$$

Example: Calculate the average acceleration of an Olympic 100 m dash sprinter who reaches a velocity of 20 m/s south at the finish line. The race was in a straight line and lasted 10 s.

$$\frac{20 \text{ m/s} - 0 \text{ m/s}}{10 \text{s}} = 2 \text{ m/s/s}$$

The sprinter's average acceleration is **2 m/s/s south.**

Net force

Forces in the Same Direction

When forces are in the same direction, add the forces together to determine the net force.

Example: Calculate the net force on a stalled car that is being pushed by two people. One person is pushing with a force of 13 N northwest, and the other person is pushing with a force of 8 N in the same direction.

$$13 \text{ N} + 8 \text{ N} = 21 \text{ N}$$

The net force is **21 N northwest.**

Forces in Opposite Directions

When forces are in opposite directions, subtract the smaller force from the larger force to determine the net force. The net force will be in the direction of the larger force.

Example: Calculate the net force on a rope that is being pulled on each end. One person is pulling on one end of the rope with a force of 12 N south. Another person is pulling on the opposite end of the rope with a force of 7 N north.

$$12 \text{ N} - 7 \text{ N} = 5 \text{ N}$$

The net force is **5 N south.**

Work

Work is done by exerting a force through a distance. Work has units of joules (J), which are equivalent to Newton-meters.

$$Work = F \times d$$

Example: Calculate the amount of work done by a man who lifts a 100 N toddler 1.5 m off the floor.

$Work = 100 \text{ N} \times 1.5 \text{ m} = 150 \text{ N•m} = 150 \text{ J}$

The man did **150 J** of work.

Power

Power is the rate at which work is done. Power is measured in watts (W), which are equivalent to joules per second.

$$P = \frac{Work}{t}$$

Example: Calculate the power of a weight-lifter who raises a 300 N barbell 2.1 m off the floor in 1.25 s.

$Work = 300 \text{ N} \times 2.1 \text{ m} = 630 \text{ N•m} = 630 \text{ J}$

$P = \dfrac{630 \text{ J}}{1.25 \text{ s}} = \dfrac{504 \text{ J}}{\text{s}} = 504 \text{ W}$

The weightlifter has **504 W** of power.

Pressure

Pressure is the force exerted over a given area. The SI unit for pressure is the pascal (Pa).

$$pressure = \frac{force}{area}$$

Example: Calculate the pressure of the air in a soccer ball if the air exerts a force of 25,000 N over an area of 0.15 m².

$pressure = \dfrac{25{,}000 \text{ N}}{0.15 \text{ m}^2} = \dfrac{167{,}000 \text{ N}}{\text{m}^2} = 167{,}000 \text{ Pa}$

The pressure of the air inside the soccer ball is **167,000 Pa.**

Density

$$density = \frac{mass}{volume}$$

Example: Calculate the density of a sponge that has a mass of 10 g and a volume of 40 cm³.

$\dfrac{10 \text{ g}}{40 \text{ cm}^3} = \dfrac{0.25 \text{ g}}{\text{cm}^3}$

The density of the sponge is $\dfrac{0.25 \text{ g}}{\text{cm}^3}$.

Concentration

$$concentration = \frac{mass\ of\ solute}{volume\ of\ solvent}$$

Example: Calculate the concentration of a solution in which 10 g of sugar is dissolved in 125 mL of water.

$\dfrac{10 \text{ g of sugar}}{125 \text{ mL of water}} = \dfrac{0.08 \text{ g}}{\text{mL}}$

The concentration of this solution is $\dfrac{0.08 \text{ g}}{\text{mL}}$.

Math Refresher

Science requires an understanding of many math concepts. The following pages will help you review some important math skills.

Averages

An **average,** or **mean,** simplifies a set of numbers into a single number that *approximates* the value of the set.

> **Example:** Find the average of the following set of numbers: 5, 4, 7, and 8.

Step 1: Find the sum.
$$5 + 4 + 7 + 8 = 24$$

Step 2: Divide the sum by the number of numbers in your set. Because there are four numbers in this example, divide the sum by 4.

$$\frac{24}{4} = 6$$

The average, or mean, is **6.**

Ratios

A **ratio** is a comparison between numbers, and it is usually written as a fraction.

> **Example:** Find the ratio of thermometers to students if you have 36 thermometers and 48 students in your class.

Step 1: Make the ratio.

$$\frac{36 \text{ thermometers}}{48 \text{ students}}$$

Step 2: Reduce the fraction to its simplest form.

$$\frac{36}{48} = \frac{36 \div 12}{48 \div 12} = \frac{3}{4}$$

The ratio of thermometers to students is **3 to 4,** or $\frac{3}{4}$. The ratio may also be written in the form 3:4.

Proportions

A **proportion** is an equation that states that two ratios are equal.

$$\frac{3}{1} = \frac{12}{4}$$

To solve a proportion, first multiply across the equal sign. This is called *cross-multiplication*. If you know three of the quantities in a proportion, you can use cross-multiplication to find the fourth.

> **Example:** Imagine that you are making a scale model of the solar system for your science project. The diameter of Jupiter is 11.2 times the diameter of the Earth. If you are using a plastic-foam ball that has a diameter of 2 cm to represent the Earth, what must the diameter of the ball representing Jupiter be?
>
> $$\frac{11.2}{1} = \frac{x}{2 \text{ cm}}$$

Step 1: Cross-multiply.

$$\frac{11.2}{1} \times \frac{x}{2}$$

$$11.2 \times 2 = x \times 1$$

Step 2: Multiply.
$$22.4 = x \times 1$$

Step 3: Isolate the variable by dividing both sides by 1.

$$x = \frac{22.4}{1}$$
$$x = 22.4 \text{ cm}$$

You will need to use a ball that has a diameter of **22.4** cm to represent Jupiter.

Percentages

A **percentage** is a ratio of a given number to 100.

> **Example:** What is 85% of 40?

Step 1: Rewrite the percentage by moving the decimal point two places to the left.

$$0.85$$

Step 2: Multiply the decimal by the number that you are calculating the percentage of.

$$0.85 \times 40 = 34$$

85% of 40 is **34.**

Decimals

To **add** or **subtract decimals,** line up the digits vertically so that the decimal points line up. Then, add or subtract the columns from right to left. Carry or borrow numbers as necessary.

> **Example:** Add the following numbers: 3.1415 and 2.96.

Step 1: Line up the digits vertically so that the decimal points line up.

$$\begin{array}{r} 3.1415 \\ + 2.96 \\ \hline \end{array}$$

Step 2: Add the columns from right to left, and carry when necessary.

$$\begin{array}{r} {}^{1\ 1} \\ 3.1415 \\ + 2.96 \\ \hline 6.1015 \end{array}$$

The sum is **6.1015.**

Fractions

Numbers tell you how many; **fractions** tell you *how much of a whole.*

> **Example:** Your class has 24 plants. Your teacher instructs you to put 5 plants in a shady spot. What fraction of the plants in your class will you put in a shady spot?

Step 1: In the denominator, write the total number of parts in the whole.

$$\frac{?}{24}$$

Step 2: In the numerator, write the number of parts of the whole that are being considered.

$$\frac{5}{24}$$

So, $\frac{5}{24}$ of the plants will be in the shade.

Reducing Fractions

It is usually best to express a fraction in its simplest form. Expressing a fraction in its simplest form is called *reducing* a fraction.

> **Example:** Reduce the fraction $\frac{30}{45}$ to its simplest form.

Step 1: Find the largest whole number that will divide evenly into both the numerator and denominator. This number is called the *greatest common factor* (GCF).

Factors of the numerator 30:
   1, 2, 3, 5, 6, 10, **15,** 30

Factors of the denominator 45:
   1, 3, 5, 9, **15,** 45

Step 2: Divide both the numerator and the denominator by the GCF, which in this case is 15.

$$\frac{30}{45} = \frac{30 \div 15}{45 \div 15} = \frac{2}{3}$$

Thus, $\frac{30}{45}$ reduced to its simplest form is $\frac{2}{3}$.

Adding and Subtracting Fractions

To **add** or **subtract fractions** that have the **same denominator,** simply add or subtract the numerators.

> **Examples:**
>
> $\frac{3}{5} + \frac{1}{5} = ?$ and $\frac{3}{4} - \frac{1}{4} = ?$

Step 1: Add or subtract the numerators.

$$\frac{3}{5} + \frac{1}{5} = \frac{4}{} \text{ and } \frac{3}{4} - \frac{1}{4} = \frac{2}{}$$

Step 2: Write the sum or difference over the denominator.

$$\frac{3}{5} + \frac{1}{5} = \frac{4}{5} \text{ and } \frac{3}{4} - \frac{1}{4} = \frac{2}{4}$$

Step 3: If necessary, reduce the fraction to its simplest form.

$\frac{4}{5}$ cannot be reduced, and $\frac{2}{4} = \frac{1}{2}$.

To **add** or **subtract fractions** that have **different denominators,** first find the least common denominator (LCD).

> **Examples:**
>
> $\frac{1}{2} + \frac{1}{6} = ?$ and $\frac{3}{4} - \frac{2}{3} = ?$

Step 1: Write the equivalent fractions that have a common denominator.

$$\frac{3}{6} + \frac{1}{6} = ? \text{ and } \frac{9}{12} - \frac{8}{12} = ?$$

Step 2: Add or subtract the fractions.

$$\frac{3}{6} + \frac{1}{6} = \frac{4}{6} \text{ and } \frac{9}{12} - \frac{8}{12} = \frac{1}{12}$$

Step 3: If necessary, reduce the fraction to its simplest form.

The fraction $\frac{4}{6} = \frac{2}{3}$, and $\frac{1}{12}$ cannot be reduced.

Multiplying Fractions

To **multiply fractions,** multiply the numerators and the denominators together, and then reduce the fraction to its simplest form.

> **Example:**
>
> $\frac{5}{9} \times \frac{7}{10} = ?$

Step 1: Multiply the numerators and denominators.

$$\frac{5}{9} \times \frac{7}{10} = \frac{5 \times 7}{9 \times 10} = \frac{35}{90}$$

Step 2: Reduce the fraction.

$$\frac{35}{90} = \frac{35 \div 5}{90 \div 5} = \frac{7}{18}$$

Dividing Fractions

To **divide fractions,** first rewrite the divisor (the number you divide by) upside down. This number is called the *reciprocal* of the divisor. Then multiply and reduce if necessary.

> **Example:**
>
> $\frac{5}{8} \div \frac{3}{2} = ?$

Step 1: Rewrite the divisor as its reciprocal.

$$\frac{3}{2} \rightarrow \frac{2}{3}$$

Step 2: Multiply the fractions.

$$\frac{5}{8} \times \frac{2}{3} = \frac{5 \times 2}{8 \times 3} = \frac{10}{24}$$

Step 3: Reduce the fraction.

$$\frac{10}{24} = \frac{10 \div 2}{24 \div 2} = \frac{5}{12}$$

Scientific Notation

Scientific notation is a short way of representing very large and very small numbers without writing all of the place-holding zeros.

> **Example:** Write 653,000,000 in scientific notation.

Step 1: Write the number without the place-holding zeros.

653

Step 2: Place the decimal point after the first digit.

6.53

Step 3: Find the exponent by counting the number of places that you moved the decimal point.

6.53000000

The decimal point was moved eight places to the left. Therefore, the exponent of 10 is positive 8. If you had moved the decimal point to the right, the exponent would be negative.

Step 4: Write the number in scientific notation.

$$6.53 \times 10^8$$

Area

Area is the number of square units needed to cover the surface of an object.

> **Formulas:**
>
> area of a square = side × side
> area of a rectangle = length × width
> area of a triangle = $\frac{1}{2}$ × base × height
>
> **Examples:** Find the areas.

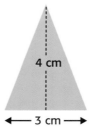

Triangle

$area = \frac{1}{2} \times base \times height$

$area = \frac{1}{2} \times 3 \text{ cm} \times 4 \text{ cm}$

$area = \textbf{6 cm}^2$

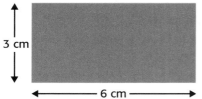

Rectangle

$area = length \times width$

$area = 6 \text{ cm} \times 3 \text{ cm}$

$area = \textbf{18 cm}^2$

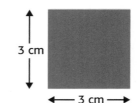

Square

$area = side \times side$

$area = 3 \text{ cm} \times 3 \text{ cm}$

$area = \textbf{9 cm}^2$

Volume

Volume is the amount of space that something occupies.

> **Formulas:**
>
> volume of a cube =
> side × side × side
>
> volume of a prism =
> area of base × height
>
> **Examples:**
>
> Find the volume of the solids.

Cube

$volume = side \times side \times side$

$volume = 4 \text{ cm} \times 4 \text{ cm} \times 4 \text{ cm}$

$volume = \textbf{64 cm}^3$

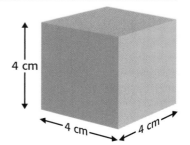

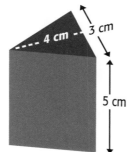

Prism

$volume = area \ of \ base \times height$

$volume = (area \ of \ triangle) \times height$

$volume = (\frac{1}{2} \times 3 \text{ cm} \times 4 \text{ cm}) \times 5 \text{ cm}$

$volume = 6 \text{ cm}^2 \times 5 \text{ cm}$

$volume = \textbf{30 cm}^3$

Making Charts and Graphs

Pie Charts

A pie chart shows how each group of data relates to all of the data. Each part of the circle forming the chart represents a category of the data. The entire circle represents all of the data. For example, a biologist studying a hardwood forest in Wisconsin found that there were five different types of trees. The data table at right summarizes the biologist's findings.

Wisconsin Hardwood Trees	
Type of tree	Number found
Oak	600
Maple	750
Beech	300
Birch	1,200
Hickory	150
Total	3,000

How to Make a Pie Chart

1 To make a pie chart of these data, first find the percentage of each type of tree. Divide the number of trees of each type by the total number of trees, and multiply by 100.

$$\frac{600 \text{ oak}}{3,000 \text{ trees}} \times 100 = 20\%$$

$$\frac{750 \text{ maple}}{3,000 \text{ trees}} \times 100 = 25\%$$

$$\frac{300 \text{ beech}}{3,000 \text{ trees}} \times 100 = 10\%$$

$$\frac{1,200 \text{ birch}}{3,000 \text{ trees}} \times 100 = 40\%$$

$$\frac{150 \text{ hickory}}{3,000 \text{ trees}} \times 100 = 5\%$$

2 Now, determine the size of the wedges that make up the pie chart. Multiply each percentage by 360°. Remember that a circle contains 360°.

20% × 360° = 72°   25% × 360° = 90°

10% × 360° = 36°   40% × 360° = 144°

5% × 360° = 18°

3 Check that the sum of the percentages is 100 and the sum of the degrees is 360.

20% + 25% + 10% + 40% + 5% = 100%

72° + 90° + 36° + 144° + 18° = 360°

4 Use a compass to draw a circle and mark the center of the circle.

5 Then, use a protractor to draw angles of 72°, 90°, 36°, 144°, and 18° in the circle.

6 Finally, label each part of the chart, and choose an appropriate title.

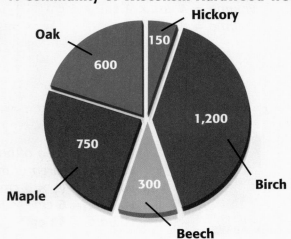

A Community of Wisconsin Hardwood Trees

Line Graphs

Line graphs are most often used to demonstrate continuous change. For example, Mr. Smith's students analyzed the population records for their hometown, Appleton, between 1900 and 2000. Examine the data at right.

Because the year and the population change, they are the *variables*. The population is determined by, or dependent on, the year. Therefore, the population is called the **dependent variable,** and the year is called the **independent variable.** Each set of data is called a **data pair.** To prepare a line graph, you must first organize data pairs into a table like the one at right.

Population of Appleton, 1900–2000	
Year	**Population**
1900	1,800
1920	2,500
1940	3,200
1960	3,900
1980	4,600
2000	5,300

How to Make a Line Graph

1 Place the independent variable along the horizontal (*x*) axis. Place the dependent variable along the vertical (*y*) axis.

2 Label the *x*-axis "Year" and the *y*-axis "Population." Look at your largest and smallest values for the population. For the *y*-axis, determine a scale that will provide enough space to show these values. You must use the same scale for the entire length of the axis. Next, find an appropriate scale for the *x*-axis.

3 Choose reasonable starting points for each axis.

4 Plot the data pairs as accurately as possible.

5 Choose a title that accurately represents the data.

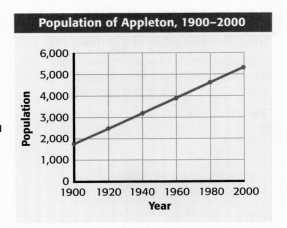

How to Determine Slope

Slope is the ratio of the change in the *y*-value to the change in the *x*-value, or "rise over run."

1 Choose two points on the line graph. For example, the population of Appleton in 2000 was 5,300 people. Therefore, you can define point *a* as (2000, 5,300). In 1900, the population was 1,800 people. You can define point *b* as (1900, 1,800).

2 Find the change in the *y*-value. (*y* at point *a*) − (*y* at point *b*) = 5,300 people − 1,800 people = 3,500 people

3 Find the change in the *x*-value. (*x* at point *a*) − (*x* at point *b*) = 2000 − 1900 = 100 years

4 Calculate the slope of the graph by dividing the change in *y* by the change in *x*.

$$slope = \frac{change\ in\ y}{change\ in\ x}$$

$$slope = \frac{3{,}500\ people}{100\ years}$$

$$slope = 35\ people\ per\ year$$

In this example, the population in Appleton increased by a fixed amount each year. The graph of these data is a straight line. Therefore, the relationship is **linear.** When the graph of a set of data is not a straight line, the relationship is **nonlinear.**

Using Algebra to Determine Slope

The equation in step 4 may also be arranged to be

$$y = kx$$

where y represents the change in the y-value, k represents the slope, and x represents the change in the x-value.

$$slope = \frac{change\ in\ y}{change\ in\ x}$$

$$k = \frac{y}{x}$$

$$k \times x = \frac{y \times x}{x}$$

$$kx = y$$

Bar Graphs

Bar graphs are used to demonstrate change that is not continuous. These graphs can be used to indicate trends when the data cover a long period of time. A meteorologist gathered the precipitation data shown here for Hartford, Connecticut, for April 1–15, 1996, and used a bar graph to represent the data.

Precipitation in Hartford, Connecticut April 1–15, 1996			
Date	Precipitation (cm)	Date	Precipitation (cm)
April 1	0.5	April 9	0.25
April 2	1.25	April 10	0.0
April 3	0.0	April 11	1.0
April 4	0.0	April 12	0.0
April 5	0.0	April 13	0.25
April 6	0.0	April 14	0.0
April 7	0.0	April 15	6.50
April 8	1.75		

How to Make a Bar Graph

1 Use an appropriate scale and a reasonable starting point for each axis.

2 Label the axes, and plot the data.

3 Choose a title that accurately represents the data.

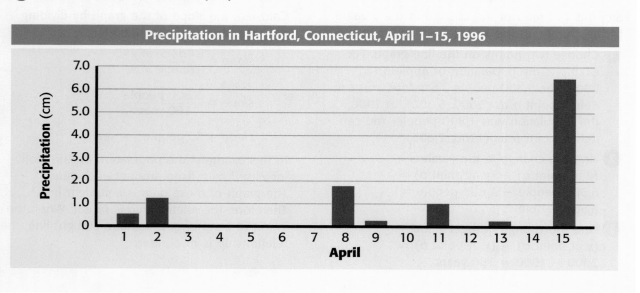

Precipitation in Hartford, Connecticut, April 1–15, 1996

Appendix

Measuring Skills

Using a Graduated Cylinder

When using a graduated cylinder to measure volume, keep the following procedures in mind:

1. Place the cylinder on a flat, level surface before measuring liquid.

2. Move your head so that your eye is level with the surface of the liquid.

3. Read the mark closest to the liquid level. On glass graduated cylinders, read the mark closest to the center of the curve in the liquid's surface.

Using a Meterstick or Metric Ruler

When using a meterstick or metric ruler to measure length, keep the following procedures in mind:

1. Place the ruler firmly against the object that you are measuring.

2. Align one edge of the object exactly with the 0 end of the ruler.

3. Look at the other edge of the object to see which of the marks on the ruler is closest to that edge. (Note: Each small slash between the centimeters represents a millimeter, which is one-tenth of a centimeter.)

Using a Triple-Beam Balance

When using a triple-beam balance to measure mass, keep the following procedures in mind:

1. Make sure the balance is on a level surface.

2. Place all of the countermasses at 0. Adjust the balancing knob until the pointer rests at 0.

3. Place the object you wish to measure on the pan. **Caution:** Do not place hot objects or chemicals directly on the balance pan.

4. Move the largest countermass along the beam to the right until it is at the last notch that does not tip the balance. Follow the same procedure with the next-largest countermass. Then, move the smallest countermass until the pointer rests at 0.

5. Add the readings from the three beams together to determine the mass of the object.

6. When determining the mass of crystals or powders, first find the mass of a piece of filter paper. Then, add the crystals or powder to the paper, and remeasure. The actual mass of the crystals or powder is the total mass minus the mass of the paper. When finding the mass of liquids, first find the mass of the empty container. Then, find the combined mass of the liquid and container. The mass of the liquid is the total mass minus the mass of the container.

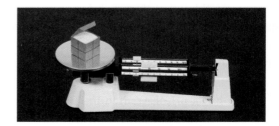

Scientific Methods

The ways in which scientists answer questions and solve problems are called **scientific methods.** The same steps are often used by scientists as they look for answers. However, there is more than one way to use these steps. Scientists may use all of the steps or just some of the steps during an investigation. They may even repeat some of the steps. The goal of using scientific methods is to come up with reliable answers and solutions.

Six Steps of Scientific Methods

 **1 Ask a Question**

Good questions come from careful **observations.** You make observations by using your senses to gather information. Sometimes, you may use instruments, such as microscopes and telescopes, to extend the range of your senses. As you observe the natural world, you will discover that you have many more questions than answers. These questions drive investigations.

Questions beginning with *what, why, how,* and *when* are important in focusing an investigation. Here is an example of a question that could lead to an investigation.

Question: How does acid rain affect plant growth?

 **2 Form a Hypothesis**

After you ask a question, you need to form a **hypothesis.** A hypothesis is a clear statement of what you expect the answer to your question to be. Your hypothesis will represent your best "educated guess" based on what you have observed and what you already know. A good hypothesis is testable. Otherwise, the investigation can go no further. Here is a hypothesis based on the question, "How does acid rain affect plant growth?"

Hypothesis: Acid rain slows plant growth.

The hypothesis can lead to predictions. A prediction is what you think the outcome of your experiment or data collection will be. Predictions are usually stated in an if-then format. Here is a sample prediction for the hypothesis that acid rain slows plant growth.

Prediction: If a plant is watered with only acid rain (which has a pH of 4), then the plant will grow at half its normal rate.

 **3 Test the Hypothesis**

After you have formed a hypothesis and made a prediction, your hypothesis should be tested. One way to test a hypothesis is with a controlled experiment. A **controlled experiment** tests only one factor at a time. In an experiment to test the effect of acid rain on plant growth, the **control group** would be watered with normal rain water. The **experimental group** would be watered with acid rain. All of the plants should receive the same amount of sunlight and water each day. The air temperature should be the same for all groups. However, the acidity of the water will be a variable. In fact, any factor that is different from one group to another is a **variable.** If your hypothesis is correct, then the acidity of the water and plant growth are *dependant variables.* The amount a plant grows is dependent on the acidity of the water. However, the amount of water each plant receives and the amount of sunlight each plant receives are *independent variables.* Either of these factors could change without affecting the other factor.

Sometimes, the nature of an investigation makes a controlled experiment impossible. For example, the Earth's core is surrounded by thousands of meters of rock. Under such circumstances, a hypothesis may be tested by making detailed observations.

 **4 Analyze the Results**

After you have completed your experiments, made your observations, and collected your data, you must analyze all the information you have gathered. Tables and graphs are often used in this step to organize the data.

Appendix

5 Draw Conclusions

After analyzing your data, you can determine if your results support your hypothesis. If your hypothesis is supported, you (or others) might want to repeat the observations or experiments to verify your results. If your hypothesis is not supported by the data, you may have to check your procedure for errors. You may even have to reject your hypothesis and make a new one. If you cannot draw a conclusion from your results, you may have to try the investigation again or carry out further observations or experiments.

6 Communicate Results

After any scientific investigation, you should report your results. By preparing a written or oral report, you let others know what you have learned. They may repeat your investigation to see if they get the same results. Your report may even lead to another question and then to another investigation.

Scientific Methods in Action

Scientific methods contain loops in which several steps may be repeated over and over again. In some cases, certain steps are unnecessary. Thus, there is not a "straight line" of steps. For example, sometimes scientists find that testing one hypothesis raises new questions and new hypotheses to be tested. And sometimes, testing the hypothesis leads directly to a conclusion. Furthermore, the steps in scientific methods are not always used in the same order. Follow the steps in the diagram, and see how many different directions scientific methods can take you.

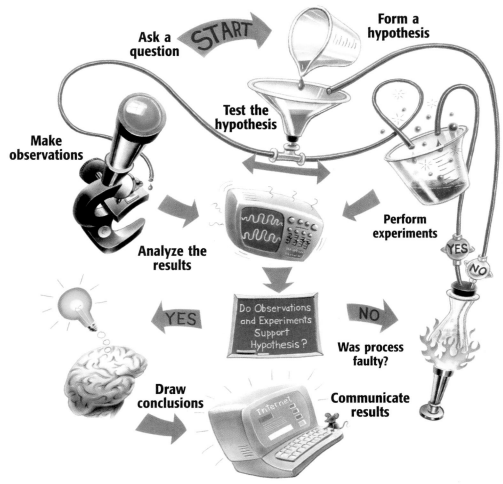

Using the Microscope

Parts of the Compound Light Microscope

- The **ocular lens** magnifies the image 10×.
- The **low-power objective** magnifies the image 10×.
- The **high-power objective** magnifies the image either 40× or 43×.
- The **revolving nosepiece** holds the objectives and can be turned to change from one magnification to the other.
- The **body tube** maintains the correct distance between the ocular lens and objectives.
- The **coarse-adjustment knob** moves the body tube up and down to allow focusing of the image.
- The **fine-adjustment knob** moves the body tube slightly to bring the image into sharper focus. It is usually located in the center of the coarse-adjustment knob.
- The **stage** supports a slide.
- **Stage clips** hold the slide in place for viewing.
- The **diaphragm** controls the amount of light coming through the stage.
- The light source provides a **light** for viewing the slide.
- The **arm** supports the body tube.
- The **base** supports the microscope.

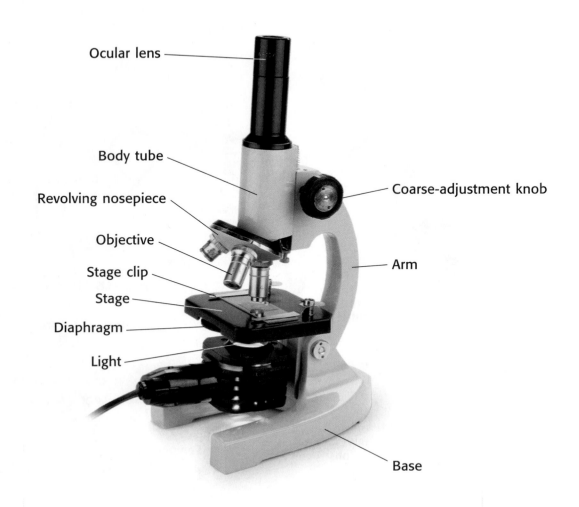

Ocular lens

Body tube

Revolving nosepiece

Objective

Stage clip

Stage

Diaphragm

Light

Coarse-adjustment knob

Arm

Base

Proper Use of the Compound Light Microscope

1. Use both hands to carry the microscope to your lab table. Place one hand beneath the base, and use the other hand to hold the arm of the microscope. Hold the microscope close to your body while carrying it to your lab table.

2. Place the microscope on the lab table at least 5 cm from the edge of the table.

3. Check to see what type of light source is used by your microscope. If the microscope has a lamp, plug it in and make sure that the cord is out of the way. If the microscope has a mirror, adjust the mirror to reflect light through the hole in the stage. **Caution:** If your microscope has a mirror, do not use direct sunlight as a light source. Direct sunlight can damage your eyes.

4. Always begin work with the low-power objective in line with the body tube. Adjust the revolving nosepiece.

5. Place a prepared slide over the hole in the stage. Secure the slide with the stage clips.

6. Look through the ocular lens. Move the diaphragm to adjust the amount of light coming through the stage.

7. Look at the stage from eye level. Slowly turn the coarse adjustment to lower the objective until the objective almost touches the slide. Do not allow the objective to touch the slide.

8. Look through the ocular lens. Turn the coarse adjustment to raise the low-power objective until the image is in focus. Always focus by raising the objective away from the slide. Never focus the objective downward. Use the fine adjustment to sharpen the focus. Keep both eyes open while viewing a slide.

9. Make sure that the image is exactly in the center of your field of vision. Then, switch to the high-power objective. Focus the image by using only the fine adjustment. Never use the coarse adjustment at high power.

10. When you are finished using the microscope, remove the slide. Clean the ocular lens and objectives with lens paper. Return the microscope to its storage area. Remember to use both hands when carrying the microscope.

Making a Wet Mount

1. Use lens paper to clean a glass slide and a coverslip.

2. Place the specimen that you wish to observe in the center of the slide.

3. Using a medicine dropper, place one drop of water on the specimen.

4. Hold the coverslip at the edge of the water and at a 45° angle to the slide. Make sure that the water runs along the edge of the coverslip.

5. Lower the coverslip slowly to avoid trapping air bubbles.

6. Water might evaporate from the slide as you work. Add more water to keep the specimen fresh. Place the tip of the medicine dropper next to the edge of the coverslip. Add a drop of water. (You can also use this method to add stain or solutions to a wet mount.) Remove excess water from the slide by using the corner of a paper towel as a blotter. Do not lift the coverslip to add or remove water.

SI Measurement

The International System of Units, or SI, is the standard system of measurement used by many scientists. Using the same standards of measurement makes it easier for scientists to communicate with one another.

SI works by combining prefixes and base units. Each base unit can be used with different prefixes to define smaller and larger quantities. The table below lists common SI prefixes.

SI Prefixes

Prefix	Symbol	Factor	Example
kilo-	k	1,000	kilogram, 1 kg = 1,000 g
hecto-	h	100	hectoliter, 1 hL = 100 L
deka-	da	10	dekameter, 1 dam = 10 m
		1	meter, liter, gram
deci-	d	0.1	decigram, 1 dg = 0.1 g
centi-	c	0.01	centimeter, 1 cm = 0.01 m
milli-	m	0.001	milliliter, 1 mL = 0.001 L
micro-	μ	0.000 001	micrometer, 1 μm = 0.000 001 m

SI Conversion Table

SI units	From SI to English	From English to SI
Length		
kilometer (km) = 1,000 m	1 km = 0.621 mi	1 mi = 1.609 km
meter (m) = 100 cm	1 m = 3.281 ft	1 ft = 0.305 m
centimeter (cm) = 0.01 m	1 cm = 0.394 in.	1 in. = 2.540 cm
millimeter (mm) = 0.001 m	1 mm = 0.039 in.	
micrometer (μm) = 0.000 001 m		
nanometer (nm) = 0.000 000 001 m		
Area		
square kilometer (km^2) = 100 hectares	1 km^2 = 0.386 mi^2	1 mi^2 = 2.590 km^2
hectare (ha) = 10,000 m^2	1 ha = 2.471 acres	1 acre = 0.405 ha
square meter (m^2) = 10,000 cm^2	1 m^2 = 10.764 ft^2	1 ft^2 = 0.093 m^2
square centimeter (cm^2) = 100 mm^2	1 cm^2 = 0.155 in.^{2}	1 in.^{2} = 6.452 cm^2
Volume		
liter (L) = 1,000 mL = 1 dm^3	1 L = 1.057 fl qt	1 fl qt = 0.946 L
milliliter (mL) = 0.001 L = 1 cm^3	1 mL = 0.034 fl oz	1 fl oz = 29.574 mL
microliter (μL) = 0.000 001 L		
Mass		*Equivalent weight at Earth's surface
kilogram (kg) = 1,000 g	1 kg = 2.205 lb*	1 lb* = 0.454 kg
gram (g) = 1,000 mg	1 g = 0.035 oz*	1 oz* = 28.350 g
milligram (mg) = 0.001 g		
microgram (μg) = 0.000 001 g		

Temperature Scales

Temperature can be expressed by using three different scales: Fahrenheit, Celsius, and Kelvin. The SI unit for temperature is the kelvin (K).

Although 0 K is much colder than 0°C, a change of 1 K is equal to a change of 1°C.

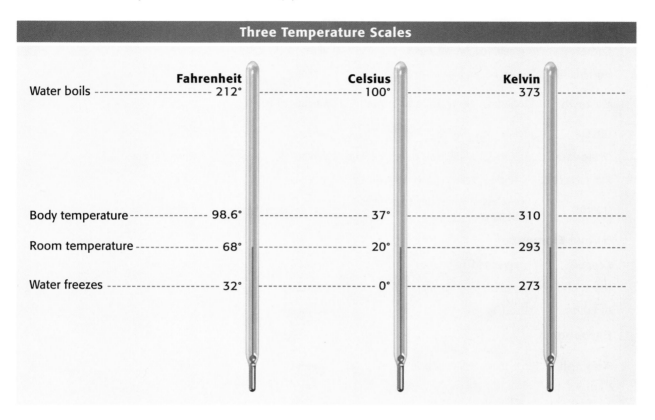

Three Temperature Scales

	Fahrenheit	Celsius	Kelvin
Water boils	212°	100°	373
Body temperature	98.6°	37°	310
Room temperature	68°	20°	293
Water freezes	32°	0°	273

Temperature Conversions Table

To convert	Use this equation:	Example
Celsius to Fahrenheit °C → °F	$°F = \left(\dfrac{9}{5} \times °C\right) + 32$	Convert 45°C to °F. $°F = \left(\dfrac{9}{5} \times 45°C\right) + 32 = 113°F$
Fahrenheit to Celsius °F → °C	$°C = \dfrac{5}{9} \times (°F - 32)$	Convert 68°F to °C. $°C = \dfrac{5}{9} \times (68°F - 32) = 20°C$
Celsius to Kelvin °C → K	$K = °C + 273$	Convert 45°C to K. $K = 45°C + 273 = 318\ K$
Kelvin to Celsius K → °C	$°C = K - 273$	Convert 32 K to °C. $°C = 32K - 273 = -241°C$

Properties of Common Minerals

	Mineral	Color	Luster	Streak	Hardness
Silicate Minerals	Beryl	deep green, pink, white, bluish green, or yellow	vitreous	white	7.5–8
	Chlorite	green	vitreous to pearly	pale green	2–2.5
	Garnet	green, red, brown, black	vitreous	white	6.5–7.5
	Hornblende	dark green, brown, or black	vitreous	none	5–6
	Muscovite	colorless, silvery white, or brown	vitreous or pearly	white	2–2.5
	Olivine	olive green, yellow	vitreous	white or none	6.5–7
	Orthoclase	colorless, white, pink, or other colors	vitreous	white or none	6
	Plagioclase	colorless, white, yellow, pink, green	vitreous	white	6
	Quartz	colorless or white; any color when not pure	vitreous or waxy	white or none	7
Nonsilicate Minerals	**Native Elements**				
	Copper	copper-red	metallic	copper-red	2.5–3
	Diamond	pale yellow or colorless	adamantine	none	10
	Graphite	black to gray	submetallic	black	1–2
	Carbonates				
	Aragonite	colorless, white, or pale yellow	vitreous	white	3.5–4
	Calcite	colorless or white to tan	vitreous	white	3
	Halides				
	Fluorite	light green, yellow, purple, bluish green, or other colors	vitreous	none	4
	Halite	white	vitreous	white	2.0–2.5
	Oxides				
	Hematite	reddish brown to black	metallic to earthy	dark red to red-brown	5.6–6.5
	Magnetite	iron-black	metallic	black	5.5–6.5
	Sulfates				
	Anhydrite	colorless, bluish, or violet	vitreous to pearly	white	3–3.5
	Gypsum	white, pink, gray, or colorless	vitreous, pearly, or silky	white	2.0
	Sulfides				
	Galena	lead-gray	metallic	lead-gray to black	2.5–2.8
	Pyrite	brassy yellow	metallic	greenish, brownish, or black	6–6.5

Appendix

Density (g/cm³)	Cleavage, Fracture, Special Properties	Common Uses
2.6–2.8	1 cleavage direction; irregular fracture; some varieties fluoresce in ultraviolet light	gemstones, ore of the metal beryllium
2.6–3.3	1 cleavage direction; irregular fracture	
4.2	no cleavage; conchoidal to splintery fracture	gemstones, abrasives
3.0–3.4	2 cleavage directions; hackly to splintery fracture	
2.7–3	1 cleavage direction; irregular fracture	electrical insulation, wallpaper, fireproofing material, lubricant
3.2–3.3	no cleavage; conchoidal fracture	gemstones, casting
2.6	2 cleavage directions; irregular fracture	porcelain
2.6–2.7	2 cleavage directions; irregular fracture	ceramics
2.6	no cleavage; conchoidal fracture	gemstones, concrete, glass, porcelain, sandpaper, lenses
8.9	no cleavage; hackly fracture	wiring, brass, bronze, coins
3.5	4 cleavage directions; irregular to conchoidal fracture	gemstones, drilling
2.3	1 cleavage direction; irregular fracture	pencils, paints, lubricants, batteries
2.95	2 cleavage directions; irregular fracture; reacts with hydrochloric acid	no important industrial uses
2.7	3 cleavage directions; irregular fracture; reacts with weak acid; double refraction	cements, soil conditioner, whitewash, construction materials
3.0–3.3	4 cleavage directions; irregular fracture; some varieties fluoresce	hydrofluoric acid, steel, glass, fiberglass, pottery, enamel
2.1–2.2	3 cleavage directions; splintery to conchoidal fracture; salty taste	tanning hides, salting icy roads, food preservation
5.2–5.3	no cleavage; splintery fracture; magnetic when heated	iron ore for steel, pigments
5.2	no cleavage; splintery fracture; magnetic	iron ore
3.0	3 cleavage directions; conchoidal to splintery fracture	soil conditioner, sulfuric acid
2.3	3 cleavage directions; conchoidal to splintery fracture	plaster of Paris, wallboard, soil conditioner
7.4–7.6	3 cleavage directions; irregular fracture	batteries, paints
5	no cleavage; conchoidal to splintery fracture	sulfuric acid

Sky Maps

Spring

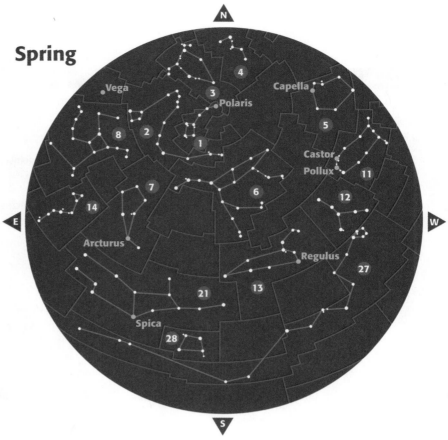

Summer

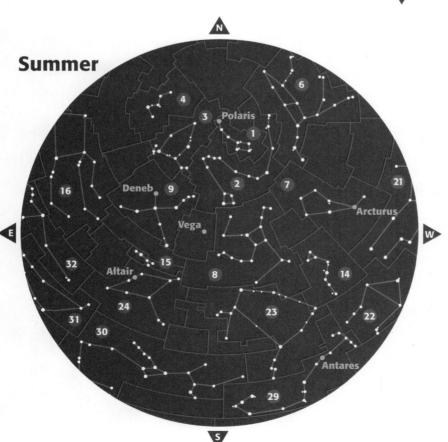

Constellations

1 **Ursa Minor**
2 **Draco**
3 **Cepheus**
4 **Cassiopeia**
5 **Auriga**
6 **Ursa Major**
7 **Bootes**
8 **Hercules**
9 **Cygnus**
10 **Perseus**
11 **Gemini**
12 **Cancer**
13 **Leo**
14 **Serpens**
15 **Sagitta**
16 **Pegasus**
17 **Pisces**

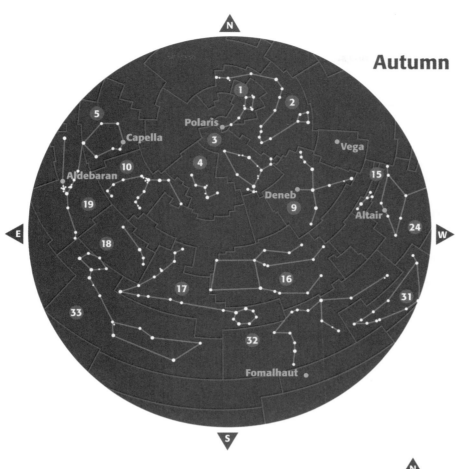

Autumn

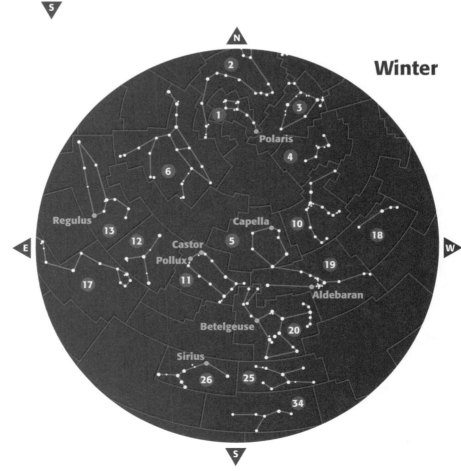

Winter

Constellations

18 **Aries**
19 **Taurus**
20 **Orion**
21 **Virgo**
22 **Libra**
23 **Ophiuchus**
24 **Aquila**
25 **Lepus**
26 **Canis Major**
27 **Hydra**
28 **Corvus**
29 **Scorpius**
30 **Sagittarius**
31 **Capricornus**
32 **Aquarius**
33 **Cetus**
34 **Columba**

Glossary

A

abiotic describes the nonliving part of the environment, including water, rocks, light, and temperature (481)

abrasion the grinding and wearing away of rock surfaces through the mechanical action of other rock or sand particles (41, 111)

absolute zero the temperature at which molecular energy is at a minimum (0 K on the Kelvin scale or -273.16°C on the Celsius scale) (716)

acceleration (ak SEL uhr AY shuhn) the rate at which velocity changes over time; an object accelerates if its speed, direction, or both change (561)

acid precipitation rain, sleet, or snow that contains a high concentration of acids (43, 155)

adenosine triphosphate (ATP), a molecule that acts as the main energy source for cell processes (290)

air mass a large body of air where temperature and moisture content are similar throughout (179)

air pollution the contamination of the atmosphere by the introduction of pollutants from human and natural sources (152)

air pressure the measure of the force with which air molecules push on a surface (137)

algae (AL JEE) eukaryotic organisms that convert the sun's energy into food through photosynthesis but that do not have roots, stems, or leaves (singular, *alga*) (384)

alluvial fan a fan-shaped mass of material deposited by a stream when the slope of the land decreases sharply (80)

anemometer an instrument used to measure wind speed (193)

angiosperm (AN jee oh SPUHRM) a flowering plant that produces seeds within a fruit (412)

Animalia a kingdom made up of complex, multicellular organisms that lack cell walls, can usually move around, and quickly respond to their environment (344)

antibiotic medicine used to kill bacteria and other microorganisms (364)

anticyclone the rotation of air around a high-pressure center in the direction opposite to Earth's rotation (182)

aquifer a body of rock or sediment that stores groundwater and allows the flow of groundwater (83)

Archaea (AHR kee uh) in a modern taxonomic system, a domain made up of prokaryotes (most of which are known to live in extreme environments) that are distinguished from other prokaryotes by differences in their genetics and in the make-up of their cell wall; the domain aligns with the traditional kingdom Archaebacteria (341)

Archimedes' principle (AHR kuh MEE DEEZ PRIN suh puhl) the principle that states that the buoyant force on an object in a fluid is an upward force equal to the weight of the volume of fluid that the object displaces (626)

area a measure of the size of a surface or a region (25)

artesian spring a spring whose water flows from a crack in the cap rock over the aquifer (85)

asexual reproduction reproduction that does not involve the union of sex cells and in which one parent produces offspring that are genetically identical to the parent (284)

asteroid a small, rocky object that orbits the sun, usually in a band between the orbits of Mars and Jupiter (266)

asteroid belt the region of the solar system that is between the orbits of Mars and Jupiter and in which most asteroids orbit (266)

astronomical unit the average distance between the Earth and the sun; approximately 150 million kilometers (symbol, AU) (241)

atmosphere a mixture of gases that surrounds a planet or moon (137)

atmospheric pressure the pressure caused by the weight of the atmosphere (620)

atom the smallest unit of an element that maintains the properties of that element (529)

B

bacteria (bak TEER ee uh) in the modern taxonomic system, a domain made up of prokaryotes that usually have a cell wall and that usually reproduce by cell division; this domain aligns with the traditional kingdom Eubacteria (341)

barometer an instrument that measures atmospheric pressure (193)

beach an area of the shoreline made up of material deposited by waves (108)

bedrock the layer of rock beneath soil (50)

Bernoulli's principle (ber NOO leez PRIN suh puhl) the principle that states that the pressure in a fluid decreases as the fluid's velocity increases (632)

binary fission (BIE nuh ree FISH uhn) a form of asexual reproduction in single-celled organisms by which one cell divides into two cells of the same size (358)

biome (BIE OHM) a large region characterized by a specific type of climate and certain types of plant and animal communities (212)

bioremediation (BIE oh ri MEE dee AY shuhn) the biological treatment of hazardous waste by living organisms (363)

biosphere the part of Earth where life exists (483)

biotic describes living factors in the environment (481)

buoyant force (BOY uhnt FAWRS) the upward force that keeps an object immersed in or floating on a liquid (626)

C

carbohydrate a class of energy-giving nutrients that includes sugars, starches, and fiber; contains carbon, hydrogen, and oxygen (289)

carnivore an organism that eats animals (485)

carrying capacity the largest population that an environment can support at any given time (491)

cartilage a flexible and strong connective tissue (465)

cell in biology, the smallest unit that can perform all life processes; cells are covered by a membrane and have DNA and cytoplasm (282, 303)

cell membrane a phospholipid layer that covers a cell's surface and acts as a barrier between the inside of a cell and the cell's environment (305)

cell wall a rigid structure that surrounds the cell membrane and provides support to the cell (310, 411)

change of state the change of a substance from one physical state to another (729)

channel the path that a stream follows (73)

chemical change a change that occurs when one or more substances change into entirely new substances with different properties (539)

chemical property a property of matter that describes a substance's ability to participate in chemical reactions (533)

chemical weathering the process by which rocks break down as a result of chemical reactions (43)

chloroplasts contain chlorophyll. Chlorophyll captures energy from the sun. Plants use this energy to make food. (411)

classification the division of organisms into groups, or classes, based on specific characteristics (334)

climate the average weather conditions in an area over a long period of time (207)

closed circulatory system a circulatory system in which the heart circulates blood through a network of vessels that form a closed loop; the blood does not leave the blood vessels, and materials diffuse across the walls of the vessels (461)

cloud a collection of small water droplets or ice crystals suspended in the air, which forms when the air is cooled and condensation occurs (174)

coelom (SEE luhm) a body cavity that contains the internal organs (446)

coevolution the evolution of two species that is due to mutual influence, often in a way that makes the relationship more beneficial to both species (495)

combustion the burning of a substance (510)

comet a small body of ice, rock, and cosmic dust that follows an elliptical orbit around the sun and that gives off gas and dust in the form of a tail as it passes close to the sun (265)

commensalism a relationship between two organisms in which one organism benefits and the other is unaffected (494)

community all of the populations of species that live in the same habitat and interact with each other (482)

compound a substance made up of atoms of two or more different elements joined by chemical bonds (530)

compound machine a machine made of more than one simple machine (668)

condensation the change of state from a gas to a liquid (173, 508)

consumer an organism that eats other organisms or organic matter (287, 446)

convection the transfer of thermal energy by the circulation or movement of a liquid or gas (143, 723)

Coriolis effect the apparent curving of the path of a moving object from an otherwise straight path due to the Earth's rotation (148)

creep the slow downhill movement of weathered rock material (123)

cyclone an area in the atmosphere that has lower pressure than the surrounding areas and has winds that spiral toward the center (182)

D

data any pieces of information acquired through observation or experimentation (13)

decomposer an organism that gets energy by breaking down the remains of dead organisms or animal wastes and consuming or absorbing the nutrients (287)

decomposition the breakdown of substances into simpler molecular substances (510)

deflation a form of wind erosion in which fine, dry soil particles are blown away (111)

delta a fan-shaped mass of material deposited at the mouth of a stream (79)

deposition the process in which material is laid down (79)

dichotomous key (die KAHT uh muhs KEE) an aid that is used to identify organisms and that consists of the answers to a series of questions (338)

differential weathering the process by which softer, less weather resistant rocks wear away and leave harder, more weather resistant rocks behind (47)

differentiation (DIF uhr EN Shee AY Shuhn) the process in which the structure and function of the parts of an organism change to enable specialization of those parts (447)

divide the boundary between drainage areas that have streams that flow in opposite directions (73)

drag a force parallel to the velocity of the flow; it opposes the direction of an aircraft and, in combination with thrust, determines the speed of the aircraft (635)

dune a mound of wind-deposited sand that keeps its shape even though it moves (112)

E

eclipse an event in which the shadow of one celestial body falls on another (259)

ecology the study of the interactions of living organisms with one another and with their environment (481)

ecosystem a community of organisms and their abiotic, or nonliving, environment (483)

element a substance that cannot be separated or broken down into simpler substances by chemical means (529)

elevation the height of an object above sea level (211)

endoplasmic reticulum (EN doh PLAZ mik ri TIK yuh luhm) a system of membranes that is found in a cell's cytoplasm and that assists in the production, processing, and transport of proteins and in the production of lipids (313)

endoskeleton (EN doh SKEL uh tuhn) an internal skeleton made of bone and cartilage (454)

endospore (EN doh SPAWR) a thick-walled protective spore that forms inside a bacterial cell and resists harsh conditions (359)

energy the capacity to do work (680)

energy conversion a change from one form of energy to another (688)

energy pyramid a triangular diagram that shows an ecosystem's loss of energy, which results as energy passes through the ecosystem's food chain (487)

erosion the process by which wind, water, ice, or gravity transports soil and sediment from one location to another (57, 70)

Eukarya in a modern taxonomic system, a domain made up of all eukaryotes; this domain aligns with the traditional kingdoms Protista, Fungi, Plantae, and Animalia (342)

eukaryote an organism made up of cells that have a nucleus enclosed by a membrane; eukaryotes include protists, animals, plants, and fungi but not archaea or bacteria (308)

evaporation (ee vap uh RAY shuhn) the change of a substance from a liquid to a gas (508)

exoskeleton a hard, external, supporting structure (452)

F

floodplain an area along a river that forms from sediments deposited when the river overflows its banks (80)

fluid a nonsolid state of matter in which the atoms or molecules are free to move past each other, as in a gas or liquid (620)

food chain the pathway of energy transfer through various stages as a result of the feeding patterns of a series of organisms (486)

food web a diagram that shows the feeding relationships between organisms in an ecosystem (486)

force a push or a pull exerted on an object in order to change the motion of the object; force has size and direction (565)

fossil fuel a nonrenewable energy resource formed from the remains of organisms that lived long ago (698)

free fall the motion of a body when only the force of gravity is acting on the body (593)

friction a force that opposes motion between two surfaces that are in contact (568, 695)

front the boundary between air masses of different densities and usually different temperatures (180)

function the special, normal, or proper activity of an organ or part (320)

fungi (FUHN JIE) a kingdom made up of nongreen, eukaryotic organisms that have no means of movement, reproduce by using spores, and get food by breaking down substances in their surroundings and absorbing the nutrients (342)

fungus an organism whose cells have nuclei, rigid cell walls, and no chlorophyll and that belongs to the kingdom Fungi (392)

G

gas a form of matter that does not have a definite volume or shape (544)

gas giant a planet that has a deep, massive atmosphere, such as Jupiter, Saturn, Uranus, or Neptune (250)

glacial drift the rock material carried and deposited by glaciers (118)

glacier a large mass of moving ice (114)

global warming a gradual increase in average global temperature (145, 228)

Golgi complex (GOHL jee KAHM PLEKS) cell organelle that helps make and package materials to be transported out of the cell (315)

gravity a force of attraction between objects that is due to their masses (574)

greenhouse effect the warming of the surface and lower atmosphere of Earth that occurs when water vapor, carbon dioxide, and other gases absorb and reradiate thermal energy (144, 228)

gymnosperm (JIM noh SPUHRM) a woody, vascular seed plant whose seeds are not enclosed by an ovary or fruit (412)

H

heat the energy transferred between objects that are at different temperatures (720)

heat engine a machine that transforms heat into mechanical energy, or work (735)

herbivore an organism that eats only plants (485)

heredity the passing of genetic traits from parent to offspring (284)

heterotroph (HET uhr oh TROHF) an organism that gets food by eating other organisms or their byproducts and that cannot make organic compounds from inorganic materials (381)

homeostasis (HOH mee OH STAY sis) the maintenance of a constant internal state in a changing environment (283)

host an organism from which a parasite takes food or shelter (366, 381)

humidity the amount of water vapor in the air (171)

humus dark, organic material formed in soil from the decayed remains of plants and animals (52)

hurricane a severe storm that develops over tropical oceans and whose strong winds of more than 120 km/h spiral in toward the intensely low-pressure storm center (187)

hypha (HIE fuh) a nonreproductive filament of a fungus (393)

hypothesis (hie PAHTH uh sis) an explanation that is based on prior scientific research or observations and that can be tested (12)

I

ice age a long period of climate cooling during which ice sheets cover large areas of Earth's surface; also known as a *glacial period* (224)

inclined plane a simple machine that is a straight, slanted surface, which facilitates the raising of loads; a ramp (666)

inertia (in UHR shuh) the tendency of an object to resist being moved or, if the object is moving, to resist a change in speed or direction until an outside force acts on the object (600)

insulation a substance that reduces the transfer of electricity, heat, or sound (733)

J

jet stream a narrow belt of strong winds that blow in the upper troposphere (150)

joule (j) the unit used to express energy; equivalent to the amount of work done by a force of 1 N acting through a distance of 1 m in the direction of the force (symbol, J) (653)

K

kinetic energy (ki NET ik EN uhr jee) the energy of an object that is due to the object's motion (681)

L

landslide the sudden movement of rock and soil down a slope (121)

large intestine the wider and shorter portion of the intestine that removes water from mostly digested food and that turns the waste into semisolid feces, or stool (467)

latitude the distance north or south from the equator; expressed in degrees (207)

law a summary of many experimental results and observations; a law tells how things work (20)

law of conservation of energy the law that states that energy cannot be created or destroyed but can be changed from one form to another (695)

law of conservation of mass the law that states that mass cannot be created or destroyed in ordinary chemical and physical changes (536)

leaching the removal of substances that can be dissolved from rock, ore, or layers of soil due to the passing of water (52)

lever a simple machine that consists of a bar that pivots at a fixed point called a *fulcrum* (663)

lichen (LIE kuhn) a mass of fungal and algal cells that grow together in a symbiotic relationship and that are usually found on rocks or trees (398)

lift an upward force on an object that moves in a fluid (633)

lightning an electric discharge that takes place between two oppositely charged surfaces, such as between a cloud and the ground, between two clouds, or between two parts of the same cloud (185)

lipid a type of biochemical that does not dissolve in water; fats and steroids are lipids (290)

liquid the state of matter that has a definite volume but not a definite shape (544)

load the materials carried by a stream; *also* the mass of rock overlying a geological structure (74)

loess (LOH ES) very fertile sediments of quartz, feldspar, hornblende, mica, and clay deposited by the wind (112)

lysosome (LIE suh SOHM) a cell organelle that contains digestive enzymes (316)

M

machine a device that helps do work by either overcoming a force or changing the direction of the applied force (657)

mass a measure of the amount of matter in an object (25, 578)

mass movement a movement of a section of land down a slope (120)

matter anything that has mass and takes up space (529)

mechanical advantage a number that tells how many times a machine multiplies force (659)

mechanical efficiency (muh KAN i kuhl e FISH uhn see) the ratio of output to input of energy or of power; it can be calculated by dividing work output by work input (660)

mechanical energy the amount of work an object can do because of the object's kinetic and potential energies (683)

mechanical weathering the breakdown of rock into smaller pieces by physical means (40)

mesosphere the layer of the atmosphere between the stratosphere and the thermosphere and in which temperature decreases as altitude increases (139)

metabolism (muh TAB uh LIZ uhm) the sum of all chemical processes that occur in an organism (284)

metamorphosis (MET uh MAWR fuh sis) a phase in the life cycle of many animals during which a rapid change from the immature form of an organism to the adult form takes place (462)

meteor a bright streak of light that results when a meteoroid burns up in the Earth's atmosphere (267)

meteorite a meteoroid that reaches the Earth's surface without burning up completely (267)

meteoroid a relatively small, rocky body that travels through space (267)

meter the basic unit of length in the SI (symbol, m) (25)

microclimate the climate of a small area (222)

mitochondrion (MIET oh KAHN dree uhn) in eukaryotic cells, the cell organelle that is surrounded by two membranes and that is the site of cellular respiration (314)

mixture a combination of two or more substances that are not chemically combined (530)

model a pattern, plan, representation, or description designed to show the structure or workings of an object, system, or concept (18)

mold in biology, a fungus that looks like wool or cotton (394)

momentum (moh MEN tuhm) a quantity defined as the product of the mass and velocity of an object (606)

motion an object's change in position relative to a reference point (559)

mudflow the flow of a mass of mud or rock and soil mixed with a large amount of water (122)

mutualism (MYOO choo uhl IZ uhm) a relationship between two species in which both species benefit (494)

mycelium (mie SEE lee uhm) the mass of fungal filaments, or hyphae, that forms the body of a fungus (393)

N

net force the combination of all of the forces acting on an object (565)

neuron (NOO RAHN) a nerve cell that is specialized to receive and conduct electrical impulses (565)

nonpoint-source pollution pollution that comes from many sources rather than from a single, specific site (88)

nonrenewable resource a resource that forms at a rate that is much slower than the rate at which it is consumed (698)

nonvascular plant the three groups of plants (liverworts, hornworts, and mosses) that lack specialized conducting tissues and true roots, stems, and leaves (412)

nucleic acid (noo KLEE ik AS id) a molecule made up of subunits called *nucleotides* (291)

nucleus in a eukaryotic cell, a membrane-bound organelle that contains the cell's DNA and that has a role in processes such as growth, metabolism, and reproduction (305)

O

observation the process of obtaining information by using the senses (11)

omnivore an organism that eats both plants and animals (485)

open circulatory system a circulatory system in which the circulatory fluid is not contained entirely within vessels; a heart pumps fluid through vessels that empty into spaces called *sinuses* (461)

organ a collection of tissues that carry out a specialized function of the body (319)

organelle one of the small bodies in a cell's cytoplasm that are specialized to perform a specific function (305)

organism a living thing; anything that can carry out life processes independently (320)

organ system a group of organs that work together to perform body functions (320)

ovary in flowering plants, the lower part of a pistil that produces eggs in ovules (430)

P

parasite an organism that feeds on an organism of another species (the host) and that usually harms the host; the host never benefits from the presence of the parasite (381)

parasitism (PAR uh SIET IZ uhm) a relationship between two species in which one species, the parasite, benefits from the other species, the host, which is harmed (495)

parent rock a rock formation that is the source of soil (50)

pascal the SI unit of pressure (symbol, Pa) (620)

Pascal's principle the principle that states that a fluid in equilibrium contained in a vessel exerts a pressure of equal intensity in all directions (636)

pathogenic bacteria (PATH uh JEN ik bak TIR ee uh) bacteria that cause disease (364)

permeability the ability of a rock or sediment to let fluids pass through its open spaces, or pores (83)

petal one of the usually brightly colored, leaf-shaped parts that make up one of the rings of a flower (429)

phase the change in the sunlit area of one celestial body as seen from another celestial body (258)

phloem (FLOH EM) the tissue that conducts food in vascular plants (424)

phospholipid (FAHS foh LIP id) a lipid that contains phosphorus and that is a structural component in cell membranes (290)

physical change a change of matter from one form to another without a change in chemical properties (537)

physical property a characteristic of a substance that does not involve a chemical change, such as density, color, or hardness (532)

phytoplankton (FIET oh PLANGK tuhn) the microscopic, photosynthetic organisms that float near the surface of marine or fresh water (384)

pioneer species a species that colonizes an uninhabited area and that starts a process of succession (513)

pistil the female reproductive part of a flower that produces seeds and consists of an ovary, style, and stigma (430)

Plantae a kingdom made up of complex, multicellular organisms that are usually green, have cell walls made of cellulose, cannot move around, and use the sun's energy to make sugar by photosynthesis (343)

plasma a state of matter that starts as a gas and then becomes ionized; it consists of free-moving ions and electrons, it takes on an electric charge, and its properties differ from those of a solid, liquid, or gas (546)

point-source pollution pollution that comes from a specific site (88)

polar easterlies prevailing winds that blow from east to west between 60° and 90° latitude in both hemispheres (148)

polar zone the North or South Pole and the surrounding region (221)

pollen the tiny granules that contain the male gametophyte of seed plants (418)

pollination the transfer of pollen from the male reproductive structures to the female structures of seed plants (421)

population a group of organisms of the same species that live in a specific geographical area (482)

porosity the percentage of the total volume of a rock or sediment that consists of open spaces (83)

potential energy the energy that an object has because of the position, shape, or condition of the object (683)

power the rate at which work is done or energy is transformed (654)

precipitation any form of water that falls to the Earth's surface from the clouds (176, 508)

predator an organism that eats all or part of another organism (492)

pressure the amount of force exerted per unit area of a surface (546, 620)

prevailing winds winds that blow mainly from one direction during a given period (209)

prey an organism that is killed and eaten by another organism (492)

producer an organism that can make its own food by using energy from its surroundings (287)

prograde rotation the counterclockwise spin of a planet or moon as seen from above the planet's North Pole; rotation in the same direction as the sun's rotation (245)

projectile motion (proh JEK tuhl MOH shuhn) the curved path that an object follows when thrown, launched, or otherwise projected near the surface of Earth (595)

prokaryote (pro KAR ee OHT) a single-celled organism that does not have a nucleus or membrane-bound organelles; examples are archaea and bacteria (306, 357)

protein a molecule that is made up of amino acids and that is needed to build and repair body structures and to regulate processes in the body (288)

protist an organism that belongs to the kingdom Protista (380)

Protista (proh TIST uh) a kingdom of mostly one-celled eukaryotic organisms that are different from plants, animals, bacteria, and fungi (342)

pulley a simple machine that consists of a wheel over which a rope, chain, or wire passes (664)

pure substance a sample of matter, either a single element or a single compound, that has definite chemical and physical properties (529)

R

radiation the transfer of energy as electromagnetic waves (143, 724)

recharge zone an area in which water travels downward to become part of an aquifer (84)

relative humidity the ratio of the amount of water vapor in the air to the maximum amount of water vapor the air can hold at a set temperature (171)

renewable resource a natural resource that can be replaced at the same rate at which the resource is consumed (701)

retrograde rotation the clockwise spin of a planet or moon as seen from above the planet's North Pole (245)

rhizoid (RIE ZOYD) a rootlike structure in nonvascular plants that holds the plants in place and helps plants get water and nutrients (414)

rhizome a horizontal, underground stem that produces new leaves, shoots, and roots (416)

ribosome a cell organelle composed of RNA and protein; the site of protein synthesis (313)

rock fall the rapid mass movement of rock down a steep slope or cliff (121)

S

saltation the movement of sand or other sediments by short jumps and bounces that is caused by wind or water (111)

satellite a natural or artificial body that revolves around a planet (257)

science the knowledge obtained by observing natural events and conditions in order to discover facts and formulate laws or principles that can be verified or tested (4)

scientific methods a series of steps followed to solve problems (10)

screw a simple machine that consists of an inclined plane wrapped around a cylinder (667)

segment any part of a larger structure, such as the body of an organism, that is set off by natural or arbitrary boundaries (459)

sepal in a flower, one of the outermost rings of modified leaves that protect the flower bud (429)

septic tank a tank that separates solid waste from liquids and that has bacteria that break down the solid waste (91)

sewage treatment plant a facility that cleans the waste materials found in water that comes from sewers or drains (90)

sexual reproduction reproduction in which the sex cells from two parents unite to produce offspring that share traits from both parents (284)

shoreline the boundary between land and a body of water (105)

small intestine the organ between the stomach and the large intestine where most of the breakdown of food happens and most of the nutrients from food are absorbed (467)

soil a loose mixture of rock fragments, organic material, water, and air that can support the growth of vegetation (50)

soil conservation a method to maintain the fertility of the soil by protecting the soil from erosion and nutrient loss (56)

soil structure the arrangement of soil particles (51)

soil texture the soil quality that is based on the proportions of soil particles (51)

solid the state of matter in which the volume and shape of a substance are fixed (543)

specific heat the quantity of heat required to raise a unit mass of homogeneous material 1 K or 1°C in a specified way given constant pressure and volume (725)

speed the distance traveled divided by the time interval during which the motion occurred (559)

spore a reproductive cell or multicellular structure that is resistant to stressful environmental conditions and that can develop into an adult without fusing with another cell (393)

stamen the male reproductive structure of a flower that produces pollen and consists of an anther at the tip of a filament (430)

states of matter the physical forms of matter, which include solid, liquid, and gas (729)

stimulus anything that causes a reaction or change in an organism or any part of an organism (283)

stratified drift a glacial deposit that has been sorted and layered by the action of streams or meltwater (118)

stratosphere the layer of the atmosphere that is above the troposphere and in which temperature increases as altitude increases (139)

structure the arrangement of parts in an organism (320)

succession the replacement of one type of community by another at a single location over a period of time (512)

surface current a horizontal movement of ocean water that is caused by wind and that occurs at or near the ocean's surface (211)

symbiosis a relationship in which two different organisms live in close association with each other (494)

T

taxonomy (taks AHN uh mee) the science of describing, naming, and classifying organisms (335)

temperate zone the climate zone between the Tropics and the polar zone (219)

temperature a measure of how hot (or cold) something is; specifically, a measure of the average kinetic energy of the particles in an object (26, 714)

terminal velocity the constant velocity of a falling object when the force of air resistance is equal in magnitude and opposite in direction to the force of gravity (592)

terrestrial planet one of the highly dense planets nearest to the sun; Mercury, Venus, Mars, and Earth (244)

theory an explanation that ties together many hypotheses and observations (20)

thermal conduction the transfer of energy as heat through a material (143, 722)

thermal conductor a material through which energy can be transferred as heat (723)

thermal energy the kinetic energy of a substance's atoms (721)

thermal expansion an increase in the size of a substance in response to an increase in the temperature of the substance (716)

Glossary **841**

thermal insulator a material that reduces or prevents the transfer of heat (723)

thermal pollution a temperature increase in a body of water that is caused by human activity and that has a harmful effect on water quality and on the ability of that body of water to support life (738)

thermometer an instrument that measures and indicates temperature (193)

thermosphere the uppermost layer of the atmosphere, in which temperature increases as altitude increases (140)

thrust the pushing or pulling force exerted by the engine of an aircraft or rocket (634)

thunderstorm a usually brief, heavy storm that consists of rain, strong winds, lightning, and thunder (184, 185)

till unsorted rock material that is deposited directly by a melting glacier (118)

tissue a group of similar cells that perform a common function (319)

tornado a destructive, rotating column of air that has very high wind speeds, is visible as a funnel-shaped cloud, and touches the ground (186)

trade winds prevailing winds that blow northeast from 30° north latitude to the equator and that blow southeast from 30° south latitude to the equator (148)

tributary a stream that flows into a lake or into a larger stream (73)

tropical zone the region that surrounds the equator and that extends from about 23° north latitude to 23° south latitude (215)

troposphere the lowest layer of the atmosphere, in which temperature decreases at a constant rate as altitude increases (139)

V

vascular plant a plant that has specialized tissues that conduct materials from one part of the plant to another (412)

velocity (vuh LAHS uh tee) the speed of an object in a particular direction (561)

vertebrate (VUHR tuh brit) an animal that has a backbone (454)

vesicle (VES i kuhl) a small cavity or sac that contains materials in a eukaryotic cell; forms when part of the cell membrane surrounds the materials to be taken into the cell or transported within the cell (315)

virus a microscopic particle that gets inside a cell and often destroys the cell (366)

volume a measure of the size of a body or region in three-dimensional space (26)

W

water cycle the continuous movement of water from the ocean to the atmosphere to the land and back to the ocean (71)

watershed the area of land that is drained by a water system (73)

water table the upper surface of underground water; the upper boundary of the zone of saturation (82)

watt the unit used to express power; equivalent to joules per second (symbol, W) (654)

weather the short-term state of the atmosphere, including temperature, humidity, precipitation, wind, and visibility (171, 207)

weathering the process by which rock materials are broken down by the action of physical or chemical processes (40)

wedge a simple machine that is made up of two inclined planes and that moves; often used for cutting (667)

weight a measure of the gravitational force exerted on an object; its value can change with the location of the object in the universe (578)

westerlies prevailing winds that blow from west to east between 30° and 60° latitude in both hemispheres (148)

wheel and axle a simple machine consisting of two circular objects of different sizes; the wheel is the larger of the two circular objects (665)

wind the movement of air caused by differences in air pressure (146)

work the transfer of energy to an object by using a force that causes the object to move in the direction of the force (651)

work input the work done on a machine; the product of the input force and the distance through which the force is exerted (657)

work output the work done by a machine; the product of the output force and the distance through which the force is exerted (657)

X

xylem (ZIE luhm) the type of tissue in vascular plants that provides support and conducts water and nutrients from the roots (424)

Glossary

Spanish Glossary

A

abiotic/abiótico término que describe la parte sin vida del ambiente, incluyendo el agua, las rocas, la luz y la temperatura (481)

abrasion/abrasión proceso por el cual las superficies de las rocas se muelen o desgastan por medio de la acción mecánica de otras rocas y partículas de arena (111)

absolute zero/cero absoluto la temperatura a la que la energía molecular es mínima (0 K en la escala de Kelvin o −273.16°C en la escala de Celsius) (716)

acceleration/aceleración la tasa a la que la velocidad cambia con el tiempo; un objeto acelera si su rapidez cambia, si su dirección cambia, o si tanto su rapidez como su dirección cambian (561)

acid precipitation/precipitación ácida lluvia, aguanieve o nieve que contiene una alta concentración de ácidos (43, 155)

adenosín trifosfato (ATP/ATP), una molécula orgánica que funciona como la fuente principal de energía para los procesos celulares (290)

air mass/masa de aire un gran volumen de aire que tiene una temperatura y contenido de humedad similar en toda su extensión (179)

air pollution/contaminación del aire la contaminación de la atmósfera debido a la introducción de contaminantes provenientes de fuentes humanas y naturales (152)

air pressure/presión del aire la medida de la fuerza con la que las moléculas del aire empujan contra una superficie (137)

algae/algas organismos eucarióticos que transforman la energía del Sol en alimento por medio de la fotosíntesis, pero que no tienen raíces, tallos ni hojas (384)

alluvial fan/abanico aluvial masa de materiales rocosos en forma de abanico, depositados por un arroyo cuando la pendiente del terreno disminuye bruscamente (80)

anemometer/anemómetro un instrumento que se usa para medir la rapidez del viento (193)

angiosperm/angiosperma una planta que da flores y que produce semillas dentro de la fruta (412)

Animalia/Animalia un reino formado por organismos pluricelulares complejos que no tienen pared celular, normalmente son capaces de moverse y reaccionan rápidamente a su ambiente (344)

antibiotic/antibiótico medicina utilizada para matar bacterias y otros microorganismos (364)

anticyclone/anticiclón la rotación del aire alrededor de un centro de alta presión en dirección opuesta a la rotación de la Tierra (182)

aquifer/acuífero un cuerpo rocoso o sedimento que almacena agua subterránea y permite que fluya (83)

Archaea/Archaea en un sistema taxonómico moderno, un dominio compuesto por procariotes (la mayoría de los cuales viven en ambientes extremos) que se distinguen de otros procariotes por diferencias genéticas y por la diferente composición de su pared celular; este dominio coincide con el reino tradicional Archaebacteria (341)

Archimedes' principle/principio de Arquímedes el principio que establece que la fuerza flotante de un objeto que está en un fluido es una fuerza ascendente cuya magnitud es igual al peso del volumen del fluido que el objeto desplaza (626)

area/área una medida del tamaño de una superficie o región (25)

artesian spring/manantial artesiano un manantial en el que el agua fluye a partir de una grieta en la capa de rocas que se encuentra sobre el acuífero (85)

asexual reproduction/reproducción asexual reproducción que no involucra la unión de células sexuales, en la que un solo progenitor produce descendencia que es genéticamente igual al progenitor (284)

asteroid/asteroide un objeto pequeño y rocoso que se encuentra en órbita alrededor del Sol, normalmente en una banda entre las órbitas de Marte y Júpiter (266)

asteroid belt/cinturón de asteroides la región del Sistema Solar que está entre las órbitas de Marte y Júpiter, en la que la mayoría de los asteroides se encuentran en órbita (266)

astronomical unit/unidad astronómica la distancia promedio entre la Tierra y el Sol; aproximadamente 150 millones de kilómetros (símbolo: UA) (241)

atmosphere/atmósfera una mezcla de gases que rodea un planeta o una luna (137)

atmospheric pressure/presión atmosférica la presión producida por el peso de la atmósfera (620)

atom/átomo la unidad más pequeña de un elemento que conserva las propiedades de ese elemento (529)

Bacteria/Bacteria en un sistema taxonómico moderno, un dominio compuesto por procariotes que normalmente tienen pared celular y se reproducen por división celular; este dominio coincide con el reino tradicional Eubacteria (341)

barometer/barómetro un instrumento que mide la presión atmosférica (193)

beach/playa un área de la costa formada por materiales depositados por las olas (108)

bedrock/lecho de roca la capa de rocas que está debajo del suelo (50)

Bernoulli's principle/principio de Bernoulli el principio que establece que la presión de un fluido disminuye a medida que la velocidad del fluido aumenta (632)

binary fission/fisión binaria una forma de reproducción asexual de los organismos unicelulares, por medio de la cual la célula se divide en dos células del mismo tamaño (358)

biome/bioma una región extensa caracterizada por un tipo de clima específico y ciertos tipos de comunidades de plantas y animales (212)

bioremediation/bioremediación el tratamiento biológico de desechos peligrosos por medio de organismos vivos (363)

biosphere/biosfera la parte de la Tierra donde existe la vida (483)

biotic/biótico término que describe los factores vivientes del ambiente (481)

buoyant force/fuerza boyante la fuerza ascendente que hace que un objeto se mantenga sumergido en un líquido o flotando en él (626)

C

carbohydrate/carbohidrato una clase de nutrientes que proporcionan energía; incluye los azúcares, los almidones y las fibras; contiene carbono, hidrógeno y oxígeno (289)

carnivore/carnívoro un organismo que se alimenta de animales (485)

carrying capacity/capacidad de carga la población más grande que un ambiente puede sostener en cualquier momento dado (491)

cartilage/cartílago un tejido conectivo flexible y fuerte (465)

cell/célula en biología, la unidad más pequeña que puede realizar todos los procesos vitales; las células están cubiertas por una membrana y tienen ADN y citoplasma (282, 303)

cell membrane/membrana celular una capa de fosfolípidos que cubre la superficie de la célula y funciona como una barrera entre el interior de la célula y el ambiente de la célula (305)

cell wall/pared celular una estructura rígida que rodea la membrana celular y le brinda soporte a la célula (310, 411)

change of state/cambio de estado el cambio de una substancia de un estado físico a otro (729)

channel/canal el camino que sigue un arroyo (73)

chemical change/cambio químico un cambio que ocurre cuando una o más substancias se transforman en substancias totalmente nuevas con propiedades diferentes (539)

chemical property/propiedad química una propiedad de la materia que describe la capacidad de una substancia de participar en reacciones químicas (533)

chemical weathering/desgaste químico el proceso por medio del cual las rocas se fragmentan como resultado de reacciones químicas (43)

chloroplasts/cloroplasto un organelo que se encuentra en las células vegetales y en las células de las algas, en el cual se lleva a cabo la fotosíntesis (411)

classification/clasificación la división de organismos en grupos, o clases, en función de características específicas (334)

climate/clima las condiciones promedio del tiempo en un área durante un largo período de tiempo (207)

closed circulatory system/aparato circulatorio cerrado un aparato circulatorio en el que el corazón hace que la sangre circule a través de una red de vasos que forman un circuito cerrado; la sangre no sale de los vasos sanguíneos y los materiales pasan a través de las paredes de los vasos por difusión (461)

cloud/nube un conjunto de pequeñas gotitas de agua o cristales de hielo suspendidos en el aire, que se forma cuando el aire se enfría y ocurre condensación (174)

coelom/celoma una cavidad del cuerpo que contiene los órganos internos (446)

coevolution/coevolución la evolución de dos especies que se debe a su influencia mutua, a menudo de un modo que hace que la relación sea más beneficiosa para ambas (495)

combustion/combustión fenómeno que ocurre cuando una substancia se quema (510)

comet/cometa un cuerpo pequeño formado por hielo, roca y polvo cósmico que sigue una órbita elíptica alrededor del Sol y que libera gas y polvo, los cuales forman una cola al pasar cerca del Sol (265)

commensalism/comensalismo una relación entre dos organismos en la que uno se beneficia y el otro no es afectado (494)

community/comunidad todas las poblaciones de especies que viven en el mismo hábitat e interactúan entre sí (482)

compound/compuesto una substancia formada por átomos de dos o más elementos diferentes unidos por enlaces químicos (94)

compound machine/máquina compuesta una máquina hecha de más de una máquina simple (668)

condensation/condensación el cambio de estado de gas a líquido (173, 508)

consumer/consumidor un organismo que se alimenta de otros organismos o de materia orgánica (287, 446)

convection/convección la transferencia de energía térmica mediante la circulación o el movimiento de un líquido o gas (143, 723)

Coriolis effect/efecto de Coriolis la desviación aparente de la trayectoria recta que experimentan los objetos en ovimiento debido a la rotación de la Tierra (148)

creep/arrastre el movimiento lento y descendente de materiales rocosos desgastados (123)

cyclone/ciclón un área de la atmósfera que tiene una presión menor que la de las áreas circundantes y que tiene vientos que giran en espiral hacia el centro (182)

D

data/datos cualquier parte de la información que se adquiere por medio de la observación o experimentación (13)

decomposer/descomponedor un organismo que, para obtener energía, desintegra los restos de organismos muertos o los desechos de animales y consume o absorbe los nutrientes (287)

decomposition/descomposición la desintegración de substancias en substancias moleculares más simples (510)

deflation/deflación una forma de erosión del viento en la que se mueven partículas de suelo finas y secas (111)

delta/delta un depósito de materiales rocosos en forma de abanico ubicado en la desembocadura de un río (79)

deposition/deposición el proceso por medio del cual un material se deposita (79)

dichotomous key/clave dicotómica una ayuda para identificar organismos, que consiste en las respuestas a una serie de preguntas (338)

differential weathering/desgaste diferencial el proceso por medio cual las rocas más suaves y menos resistentes al clima se desgastan y las rocas más duras y resistentes al clima permanecen (47)

differentiation/diferenciación el proceso por medio del cual la estructura y función de las partes de un organismo cambian para permitir la especialización de esas partes (447)

divide/división el límite entre áreas de drenaje que tienen corrientes que fluyen en direcciones opuestas (73)

drag/resistencia aerodinámica una fuerza paralela a la velocidad del flujo; se opone a la dirección de un avión y, en combinación con el empuje, determina la velocidad del avión (635)

dune/duna un montículo de arena depositada por el viendo que conserva su forma incluso cuando se mueve (112)

E

eclipse/eclipse un suceso en el que la sombra de un cuerpo celeste cubre otro cuerpo celeste (259)

ecology/ecología el estudio de las interacciones de los seres vivos entre sí mismos y entre sí mismos y su ambiente (481)

ecosystem/ecosistema una comunidad de organismos y su ambiente abiótico o no vivo (483)

element/elemento una substancia que no se puede separar o descomponer en substancias más simples por medio de métodos químicos (529)

elevation/elevación la altura de un objeto sobre el nivel del mar (211)

endoplasmic reticulum/retículo endoplásmico un sistema de membranas que se encuentra en el citoplasma de la célula y que tiene una función en la producción, procesamiento y transporte de proteínas y en la producción de lípidos (313)

endoskeleton/endoesqueleto un esqueleto interno hecho de hueso y cartílago (454)

endospore/endospora una espora protectiva que tiene una pared gruesa, se forma dentro de una célula bacteriana y resiste condiciones adversas (359)

energy/energía la capacidad de realizar un trabajo (680)

energy conversion/transformación de energía un cambio de un tipo de energía a otro (688)

energy pyramid/pirámide de energía un diagrama triangular que muestra la pérdida de energía en un ecosistema, producida a medida que la energía pasa a través de la cadena alimenticia del ecosistema (487)

erosion/erosión el proceso por medio del cual el viento, el agua, el hielo o la gravedad transporta tierra y sedimentos de un lugar a otro (57, 70)

Eukarya/Eukarya en un sistema taxonómico moderno, un dominio compuesto por todos los eucariotes; este dominio coincide con los reinos tradicionales Protista, Fungi, Plantae y Animalia (342)

eukaryote/eucariote un organismo cuyas células tienen un núcleo contenido en una membrana; entre los eucariotes se encuentran protistas, animales, plantas y hongos, pero no arqueas ni bacterias (308)

evaporation/evaporación el cambio de una substancia de líquido a gas (508)

exoskeleton/exoesqueleto una estructura de soporte, dura y externa (452)

F

floodplain/llanura de inundación un área a lo largo de un río formada por sedimentos que se depositan cuando el río se desborda (80)

fluid/fluido un estado no sólido de la materia en el que los átomos o moléculas tienen libertad de movimiento, como en el caso de un gas o un líquido (620)

food chain/cadena alimenticia la vía de transferencia de energía través de varias etapas, que ocurre como resultado de los patrones de alimentación de una serie de organismos (486)

food web/red alimenticia un diagrama que muestra las relaciones de alimentación entre los organismos de un ecosistema (486)

force/fuerza una acción de empuje o atracción que se ejerce sobre un objeto con el fin de cambiar su movimiento; la fuerza tiene magnitud y dirección (565)

fossil fuel/combustible fósil un recurso energético no renovable formado a partir de los restos de organismos que vivieron hace mucho tiempo (698)

free fall/caída libre el movimiento de un cuerpo cuando la única fuerza que actúa sobre él es la fuerza de gravedad (593)

friction/fricción una fuerza que se opone al movimiento entre dos superficies que están en contacto (568, 695)

front/frente el límite entre masas de aire de diferentes desidades y, normalmente, diferentes temperaturas (180)

function/función la actividad especial, normal o adecuada de un órgano o parte (320)

fungi/fungi un reino formado por organismos eucarióticos no verdes que no tienen capacidad de movimiento, se reproducen por esporas y obtienen alimento al descomponer substancias de su entorno y absorber los nutrientes (342)

fungus/hongo un organismo que tiene células con núcleos y pared celular rígida, pero carece de clorofila, perteneciente al reino Fungi (392)

G

gas/gas un estado de la materia que no tiene volumen ni forma definidos (544)

gas giant/gigante gaseoso un planeta con una atmósfera masiva y profunda, como por ejemplo, Júpiter, Saturno, Urano o Neptuno (250)

glacial drift/deriva glacial el material rocoso que es transportado y depositado por los glaciares (118)

glacier/glaciar una masa grande de hielo en movimiento (114)

global warming/calentamiento global un aumento gradual de la temperatura global promedio (145, 228)

Golgi complex/aparato de Golgi un organelo celular que ayuda a hacer y a empacar los materiales que serán transportados al exterior de la célula (315)

gravity/gravedad una fuerza de atracción entre dos objetos debido a sus masas (574)

greenhouse effect/efecto de invernadero el calentamiento de la superficie y de la parte más baja de la atmósfera, el cual se produce cuando el vapor de agua, el dióxido de carbono y otros gases absorben y vuelven a irradiar la energía térmica (144, 228)

gymnosperm/gimnosperma una planta leñosa vascular que produce semillas que no están contenidas en un ovario o fruto (412)

H

heat/calor la transferencia de energía entre objetos que están a temperaturas diferentes (720)

heat engine/motor térmico una máquina que transforma el calor en energía mecánica, o trabajo (735)

herbivore/herbívoro un organismo que sólo come plantas (485)

heredity/herencia la transmisión de caracteres genéticos de padres a hijos (284)

heterotroph/heterótrofo un organismo que se alimenta comiendo otros organismos o sus productos secundarios y que no puede producir compuestos orgánicos a partir de materiales inorgánicos (381)

homeostasis/homeostasis la capacidad de mantener un estado interno constante en un ambiente en cambio (283)

host/huésped el organismo del cual un parásito obtiene alimento y refugio (366, 381)

humidity/humedad la cantidad de vapor de agua que hay en el aire (171)

humus/humus material orgánico obscuro que se forma en la tierra a partir de restos de plantas y animales en descomposición (52)

hurricane/huracán tormenta severa que se desarrolla sobre océanos tropicales, con vientos fuertes que soplan a más de 120 km/h y que se mueven en espiral hacia el centro de presión extremadamente baja de la tormenta (187)

hypha/hifa un filamento no-reproductor de un hongo (393)

hypothesis/hipótesis una explicación que se basa en observaciones o investigaciones científicas previas y que se puede probar (12)

I

ice age/edad de hielo un largo período de tiempo frío durante el cual grandes áreas de la superficie terrestre están cubiertas por capas de hielo; también conocido como período glacial (224)

inclined plane/plano inclinado una máquina simple que es una superficie recta e inclinada, que facilita el levantamiento de cargas; una rampa (666)

inertia/inercia la tendencia de un objeto a no moverse o, si el objeto se está moviendo, la tendencia a resistir un cambio en su rapidez o dirección hasta que una fuerza externa actúe en el objeto (600)

insulation/aislante una substancia que reduce la transferencia de electricidad, calor o sonido (733)

J

jet stream/corriente en chorro un cinturón delgado de vientos fuertes que soplan en la parte superior de la troposfera (150)

joule/joule la unidad que se usa para expresar energía; equivale a la cantidad de trabajo realizada por una fuerza de 1 N que actúa a través de una distancia de 1 m en la dirección de la fuerza (símbolo: J) (653)

K

kinetic energy/energía cinética la energía de un objeto debido al movimiento del objeto (681)

L

landslide/derrumbamiento el movimiento súbito hacia abajo de rocas y suelo por una pendiente (121)

large intestine/intestino grueso la porción más ancha y más corta del intestino, que elimina el agua de los alimentos casi totalmente digeridos y convierte los desechos en heces semisólidas o excremento (467)

latitude/latitud la distancia hacia el norte o hacia el sur del ecuador; se expresa en grados (207)

law/ley un resumen de muchos resultados y observaciones experimentales; una ley dice cómo funcionan las cosas (20)

law of conservation of energy/ley de la conservación de la energía la ley que establece que la energía ni se crea ni se destruye, sólo se transforma de una forma a otra (695)

law of conservation of mass/ley de la conservación de la masa la ley que establece que la masa no se crea ni se destruye por cambios químicos o físicos comunes (536)

leaching/lixiviación la remoción de substancias que pueden disolverse de rocas, menas o capas de suelo debido al paso del agua (52)

lever/palanca una máquina simple formada por una barra que gira en un punto fijo llamado *fulcro* (663)

lichen/liquen una masa de células de hongos y de algas que crecen juntas en una relación simbiótica y que normalmente se encuentran en rocas o árboles (398)

lift/propulsión una fuerza hacia arriba en un objeto que se mueve en un fluido (633)

lightning/relámpago una descarga eléctrica que ocurre entre dos superficies que tienen carga opuesta, como por ejemplo, entre una nube y el suelo, entre dos nubes o entres dos partes de la misma nube (185)

lipid/lípido un tipo de substancia bioquímica que no se disuelve en agua; las grasas y los esteroides son lípidos (290)

liquid/líquido el estado de la materia que tiene un volumen definido, pero no una forma definida (544)

load/carga los materiales que lleva un arroyo; también, la masa de rocas que recubre una estructura geológica (74)

loess/loess sedimentos muy fértiles de cuarzo, feldespato, hornblenda, mica y arcilla depositados por el viento (112)

lysosome/lisosoma un organelo celular que contiene enzimas digestivas (316)

M

machine/máquina un aparato que ayuda a realizar un trabajo, ya sea venciendo una fuerza o cambiando la dirección de la fuerza aplicada (657)

mass/masa una medida de la cantidad de materia que tiene un objeto (25, 578)

mass movement/movimiento masivo un movimiento hacia abajo de una sección de terreno por una pendiente (120)

matter/materia cualquier cosa que tiene masa y ocupa un lugar en el espacio (529)

mechanical advantage/ventaja mecánica un número que dice cuántas veces una máquina multiplica una fuerza (659)

mechanical efficiency/eficiencia mecánica la relación entre la entrada y la salida de energía o potencia; se calcula dividiendo la salida de trabajo por la entrada de trabajo (660)

mechanical energy/energía mecánica la cantidad de trabajo que un objeto realiza debido a las energías cinética y potencial del objeto (683)

mechanical weathering/desgaste mecánico el rompimiento de una roca en pedazos más pequeños mediante medios físicos (40)

mesosphere/mesosfera la capa de la atmósfera que se encuentra entre la estratosfera y la termosfera, en la cual la temperatura disminuye al aumentar la altitud (139)

metabolism/metabolismo la suma de todos los procesos químicos que ocurren en un organismo (284)

metamorphosis/metamorfosis una fase del ciclo de vida de muchos animales durante la cual ocurre un cambio rápido de la forma inmadura del organismo a la adulta (462)

meteor/meteoro un rayo de luz brillante que se produce cuando un meteoroide se quema en la atmósfera de la Tierra (267)

meteorite/meteorito un meteoroide que llega a la superficie de la Tierra sin quemarse por completo (267)

meteoroid/meteoroide un cuerpo rocoso relativamente pequeño que viaja en el espacio (267)

meter/metro la unidad fundamental de longitud en el sistema internacional de unidades (símbolo: m) (25)

microclimate/microclima el clima de un área pequeña (222)

mitochondrion/mitocondria en las células eucarióticas, el organelo celular rodeado por dos membranas que es el lugar donde se lleva a cabo la respiración celular (314)

mixture/mezcla una combinación de dos o más substancias que no están combinadas químicamente (530)

model/modelo un diseño, plan, representación o descripción cuyo objetivo es mostrar la estructura o funcionamiento de un objeto, sistema o concepto (18)

mold/moho en biología, un hongo que tiene la apariencia de lana o algodón (394)

momentum/momento una cantidad que se define como el producto de la masa de un objeto por su velocidad (606)

motion/movimiento el cambio en la posición de un objeto respecto a un punto de referencia (559)

mudflow/flujo de lodo el flujo de una masa de lodo o roca y suelo mezclados con una gran cantidad de agua (122)

mutualism/mutualismo una relación entre dos especies en la que ambas se benefician (494)

mycelium/micelio una masa de filamentos de hongos, o hifas, que forma el cuerpo de un hongo (393)

N

net force/fuerza neta la combinación de todas las fuerzas que actúan sobre un objeto (565)

nonpoint-source pollution/contaminación no puntual contaminación que proviene de muchas fuentes, en lugar de provenir de un solo sitio específico (88)

nonrenewable resource/recurso no renovable un recurso que se forma a una tasa que es mucho más lenta que la tasa a la que se consume (698)

nonvascular plant/planta no vascular los tres tipos de plantas (hepáticas, milhojas y musgos) que carecen de tejidos transportadores y de raíces, tallos y hojas verdaderas (412)

nucleic acid/ácido nucleico una molécula formada por subunidades llamadas *nucleótidos* (291)

nucleus/núcleo en ciencias físicas, la región central de un átomo, la cual está constituida por protones y neutrones (305)

O

observation/observación el proceso de obtener información por medio de los sentidos (11)

omnivore/omnívoro un organismo que come tanto plantas como animales (485)

open circulatory system/aparato circulatorio abierto un aparato circulatorio en el que el fluido circulatorio no está totalmente contenido en los vasos sanguíneos; un corazón bombea fluido por los vasos sanguíneos, los cuales se vacían en espacios llamados *senos* (461)

organ/órgano un conjunto de tejidos que desempeñan una función especializada en el cuerpo (319)

organelle/organelo uno de los cuerpos pequeños del citoplasma de una célula que están especializados para llevar a cabo una función específica (305)

organism/organismo un ser vivo; cualquier cosa que pueda llevar a cabo procesos vitales independientemente (320)

organ system/aparato (o sistema) de órganos un grupo de órganos que trabajan en conjunto para desempeñar funciones corporales (320)

ovary/ovario en las plantas con flores, la parte inferior del pistilo que produce óvulos (320)

P

parasite/parásito un organismo que se alimenta de un organismo de otra especie (el huésped) y que normalmente lo daña; el huésped nunca se beneficia de la presencia del parásito (381)

parasitism/parasitismo una relación entre dos especies en la que una, el parásito, se beneficia de la otra, el huésped, que resulta perjudicada (495)

parent rock/roca precursora una formación rocosa que es la fuente a partir de la cual se origina el suelo (50)

pascal/pascal la unidad de presión del sistema internacional de unidades (símbolo: Pa) (620)

Pascal's principle/principio de Pascal el principio que establece que un fluido en equilibro que esté contenido en un recipiente ejerce una presión de igual intensidad en todas las direcciones (636)

pathogenic bacteria/bacteria patogénica bacteria que causa una enfermedad (364)

permeability/permeabilidad la capacidad de una roca o sedimento de permitir que los fluidos pasen a través de sus espacios abiertos o poros (83)

petal/pétalo una de las partes de una flor que normalmente tienen colores brillantes y forma de hoja, las cuales forman uno de los anillos de una flor (429)

phase/fase el cambio en el área iluminada de un cuerpo celeste según se ve desde otro cuerpo celeste (258)

phloem/floema el tejido que transporta alimento en las plantas vasculares (424)

phospholipid/fosfolípido un lípido que contiene fósforo y que es un componente estructural de la membrana celular (290)

physical change/cambio físico un cambio de materia de una forma a otra sin que ocurra un cambio en sus propiedades químicas (537)

physical property/propiedad física una característica de una substancia que no implica un cambio químico, tal como la densidad, el color o la dureza (532)

phytoplankton/fitoplancton los organismos microscópicos fotosintéticos que flotan cerca de la superficie del agua dulce o marina (384)

pioneer species/especie pionera una especie que coloniza un área deshabitada y empieza un proceso de sucesión (513)

pistil/pistilo la parte reproductora femenina de una flor, la cual produce semillas y está formada por el ovario, estilo y estigma (430)

plantae/plantae un reino formado por organismos pluricelulares complejos que normalmente son verdes, tienen una pared celular de celulosa, no tienen capacidad de movimiento y utilizan la energía del Sol para producir azúcar mediante la fotosíntesis (343)

plasma/plasma en ciencias físicas, un estado de la materia que comienza como un gas y luego se vuelve ionizado; está formado por iones y electrones que se mueven libremente, tiene carga eléctrica y sus propiedades difieren de las propiedades de un sólido, líquido o gas (546)

point-source pollution/contaminación puntual
contaminación que proviene de un lugar específico
(88)

polar easterlies/vientos polares del este vientos
preponderantes que soplan de este a oeste entre
los 60° y los 90° de latitud en ambos hemisferios
(148)

polar zone/zona polar el Polo Norte y el Polo Sur
y la región circundante (221)

pollen/polen los gránulos diminutos que con-
tienen el gametofito masculino en las plantas con
semilla (418)

pollination/polinización la transferencia de polen
de las estructuras reproductoras masculinas a las
estructuras femeninas de las plantas con semillas
(421)

population/población un grupo de organismos de
la misma especie que viven en un área geográfica
específica (482)

porosity/porosidad el porcentaje del volumen
total de una roca o sedimento que está formado
por espacios abiertos (83)

potential energy/energía potencial la energía
que tiene un objeto debido a su posición, forma o
condición (683)

power/potencia la tasa a la que se realiza un trabajo o a la que se transforma la energía (654)

precipitation/precipitación cualquier forma de
agua que cae de las nubes a la superficie de la
Tierra (176, 508)

precipitation/precipitación cualquier forma
deagua que cae de las nubes a la superficie de la
Tierra (508)

predator/depredador un organismo que se alimenta de otro organismo o de parte de él (492)

pressure/presión la cantidad de fuerza ejercida en
una superficie por unidad de área (546, 620)

prevailing winds/vientos prevalecientes vientos
que soplan principalmente de una dirección durante
un período de tiempo determinado (209)

prey/presa un organismo al que otro organismo
mata para alimentarse de él (492)

producer/productor un organismo que puede
elaborar sus propios alimentos utilizando la energía
de su entorno (287)

prograde rotation/rotación progresiva el giro en
contra de las manecillas del reloj de un planeta o
de una luna según lo vería un observador ubicado
encima del Polo Norte del planeta; rotación en la
misma dirección que la rotación del Sol (245)

projectile motion/movimiento proyectil la
trayectoria curva que sigue un objeto cuando es
aventado, lanzado o proyectado de cualquier otra
manera cerca de la superficie de la Tierra (595)

prokaryote/procariote un organismo unicelular
que no tiene núcleo ni organelos cubiertos por una
membrana, por ejemplo, las arqueas y las bacterias
(306, 357)

protein/proteína una molécula formada por ami-
noácidos que es necesaria para construir y reparar
estructuras corporales y para regular procesos del
cuerpo (288)

protist/protista un organismo que pertenece al
reino Protista (380)

Protista/Protista un reino compuesto principalmente por organismos eucarióticos unicelulares que
son diferentes de las plantas, animales, bacterias y
hongos (342)

pulley/polea una máquina simple formada por
una rueda sobre la cual pasa una cuerda, cadena o
cable (664)

pure substance/substancia pura una muestra de
materia, ya sea un solo elemento o un solo compuesto, que tiene propiedades químicas y físicas
definidas (529)

R

radiation/radiación la transferencia de energía en
forma de ondas electromagnéticas (143, 724)

recharge zone/zona de recarga un área en la que
el agua se desplaza hacia abajo para convertirse en
parte de un acuífero (84)

relative humidity/humedad relativa la proporción
de la cantidad de vapor de agua que hay en el aire
respecto a la cantidad máxima de vapor de agua que
el aire puede contener a una temperatura dada (171)

renewable resource/recurso renovable un recurso
natural que puede reemplazarse a la misma tasa a
la que se consume (701)

retrograde rotation/rotación retrógrada el giro
en el sentido de las manecillas del reloj de un planeta o de una luna según lo vería un observador
ubicado encima del Polo Norte del planeta (245)

rhizoid/rizoide una estructura parecida a una
raíz que se encuentra en las plantas no vasculares;
mantiene a las plantas en su lugar y las ayuda a
obtener agua y nutrientes (414)

rhizome/rizoma un tallo horizontal subterráneo
que produce nuevas hojas, brotes y raíces (416)

ribosome/ribosoma un organelo celular compuesto de ARN y proteína; el sitio donde ocurre la
síntesis de proteínas (313)

rock fall/desprendimiento de rocas el movimiento rápido y masivo de rocas por una pendiente empinada o un precipicio (121)

S

saltation/saltación el movimiento de la arena u otros sedimentos por medio de saltos pequeños y rebotes debido al viento o al agua (111)

satellite/satélite un cuerpo natural o artificial que gira alrededor de un planeta (257)

science/ciencia el conocimiento que se obtiene por medio de la observación natural de acontecimientos y condiciones con el fin de descubrir hechos y formular leyes o principios que puedan ser verificados o probados (4)

scientific methods/métodos científicos una serie de pasos que se siguen para solucionar problemas (10)

screw/tornillo una máquina simple formada por un plano inclinado enrollado a un cilindro (667)

segment/segmento cualquier parte de una estructura más grande, como el cuerpo de un organismo, que se determina por límites naturales o arbitrarios (459)

sepal/sépalo en una flor, uno de los anillos más externos de hojas modificadas que protegen el capullo de la flor (429)

septic tank/tanque séptico un tanque que separa los desechos sólidos de los líquidos y que tiene bacterias que escomponen los desechos sólidos (91)

sewage treatment plant/planta de tratamiento de residuos una instalación que limpia los materiales de desecho que se encuentran en el agua procedente de cloacas o alcantarillas (90)

sexual reproduction/reproducción sexual reproducción en la que se unen las células sexuales de los dos progenitores para producir descendencia que comparte caracteres de ambos progenitores (284)

shoreline/orilla el límite entre la tierra y una masa de agua (105)

small intestine/intestino delgado el órgano que se encuentra entre el estómago y el intestino grueso en el cual se produce la mayor parte de la descomposición de los alimentos y se absorben la mayoría de los nutrientes (467)

soil/suelo una mezcla suelta de fragmentos de roca, material orgánico, agua y aire en la que puede crecer vegetación (50)

soil conservation/conservación del suelo un método para mantener la fertilidad del suelo protegiéndolo de la erosión y la pérdida de nutrientes (56)

soil structure/estructura del suelo la organización de las partículas del suelo (51)

soil texture/textura del suelo la cualidad del suelo que se basa en las proporciones de sus partículas (51)

solid/sólido el estado de la materia en el cual el volumen y la forma de una sustancia están fijos (543)

specific heat/calor específico la cantidad de calor que se requiere para aumentar una unidad de masa de un material homogéneo 1 K o 1°C de una manera especificada, dados un volumen y una presión constantes (725)

speed/rapidez la distancia que un objeto se desplaza dividida entre el intervalo de tiempo durante el cual ocurrió el movimiento (559)

spore/espora una célula reproductora o estructura pluricelular que resiste las condiciones ambientales adversas y que se puede desarrollar hasta convertirse en un adulto sin necesidad de fusionarse con otra célula (393)

stamen/estambre la estructura reproductora masculina de una flor, que produce polen y está formada por una antera ubicada en la punta del filamento (430)

states of matter/estados de la material las formas físicas de la materia, que son sólida, líquida y gaseosa (729)

stimulus/estímulo cualquier cosa que causa una reacción o cambio en un organismo o cualquier parte de un organismo (283)

stratified drift/deriva estratificada un depósito glacial que ha formado capas debido a la acción de los arroyos o de las aguas de ablación (118)

stratosphere/estratosfera la capa de la atmósfera que se encuentra encima de la troposfera y en la que la temperatura aumenta al aumentar la altitud (139)

structure/estructura el orden y distribución de las partes de un organismo (320)

succession/sucesión el reemplazo de un tipo de comunidad por otro en un mismo lugar a lo largo de un período de tiempo (512)

surface current/corriente superficial un movimiento horizontal del agua del océano que es producido por el viento y que ocurre en la superficie del océano o cerca de ella (211)

symbiosis/simbiosis una relación en la que dos organismos diferentes viven estrechamente asociados uno con el otro (494)

taxonomy/taxonomía la ciencia de describir, nombrar y clasificar organismos (335)

temperate zone/zona templada la zona climática ubicada entre los trópicos y la zona polar (219)

temperature/temperatura una medida de qué tan caliente (o frío) está algo; específicamente, una medida de la energía cinética promedio de las partículas de un objeto (26, 714)

terminal velocity/velocidad terminal la velocidad constante de un objeto en caída cuando la fuerza de resistencia del aire es igual en magnitud y opuesta en dirección a la fuerza de gravedad (592)

terrestrial planet/planeta terrestre uno de los planetas muy densos que se encuentran más cerca del Sol; Mercurio, Venus, Marte y la Tierra (244)

theory/teoría una explicación que relaciona muchas hipótesis y observaciones (20)

thermal conduction/conducción térmica la transferencia de energía en forma de calor a través de un material (143, 722)

thermal conductor/conductor térmico un material a través del cual es posible transferir energía en forma de calor (723)

thermal energy/energía térmica la energía cinética de los átomos de una sustancia (721)

thermal expansion/expansión térmica un aumento en el tamaño de una sustancia en respuesta a un aumento en la temperatura de la sustancia (716)

thermal insulator/aislante térmico un material que reduce o evita la transferencia de calor (723)

thermal pollution/contaminación térmica un aumento en la temperatura de una masa de agua, producido por las actividades humanas y que tienen efecto dañino en la calidad del agua y en la capacidad de esa masa de agua para permitir que se desarrolle la vida (738)

thermometer/termómetro un instrumento que mide e indica la temperatura (193)

thermosphere/termosfera la capa más alta de la atmósfera, en la cual la temperatura aumenta a medida que la altitud aumenta (140)

thrust/empuje la fuerza de empuje o arrastre ejercida por el motor de un avión o cohete (634)

thunderstorm/tormenta eléctrica una tormenta fuerte y normalmente breve que consiste en lluvia, vientos fuertes, relámpagos y truenos (184, 185)

till/arcilla glaciárica material rocoso desordenado que deposita directamente un glaciar que se está derritiendo (118)

tissue/tejido un grupo de células similares que llevan a cabo una función común (319)

tornado/tornado una columna destructiva de aire en rotación cuyos vientos se mueven a velocidades muy altas; se ve como una nube con forma de embudo y toca el suelo (186)

trade winds/vientos alisios vientos preponderantes que soplan hacia el noreste a partir de los 30° de latitud norte hacia el ecuador y que soplan hacia el sureste a partir de los 30° de latitud sur hacia el ecuador (148)

tributary/afluente un arroyo que fluye a un lago o a otro arroyo más grande (73)

tropical zone/zona tropical la región que rodea el ecuador y se extiende desde aproximadamente 23° de latitud norte hasta 23° de latitud sur (215)

troposphere/troposfera la capa inferior de la atmósfera, en la que la temperatura disminuye a una tasa constante a medida que la altitud aumenta (139)

V

vascular plant/planta vascular una planta que tiene tejidos especializados que transportan materiales de una parte de la planta a otra (412)

velocity/velocidad la rapidez de un objeto en una dirección dada (561)

vertebrate/vertebrado un animal que tiene columna vertebral (454)

vesicle/vesícula una cavidad o bolsa pequeña que contiene materiales en una célula eucariótica; se forma cuando parte de la membrana celular rodea los materiales que van a ser llevados al interior la célula o transportados dentro de ella (315)

virus/virus una partícula microscópica que se introduce en una célula y a menudo la destruye (366)

volume/volumen una medida del tamaño de un cuerpo o región en un espacio de tres dimensiones (26)

W

water cycle/ciclo del agua el movimiento continuo del agua: del océano a la atmósfera, de la atmósfera a la tierra y de la tierra al océano (71)

watershed/cuenca hidrográfica el área del terreno que es drenada por un sistema de agua (310)

water table/capa freática el nivel más alto del agua subterránea; el límite superior de la zona de saturación (82)

watt/watt (o vatio) la unidad que se usa para expresar potencia; es equivalente a un joule por segundo (símbolo: W) (654)

weather/tiempo el estado de la atmósfera a corto plazo que incluye la temperatura, la humedad, la precipitación, el viento y la visibilidad (171, 207)

weathering/meteorización el proceso por el cual se desintegran los materiales que forman las rocas debido a la acción de procesos físicos o químicos (40)

wedge/cuña una máquina simple que está formada por dos planos inclinados y que se mueve; normalmente se usa para cortar (667)

weight/peso una medida de la fuerza gravitacional ejercida sobre un objeto; su valor puede cambiar en función de la ubicación del objeto en el universo (578)

westerlies/vientos del oeste vientos preponderantes que soplan de oeste a este entre 30° y 60° de latitud en ambos hemisferios (148)

wheel and axle/eje y rueda una máquina simple que está formada por dos objetos circulares de diferente tamaño; la rueda es el mayor de los dos objetos circulares (665)

wind/viento el movimiento de aire producido por diferencias en la presión barométrica (146)

work/trabajo la transferencia de energía a un objeto mediante una fuerza que hace que el objeto se mueva en la dirección de la fuerza (651)

work input/trabajo de entrada el trabajo realizado en una máquina; el producto de la fuerza de entrada por la distancia a través de la que se ejerce la fuerza (657)

work output/trabajo producido el trabajo realizado por una máquina; el producto de la fuerza de salida por la distancia a través de la que se ejerce la fuerza (657)

X

xylem/xilema el tipo de tejido que se encuentra en las plantas vasculares, el cual provee soporte y transporta el agua y los nutrientes desde las raíces (424)

Index

Index

Index

Index

Index

Index

Index

Index

Acknowledgments

continued from page ii

John Brockhaus, Ph.D.
Director of Geospatial Science Information Program
Department of Geography and Environmental Engineering
United States Military Academy
West Point, New York

Howard L. Brooks, Ph.D.
Professor of Physics & Astronomy
Department of Physics & Astronomy
DePauw University
Greencastle, Indiana

Dan Bruton, Ph.D.
Associate Professor
Department of Physics and Astronomy
Stephen F. Austin State University
Nacogdoches, Texas

Wesley N. Colley, Ph.D.
Lecturer
Department of Astronomy
University of Virginia
Charlottesville, Virginia

Joe W. Crim, Ph.D.
Professor and Head of Cellular Biology
Department of Cellular Biology
University of Georgia
Athens, Georgia

Simonetta Frittelli, Ph.D.
Associate Professor
Department of Physics
Duquesne University
Pittsburgh, Pennsylvania

L. Lee Grismer, Ph.D.
Professor
Department of Biology
La Sierra University
Riverside, California

P. Shiv Halasyamani, Ph.D.
Associate Professor of Chemistry
Department of Chemistry
University of Houston
Houston, Texas

David S. Hall, Ph.D.
Assistant Professor of Physics
Department of Physics
Amherst College
Amherst, Massachusetts

Deborah Hanley, Ph.D.
Meteorologist
State of Florida
Department of Agriculture and Consumer Services
Division of Forestry
Tallahassee, Florida

David Hershey, Ph.D.
Education Consultant
Hyattsville, Maryland

William H. Ingham, Ph.D.
Professor of Physics
James Madison University
Harrisonburg, Virginia

Steven A. Jennings, Ph.D.
Associate Professor
Department of Geography and Environmental Studies
University of Colorado
Colorado Springs, Colorado

Linda Jones
Program Manager
Texas Department of Public Health
Austin, Texas

Lee B. Kats, Ph.D.
Professor of Biology
Natural Science Division
Pepperdine University
Malibu, California

Jamie Kneitel, Ph.D.
Postdoctoral Associate
Department of Biology
Washington University
St. Louis, Missouri

David Lamp, Ph.D.
Associate Professor of Physics
Physics Department
Texas Tech University
Lubbock, Texas

Mark Mattson, Ph.D.
Director, College of Science and Mathematics Learning Center
James Madison University
Harrisonburg, Virginia

Nancy L. McQueen, Ph.D.
Professor of Microbiology
Department of Biological Sciences
California State University, Los Angeles
Los Angeles, California

Madeline Micceri Mignone, Ph.D.
Assistant Professor
Natural Science
Dominican College
Orangeburg, New York

Richard F. Niedziela, Ph.D.
Assistant Professor of Chemistry
Department of Chemistry
DePaul University
Chicago, Illinois

Eva Oberdoerster, Ph.D.
Lecturer
Department of Biology
Southern Methodist University
Dallas, Texas

Michael H. Renfroe, Ph.D.
Professor of Biology
Department of Biology
James Madison University
Harrisonburg, Virginia

Dork Sahagian, Ph.D.
Research Professor
Department of Earth Sciences
Institute for the Study of Earth, Oceans, and Space
University of New Hampshire
Durham, New Hampshire

Patrick K. Schoff, Ph.D.
Research Associate
Natural Resources Research Institute
University of Minnesota at Duluth
Duluth, Minnesota

Fred Seaman, Ph.D.
Retired Research Associate
College of Pharmacy
The University of Texas at Austin
Austin, Texas

H. Michael Sommermann, Ph.D.
Professor of Physics
Physics Department
Westmont College
Santa Barbara, California

Vatche P. Tchakerian, Ph.D.
Professor
Department of Geography & Geology
Texas A&M University
College Station, Texas

Richard S. Treptow, Ph.D.
Professor of Chemistry
Department of Chemistry and Physics
Chicago State University
Chicago, Illinois

Richard P. Vari, Ph.D.
Research Scientist and Curator
Department of Vertebrate Zoology
National Museum of Natural History
Washington, D.C

Dale Wheeler
Associate Professor of Chemistry
A. R. Smith Department of Chemistry
Appalachian State University
Boone, North Carolina

Teacher Reviewers

Diedre S. Adams
Physical Science Instructor
West Vigo Middle School
West Terre Haute, Indiana

Barbara Gavin Akre
Teacher of Biology, Anatomy-Physiology, and Life Science
Duluth Independent School District
Duluth, Minnesota

Laura Buchanan
Science Teacher and Department Chair
Corkran Middle School
Glen Burnie, Maryland

Sarah Carver
Science Teacher
Jackson Creek Middle
  School
Bloomington, Indiana

Robin K. Clanton
Science Department Head
Berrien Middle School
Nashville, Georgia

Karen Dietrich, S.S.J., Ph.D.
*Principal and Biology
  Instructor*
Mount Saint Joseph Academy
Flourtown, Pennsylvania

Trisha Elliott
*Science and Mathematics
  Teacher*
Chain of Lakes Middle
  School
Orlando, Florida

Liza M. Guasp
Science Teacher
Celebration K–8 School
Celebration, Florida

Meredith Hanson
Science Teacher
Westside Middle School
Rocky Face, Georgia

Ronald W. Hudson
Science Teacher
Batchelor Middle School
Bloomington, Indiana

Denise Hulette
Science Teacher
Conway Middle School
Orlando, Florida

James Kerr
*Oklahoma Teacher of the Year
  2002–2003*
Union Public Schools
Tulsa, Oklahoma

M. R. Penny Kisiah
*Science Teacher and
  Department Chair*
Fairview Middle School
Tallahassee, Florida

Laura Kitselman
*Science Teacher and
  Coordinator*
Loudoun Country Day
  School
Leesburg, Virginia

Debra S. Kogelman, MAed.
Science Teacher
University of Chicago
Laboratory Schools
Chicago, Illinois

Deborah L. Kronsteiner
Science Teacher
Spring Grove Area Middle
  School
Spring Grove, Pennsylvania

Jennifer L. Lamkie
Science Teacher
Thomas Jefferson Middle
  School
Edison, New Jersey

Rebecca Larsen
Science Teacher
Fernandina Beach Middle
  School
Fernandina Beach, Florida

Sally M. Lesley
ESL Science Teacher
Burnet Middle School
Austin, Texas

Stacy Loeak
*Science Teacher and
  Department Chair*
Baker Middle School
Columbus, Georgia

Augie Maldonado
Science Teacher
Grisham Middle School
Round Rock, Texas

Bill Martin
Science Teacher
Southeast Middle School
Kernersville, North
  Carolina

Maureen Martin
Green Team Science Teacher
Jackson Creek Middle
  School
Bloomington, Indiana

Susan H. Robinson
Science Teacher
Oglethorpe County Middle
  School
Lexington, Georgia

Elizabeth J. Rustad
Science Department Chair
Coronado Elementary
Gilbert, Arizona

Helen P. Schiller
Instructional Coach
The School District of
  Greenville County
Greenville, South Carolina

Mark Schnably
Science Instructor
Thomas Jefferson Middle
  School
Winston-Salem, North
  Carolina

Stephanie Snowden
Science Teacher
Canyon Vista Middle
  School
Austin, Texas

Marci L. Stadiem
Science Department Head
Cascade Middle School
Seattle, Washington

Anne Stephens, MA
Science Teacher
Marsh Junior High School
*Co-Director, Hands-on
  Science Lab*
College of Natural Sciences
California State University,
  Chico
Chico, California

Martha Tedrow
Science Teacher
Thomas Jefferson Middle
  School
Winston-Salem, North
  Carolina

Martha B. Trisler
Science Teacher
Rising Starr Middle School
Fayetteville, Georgia

Sherrye Valenti
Curriculum Leader
Science Department
Wildwood Middle School
Wildwood, Missouri

Gayle Van Fossen
Science Teacher
George V. LeyVa Middle
  School
San Jose, California

Louise Whealton
Science Teacher
Wiley Middle School
Winston-Salem, North
  Carolina

Angie Williams
Teacher
Riversprings Middle School
Crawfordville, Florida

Lab Testing

Barry L. Bishop
Science Teacher
San Rafael Junior High
  School
Ferron, Utah

Daniel Bugenhagen
Science Teacher
Yutan Junior-Senior High
  School
Yutan, Nebraska

Gladys Cherniak
Science Teacher
St. Paul's Episcopal School
Mobile, Alabama

Kenneth Creese
Science Teacher
White Mountain Junior
  High School
Rock Springs, Wyoming

Georgiann Delgadillo
Science Teacher
East Valley School District
Continuous Curriculum
  School
Spokane, Washington

Alonda Droege
Science Teacher
Pioneer Middle School
Steilacom, Washington

Vicky Farland
Science Teacher
Crane Junior High School
Yuma, Arizona

Rebecca Ferguson
Science Teacher
North Ridge Middle School
North Richland Hills, Texas

Susan Gorman
Science Teacher
North Ridge Middle School
North Ridge, Texas

C. John Graves
Science Teacher
Montforton Middle School
Bozeman, Montana

Dennis Hanson
Science Teacher
Big Bear Middle School
Big Bear Lake, California

Norman Holcomb
Science Teacher
Marion Elementary School
Maria Stein, Ohio

Kerry Johnson
Science Teacher
Isbell Middle School
Santa Paula, California

Michael E. Krai
Science Teacher
West Hardin Middle School
Cecilia, Kentucky

Jane Lemons
Science Teacher
Western Rockingham
   Middle School
Madison, North Carolina

Maurine Marchani
Science Teacher
Raymond Park Middle
   School
Indianapolis, Indiana

Jason P. Marsh
Biology Teacher
Montevideo High School
   and Montevideo Country
   School
Montevideo, Minnesota

Edith McAlanis
Science Teacher
Socorro Middle School
El Paso, Texas

Jan Nelson
Science Teacher
East Valley Middle School
East Helena, Montana

Joseph W. Price
Science Teacher
H.M. Browne Junior High
   School
Washington, D.C.

Terry Rakes
Science Teacher
Elmwood Junior High
   School
Rogers, Arizona

Elizabeth Rustad
Science Teacher
Crane Junior High School
Yuma, Arizona

Bert Sherwood
Science Teacher
Socorro Middle School
El Paso, Texas

David M. Sparks
Science Teacher
Redwater Junior High
   School
Redwater, Texas

Larry Tackett
Science Teacher
Andrew Jackson Middle
   School
Cross Lanes, West Virginia

Elsie Waynes
Science Teacher
Terrell Junior High School
Washington, D.C.

Sharon Woolf
Science Teacher
Langston Hughes Middle
   School
Reston, Virginia

John Zambo
Science Teacher
E. Ustach Middle School
Modesto, California

Gordon Zibelman
Science Teacher
Drexel Hill Middle School
Drexel Hill, Pennsylvania

Answer Checking

Hatim Belyamani
Austin, Texas

John A. Bennner
Austin, Texas

Catherine Podeszwa
Duluth, Minnesota

Credits

PHOTOGRAPHY

Abbreviations used: (t) top, (c) center, (b) bottom, (l) left, (r) right, (bkgd) background

Front Cover (tl) Andy Small/Corbis; (tr) SPL/Photo Researchers, Inc.; (c) Gallo Images-Roger De La Harpe/Getty Images; (b) Yva Momatiuk/John Eastcott/Minden Pictures

Skills Practice Lab Teens Sam Dudgeon/HRW

Connection to Astronomy Corbis Images; **Connection to Biology** David M. Phillips/Visuals Unlimited; **Connection to Chemistry** Digital Image copyright © 2005 PhotoDisc; **Connection to Environment** Digital Image copyright © 2005 PhotoDisc; **Connection to Geology** Letraset Phototone; **Connection to Language Arts** Digital Image copyright © 2005 PhotoDisc; **Connection to Meteorology** Digital Image copyright © 2005 PhotoDisc; **Connection to Oceanography** © ICONOTEC; **Connection to Physics** Digital Image copyright © 2005 PhotoDisc

Table of Contents iii (tr), Sam Dudgeon/HRW; iii (br), © Lawrence Livermore National Laboratory/Photo Researchers, Inc.; v (tl), Glenn M. Oliver/Visuals Unlimited; v (b), Tom Bean/CORBIS; iv (tl), Ron Niebrugge/Niebrugge Images; iv (bl), Bob Krueger/Photo Researchers, Inc.; vi (tl), Peter Van Steen/HRW; vi (bl), NASA; vii (tl), Michael Fogden/Bruce Coleman, Inc.; vii (bl), NASA/Peter Arnold, Inc.; viii (tl), Wolfgang Bayer; ix (tl), © Gary Randall; ix (bl), CNRI/Science Photo Library/Photo Researchers; x (tl), © Stan Osolinski/Getty Images; x (b), PhotoDisc/Getty Images; xi (tl), © David B. Fleetham/Getty Images; xii (t), Kim Heacox/DRK Photo; xii (bl), Tom Addison/Addison Fitzgerald Studios/HRW; xiii (tl), age fotostock/Fabio Cardoso; xiii (bl), NASA; xiv (tl), Larry L. Miller/Photo Researchers, Inc.; xiv (bl), © Galen Rowell/CORBIS; xv (tl), © Royalty Free/CORBIS; xv (bc), John Langford/HRW; xvi (b), Sam Dudgeon/HRW; xvii (tr), Sam Dudgeon/HRW; xviii (tr), Sam Dudgeon/HRW; xix (b), Sam Dudgeon/HRW; xxi (tr), Victoria Smith/HRW; xxii (bl), Victoria Smith/HRW; xxiv (bl), Victoria Smith/HRW

Safety First! xxviii, Sam Dudgeon/HRW; xxix(t), John Langford/HRW; xxix(bc), xxx(br) & xxx(tl), Sam Dudgeon/HRW xxx(bl), Stephanie Morris/HRW; xxxi(tl), Sam Dudgeon/ HRW xxxi(tr), Jana Birchum/HRW; xxxi(b), Sam Dudgeon/HRW

Chapter One 4 Peter Van Steen/HRW Photo; 5 (t) Peter Van Steen/HRW; 5 (b) Victoria Smith/HRW; 7(t) Mike Segar/Reuters Photo Archive; 7(b) CORBIS/ Annie Griffiths Belt; 8 (t) Annie Griffiths/Westlight/Corbis; 8 (b) AP Photo/Knoxville News-Sentinel; 9 Aurora Photos; 11 Peter Van Steen/HRW; 12 Courtesy of Dr. David Gillette; 16 Paul Fraughton/HRW; 18 (l) Sam Dudgeon/HRW; 18 (r) Jim Sugar Photography/CORBIS; 20 (l) AKG-Images; 20 (r) Image Copyright ©2001 PhotoDisc, Inc.; 21 Victoria Smith/HRW; 22 CENCO; 22 (zoom) Robert Brons/Getty Images/ Stone; 23 Victoria Smith/HRW; 25 (b) Peter Van Steen/HRW; 26 (l) Peter Van Steen/HRW; 26(r) Peter Van Steen/HRW; 30 Paul Fraughton/HRW 31 (R) Image Copyright ©2001 PhotoDisc, Inc.34 (tr), The Stuart News, Carl Rivenbark/AP/Wide World Photos; 35, AFP/CORBIS; 35 (b), AFP/CORBIS

Unit One 36 (bl), Detail of The Age of Reptiles, a mural by Rudolph F. Zallinger. ©1996, 1975,1985,1989, Peabody Museum of Natural History, Yale University, New Haven, Connecticut, USA.; 36-37 (bc), Price, R.-Survi OSF/Animals Animals/Earth Scenes; 36 (c), Peter Essick/Aurora; 36 (bl) Tom Bean/CORBIS; 37 (tr), John Eastcott/YVA Momatiuk/DRK Photo; 37 (c), Stock Montage, Inc.; 37 (cr), © Lauree Feldman/Index Stock Imagery, Inc.; 37 (bl), Hong Kong Airport Authority/AP/Wide World Photos; 37 (inset), Corbis Images

Chapter Two 38-39, Johny Sundby/Zuma Press/NewsCom; 40, SuperStock; 41 (tc), Visuals Unlimited/Martin G. Miller; 41 (tl), Ron Niebrugge/Niebrugge Images; 41 (tr), Grant Heilman/Grant Heilman Photography; 42 (t), John Sohlden/Visuals Unlimited; 44 (b), Laurence Parent; 44 (b), C. Campbell/Westlight/Corbis; 45, Bob Krueger/Photo Researchers, Inc.; 46 (b), B. Ross/Westlight/Corbis; 48 (bl), Digital Image copyright © 2005 EyeWire; 48 (br), David Cumming; Eye Ubiquitous/ CORBIS; 49, Corbis Images; 50, The G.R. "Dick" Roberts Photo Library; 53, Tom Bean/Getty Images/Stone; 54 (t), Bill Ross/Westlight/Corbis; 54 (b), Bruce Coleman, Inc.; 55, Lee Rentz/Bruce Coleman, Inc.; 56 (bl), Grant Heilman Photography, Inc.; 56 (br), Charlton Photos, Inc.; 57, Kevin Fleming/CORBIS; 58 (tr), Mark Lewis/ImageState; 58 (tl), Paul Chesley/Getty Images/Stone; 58 (br), Tom Hovland/Grant Heilman Photography, Inc.; 58 (bl), AgStockUsa; 59, Bettmann/ CORBIS; 60, 61 Sam Dudgeon/HRW; 62, B. Ross/Westlight/Corbis; 63, Bob Krueger/Photo Researchers, Inc.; 66 (tr), M.A. Kessler/Earth Sciences Department, University of California at Santa Cruz; 66 (tl), © W. Ming/UNEP/Peter Arnold, Inc.; 67 (t), Michael Murphy/By permission of Selah, Bamberger Ranch; 67 (b), Michael Murphy/By permission of Selah, Bamberger Ranch

Chapter Three 68-69, Owen Franklin/CORBIS; 70, Tom Bean/DRK Photo; 72, E.R.I.M./Stone; 73, (tr) Jim Wark/Peter Arnold; 73 (tl), Nancy Simmerman/Getty Images/Stone; 75, Frans Lanting/Minden Pictures; 75 (cr), Laurence Parent; 76 (t), The G.R. "Dick" Roberts Photo Library; 76, Galen Rowell/Peter Arnold, Inc.; 77 (t), Nancy Simmerman/Getty Images/Stone; 78, Glenn M. Oliver/Visuals Unlimited; 79 (t), The Huntington Library/SuperStock; 79 (b), Earth Satellite Corporation/Science Photo Library/Photo Researchers, Inc.; 80 (t), Visuals Unlimited/Martin G. Miller; 80

(b), Earth Satellite Corporation; 81, Jerry Laizure/AP/Wide World Photos; 86, Rich Reid/Animals Animals/Earth Scenes; 87, Leif Skoogfers/Woodfin Camp & Associates, Inc.; 88, Digital Image © 2005, Eyewire/Getty Images; 89, Morton Beebe/CORBIS; 93, Getty Images/Stone; 94, Victoria Smith/HRW; 96, Martin Harvey; Gallo Images/CORBIS; 97 (t), The Huntington Library/SuperStock; 97 (b), Jim Wark/Peter Arnold; 100 (t), David R. Parks; 100 (br), Martin Harvey; Gallo Images/CORBIS; 101 (tr), Photo by Sam Kittner, courtesy of Rita Colwell/National Science Foundation; 101 (b), Anwar Huq, UMBI

Chapter Four 103, John Kuntz/Reuters NewMedia Inc./CORBIS; 104, Aaron Chang/Corbis Stock Market; 105 (t), Tom Bean; 105 (b), CORBIS Images/HRW; 106 (tc), The G.R. "Dick" Roberts Photo Library; 106 (br), Jeff Foott/DRK Photo; 106 (bl), CORBIS Images/HRW; 107 (tl), Breck P. Kent; 107 (tr), John S. Shelton; 108 (c), © Panorama Stock/Digital Vision/gettyimages; 108 (b), Jonathan Weston/ImageState; 108 (t), SuperStock; 109, InterNetwork Media/Getty Images; 111, Jonathan Blair/ CORBIS; 112, © John Warden/Getty Images; 114, Tom Bean/CORBIS; 116 (b), Getty Images/Stone; 116 (t), Visuals Unlimited/Glenn M. Oliver; 118, 119, Tom Bean; 120 (l), Sam Dudgeon/HRW; 120 (r), Sam Dudgeon/HRW Photo; 121 (b), Sebastian d'Souza/AFP/CORBIS; 121 (t), Jacques Jangoux/Getty Images/Stone; 122 (t), Jebb Harris/Orange County Register/SABA/CORBIS; 122 (b), Mike Yamashita/Woodfin Camp & Associates; 123, Visuals Unlimited/John D. Cunningham; 124, Sam Dudgeon/HRW; 126, Tom Bean/CORBIS; 127, Aaron Chang/Corbis Stock Market; 130 (bl), Geological Survey of Canada, Photo #2002-581, Photographer Dr. Rejean Couture; 130, Charles H. Stites/The Lost Squadron Museum; 130 (t), Louis Sapienza/ The Lost Squadron Museum; 131 (r), ©National Geographic Image Collection/ Marla Stenzel; 131 (l), Martin Mejia/AP/Wide World Photos

Unit Two 132 (t), Ronald Sheridan/Ancient Art & Architecture Collection; 132 (c), The Huntington Library, Art Collections, and Botanical Gardens, San Marino, California/SuperStock; 133 (tl), NASA; 133 (tr), Sam Dudgeon/HRW; 133 (cr), SuperStock; 133 (bc), Lawrence Livermore Laboratory/Photo Researchers, Inc.; 133, S.Feval/Le Matin/Corbis Sygma

Chapter Five 134-135, Robert Holmes/CORBIS; 137, Peter Van Steen/HRW; 139 (t), SuperStock; 139 (b), NASA; 140, Image Copyright ©2005 PhotoDisc, Inc.; 141, Patrick J. Endres/Alaskaphotographics.com; 146, Terry Renna/AP/Wide World Photos; 147 (b), Moredun Animal Health Ltd./Science Photo Library/Photo Researchers, Inc.; 150 (t), NASA/Science Photo Library/Photo Researchers, Inc.; 152 (c), Argus Fotoarchiv/ Peter Arnold, Inc.; 152 (r), David Weintraub/Photo Researchers, Inc; 152 (l), Digital Image copyright © 2005 PhotoDisc/Getty Images; 153 (bl), Steve Starr/CORBIS; 153 (r), Corbis Images; 155, Simon Fraser/SPL/Photo Researchers, Inc.; 156 (t), Goddard Space Flight Center Scientific Visualization Studio/NASA; 156 (b), Goddard Space Flight Center Scientific Visualization Studio/NASA; 157, Tampa Electric; 158, Francis Dean/The Image Works; 159, Tampa Electric; 160, 161, Sam Dudgeon/HRW; 163 (t), Goddard Space Flight Center Scientific Visualization Studio/NASA; 166 (b), James McInnis/Los Alamos National Laboratories; 166 (t), Jonathan Blair/CORBIS; 167 (r), Fred Hirschmann; 167 (bl), Fred Hirschmann

Chapter Six 168-169, Tim Chapman/Miami Herald/NewsCom; 172, Sam Dudgeon/ HRW; 173, Victoria Smith/HRW; 174 (tc), NOAA; 174 (tr), Joyce Photographics/Photo Researchers, Inc.; 174 (tl), Corbis Images; 176, Gene E. Moore; 176 (tl), Gerben Oppermans/Getty Images/Stone; 177 (c), Corbis Images; 177 (t), Victoria Smith/ HRW; 179, Image Copyright ©2005 PhotoDisc, Inc.; 179 (t), Reuters/Gary Wiepert/ NewsCom; 182, NASA; 184, William H. Edwards/Getty Images/The Image Bank; 185 (br), Jean-Loup Charmet/Science Photo Library/Photo Researchers, Inc.; 186 (all), Howard B. Bluestein/Photo Researchers, Inc.; 187 (t), Red Huber/Orlando Sentinel/ SYGMA/CORBIS; 187 (b), NASA; 188 (t), NASA/Science Photo Library/Photo Researchers, Inc.; 189, Dave Martin/AP/Wide World Photos; 190 (b), Joe Raedle/ NewsCom; 190 (t), Will Chandler/Anderson Independent-Mail/AP/Wide World Photos; 191 (b), Jean-Loup Charmet/Science Photo Library/Photo Researchers, Inc.; 191 (c), NASA/Science Photo Library/Photo Researchers, Inc.; 192, Graham Neden/ Ecoscene/CORBIS; 193, Sam Dudgeon/HRW; 193 (br), G.R. Roberts Photo Library; 193 (t), Guido Alberto Rossi/Getty Images/The Image Bank; 194, National Weather Service/NOAA; 197, Sam Dudgeon/HRW; 198 (tl), Lightscapes Photography, Inc./ CORBIS; 199 (b), Corbis Images; 202 (tr), Joyce Photographics/Photo Researchers, Inc.; 203 (t), Michael Lyon; 203 (bl), Corbis Images

Chapter Seven 204-205, Steve Bloom Images; 206 (bkgd), Tom Van Sant, Geosphere Project/Planetary Visions/Science Photo Library/Photo Researchers, Inc.; 206 (tl), G. R. Roberts, © Natural Sciences Image Library; 206 (tr), Index Stock; 206 (c), Yva Momatiuk & John Eastcott; 206 (bl), Gary Retherford/Photo Researchers, Inc.; 206 (br), SuperStock; 207 (tr), CALLER-TIMES/AP/Wide World Photos; 207 (tc), Doug Mills/AP/Wide World Photos; 209 (b), Tom Van Sant, Geosphere Project/Planetary Visions/Science Photo Library/Photo Researchers, Inc.; 210 (bl), Larry Ulrich Photography; 210 (br), Paul Wakefield/Getty Images/Stone; 213, Index Stock; 214 (br), Tom Van Sant/Geosphere Project, Santa Monica/Science Photo Library/Photo Researchers, Inc.; 215 (tl), Carlos Navajas/Getty Images/The Image Bank; 215 (tr), Michael Zuber/Bruce Coleman, Inc.; 216, Nadine Zuber/Photo Researchers, Inc.; 217, © Sergio Pitamitz/CORBIS; 218 (br), Tom Van Sant/Geosphere Project, Santa Monica/Science Photo Library/Photo Researchers, Inc.; 219 (b), Tom Bean/Getty Images/Stone; 219 (t), CORBIS Images/HRW; 220 (l), © Gordon Whitten/CORBIS; 220 (t), Fred Hirschmann; 221 (b), Harry Walker/Alaska Stock; 221 (tr), Tom Van Sant/Geosphere Project, Santa Monica/Science Photo Library/Photo Researchers, Inc.; 222, SuperStock; 226 (br), Roger Werth/Woodfin Camp & Associates; 227 (b), D. Van Ravenswaay/Photo Researchers, Inc.; 232, Gunter Ziesler/Peter Arnold, Inc.; 233, SuperStock; 236, Roger Ressmeyer/CORBIS; 236 (b), Terry Brandt/Grant Heilman Photography, Inc.; 237 (t), Courtesy of The University of Michigan

STAFF CREDITS

The people who contributed to *Holt Science & Technology* are listed below. They represent editorial, design, production, eMedia, permissions, and marketing.

Chris Allison, Melanie Baccus, Wesley M. Bain, Juan Baquera, Angela Beckmann, Ed Blake, Sara Buller, Marc Burgamy, Rebecca Calhoun, Kimberly Cammerata, Soojinn Choi, Eddie Dawson, Julie Dervin, Michelle Dike, Lydia Doty, Jen Driscoll, Leigh Ann García, Catherine Gnader, Diana Goetting, Tim Hovde, Wilonda Ieans, Jevara Jackson, Simon Key, Jane A. Kirschman, Cathy Kuhles, Laura Likon, Denise Mahoney, Michael Mazza, Kristen McCardel, Richard Metzger, Micah Newman, Janice Noske, Joeleen Ornt, Cathy Paré, Jenny Patton, Laura Prescott, Bill Rader, Peter D. Reid, Curtis Riker, Michael Rinella, Jeff Robinson, Audrey Rozsypal, Beth Sample, Margaret Sanchez, Kay Selke, Elizabeth Simmons, Chris Smith, Dawn Marie Spinozza, Sherry Sprague, Jeff Streber, JoAnn Stringer, Roshan Strong, Jeannie Taylor, Bob Tucek, Tam Voynick, Clay Walton, Kira J. Watkins, Ken Whiteside, Holly Whittaker, David Wisnieski, Monica Yudron, Patty Zepeda